OXFORD HISTORY OF
MODERN EUROPE

General Editors

ALAN BULLOCK *and* F. W. D. DEAKIN

Oxford History of Modern Europe

SPAIN 1808-1939
By RAYMOND CARR

THE RUSSIAN EMPIRE 1801-1917
By HUGH SETON-WATSON

to act as his guarantor to the radicals.[1] Lamartine, and his colleagues in the Provisional government, were conscious, perhaps too conscious, of their precarious position; their aim was to avert a more radical revolution, and they tried to stave it off by harmless radical gestures. Such had been the abolition of the death penalty. Such was Lamartine's declaration of revolutionary foreign policy. To satisfy radical opinion in France he repudiated the treaties of 1815; to reassure the statesmen of Europe he announced that France would continue to recognize them: 'the treaties of 1815 have no legal existence in the eyes of the French republic; nevertheless the territorial provisions of these treaties are a fact which the republic admits as basis and starting-point in its relations with other nations'. The only threat of war was in case of interference with Switzerland or with 'the independent states of Italy'.[2] Not content with these cautious phrases, Lamartine apologized beforehand for the Manifesto to the British ambassador and even sent a private message to the duke of Wellington: 'The Provisional Government will make a forceful declaration to the nations of Europe, but the Duke of Wellington will understand its real sense'.[3] Still, despite these apologies, Lamartine's circular was a dramatic act—the first official announcement by the government of a Great Power that the Vienna settlement had no moral validity. Without meaning to do so, Lamartine had put international relations on a *de facto* basis.

The old world of the Holy Alliance had a last moment of life after the Paris revolution before being itself swept away. Metternich to the end thought of 'the revolution' as something external and remarked cheerfully: 'the situation is just what it was in 1792.' He wished to repeat the blunder of 1792, that is, to demand from France a declaration of respect for the existing treaties.[4] Though Frederick William IV and Tsar Nicholas talked of a united resistance to the spread of revolution, they were not to be drawn into any plan of action. Certainly, if there were to be a revolutionary war, the Russians would prefer it to be fought on the Rhine, not in Poland. In the former case, Russia would provide merely an auxiliary corps; in the latter case she would fight alone, as in 1812, and might

[1] Lamartine, *Histoire de la révolution de 1848*, ii. 7.   [2] Ibid., ii. 28–35.
[3] Spencer Walpole, *Life of Lord John Russell*, ii. 32.
[4] Draft of Four-Power declaration, 7 Mar. 1848.

...o raise the masses with a promise of social revolution.
...other hand, the Russians knew that Austria could
...ate nothing and doubted whether Prussia could con-
...much; the entry of a Russian army into Germany
mig... well touch off the revolution. Therefore the tsar encouraged the conservatism of others without pledging himself
to the conservative cause; Russian self-interest, not abstract
principle, was his guiding motive.[1] As for Frederick William,
his mind was already in a high ferment of contradictions. He
wished to act in unison with Russia, but also in unison with
Great Britain; and if the two would not act together, then he
would not act at all.[2]

British policy had, of course, long been out of step with the
rigidity of the Holy Alliance; and the February revolution in
Paris completed the estrangement. All the Powers had resented
Louis Philippe, most because he was too liberal a monarch,
Great Britain because he was not liberal enough; by the end of
the July Monarchy France was on worse terms with Great
Britain than with any other Power. Russell, the prime minister,
and Palmerston, the foreign secretary, were both on intimate
terms with the leaders of the French opposition; and both were
ready to believe Lamartine's pacific assurances. Besides, Palmerston hoped to repeat on a larger scale the greatest success
in British policy since the congress of Vienna—the 'appeasement' of 1830 in the Belgian question by which French sentiment had been satisfied without a disturbance of the Balance
of Power. Therefore, while Metternich was demanding that
France should give guarantees to Europe, Palmerston proposed
that Europe should give guarantees to France. On 4 March he
asked the three 'Northern Courts' to consider 'whether important advantages might not be gained to the cause of Peace' by
giving France the assurance that 'so long as France is not
aggressive, no aggression will be made upon her'.[3] Though all
these moves soon became out of date with the spread of revolution to central Europe, they already sketched the attitude of
the Powers in the following years. France was resentful against

[1] Meyendorff (Russian ambassador at Berlin) to Nesselrode (Russian chancellor), 2 Mar., 8 Mar. 1848. Hoetzsch, *Peter von Meyendorff*, ii, nos. 218, 219.

[2] It is often forgotten that, though Frederick William wrote ceaseless hysterical
letters to the tsar, he also wrote ceaseless hysterical letters to Queen Victoria.

[3] Palmerston to Bloomfield (St. Petersburg), Ponsonby (Vienna), Westmorland
(Berlin), 4 Mar. 1848.

the existence of the settlement of 1815, yet without any concrete grievance; Great Britain believed that peace could be preserved by conciliating French feeling; Russia wished to push the two German powers into a defence of conservatism without being committed herself; Austria was willing to be pushed forward if she could have an assurance of Russian support; and Prussia clung indecisively to Great Britain and Russia, tempted by a revision of Europe, fearful that it would be executed at her expense.

On 13 March the revolution spread from France to central Europe. Metternich fell from power in Vienna, and with him the prestige of Austria. 'The system of 1815' was at an end. On 18 March Frederick William IV gave way before the rioters in Berlin and agreed to make liberal concessions; three days later he proclaimed, 'Prussia merges into Germany', and promised to protect Germany 'against the imminent double danger', that is, against Russia as much as against France. The promise did not long hold its force. Still, what took place in Prussia or elsewhere in Germany was primarily an internal affair. The two great grievances of radical sentiment were Poland and Italy; and these two gave the pattern to the diplomacy of the revolutionary year. Poland hardly stirred. Russian Poland had been firmly gripped by a Russian army ever since the defeat of the revolt in 1831; Galicia, Austrian Poland, was still exhausted from the revolt of 1846 and produced only some disturbances in Cracow, which were finally subdued on 25 April. Only the liberal government in Prussia did something for the Poles. The Polish leaders imprisoned in Berlin since 1846, with Mieroslawski at their head, were released; and the Poles were promised 'a national reorganization' of the Grand Duchy of Posen, Prussia's share of the partitions. Italy, on the other hand, liberated itself. Venice and Milan both drove out the Austrian troops and set up provisional governments (23 March); both appealed for help to Charles Albert, king of Sardinia.

Between Charles Albert and Frederick William IV there were many points of similarity. Both combined romantic conservatism with a shrewd calculation of state-interest; both, on occasion, would pretend to liberalism while inwardly loathing it. For a moment, towards the end of March 1848, it looked as though both would follow the same pattern. To save their

thrones they would put themselves at the head respectively of
Italian and of German nationalism. Sardinia would go to war
with Austria for the sake of Lombardy and Venetia; Prussia
would go to war with Russia for the sake of Poland. Radical
France would stand behind both, as Russia had stood behind
the Holy Alliance; and both would enjoy British benevolence,
if not more. This liberal dream was never realized. Prussia and
Sardinia took opposite paths. Charles Albert felt himself the
more menaced by radicalism—if he did not go to war there
would be an immediate republican outbreak in Genoa. Besides,
he had a weaker opponent: Austria seemed already in disintegration, and he could attack her without the risk of needing
French help. His famous phrase, 'Italy will do it herself', was
a judgement of fact (though a wrong one), not an expression
of hope. On 24 March therefore Charles Albert resolved on
war. The Italian question ceased, for the moment, to be a
question of diplomacy.

German liberal feeling ran as strongly against Russia as did
Italian feeling against Austria. The Italians could treat Metternich as the centre of reaction; the Germans turned more
readily against a non-German power. Arguing from the analogy
of the French Jacobins and the Reign of Terror, many German
liberals believed that Germany could be united only by a
foreign war; and in the revolutionary circumstances that must
be a war against Russia for the liberation of Poland. Arnim-
Suckow, the routine diplomat who had become Prussian
Foreign Minister on 21 March, was ready to champion this
policy; and, since he had recently been ambassador in Paris,
he imagined that he could draw France along with him.
Frederick William, once he recovered from his panic of 18
March, was, however, resolved not to go against Russia. As
early as 22 March he said to a leading liberal, Max von
Gagern, who had urged him to liberate Poland: 'By God, I
shall never, never under any circumstances, draw the sword
against Russia.'[1] There were other differences from Italy apart
from the obstinacy of the king. Austria, though weak and
chaotic, had challenged the Italian revolution. Russia, though
her army was assumed to be formidable, avoided any challenge
to the German, or even to the French, revolution, once the

---

[1] Pastor, *Leben des Freiherrn Max von Gagern*, p. 234. For the Polish question,
Namier, *1848: the Revolution of the Intellectuals*, pp. 43–65.

question of Poland had been raised. On the news of the February revolution Tsar Nicholas had told his officers to saddle their horses. A month later he was telling an unofficial French representative that it would be easier for him to get on with a republic than with a constitutional monarchy: 'The republic and absolute monarchy are both concerned with the good of the people. Constitutions on the other hand are only made for the advantage of a few individuals.'[1] The directors of Russian policy were themselves mostly Germans—Meyendorff, the ambassador at Berlin, a Baltic baron; Nesselrode, the chancellor, a Lutheran, who never learnt to speak Russian. Perhaps for this reason they appreciated the more readily that Germans and Poles would quarrel, if Russia kept out of the way.[2]

This was much deeper than a diplomatic calculation. The rulers of Russia were unanimously convinced that the revival of an independent Poland would mean the end of Russia as a Great Power. Meyendorff told Stratford Canning: 'Poland as the Poles understand it extends to the mouths of the Vistula and the Danube and to the Dnieper at Smolensk as at Kiev. This Poland forms a bastion into Russia, destroys her political and geographical unity, pushes her back into Asia, sets her back 200 years.' And he added: 'to forbid the establishment of this Poland every Russian will take up arms as in 1812'.[3] Nesselrode had the same conviction. He wrote to Meyendorff on 27 April: 'To repulse an attack on the part of the Poles is to everybody's taste. For that there would be a levée en masse, even if this attack were supported by the entire world. But an army sent abroad to restore the fallen thrones or to support Germany against France, would not be popular here.'[4] Certainly the Russians threatened to intervene if there were a serious Polish movement either in Prussian Poland or in Galicia;[5] otherwise, in the tsar's words: 'A musket should not be shouldered unless Russia was attacked.'[6]

Russia refused to be provoked; even more decisive, France refused to provoke her. Lamartine's Manifesto to Europe had not even mentioned Poland, an astonishing omission after the

---

[1] Bapst, *Origines de la guerre de Crimée*, p. 8.
[2] *Meyendorff*, ii, no. 226.   [3] Ibid., no. 229.
[4] Nesselrode to Meyendorff, 27 April 1848. *Lettres et papiers*, ix. 87.
[5] So Nicholas warned an Austrian representative early in April. Guichen, *Les grandes questions européennes*, i. 79.
[6] Bloomfield to Palmerston, no. 89, 18 Apr. 1848. F.O. 65/348.

resolutions of sympathy for Poland passed annually even by the Chamber of the July Monarchy. Lamartine defined his policy in reply to a Polish deputation: 'We love Poland, we love Italy, we love all the oppressed nations, but most of all we love France.'[1] Though he hoped for an alliance with Prussia, he wanted it on a pacific basis, not as an alliance against Russia; and the special representative whom he sent to Berlin was one of the few Frenchmen unsympathetic to Poland— Circourt, a legitimist noble married to a Russian. Circourt's task was to discourage the Prussian government from offending Russia and, at the same time, to supply Lamartine with material which might discredit the Poles in French public opinion. To satisfy this opinion Lamartine had to allow the Polish exiles in Paris to leave for Berlin and even to demand that they should be sent on to Posen; but he was determined to go no further. The crisis, if it can be dignified with that name, came at the end of March. Arnim asked Circourt what France would do if the Poles attacked Russia from Prussian soil, and the Russians then invaded Posen. What he wanted was 'a solemn declaration of alliance and political solidarity concerning the restoration of Poland' and 'the despatch, if asked for, of a French squadron to the Baltic'.[2] Lamartine used the excuse of the confusion in Paris to avoid giving an official reply. His secretary merely sent Circourt a phrase to be used in conversation: 'If Russia attacked Prussia and invaded her territory seizing Posnania, France would give Prussia armed support.'[3] This letter did not reach Circourt until 15 April and by then Arnim was taking the condescending line that Prussia might possibly second French designs in Poland if offered sufficient inducement.

British prompting may have helped to turn Arnim from his brief liberal enthusiasm. Stratford Canning, an outstanding British diplomat, had been sent by Palmerston on a roving tour of Europe preparatory to returning to Constantinople; and at the end of March he reached Berlin. Arnim asked for 'the countenance and support of England'; Frederick William asked for Stratford Canning's support against Arnim and his

---

[1] Lamartine, *Trois mois au pouvoir*, p. 133.
[2] Circourt to Lamartine, 31 Mar. 1848. Circourt, *Souvenirs d'une mission à Berlin*, i. 326–9.
[3] Champeaux to Circourt, 4 Apr. 1848. Circourt, i. 329.

Polish policy. Though Stratford Canning had no precise instructions, he knew Palmerston's view that the preservation of peace was 'one of the first objects to the attainment of which the efforts of enlightened Statesmen ought to be directed'; and he preached peace to everybody, winning even Meyendorff's approval.[1] Still, the British minister at Turin had also preached peace to Charles Albert, in that case without effect. The decisive factor was the conflict between Germans and Poles in Posnania, which broke out in the middle of April. Instead of liberating the Poles, Prussian forces were soon fighting them; on 6 May Mieroslawski, who had tried to raise the Poles, relinquished his command. By the end of April Arnim was telling Circourt that France would have to fight her way across Germany if she wished to help Poland: 'Germany believes that restoring Poland would help France to take her neighbours between two fires';[2] and on 14 May Circourt wrote to Lamartine: 'we shall go to war for Posen and we shall make peace by surrendering Strasbourg'.[3] The prophecy was too soon by ninety years. Early in April Lamartine spoke so slightingly to a Polish deputation that the tsar ordered the Russian chargé d'affaires to stay in Paris as a sign of his approval. The open collapse of Polish hopes early in May provoked a radical revolt in Paris on 15 May. The only act of the Provisional Government then set up was to declare: 'it will immediately order the Russian and German governments to restore Poland and, if they fail to obey this order, it will immediately declare war on them'. Barbès and his fellow radicals were turned out of the Hôtel de Ville after a couple of hours, and when they fell the liberation of Poland went with them. So long as Tsardom lived, great Poland, the Poland of 1772, was never to be advocated again even by the most temporary of French governments. On 23 May Lamartine, no longer foreign minister, defended his foreign policy in the Assembly; in its order of the day the Assembly declared in favour of 'a pact of fraternity with Germany, the reconstruction of a free independent Poland, and the liberation of Italy'. It did not, however, prescribe any action by which any of these might be achieved.

Prussian policy and German feeling had thus turned against

---

[1] His dispatches are quoted in Namier, pp. 62–63.
[2] Circourt to Lamartine, 27 Apr. 1848. Circourt, ii. 73.
[3] Circourt to Lamartine, 14 May 1848. Circourt, ii. 206.

Poland, and to a certain extent against France, instead of against Russia. Still, another outlet had been discovered unexpectedly for the activity in foreign affairs which was held essential to German unity. This was the question of the Elbe duchies, Sleswick and Holstein, the question, as it turned out, round which Germany was to be made. Though the two duchies regarded themselves as 'forever united', only Holstein was a member of the German confederation; both were under the suzerainty of the king of Denmark, Holstein exclusively German in character, Sleswick German in its southern part. To these national and historical complications a personal complication was now added: the male line in Denmark was running out, and the duchies claimed to follow the Salic law, while Denmark accepted a female succession. Against this, Danish radicalism—also astir in 1848—proposed to break the loose feudal connexion with the duchies and to incorporate them, or a large part of them, directly into Denmark. Still these topics merely provided the setting; essentially the duchies raised the question whether the German nation could assert its will as a Great Power. This could not be a question between the Germans and Denmark alone. The duchies had been secured to the crown of Denmark by international agreement; and in the eighteenth century they had been a vital point for European diplomacy. Great Britain, Russia, and even France had insisted on the duchies remaining in Danish hands so that the entrance to the Baltic should not be controlled by a Great Power. By the middle of the nineteenth century the Baltic had ceased to be a vital factor in the Balance of Power, a change heavy with consequences for the rise of Germany. Great Britain, with the development of steam-power, no longer depended on timber and ship's stores from the Baltic; Russia, shifting the weight of her exports from timber to wheat, moved her economic centre from the Baltic provinces to the Ukraine and her lifeline from the Sound to the Straits. As early as May 1848 the Russian council of ministers decided that, while Poland and Turkey were vital issues for Russia, the Elbe duchies were not.[1]

British policy did not admit the changed circumstances so clearly or so consciously; indeed, though the Baltic itself was no longer important, a vital British interest was still involved—

[1] Schiemann, *Geschichte Rußlands unter Kaiser Nikolaus I.*, iv. 164.

not to have a Great Power on the shores of the North Sea. Here too was a fundamental point for the future. Great Britain —the Power most sympathetic to liberal nationalism in general and, because of the influence of Prince Albert and his German relatives, the Power most sympathetic to German nationalism in particular—was the leading opponent of this national senti-ment in the only international question which concerned it. In the quarter of a century after the revolutions of 1848 Italy was united with British sympathy and support; Germany without them. This difference had many causes. Many British statesmen, Palmerston for instance most strongly, feared that a united Germany would put up tariff barriers against British goods; again, British sentiment disliked the military measures by which Germany was united—the Italians did much better to unite their country by losing wars. But from start to finish Sleswick and Holstein were the decisive factor. It was almost as though Italian nationalists had regarded Malta as their first essential aim. The British did not threaten to go to war themselves; they threatened Germany with war from others: from Russia or from France. The British assumed that in every European question, except possibly Belgium, the interests of others were more vitally affected than their own. Usually this was true; in the duchies it was not, as the later failure of British policy was to show.

The question of the duchies became international as part of the general revolution. On 24 March the Estates of the two duchies broke with Denmark and appealed to the German Confederation for support. In practice this appeal could be directed only to Prussia, which had the force for a 'federal execution'. It was an appeal which a liberal Prussian govern-ment could not refuse; even Frederick William, torn between leading Germany and offending Russia, welcomed an alterna-tive to Poland. On 10 April Prussian troops crossed the frontier of the duchies; by the end of April they had expelled the Danes from the duchies and on 2 May entered Jutland, an intrinsic part of the Danish monarchy. Though the Russians were indignant at this subversive policy, they had no intention of fighting for Denmark the war which they had avoided over Poland. Moreover Russia, despite her professions of conserva-tive principle, was less involved in the treaty-structure of Europe than any other Power; herself resting on national sentiment and military strength, she was ready to accept the national principle elsewhere, except, of course, in Poland. As a result Nesselrode was the first to propose the division of Sleswick along the national line—a proposal that would have settled the Sleswick question in a week, had it not been for the conflicting claims of Germany and Denmark, claims based on history and law, not on nationality.[1] Russia stood aside and left Palmerston to mediate alone between Denmark and the Germans. In the idealistic atmosphere of 1848, the German liberals thought that they were acquiring a mediator favourable to their cause; Palmerston, on his side, thought that he was doing a sufficient service to Germany by saving her from a war with France and Russia.

Palmerston took up, with some hesitation, Nesselrode's suggestion of a division at the national line. This was rejected by the Danes, now bent on asserting the 'integrity' of the Danish monarchy. Since the only British weapon was the threat that other Powers would intervene and since, as the Danes knew, no Power would intervene against Denmark, Palmerston was helpless; and this helplessness made him the more annoyed with the Germans for their persistence in claims which he had recognized as just. British policy was thus reduced to vague insistence on peace, or at least an armistice; but it did not in fact contribute much to the actual armistice negotiations conducted between Prussia and Denmark in July. The sole motive of these was Frederick William's increasing abhorrence of his association with the liberal German cause; though he would have liked to acquire the duchies, he was determined, absurdly enough, not to acquire them with liberal approval. Therefore he pushed on negotiations which would postpone the question of the duchies to a less revolutionary future. The first armistice, negotiated in July, was rejected by the Prussian commander in the duchies; he was brought to heel by direct orders from the king, and a second armistice was concluded at Malmö on 26 August. This provided for the withdrawal of both Danish and Prussian troops from the duchies and for their temporary administration by a joint Prusso-Danish commission. The German central Power was disregarded, the German 'national' cause betrayed. This provoked the decisive crisis in the German

---

[1] Nesselrode to Meyendorff, 8 May 1848. *Lettres et papiers*, ix. 93. Bloomfield to Palmerston, no. 131, 5 May 1848, F.O. 65/349.

national assembly at Frankfurt in September; and when a majority was finally found in the assembly to acquiesce in the armistice, it had to be supported against the Frankfurt radicals by force of Prussian arms.

The armistice of Malmö was certainly the central event in the German revolution of 1848. It is often said that it was imposed on Prussia by foreign pressure; and from this the conclusion is drawn that, since France and Russia would not tolerate the unification of Germany by consent, the only alternative was unification by force. There is little to support this view. Frederick William's motive was shame at the tsar's moral disapproval, not fear of Franco-Russian intervention. When Nicholas described Frederick William's conduct as *infamous*,[1] he posed for Prussia the problem which was to shape her policy for the next twenty years: how could Sleswick be won, how could Germany be united without a breach with Russia? Nicholas, in fact, reversed the trick which Metternich had played on him for years in the Near East: by evoking the principle of monarchical solidarity he distracted Frederick William from the concrete object of policy in the Elbe duchies. Palmerston may have threatened that Russia would intervene; the threat was never made by the Russians themselves.

The threat from France was even more remote. It is true that when Lamartine handed over the foreign ministry to Bastide in May a change of spirit came over French foreign policy. Lamartine, because of his equivocal past, had to talk revolution in foreign affairs; Bastide, a republican beyond reproach, did not need to worry about his reputation. Besides, with the June days in Paris and the setting-up of Cavaignac's dictatorship, extreme radical opinion no longer counted. Bastide was the first Frenchman of the left to realize that a general upset of the Vienna settlement would not be to French advantage; in his brief tenure of the foreign ministry (May to December 1848) he anticipated the statesmen of the Third Republic. Thus, though he sent Arago, a good republican, to Berlin instead of Circourt he instructed him to drop the Polish question and to keep quiet: 'do not publish anything in the papers and do not excite people'. On 16 June Bastide wrote to his representative at Frankfurt concerning Sleswick: 'From the point of view of legality, of treaties, of the territorial *status quo*,

[1] Bloomfield to Palmerston, no. 144, 12 May 12 1848, F.O. 65/349.

of nationality, of honest and considered policy, the German diet has got on a false road'; thus, in Bastide's view, the principle of nationalism had sunk to fourth place. Again, on 31 July, he wrote to Arago: 'German unity would make of this people of more than thirty-five million a power very much more redoubtable to its neighbours than Germany is to-day, and therefore I do not think we have any reason to desire this unity, still less to promote it.'

This theoretical disapproval was far removed from action. Though Cavaignac and Bastide made approaches to Russia —not unsuccessfully—these had no practical purport; they were merely intended to guard against a revival of the 'Holy Alliance' by convincing the tsar that republican France did not mean to launch a revolutionary crusade. Besides, Bastide's practical receipt for checking German unity was to back Prussia. Believing, as all Frenchmen did, that Austria was still stronger than Prussia, he regarded any increase in Prussian strength as an increase in German disunity; hence he never contemplated threatening Prussia in regard to Sleswick, despite his concern for 'treaties and the territorial *status quo*'.[1]

The prospect of a general European war, evoked by Palmerston to justify the armistice of Malmö, was in fact a turnip-ghost; and some of the Frankfurt liberals realized that, so far as foreign Powers counted, humiliation was being forced on them by Great Britain, not by France or Russia. Moreover, the acceptance of the armistice by Prussia caused a breach between Frederick William and the German liberals. Yet as Cowley, the British representative at Frankfurt, argued, German unification under a liberal Prussia would be 'the safest and the easiest way'.[2] The creation of a 'lesser Germany' would have given Great Britain a substitute for the 'natural alliance' with Austria, an ally both stronger and more congenial. British policy helped to prevent this outcome for the sake of Sleswick; it served the turn of France and Russia without these powers

[1] This summary of Bastide's policy is based on three articles by Paul Henry in *Revue historique*, vols. 178, 186, 188. The argument that German action in Sleswick, and therewith German unity, were forbidden by Russia and France was advanced by Erich Marcks in *Historische Zeitschrift*, vol. 142, and more elaborately by A. Scharff, *Die europäischen Großmächte und die deutsche Revolution*.

[2] Cowley to Palmerston, 3 Dec. 1848. Cowley wished to second Gagern's plans for uniting Germany under Prussia by using British influence with the German princes; Palmerston forbade it.

lifting a finger. The half-conscious realization of this contradiction made Palmerston and other British statesmen impatient with 'the parcel of children' at Frankfurt. When Palmerston a little later said to Bunsen, the Prussian minister in London: 'There is nothing to be said against the idea of a German Reich except that no one seems able to bring it about',[1] he was really condemning those who thought Sleswick an essential part of a united Germany.

There was a deeper consideration. German unification was not part of radical mythology, least of all the liberation of Sleswick. The German question, in all its aspects, took European statesmen by surprise; and they treated it in a casual manner, without urgency. It is difficult to believe that even Palmerston took seriously the danger of a general war arising from the conflict between Denmark and Prussia. Apart from the Russian obsession with Poland, everyone in 1848 regarded Italy as the decisive theatre of events; and what men think is more important in history than the objective facts. The universal error of the two generations after the congress of Vienna was to exaggerate the strength of France among the Great Powers. Once this error was made, Italy as a field of French expansion received exaggerated importance also. Besides, it was genuinely more difficult for French radicals to drop their revolutionary past in Italy than elsewhere. Hard geographical reality stood between France and Poland; nothing seemed to stand between France and Italy except a French reluctance to launch a great war. And, on the other side, control of Italy was fundamental to the existence of Austria as a Great Power, or so Austrian statesmen argued; this was a very different question from the future of Sleswick or even from the independence of Denmark. Hence it was in Italy that British policy was most active and displayed most initiative.

The early days of the Austro-Sardinian war offered results suited to British policy. Though Palmerston had urged Charles Albert not to go to war, he was satisfied with Charles Albert's programme, once the war had started. 'Italy will do it herself' was exactly what the British wanted: to get Austria out without letting the French in. British statesmen continued to express themselves in favour of the maintenance of Austria as a Great Power; but they thought she would be stronger without

---

[1] Quoted in Precht, *Englands Stellung zur deutschen Einheit.*

Lombardy and Venetia than with them, stronger, that is, to hold a balance against Russia in the Near East, which was Austria's essential function in British eyes. They wished Austria's defeat to be complete for her own sake; and they wished it to be speedy so that all northern Italy could be consolidated in a single state before France had time to intervene. The bewildered remnant of officials who ran the Austrian empire after the fall of Metternich did not understand such subtleties. When Stratford Canning arrived in Vienna at the end of April and made the usual conventional remarks about the need for Austria as a Great Power, Pillersdorf, the elderly official who was temporarily in charge of foreign affairs, took these remarks seriously; he even supposed that with the cover of a few liberal phrases Great Britain might come to Austria's rescue in Italy. Hummelauer, British expert in the foreign ministry, was therefore sent to London to obtain British help on almost any terms; convinced as the Austrians were that they would be attacked by France at any moment, they were ready to jettison most of their Italian possessions if this would win some sort of British guarantee for the remainder. On 23 May Hummelauer met Palmerston and offered Lombardy-Venetia full autonomy; when Palmerston rejected this as inadequate Hummelauer increased the offer on 24 May—Lombardy should become independent and only Venetia remain under Austrian suzerainty.

This offer, too, was rejected by the British cabinet as inadequate. On 3 June the British government gave Hummelauer a formal reply: they would be prepared to mediate between Austria and Sardinia if the Austrians were willing to surrender not only Lombardy but 'such portions of the Venetian Territory as may be agreed upon between the respective Parties'. Palmerston told his colleagues that this phrase had no serious meaning: 'such portions . . . will of course be the whole.' On the other hand he, and Prince Albert, represented it to Hummelauer as a considerable concession to Austria; and Hummelauer returned to Vienna with the shadowy comfort that, in case of further military defeat, something might be saved from the wreck. Palmerston was not deceiving either party. As in the Sleswick question, his overriding concern was to end the war; what happened round the conference-table could be settled later. It was more important that the parties

should negotiate than that they should reach agreement—a
common theme in British diplomacy. Still, so far as Palmerston
had an Italian policy in the summer of 1848, it was to set up a
united kingdom of northern Italy, with Austrian consent, before
the French had time to intervene.

Though the French too talked of mediation, they meant it
in an opposite sense. Throughout 1848 the French politicians
were mainly concerned to find excuses for not intervening in
Italy. No doubt this sprang fundamentally from the deep
unstated French reluctance against starting a great European
war; but even this was in its way an excuse—resolute French
action early in 1848 could probably have got the Austrians
out of Italy without much risk. There was too the bewilderment at discovering that France could only support the
'national principle' in Europe at the risk of creating two neighbours mightier than herself. In the foreground was the practical
objection that the Italian movement was led by the house of
Savoy. The French republicans argued, sincerely enough, that
they could not be expected to assist the aggrandizement of a
monarchy: this too was an excuse at bottom, since they also
did nothing to assist the republic of Venice. It was more concrete and more serious that the king of Sardinia, though leading
Italy, also held Savoy and Nice, the most flagrant symbols of
France's humiliation in 1815. Savoy and Nice represented an
injustice both on national grounds and on grounds of 'the
natural frontiers'; whereas on the German side there was no such
clear-cut grievance—hence the vague phrases, never defined,
about 'the Rhine'.

Every national movement needs some defined grievance if
it is to take on practical form. The topic of grievance may be
a prize in itself, as Sleswick and Holstein were a prize from the
geographic point of view; or as political speculators tried to
make out that the later French grievance over Alsace and Lorraine was provoked by French need for iron-ore. But fundamentally these centres of grievance—Sleswick, the Straits, south
Tyrol—were the focus for national sentiment; and a nation
made greater sacrifices for them than they were worth. Hence
the greatest problem in French policy towards Italy turned on
this trivial point: it was impossible for the French to aid Italy
without demanding Savoy and Nice for themselves. In 1848
the French rulers already knew this; the Italians, or at least

the Piedmontese, knew it; and the king of Sardinia knew it most of all. The only French action on the Italian side in 1848 was an abortive radical attack on Savoy; this was hardly an encouragement to more official co-operation. Bastide fumbled at a solution: if Austria could be persuaded to withdraw from Italy voluntarily, then Lombardy and Venice could become republics, the kingdom of Sardinia would not profit, and the question of Savoy and Nice need not be raised. Hence he made tentative suggestions to mediate between Austria and the provisional government in Lombardy, not between Austria and Sardinia; and the purpose of this mediation was to be 'a free and independent Lombardy', not the aggrandizement of the house of Savoy. Thus, though both Great Britain and France claimed to be sympathetic to Italy, French policy aimed at the one thing which Palmerston was anxious to prevent.

Both Great Powers were thwarted by the actions of the Italians themselves. Lombardy and Venetia voted for union with Sardinia (29 May and 4 July); this defeated the French plan for independent republics. The provisional government in Milan not only refused separate negotiations with the Austrians; it also insisted that any offer of independence must extend 'to the whole of Austrian Italy (including South Tirol)'. This defeated Palmerston's hope of transferring the dispute to the conference table. Great Britain and France were thus forced together. Bastide decided that he must put up with the union of Lombardy and Sardinia, so long as he could prevent the inclusion of Venetia (19 July); this was the exact proposal that Hummelauer had made to Palmerston on 24 May. Palmerston intended to reply that he would join France in mediating, on condition that part of Venetia should be included in the proposed surrender of Austrian territory—the answer which he had made to Hummelauer on 3 June. Meanwhile, military events had taken an unexpected course. In the middle of June the Austrian empire had at last acquired a resolute government; and in Wessenberg, the new foreign minister, a diplomat of experience and courage. Recognizing that in Italy it was a case of all or nothing, the new government decided to risk the fortunes of war; and their hopes were not disappointed. On 25 July Radetzky, the Austrian commander, routed the Sardinian army at Custoza. Though Italy had failed to do it herself, Charles Albert was no more inclined for French help in defeat than he had been in victory. He abandoned Milan without a struggle, withdrew his army behind the Sardinian frontier, and concluded an armistice of simple military character on 9 August.

Had Sardinia alone been in question, this would have been the end of the Italian affair. But with Charles Albert out of the way, appeals to France from the republicans in Lombardy and Venice were the more plausible and pressing. Normanby, the British ambassador at Paris, felt the crisis. Without waiting for instructions, he took up the French suggestion of 19 July and proposed Anglo-French mediation on the basis of the Hummelauer plan of 24 May. Cavaignac and Bastide snatched at the chance of avoiding war and accepted the proposal (5 Aug.); two days later Palmerston confirmed it. It remained to get the mediation accepted by the two contending parties. The Sardinian government, already at odds with Charles Albert for his hasty armistice, at once welcomed the chance of reopening the Italian question. Wessenberg temporized for a fortnight; then replied that mediation was unnecessary and the Hummelauer plan, in any case, out of the question. At the same time Radetzky prepared to attack Venice. The French government had reached its moment of decision—whether the Republic would honour its unbroken series of declarations in favour of Italian independence. Cavaignac and Bastide grasped at a way out—a joint Anglo-French occupation of Venice, imposing concessions on Austria as in 1831 Great Britain and France had imposed concessions on Holland in the Belgian question. Under pressure of events these two inexperienced amateurs had formulated the 'liberal alliance' between Great Britain and France, which was thereafter to make the Crimean war and to secure the liberation of Italy. The alliance now and afterward was intended to bridle French extremism; it rested on distrust and fear. British governments distrusted French governments; and these feared their own public opinion. No concrete British interest was involved (except later in the Near East). For the sake of peace and the *status quo*, Great Britain had to accept attacks on the *status quo* or even to go to war; not surprisingly the British tried to escape from this contradiction by claiming idealistic motives for their foreign policy. In reality British policy would never have bestirred itself for Italian nationalism, had it not been for fear of an explosion from France. Palmerston was ready to co-operate with France even in 1848: 'If France is to act anywhere in Italy, she ought to be tied up by a previous agreement with us' (30 Aug.). The Whig cabinet refused to follow him: they saw only that they would be tied up by an agreement with the French. Though some of them were enthusiastic for Italy, they depended on a minority in the house of commons and as well were ceaselessly hampered by the queen's Germanic sympathy with Austria.

The French therefore had to make up their minds unaided. On 1 September they decided to occupy Venice alone and to impose armed mediation on Austria; on 2 September they decided to wait a little longer; on 7 September Bastide said to the Austrian representative: 'We find ourselves, or to speak more accurately we have put ourselves in a very embarrassing position.' The days of French idealism were over; the great revolutionary war would not be launched. This time the Italian affair should really have ended. But events do not follow such clear-cut patterns. On 2 September Wessenberg also lost his nerve: he accepted Anglo-French mediation, though not on the basis of the Hummelauer plan. This suited the French admirably: it saved their reputation, yet prevented the union of Lombardy and Sardinia. Wessenberg's eyes were, however, still focused on Great Britain. He wanted to win British support against France, not to make this support unnecessary. But Wessenberg's day, the brief period of a liberal Austrian Empire, was ending. At the beginning of October Felix Schwarzenberg arrived from Radetzky's headquarters and took over control of foreign policy; on 21 November he became prime minister and minister of foreign affairs. Schwarzenberg was the first of the 'realists' who were to shape European affairs for the next thirty years; he judged, or so he claimed, from facts, not from principles. As he said to the French representative: 'what does the difference in the form of Government matter to-day. . . . There is something above that, it is the maintenance of peace and the re-establishment of order.' Almost his first act was to draft a letter for Bastide (5 Oct.), arguing that France and Austria had a common interest in preventing a united kingdom of northern Italy; with his attention already focused on Prussia, he might have added in preventing a united Germany also. Here too was the first sketch of another programme: 'the conservative alliance' of France and Austria, an alliance based on interest, not on principle. The idea was too daring for Bastide and Cavaignac. They drifted on, at one moment threatening war for the sake of Venice, at another violently refusing to promise armed aid to Sardinia. But their days too were numbered. On 10 December Louis Napoleon was elected President of the French Republic by an overwhelming majority; on 29 December he took the oath to the constitution and established himself in the palace of the Elysée. Another 'realist' had arrived.

II

THE DIPLOMACY OF REACTION

1849–50

BY the end of 1848 order had been restored in the great capitals of Europe. Vienna had been reduced by armed force in November; the liberals of Berlin had capitulated without a struggle; in France the election of Louis Napoleon seemed to have completed the work of the 'June days'—the President was 'the guardian of order'. All that remained of the revolution was disorder in Rome; Sardinia resentful though defeated; a radical government in Hungary apparently on the point of military collapse; and the German National Assembly in Frankfurt, still manufacturing plans for national unity, though without material force. Though it took longer than expected to complete the restoration of order, this was not from the strength of the revolutionary remnants. It was rather from conflicts between the guardians of order themselves. The new rulers of Europe were despotic, not conservative. Relying at home on military force, they thought in terms of force in foreign affairs; and, far from believing in any European order, drew new maps of Europe as wildly as any revolutionary. The only one still to feel any loyalty to Metternich's 'system' was the ruler against whom it had been devised—the Tsar Nicholas; and he ended by regretting his belief.

The changed spirit was shown most clearly in Louis Napoleon. He had been elected President with the support of the Party of Order; and his election was a defeat for the radicals and republicans. His foreign minister, Drouyn de Lhuys, had served Louis Philippe and had the Orleanist preference for a conservative alliance with Austria. In his view the disunity of Germany and Italy was in France's interest. He wrote in 1849: 'French superiority rests on her national unity. . . . Everything which promotes the division of the great races is useful for us.'[1] Louis Napoleon could never accept this creed. He

[1] Drouyn de Lhuys to Tocqueville, 25 Aug. 1849.

was convinced that his uncle had fallen when he opposed the national will of Germany and Italy; and his mind ran over with vague schemes for redrawing the map of Europe. His name alone was a greater challenge to the congress settlement than all the words of Lamartine's Manifesto; whatever other Frenchmen might argue, a Bonaparte could never accept the congress of Vienna. If there was a stable point in his unstable mind, it was resentment against Austria, the country of Metternich and of stability. Louis Napoleon was neither a revolutionary nor a warmonger. He wished to accomplish a revolutionary foreign policy without calling on the spirit of revolution, and to remodel Europe without a war. Hence his favourite dream was 'a general Congress of the great powers of Europe', which should settle every question in dispute by peaceful agreement. He was a mixture of idealist and conspirator; consistent only in one thing—he could never resist the temptation to speculate. He plunged in politics, as contemporary capitalists plunged in railway ventures. Though he hated war and feared its risks, in the last resort he always came down on the side of action. In this he supposed he was interpreting French sentiment. As he said to Hübner, the Austrian minister: 'There is an urge for expansion in France which must be reckoned with.' In reality the urge was within himself; hence all the contradictions of his policy.

Though Louis Napoleon and the 'legitimate' monarchies had opposite origins, there was a similarity in their aims and methods. Schwarzenberg and his colleagues, though ministers of a Habsburg emperor, were revolutionary in home affairs— more so indeed than Louis Napoleon who had only to conserve the fruits of a revolution carried out sixty years before. Frederick William IV, though a Hohenzollern, had the same romantic cast of mind as Louis Napoleon—dreaming great things, shrinking from carrying them out, and in practical outcome very much of a conspirator. The events of 1848 had destroyed for good the stable fragility of Metternich's German Confederation; after 1848 both Prussia and Austria were 'on the make'. Schwarzenberg was persuaded by Bruck, his minister of commerce, to promote 'the Empire of seventy millions', by which the whole of the Austrian Empire should be united with the German Confederation; then Austria would dominate Germany and, through Germany, Europe. Frederick William IV, on his side, was bewitched by the idea of a 'narrower' and a 'wider' German confederation—the first, excluding all the Austrian lands, a real union under Prussia; the second a vague alliance with the Habsburg monarchy. Both projects were revolutionary, involving an upheaval in Germany; yet the rulers of Austria and Prussia strove to achieve them without appealing to German sentiment, that is, without using revolutionary means. For instance, the scheme for a narrower and a wider Confederation had been launched by Gagern and the moderate liberals of Frankfurt; but Frederick William took it up only when it was presented to him in a romantic, conservative form by Radowitz, a Roman Catholic noble and his boyhood friend.

The plans of Radowitz and Schwarzenberg both involved a destruction of the Balance of Power as it had been established at the congress of Vienna. Germany, whether united under Austria or under Prussia, would be a more formidable neighbour to France than the impotent German Confederation. German strength might guarantee Austria's hold in Italy, might even—as the radicals of 1848 had demanded—grasp at Alsace. Since the German Confederation seemed beyond restoration, even the most conservative Frenchmen were tempted to play one rival against the other. In April 1849 Drouyn de Lhuys said that France would welcome the aggrandizement of Prussia if this involved the destruction of the Holy Alliance:[1] yet the Holy Alliance, the union of the 'three Northern Courts', had given France more than thirty years of security on her eastern frontier. But the projected upheaval in Germany was not directed only against France. Both Bruck's and Gagern's plans were designed to make German influence supreme in the valley of the Danube, in the Balkans, and therefore ultimately at the Straits and in the Black Sea. Bruck's 'Empire of seventy millions' was intended as preliminary to a customs union which should embrace all Europe between the frontiers of France and Russia. Gagern said of his projects for German unity, in words that were endorsed by Radowitz: 'It is not enough to warm ourselves at our own firesides. We want a unity that can incorporate, like satellites in our planetary system, all the peoples in the Danube basin who have neither ability nor claim to independence.'[2]

---

[1] Meinecke, *Radowitz und die deutsche Revolution*, p. 255.
[2] Meinecke, *Radowitz*, p. 191. The view that Germany should dominate the

All plans for German unity were essentially anti-Russian. The dilemma of Russia was that if, to defend herself against liberal plans for unity, she aided Schwarzenberg and Frederick William IV, this would promote the same plans in more ruthless form. One element in Germany hated these plans: had no desire to bar the way against Russia in the Near East and little desire to quarrel with France in Italy or even on the Rhine. This was the Prussian gentry—the Junkers, who supplied Prussia with its army officers, with many of its administrators and with some of its statesmen. The Junkers hated Austria and disliked German nationalism; they had strong links of class with Tsarist Russia and a common hostility to the Poles. In personal terms they regarded Radowitz as a foreigner and Frederick William IV as mentally unbalanced, which indeed he was. The struggle in Germany in 1849 and 1850 was therefore as much a struggle between Radowitz and the Junkers for the soul of Frederick William as a conflict between Prussia and Austria.

The events of the early part of 1849 cleared the ground for the struggle over Germany. They demonstrated the principle, shown afresh after 1863, that—once Poland, Italy, and the Near East were out of the way—all energy would go into the German question. Affairs in Italy were much in the nature of an epilogue. The danger of a French intervention had disappeared in September 1848 and was not renewed by the election of Louis Napoleon: his line was 'to play himself in', to establish his standing as a guardian of order and the *status quo* before revealing the conspirator beneath. The mediating Powers, Great Britain and France, were pledged to promote a peace conference at Brussels between Sardinia and Austria; but Schwarzenberg would not authorize Austrian attendance at the conference, unless the mediating Powers would commit themselves against any territorial changes. Both refused. Louis Napoleon, though hostile to Sardinian ambition, could not begin his public life by endorsing a frontier of 1815; besides, he could never renounce an opportunity of manœuvre. Palmerston, though admitting that Austria could not be expected to surrender territory, would not make a declaration which would drive Sardinia to despair. The deadlock had much the same

peoples of eastern Europe was, of course ,shared by the German radicals, including Marx and Engels.

result. The Sardinian chamber was dominated by radical opinion; and in March 1849 Charles Albert was driven to renew the war against Austria. Within a week he was defeated at Novara (23 Mar.) and abdicated. Once more there were Italian appeals to Paris, once more rumours of French intervention.

But revolutionary policy was over, and Bonapartist policy had not begun. Palmerston, more firmly restrained by the cabinet than in August 1848, refused to support any French action; and the French had no enthusiasm to act. Schwarzenberg, on his side, knew that he must respect the independence of Sardinia, in order to keep the French out of northern Italy. The peace negotiations turned therefore solely on the size of the indemnity which Sardinia should pay; and, after an occasional alarm, peace was made at Milan on 6 August on the basis of the *status quo*. Though Austria had triumphed, she received a setback in the moment of victory. Victor Emanuel, who had succeeded to the Sardinian throne on his father's abdication, was certainly determined to subdue Sardinian radicalism; when the chamber refused to ratify the treaty of peace, he dissolved it, appealed to moderate opinion in the proclamation of Moncalieri (20 Nov.) and was rewarded by the election of a chamber which ratified the treaty in silence by 112 votes to 17 (9 Jan. 1850). But Victor Emanuel was not drawn into the Austrian system. A soldier and a man of action, not a dreamer like his father, he was humiliated by military defeat and meant to renew the war against Austria in more favourable circumstances. Hence, despite his authoritarian character, he maintained the Constitution granted by his father and even favoured the Sardinian liberals. In his way Victor Emanuel too was one of the new realists, another who would pursue revolutionary aims while seeking to avoid revolutionary means.

Italy produced one last strange outcome from the year of revolutions. Rome had turned against the pope only in November 1848 and had become a republic, under Triumvirs led by Mazzini, only in February 1849. With the second defeat of Sardinia, intervention against the Roman republic was expected from Austria, from Naples, or even from Spain. The French government decided to anticipate these interventions by intervening itself; its prime motive was undoubtedly to challenge the Austrian monopoly in Italy. As most of the ministers were former Orleanists, they supposed they were echoing the French occupation of Ancona in 1832. Louis Napoleon acquiesced in the decision of his government in a general spirit of speculation: it is impossible to know whether his original intention was to save the republic or to restore the pope. General Oudinot, with a detachment of the army of the Alps, which had been originally designed to liberate northern Italy and later to protect the republic of Venice, was dispatched to Roman territory; on 30 April his forces clashed with the republican troops led by Garibaldi. The first military action of revolutionary France after thirty-four years of apprehension was taken against a republic led and defended by idealists, and in favour of the most obscurantist tyranny in Europe. There was an outcry in the French national assembly against this betrayal of republican principle; and a special representative, de Lesseps, was sent to negotiate with Mazzini. On 31 May they reached agreement, by which the Roman republic accepted the protection of France. But Louis Napoleon had felt the humiliation to French arms, implied in the check at the gates of Rome, more deeply than the betrayal of republicanism; and besides, the elections to the new legislative assembly in France (13 May) returned an anti-republican, clericalist majority. Reinforcements and orders for energetic action were sent to Oudinot; he repudiated de Lesseps's treaty and launched a full-scale attack which brought about the fall of the Roman republic at the end of June.

The result was most unwelcome to Louis Napoleon, despite the clericalist support which it brought him in France. His first action in foreign affairs had been to restore the temporal power of the pope, against which he himself had conspired in 1831. He attempted to dissociate himself from the papal reaction by blaming his ministers and by publishing a letter of protest which he wrote to his adjutant Edgar Ney in August. It was useless to recommend lay administration and the Napoleonic code, unless these could be enforced by threats; and Louis Napoleon could not use the threat to withdraw from Rome either now or afterwards. Louis Napoleon's Roman policy, throughout his reign, showed his methods at their worst: a revolutionary aim, in this case, the satisfying of Italian feeling over Rome, without the use of revolutionary means, that is, without a breach with the pope. When one state is completely

dependent on another, it is the weaker which can call the tune:
it can threaten to collapse unless supported, and its protector
has no answering threat to return. Louis Napoleon became and
remained the prisoner of papal policy; and perhaps nothing did
more to drive him towards adventure elsewhere than the self-
reproach caused by the Roman blunder.

A greater radical state than Rome was also reduced in the
summer of 1849; and intervention on a greater scale followed
the French example. In the preceding winter it had seemed that
the Austrian army would make easy headway in Hungary, the
last centre of disaffection in the Habsburg monarchy. The hope
was disappointed. In April 1849 the Austrian forces were once
more expelled from Hungary; the Habsburgs were declared
deposed; and Hungary became an independent state with
Kossuth as governor. Hungary had tried to win the support of
liberal Europe in the previous year, while still nominally part
of the Austrian empire; these appeals met with a friendly response only from the German national assembly at Frankfurt,
and in any case liberal Germany needed support from Hungary
rather than being able to offer it. The appeals were now
renewed under less favourable circumstances. France, which
had failed to do anything for Poland or for Italy, and which
was now engaged in suppressing the Roman republic, could not
be expected to act for a cause less known and more remote;
Palmerston never varied from the doctrine that the preservation of the Austrian empire was essential to the Balance of
Power. All Kossuth secured was an alliance with the republic
of Venice, itself on the point of dissolution.

Schwarzenberg, on the other hand, was able at last to display
the Holy Alliance in action, though a Holy Alliance without
Prussia. In May 1849 Prussia indeed offered her help against
the Hungarian revolution; there was a price attached—that
Austria should recognize Prussia's supremacy in the 'narrower'
Germany. Schwarzenberg was, however, concerned to restore
Austrian greatness so that she could recover her place in Germany, not so that she should abdicate it. His negative response
first showed the dual nature of Austro-Prussian relations:
despite their sympathy and common interests in European
affairs, they were in ceaseless conflict within Germany. When
Germany was tranquil, as before 1848, there was a genuine
Austro-Prussian solidarity; when Germany was in turmoil, both

Powers put Europe and even their own international interests in the background. Even in the dangerous circumstances of May 1849 Schwarzenberg rejected an alliance with Prussia against 'the revolution', rather than yield anything to her German ambitions. There was a further, and decisive, factor. While Prussia demanded a price in Germany for her help, Russia did not demand a price in the Near East. The tsar offered help against 'the revolution' without conditions. The prime motive of this offer was undoubtedly conservative solidarity; the tsar and his ministers had talked so much of their principles that they could scarcely avoid acting on them. Till now, they had been restrained by fear of provoking French action elsewhere; in Nesselrode's words, non-intervention had been the price which Russia had had to pay in order to keep France neutral.[1] The French intervention at Rome belatedly freed Russian hands. The fates of Italy and Hungary were, as often, intertwined. Nicholas I recognized the French republic on 8 May, the day on which he announced his intervention in Hungary.

Of course there were practical considerations behind Russia's action. The greatest of these was apprehension for Poland: many Polish exiles were fighting in the Hungarian army, and its two best generals were Poles.[2] If the Hungarians were victorious, the revolution would spread at least to Galicia, Austria's share of Poland; and the whole Polish question would soon be reopened. There was apprehension, too, for Russian interests in Turkey: the Russians did not wish the revolutionary example to spread from Hungary to the Danubian principalities, Moldavia and Wallachia. In July 1848 Russian troops had occupied these two principalities, on the first stirrings of a revolutionary movement there; and on 1 May 1849, at the moment of intervening in Hungary, Russia concluded a treaty with Turkey, providing for a joint occupation of the principalities until order was restored. Thus Russian action in Hungary was designed to protect her interests at the mouth of the Danube; and Russian troops remained in the principalities until the beginning of 1851.

More generally still, the Russians acted in order to preserve Austria as a Great Power and so to restore the balance in Germany. This was not a Russian 'option' for Austria; the object

---

[1] Nesselrode to Meyendorff, 1 April 1849. *Lettres et papiers*, ix. 228.
[2] So also was the general who commanded the Sardinian army in the Novara campaign.

was to restore the German balance, not to overthrow it. On 28 April, as an essential part of the diplomatic preparations for intervening in Hungary, Nicholas wrote to Frederick William IV, promising him support against the German radicals, on condition that he withdrew altogether from the Sleswick affair;[1] and at the same time Nesselrode insisted to Schwarzenberg on the need for Austrian co-operation with Prussia.[2] Russia was equally opposed to the Austrian and the Prussian plans for uniting Germany; she alone wished to see restored the system of Metternich. This judgement sprang primarily from anxiety over Poland and from the natural dislike of having a mighty neighbour. So far as the Near East was concerned, the Russians rather casually assumed that Austria would be too weak and too dependent on them to bar the way against Russian plans, if indeed these ever matured. No doubt the Russians counted vaguely on Austrian gratitude; though in international affairs there is no way by which a Power can assure future reward in exchange for a present service. Later, in 1854, when the Eastern question dominated the European scene, Russia was held to have committed a supreme blunder in restoring Austria, the principal obstacle to her success.

The judgement posed a false choice. The alternative to supporting Habsburg absolutism was a great national Hungary and, probably, a great national Germany, not the disintegration of the Austrian empire into impotent fragments. In the Crimean war Austria repaid Russia with a malevolent neutrality. In 1878, when the defeat of Kossuth had been undone and when Andrássy, Kossuth's associate, directed Habsburg policy, Austria-Hungary threatened war; and in 1914, when German and Hungarian nationalism were supreme in central Europe, Russia had to fight a war for existence—a war repeated under still less favourable circumstances in 1941. Still, these were distant calculations. The Russian rulers, like the statesmen of other countries, judged according to the moment, not in terms of far-fetched schemes. In 1849 they thought only of Poland and Germany; with their troops actually in the principalities, they were not likely to worry about the future of the Eastern question. On the other hand, Palmerston, to whom

[1] Nicholas I to Frederick William IV, 28 Apr., 1849. *Meyendorff*, ii, no. 291.
[2] Nesselrode to Medem (Russian ambassador to Austria), 30 Apr. 1849. *Meyendorff*, ii, no. 292.

Poland meant nothing and Germany very little, thought of
Austria and Russia exclusively in terms of the Near East; and
it is therefore not surprising that, despite his liberal principles,
he welcomed Russia's action in restoring Austria as a Great
Power. His motives are obvious; and it is certainly not necessary
to argue that he was a hypocrite who secretly favoured the
victory of reaction or even, more crudely, that he was in
Russian pay.[1]

The Russian forces entered Hungary in May; they were completely successful by the middle of August. Kossuth and his
principal supporters escaped to Turkey. The intervention had
been carried through without any difficulties from the western
Powers; and the Russians could congratulate themselves that
they had restored the system of the Holy Alliance without provoking a new liberal alliance in return. This success was ruined
by a Russian blunder, itself caused by an echo from Poland,
always Russia's blind spot. Nicholas had preached clemency for
the defeated Hungarians and much resented the Austrian
measures of repression. But among the refugees in Turkey were
four outstanding Poles (and some 800 others). On 6 September
1849 the tsar demanded the extradition of the four Polish
generals; Austria followed suit by demanding the extradition of
4,000 Hungarians. When the demands were refused, the Russian
and Austrian ambassadors broke off relations. The Eastern
question seemed to be reopened. The Turks played the crisis with
their customary adroitness. On the one hand they appealed for
support to Stratford Canning and to General Aupick, the French
ambassador; and they were not disappointed. On the other
hand, they secretly appealed to the tsar by dispatching a
special envoy, Fuad Effendi, long a Russian favourite; here,
too, they were not disappointed. Nicholas had recovered from
his anti-Polish outburst; instead he was infuriated by the
Austrian execution on 6 October of thirteen Hungarian generals,
most of whom had surrendered to the Russian army. On
16 October Fuad and Nesselrode reached an amicable conclusion; Austria, deserted by Russia, had to give way in her turn.
But meanwhile both Great Britain and France had been

[1] The latter is a contemporary version launched by Karl Marx in his newspaper
articles, collected as *The Eastern Question*. He learnt it from the pro-Turk lunatic
David Urquhart. Present-day Marxism favours the more sophisticated first explanation. The only ground for it is that, according to Russian reports, Palmerston said
that if the Russians were going to act in Hungary, they should act quickly.

forced into action. On 29 September, when Stratford Canning's appeal reached London, Palmerston wrote to Lord John Russell: 'With a little manly firmness we shall successfully get through this matter.' After his Italian experiences, Palmerston was afraid that 'the Broadbrims of the Cabinet' would restrain him; but for once the cabinet agreed on action—liberal sympathy with the refugees combined with apprehension over the Near East to overcome pacificism and timidity. On 6 October the Mediterranean fleet was instructed to proceed to the neighbourhood of the Dardanelles. Even more important was the response from France. In June Louis Napoleon had escaped from the control of the Party of Order, who had won the elections, by calling in some of the moderate republicans, who had lost it. Among these, Alexis de Tocqueville had become foreign minister. Like many daring thinkers, Tocqueville was timid when it came to action. He had diagnosed the decline of France and perhaps exaggerated it; at any rate he was the first Frenchman to advocate that a great united Germany should be built up to protect France against Russia—a view so gloomy that it won acceptance in France only in 1942.[1] Besides, Tocqueville was resentful that Palmerston had refused to respond to a hysterical proposal for supporting Sardinia which Tocqueville had made, from anxiety and inexperience, in July. Tocqueville therefore proposed to refuse to co-operate with the British in the Near East; and he supported his refusal with an argument which was later often employed against any determined action by France as a Great Power: 'England would risk her fleet, we our existence.' But when he arrived at the council of ministers, he found that Louis Napoleon had made up his mind and that the order to the French Mediterranean fleet had already gone.[2] The Anglo-French alliance of the Crimean war was born in October 1849. The decision revealed Louis Napoleon's character. Schwarzenberg might talk of their common interest in restoring order, Nicholas I of his sympathy for the republic; these were gestures, mere words. Great Britain offered action; and only action could overthrow the settlement of the congress of Vienna. Though British interest in action was confined to the

[1] The full text of Tocqueville's *Souvenirs* was first published in 1942 (English translation 1948).

[2] Tocqueville attributed the President's decision to the influence of his mistress, Miss Howard. This attribution of unworthy motives (in this case unfounded, as Tocqueville later admitted) is characteristic of the intellectual in politics.

Near East, as events were to show, an Anglo-French alliance cemented there would free Louis Napoleon's hands for action elsewhere. Russian restlessness in the Near East—or rather suspicion of this restlessness—opened the door to a general reconstruction of Europe.

The Near Eastern crisis of October 1849 was shortlived. Nicholas had already withdrawn his demands on Turkey before the British and French fleets moved. Though he had had unofficial warning of the Anglo-French action, he could claim to have yielded spontaneously from generosity. In more ways than one the crisis ended in Russia's favour. On 1 November Admiral Parker, commanding the British squadron, entered the Dardanelles, under stress of weather, for shelter; though he did not 'pass' the Straits, this was a forced interpretation of the Convention of 1841. Palmerston at once apologized, in order not to set a precedent by which the Russian fleet, always near at hand, might enter the Bosphorus; and Nesselrode regarded this sealing of the Dardanelles as a triumph.[1] Moreover, in November, during the crisis, the Turks proposed a formal defensive alliance with Great Britain. Palmerston refused. Turkey, he believed, must build up her own strength, if she was to merit foreign aid. Besides, he still had faith in Nicholas's professions of conservative principle. At the end of 1849, Bloomfield, British ambassador in Russia, wrote: 'I think we may reasonably expect that at all events during the reign of the Emperor Nicholas no attempt will be made by Russia to subvert the Ottoman Empire.'[2] Finally, an impulsive action by Palmerston disrupted the growing Anglo-French alliance and almost put a Franco-Russian alliance in its place. In January 1850 Admiral Parker, on his way back from the Dardanelles, called in at Athens to enforce the dubious claims of a British subject, Don Pacifico. Greece appealed to France and Russia, the two other protecting powers (by the treaty of London in 1832). Palmerston behaved impatiently, and his representative in Athens even more so. The Russians wisely left France to take the lead; and when Palmerston refused French mediation, Drouyn de Lhuys, at this time French ambassador, was withdrawn from London. By the time the sordid business was settled (26 Apr. 1850) not much was left of the alliance of 'the liberal Powers'.

[1] Nesselrode to Nicholas I, 20 Nov. 1850, *Lettres et papiers*, x. 6.
[2] Bloomfield to Palmerston, no. 37, 24 Jan. 1850, F.O. 65/276

It was Germany, however, which seemed to show Russian security and predominance at its greatest. Prussia had wasted the opportunity of Austrian distractions in Italy and Hungary. Frederick William was all along the determining factor in Prussian policy; and his determination was contradictory. He wanted a united Germany, with himself at its head; and he wanted this with Austrian agreement. His impossible dream was that Austria should abdicate voluntarily; sooner than give up the dream he would give up the reality. Thus, one of his reasons for breaking with his liberal ministers in November 1848 was their proposal to support Sardinian claims against Austria in the abortive conference at Brussels; yet in essence Prussia and Sardinia had similar aims. Again in April 1849, he refused the German crown when it was offered to him by the Frankfurt parliament; yet immediately afterwards tried to obtain it by the free agreement of the German princes. In May 1849 the German princes, threatened by radical revolts, would have agreed to anything. Radowitz took on the task of achieving German unity on a conservative basis. He drafted a German constitution and concluded the Alliance of the Three Kings with Hanover and Saxony (28 May). This, like all later attempts at unification by agreement, was nullified by a reserve: Saxony and Hanover insisted that negotiations must begin anew if agreement could not be reached with Bavaria and Austria.

Still worse, Prussia drifted once more into the affair of the Elbe duchies. In March 1849 the Danes had denounced the armistice and renewed the war. Prussia was in an absurd position in that, though trying to stand aside, there was a Prussian contingent with the federal forces and that these forces were commanded by a Prussian general. Both Russia and Great Britain renewed their pressure on Prussia—Russia by sending a fleet to Danish waters, Great Britain by the threat to stand aside if Prussia were attacked by Russia and France. Both threats were empty. The tsar did not intend 'to drive Frederick William blindly into the arms of the German party'; in any case his forces were fully absorbed by the intervention in Hungary. France was taken up with the intervention in Rome; and her government was far too unstable to be an attractive ally for Russia or even for Great Britain. But once again Russian disapproval was too much for Frederick William. Prussia gave way and signed a further armistice, still more favourable to the

Danes, on 10 July 1849. Prussia had been again discredited in German eyes. Moreover, Palmerston was permanently estranged. Though he recognized that Germany under Prussia 'would be the best solution and a solid barrier between the great Powers of the continent',[1] he was indignant at Frederick William's behaviour: instead of going against British interests in Sleswick, Prussia ought to have united Germany on a liberal basis.

By August 1849, when Hungary was subdued, Prussia had missed her chance. Schwarzenberg would have liked to move against her at once; but he was uncertain of Russia and even of Francis Joseph, who had a family meeting with Frederick William at Teplitz, on 9 September. He therefore offered a compromise by which Austria and Prussia should jointly administer the German Confederation until 1 May 1850; and Bernstorff, the Prussian minister at Vienna, accepted this 'interim' on his own initiative on 30 September. Bernstorff supposed that Schwarzenberg had agreed to 'the decisive hegemony of Prussia in northern and central Germany'.[2] In reality Schwarzenberg had merely postponed the struggle until a more favourable moment—the first of many occasions on which one side or the other papered over the cracks. Prussian policy continued to follow Bernstorff's delusion. Radowitz developed the limited Union under Prussia; he forced a constitution through the Union parliament at Erfurt, and in May 1850 held a grandiose, though futile, congress of German princes at Berlin. Schwarzenberg answered, when the interim ran out, by proposing to summon the old Federal Diet at Frankfurt. Once more the tsar was called in. At the end of May 1850 Prince William of Prussia and Schwarzenberg both visited Nicholas at Warsaw. Nicholas repeated his former themes: instead of quarrelling, Austria and Prussia should repudiate their constitutions and unite against the revolution; Prussia should make peace with Denmark; he would support whichever was attacked. Moreover, 'the aggressor is not always the one who attacks, but the one who causes the quarrel'; and he would favour whichever Power was nearest to the treaties (though he characteristically added that he did not understand what these were).

---

[1] So he told Drouyn de Lhuys rather tactlessly on 27 July 1849. Guichen, *Les grandes questions européennes*, i. 367.

[2] Ringhoffer, *Im Kampf um Preußens Ehre*, p. 113.

Since Schwarzenberg had never operated the Austrian con-stitution of March 1849, and now meant to repudiate it, he had the best of the argument. Nicholas even said that he would have no objection to 'the Empire of seventy millions', if Prussia agreed to it. Still this was not an option for Austria; it was the old insistence on compromise.

Prussia so far followed the tsar's advice as to make peace with Denmark on 2 July. Schwarzenberg, on his side, produced a plausible compromise: he would divide Germany with Prussia, on condition Frederick William abandoned the Erfurt Union and destroyed the Prussian constitution. This was prob-ably little more than conservative window-dressing to please the tsar. At this very time Schwarzenberg asked the tsar's per-mission to annex the county of Glatz (lost by Austria to Prussia in 1742) and is said to have been 'furious' when it was refused.[1] Much as Frederick William disliked the Prussian constitution, he would not renounce it on Austrian bidding. The decisive crisis seemed to be approaching. The underlying issue was, of course, whether Austria or Prussia should dominate Germany; the occasion was given by Holstein and by Hesse—the one a point of some importance, the other a trumpery quarrel. The Elbe duchies had continued to resist the Danes, even when abandoned by Prussia; when Sleswick was finally reduced, resistance continued in Holstein. The Danes played the German Confederation against the Germans of Holstein; that is, since Holstein was a member of the German Confederation, the king of Denmark asked for a 'federal execution' against his rebellious subjects. Austria had revived the German Confederation, Prussia stood aloof from it; therefore federal execution would mean Austrian troops in north Germany, very much Prussia's 'sphere of interest'. Hesse was a simpler matter—one of the usual German squabbles between a petty prince and his estates. The elector had been a member of the Prussian Union, but had slipped over to the Confederation and asked also for federal execution; apart from the conflict of authorities, this touched Prussia on a sensitive point, for the Prussian military road, con-necting Rhenish Prussia with the rest of the kingdom, ran through Hesse. Both sides made gestures of war. On 26 Septem-ber 1850 Radowitz—the only man who believed wholeheartedly in the line that Prussia had followed—became Prussian foreign

[1] Srbik, *Deutsche Einheit*, ii. 50.

minister; on 12 October Schwarzenberg concluded a war-alliance with the kings of Bavaria and Württemberg.

In July 1850 the three Great Powers outside Germany—France, Great Britain, and Russia—had signed a protocol, recognizing the Danish rule of inheritance in the duchies;[1] Prussia estranged all three by her equivocal policy. This might not have been decisive, if Frederick William had been willing to manœuvre between the Powers. Certainly Louis Napoleon was eager enough to promote trouble in Germany. As early as November 1849 he had suggested to the tsar that Russia should turn her back on Germany and concentrate on the Near East, her real centre of interest: Russia might have Constantinople, Great Britain would content herself with Egypt, and France would find compensation on the Rhine.[2] As the tsar did not respond favourably, Louis Napoleon tried Prussia. In January 1850 he sent his personal friend and fellow conspirator, Persigny, to Berlin. Persigny was well described as 'travelling in imperialism'. He spoke approvingly of Prussia's 'revolutionary' course and hinted at French support in exchange for territory on the Rhine. Later, in June, Louis Napoleon himself told Hatzfeldt, the Prussian minister, that it would be impossible for France to stay neutral if Russia intervened and that he would support whichever German power offered him the most; he too pointed at the Bavarian palatinate. He received the answer that was to be so often repeated: Prussia could not win the leadership of Germany at the price of surrendering German territory to France. Schwarzenberg was less scrupulous: he told the French representative that he would have no objection to surrendering Rhenish Prussia to France in exchange for an agreement over German affairs.[3] Perhaps Schwarzenberg, like Bismarck later, believed in playing on Louis Napoleon's greed; but his hint showed a reality—Austria was in truth more indifferent to German opinion. Louis Napoleon did not respond to Austria's offer; when he aspired to a 'revolutionary' policy, he had to

[1] It is suggested by Precht (*Englands Stellung zur deutschen Einheit*) that Palmerston signed the protocol as a sort of apology for his bad behaviour over Don Pacifico in Greece. This, though an ingenious linking-up of the German and Eastern questions, ignores the fact that the duchies were themselves a British interest.

[2] So Nicholas told Rauch, the Prussian military plenipotentiary. No doubt therefore he exaggerated the story in order to frighten the Prussians into conservatism.

[3] De la Cour (Vienna) to de la Hitte, 26 Aug. 1850.

make it with a 'revolutionary' Power. This was exactly the role which Frederick William rejected. In his own dithyrambic words: 'I shall never use revolutionary means, never make an alliance with France or Sardinia, never associate with Reds or Gotha-ers,[1] with murderers of Kings and makers of Emperors.'[2] Here was the dilemma; so far as French politicians did not come under Frederick William's elegant description, they had no interest in supporting Prussian expansion. In October 1850 French conservative diplomats were concentrating on Holstein, in order to restore good relations with Great Britain, shaken by the Greek affair. Drouyn de Lhuys in London even proposed a triple alliance of France, Russia, and Great Britain to restore order in Holstein—a proposal evaded, though for different reasons, both by Palmerston and by the tsar.

Thus partly from force of circumstance, partly from lack of will, Prussia remained isolated; and the more vulnerable in that the policy of Radowitz was repugnant to the majority of Prussian ministers. Once more there was an appeal to the tsar. Schwarzenberg went to Warsaw in order to obtain a free hand against Prussia. Brandenburg, the Prussian prime minister, went to accept belatedly Schwarzenberg's offer of July: parity in Germany, in exchange for Prussia's adopting the reactionary course. This was not a surrender on Brandenburg's part: conservative though proud, he was anxious for foreign help in order to rescue Frederick William (of whom he was the illegitimate uncle) from his infatuation with Radowitz. The opportunity had passed, if it had ever existed. What tipped the scale was a report that Radowitz had threatened war if federal troops entered Hesse: in the tsar's eyes, this was the act of aggression against which he had promised to take sides. On 28 October Nesselrode and Schwarzenberg agreed, by an exchange of notes, that Russia would give Austria moral support if Prussia opposed federal execution in Hesse; and that she would regard Prussian resistance in Holstein as a *casus belli* for herself. To the end, Prussia's position was bedevilled by her equivocations over the Elbe duchies.

Brandenburg returned to Berlin. On 2 November the Prussian council of ministers, following his lead, decided by a majority

---

[1] The liberal supporters of Heinrich von Gagern.

[2] Frederick William IV to Bunsen, 14 Nov. 1850. Poschinger, *Preußens auswärtige Politik 1850–1858*, i. 18.

to give way and to negotiate further with Austria. Radowitz resigned; and, on the sudden death of Brandenburg, Manteuffel, who was at once more conservative and more timid, was put in charge of foreign affairs.[1] The decision was determined essentially by the lack of conviction, which had all along confused Prussian policy; this confusion was now hidden under excuses of weakness. But Prince William, who understood military affairs, insisted that Prussia was the stronger; and this opinion was shared by the Russian generals who had seen the Austrian army engaged in Hungary. Paskievich, the Russian commander-in-chief, even believed that Prussia would be a match for Russia and Austria combined.[2] All reports agree that there was enthusiasm for war in Prussia, none in Austria; this very fact made the war repugnant to Frederick William and his ministers. It was irrelevant that the Prussian army was superior in number and perhaps in fighting quality to that of Austria and her associates; what was lacking in Berlin was the fighting will. Yet, having decided to surrender, Frederick William and his ministers wanted that impossibility, a surrender with honour. On 6 November the Prussian army was mobilized. Two days later four Austrian soldiers were wounded, and a Prussian horse killed, at Bronzell in Hesse; it was the first time Austria and Prussia had exchanged shots since 1778. Radowitz was sent to London, more to console him than with any serious purpose. He was empowered to offer the British government reductions in the Zollverein tariff in exchange for an alliance—certainly a crude appeal to British materialism. Radowitz had, of course, no success. He found the British ministers impatient over Holstein, and the more liberal of them angry that Frederick William had not led the constitutional movement in Germany. Palmerston said that he would not co-operate with Prussia unless France made a third—in view of the French attitude, no doubt merely an adroit excuse. For on 12 November Louis Napoleon opened the French legislative assembly with a presidential message that France would remain neutral in German affairs unless the treaties of 1815 were threatened—strange condition in the mouth of a Bonaparte. It was little consolation against this that Louis Napoleon prompted anonymous newspaper articles in favour of Prussia. Though the 'liberal alliance'

---

[1] He became prime minister and foreign minister in December after his return from Olomouc.　　　[2] Schiemann, *Kaiser Nikolaus*, iv. 226.

did nothing to stiffen Prussia, it was not altogether fruitless. Apprehension of it helped to force Schwarzenberg towards compromise.[1] Moreover the movement of French troops in Alsace, slight as it was,[2] inspired Frederick William with the idea of a conservative crusade against France[3] and thus gave him a rival enthusiasm to the admiration for Radowitz, which still lurked in his mind.

The way was clear for Manteuffel's policy of surrender. He urged a personal meeting on Schwarzenberg; and on 27 November Schwarzenberg accepted. The outcome of the meeting was the agreement of Olomouc[4] on 29 November. Peaceful solution is said, on doubtful authority, to have been forced on Schwarzenberg by the young Emperor Francis Joseph; it is more significant that Meyendorff, now Russian ambassador at Vienna, attended the meeting and composed a commemorative plaque for the house in which it took place.[5] The essence of Russian policy had been an insistence that both Austria and Prussia should return to the treaty settlement of 1815; and once Prussia was prepared to give way Austria would have become the 'aggressor' if she had demanded more. In fact, Frederick William's subservient letters had already alarmed the Tsar that Prussia might destroy the German balance by giving way too much. In any case Schwarzenberg had all along been more concerned to defeat Prussia's projects in Germany than to promote Austrian ones which were those of the ex-radicals in his ministry rather than his own. The agreement of Olomouc was therefore purely negative. Prussia gave up the Erfurt Union, agreed to federal execution in Hesse and ultimately in Holstein, and returned to the old Confederation; the plans for including the entire Austrian empire were left to 'free conferences' at Dresden. This was a return without enthusiasm or belief to the old order. Prussia had accepted without war the conditions which it took Austria two campaigns to force upon Sardinia. If, following the Sardinian pattern, Frederick William had abdicated, his brother William would no doubt have taken the path of military resentment and perhaps even of liberalism. As

[1] Meyendorff to Nesselrode, 27 Nov. 1850. *Meyendorff*, ii, no. 363.

[2] 40,000 men in November; it was intended to increase this to 60,000 by December and to have 80,000 to 115,000 by the New Year.

[3] Frederick William IV to Francis Joseph, 26 Nov. 1850. *Preußens auswärtige Politik 1850–1858*, i. 31.

[4] Obsolcte German name: Olmütz.   [5] *Meyendorff*, ii, no. 365.

it was, Frederick William spent the rest of his reign repenting the sins that led to Olomouc, not the humiliation that took place there.

The limits of Austria's success were shown in the new year when the conference on German affairs met at Dresden. Prussia would not agree to the incorporation of all Austria in the Confederation; and she was supported by the smaller states. It was useless this time for Schwarzenberg to appeal to the tsar; though Nicholas was prepared to accept anything on which Austria and Prussia agreed, he would not dictate agreement. Firm protest against modifying the settlement of 1815 came from France, a protest seconded by Great Britain. Louis Napoleon even sent a special envoy to St. Petersburg to enlist Russian support. Once more Nicholas took the conciliatory line: though he would not join the French protest, he was annoyed at the Anglo-French co-operation which Austrian policy had provoked and warned Schwarzenberg that he must not count on Russian support if France went to war.[1] In March 1851 Manteuffel discovered an acceptable compromise. Prussia was anxious to co-operate with Austria in European affairs, though determined not to yield anything of her German position; hence, while refusing the inclusion of the Austrian empire in Germany, Manteuffel proposed a secret alliance which should guarantee the whole of Austrian territory. After some delay, Schwarzenberg accepted: the project of including the Empire in the German confederation was primarily a matter of domestic politics, to display that Austria was entirely a German state, and Schwarzenberg did not trouble much about these internal questions.

The Austro-Prussian alliance, signed on 16 May, was essentially an alliance against 'the revolution'. Frederick William even wished to include in the preamble that it was directed against the danger of new convulsions in France and against 'the general upheaval which may be brought about by the not improbable attempts of the revolutionary party throughout Europe'.[2] Schwarzenberg did not favour this reflection on Louis Napoleon's stability; and the alliance was concluded in general terms, to last three years. Though it sprang from Prussian

---

[1] Nesselrode to Meyendorff, 16 Mar., 12 Apr., 1851. *Lettres et papiers*, x. 34, 40; Bapst, *Origines de la guerre de Crimée*, pp. 188–90.
[2] Frederick William IV to Manteuffel, 24 Apr. 1851. *Preußens auswärtige Politik 1850–1858*, i. 155.

initiative, the alliance was sheer gain for Austria. 'The revolution' disturbed Frederick William's conscience; it threatened Austria's existence. In practical terms the alliance was simply a Prussian guarantee of Austria's territory in Italy; Austria was incapable of providing a similar guarantee for Prussian territory on the Rhine, even if Prussia had required one. The alliance sprang from concrete need on the one side, from emotional principle on the other—always a shaky basis for international co-operation. Even Frederick William recognized this when he limited the alliance to three years; by then he would have atoned for his revolutionary sins, and his conscience would be clear.

The Austro-Prussian alliance seemed a revival of the Holy Alliance, more effective than the original. It was a revival with a difference. Nicholas refused to make a third in the alliance, so as not to provoke a western alliance in return; he would not even agree to a meeting of the three rulers.[1] In his own words, he would not repeat the blunder of Münchengrätz in 1833, which had provoked Palmerston's Quadruple Alliance of 1834. Thus Nicholas carried a stage farther the attitude which he had taken up at the outbreak of the revolutions of 1848: though he welcomed Austria and Prussia as a buffer against France, he would not go to their assistance. Besides, the abject failure of the Polish movement seemed to give Russia unchecked freedom of action: there was no need for her to join a revived Holy Alliance against a danger which had proved so trivial. All that remained of Münchengrätz, so far as Russia was concerned, was the promise not to disturb the *status quo* in the Near East; and this promise had been the counterpart for help in Poland which was no longer required. Nicholas and his advisers had no conscious or defined aims in the Near East; they merely assumed that the situation had changed radically in their favour. The revolution had been defeated; the Austro-Prussian alliance checked France in Italy; yet Austria, on her side, was checked by the danger from the revolution and from France. The new Balance seemed to work exclusively for Russia: the powers of Europe cancelled each other out, and Russia was left with a free hand in the Near East. Certainly Nicholas assumed that he would have to bargain either with France or with Great

[1] Nicholas met Frederick William at Warsaw, and Francis Joseph at Olomouc in May; Frederick William and Francis Joseph met at Ischl in August.

Britain; a principal factor in his remaining out of the Austro-Prussian alliance was his conviction that he could 'do business' with Louis Napoleon. But Nicholas assumed that he would bargain from strength; for him, as for everyone else, the overriding impression of the years of revolution had been Russian power. It never occurred to him, nor indeed to anyone else, that before the three years of the Austro-Prussian alliance ran out it would be Russia which needed protection and that Nicholas would be left regretting the vanished union of 'the three Northern Courts'.

III

THE END OF THE HOLY ALLIANCE

1852-3

1851 was the year of Peace in Europe, symbolized by the Great Exhibition in London. English radicals attributed this peace to the triumphs of industrialism; in reality it rested on the revived Holy Alliance. The crowds which went to the Crystal Palace cheered Kossuth later in the year; they did not appreciate the connexion—it was because Kossuth was in exile that the Great Exhibition could be held. Every trouble seemed to be dying away. In Germany, a federal execution imposed the elector of Hesse on his subjects; and the diet, after some fumbling, devised a meaningless constitution. Danish authority was reasserted in Holstein. In June 1851 Nesselrode settled the question of the succession with the Danes; and this solution was accepted by the Great Powers in the London protocol of May 1852. Austria and Prussia co-operated somewhat grudgingly at the federal diet. Nesselrode remarked complacently of Bismarck and Thun, the Prussian and Austrian representatives: 'The good God certainly did not create these two men to solve the German question.'[1] In December 1851 Louis Napoleon destroyed the republican constitution and established himself as dictator; at the end of December the still-born Austrian constitution was formally revoked. Early in 1852 the Whig government in England gave place to a Tory government under Derby, with Malmesbury as foreign secretary. Reaction seemed to have triumphed; peace to be more secure than it had been for many years.

The only anxiety was the shadow of the Second Empire. Louis Napoleon could not remain content with the position of Prince President; and once he became emperor he would not remain content with the existing settlement of Europe. He himself said to Cowley, the British ambassador: 'I have every inten-

---

[1] Nesselrode to Meyendorff, 26 Feb. 1852. *Lettres et papiers*, x. 169.

tion of observing these Treaties—but you should recollect how galling they are to France';[1] and Nesselrode warned the tsar that a dangerous time was approaching: 'Napoleon's absence of principles makes it impossible to establish true relations of confidence, makes vigilance a law and puts Europe perpetually on the alert. It is peace, but armed peace with all its expenses and uncertainty. Only the union of the Great Powers is capable of maintaining it.'[2] Still, this improved Russia's position: a solidarity against France was necessarily a solidarity in Russia's favour. A real French effort against the treaties of 1815 must mean French action on the Rhine; and the threat of this made Prussia and Austria dependent on Russian support. In March 1852, only three months after the *coup d'état*, the independence of Belgium seemed to be threatened. Louis Napoleon found plenty to complain of in the Belgian press; and Bonapartist publicists were already airing the idea of a Zollverein with Belgium, if not of political union. The Russians saw a chance to improve their standing with the British, and pushed in officiously, assuring Malmesbury in April 1852 that they would send 60,000 men to defend Belgian independence. Malmesbury, timid and inexperienced, welcomed the offer; and the Russians supposed that they had consolidated the union of the four Great Powers. They underrated the cleverness of Louis Napoleon: as in domestic affairs, he would destroy the conservative union against him by sap, not by storm. Though inferior to his uncle in almost every way, he had one essential quality which the great Napoleon lacked: he had infinite patience. The Russians misunderstood, too, the spirit of British policy: unless the Bonapartist danger actually matured into action, the very name and existence of Napoleon made it more conciliatory, more anxious to stand well with France, than it had been in the days of the pacific Louis Philippe.

Russian confidence was also improved by the death of Schwarzenberg in April 1852. Schwarzenberg had persisted in remaining on good terms with Louis Napoleon even after the *coup d'état*, ostensibly in order to keep France on the counter-revolutionary course, really in order to shake himself free of Russia. Buol, who succeeded Schwarzenberg, lacked daring for

---

[1] Cowley to Malmesbury, 11 Nov. 1852.
[2] Nesselrode's review to the tsar of the year 1852. Zaionchkovski, *Vostochnaya Voina*, i (ii), no. 89.

this policy and proposed that the Powers should demand from Louis Napoleon a guarantee of his peaceful intentions before recognizing the empire when it came. This suited the Russians, who accepted the proposal on 13 May; and Frederick William IV followed with conservative zeal on 22 May. The British would not join: even a tory government, even Malmesbury, saw the folly of demanding guarantees which would be either refused or else ineffective. As Queen Victoria wrote: 'We have no means of making Louis Napoleon say what he will not.'[1] When in October Louis Napoleon made his famous declaration at Bordeaux: 'Mistrustful people say, the Empire means war, but I say, the Empire means peace', the British took the line that this was guarantee enough. All that remained of the conservative alliance was a protocol, signed by the four Great Powers on 3 December 1852; they noted Napoleon's pacific declaration and promised each other to favour the territorial *status quo* in the future as they had done in the past.

Even this superficial unity did not survive the actual recognition. The British, though they had raised the first qualms against the 'III' of the title, recognized the new Emperor immediately and without reserves.[2] Buol meanwhile had taken fright at the prospect of a Franco-Russian reconciliation, engineered by the British, at Austria's expense. To ward off this imaginary danger, he stirred up the tsar's legitimist principles and proposed that Napoleon III should be greeted only as 'friend', not as 'brother'. The appeal worked. The tsar noted: 'Brother! this relationship does not exist between us and Napoleon.' Though Frederick William IV was in great alarm at 'the revolution incarnate', fear drove him in the other direction. He was resolved not to provoke Napoleon by denying him the title of brother. When Buol learnt this, he also lost his nerve: he could not let Prussia get ahead in the competition for Napoleon's favour. Hence, when it came to the point, only the Russian ambassador greeted Napoleon III as friend. Some of Napoleon's radical advisers, in particular Persigny, wanted to seize the opportunity for a breach with Russia; but Napoleon would not start his reign

---

[1] Victoria to Malmesbury, 2 Dec. 1852. *Letters of Queen Victoria*, first series, ii. 492.

[2] The British were outpaced only by the kingdom of the Two Sicilies, the most legitimist government in Europe, which had held out against recognizing Louis Philippe. The Neapolitan government had now the futile dream of competing with the kingdom of Sardinia for French, and even for Italian, favour.

with a purely personal quarrel and passed off the Russian gesture with the adroit remark: 'God gives us our brothers; we choose our friends.'[1] All the same Buol had got his way: there was a coolness between the rulers of Russia and of France. It was, however, more important and more significant that the solidarity of the three 'Northern Courts' had dissolved at the first whiff of the French empire. In fact the muddle over the form of address symbolized the approaching end of the Holy Alliance and especially of the conservative partnership between Russia and Austria, on which the security of both empires depended.

For, by the end of 1852, real trouble was approaching in the Near East. Louis Napoleon, in his endless search for prestige, had earlier hit on the idea of backing the claims of the Latin monks for control of the Holy Places; this had the additional advantage of pleasing his clerical supporters in France. The tsar's prestige was challenged: he was much more genuinely the head of the Greek Church than Louis Napoleon was the protector of the Latins. A period of political auction followed, each side bidding by threats. The Turks, in their usual manner, tried to cheat both sides. Throughout 1851 they made concessions to the Latins and then secretly contradicted these to the Greeks. In April 1852 the French ambassador returned to Constantinople on the *Charlemagne*, a ninety-gun screw-driven ship, and insisted on its sailing through the Dardanelles; in July a French squadron threatened to bombard Tripoli. The Turks came to the conclusion that 'a French fleet would beat a Russian fleet even united with a Turkish one';[2] they gave the practical decision over the Holy Places to the Latins, and this was known all over the Near East by the end of 1852. The French success was not merely a challenge to the tsar's religious prestige; it threatened the basis of Russia's policy towards Turkey. However much the Russians might talk about the coming collapse and partition of the Turkish empire, their practical policy for the past twenty years had been the maintenance of the Ottoman empire as a buffer state securing the Black Sea; the essential condition of this policy was that Turkey should fear Russia more than any other Power. Now the Turks had shown that they

---

[1] There are many versions of this famous remark. Probably Napoleon said: 'Si l'on subit ses frères, on choisit ses amis'; but this does not translate easily into English.   [2] Rose (Constantinople) to Russell, 28 Dec. 1852.

feared France more than Russia; and the Russians had an immediate vision of a French fleet in the Black Sea. The tsar would have reacted, no doubt, to such a challenge from any Great Power; but he would not have reacted so violently if the challenge had not come from France—after all he had tolerated a pretty strong British influence at Constantinople in the preceding decade. In his eyes (and not in his alone) the struggle between France and Russia was merely a cover for the far greater struggle between conservatism and 'the revolution'. So long as Russia was herself invulnerable, she could sustain the cause of monarchy in Europe; if her Black Sea flank was open, the revolution might triumph in Germany and Italy. When the tsar flung himself into the Turkish conflict, he genuinely supposed that he was serving a European cause as well as his own.

He also supposed that this European cause would make his victory easier and more certain. Nesselrode warned him that neither England nor Austria would support Russia in a war against France;[1] but Nicholas thought that he could deal with France so long as the others stayed neutral, and he was confident of their neutrality. In December 1852 a coalition ministry had been formed in England under Lord Aberdeen; and he was not merely the man who had listened favourably to the tsar's plans for partitioning Turkey in 1844—much more important, he was terrified of French aggression and of French power. Nicholas, who prided himself on his gifts in diplomacy, thought to give the British even greater security by renewing the talk of partition; this was to assure them that their interests would be protected even if the Ottoman empire collapsed. In January 1853 Nicholas aired his ideas of partition to the British ambassador, Seymour: the Danubian principalities to be under Russian protection; Constantinople to be a free city; the British to take Egypt and, if they wished, Crete. Of course Nicholas was not being perfectly honest in these proposals; it is impossible to be so, when speculating in the void about the future. He said nothing about the share he meant to give Austria, nor about his plan for a Russian garrison at the Bosphorus and an Austrian garrison at the Dardanelles; more important, in a private plan that he scribbled down at the same time, he proposed to give Crete to France. Still, these details were not im-

[1] Nesselrode to Nicholas I, 20 Dec. 1852. Zaionchkovski, i (ii), no. 97.

portant. The British government rejected the 'offer' as meaning-less, not because it was inadequate. In Nesselrode's words, it was a principle of British policy 'never to take engagements for a more or less uncertain future, but to await the event in order to decide what line to adopt'. Nor did the tsar take the British reply as a rebuff: he had not intended a concrete immediate plan, therefore there was nothing to reject. He genuinely sup-posed that he had increased British confidence in himself. On the outbreak of war in the following year the 'Seymour Con-versations' were published by the British government, together with the partition plan of 1844; and the myth was then estab-lished that Russia was aiming at the dismemberment of the Turkish empire. This was not the case: whatever distant plans the tsar might form, the practical object of Russian policy at the beginning of 1853 was to restore at Constantinople the pre-dominant influence which had been lost by the French success over the Holy Places.

The tsar did not trouble to calm Austria with similar pro-jects of partition; he supposed that Austria was dependent on him already. Besides, in January 1853, Austria set the pace at Constantinople for a Russian intervention. A Turkish army was threatening to invade Montenegro. Austria could not allow this, for fear of the effect on her own South Slav subjects. Count Leiningen was therefore sent to Constantinople with a ten-day ultimatum that the conflict with Montenegro be brought to an end. The Turks saw other, graver troubles approaching; also, they could acknowledge Austrian interest in Montenegro with-out accepting, as a consequence, any general protectorate over their Christian subjects. Austria did not threaten the indepen-dent existence of the Ottoman empire; the Turks could safely give way. The tsar saw only the precedent. He promised Francis Joseph full support in case of war against Turkey; and prepared to repeat Austria's success on a greater scale. A special mission was sent to Constantinople at the end of February 1853; the envoy was Prince Menshikov, chosen as a 'pure Russian' in order to convince Russian opinion of the tsar's genuine con-cern for the Holy Places. A conflict of prestige with France had, in fact, to be tied up with religious sentiment before it could appeal to an Orthodox and obscurantist public indifferent to the danger from 'the revolution'. Menshikov was not merely to undo the French victory over the Holy Places; he was to achieve a more general and more striking success. After some fumbling, the Russian diplomats hit on the idea of enforcing Russia's protectorate over the Orthodox peoples of Turkey, a claim allegedly based on the treaty of Kutchuk Kainardji, signed in 1774.[1] As usual the tsar did not know what was in the treaty that he was seeking to enforce; he explained later that 'his conduct would have been different but for the error into which he had been led'.[2] Even Nesselrode did not look carefully at the treaty of 1774, though some of the Russian diplomats knew that they were running a forced claim. These technicalities were of little moment. The tsar wanted a victory of prestige over the Turks; and the religious protectorate was the first idea that came to hand. If the Turks did not like this, Menshikov was to offer them an alliance against France—an alternative equally unwelcome.

Menshikov supposed that he would easily carry the day with a show of force. There were rumours of mobilization in southern Russia and a flamboyant review of the Russian fleet at Sebastopol. Menshikov's first demand (2 Mar.) was for the dismissal of Fuad, the man who had given the Latins the keys of the Holy Places. This put Rose, the British chargé d'affaires, in a panic; he telegraphed direct to Malta asking that the fleet be sent to Constantinople. The British admiral passed the appeal on to London; and there a group of ministers, who were to become the 'inner cabinet' of the Crimean war,[3] decided not to respond to Rose's call. Only Aberdeen was ready to stomach any

[1] In article VII of the treaty of Kutchuk Kainardji the Porte 'promises to protect the Christian religion and its churches', and 'also allows the Russian ministers to make representations in regard to the new church at Constantinople'. There was clearly no general right of protection by Russia, though one crept in by custom. In 1849 Palmerston argued that Russia could make complaints, but that the sultan could disregard them; and Brunnow admitted to Nesselrode that Palmerston was right.

The idea of appealing to Kutchuk Kainardji in 1853 was suggested to the Russians, strangely enough, by Reshid, who was at that time working with them against France. Brunnow said that the real basis of Russian influence 'consists in facts, not words. Russia is strong, Turkey is weak; that is the preamble of all our treaties.' Nesselrode took up Reshid's suggestion without consulting Brunnow; and neither he nor Nicholas I seems to have realized the shakiness of their legal position until the beginning of 1854.

[2] Seymour (St. Petersburg) to Clarendon, no. 176, 21 Feb. 1854.

[3] Aberdeen, prime minister; Lord John Russell, leader of the house of commons; Clarendon, foreign secretary; Palmerston, home secretary, invited on Clarendon's suggestion as the most formidable authority on foreign affairs. Palmerston and Aberdeen had both been foreign secretary; Russell was to be later. Russell was a former prime minister, Palmerston a future one. The result was to show that there is nothing more disastrous than a committee of extremely able men.

Russian demand;[1] the others relied on the tsar's good faith and still blamed 'the restless ambition and energy of France' for all the trouble.[2] The news of Rose's appeal also reached Paris. At the council of ministers on 19 March Drouyn de Lhuys, foreign minister, argued that any French action would increase European suspicions and that they should wait for England to take the lead; Persigny answered that British public opinion would force the British government into opposing Russia and that this was the moment to launch 'the war of peoples against the kings'. Napoleon III could not resist the appeal of adventure; and the French fleet was ordered to Salamis. No doubt Napoleon III had to sustain his prestige against Russia; but he acted the more promptly because he saw the chance of renewing the Anglo-French co-operation of October 1849.

For the moment he was disappointed. Cowley told Drouyn that if the independence of the Ottoman empire were menaced 'it was the fault of France'.[3] Events in Constantinople soon changed this line. Stratford Canning, now Lord Stratford de Redcliffe, had been sent hastily back to Constantinople; he came with the mission of settling the dispute over the Holy Places in a sense favourable to Russia. This was attained, thanks largely to Stratford's advice, early in May.[4] Menshikov then put forward his further demand for a Russian protectorate over the Orthodox subjects of the Porte; his real object was not so much to snub the French (this had been achieved) as to end 'the infernal dictatorship of this Redcliffe'. Instead he forced the Turks back under Stratford's guidance. They held out against Menshikov's demand; and on 21 May he departed, taking the Russian diplomatic staff with him. The Turks were bound to refuse, if the Ottoman Empire was to remain an independent power; and Stratford was bound to advise them as he did, so long as the independence of Turkey was part of British policy.

[1] He said to Brunnow: 'Whether right or wrong we advise the Turks to yield.' Brunnow to Nesselrode, 21 Feb. 1853. Zaionchkovski, i (ii), no. 102.

[2] Clarendon to Seymour, 8 Mar. 1853.

[3] Cowley to Clarendon, no. 161, 19 Mar. 1853.

[4] Stratford was sent to Constantinople partly in the belief that he would be less of a danger to the government than in London. The myth was later established that he followed an independent policy and forced the British government into war. The myth has been exploded by Temperley, *England and the Near East: the Crimea.* The irritation of, say, Clarendon against Stratford was really that of a man in a state of muddle and hesitation against the man who presented the issues clearly and without pretence.

On the other hand, once it was admitted that Turkey was not truly independent (and every event of the Crimean war proved it), the Russians were justified in their demands for the sake of their own security: Turkey was tolerable as a buffer state only so long as she feared Russia more than any other Power. In seeking to maintain Turkish independence, Great Britain and France were fighting for a pretence, which they knew to be such; but it was a pretence which had to be kept up for lack of an alternative. Menshikov's threats changed British policy decisively. Even Aberdeen thought the demands 'unreasonable'. Russell and Palmerston urged strong action to counter Russia; Clarendon was more concerned to restore confidence in the government.[1] On 2 June the British fleet was ordered to Besika bay, outside the Dardanelles. It was joined by the French fleet a few days later; the Anglo-French alliance thus came into being literally by a side wind.

This development was unwelcome to the tsar, rather than alarming. He had often faced Anglo-French opposition at Constantinople; and he still felt secure of the Holy Alliance. He said to the French ambassador: 'The four of you could dictate to me; but that will never happen. I can count on Vienna and Berlin.'[2] The tsar had ordered the occupation of the Danubian principalities on Menshikov's return at the end of May; he saw no reason to draw back in this auction of threats and the Russian forces crossed the Pruth on 2 July. Palmerston again proposed resolute action, by sending the fleet through the Straits; he was overruled by the cabinet. Napoleon III on his side was dreaming of a dramatic act of mediation by which he might win Russian favour; and therefore also opposed action. The alternative to action was diplomacy, and the two Powers tried to involve 'Europe', that is, in practice, Prussia and Austria. Therewith began the characteristic diplomatic pattern of the Crimean war: the attempt by the two conflicting sides to involve the central Powers and so to achieve a decision. Both Prussia and Austria aimed at neutrality, Prussia because she had no interests at stake, Austria because she had too many. Prussia's only concern was not to become the battlefield in the

[1] He wrote to Seymour on 31 May that there was a *universal* conviction that the government had left Turkey to Russia's mercy and that therefore a strong line was now necessary.

[2] Bunsen to Manteuffel, 29 June 1853. *Preußens auswärtige Politik 1850–1858*, ii. 110.

struggle between conservatism and 'the revolution'; unless she chose to involve herself in war on a grand scale, Russia was not likely to threaten her in Poland nor France on the Rhine. Austria, on the other hand, had immediate and pressing alarms. If she sided with Russia, or even refused to side against her, France could explode Italy, or so the Austrians believed. The symbol of this threat was a prolonged tour of Italy in the autumn of 1853 by Brenier, a former French foreign minister, making ostentatious preparations for a French league. Even more urgent, Austria, mainly dependent on the Danube for her trade with the outer world, could not tolerate the Russians in the principalities; no Russian offer of the western Balkans could atone for this, even if it had been attractive—and it was not. Yet Austria shrank from a war with Russia, in which she would bear the full brunt. What she wanted was an impossibility: that Nicholas should drop his demands on Turkey without being humiliated. Hence the Austrian efforts to devise plans which should satisfy the tsar and yet secure the independence of Turkey, a policy which ended in deceiving, or attempting to deceive, both sides. While Prussia merely refused to support either side, Austria had to pretend to support the western Powers, yet never give them real support.

In the summer of 1853 this was still in the future: both Russia and the western Powers had illusions as to what they could expect from Prussia and Austria. The first manifestation of 'Europe' was the Vienna note, devised by the representatives of the Four Powers under Buol's guidance, and agreed on 1 August. The note embodied the concessions which in the opinion of the Four Powers Turkey could make to Russia without risking her independence.[1] It had been submitted beforehand

[1] On 20 July the Turks made a last offer to Russia, which came to be called 'the Turkish ultimatum'. They recited the concessions which the Sultan had made to the Christians and cited the four other Powers as witnesses to Turkey's bond 'in perpetuity'. Clarendon proposed that the four Powers, negotiating at Vienna, should confirm this offer; Europe would thus become the guarantor of Turkey's good faith. Napoleon III, however, insisted that the dispute was essentially between France and Russia; and Buol accepted this claim. The Vienna note therefore laid down that the Porte would not alter the conditions of the Christians 'without previous understanding with the Governments of France and Russia'. The Turks objected to this Franco-Russian protectorate and, still more, that they had not been treated on an equality with Russia. Though they demanded 'amendments' in order to bring the note into line with their ultimatum, their real object (which they attained) was a straight rejection.

Nesselrode's 'violent interpretation', which he gave to a German newspaper,

to the Russians, but not to the Turks.[1] Nesselrode accepted
the note on 5 August; the Turks discussed it for a fortnight and
then insisted on amendments.[2] This was a strange situation, in
which Russia accepted and Turkey rejected a scheme devised
by Europe for Turkey's protection against Russia. Within a
fortnight it turned out that the Turks had been right and that
the diplomats at Vienna had bungled their job. Nesselrode was
anxious to show that Russia had won the battle of prestige,
therefore he gave out a statement on 7 September, claiming that
the Vienna note gave to Russia the protection of the Orthodox
peoples of Turkey. This 'violent interpretation' killed the Vienna
note. Great Britain and France were driven back to action; they
had to show that they were in earnest in resisting Russian en-
croachments. On 22 September Walewski, the French ambassador, proposed to Clarendon that the fleets should pass the
Dardanelles; and this was authorized on the following day by
Aberdeen and Clarendon, without consulting any other ministers. Various excuses were given for this measure. Aberdeen
made out that it was to protect British subjects at Constantinople; Clarendon that it was an answer to Nesselrode; Napoleon III even claimed that it was to make the Turks more
moderate. In reality, it was simply the turn of the maritime
powers to 'move'; and by definition they could only move
their fleets.[3] As a matter of fact, the move was not at once

claimed that the Vienna note guaranteed 'the maintenance of the privileges and
immunities of the Orthodox Greek Church in the Ottoman Empire' and compelled
Turkey 'to take account of Russia's active solicitude for her co-religionists in
Turkey'. In other words, he repeated the unfounded Russian interpretation of the
treaty of Kutchuk Kainardji and made out that this had now been endorsed by
the Great Powers.

The 'Buol Project', put forward on 23 Sept. after the meeting at Olomouc,
reaffirmed the Vienna note, together with a Russian repudiation of Nesselrode's
'violent interpretation': 'The Cabinet of St. Petersburg gives a new assurance that
it will in no way exercise for itself the protection of a Christian cult inside the
Ottoman Empire . . . and that Russia only reserved to herself the duty of watching
that the engagement contracted by the Ottoman Empire in the Treaty of Kainardji
be strictly executed.'

[1] The telegraph lines from western Europe extended only to Vienna; there was
no telegraphic link with Constantinople. The diplomats at Vienna were therefore
being ceaselessly urged to agreement by their respective capitals; and could do so
only by ignoring Constantinople.

[2] Stratford was much blamed for the Turkish refusal; and his critics were not
silenced even when the Turks were shown to be right.

[3] There was also an urgent practical motive for action: the fleets could not
remain in the exposed anchorage at Besika bay when the autumn gales began to
blow. On the other hand, they could not enter the Dardanelles without violating

decisive: Stratford deliberately failed to carry out the order to summon the fleet when he received it, in the hope that a further attempt at mediation might succeed.

This last attempt was the meeting of the tsar and Francis Joseph at Olomouc at the end of September. The tsar was now in retreat: he repudiated Nesselrode's 'violent interpretation' and agreed that Austria should guarantee his good faith—after all, he could always try again later when western opposition had declined. Besides, this moderation was a bait: Nicholas now wanted the alliance of 'the three Northern Courts' which he had evaded in 1851. Faithful to his old illusion, he thought to win Austria with new plans of partition; once more he talked of Constantinople as a Free City, offered the western Balkans to Austria, and even suggested a joint protectorate of the Danubian principalities, anything, in fact, to break the solidarity of 'Europe'. Nothing could be more alarming to the Austrians than to have the Russians permanently on the Danube even as partners. Francis Joseph said sulkily: 'we should have to police these states and that is unworkable.' He would agree to an alliance only if Prussia made a third. But when Frederick William IV met the two emperors at Warsaw, he proved evasive; his policy was 'strong neutrality'. Neither of the two German rulers could bring himself to point out that Russia's withdrawal from the principalities was the first condition of any co-operation; and withdrawal would have made co-operation unnecessary. The result therefore was 'completely Null'. Finally Nicholas tried a direct attack on the Prussians at Potsdam, offering a guarantee against French aggression; he still could not understand that Russia, not Prussia, was threatened.[1] Once the Eastern question was raised, the Holy Alliance was a ghost, no more.

Even the ghost gave the western Powers a fright, though it frightened them in opposite directions. Napoleon wanted to accept in good faith the moderation which Nicholas had shown at Olomouc and to call off the conflict on the basis of a new version of the Vienna note which Buol had devised. The British were convinced that Austria and Russia had planned a partition of Turkey, and they resolved, in Palmerston's words, 'to

the convention of 1841; therefore some excuse of policy or exceptional need had to be found for this breach of international agreement.

[1] Eckhart, *Die deutsche Frage und der Krimkrieg*, p. 8; and Borries, *Preußen im Krimkrieg*, p. 63, with report by William, prince of Prussia, p. 344.

play old Gooseberry with the wouldbe Partitionists'.[1] On 8 October the British cabinet, meeting for the first time in six weeks, turned down the 'Buol project' and sent peremptory orders to Stratford to bring the fleet up to Constantinople; their action was a 'Brag', designed both to satisfy British public opinion and to convince Napoleon of the reality of the British alliance. This latter object succeeded: if Napoleon had to choose between Russia and England, he would choose England. Regretfully he dropped the 'Buol project' and ordered his fleet to follow the British. The action had even more decisive results at Constantinople. On 4 October, the Sultan, driven on by his public opinion, had declared war on Russia; pressed hard by Stratford, he had agreed not to open hostilities. But when the allied fleets passed the Straits, there was no holding the Turks; on 23 October Turkish troops crossed the Danube and killed some Russians.

For the last time the Turks fell out of favour. Clarendon spoke of 'the beastly Turks' and Napoleon III hoped for a Russian victory to bring the Turks to their senses. At Vienna Buol drafted the last of many attempts at compromise—the protocol of 5 December signed by the representatives of the four Powers.[2] Like the Holy Alliance of October, this, too, was a pretence: Austria and, still more, Prussia agreed to it with the intention of warning the tsar that 'Europe' was against him, yet neither German Power meant to commit itself to action. In any case the protocol of 5 December was stillborn. On 30 November the Russians got the victory which Napoleon had hoped for them—unfortunately at sea, not on land. They destroyed a squadron of the Turkish fleet at Sinope. This was an affront to the maritime Powers, with their fleets at Constantinople supposedly to protect the Turks. The 'massacre' of Sinope was decisive in its effect on British public opinion; it was the symbol which removed all doubts. Palmerston resigned on 16 December, ostensibly on the issue of parliamentary reform;[3] and Russell threatened to follow him. The cabinet still hesitated;

[1] Palmerston to Clarendon, 21 Sept. 1853. Clarendon also thought that a revived Holy Alliance had been prevented only by the 'manly and resolute' conduct of Manteuffel.

[2] This reminded the tsar of his promises not to infringe Turkish integrity nor to weaken the Sultan's authority over his Christian subjects; and at the same time called on the Sultan to renew his concessions to the Christians.

[3] He withdrew his resignation on 25 Dec.

they were pushed into decision by a threat from Napoleon that, if necessary, he would act alone.[1] The maritime Powers were drawn along from first to last by the need to prove to each other their mutual good faith. The British had led the way up the Straits in October; now the French pulled the British fleet into the Black Sea. The two fleets were to protect the Turkish ships and to confine the Russian navy to its base at Sebastopol. When these instructions were communicated to Nesselrode on 12 January 1854, it was next door to a declaration of war.

The tsar supposed that the time had come to invoke the Holy Alliance in earnest. What he wanted from Prussia and Austria was their armed neutrality: this would give him security on his western frontiers and so enable him to concentrate his forces on the Danube and in southern Russia. A special envoy, Orlov, was sent to Vienna with the old offer—Russia would not change things in the Balkans without Austria's consent. This was not enough: Russia must not interfere in the Balkans on any conditions. Buol tried to ride off with the excuse that armed neutrality would provoke French action in Italy. Francis Joseph was franker. He insisted that Russian troops should not cross the Danube and added: 'Only if the tsar gives us a formal guarantee of the maintenance of the Turkish empire and promises to put the frontier peoples, back in the position where they actually are under Turkish suzerainty can I consent.'[2] As always, Russian inaction in the Balkans was the essential condition for the Holy Alliance; and in the circumstances of the moment Nicholas could not agree to this condition for the sake of his prestige. Prussia also refused to satisfy the tsar's demand, though for an opposite reason. Whereas Austria would not respond because she dared not remain neutral in the Eastern question, Prussia refused because she intended to remain neutral at all costs. Frederick William IV had devised an extraordinary plan of getting something for nothing. He was proposing to promise his neutrality to Great Britain, if the British would in exchange guarantee him against French interference either in Germany or in Poland and would also help to promote Prussian hegemony in Germany. This was a futile offer to make to the

---

[1] He repudiated the threat a few days later when it had served its purpose. Temperley, *England and the Near East: the Crimea*, appendix vii, pp. 515–16.

[2] Orlov to Nesselrode, 3 Feb. 1854. Zaionchkovski, ii (iii), no. 124.

British: they wanted Prussia as an ally against Russia, not as a buffer for her protection. But since Frederick William was engaged, as he thought, in trading his neutrality to the British, he would not trade it to the tsar. This was more reasonable than it seemed. Unless he had a British guarantee against France, he dared not make any promise to Russia, not even the promise of neutrality. This was indeed the essence of the situation. Once Russia was involved in the Near East, she could not protect Prussia and Austria against 'the revolution'; the Holy Alliance had ceased to exist.

This was obvious to Napoleon III; with it, his object was achieved. On 29 January 1854 he wrote to the tsar suggesting direct negotiations between Russia and Turkey, the very thing which 'Europe' had been resisting since the Vienna Note. Napoleon was indifferent to the Holy Places, once the Holy Alliance was out of the way; and even before the Crimean war started, he was already thinking of the Franco-Russian alliance with which it ended. The tsar could not retreat so easily in the struggle for prestige, and he returned a defiant answer on 9 February: 'Russia would be in 1854 what she had been in 1812.' Besides, there was, now as always, an implied reservation in Napoleon's offer to Russia: he meant to remain on good terms with Great Britain. Yet she also stood in Russia's way at Constantinople; an entente with France only made sense in Russian eyes if Great Britain and France were estranged. Napoleon was, in fact, asking for what he got in later years: Russia should drop her Turkish ambitions as too difficult to accomplish, yet should acquiesce in French ambitions in western Europe. This programme was possible after the defeat of Russia, not before. The Crimean war had to be fought, in order to bring Nicholas I to see that the Holy Alliance no longer existed.

On 27 February the two western Powers sent an ultimatum to Russia demanding her withdrawal from the principalities. When she refused, the war was virtually under weigh. In one sense, it was predestined and had deep-seated causes. Neither Nicholas nor Napoleon nor the British government could retreat in the conflict for prestige once it was launched. Nicholas needed a subservient Turkey for the sake of Russian security; Napoleon needed success for the sake of his domestic position; the British government needed an independent Turkey for the security of the eastern Mediterranean. Yet none of the three

had conscious plans of aggression, not even Napoleon, despite
his welcome of disturbance for its own sake. The British fears
that Russia planned the dismemberment of Turkey were as ill
founded as Russia's fears that the western Powers threatened
her security in the Black Sea. Mutual fear, not mutual aggression, caused the Crimean war. Nevertheless it was not a war
without a purpose. At bottom, it followed from the events of
1848. British opinion would never have turned so harshly
against Russia had it not been for Austria's victory in Italy and,
still more, Russia's intervention in Hungary. The Crimean war
was fought for the sake of Europe rather than for the Eastern
question; it was fought against Russia, not in favour of Turkey.
But there was a deep-seated, unspoken disparity between the
aims and outlook of the two western allies. Both resented the
Russian preponderance which had, they thought, caused the
failure of the revolutions of 1848; but only Napoleon III hoped
to reverse the verdict. The British certainly wished for no new
revolutions; they fought Russia out of resentment and supposed
that her defeat would strengthen the European Balance of
Power. Napoleon, on the other hand, thought that her defeat
would destroy the Balance. Hence, though the more ambitious,
he was the less bellicose. He was quite ready to call off the
struggle once Russia abandoned interest in central Europe.

The real stake in the Crimean war was not Turkey. It was
central Europe; that is to say, Germany and Italy. The British
hoped to substitute 'the Concert of Europe' for the hegemony of
Russia; they failed. Napoleon III wished to substitute his own
hegemony; and for a few years supposed that he had succeeded.
As events turned out, the central Powers evaded commitment;
and for this reason the Crimean war was indecisive. This was
in itself the decision. The Crimean war was fought to remake
the European system. The old order of the Holy Alliance was
destroyed; but no new system took its place—neither the liberal
Concert of British ideal nor the revolutionary association of
Napoleon's dreams. Instead there opened a period of European
anarchy which lasted from the Crimean war until the next
great struggle in the Near East.

IV

THE CRIMEAN WAR

1854–6

WHEN the British and French governments moved their fleets stage by stage from the Mediterranean to the roads of Sebastopol, they had no intention of fighting Russia unaided. They had expected Russia to give way; failing that, they had counted on translating the 'Concert of Europe' into a war alliance. The events of March 1854 disillusioned them. In Austria a strong party, led by Buol, the foreign minister, favoured alliance with the western Powers. Not only would this protect Austrian interests on the lower Danube; it would also give her security in Italy. Buol's policy was hamstrung by the opposition of the Austrian generals. They saw clearly that, since Russia and the maritime Powers could not get at each other, the whole weight of Russia's military power would be flung against Austria, if she entered the war. Their calculations no doubt exaggerated Russia's strength; all the same, their fundamental objection was sound—for Austria the war would be a struggle for existence, not a war of limited objectives. The situation would be different if Prussia could be brought to co-operate: at the least, this would secure Austria against an attack from Prussia in Germany and, if it came to a war, Prussia could threaten Russia decisively. On 22 March 1854 Buol agreed somewhat reluctantly to postpone alliance with the western Powers until he had reached agreement with Prussia.

The Prussians, on their side, desired agreement with Austria, though for the opposite reason. Austria wished to pull Prussia into war; Prussia wished to tie Austria down to neutrality. For, just as Austria would have to bear the brunt of war for the sake of the western Powers, Prussia would have to bear the brunt for the sake of Austria; and this in a war where no Prussian interest was at stake. Bismarck, the most daring of Prussian diplomats, though still in a subordinate position, therefore advocated rigid neutrality. This was too clear-cut for Frederick William IV; to his mind there was a Prussian interest at stake, in so far as Austria was endangered by 'the revolution'.[1] This argument operated only against France, not against Russia (unless the Russians dared to raise Poland); it was irrelevant to the circumstances of the Crimean war. Thus, for all practical purposes, Frederick William IV too was resolved on neutrality. In his own dithyrambic words: 'not a vacillating and indecisive neutrality, but sovereign neutrality—genuinely impartial, independent and self-confident'.[2] It is true that there was also in Prussia a party which favoured co-operation with the western Powers, a party led by Prince William, the heir-apparent. This party caused much diplomatic turmoil and even a political crisis early in March; the crisis was not finally resolved until Prince William went into semi-exile early in May. But fundamentally the issue was never in doubt, despite the alarm of the pro-Russian conservatives. Though Frederick William pressed his alliance on the British, this was to secure his neutrality by detaching Great Britain from France, not to involve Prussia in war. In the last resort this most erratic man never wavered from the principle that he had laid down even in 1848: never, under any circumstances, would he fight against Russia.

By the end of March the western Powers could wait no longer. On 31 March they declared war on Russia; on 10 April they concluded a formal alliance. Napoleon III had achieved his first ambition, despite the clause by which the allies renounced any gains for themselves. Great Britain and France were allies. But though allies and theoretically at war, they were still a long way from fighting. Their strategy, like their diplomacy before it, assumed that Russia was actively threatening Turkey; therefore their only action was to send an expeditionary force to protect Constantinople. In reality the boasted Russian power began to dwindle as soon as it was exposed to practical test: the 800,000 men which the tsar was supposed to have always available turned into 350,000 raised after immense exertions. Far from threatening Constantinople, the Russians were already finding it difficult to maintain themselves on the Danube; the

[1] He wrote to Bunsen on 29 Jan. 1854: 'I shall not allow Austria, the inconvenient, intriguing, malevolent Austria, to *be attacked by the Revolution, without drawing the sword on her behalf*, and this from pure love of Prussia, *from self-preservation*.'

[2] Frederick William IV to Manteuffel, 27 Feb. 1854. Eckhart, *Die deutsche Frage und der Krimkrieg*, p. 38.

more so, when they had to look over their right flank at Austria's doubtful moves. Decision still seemed to wait upon Vienna. Russia would not advance into the Balkans and the allies could not advance beyond Constantinople; therefore only Austria could turn the war into a reality. On the other hand, since the allies were now committed theoretically to war, there was no urgency for the Austrians to do anything.

This gave Frederick William the chance to renew his offers to Austria. He would make an alliance with her, would even guarantee her territory in Italy, on condition that she did not make an alliance with any non-German power. This was Frederick William's old dream of an alliance against 'the revolution'. Buol answered with a clause that Prussia should support Austria in the Danubian principalities if Russia refused to withdraw. This clause seemed to commit Prussia to the eastern war. Frederick William was won over by a private message from Francis Joseph that a conflict over the principalities was 'not yet in question'. Prussia, in fact, risked war in the future for the sake of keeping Austria neutral in the present. The treaty of alliance between Prussia and Austria, signed on 20 April, seemed a complete Austrian victory. She got Prussian backing in Italy and on the lower Danube; Prussia ran risks for no interest of her own. In reality the Prussians were gambling on a certainty. They were assuming that Russia would fight a defensive war; and, with the Austrian army mobilizing in Galicia and the allied fleets controlling the Black Sea, there was no other war she could fight. At first Austria seemed to have things all her own way. The Austro-Prussian treaty was forced through the German diet with Prussian backing; and all Germany was thus committed to supporting Austria on the Danube. Early in May Frederick William tried to turn Austria from her anti-Russian line by raising again the revolutionary alarm, in which only he believed; his efforts were entirely unsuccessful. On 3 June the Austrians made the formal demand to Russia that she should evacuate the principalities. This was a decisive step. In less than six months the Austrians had moved from refusing to promise neutrality to an open threat of hostilities. For the first time the Russians saw clearly that Austria might oppose them in the Balkans; and the phrase was first heard in St. Petersburg that the road to Constantinople lay through Vienna. But war with Austria was beyond Russia's present strength. Indeed, faced by the Turkish and allied armies and without a firm promise of Austrian neutrality, the Russians would have had to withdraw from the principalities, even if Austria had not presented an ultimatum. The way was made easy for them by Frederick William. Three days before meeting Francis Joseph in order to discuss measures against Russia (9 June), he wrote to the tsar, advising his 'cher et bon Nix' in what terms to yield;[1] and the tsar followed Prussia's advice 'for the last time'. On 29 June, in reply to the Austrian demand, he offered to withdraw from the principalities, on condition that Austria would prevent the western Powers from entering them. This was an inadequate answer; and the Austrians prepared seriously for war. In fact, the Russians intended to evacuate the principalities in any case, since they could not withstand the mounting pressure from the Turkish army.

The shadow of war gave Buol the excuse to ask the western Powers their war-aims. Moreover, if Austria was to be involved in war, she needed an alliance with the western Powers and, above all, assurance that the war would not be fought in a revolutionary spirit. This suited Drouyn de Lhuys: conservative in outlook, he doubted the willingness of the French to fight a great war and was eager enough to bar the way against Napoleon's revolutionary projects. In his own words, he wished 'to master the revolution without the help of Russia and to check Russia without the help of the revolution'.[2] The British, on the other hand, did not wish to be committed to anything. Though their war-aim was to reduce the preponderance of Russia, they had no idea how this could be translated into practical terms; besides, they shrank from defining their war-aims when victory might later enable them to demand more. Their concern was to win the war, Drouyn's to make it unnecessary. He negotiated with Buol about war-aims behind the backs of the British. The result was the Four Points which henceforth dominated the diplomacy of the war.

It was characteristic of the Crimean war that its aims should be defined in the negative. The Four Points laid down that stable relations could not be established between Russia and Turkey unless (1) the Russian protectorate of the principalities were replaced by a European guarantee; (2) the navigation of

---

[1] Frederick William to Nicholas I, 6 June 1854. *Preußens auswärtige Politik 1850–1858*, ii. 440.   [2] Hübner (Paris) to Buol, 15 July 1854.

the Danube were 'freed'; (3) the Straits convention of 1841 were revised 'in the interests of the Balance of Power in Europe'; (4) the Russians abandoned their claim to a protectorate over the Christian subjects of Turkey and instead the five Great Powers obtained from the Turkish government security for the Christians. Point 4, the original cause of conflict, had already been conceded by the Russians when they accepted the Vienna note in August 1853 and when Nicholas I repudiated at Olomouc Nesselrode's 'violent interpretation' of it. The first and second Points were tacitly conceded, when the Russians withdrew from the principalities in August 1854. The Crimean war was therefore fought over Point 3; since a mere revision of the Straits convention was not enough, the decisive conflict came over the question of Russian naval power in the Black Sea. Though this affected Turkey and the Near East, its basis was 'the interest of the Balance of Power in Europe'.

Drouyn and Buol drafted the Four Points early in July. On 19 July the Points were presented to the British cabinet, which refused to be committed to them. Meanwhile, Drouyn and Buol also drafted a treaty of alliance in case Austria became involved in war over the principalities. This was more attractive to the British; they wanted Austria as an ally, and therefore had no objection to signing a treaty of alliance with her. On 29 July the British cabinet accepted the treaty of alliance and at the same time agreed to the Four Points as a condition of it. By the time that British approval reached Vienna, the news of Russia's withdrawal from the principalities had arrived also. On 5 August Buol refused to sign the treaty. Drouyn, in desperation, tried to catch him by agreeing to the Four Points without the treaty; and the British ambassador, who had been told to keep in step with his French colleague, agreed also. Notes accepting the Four Points were exchanged on 8 August. On the same day Buol received from Gorchakov, the new Russian ambassador, the formal announcement of Russia's withdrawal from the principalities. A few days later Austrian troops occupied the principalities after agreement with the Turks. Austria had both expelled the Russians from the principalities and limited the war-aims of the allies without herself lifting a finger. Buol even supposed that he had added the principalities permanently to the Austrian empire.

Russia's withdrawal left the western allies at a loss. They had

gone to war in order to check Russia's aggression on Turkey;
and this aggression had ceased. They were thus faced with the
problem—how to check an aggressive Power when it is not
being aggressive? Russia had not obliged the allies by waiting
in the principalities to be attacked: where now were they to
attack her? and what terms were they to impose on Russia if
the attack was successful? The French had tried diplomacy in
order to avoid military action; the British now pressed for
military action in order to escape diplomacy. The British had
one great asset: though Napoleon was at heart little more
bellicose than his ministers, he dared not let this appear for the
sake of his prestige—in case of doubt, a Bonaparte had to choose
the warlike course. Besides, with the diplomatic failure of
8 August there was no further excuse for delay: since the allies
were at war, they had to start fighting. A mere pursuit of the
Russians across the Danube would achieve nothing. From the
beginning of the war, Napoleon had urged the resurrection of
Poland and continental war against Russia on a grand scale;
but, apart from the British reluctance to be involved in a revolutionary war,[1] the allies had not the military resources for such
a war nor could they launch it so long as Prussia and Austria
barred the way. The only solution for the maritime powers was
an 'amphibious' operation in the Black Sea; if they could carry
Sebastopol by a *coup de main*, they would destroy Russian naval
power in the Black Sea and achieve the essential third 'Point'
without negotiation. Later the French were to argue that the
Crimean expedition had served purely British interests; an
argument true only if France was concerned solely with the disruption of Europe and not with the security of Turkey. In
reality France was concerned with both; and the contradictions
of her policy sprang from the fact that she was pursuing simultaneously a conservative and a revolutionary foreign policy.

The allied expedition to the Crimea was at first successful.
In the middle of September the allies landed over 50,000 men
as against the total Russian force in the Crimea of 35,000. On

---

[1] This reluctance was not universal. Palmerston wrote to Clarendon on 6 Apr.
1854: 'Prussia might get the German Provinces on the Baltic in exchange for the
Polish Part of the Duchy of Posen in the event of a Restoration of the Kingdom of
Poland; and such a Restoration not under Russian rule, would probably be the
best security for the future independence of Germany. . . . Austria to get the
Principalities giving up in exchange her Italian Provinces, and Turkey being
indemnified by the Crimea, the eastern shores of the Black Sea and Georgia.'

20 September a Russian attempt to check the allied advance was defeated at the battle of the Alma. A few days later the rumour reached western Europe that Sebastopol had fallen. The rumour was false; the allies had missed their chance and were tied down to a long and exhausting siege. In the middle of October Raglan, the British commander, wrote: 'in the Crimea we hold only the position on which we stand';[1] and Clarendon, gloomy as usual, expected '*a monster catastrophe*', a mixture of Afganistan and Corunna.[2] These expectations of defeat proved as unfounded as the earlier expectations of success. The two Russian attempts to drive the allies out of the Crimea failed at Balaklava (25 Oct.) and at Inkerman (5 Nov.). Military action, which had been designed to break the diplomatic deadlock, had ended in equal deadlock. The allies could not take Sebastopol; the Russians could not expel the allies. This military deadlock, with all the horrors of disease and medical incompetence, remained unbroken from November 1854 until June 1855. Diplomacy returned to the centre of the stage; and diplomacy meant Austria once more. The allies had intended to free themselves from Austria by a military victory; now in order to stay in the Crimea at all, they needed the threat of Austrian action so as to keep the bulk of the Russian army pinned down in Galicia. The Russians, on the other hand, could achieve nothing in the Crimea, and might be tempted to free their hands by attacking Austria, or at the very least to demand a formal neutrality. Both sides wanted to involve Austria in order to break the deadlock; Buol's answer was to try to break the deadlock so that Austria should not be involved.

Buol's object was to repeat in more permanent form the policy which had been successful in August: on the one hand he would compel Russia to yield by threatening co-operation with the western Powers; on the other, he would offer co-operation to the western Powers in such terms as would make it easy for the Russians to yield. Therefore, throughout the autumn, he lured the western Powers with prospects of an alliance, yet held out until he felt safe that the alliance would not involve Austria in war. The essential issue was whether Russia would accept the Four Points. On 26 August the Russians

---

[1] Raglan to Newcastle, 23 Oct. 1854. Martineau, *Life of Henry Pelham, fifth Duke of Newcastle*, p. 174.
[2] Clarendon to Cowley, 17 Nov. 1854.

had rejected the Four Points and had even talked of war with Austria; Buol, on his side, sang small and said merely: 'the Russians have not accepted our challenge'. But once the allies were established in the Crimea, he dared not let the situation drift: Russia had to be brought to accept the Four Points, so that Austria could safely make an alliance with the western Powers in order to enforce them. On 22 October the Austrian army was mobilized for war: since the campaigning season had passed, this mobilization was diplomatic, not military. Still, the threat of Austrian action put Frederick William once more into a panic. On 24 October he wrote to the tsar, imploring him to accept the Four Points as the only way of avoiding a general war: 'the green table of the conference room is the sheet-anchor of the world.' Nesselrode also urged the Four Points on the tsar; and early in November the Russians prepared to give way. The pattern of the withdrawal from the principalities was repeated: the Russians jettisoned diplomatic pretensions in order to divide the European coalition which seemed to be forming against them. Frederick William on his side did his best for the Russians. He offered to guarantee the Austrian troops in the principalities against a Russian attack (a safe enough offer to make), on condition that Austria did not make an alliance with the western Powers. Buol accepted this offer on 26 November, only to break the bargain within a week.

For Austria's weakness in Italy still weighed heavily upon him. If he professed himself satisfied with the Russian acceptance of the Four Points, he might be threatened instead by France; therefore he dared not compromise with the Russians without compromising with the western Powers as well. On 20 November it became known in Vienna that the Russians would accept the Four Points; on 21 November the Austrians revoked their general mobilization—it had served its turn. Immediately Buol began to press upon the western Powers the draft treaty which he had rejected in August. Here, too, the pattern was repeated: the British were reluctant to be committed, the French made the Austrian alliance their condition for continuing the war. The British were now caught by their own initiative in going to the Crimea; they could not maintain themselves there without French support, and the French had a decisive argument that they were contributing the bulk of the armed forces. Besides, the French were able to make out that the treaty would lure Austria into war. Article V of the draft treaty provided that, if peace was not assured by the end of the year on the basis of the Four Points, the three allies would deliberate 'as to the best means of securing the object of their alliance'. This clause was made futile before the alliance was concluded. For the treaty of alliance was signed, on Buol's prompting,[1] on 2 December; and the Russians had accepted the Four Points unconditionally on 29 November.

For the moment Napoleon was delighted with his bargain. When the news of the alliance arrived in Paris, Napoleon 'embraced the Empress and held her for a long time pressed to his heart'.[2] Benedetti, the French representative at Constantinople, wrote triumphantly: 'you have inflicted a mortal blow on the Holy Alliance'.[3] In return for the alliance, the French, though not the British, were prepared to pay the price which the Austrians had long demanded—security in Italy. On 22 December France and Austria concluded a secret treaty agreeing to maintain the *status quo* in Italy and providing that, in case of military co-operation in the Near East, their troops would also co-operate in Italy. The whole arrangement seemed a triumph for Buol. He had secured the great prize which had evaded even Metternich: alliance with a Napoleon which would check Russia and yet not endanger Austria as a Great Power. Drouyn, on his side, was equally delighted. By the alliance of 2 December he had, as he thought, forced a breach between Austria and Russia; by the treaty of 22 December over Italy he had forced a breach between Napoleon and 'the revolution'. The new system had two fatal flaws, which reinforced each other. One was Austria's position between France and Russia: with so much at stake both on the Danube and in Italy, she dared not go decisively against either. The other was in the tenacity of Napoleon: however great his need for the Austrian alliance, he would never permanently renounce his plans for remaking the map of Europe.

[1] In order to appease the Russians, Buol launched the story that he had been compelled to sign the treaty by an ultimatum from the western Powers; and this myth was accepted by all historians until exposed by Eckhart, *Die deutsche Frage und der Krimkrieg*, pp. 125–32. In reality it was Buol who insisted on the alliance; and the western Powers, especially the British, who were reluctant. Westmorland merely wrote to Clarendon, 2 Dec. 1854: 'there never was a *hitch* about the signature.'   [2] Hübner, *Neuf ans de souvenirs*, i. 284.

[3] Benedetti to Thouvenel, 10 Dec. 1854. Thouvenel, *Pages de l'histoire du second empire 1854–1866*, pp. 26–27.

The 'reversal of alliances' was, in fact, itself reversed within a month; and that as a consequence of the Italian treaty of 22 December. Maintaining the *status quo* in Italy meant, in practice, demanding securities from Sardinia that she would not take advantage of Austria's preoccupations in the Near East. Here the British had urgent motives for seconding French policy: with their own shortage of trained men, they cast longing eyes on the Sardinian army, small but undeniably efficient. If a Sardinian contingent were sent to the Near East, this would strengthen the allied forces and at the same time give Austria practical security in Italy. This project had been put to Cavour, the Sardinian prime minister, as early as 14 April 1854: he had replied that, if Austria declared war on Russia, he would at once give her security by sending 15,000 men (one-third of the Sardinian army) to the Near East.[1] Cavour ignored his colleagues when he made this reply; after the humiliating defeat of 1849, they wanted some striking satisfaction of Sardinian 'honour' in exchange for their military contribution. He, on the other hand, recognized that alliance between France and Austria meant the end of all Italian hopes; and he wished to keep the favour of the western Powers, even if this involved indirectly co-operation with Austria. In April this paradox was too daring for Cavour's colleagues; and he was overruled. The question slept. Serious fighting did not begin until the autumn; and the British did not renew their approach.

At the end of November they tried again.[2] On 13 December the request for troops reached the Sardinian cabinet. Cavour was again for agreeing at once; the foreign minister, Dabormida, insisted on imposing conditions. The western allies should prevail on Austria to raise the sequestration on the property of Lombard refugees in Piedmont[3] and they should agree 'to take

---

[1] Hudson to Clarendon, 14 Apr. 1854. Hudson seems to have made this proposal on his own initiative; the French, at this time set on a conservative partnership with Austria, were much offended at not having been consulted.

[2] Clarendon's letter to Hudson of 29 Nov. did not reach him until 13 Dec. It is possible that Cowley, the ambassador in Paris, who did not share the British enthusiasm for Italy, held up the letter, so as to give the French time to settle Italian affairs with Austria.

[3] This had been a cause of dispute between Sardinia and Austria since 1849. In that civilized age it was thought a reasonable demand that political refugees should be allowed to draw enormous revenues from their estates while conducting revolutionary propaganda against the ruler of the country in which the estates lay.

the state of Italy into consideration at the time of peace'. The British government would have agreed to these conditions if it had been negotiating alone. But by now the French needed an agreement with Sardinia in order to fulfil their bargain with Austria; and clearly this agreement could not be concluded in an anti-Austrian spirit. The French therefore insisted that Sardinian aid must be given without conditions. The deadlock persisted for a fortnight. Dabormida suggested that the allies might put their promises in secret articles or in the form of a 'reverse note'; the French would make no concessions. They even threatened to go over to the 'conservative' side by second-ing Austrian complaints against the Sardinian press. Victor Emanuel would not face this risk; besides, being primarily a soldier, he wished to enter the war on any terms in order to restore the prestige of his army. On 9 January 1855 he deter-mined that, since his liberal ministers would not make the alliance, he would call on the conservatives and thus pass over to the Austrian camp. When Cavour learnt this he made the first dramatic decision of his career: to save Sardinia from the conservatives, he would sign the alliance without conditions. Dabormida resigned; and Cavour took over the foreign ministry on 10 January. The only trace of satisfaction for Sardinia was a formal declaration by the British and French ministers that they could sign 'no note secret or public'; this was at least evidence that the demand had been made. Thereupon Sardinia acceded unconditionally to the Anglo-French alliance; a military con-vention followed on 26 January.

Sardinia had been tamed; this, too, seemed a triumph for Buol and for the French conservatives. In reality the alliance of 10 January 1855 with Sardinia was as much a success for 'liberalism' as the treaties of 2 and 22 December 1854 with Austria had been a success for conservatism. Though Great Britain and France had not promised to back the cause of Italy, Cavour had not promised to give it up. Moreover, he now had the chance of competing with the Austrians on practical terms; in realist fashion, this was a competition that he could win. Like the Prussians, though for opposite reasons, he gambled on Austrian neutrality. The Prussians did not want to fight against Russia; Cavour did not want to fight side by side with Austria. Austrian neutrality was the safeguard against both dangers. By the end of the war in 1856 Prussia was secure in Russian favour, and Sardinia was secure in the favour of Great Britain and France.

Austria's alliance with the western Powers alarmed Frederick William IV even more than it did Victor Emanuel. He too re-entered the field as an amateur diplomat. Austria's action, coming so soon after the agreement of 26 November, seemed to him 'treachery'; and he thought of mobilizing forces in Silesia which, ostensibly directed against Russia, should really threaten Austria. This was too risky; it would involve a breach with the western Powers. His next impulse was to try to outbid Austria in the competition for western favour. He, too, offered his alliance to Great Britain and France, but again on the old conditions: no French troops in Germany, and a guarantee against any raising of the Polish question. In return for this, as Gerlach, his conservative friend, contemptuously said, 'Prussia will mobilize an army which will do nothing'. This was the essential difference between Prussia and Austria. An Austrian mobilization inevitably threatened Russia and diverted her military resources from the Crimea. Prussia would never go to war against Russia and therefore her mobilization would merely place a strong buffer of protection between Russia and the western Powers. Not surprisingly Drouyn de Lhuys said of the Prussian envoy: 'He brings us nothing except his king's tears.' So long as the Near East dominated events, Prussia, by her in-difference, would appear to be a second-rate Power; once interest shifted back to Europe, this indifference would prove to have been her strength. This was already shown in the early days of 1855. In January Austria, as part of her policy of aiding the western Powers without actually going to war, proposed at the German diet that the federal forces should be mobilized in order to enforce the Four Points. Bismarck, Prussia's representa-tive, replied that Germany's only interest, the freedom of the Danube, was already secured; and he turned the proposal into a general defence of German neutrality (8 Feb.)[1] In this way not only Prussia, but the rest of Germany under Prussia's leader-ship, ceased to be a threat to Russia and became instead a barrier against France. It was the first foretaste of Bismarck's later policy—the defence of Austria as a German, but not as a

---

[1] With characteristic ruthlessness Bismarck even suggested to the Russians that they should invoke the federal act against Austria as having given a foreign power ground of complaint.

Balkan power. By the end of March 1855 Frederick William IV, after many hysterical alarms, had returned to the policy with which he had started—independent neutrality.

The British and French governments had never taken the diplomacy of Frederick William seriously. Their overriding concern was with Austria. Drouyn was now inescapably tied to the proposition that, by negotiating over terms of peace, he could draw Austria into war; and the British were prepared to try the idea of taking Sebastopol by diplomacy, since they could not take it by military means. The treaty of 2 December had been intended to commit Austria to war; instead it had committed the allies to negotiating on the basis of the Four Points. But what did they, or rather Point 3 mean? The British wanted a precise definition that Point 3 involved the demolition of Sebastopol and of the other Russian fortresses on the Black Sea and the limitation of Russia's Black Sea fleet to four ships. Drouyn at once protested that the Austrians would take fright at such an extreme demand and would back out of their alliance;[1] he might have added that it was absurd to make it until Sebastopol had fallen, and then it would be unnecessary. To reconcile British resolution and Austrian evasiveness, the western Powers hit on an extraordinary device. They bound themselves to each other to enforce the severe British interpretation of Point 3 (notes of 17 and 19 Dec.); ten days later (protocol of 28 Dec.) they agreed with Austria on a weak interpretation. This merely said that 'Russian predominance in the Black Sea should be brought to an end'. The allies were hoping that Russia would get them out of their difficulty. The Russians, they imagined, would object to the weak interpretation, and Austria would then go to war to enforce the strict one. The Russians, of course, did nothing of the kind, particularly when Buol impressed upon them that nothing more than the weak interpretation was at stake. On 7 January 1855 Gorchakov, the Russian ambassador at Vienna, accepted Point 3 as defined in the protocol of 28 December. Once more the allies, hoping to lure Austria into war, had been themselves lured into negotiations. They were committed to attending a formal peace conference at Vienna.

The French now swung around again. They had promoted negotiations in order to avoid war; now they decided on war in

[1] Cowley to Clarendon, 12 Dec. 1854.

order to avoid negotiations. Napoleon himself was insistent that
imperial honour would not be satisfied unless Sebastopol was
taken; and the French therefore aimed to evade the peace conference until there was victory in the Crimea. Napoleon, however, was impatient: he could not wait indefinitely without
either military or diplomatic success. On 16 February he
dramatically announced that he would go himself to the Crimea
and take the supreme command. This threw everyone into a
panic. The gang of Bonapartist adventurers who ran France
were afraid that the empire would collapse during Napoleon's
absence, certainly if he failed; the British were afraid that
Napoleon might do a deal with the Russians over their heads—
an alarm later justified by the similar way in which he ended
the war with Austria in 1859. The French ministers therefore
became as urgent for the conference as previously they had been
dilatory; Drouyn even proposed to be satisfied with a 'limitation' of the Russian Black Sea fleet to its existing numbers. This
was rejected by the British government; but they, too, had their
motives for urging on the conference. On 30 January 1855
Aberdeen's government was overthrown because of its incompetent conduct of the war; and when Palmerston formed a
government (6 Feb.) he was at first the prisoner of the Peelites.
They insisted on early negotiations and even on the dropping
of the demand for the destruction of Sebastopol; to satisfy them,
it was agreed to send Lord John Russell to Vienna as British
plenipotentiary. Russell had been among the most bellicose of
British ministers; on the other hand, a competition between
himself and Palmerston had now opened for the leadership of
the whig-liberal party. His determination to appear as the
apostle of peace was paradoxically enough increased by the
resignation of the Peelites on 22 February; for now Palmerston's
government became truly a government to make war, and
Russell's only chance of eclipsing Palmerston was to return from
Vienna, in Palmerston's words, 'with an olive-branch round his
temples'.[1] Finally, the Russians, too, were increasingly conciliatory. Their economic resources were becoming strained;
and the death of Nicholas I on 2 March removed the greatest
obstacle to concession. His successor, Alexander II, was resolved
from the first to think only of Russia's interests and not to
shoulder the struggle against 'the revolution'.

[1] Palmerston to Clarendon, 10 Feb. 1855.

The peace conference opened at Vienna on 15 March. Russell soon realized that the Russians would not agree to any real limitation of their fleet; he therefore proposed that they should be asked how Point 3 could be achieved—in other words, the Russians were to define the allied war-aims. Gorchakov, though bewildered, agreed to write to St. Petersburg; and the conference was suspended on 2 April. Meanwhile the British had hit on the idea of inviting Napoleon to Windsor in order to postpone his journey to the Crimea. Drouyn thought to exploit the breathing-space by himself going to Vienna and making a triumphant peace. He produced yet another interpretation of Point 3: the Black Sea should be 'neutralized', that is, Russian and Turkish ships equally excluded. On 30 March he agreed with the British government that neutralization or limitation and nothing else should be proposed. But when the conference reopened on 17 April, Russell and Drouyn discovered that Russia would not accept nor Austria go to war for either scheme. Buol then produced another scheme of his own: the Russians should be allowed as large a fleet as they had before the war, and the British and French should be allowed to send ships into the Black Sea as a 'counterpoise'. Drouyn was terrified of losing the Austrian alliance on which he based all his policy; Russell was terrified of losing the alliance of France; both were terrified of failing to return as peace-makers. Despite the orders of their respective governments, they therefore accepted 'counterpoise', and returned to London and Paris in order to advocate it.

The first impulse of the British government was to reject the scheme out of hand; then they reflected that they must not break with France. By 3 May the British cabinet came reluctantly round to the view that they would have to follow Drouyn's lead. But Drouyn was no longer leading. On 16 April Napoleon had come to England; he was welcomed enthusiastically, and this convinced him that the British alliance was worth a serious war. Moreover, on British prompting, he gave up the idea of going to the Crimea. The Bonapartist supporters were now as keen on war, for the sake of prestige, as previously they had been bent on peace. The decision not to go to the Crimea was made on 26 April; Drouyn arrived in Paris on 30 April, four days too late. Napoleon at first hesitated, and Drouyn almost talked him round. But on 4 May he had a decisive meeting with Drouyn, at which Cowley, the British ambassador, and Marshal Vaillant, the minister of war, were also present. Cowley, though without instructions from his government, showed that Buol's proposals would leave Russia as strong as she had been before the outbreak of war. Vaillant declared: 'anything more dishonourable to the Army could not well be imagined'.[1] Military prestige, together with the British alliance, carried the day. Counterpoise was rejected; and Drouyn resigned.[2] Napoleon had not meant to break with Austria; he said to Cowley: 'I don't think of making peace, but I want to manœuvre in order to have Austria with us.'[3] As to Walewski, the new foreign minister, he was 'at bottom for *paix à tout prix*'.[4] In reality a decision could no longer be postponed. When the peace conference resumed on 4 June, Gorchakov rejected any limitation of the Russian fleet; and the western representatives at once broke off. If treaties meant anything, Austria should now have gone to war; instead the Austrian army was demobilized on 10 June. The conservative alliance of Austria and France had lasted less than six months; Palmerston was not far wrong when he called it 'a stillborn child'.

The liberal alliance of Great Britain and France remained; and the pattern of September 1854 was repeated. Since diplomacy had failed, the allies once more tried war. The Austrian demobilization of 10 June had come too late to help the Russians; their army in Galicia could not be transferred to the Crimea in time to meet the allied attack. The allies took the offensive against Sebastopol in June; and it fell on 8 September. The Crimean war had been won; but the allies were as far as ever from knowing what to do with their victory. They were at a loss where to attack Russia next; and equally at a loss what terms to demand after further victories. The British wished simply to continue the existing course of war without war-aims: more amphibious attacks in the Black Sea and in the Baltic,[5]

---

[1] Cowley to Clarendon, 4 May 1854.

[2] Russell took the view that, since Napoleon had rejected counterpoise, he was no longer bound to it; and therefore remained in the cabinet, more bellicose than ever. But when Buol, after the breakdown of the conference, revealed that Russell had supported counterpoise, British opinion was in an uproar and Russell was forced to resign. It was the irremediable catastrophe of his political career.

[3] Cowley to Clarendon, no. 584, 20 May 1854.

[4] Cowley to Clarendon, 18 May 1854.

[5] With a Baltic expedition in view, the British and French concluded an alliance with Sweden in November.

until Russia was cut off from salt water altogether. Palmerston cheerfully contemplated 'licking the Russians' by October 1856.[1] This programme did not suit Napoleon III. French public opinion was weary of the war; and would not be satisfied with the capture of fortresses in Georgia and Circassia. The French had ceased to be a warlike nation; it was the great delusion of the Second Empire that they would recover their enthusiasm for war if they were offered a 'revolutionary' programme, revising the map of Europe from one end to the other. Napoleon was urgent to raise the question of Poland; after all, the restoration of Poland made good sense, if Russia was to be excluded from Europe. The British could not tolerate this proposal. However much Napoleon and Walewski might dress up their Polish plans in the modest form of restoring the constitution granted to 'Congress Poland' by the congress of Vienna, the raising of the Polish question would drive Austria and Prussia back to Russia, revive the Holy Alliance, and thus launch a 'revolutionary' war in Italy and on the Rhine. It was certainly not the British object to restore the Empire of Napoleon I; and since Napoleon III shrank from war without the British alliance, his only way out was to make peace.

Two paths to peace were open for French diplomacy. One was the path, already tried, of invoking 'Europe' against Russia, that is, of again involving Austria; the other was of a direct settlement with Russia behind the backs of the British. An influential party, led by Morny, Napoleon's half-brother, favoured the latter course. Morny, the greatest speculator of the Second Empire, already saw in Russia 'a mine to be exploited by France';[2] he imagined that Russia, in return for French capital, would give France a free hand in Europe. Morny made secret contact with Gorchakov and tried to win him for a deal. France and England, he said, 'will soon be astonished how little they care for each other'; and the proposed limitation of Russian power in the Black Sea, supposedly so humiliating, was negligible—such clauses never lasted long. Gorchakov was the leading representative of the new line in Russian policy, the line of considering only Russian interests even at the risk of aiding the revolution in Europe;[3] and he would have responded to Morny's

---

[1] Palmerston to Clarendon, 16 Oct. 1855.
[2] Morny to Walewski, 8 Aug. 1856.
[3] When Gorchakov was appointed to Vienna, Nesselrode objected on the

approach. The idea was too daring for Alexander II and Nesselrode; though they too had abandoned the Holy Alliance, their alternative was sullen isolation, not an alliance with Napoleon III. Morny's move, however, reached Buol's ears and alarmed him: a Franco-Russian deal over Austria's head, and at her expense, had been his greatest fear. He therefore proposed to the French to formulate a more stringent version of the Four Points and to impose these upon Russia by an Austrian ultimatum; in return, Great Britain and France should join with Austria in guaranteeing the integrity of Turkey. This offer was accepted by the French; they were thus back on the old line of Drouyn de Lhuys. The British, too, took their old line: though they much disliked Austria dictating terms of peace without having fought in the war, they could think of no terms of their own and therefore acquiesced, meaning to formulate objections when Austria and France had reached agreement.

The intrigues of November 1855 were a fitting end to a war in which diplomacy had only occasionally been interrupted by battles. The French ascertained through Morny what terms the Russians were likely to accept; they then suggested these terms to Buol; and finally presented them to the British as the terms which Buol was willing to impose upon the Russians. The terms agreed by Buol and Bourqueney, the French ambassador, on 14 November were in essence the Four Points, defined rather more closely. Buol improved the first point in Austria's favour by stipulating that Russia should surrender part of Bessarabia so as to be altogether cut off from the Danube. The third point was turned into Drouyn's project of 'neutralizing' the Black Sea; since the Russian fleet there had ceased to exist, this was a concession to Russia, implying as it did that the Turkish fleet would cease to exist also. Moreover, neutralization was to be laid down only in a separate treaty between Russia and Turkey. When the British were told of these terms, they were tempted to reject them altogether—no real security against Russia in the Black Sea, no mention of the Baltic. Palmerston wrote: 'we stick to the great Principles of Settlement which are required for the future security of Europe. . . . If the French government

grounds of his incompetence. Nicholas I replied: 'I have nominated him because he is Russian.' Meyendorff, his predecessor, had been, like Nesselrode himself, a German.

change their opinion, responsibility will rest with them, and the People of the two countries will be told of it.'[1] Clarendon, despairing as ever, thought that France would make a separate peace and that Great Britain could not continue the war alone.[2] After much bitter exchange he extracted some concessions from Walewski: neutralization of the Black Sea should be put in the general treaty, and the allies should specify as Point 5 their intention to demand further 'particular conditions'—but Austria was not to be asked to support these conditions. This was a new version of the old tactic by which Austria was to be lured into supporting terms to which she had not agreed. Yet even now Austria did not intend to go to war; all she offered was to break off diplomatic relations or, in Buol's words, 'la guerre sans la bataille'.

The Austrian ultimatum, grudgingly agreed to by the British, was sent off to St. Petersburg on 15 December. The Russians tried to bargain, as they had over their original acceptance of the Four Points; their temporizing answer was rejected by Buol on 5 January 1856—now that they were defeated he had no objection to humiliating them. The decisive Russian crown council was held on 15 January. As well as the Austrian ultimatum, Alexander II had also urgent letters from Frederick William IV 'imploring' him to give way, and warning him that, though Prussia did not support the ultimatum,[3] she might not be able to remain neutral if France threatened her with war on the Rhine. The Holy Alliance was indeed dissolved. Still, the Russians would not have had to give way, if they had not worn themselves out in their defence of Sebastopol; there they had defeated themselves, and they accepted terms of defeat because they could no longer contend with the allies, not because they were faced with new enemies. At the last moment Gorchakov telegraphed from Vienna, urging that the Austrian terms be rejected and that instead a direct appeal be made to France;[4]

---

[1] Palmerston to Clarendon, 1 Dec. 1855.

[2] Clarendon to Palmerston, 18 Nov. 1855.

[3] Characteristically, and falsely, Frederick William told the French that he had supported the ultimatum at St. Petersburg; and even drafted a semi-public letter to the tsar to bolster up this story.

[4] The appeal might well have been successful. In the anxious period of waiting between the first and second Russian replies (5 Jan. and 16 Jan.) Napoleon III wrote to Queen Victoria, advocating direct negotiations with the Russians and the offer of concessions by the allies.

Nesselrode suppressed the telegram and won the council for unconditional acceptance of the Austrian terms. All the same Gorchakov had made his name; it was the telegram of 15 January which led to his nomination as vice-chancellor and began his policy of *entente* with France.

The diplomatic battle was over for everyone except the British. They had still to fight a prolonged engagement with Walewski over the 'particular conditions', which they wished Russia to accept in the preliminary peace. Walewski was now bent on conciliating the Russians and described this demand as 'a second ultimatum'. There was a last discreditable compromise: the 'particular conditions' were accepted as *sine quibus non* by Walewski, and the Russians were even told of this, but they were left out of the preliminary peace.[1] The British got their way on a more important point. They wanted to impose terms on the Russians, not to conciliate them; they therefore insisted on an early meeting of the peace congress, so as to be free to threaten a renewal of war in the spring. With this the peace preliminaries were signed on 1 February 1856. The Crimean war was over. It had cost the lives of nearly half a million men,[2] a larger total than that of any other European

---

[1] It would be futile to speculate whether Walewski meant ultimately to cheat the British or the Russians or both. Like the endless compromises earlier devised by Drouyn, all of which implied a deception of one or other party, this compromise too was a translation into diplomatic terms of the hope that something would turn up. Walewski, Drouyn, Morny, and the rest of Napoleon's 'swell mob' (Clarendon's phrase), introduced into international affairs the methods of lying and dishonesty which had made the *coup d'état*; they knew no other methods. With no conscience and no policy, Walewski and the others thought simply of escaping from the particular problem of the moment, regardless whether it would create a greater problem later.

Contrary to the common view, diplomacy is an art which, despite its subtlety, depends on the rigid accuracy of all who practise it. To have a great state ruled and run by liars was a unique problem with which the statesmen of Europe were unfitted to deal. French policy could not be pinned down by negotiating with the foreign minister, whether Drouyn or Walewski; decisions could be obtained only from Napoleon, who—with all the dishonesty of his gangster-followers—had also a quality of resolution which made him their chief. But Napoleon was equally unreliable; and the bewildering diplomacy of the 'fifties and 'sixties is explained in large part by this fact. One of the parties in a game with complicated rules made it more complicated by persistent cheating, even on unimportant points. If indeed there was a decline in international morality, the origins of this are to be found in Napoleon and his associates, not in Bismarck. He only applied the maxim *à corsaire, corsaire et demi*.

[2] The French lost nearly 100,000 men; the British 60,000; the Russians over 300,000. Two-thirds of the total casualties were from disease and hardship, not from battle.

war fought in the hundred years after the congress of Vienna. In the Near East the outcome of the war seemed confused and disappointing; in Europe it was decisive. The war shattered both the myth and the reality of Russian power. Whatever its origin, the war was in essence an invasion of Russia by the west;[1] of the five invasions of Russia in modern times,[2] it was by far the most successful. After 1856 Russia carried less weight in European affairs than at any time since the end of the Great Northern war in 1721; and the predominance which she had exercised at Berlin and Vienna before 1854 she was never to wield again until 1945. The rulers and peoples of Europe west of the Vistula were free to make of Europe what they would. If Russia was indeed the tyrant of Europe, then the Crimean war was a war of liberation. This liberation delivered Europe first into the hands of Napoleon III, then into those of Bismarck.

[1] Even Kinglake, an enthusiast for the war, called his history *The Invasion of the Crimea*.

[2] Napoleon in 1812; the British and French in 1854; the Germans in 1916–18; the entente Powers in 1919–20; Hitler in 1941.

V

THE CONGRESS OF PARIS AND ITS CONSEQUENCES

1856–8

THE peace congress which met at Paris from 25 February until 16 April was in theory the first European meeting since the congress of Verona in 1822—all intermediate meetings had been conferences, limited to specific subjects. As a matter of fact it was more successful as a conference, settling the particular questions of the Near East, than as a congress discussing the affairs of all Europe. Since the Russians had already accepted the Austrian ultimatum and even, indirectly, the 'particular conditions', there was no fundamental struggle over the terms of peace. Contrary to British expectations, the Russians swallowed the neutralization of the Aaland islands, the most important 'particular condition'; they jibbed only at ceding territory in Bessarabia. They put forward the plausible argument that they should retain Bessarabia in compensation for the Turkish fortress of Kars which they had captured just before the armistice. Bessarabia was Austria's affair; and Kars, the gateway to Asiatic Turkey, was Great Britain's. Napoleon III cared for neither and was eager to conciliate Russia. The British, who had no such desire, stood firm;[1] and the Russians had to give way. This was a preliminary warning that Napoleon, though anxious to win Russia, would not do so at the expense of the British alliance. Apart from this there was no serious conflict; and the peace treaty was signed on 30 March.

The treaty 'solved' the problem of relations between Russia and Turkey in three ways: the Turks gave a voluntary promise

[1] Clarendon, the British representative, only after a stern telegram from the British cabinet. Clarendon, as usual, lost his nerve, particularly when he saw that Napoleon was bent on peace. Palmerston, as usual, believed that resolution would carry the day. Besides, 'if Russia is allowed to consider this an open question . . . what is the use of making any treaty with her?' Palmerston to Clarendon, 29 Feb. 1856.

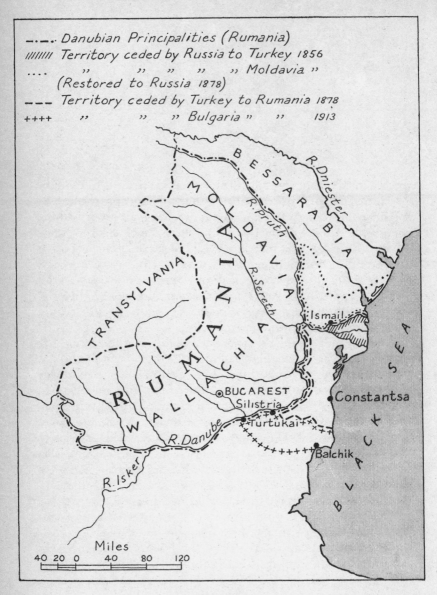

_._._. Danubian Principalities (Rumania)
////////// Territory ceded by Russia to Turkey 1856
....   ,,   ,,   ,,   ,,   ,, Moldavia ,,
    (Restored to Russia 1878)
___ Territory ceded by Turkey to Rumania 1878
++++   ,,   ,,   ,, Bulgaria ,,   ,,   1913

RUMANIA

to reform; the Black Sea was neutralized; the Danubian princi-palities were made independent of Russia. Of these three methods, the first counted for nothing; the Turks never put their promises into execution. Neutralization of the Black Sea was the prized achievement of 1856; it seemed to provide what the western Powers had long sought—a barrier against Russia without effort from themselves. In reality, like all disarmament clauses in a peace treaty, it was an attempt to perpetuate an existing Balance of Power when that balance should have changed: the Russians were to promise to behave for all time as though the British and French fleets were in the Black Sea when in fact they had gone away. Neutralization lacked a sanc-tion other than Russian good faith; and if this could be relied on, neutralization was unnecessary. No such compulsory dis-armament had ever been imposed upon a Great Power, except by Napoleon I on Prussia in 1807; and the allies would not have presented such terms to any Power whom they regarded as truly European. At bottom, the British and to a lesser extent the French regarded Russia as a semi-Asiatic state, not much above the level of Turkey and not at all above the level of China.[1] The view was not without truth; the Russians resented it the more for that reason and made the abolition of the Black Sea clauses the principal object of their diplomacy.[2]

The freeing of the Danubian principalities, which led ulti-mately to an independent Rumania, was the real achievement of the treaty of Paris. This independence rested on a real sanc-tion—the jealousy of Russia and Austria. The Austrians had got the Russians out by threat of war in August 1854; but, since they would not pay the price for western support by withdrawing from Lombardy and Venetia, they did not get themselves in. The Austrian troops which were still occupying the principali-ties had to be withdrawn on the conclusion of peace. The principalities caused new disputes after the peace congress: the frontiers of Bessarabia had to be defined, the status of the

[1] When Walewski objected that the demand to have consuls in the Black Sea ports controlling Russian disarmament was humiliating to Russia, Cowley replied that it had been imposed upon China by treaty. Cowley to Clarendon, no. 1551, 28 Nov. 1855.

[2] Palmerston answered Russian complaints (to Clarendon, no. 6, 26 Feb. 1856): 'It is no doubt humiliating to be compelled by force of arms to submit to Condi-tions which without such compulsion she would have refused; but Russia has brought this humiliation upon herself.' France did not bring this humiliation upon herself by waging war on all Europe for more than twenty years.

principalities—whether united, whether independent of Turkey —had to be settled. Fundamentally Rumania had come into existence as a genuine buffer-state, guaranteed by the rivalry of her two great neighbours, and a barrier against either a Russian invasion of the Balkans or an Austrian domination of the Danube. Whereas the clauses neutralizing the Black Sea lasted only fifteen years, independent Rumania survived until 1941.

When the Near East had been settled, the congress turned itself, less successfully, into a great European gathering. Though the British had always been the principal advocates of 'the Concert of Europe', they insisted on excluding Prussia from the peace negotiations, in resentment at her policy of neutrality; even when these were concluded the Prussians got in only on the technical ground that, as signatories of the Straits convention of 1841, they must acquiesce in its revision. It was dangerous for the British to lay down the principle that only Powers which had taken part in a war were entitled to make peace; in later years, the argument could easily be turned against themselves. Prussia's position appeared humiliating: she entered the congress late, under Austrian patronage, and her representatives had to wait in an ante-room, while Clarendon had a last fling against them. In reality Prussian policy had scored a great success: Prussia had steered herself through the Crimean war without alienating either side, and Manteuffel was already prophesying an alliance between Russia and France, in which Prussia would make a third.[1]

Napoleon wanted to follow the signature of the peace treaty by a discussion which should ramble over all Europe; this had been his dream ever since 1849. The excuse was to be the presence of armies of occupation on foreign soil. The Austrians were already committed to withdrawing their forces from the Danubian principalities; Poland, Greece, Italy made up the rest of the list. Orlov, the principal Russian representative, objected that any mention of Poland would offend Alexan-

[1] So he told the Sardinian minister at Berlin, no doubt with the intention of encouraging Sardinia to embarrass Austria on the other side. Launay to Cibrario, 16 Feb. 1856. *Cavour e l'Inghilterra*, i, no. 242. The legend became later established that Prussia had followed a policy of subservience to Austria, and was rescued from it only by Bismarck. This legend is sustained by the anxious dispatches which Bismarck wrote to Manteuffel during the Crimean war. In fact Manteuffel knew what he was doing without Bismarck's prompting; and Bismarck's own policy later was less original than he liked to make out. At best he conducted with more daring a policy that had been long defined.

der II and turn him against the liberal concessions that he was proposing to make there; Poland was therefore passed over in silence. The foreign troops in Greece were British and French;[1] and it did not become the congress to attack the two victorious Powers. Only Italy remained; and Napoleon turned the discussion the more readily against Austria to distract attention from the French troops in Rome. Besides he had failed to satisfy any of Cavour's practical demands, designed to set the Italian question in motion;[2] therefore was the more willing to give Cavour an opportunity of speaking his mind. The sensation of the session of 8 April was, however, Clarendon, not Cavour. Clarendon no doubt wanted to work off the irritation against Austria which he had been accumulating since the beginning of the war; besides, an attack on clerical rule in Rome as 'a disgrace to Europe' was an easy way of winning the favour of English Protestants.[3]

Though the speeches of 8 April did nothing for Italy and were poor consolation for Cavour, they were a deadly blow to Austria: the Powers generally, and not merely Lamartine, transient foreign minister of a provisional government, had ceased to believe in the moral validity of the treaties of 1815 and hence in Austria's European mission. Ever since 1849 Austria had based her rule in Italy on the right of the stronger; now the Powers took her at her word. Buol attempted a counterstroke. A guarantee of Turkey by Austria and the western Powers had been part of every negotiation over peace terms since the drafting of the original Four Points; and Buol had renewed this condition when preparing the ultimatum to Russia in December 1855. He now called for its fulfilment; and Napoleon had to

---

[1] They had gone there in May 1854 in order to compel Greece to remain neutral during the Crimean war.

[2] Such as that the duke of Modena and the duchess of Parma (Austrian satellites) should become rulers of Moldavia and Wallachia, and their Italian lands given to Sardinia. This would both benefit Austria and yet disturb the Italian *status quo.* Later Cavour suggested that the duchess of Parma should marry the duke of Carignan, a member of the house of Savoy; and that the married pair should rule the united principalities.

[3] Protestant feeling against the pope played an important part in winning British support for Italian unity, especially among tories who did not otherwise favour the nationalist cause. Thus Shaftesbury was Cavour's most reliable instrument in British politics. The same feeling, of course, did something later to win British favour for Protestant Prussia against Roman Catholic Austria and even against France, which combined Roman Catholicism and atheism, both distasteful to Protestant tories.

agree, much against his will. On 15 April, France and Great Britain signed a treaty, guaranteeing the independence and integrity of the Ottoman empire, though not specifically against Russia—the one concession which Napoleon obtained. Austria at last committed herself in peace to the cause which she had refused to defend in war; since the danger had passed, the risk seemed small. In return Buol supposed that he had barred the way against an alliance between Russia and France; still more important, he supposed that since Napoleon was committed to supporting the *status quo* in the Near East he could not work against it in Italy. This was an echo in reverse of Metternich's persistent hope that, if he committed Russia to conservatism in Europe, she must be conservative in the Near East also. The disappointment of the one hope caused the Crimean war; of the other the Italian war of 1859.

Buol was not, however, the only one to be mistaken in his calculations. The congress of Paris proved a disappointment to nearly all who attended it: only the Prussians, who came late and expected nothing, had their hopes fulfilled. The British were sharply aware that they had not got their way: in fact they exaggerated the ease with which Russia would recover from her defeat.[1] Cavour is often made out to have scored a triumph at the congress; but, short of being excluded, he could hardly have done worse. He got none of the concessions which even he had originally regarded as essential in return for taking part in the war. Nothing was changed in Italy. Austria was not, to all appearance, estranged from the western Powers; Sardinia was not treated as a Great Power and was not even given the chance of adhering to the treaty of guarantee of 15 April. It is true that Sardinia's military assistance had won British gratitude; and during the congress when the British were still full of fight, both Clarendon and Palmerston talked of supporting Sardinia in the coming war against Austria.[2] This enthusiasm did not

---

[1] Palmerston wrote to Clarendon, 7 Mar. 1856: 'The treaty will leave Russia a most formidable Power able in a few years when she shall by wiser internal Policy have developed her immense Natural Resources to place in danger the great Interests of Europe. But the future must look after itself.'

[2] After the session of 8 Apr. Cavour said to Clarendon: 'Italy has nothing to hope from diplomacy.' Clarendon: 'You are perfectly right, but you must not say so.' Cavour: 'You would be forced to help us.' Clarendon: 'Certainly; and it would be gladly and with great energy.' Cavour to D'Azeglio, 11 Apr. 1856. *Cavour e l'Inghilterra*, i, no. 521. Palmerston told Cavour: 'He might say to the Emperor that for every step he might be ready to take in Italian affairs he would

last. Clarendon was no sooner back in England than he took offence at Cavour's relations with members of the opposition; and within a year (April 1857) the British government were demanding that Cavour should lessen the tension in Italy by declaring his respect for the treaty settlement of 1815. In any case French policy, not British, would decide the future of Italy; and there is no reason to suppose that Napoleon's later attitude would have been different had Sardinia followed Prussia's example and remained neutral during the Crimean war. In 1856 Napoleon was still a long way from launching a war of Italian liberation; when he did so, it was not because of Sardinia's contribution to the Crimean war. The only defence for Cavour must be found in home policy: at least he prevented the war being fought by a conservative Sardinian government and thus kept open a door for the future. But the Crimean war was not the moment when opportunity knocked so far as Italy was concerned.

Most of all the congress of Paris was not the moment when opportunity knocked for a Napoleonic reconstruction of Europe. It was no doubt highly flattering to Napoleon III that the congress met at Paris and under his aegis. But nothing was changed from the days of the congress of Vienna except the meeting-place of the congress. Who, in the forty years that had passed since Waterloo, would ever have foretold that in a congress, meeting at Paris and presided over by an illegitimate son of the great Napoleon (Walewski), nothing should have been said about Poland and nothing done about Italy? The congress of Paris was not a European acknowledgement of the Second Empire; it was an acknowledgement of France as a conservative Power, an assertion in fact that the Second Empire was not the First. Napoleon III had accomplished something beyond the reach of Napoleon I: he had achieved alliance with Great Britain. But it had been accomplished at the price of abandoning Napoleonic designs in Europe: he had failed to extend the war from the Near East to Italy and the Rhine. Napoleon III was aware of his failure; and he had thought too of a solution. While retaining the British alliance, he would escape from its

probably find us ready to take one and a Half.' Palmerston to Clarendon, 30 Apr. 1856. And again (to Clarendon, 27 May 1856): 'Buol must be made to understand that in the next war between Austria and Sardinia, if it is brought about as it will be by the fault of Austria, Sardinia will not be left alone as she was last time.' The last phrase (a favourite of Palmerston's) might, of course, be only a threat of French intervention.

control by building an alliance with Russia. The congress of Paris was to be a new Tilsit; and the symbol of the congress was a resounding kiss given to Orlov by Princess Mathilde, Napoleon III's cousin, and overheard by Hübner, the Austrian representative. As Tilsit, too, the congress was a deception. At Tilsit Napoleon I had just conquered all Europe; and Alexander I represented the only Great Power left standing on the Continent. When they schemed great plans of partition, they had no obstacle except their mutual jealousies. At Paris Russia had just been excluded from Europe; and Napoleon III had not begun to conquer it. The Second Empire was pretence from start to finish; and in nothing more so than in the pretence that Austria, Prussia, and Great Britain had ceased to exist as Great Powers. Besides, the project of alliance between France and Russia rested on pretence towards each other. Napoleon expected that the Russians would treat their defeat in the Near East as permanent and yet would acquiesce in his overthrowing the *status quo* in western Europe; the Russians hoped that Napoleon would remain conservative in western Europe and would yet acquiesce in their destroying the peace settlement in the Near East. Of the two the Russian hope was the more preposterous. After 1856 the Russians were genuinely indifferent to the fate of Austria in Italy, though not to that of Prussia on the Rhine; Napoleon III could not be indifferent to the settlement in the Near East, for it was his own work. Thus the congress of Paris ushered in the great age of European deceptions, not an age of European peace.

For most of the Powers the Crimean war had been an indecisive engagement and the congress of Paris brought no great change. In Napoleon's own words: 'what should have been a great political revolution had been reduced to a simple tournament'.[1] For Russia the war had been a decisive defeat, and the congress was a setback without parallel. Therefore Russian policy after the congress of Paris had a singleness of purpose lacking in that of other Powers: it was bent on the revision of the treaty of Paris to the exclusion of all else. Before 1854 Russia had perhaps neglected her national interests for the sake of general European concerns; now, for fifteen years, she neglected everything in Europe for the sake of her national interests. Or

[1] Napoleon III to Walewski, 24 Dec. 1858. Valsecchi, *L'unificazione italiana e la politica europea 1854–1859*, p. 336.

rather for the sake of her national honour. In the eighteenth, and even in the early nineteenth century, the Black Sea and the Near East had been the decisive sphere of Russia's imperial ambitions. They were ceasing to be so. Russia's imperial future lay in Asia; her only concern in the Black Sea was defensive. The Balkans offered trivial prizes compared to those of central Asia and the Far East. But this could not be appreciated by a tsar and by statesmen who had suffered the humiliation of loss of territory and of a compulsory neutralization of the Black Sea. Russian diplomacy concentrated for a generation on the wrong object. Gorchakov, who took over foreign affairs from Nesselrode in May 1856, symbolized the new policy. He defined it in simple terms to Kiselev, his ambassador in Paris: 'I am looking for a man who will annul the clauses of the treaty of Paris, concerning the Black Sea question and the Bessarabian frontier; I am looking for him and I shall find him.'[1] Gorchakov's mind was shaped by his experiences of the Vienna conferences; he had tried there to negotiate directly with the French over the heads of the Austrians, and he was convinced that the aim of Russian policy should be to separate Austria and France. This was not difficult: there was nothing Napoleon III would like better than to escape with Russian assistance from the Austrian alliance which had been forced upon him by his conservative advisers. But Gorchakov failed to understand that Napoleon would not be so easily parted from the British; the Napoleonic dream was of a reconstruction of Europe *à trois*—a new Tilsit indeed, but with a British representative on the raft and not (as legend has it) hiding underneath it.

The Russian mistake was shared by Morny, who went to St. Petersburg as ambassador in a blaze of glory. Morny had strong economic reasons for disliking the British connexion; he wished France to replace Great Britain as the financier of Russia.[2] Although he was without sympathy for Napoleon's schemes of revising the map of Europe, he hoped to prevent these by tying Napoleon to the Russian alliance; at the same time, knowing Napoleon's obstinacy, he had to make out that this alliance would open the door to treaty revision. As a result

<hr />

[1] Zablochii, *Kiselev*, iii. 37.

[2] Morny's career is disturbing for the theory that 'finance-imperialism' started only in the eighteen-eighties. Morny had obtained a large railway concession for his 'Grande Société' in 1851. This gave him plenty of opportunity for speculation on the Bourse, though it built few railways in Russia.

he both misled the Russians as to Napoleon's eagerness for their alliance and misled Napoleon as to what he might get out of it. No sooner was the congress over than the Russians, encouraged by Morny, began to cheat in the execution of the treaty. They claimed that Serpents' Island at the mouth of the Danube, which had not been mentioned in the peace treaty, was still theirs; and they took advantage of a misunderstanding to claim Bolgrad, which stood on an arm of the Danube.[1] The British, however, were still in that shortlived mood of confident belligerence which often follows their victory in war. They sent their fleet back into the Black Sea and landed a Turkish garrison on Serpents' Island before the Russians were aware that anything was happening. Bolgrad was more difficult. It was beyond the range of simple sea-power. Besides, Napoleon wanted to meet the Russian claim. He had a guilty conscience about the treaty of 15 April with Austria and Great Britain. This had implied lack of faith in Russia just when he was trying to get on good terms with her; and he thought that the best way of obliterating this disloyalty towards Russia was by acting disloyally towards his allies in the question of Bolgrad.[2] The Russians made the most of this situation. As well, with the British fleet in the Black Sea and the Austrians still in the principalities, they were genuinely frightened: intending to evade the conditions of peace themselves, they suspected the British and Austrians of intending to do the same. When Gorchakov asked Napoleon to protect Russia from Austria and Great Britain, he was not merely trying to separate the allies; he really supposed that Russia needed protection.

To win over Napoleon, Gorchakov offered to give up Bolgrad in exchange for any compensation that Napoleon cared to name; in addition, Napoleon should sign a secret treaty with Russia, guaranteeing the execution of the treaty of Paris. Since the treaty had been made as a consequence of Russia's defeat, this seemed a surprising suggestion; its meaning became clear when Gorchakov specified that Napoleon should keep the

[1] This was a characteristic piece of Russian sharp practice. At the congress the Russians had asked to retain Bolgrad as centre of the Bulgarian colony in Bessarabia, and the request was granted; this was certainly the Bolgrad that they now claimed. But the only map submitted to the congress showed a different, unimportant Bolgrad not on the Danube; and it was this Bolgrad which the Powers thought that they were leaving to Russia.

[2] Cowley to Clarendon, 26 June 1856.

Straits closed against the British and should compel the Austrians to evacuate the principalities. Fear and guile were characteristically mixed; and it was small consolation that the neutralization of the Black Sea was to be reaffirmed. To make the proposition more attractive Morny wrote: 'Russia is the only power who will ratify in advance any aggrandizement of France. *I have already received the assurance of this.*'[1] Morny and Gorchakov had asked too much. It was one thing for Napoleon to abandon Austria; to abandon Great Britain quite another. He said to Kiselev: 'Could not the three of us agree? Together we could rule Europe.' Besides, Morny was not the only member of Napoleon's private circle; Persigny, now ambassador at London, had even stronger claims on Napoleon's gratitude. Persigny was always the man of the British alliance, if only to distinguish himself from Morny and Drouyn. He insisted that Walewski and Morny were repeating the mistake of Louis Philippe, when they quarrelled with England—a comparison always alarming to Napoleon.

Early in November 1856 Persigny came over to Compiègne and, aided by Cowley, carried the day. Napoleon agreed to the British proposal that the congress should be resumed solely to answer the question: 'which Bolgrad did the Congress intend to give to Russia?' Further Napoleon sent a secret message to Cavour that Sardinia should vote on the British side; this, with Great Britain, Austria, and Turkey, gave an anti-Russian majority, and Napoleon could vote ineffectively for Russia. The Prussians had intended to refuse to attend the meeting; they were told by the Russians that this was conduct unworthy of a Great Power and, when they learnt that Napoleon had safely rigged things, they came to give an ineffective vote for Russia also. Morny did not give up altogether. He asked that, since Napoleon would not sign a secret treaty with Russia, he should at least write a private letter to the tsar, promising to enforce the treaty of Paris. Even this was too much for Napoleon; and all the Russians got, when they had lost Bolgrad, was a dispatch from Walewski, affirming French loyalty to the treaty of Paris. The dispatch was harmless enough to be shown to the British.

While the Russians pressed for a secret treaty directed against the British, they failed to offer Napoleon anything in regard to Italy—the only point which might have attracted him. Quite

[1] Charles-Roux, *Alexandre II, Gortchakoff et Napoléon III*, p. 163.

the reverse, in the autumn of 1856, they showed disapproval of his Italian policy. Napoleon, and the British too for that matter, were still fumbling for some means with which to 'open' the Italian question. Cavour was not yet ready to challenge Austria; the only opening therefore seemed to be to complain of mis-government in Naples—and there was plenty of ground for complaint. In October 1856 Great Britain and France broke off diplomatic relations with Naples and threatened to follow this up with a fleet demonstration. Since neither of them was prepared to go beyond this and since the British, in addition, were afraid that a revolution in Naples might end up with Murat, Napoleon's cousin, on the throne, the fleet demonstra-tion never took place. But enough had been done to provoke a Russian protest. Alexander II said to Morny: 'This disturbs the principles which all governments have an interest to preserve and outside which there is no stability.' Though the Naples affair had no sequel, it already exposed the contradiction which would ultimately destroy the Franco-Russian entente. The Russians insisted that Napoleon should 'make a step' towards Alexander II for the sake of the entente, that is, he should give up his revisionist plans; also, they expected him 'to make a step' away from the British. Napoleon, on the other hand, expected the Russians to second his revisionist plans and to acquiesce in the Anglo-French alliance. After all, he wanted the entente in order to make things easier for his plans in Italy; and for these the alliance with Great Britain was even more necessary. Napoleon, in fact, was anti-Austrian; the Russians, obsessed with the Black Sea, saw Great Britain as their principal opponent.

The choice of allies was presented still more sharply to Napoleon in the course of 1857. Bolgrad had been a trivial affair, a mere trial of strength. The future of the Danubian principalities presented a question of a different order. The congress of Paris had failed to agree whether they should be united. The French had favoured union, in accordance with Napoleon's general support of nationalism; and they had been seconded rather half-heartedly by Clarendon. The Turks and the Austrians had opposed union. The Turks feared that a united Rumania would soon end its theoretical dependence on Turkey; the Austrians dreaded even more the effect of a Rumanian national state on the millions of Rumanians within the Habs-burg empire. The Russians had at first sat silent; after all, a

united Rumania would be a barrier also against them. But
when they saw the chance of dividing France from Austria and
Turkey, they came down on the side of union. Since the congress
could not agree, it took the usual weak line of international
gatherings and decided to leave the question to a commission,
which was to ascertain the wishes of the inhabitants. By the
time the commission got to work, the British government had
repented of Clarendon's support of union. As the Bolgrad affair
showed, they could count only on Austria and Turkey, not on
France, to enforce the treaty against Russia. Besides, Stratford,
at Constantinople, had never approved of dismembering Turkey
for the sake of French favour; and he encouraged every Turkish
device to rig the elections in the principalities against union. In
July 1857 the elections in Moldavia were conducted with
shameless dishonesty. Thouvenel, the French ambassador, demanded that they should be annulled; and when this was
refused broke off diplomatic relations with the Porte. He was
followed by the Russian ambassador; and this time the Franco-
Russian side had a majority. Sardinia supported the cause of an
anti-Austrian nationalism for obvious reasons; and the Prussians
were delighted to make a third in the Franco-Russian alliance
that they anticipated.

These expectations were once more disappointed by the
efforts of Persigny and by Napoleon's determination not to
follow the example of Louis Philippe. Persigny argued that it
was not in France's interest to dismember European Turkey;
besides, if France was to draw the sword, it should be for some
great principle, such as 'the Rhine provinces, Italy, Poland, or
Hungary'. Napoleon on his side clung to the idea that England,
France, and Russia should settle the affairs of Europe together.
By July 1857 the British had a pressing motive to avoid a new
crisis in the Near East: the Indian Mutiny had broken out, and
it was obvious that British forces would be fully occupied in
India for a long time. Napoleon was therefore a welcome
visitor at Osborne from 6 to 10 August. Though he had no luck
with Prince Albert when he aired his 'fixed idea' of a general
revision of the map of Europe, he was able to settle the dispute
over the principalities. The 'Pact of Osborne'[1] provided that the

---

[1] It is characteristic of Napoleonic diplomacy that there was no 'Pact of Osborne'. Palmerston drew up a memorandum, which Walewski accepted as accurate, though he refused to sign it. Thereafter Walewski made statements of what

election in Moldavia should be annulled; in return the French dropped their support of full union in favour of an 'administrative union', which should leave the two principalities still politically separate. The British disavowed Stratford; and Napoleon disavowed French policy. As a matter of fact, the problem of the principalities now passed to the inhabitants themselves; and they settled it by the beginning of 1859 in favour of union.[1]

Napoleon's visit to Osborne in August was followed by a much more grandiose affair in September: his meeting with Alexander II at Stuttgart. This was the first time that Napoleon had met a continental ruler of any importance; though a triumph for him, it was a modest affair when compared to Napoleon I's meeting with Alexander I at Erfurt in 1808. The Russians came on the hunt for solid agreements; Napoleon for his favourite pursuit of rambling conversations on the future of Europe. Gorchakov proposed to guarantee France against a renewal of the Holy Alliance and asked in return that the two Powers should settle every question by direct negotiation; as an additional inducement, Napoleon might be offered a free hand in Africa or Asia and a vague suggestion that Russia was not bound to the *status quo* in Europe. As well, Gorchakov raised his old proposal that France should guarantee the treaty of Paris. Walewski, when it came to his turn, wanted things arranged rather differently: a clear Russian declaration of readiness to revise the settlement of 1815 and a Russian promise to work with France if the Turkish empire fell to pieces. In the end the two foreign ministers avoided any written agreement. Gorchakov had no interest except in an agreement which could be used to separate England and France; Walewski, who disliked Napoleon's Italian dreams, was no doubt glad to escape anything that would encourage them. After the meeting was over Gorchakov said complacently: 'It is above all in the future that Stuttgart will bear its true fruits.'[2] By this he meant only that he and Walewski were still looking round for means with which to cheat each other.

had happened at Osborne, quite in contradiction to Palmerston's memorandum; this was his usual diplomatic method.

[1] The elections, when reasonably honest, went overwhelmingly in favour of the Union candidates; and the two representative bodies then solved the practical problem by electing the same hospodar or prince.

[2] Baudin (French chargé d'affaires at St. Petersburg) to Walewski, 16 Oct. 1857. Schüle, *Rußland und Frankreich 1856–59*, p. 155.

The two emperors did rather better. As Napoleon was the dominant personality he got his way, and the conversation rambled over the map of Europe. Alexander had come in hope of an anti-British agreement over the Danubian principalities; instead he was invited to acquiesce in the pact of Osborne and, having withdrawn his ambassador from Constantinople to please Napoleon, now had to send him back to please the British. Apart from this, the two emperors did not discuss the affairs of the Near East. Napoleon murmured 'Poland'; Alexander said that he wished Poland to prosper 'under the sceptre of the Emperor of Russia'. With equal vagueness Napoleon mentioned Italy. Alexander replied that 'he would not repeat the mistake of 1849'; this was the most concrete statement of the meeting, but it did not amount to much—even in 1849 Russia had aided Austria only in Hungary, not in Italy. Besides, Alexander went on to ask Napoleon to renew diplomatic relations with Naples; this was not at all the repudiation of the settlement of 1815 for which Napoleon had hoped. In short, Napoleon disliked the Russian programme in the Near East; the Russians disliked his programme in Italy. Therefore both sides steered clear of practical proposals and were content with the demonstration of imperial solidarity. The Russians had broken the isolation which had been the penalty of defeat; Napoleon had ended the humiliation of being a *parvenu*. But in essence their boasted entente rested on the condition that neither would take practical advantage from it.

The Stuttgart meeting alarmed the other partners in the former Holy Alliance. Frederick William took the characteristic course of avoiding commitment to either side. He refused to go to Stuttgart so as not to give the meeting the appearance of a combination against Austria. On the other hand, he refused to invite Alexander II and Francis Joseph to visit him at Berlin, since 'the Holy Alliance is dead, at least for the life-time of Alexander II'. The tsar, after much Austrian importuning, agreed to meet Francis Joseph at Weimar, on condition Buol was not present (1 Oct.). The meeting was not a success. Alexander said: 'We shall judge Austria by acts, by facts'; and Russian policy after the meeting was more demonstratively pro-French than ever in the countless trivialities which arose in the Near East. Certainly the Russians always made a reserve in their dealings with Napoleon: they needed Prussia as a protecting bulwark for Poland and did not intend to abandon her to French encroachment. But at this time Napoleon had no such projects: in fact, since his policy was anti-Austrian, he favoured the aggrandizement of Prussia in Germany. France and Russia made the complacent claim that they were 'natural allies';[1] if this phrase had any practical meaning, it could only be translated into a common hostility to Austria. But even this had to be kept a matter of sentiment. So far as principles still counted for anything, Russia favoured Austria's position in Italy; so far as treaties had any meaning, France was the ally of Austria in the Near East. The two 'natural allies' had drifted into their entente with the idea of bluffing Austria. Napoleon hoped that she would surrender Lombardy voluntarily for the sake of the Near East; Alexander that she would abet Russia's repudiation of the neutralization of the Black Sea for the sake of Italy. When Austria held firm on both points, the allies had to pretend to take their alliance seriously. Here Napoleon had the decisive advantage of his alliance with Great Britain. The British would acquiesce in his Italian plans; and they would enforce the neutralization of the Black Sea, even if he appeared to give it up. The Russians, on the other hand, had only their intimacy with Prussia; this, though invaluable with regard to Poland, was useless in the Near East. Hence it is not surprising that Napoleon won easily in the competition to turn the Franco-Russian entente to practical use.

[1] Gorchakov first used the phrase in regard to France and Russia on 5 Sept. 1856.

VI

THE ITALIAN WAR AND THE DISRUPTION OF THE SETTLEMENT OF VIENNA

1858–61

THE Italian question had obsessed Napoleon ever since he became president in 1848. This was, in part, a matter of sentiment. He had begun there; and so had the imperial career of his uncle. Frenchmen knew Italy; Germany was strange and unsympathetic to them. The liberation of Italy appealed to Frenchmen as even the recovery of the left bank of the Rhine did not. Emphasis on Italy was also for Napoleon a matter of calculation. He believed that his position would never be secure 'until the Empire has had its original, hereditary and predestined illness, the reaction against the treaties of 1815'. He imagined, or so he alleged, that, once the settlement of 1815 was overthrown in Italy, it would crumble elsewhere in Europe without a further war.[1] Since Metternich had held the same view (though of course drawing an opposite conclusion), this was a plausible or even a reasonable theory. Before the great development of German industry was launched in the middle of the nineteenth century, Italy certainly counted for more in the European Balance of Power than she did later. All the same, Italy did not count that much even in 1858; and Napoleon put so much emphasis on Italy because he shrank, perhaps unconsciously, from the trial of strength on the Rhine which was already beyond French power. Yet the destruction of French hegemony in central Europe was the decisive feature of the settlement of Vienna; and Italy was, at best, a back-door into central Europe. Men try to enter by the back-door when the front-door is too stalwart for them to move; and Napoleon's

---

[1] Napoleon III to Walewski, 24 Dec. 1858. Walewski was, of course, an opponent of the Italian adventure; and Napoleon therefore put the arguments in its favour more strongly than he felt them even himself.

Territory ceded by Austria 1859...
  „   „   „   „   1866...
Territory ceded to France 1860...
Territory promised to Italy by..... Treaty of London (1915)

SAVOY

TYROL

LOMBARDY

1859

Turin

Milan

PIEDMONT

VENETIA

1866

Trieste

NICE

PARMA

Venice

Fiume

Genoa

1860

MODENA

STATES

OF

THE

CHURCH

1860

ADRIATIC SEA

KINGDOM OF SARDINIA

CORSICA

1860

Florence

TUSCANY

1870
PAPAL
Rome
STATE

Naples

1860

THE TWO SICILIES

TYRRHENIAN

SEA

Miles
40 20 0   40   80   120

ITALY

concentration on Italy was a confession of French weakness. Where Italy might count decisively was in a struggle for the hegemony of the Mediterranean; but to enter this struggle was a further confession that France shrank from the conflict for central Europe on which her greatness depended. These deep-seated causes of the Italian obsession were, of course, often over-laid with tactical arguments; and after the congress of Paris there was a tactical argument of great weight—Austria was isolated, and Prussia was not.

Yet despite this advantage Napoleon might well have drifted on, bemusing himself with vague plans of European reconstruc-tion, had he not been pushed into action by an economic crisis and an Italian revolutionary. The economic crisis of 1857—the first since the year of revolutions—was a grave challenge to the stability of the Second Empire. Napoleon had justified his arbi-trary rule with the argument that, by guaranteeing social order, it secured prosperity. Now the prosperity vanished. The French middle classes were discontented for the first time since 1851; and the elections of May 1857 returned five avowed opponents of the Empire, despite every exertion of official influence. Napoleon was convinced that he could avoid political conces-sions at home only by a striking success in foreign policy; to stave off revolution in France he must launch the revolution abroad. On 1 January 1858 he wrote to the tsar, expressing the hope that 'a great chance might occur in which they could march side by side'; it was the first warning of the Italian storm. Even now Napoleon needed a further decisive impulse from without. It came on 14 January 1858, when Orsini, an Italian revolutionary, attempted to assassinate him. The Orsini affair was the turning-point in the history of the Second Empire as much as the plot of Georges Cadoudal had been in the career of Napoleon I. The official Bonapartists, from the empress down-wards, were only concerned with the security of the régime; for them Orsini was a criminal and nothing more. For Napoleon III Orsini was a hero; and he treated him as one. Though he had to acquiesce in Orsini's execution, he published his last letter, with its appeal for the liberation of Italy, and urged Cavour to reproduce it in the Sardinian press. Nothing could better illu-minate Napoleon's character than this patronage of a revolu-tionary conspiracy even when directed against his own life.

Napoleon was now convinced that the policy which he had

inherited from Lamartine and Cavaignac, of condemning the settlement of 1815 without attempting to destroy it, the policy in fact of the 'liberal' alliance with England, was impossible. He must either go back to a conservative alliance with Austria or forward to a revolutionary alliance with Italian nationalism; and his own preference was clear. He said: 'Austria is a cabinet for whom I have always felt, and still feel, the most lively repugnance. . . . My hope is that I shall never be pushed into an alliance with her.'[1] Intimacy with Great Britain was the first casualty of the Orsini plot. Orsini had made his preparations in England, and Napoleon demanded stronger British measures against foreign conspirators; when Palmerston attempted to meet this demand he was defeated in the house of commons (19 Feb.) and resigned. Derby's tory ministry, with Malmesbury as foreign secretary, accepted estrangement from France and was avowedly sympathetic to Austria's position in Italy. The breach was not closed even when Queen Victoria and Prince Albert visited Napoleon at Cherbourg in August, especially as Albert took alarm at the new French battleships, driven by steam, which Napoleon rashly displayed. British susceptibilities had no longer a restraining influence on French policy.

The Orsini plot was equally decisive in its effect on French relations with Sardinia. Napoleon demanded drastic restrictions on the Sardinian press; and he threatened to join hands with Austria in order to suppress nationalist agitation in Italy. It was the crisis of Cavour's career. An Austro-French alliance had always meant the doom of Italian hopes, even when, as in 1854, it had been confined to the Near East; and in January 1855 Cavour had flung himself unconditionally into the Crimean war in order to prevent an exclusive Austro-French partnership. The new alliance of which Napoleon talked would have been far more disastrous, for it would have been directed to the repression of Italy; and the events of 1849, from the abortive conference at Brussels to the peace following the second Austro-Sardinian war, had shown that Great Britain could do nothing for Italy if Austria and France were in agreement. Cavour had to outbid Austria by holding before Napoleon's eyes the advantages of a revolutionary policy; it was his strongest point that these advantages were never far from Napoleon's thoughts.

---

[1] Villamarina (Paris) to Cavour, 6 Feb.; Della Rocca (Paris) to Victor Emanuel, 13 Feb. 1858. *Carteggio Cavour–Nigra*, i, nos. 14 and 18.

There was a further consideration. Ever since taking office in 1852, Cavour had been determined to save the cause of moderate liberalism and monarchy by unifying Italy under the house of Savoy; he could not now mollify Napoleon by surrendering his liberal system and limiting the Sardinian press. Cavour had to go forward with Napoleon in order to preserve the Sardinian constitution. Not that he was unwilling to do so. He had always recognized that the Italian question was a problem in international relations, not in domestic politics; this was his great cleavage from the revolutionaries and his decisive contribution to Italian history. Italy could not make herself; she could only be made (and afterwards sustained) by exploiting the differences between the Great Powers.

Cavour offered Napoleon two temptations, dynastic and national. He was ready to marry Victor Emanuel's daughter to Napoleon's disreputable cousin, Prince Jerome; he would restore 'the natural frontiers' by surrendering Savoy, once France had helped to defeat Austria and to set up a kingdom of Upper Italy 'from the Alps to the Adriatic'. These terms suited Napoleon's every dream. After some preliminary sounding, Cavour and Napoleon met secretly at Plombières on 20 July to settle their future programme. There was to be first the marriage of Prince Jerome; then a common war against Austria. Italy would become a federation of four states under the presidency of the pope—Upper Italy under the house of Savoy; the papal states; the kingdom of the Two Sicilies; and a new kingdom of central Italy to be made out of the remnants. Napoleon hoped that this scheme would enable him to escape from his Roman entanglement. Cavour did not take it very seriously: for him, as for Bismarck later, the important thing was to get things moving, not to settle the future—that could be settled when it came. Napoleon characteristically remarked that the question of Savoy was secondary and could be arranged later. This was in one sense, a dishonest remark. Recovery of 'the natural frontiers' was essential for the sake of French public opinion. In a deeper sense, however, it represented Napoleon's own outlook: he genuinely believed that French security was to be found in liberating Italy, not in altering frontiers. Unfortunately, he had to claim the natural frontiers, so as to be allowed to carry out the work of liberation; and the achievement of the one largely destroyed the value of the other.

At Plombières Cavour and Napoleon also discussed their future tactics and arranged a division of labour. Cavour was to devise a 'respectable', that is to say a non-revolutionary, cause for war with Austria; Napoleon was to ensure that she was diplomatically isolated.[1] These tactical problems turned out to be more difficult than the conspirators had imagined. It was impossible to devise a respectable cause for war with Austria; Sardinia had no serious grievance against her except that she was a non-Italian state, ruling over Italians. Every right of treaty and law was on Austria's side; the only argument against her was the 'revolutionary' argument of nationality. When the war came, Sardinia did not even have the excuse of risings in Lombardy and Venetia which she had had in 1848; and, from a detached diplomatic standpoint, the war of 1859 was a war of uncompromising and unprovoked aggression, which must have been condemned by an international authority, had any been in existence. This is, no doubt, an argument against having an international authority; but it could not make Cavour's diplomatic task easy, let alone successful.

Napoleon for some time did no better. He had told Cavour at Plombières that 'he had the formal and repeated promise of Alexander II not to oppose his Italian plans'; this promise eluded him when it came to putting anything on paper. Moreover, he had not told Walewski of his visit to Plombières or of his plans for the future, and now negotiated behind the back of his official diplomatists, much as Louis XV had done in the days of Bourbon decay. Prince Jerome, eager for a young wife as well as for a revolutionary war, acted as Napoleon's secret agent. In September he went to Warsaw to negotiate with Alexander II.[2] He asked for a formal treaty by which Alexander II should agree to go to war if Prussia went to Austria's assistance; all he got was a verbal promise that Alexander would treat Austria and Prussia as Austria had treated him during the Crimean war—in practice, this was to be no more than an observation corps of 70,000 men on the Austrian frontier.[3] The

[1] Cavour to Victor Emanuel, 24 July 1859. *Carteggio Cavour–Nigra*, i, no. 51. Though it is usual to speak of 'the Pact of Plombières', nothing was signed; the 'pact' is merely Cavour's draft for an agreement which was concluded, with important changes, only on 19 Jan. 1859.

[2] It was a striking gesture of conciliation to greet the tsar in the capital of Poland, especially as Prince Jerome, the messenger, had attacked Russia's treatment of Poland in the French senate.

[3] Prince Jerome, on his return, made out that he had got everything he asked

two cousins were not discouraged by this failure. On Jerome's return they drafted a treaty, by which Russia should engage to immobilize 150,000 Austrian troops in Galicia—this was, after all, nearer the Crimean figure. In addition, Russia should, guarantee France against attack from Prussia; and France should guarantee Russia against attack from England. Two years previously this offer would have been attractive to Russia; now, with Italy blowing up and the Near East quiet, it had no meaning. Napoleon and his cousin recognized this. They therefore devised an entirely different treaty in the form of secret articles. These provided for nothing less than a joint war against Austria with a grand revision of the map of Europe at the end of it. Alexander should underwrite Napoleon's pact with Cavour for the future of Italy; Galicia should go to Russia and be united with congress Poland (this was a roundabout way of 'doing something for the Poles'); Hungary should be independent; the Black Sea clauses should be revised, while Alexander should give a guarantee that this revision was 'not a threat to the Porte or a danger to Constantinople'.

These terms threatened just what the Russians wished to avoid—a general upheaval in Europe with little gain to themselves in the Near East. They wanted the opposite: a revision of the treaty of Paris without a serious revision of the settlement of 1815. Early in November they returned a cool answer. Russia would support France diplomatically and even agree to territorial changes in Italy; in exchange France must regard the clauses of the treaty of Paris concerning both the Black Sea and Bessarabia 'as abolished' and should help Russia to secure their international annulment. This was far from suiting the Bonaparte cousins. Napoleon III tried the line of conciliatory vagueness that was his stock-in-trade. He wrote to Alexander II, explaining that he could not unilaterally abolish the treaty of Paris, but added: 'since we count on each other, it is clear that each agrees to support at the peace and to bring to success as much as he can the interests of his ally'. In other words, Russia was to back France in the Italian war with the vague hope that something would turn up at the peace conference. Prince Jerome was a little more concrete. He drafted a new clause by which Russia should agree generally to support

for, including even a Russian fleet in the Mediterranean. Nigra to Cavour, 6 Oct. 1858. *Carteggio Cavour–Nigra*, i, no. 104.

revision of the settlement of 1815 in exchange for French support for revision of the clauses of 1856 relating to the Black Sea. Even now Russia was being asked to swallow general revision in the west, yet was offered nothing in regard to Bessarabia.

On 2 January 1859 Walewski, still foreign minister, at last learnt of the negotiations with Russia. By now thoroughly conservative, he disliked the revisionist programme both east and west. Though he could not get Napoleon to drop the Italian affair, he persuaded him to conduct it in a respectable manner and to exclude Prince Jerome from the Russian negotiations. Walewski offered the Russians a vague hope of treaty revision at some time in the future,[1] in exchange for their benevolent neutrality in the coming war. Alexander II and Gorchakov knew that they were being tricked; and Gorchakov would have liked to break off. Alexander, however, was obsessed with the treaty of Paris and recognized that war in Italy was the essential first step towards its revision; he therefore fell back on the usual manœuvre of those who are at a loss in diplomacy and relied on a scamp's good faith. He wrote to Kiselev in Paris: 'I believe that Napoleon will do what he has promised, i.e. annul the treaty of Paris, which is a perpetual nightmare to me.' On 3 March 1859 France and Russia finally signed a secret treaty in the vaguest terms. In the Italian war Alexander II 'would adopt the political and military attitude most suited to display a benevolent neutrality towards France'. Nothing was said about the future revision of treaties, either east or west. So far as it went the treaty was a triumph for Napoleon; indeed it alone made possible the liberation of Italy. Though it did not hold out much prospect of Russia's support, it secured him against her opposition. He was free to overthrow the existing settlement in Italy if he felt himself strong enough to do so; whereas the Russians, by failing to include any stipulation concerning the treaty of Paris, were still not free to overthrow the settlement in the Near East, for which, in any case, they lacked the strength. In short, the Russians hoped to cheat Napoleon at some time in the future; they therefore gave Napoleon an immediate opportunity to cheat them.

Napoleon had thus arrived somewhat belatedly at an agreement with Russia. His relations with both Prussia and Great

---

[1] 'Their Majesties will agree on the modification of the existing treaties to be made in the common interest of Their Empires at the conclusion of peace.'

Britain, however, went badly during 1858. Ever since the congress of Paris, Frederick William IV had been inclining to the Franco-Russian side: resentment against Austrian 'perfidy' was his guiding motive. Any monarchist qualms against association with a Bonaparte were quietened by the thought that the Russian tsar would make a third in the partnership. In fact, entry into the Franco-Russian alliance was the programme of the Prussian reactionaries, violently advocated by Bismarck, practised more delicately by Manteuffel. During 1858 Frederick William's health broke down and finally he became totally incapacitated. His brother William succeeded him as regent. Though Prince William had been reputed a reactionary in 1848 and was to be so regarded again in later life, he had advocated a 'liberal' foreign policy during the Crimean war and had been disgraced for it. He had wanted a breach with Russia and close alliance with the western Powers, especially with Great Britain; this policy reflected the outlook of Prussian officials from the Rhineland for whom Poland was a matter of indifference. Besides, it is in the nature of an heir apparent to oppose the policy of the reigning monarch. In November 1858, when he became regent, Prince William still regarded himself as a liberal, destined to inaugurate 'the new era'. He shook off Manteuffel. Schleinitz, the new foreign minister, was a courtier without policy, anxious to please the regent, even more anxious to keep out of trouble. The regent pinned his faith to an alliance with Great Britain; he intended this to be a stabilizing alliance against France and Russia, the restless Powers on the circumference. Moreover William, in his liberal mood, wished to satisfy national sentiment in Germany; and this demanded solidarity with Austria, despite the fact that she was still governed despotically. German liberals believed that a 'German' cause was at stake in Italy, just as earlier they had insisted that a German cause was at stake on the Danube. The Austro-Prussian alliance, ineffective during the Crimean war, seemed now within sight of accomplishment. But the regent wanted a reward. Exactly like Frederick William IV during his brief liberal period in 1848, he intended to use German sentiment in order to improve Prussia's position; and his condition for aiding Austria was that Prussia should be put in supreme command of the German federal forces fighting on the Rhine. Since Austria's strength was entirely absorbed in Italy, this seemed a reasonable demand, though it would in fact have made Prussia dominant in Germany; it never occurred to William that Austria would be unyielding in Germany, as well as in Italy and the Near East.

Alliance with Prussia was the policy of the British court—of Queen Victoria and the prince consort; and it was secretly favoured by the tory ministers. But they were a minority government; and they knew that British opinion would never tolerate a war to keep Austrian rule in Italy. They therefore had to profess a policy of impartial neutrality, giving academic support to the treaties of 1815 and urging conciliation on both sides. On 12 February 1859 Malmesbury invited Cavour to state his grievances against Austria; at the same time he asked Buol to make some unspecified concessions in Italy. In short, British policy tried to turn the crisis from a fundamental conflict between two principles into a mere diplomatic dispute between two states. Even within these limits British policy was futile. As Cowley recognized, the only effective way of preventing war between Austria and Sardinia would have been for Great Britain to promise to support whichever was attacked;[1] since the British government was committed to neutrality. it had nothing to offer except moral disapproval.

Still, even this made Napoleon hesitate. His real fear was of war on the Rhine; and Prussia determined his Italian policy throughout the crisis. He hoped that Russia might help to keep Prussia neutral by a mixture of promises and threats; but this was a feeble hope—as Napoleon knew, Russia's alliance was directed exclusively against Austria. But if Great Britain remained neutral, Prussia might follow her example, and in order to win this neutrality, Austria had to be made to appear the aggressor—not an easy task, since the sole object of Austrian policy was to retain what she possessed. The treaty of alliance between France and Sardinia had at last been signed on 19 January;[2] immediately after it, Napoleon began to blow cold—to urge caution on Cavour and even to suggest that the war would have to be put off until the following year. The hesitation in Napoleon's mind was reflected in the conflict at the French court, Prince Jerome pulling one way, Walewski the

[1] Cowley to Malmesbury, 8 Apr. 1859.

[2] The treaty was antedated in order to conceal the fact that it was the price paid by Prince Jerome for his wife. It differed from the 'pact of Plombières' in providing that Nice, as well as Savoy, should be ceded to France and in dropping the project of an Italian federation.

other. So far as the emperor was concerned, the hesitation was purely tactical; at heart he was resolved on the Italian war, as on nothing before or afterwards. He told Cavour that he would compel Austria to bid ever higher, answering every concession with the phrase, 'and then?'; and the two continued their division of labour—Napoleon was to appear conciliatory, Cavour was to stir up Italy against Austria.[1] For, since neither could devise an excuse for the war, they had to count on Austria to provide one for them.

While Cavour and Napoleon had a cause for war, but no excuse, the British government had to make out that there were excuses, but no cause. The tension between France and Austria had to be ascribed to a 'misunderstanding', which could be removed by conciliatory diplomacy. Cowley, urged on by Walewski, offered himself as intermediary. Napoleon complained of the state of Italy and of his own troubles in the papal states; Cowley, armed only with these vague grievances, went to Vienna at the end of February. Buol and Francis Joseph did not intend to yield a scrap of their treaty rights, but they wanted to keep Cowley in a good temper. They therefore welcomed the peace plan which Cowley had resourcefully devised: the Great Powers would agree to 'neutralize' Piedmont; in return Austria would renounce her rights of interference in the central Italian states. In this way Italy would be made independent of the Great Powers. The plan had no chance of success. Piedmont would have refused to be neutralized. On the other side, the Austrian offer was a fraud. Buol said that Austria could not desert the Italian states, but that she would renounce her treaties with them, if they asked her to do so. Yet even before Cowley left Vienna, Buol wrote to the Italian states, instructing them not to ask for the abrogation of these treaties.[2] The Cowley mission certainly brought a temporary improvement to Austria's position by making the British government believe erroneously in Austrian goodwill; his plan must have proved unworkable if it had ever been tried.

It was, however, not put to the test of facts. Hardly had Cowley returned to Paris than his individual mediation was swept aside by a Russian proposal for a European congress to

---

[1] Nigra to Cavour, 12, 22 Mar. 1859. *Carteggio Cavour–Nigra*, ii, nos. 304, 349.

[2] Valsecchi, *La mediazione europea e la definizione dell' aggressore alla vigilia della guerra del 1859*, p. 32.

settle the affairs of Italy (18 Mar.). This was a logical consequence of the Franco-Russian treaty of 3 March.[1] The Russians
were committed to localizing the war in Italy; this meant in
practice preventing Prussia from attacking France on the Rhine.
But the Russians were all along resolved not to be dragged into
war with Prussia for the sake of their friendship with France;
therefore their only safe course was to manœuvre themselves
on to a common footing of neutrality with Prussia and Great
Britain. There was a further consideration: as soon as the
Franco-Russian treaty of 3 March was signed the Russians
realized the trick Napoleon had played on them—he had a free
hand in Italy, they were still tied in the Near East. The congress
was a method of recovering their freedom. Even though it was
ostensibly confined to Italy, they could drag in the Near East,
just as in the reverse way Italian affairs had been dragged into
the congress of Paris in 1856; and Napoleon could not well have
escaped supporting them. Napoleon in fact tolerated the congress as a means of driving Austria to war; the Russians hoped
both to humiliate the Austrians and to avoid the war—thus
defeating Austria and France at the same time.

The Austrians saw that the congress involved their humiliation. It had taken eighteen months of war to compel the
Russians to attend the congress of Paris; Austria was being
asked to attend a congress and inevitably to acquiesce in a
weakening of her Italian position before a shot had been fired.
The only way out was to inflict a preliminary humiliation on
Sardinia, which should make it appear that she and not Austria
was the defeated party in the war that had not been fought. The
Austrian weapon was a demand that Sardinia should be compelled to disarm before the congress met; this would establish
the Austrian thesis that Sardinia was the sole cause of the disturbance in Italy. Cavour answered by demands that would
treat Austria and Sardinia as equals—withdrawal of both
armies from the frontiers, general disarmament on condition
that Sardinia was admitted to the congress. The technicalities
were of no importance; for this was not a diplomatic conflict—
it was the first open clash between the two principles of treaty-
rights and national liberty. Since all the rights of treaties and
of international law were on the side of Austria, Cavour was on

---

[1] It is often said that the Russians proposed the congress on French promptings;
but there seems no evidence of this.

weak technical ground; and after a month of manœuvring he seemed to be losing the game. Even a visit by Cavour to Paris could not rid Napoleon of his fear of Prussian intervention; and in mid-April Napoleon ordered Cavour to accept a final British proposal that Sardinia should disarm, on condition of being admitted to the congress. On 19 April Cavour agreed; the opportunity, he believed, had been lost.

But this outcome did not suit the Austrians. They wished Sardinia to be disarmed by Austrian threats, not by British persuasions, still less by French promises for the future. The Sardinian obstinacy since the middle of March had certainly made Prussia and Great Britain more favourable to Austria; and the Austrian government made the astonishing blunder of supposing that this favour would continue if they went over to an aggressive policy. On 12 April they drafted an ultimatum demanding the disarmament of Sardinia, which they then submitted to Prussia and Great Britain. On 19 April the Austrian statesmen met again for a decision. Though they probably did not know that Cavour had agreed to give way, they knew that he and Napoleon were weakening; and they were afraid that they were losing their chance. Men always learn from their mistakes how to make new ones. The Austrian mistake in the Crimean war seemed to have been the hesitation to go to war; therefore they determined this time to force war on. They actually hoped that Cavour would reject their ultimatum, so that Sardinia could be broken in isolation; if, against expectation, Napoleon went to Sardinia's help, they counted confidently on Prussian, and even on British, support.[1] Once the Austrian ultimatum was launched, Cavour had only to let it take its course. He rejected the Austrian demand on 26 April; Austrian troops crossed the Sardinian frontier on 29 April; and on 3 May Napoleon announced his intention of going to Sardinia's aid. In this way the Austrians solved the problem which had baffled Napoleon and Cavour: they opened the door for the destruction of the settlement of 1815 and for the national reconstruction of central Europe.

The war of 1859 was unique in modern history: it was the

---

[1] The myth became somehow established (perhaps by Buol himself) that the ultimatum was sent by the Austrian generals without Buol's knowledge. In fact it was proposed by Buol and approved by the full council of ministers. The records have been published by Engel von Janosi, L'ultimatum austriaco del 1859.

only war which did not spring in part from mutual apprehension. Even aggressive wars have usually an element of prevention. Napoleon I had some grounds for thinking that Alexander I was preparing to attack him when he invaded Russia in 1812; the Germans had some grounds for feeling 'encircled' when they launched both the First and the Second World wars in the twentieth century; even Bismarck could plausibly, and perhaps convincingly, claim that he was merely getting his blow in first against both Austria and France. In 1859 neither France, nor even Sardinia, had any ground whatever for fearing an attack from Austria; and they could not have attacked her, unless she had given them the occasion. Both sides mobilized, not from fear, but to force the other side into war. The only genuine fear of 1859 was Austria's fear of internal revolution; and even this was much exaggerated. On the other hand, though the war lacked justification on any basis of international law, no war has been so unanimously approved by posterity. Over other wars of national liberation—Bismarck's wars, the wars of the Balkan peoples against Turkey, the Czech and South Slav struggles against the Habsburg monarchy—there is still controversy; over the war of 1859 none. The historian cannot be expected to explain this paradox; while himself approving of the war, he can only record that it was incompatible with any known system of international morality.

Napoleon had obtained his aim of a war localized in Italy; the overriding question was whether he could keep it localized. He was prepared to guarantee the integrity of German federal territory in exchange for a Prussian promise of neutrality; and Alexander II offered to underwrite Napoleon's word.[1] The Prussian government refused the offer. They dared not cut themselves off from German national feeling; besides, they were still dreaming that Austria would surrender the leadership in Germany to them in exchange for military support. Napoleon would have liked the Russians to keep Prussia neutral by a threat of war; this was the one thing that they would not do. If Prussia entered the war the Russians intended to attack not her, but Austria; after all it would have been an admirable outcome for them, if Prussia had defeated France in the west, while they overthrew the settlement of the congress of Paris in the Near

---

[1] Bismarck (St. Petersburg) to Schleinitz, 30 Apr. 1859. *Auswärtige Politik Preußens 1858–1871*, i, no. 353.

East. Besides, they wanted to keep the Prussian threat alive in case Napoleon broke his bargain and conducted the war in Italy in a revolutionary manner. It was already disturbing that Cavour, and even Napoleon, were planning with Kossuth a revolution in Hungary; the connexion between Hungary and Poland was never out of the tsar's mind. In short, what kept Prussia out of the war was expectation of the offer from Austria which never came of supremacy in Germany, and not Russian threats.

A localized war needs quick victories. Napoleon's victories, though quick, were not decisive. On 4 June the Austrians were defeated at Magenta and so driven from the plains of Lombardy. On 24 June they attempted to break out from the fortresses of the Quadrilateral and were again defeated at Solferino; but their armies were still intact and further battles would be necessary if Napoleon was to fulfil his programme of Italy 'free from the Alps to the Adriatic'. Meanwhile German sentiment and with it the prince regent of Prussia were becoming increasingly restive. On 24 June the Prussian army was mobilized, and the Prussian government determined to offer armed mediation on the basis of the treaties of 1815. Schleinitz, who disliked this course, could only postpone the decision by proposing to invite the co-operation of Russia and Great Britain. From Russia Napoleon got no promises of support, but only promptings to end the war before it got out of hand. The British situation had changed in Napoleon's favour in the middle of June, when the tory government was defeated and the first 'Liberal' government formed, with Palmerston as prime minister and Lord John Russell as foreign secretary. But this was not the purely Palmerstonian government which had carried the Crimean war to a resolute conclusion. The 'two dreadful old men' were the prisoners of the Peelites and Cobdenites, who together dominated the cabinet. Palmerston and Russell would certainly have liked to support Napoleon's programme; hampered by the cabinet and the queen, they could be little less neutral than the tories who had preceded them. This was not, however, appreciated by the Austrian government. Rechberg, who had taken Buol's place in May, was a disciple of Metternich with all his master's suspicion of British policy; and, as well, he augured nothing good from a Prussian government that claimed to act in accordance with liberal and national sentiment. In short, Napoleon feared that Prussia was about to intervene against him and that Great Britain would do nothing to help him; the Austrians feared that Prussia, Russia, and Great Britain were about to come together on a programme of mediation, hostile to Austrian interests.

There followed one of those strokes by which Napoleon showed his training as a conspirator. On 5 July he proposed an armistice to Francis Joseph; on 11 July the two emperors met at Villafranca; on 12 July a preliminary peace was signed. Napoleon dazzled and bemused Francis Joseph with talk of 'European mediation'. He produced terms which in fact he himself had proposed to the British; alleged that the British meant to put them forward as the basis for mediation; and even created the impression that Prussia would accept this basis. His own offer was simple: he would leave Venetia to Austria, if she would surrender Lombardy without the fortresses of the Quadrilateral. Francis Joseph had been disillusioned and embittered by the failure of Prussia and Great Britain to support him at the outbreak of war; and now believed Napoleon's story. Besides, in his obsession with treaty rights, he preferred to surrender Lombardy as the result of military defeat rather than at the verdict of a European conference. Napoleon, on his side, wanted peace at almost any price in order to escape the risk of war on the Rhine. He hoped to repeat the manœuvre with which he had ended the Crimean war. Then he had become reconciled with Russia at the expense of the neutral Power Austria. Now he would be reconciled with Austria at the expense of all the neutral Powers and even at the expense of his own ally Sardinia. Russia would not get a reward in the Near East; Prussia would not get a reward in Germany.[1] Sardinia, without the fortresses of the Quadrilateral, would be more dependent than ever on French support. Austria and France would remain dominant in Italy; the British therefore would be denied their aim of an independent peninsula.

A conservative partnership between Austria and France had long been the dream of sensible men in both countries from Talleyrand and Metternich in 1815 to Drouyn de Lhuys and Hübner during the Crimean war. It alone could have stabilized

---

[1] This gave great satisfaction to Francis Joseph also. On his return to Vienna he said: 'The one thing that consoles me is that Prussia has been made to look foolish.'

Germany and the Near East. But the reconciliation at Villafranca could be permanent only if the cession of Lombardy by
Austria settled the Italian question—an even more modest
version of the pretence that Napoleon had kept up during his
negotiations with Cavour that his only concern was with a
'kingdom of upper Italy'. In fact, quite apart from Venetia,
there remained the problem of the petty states in central Italy;
of the papal states; and of the kingdom of the Two Sicilies.
During the war the states of central Italy had revolted and
expelled their rulers; this 'revolutionary' display had disturbed
the tsar's conscience and had been among the causes which led
Napoleon to end the war. Francis Joseph, always concerned
with family rights, insisted that the Italian princes be restored;
Napoleon agreed on condition that they were not restored by
force.[1] In addition the pact of Villafranca provided for the
creation of an Italian federation, including Venetia; and ultimately for a European Congress to confirm the new order in
Italy. This last represented Napoleon's hope, perpetually disappointed, of somehow escaping from the occupation of Rome
—'the only *mistake* I repent of in my political career'.[2]

The great weakness of Villafranca lay in Napoleon's own
character. Though he had been upset by the carnage of the
battlefield and had taken fright at the prospect of war with
Prussia, he remained an adventurer: once back in Paris, he
began to plan new surprises in Italy. Besides, the pact of Villafranca suffered from there being only two parties to it. Russia
could conspire with France to revise the settlement of 1856 at
the expense of Austria and Great Britain; the settlement of 1859
could be revised only to the humiliation of France. Within a
few weeks Francis Joseph found that he had been defrauded.
The princes of central Italy had no chance of returning to
their states; and Napoleon looked on calmly at the mounting
nationalist agitation. The French and Austrian representatives
turned the preliminary terms into a formal treaty at Zurich
(10 Nov.); but nothing was left of the friendship of the two
emperors. Each side prepared for a new bout of the Italian

---

[1] Francis Joseph refused to allow this condition in writing; but he acquiesced
in it verbally, believing that the grand duke of Tuscany at any rate could restore
himself by his own resources. In other words, he was not deceived by Napoleon,
but deceived himself. Prince Jerome's report, 11 July 1859. *Carteggio Cavour–Nigra*,
ii, no. 481.

[2] Nigra to Cavour, 13 July 1860. Ibid., iv, no. 966.

question. Austria tried to be reconciled with Russia; Napoleon tried to secure himself from a new Prussian threat. This engagement was easily won by the French. Rechberg talked rather vaguely to the Russians of a revision of the treaty of Paris and even suggested a partition of the Ottoman empire, with Austria monopolizing the valley of the Danube. The Russians did not take the offer seriously. Gorchakov wrote: 'We shall have some smiles from Austria, some consoling words, but we shall keep our acts for those who can serve Russian interests effectively.' In theory Alexander II supported the legitimacy of princes; when it came to the point he was prepared to allow Napoleon a second round in Italy in the hope of himself achieving something in the Near East.

The limiting factor in Russian policy was fear of a general war, and especially of having to choose between Prussia and France. In the autumn of 1859 Alexander at last secured the neutrality of Prussia which had escaped him during the recent war. The prince regent, left high and dry in the middle of a mobilization, resented the contemptuous treatment he had received from Austria. Besides, having been in effective power for nearly a year, he was beginning to act as the ruler of Prussia and no longer as an heir with romantic notions. He took Poland more seriously and was less moved by Austria's 'German mission', whether in Italy or on the Danube. Hence there followed a reconciliation with Russia. William and Alexander met at Breslau in October, a decisive turn from the liberal 'new era', which was reflected at home in the appointment of Roon as minister of war in December. Emotionally William would have liked to win Alexander for the Holy Alliance; when this met with no response, he dropped instead his own hostility to France. Gorchakov boasted to the French ambassador: 'We are leading Prussia to you.' William and Schleinitz did not swallow the full Russian policy, which was also urged on them by Bismarck, their representative at St. Petersburg: they would not make a third in the Franco-Russian alliance. But they accepted Russia's guarantee against a French attack on the Rhine; and agreed in return to be neutral in the affairs of Italy.

The Russians did not perform these services for nothing. As ever, they hoped to divide Napoleon from England; and, as ever, Napoleon hoped to disappoint them. The British change of government in June 1859 certainly ended any prospect of an

Anglo-Austrian entente; but it did not automatically renew the good relations with France of Palmerston's previous government. Russell was suspicious of all foreign governments; and Palmerston was more suspicious than he had been before. Curiously enough Napoleon earned a double distrust in England from the war of 1859: fear of his warlike intentions, from his having started the war; belief that he was unreliable, from his having ended it. Palmerston and Russell were determined to wreck the agreement of Villafranca from the moment that it was made. Their first intention was to attend the congress projected at Villafranca, in order to force a radical revision of the Franco-Austrian agreement; when it became clear in the autumn that the congress would be summoned only to confirm this agreement, they planned to wreck it by staying away. Thus British policy aimed to destroy for the sake of Italy the Franco-Austrian entente, which it had previously laboured to create for the sake of the Near East. Napoleon saved the British the trouble; at the end of 1859 he decided to wreck the pact of Villafranca himself. His concern was not primarily with the duchies of central Italy; it was with opinion inside France. The war of 1859, with its half-hearted end, had brought him little prestige; above all, since he had not liberated Venetia, it had not brought him Savoy and Nice. Now he hoped that some new spin of the Italian wheel would at last enable him to begin the march to 'the natural frontiers'.

On 22 December 1859 one of Napoleon's literary dependents published a pamphlet, *The Pope and the Congress*, advocating the virtual disappearance of the temporal power. The Austrian government demanded that Napoleon disavow its argument; when he refused, they jettisoned the proposed congress. Once more Austrian impatience had opened the door to the revolution. On 4 January 1860 Walewski, defender of a conservative foreign policy, resigned; Napoleon had gone over to a policy of adventure. A period of dreaming and vague projects might have followed; but a fortnight later Cavour (who had resigned in protest against Villafranca) returned to power in Turin, and it was his task, as in the previous year, to drag Napoleon into action. Where Napoleon was still talking vaguely of 'delivering Venetia' by some impossible turn of events in the Near East,[1] Cavour was setting the pace in central Italy. Napoleon tried to

[1] Nigra to Cavour, 13 Feb. 1860. *Carteggio Cavour–Nigra*, iii, no. 543.

impose his veto on straight incorporation with the kingdom of Sardinia; Cavour answered with plebiscites—the one argument which Napoleon could not reject. Thus Napoleon, even if he shrank from the crisis, had to demand Savoy and Nice, as the only compensation for the increase in Sardinia's power and his own consequent loss of prestige. On 13 March 1860 the French plan was officially announced to the Great Powers; on 24 March Cavour signed the treaty ceding Savoy and Nice to France.

The annexation of Savoy was a turning-point in the history of the Second Empire. Until then it had been plausible to argue that Napoleon was seeking glory by liberating others, not by the direct aggrandizement of France; now he had taken up the revolutionary policy of the natural frontiers, which seemed to lead directly to a French hegemony of Europe. The British government could not oppose by war a course of events that was helping on the unification of Italy; but they never recovered the faith in Napoleon III which they lost in March 1860. Palmerston said to Cavour's representative: 'We can have no illusions on the subject. The emperor has vast conceptions which he plans to realize and which will force us to make war';[1] and John Russell, always more impetuous, regretted that Prussia had not gone to war against France in the previous year.[2] No action followed these hard words. The Austrian government were delighted at the British discomfiture and at the proof of all their forebodings. The Prussian government would have seconded the British protest, if they could have had in return a promise of support on the Rhine; this was not forthcoming. Besides, the Prussians were being hard-pressed from St. Petersburg to recognize the annexations at once. The Russians, as usual, had once again jettisoned their principles in the hope that further turmoil in western Europe would open the way to treaty revision in the Near East. Most of all, the Prussian attitude was determined by the consideration that resistance to France involved co-operation with Austria; and even the prince regent would not envisage this co-operation unless it brought him the military hegemony of Germany.[3]

As a result, though the annexation of Savoy gave the decisive

---

[1] D'Azeglio (London) to Cavour, 1 Apr. 1860. *Cavour e l'Inghilterra*, ii (ii), no. 1128.

[2] Bernstorff (London) to Schleinitz, 10 Mar. 1860. *Auswärtige Politik Preußens 1858–1871*, ii (i), no. 94.

[3] Prussian Crown Council, 26 Mar. 1860. Ibid., no. 116.

blow to the settlement of 1815, it passed over without a serious diplomatic crisis. To outward appearance, and much to Russia's disappointment, even the estrangement between England and France did not prove lasting. At a rumour of troop movements in southern Russia, the British protested with French approval; and in July 1860 the two western Powers intervened to protect the Christians of Syria—much to the annoyance of both Russia and Austria. Worst of all, events in central Italy, instead of ending the Italian revolution, began it in earnest. The princes of central Italy had been dislodged by internal revolts; and Cavour's representatives had come in ostensibly to restore order, not to provoke revolution. The kingdom of the Two Sicilies was a different matter; though there was rebellion in Sicily, the Neapolitan troops were strong enough to subdue it if they were left undisturbed. Cavour, with all his daring, could not risk an open war between Sardinia and Naples; on the other hand, if he did nothing, he might be faced with radical revolution in northern Italy. Radical energy had to be discharged somewhere: better against Sicily and Naples, than against Cavour himself, or even against Venetia and Rome—the one involving war with Austria, the other with France. The radicals were ready to compromise with Cavour. Though Mazzini held on his republican course, the fighting revolutionary Garibaldi agreed to be diverted to Sicily; and sailed with his thousand early in May. In August, having carried the island, he crossed to the mainland.

Cavour did nothing to interfere with Garibaldi, despite the protests of the three 'Northern Courts'; Napoleon did nothing to interfere with Cavour, despite the protests even of his own foreign minister. Though full of warnings to Cavour that he could not support Italy against all Europe, Napoleon always came down on the side of adventure when it came to a decision. In his own words to Thouvenel, his new foreign minister: 'he could not condemn principles which he might need to apply and invoke himself later'.[1] Napoleon was that strange thing, a procrastinating adventurer; and, no doubt, had he been in Cavour's place, he would have pretended to disavow Garibaldi. He said to Nigra: 'in acting otherwise you would make the same mistake as if I let people allege that I wanted the Rhineland'.[2]

---

[1] Nigra to Cavour, 18 Aug. 1860. *Carteggio Cavour–Nigra*, iv, no. 1059.
[2] Nigra to Cavour, 13 July, 1860. Ibid., no. 966.

Cavour, however, had a pressing motive for action. By launching Garibaldi he had given the revolution a chance to organize itself; now he had to show that he could do for Italy as much as the radicals were promising. Victor Emanuel in fact had to outbid Garibaldi, not to work against him. In July, while Garibaldi was still in Sicily, Cavour planned to annex Naples in order to preserve 'the national and monarchical character of the Italian movement'; otherwise Garibaldi would sweep up the peninsula and provoke an international crisis by attacking Venetia.[1] Garibaldi was too quick for Cavour: he crossed to the mainland before the regular Italian army was ready to move. Cavour then planned the same manœuvre with the states of the Church; and Napoleon acquiesced, on condition that Rome itself was not touched. 'Diplomacy will make great cries, but will let you act'.[2] Cavour stirred up revolts in the papal states; and on 11 September Victor Emanuel marched, ostensibly to restore order. The greatest difficulty was still ahead: to persuade Garibaldi to recognize the authority of Victor Emanuel over southern Italy. Here Cavour and the Italian monarchy were rescued by the strength of the Neapolitan army. Garibaldi, with his red shirts, could carry the open country; he was helpless against an army in prepared positions, and was glad enough to see the arrival of regular troops. On 26 October he met Victor Emanuel with the words: 'Hail to the King of Italy.' Therewith Italy was virtually made. In the following March a parliament drawn from all Italy, except Venetia and Rome, decreed that Victor Emanuel should be king of Italy 'by the grace of God and the will of the people'. The house of Savoy and the revolution had cemented their alliance.

This last stage was not completed without international alarms. On the news of Garibaldi's expedition, the British government feared that Cavour had purchased Napoleon's complaisance by promising to cede Genoa as he had ceded Savoy. They offered Cavour a defensive alliance on condition that he would not cede Genoa nor attack Venetia; and threatened, in case of refusal, to support the king of the Two Sicilies or even to ally themselves with Austria. Though Cavour

---

[1] Cavour to Nigra, 1 Aug. 1860. *Carteggio Cavour–Nigra*, iv, no. 1022.

[2] Cavour to Nigra, 28 Aug. 1860. Ibid., no. 1079. This is more authentic than the traditional version: 'do it, but do it quickly'. Napoleon himself made 'a great cry' by withdrawing his minister from Turin in protest against the attack on the states of the Church which he had secretly approved.

did not take up their offer of an alliance, he said enough to calm their fears; and henceforth the British made things easy for him. Still, this support only helped Cavour to disregard the warnings from France; the British could be of no real assistance against an attack from Austria, and that would come if the Austrians, late in the day, managed to revive the Holy Alliance with Russia and Prussia. This was the great issue of the summer of 1860—whether the Holy Alliance could be revived before the unification of Italy was complete.

There were serious reasons for expecting it. The king of the Two Sicilies had been the symbol of counter-revolution ever since the congress of Ljubljana (Laibach) in 1821; now both Alexander II and the prince regent of Prussia watched Garibaldi's campaign with mounting disapproval. William would have liked to pursue a firm conservative policy with Russian support; but Russia would not break with France, and Prussia would not co-operate with Austria. To William's urging of a Russo-Prussian alliance, Alexander replied that France should make a third in it. William asked, 'Against whom the alliance?'; and though the answer was never given, it was obvious enough —it was to disrupt Austria's position in the Near East.[1] At the end of June William met Napoleon at Baden-Baden in order to please the Russians; but instead of acquiescing in Napoleon's expansionist plans, he made the meeting a demonstration of German solidarity against France by inviting all the leading German princes. Napoleon commented: 'William behaved like a bashful girl, who is afraid of her lover's bad reputation and therefore avoids being alone with him'—in view of Napoleon's record, not an unreasonable attitude.

If Prussia would not support French plans, the obvious alternative (much favoured by the British government) was to work with Austria against them; but this was equally impossible. William and Francis Joseph met at Teplitz from 25 to 27 July, in the hope of repeating the reconciliation of Olomouc, this time, however, without the humiliation of Prussia. The two agreed on a programme of defence against French aggression; and William threw in the defence of German federal territory, including Tyrol and Trieste, against Sardinia. His price was the command of all German forces; a price at once brushed aside

---

[1] Bismarck to the prince regent, 14 June 1860. Raschdau, *Bismarcks Berichte aus Petersburg und Paris*, i. 113–17.

by the Austrians. Rechberg said: 'When Francis Joseph had just lost a valuable province, he could not make new moral surrenders voluntarily.'[1] The Austrians, in truth, never took the Prussian demands seriously; they could not understand, right down to the outbreak of war in 1866, that Prussia was genuinely bent on equality, if not more, in Germany. Therefore at the end of July 1860 Francis Joseph and Rechberg believed that the Holy Alliance was really in sight. There was an excuse for this. The invasion of Naples, combined with the Anglo-French expedition to Syria, gave Russian feeling a shortlived turn against France. Napoleon's birthday on 15 August was ignored at St. Petersburg, and the birthday of Francis Joseph on 18 August was celebrated there for the first time since the Crimean war.

Before the three monarchs could meet, Russia had been pulled back by France, and Prussia by Great Britain. Thouvenel realized that something must be done to restore Russian faith in the entente with France. At the end of September he sent a memorandum on French policy to Gorchakov. The memorandum was in two parts. In regard to Italy, France promised to stay neutral if Sardinia invaded Venetia—on condition that Prussia and the German states remained neutral also; but whatever the fortunes of war or of the future, Sardinia must retain Lombardy and France must retain Savoy. There was a significant omission: France did not promise to remain neutral if Austria intervened in Italy in order to protect the king of the Two Sicilies or the pope. The crusade against the revolution was still barred. The second part of the memorandum concerned the Near East. If 'a catastrophe' took place there, France would settle its future with Russia before approaching the other Powers; and that on the basis that no Great Power should acquire territory nor the Balance of Power in Europe be disturbed. This self-denying ordinance was not, however, to apply to the recovery of Bessarabia by the Russians. These shadowy plans delighted Alexander II and Gorchakov. They had no serious interest in a conservative crusade and thought that they had done enough if they gave Austria some security in Venetia. Their real love, as Nicholas I had shown before them, was for interminable speculation over the future of the Ottoman empire;

[1] Werther (Vienna) to Schleinitz, 23 July 1860. *Auswärtige Politik Preußens 1858-1871*, ii (i), no. 232.

and this Napoleon, himself a great projector, was prepared to offer. Besides, Thouvenel's plan gave the Russians security against their real dread—a domination of the Near East by Great Britain and Austria at their expense. As it was, they were to have Bessarabia; yet Austria would be excluded from Rumania and the British from Egypt or the Dardanelles. Alexander II said to the French ambassador: 'It is with you and you alone that I wish to negotiate.' Gorchakov actually wished to invite Thouvenel to Warsaw; since he would not also invite Russell, this would have been a continental bloc against Great Britain, and Thouvenel evaded the invitation.

Prussia meanwhile had drawn closer to Great Britain. With Austria unyielding and Russia friendly to France, this seemed the only means of security on the Rhine. Early in October William met Queen Victoria at Coblenz, the high-water mark of Anglo-Prussian friendship in the 'new era'. Russell told Schleinitz that he did not object to a Prussian protest at Turin, provided there was no united front of the conservative Powers. Schleinitz, in return, urged Russell to abandon the clauses of the treaty of Paris neutralizing the Black Sea: in this way Russia would be reconciled, and a truly pacific union could be built up against France. He met with an abrupt refusal.[1] Yet there was sense in his argument. It was not possible to maintain both the treaty of Vienna and the treaty of Paris. If the British wished to resist Napoleon's expansion in the west, they would have to accept treaty revision in the Near East; if they were immovable in the Near East, then they would be helpless against Napoleon. By failing to make up their minds to either course, the British had to tolerate upheaval in western Europe and lost the neutralization of the Black Sea into the bargain.

The meeting of the three monarchs at Warsaw from 25 to 27 October turned out to be far from a revival of the Holy Alliance. Gorchakov communicated only the Italian part of the French memorandum and declared himself satisfied with it. This ruined the conference for the Austrians. They had come expecting a conservative crusade against the Italian revolution; instead they, and the Prussians as well, were being asked to

---

[1] Palmerston wrote to Russell, 15 Oct. 1860, that he would never be a party to modifying the treaty of 1856 'unless it had become inevitable as the consequence of a war, the Results of which enabled Russia to dictate her own Terms to the Rest of Europe—but we are not likely at present to be brought to that'.

remain neutral unless Sardinia actually attacked Venetia. In return, they were to receive nothing; and they guessed correctly that the reward was to be paid exclusively to Russia. Neither Austria nor Prussia would join a Franco-Russian entente for settling the Near East to the exclusion and at the expense of Great Britain—Austria for the sake of the Near East, Prussia for the sake of the British. As a result the Warsaw meeting produced only negations: Austria did not get a free hand in Italy, Russia did not get a free hand in the Near East. Alexander II took the excuse of his mother's death to break the meeting off abruptly; and the three monarchs parted, not to meet again until 1873, when Europe had taken on a very different shape.

The Warsaw meeting had one result of an unexpected kind. The British government feared the revival of a conservative bloc. Even now they could not believe that Austria would be so obstinate as to miss a united demonstration against Italy by refusing to make concessions in the Near East. Therefore, instead of waiting for the accomplished fact, the British government for once ran ahead of events: to prevent treaty revision in the Near East they welcomed the revision that was still in process in Italy. On 27 October, while the 'Holy Alliance' was still in session, Russell sent off his famous dispatch, approving of Italian unification and justifying it by an appeal to the will of the people. This was a more revolutionary document than Lamartine's circular of March 1848. Lamartine had denounced the settlement of Vienna only in the name of France; Russell denounced it (or any other treaty settlement) in the name of any people who felt themselves strong enough to overthrow it. Russell's dispatch certainly established Italy in 'the comity of nations'. Napoleon had to accept its doctrines, despite his objections to Cavour's behaviour. When Naples was formally annexed, the tsar withdrew his representative from Turin in protest; Prussia refused to join in this futile gesture. In fact, Austria was left in helpless and empty isolation.

The unification of Italy completed what the Crimean war had begun: the destruction of the European order. Metternich's system depended on Russia's guarantee; once that was withdrawn, the system could be overthrown. Napoleon supposed that a new system, his own, was taking its place. This was to misunderstand the events of 1859 to 1861. Certainly Italy owed most to French armies and to British moral approval; but these could not have been effective without two other factors—Russian resentment against the treaty of Paris, and Prussian resentment against the Austrian hegemony in Germany. If Russia had followed a policy less consistently hostile to Austria, if Prussia had carried the war to the Rhine in 1859, Italy could not have been made. After 1861 Russia still aimed at the overthrow of the settlement of 1856; Prussia still aimed at equality, if not hegemony, in Germany. Both continued to work against Austria; this was no guarantee that they would continue to work in favour of France. And, in fact, the leadership of Europe which Napoleon seemed to have gained from the Italian affair was lost within two years over the question of Poland.

VII

THE POLISH CRISIS, AND THE END OF
THE FRANCO-RUSSIAN ENTENTE

1861–3

M<small>IDDLE-CLASS</small> liberalism reached its high-water mark in 1861. Italy had been united under a constitutional monarchy, with a parliament elected by limited suffrage. In Prussia the death of Frederick William IV seemed to remove the last obstacle to the liberal 'new era'. Austria received a parliament and something like a liberal constitution in the February Patent, devised by Schmerling. The tsar issued the edict emancipating the serfs in March; and he followed this up by attempting to conciliate national sentiment in Poland. Press censorship seemed to be dying everywhere; even in France there was a mounting freedom of discussion in the legislative body. In retrospect Napoleon came to regard the Free Trade treaty with England of March 1860 as a greater triumph than the liberation of Italy. His zest for adventure was dwindling; and by now he treated his two ententes with Great Britain and Russia as measures of security rather than as instruments for remaking Europe. Physically he was in decline; and what remained of his energy was turned away from Europe—to Syria, to China, and—most of all—to the new 'imperialist' speculation in Mexico, which came to fruition in 1862. It is commonly held that European tension is increased by rivalries overseas; in reality, the peace of the Continent is usually more secure when European restlessness can be discharged, in Guizot's phrase, 'against the barbarians', whether of China, Africa, or America.

The calm of 1861 was illusory. Paradoxically enough only France, the traditionally restless Power, was reasonably satisfied; apart from Rome, still occupied by French troops, Napoleon had no pressing worries. The three 'conservative' Powers were all discontented; even Austria had become a revisionist

Power through her dream of undoing the unification of Italy. This was not, of course, apparent to contemporaries, not apparent even to Napoleon. Thanks to the annexation of Savoy, the British government, which had cheerfully worked with Napoleon in his adventurous days, were incurably suspicious just when he had become pacific and conservative. Palmerston wrote in February 1861: 'the whole drift of our policy is to prevent France from realising her vast schemes of expansion and aggression in a great number of Quarters'.[1] Towards the end of 1860 Russell launched the idea that Austria should sell Venetia to Italy and thus free her hands to resist Napoleon on the Rhine. The Austrians made the usual reply that the emperor could give up provinces only after defeat in war; they had indeed always held out against giving up Venetia even in exchange for Rumania. The British government also urged Prussia not to press her claims to the leadership of Germany; here too they met with no response. Instead relations between Austria and Prussia took a decisive turn for the worse in April 1861.

The two foreign ministries had been trying to formulate an agreement ever since the meeting of Francis Joseph and the prince regent at Teplitz in July 1860; the terms proved elusive. Prussia offered a defensive alliance against France on the Rhine, an alliance which she would extend to Venetia; but Austria must not provoke France by reclaiming Lombardy even in the event of a victorious war against Sardinia. Moreover, Prussia made the alliance conditional on a military convention, giving her the control of all German armed forces. Early in April Rechberg broke off negotiations: the Prussian terms, he complained, would not give Austria Italy, yet would make her lose Germany.[2] The deadlock between the two German Powers, implicit since the Crimean war or even since the agreement of Olomouc, was thus clearly stated. The Austrians insisted that Prussia should serve the 'conservative' cause—on the Rhine, the Danube, or the Po—without thought of reward; the Prussians demanded that Austria should surrender the hegemony of Germany for the sake of security in northern Italy and the Near East. For, as Rechberg also complained, the Prussians still

[1] Palmerston to Russell, 8 Feb. 1861.
[2] Werther to Schleinitz, 7 Apr. 1861. *Auswärtige Politik Preußens 1858–1871*, ii (ii), no. 370.

BALTIC SEA

Gulf
of
Danzig

DANZIG

WEST PRUSSIA

EAST
PRUSSIA

R.Dubisa

R.Russ

R.Vistula

R.Niemen

R.Netze

TORUN

R.Warthe

POSEN

POSEN

R.Vistula

R.Bug

CONGRESS

WARSAW

R.Warthe

R.Prosna

R.Vistula

R.Pilitsa

POLAND

R.Bug

R.Oder

SILESIA

R.Vistula

R.San

CRACOW

LVOV

GALICIA

Miles

40   20   0   40   80   120

POLAND

thought that they were not in serious danger from France, whereas they regarded Austria as threatened by both France and Russia. The breach of April 1861 was decisive. Competition for the headship of Germany started in earnest from this moment; and negotiations for an alliance were never seriously renewed until 1879.

In July 1861 the trimming Schleinitz made way for Bernstorff at the Prussian foreign ministry; this was a preparation for the coming struggle. Schleinitz had clung obstinately to the line of 'the free hand'; so far as he had a positive policy, he looked forward ineffectively to a stabilizing alliance with Austria and Great Britain against the two restless Powers on the circumference. Alliance with Austria was played out after the breach of April 1861; and alliance with Great Britain was equally futile. One of the greatest factors in the European balance in the early 'sixties was the American civil war; between 1861 and 1865 British military resources were locked away in Canada, and when British statesmen thought of war in these years it was with the United States, not with any continental Power. Isolation, with all its momentous consequences, was imposed on Great Britain by her imperial commitments. Bernstorff, who had been Prussian minister in London, knew something of this; besides, though a conservative, he was a disciple of Radowitz (he had represented Prussia at Vienna during the crisis of 1849–50) and was eager to renew the struggle with Austria. He believed that the only way to win public opinion was to champion the 'German cause' in Sleswick-Holstein; and since both Russia and Great Britain were on the side of Denmark, the only course for Prussia was alliance with France—'the leading Power among the Great States'. If France would give Prussia a free hand in Germany, she might be given in return a free hand in the Near East.[1] This plan overrated Prussia's importance: a free hand in the Near East was not hers to give. She could offer France a free hand only on the Rhine; and this was the one place where she could not make concessions. Bernstorff also ignored the decisive fact that King William would never swallow an alliance with France against, or even without Russia. In October, after much evasion, William was driven into visiting Napoleon at Compiègne; instead of seeking an alliance he spent his time

---

[1] Memorandum by Bernstorff, Oct. 1861. Ringhoffer, *Im Kampfe für Preußens Ehre*, p. 426.

warding off Napoleon's advances. He emphasized the Polish interests which bound him to Russia; and insisted that he would not be the Victor Emanuel of Germany.[1]

Despite the lack of an ally, Bernstorff took up Radowitz's programme of 1849. He had indeed no choice; for, in the liberal atmosphere of the day, plans for reforming Germany were in the air, and unless Prussia took the lead, she would be led. On 2 February 1862 Austria, supported by the four German kingdoms, proposed a conference to discuss a stronger executive and a delegate-assembly for the Confederation. On 21 February Bernstorff, rejecting this proposal, defended the right of individual states to form closer alliances within the Confederation; and he added the warning that 'this time we are resolved not to avoid war as in 1850, but to accept it, if it is forced on us from the other side'. Both sides had, in reality, issued their defiance rather too soon. A struggle for the hegemony of Germany was hardly possible while the Franco-Russian entente remained in existence. This entente had been much shaken by Russia's breach with the new kingdom of Italy; and it had not been strengthened by the enthusiasm with which Alexander's concessions to Poland were welcomed in France. Napoleon had had to explain in a personal letter to the tsar why he could not openly disavow French sympathy for Poland; he could only promise that it would not be translated into acts (May 1861). Thereafter the situation in Russian Poland improved; and there seemed a chance in 1862 that Alexander II might bring off the miracle of satisfying Polish (and French) sentiment without sacrificing Russian interests. Poland went into the background, the Near East came once more to the front—the ideal condition for the Franco-Russian entente. There were mounting disorders in European Turkey. In July the Turkish garrison bombarded Belgrade. Russia needed French friendship; and paid the price for it by recognizing the kingdom of Italy unconditionally.[2]

[1] Note by William I, 11 Oct. 1861. *Auswärtige Politik Preußens 1858–1871* ii (ii), no. 414.

[2] In Feb. 1862 Bernstorff had offered to recognize Italy and to remain neutral in case of war between Italy and Austria, if Italy would remain neutral in case of war between Prussia and France. The Italians had at first accepted this offer; then drew back in fear that Napoleon III might take offence and support Austria against them. *Auswärtige Politik Preußens 1858–1871*, ii (ii), nos. 444 and 448. The Russians, though full of complaint at this abortive negotiation, themselves recognized Italy in July without consulting or even warning Berlin.

In return France agreed with Russia on a protocol in August, providing that Serbia should become practically independent of Turkey without falling under Austrian influence. This was far from the large-scale revision in the Near East for which the Russians always hoped. Still, it revived the negative side of the Franco-Russian entente: Austria was not to be allowed to take advantage of Russia's weakness, hence too she would not get Russian backing in Germany or Italy. In October 1862 Napoleon III could survey Europe for the last time as the man of destiny.

The man who would overthrow him had already arrived. On 24 September Bismarck became prime minister of Prussia. This was primarily an event in Prussian domestic politics, not in international affairs. Bismarck had been called in to defeat the Prussian parliament, not to change the course of foreign policy; and, contrary to the impression which he gave later, his policy continued that of his predecessors. Like Manteuffel, he built on the sympathies of Russia; like Bernstorff, he speculated on friendship with France; like Radowitz, he wanted Prussia to dominate a 'lesser Germany'; like every Prussian minister except for a few old-fashioned conservatives, he would be content with nothing less than equality with Austria. He inherited from Bernstorff the conflict with Austria over the plans for reforming Germany; and this conflict threatened to become acute, since Austria intended to propose at the diet a meeting of delegates from the state-parliaments to discuss reform. On 5 December Bismarck delivered a delayed-action ultimatum to Károlyi, the Austrian minister in Berlin. Austria should accept Prussia as equal in Germany, removing her centre of gravity to Hungary[1] and receiving in return Prussia's guarantee of her vital interests in Italy and the Near East; otherwise 'you are inviting catastrophe'.[2] This conversation, too, has been treated as epoch-making; in reality, stripped of Bismarck's forceful phrases, it did no more than repeat the alternatives which Schleinitz had posed to Austria in April 1861. Where Bismarck differed from his predecessors was in position, not in policy. They had been dependent on the king; now, owing to the constitutional struggle in Prussia, the king was dependent on him, and support for

---

[1] Not to Budapest, as in the traditional version.
[2] Károlyi (Berlin) to Rechberg, 5 Dec. 1862; Bismarck to Werther, 13 Dec. 1862. *Auswärtige Politik Preußens 1858–1871*, iii, nos. 60 and 71.

Bismarck's foreign policy was the price which William had to pay for defeating the Prussian parliament.[1]

Though Bismarck followed the same course as his predecessors, he despised their hesitations; always arrogant and impatient, he sought a quick success in foreign policy to counteract his unpopularity at home. He had advocated for years that Prussia should make a third in the Franco-Russian entente; now he at once tried to operate this line. On 21 December he told the French minister of the coming conflict with Austria and asked what Napoleon III would do 'if things hot up in Germany'.[2] Bismarck's question came two months late. Thouvenel, as foreign minister, had been a sincere executant of Napoleon's own policy —friendly to Italy, friendly to Russia, and ready to support Prussia in Germany. In the summer of 1862 he had tried to solve the Roman question by agreement with the Italian government: if the capital of Italy were moved to Florence the French troops would be withdrawn from Rome. The proposal rested on an equivocation: Thouvenel regarded it as an Italian renunciation of Rome, the Italians as a first step towards its acquisition. As such the French clericals also regarded it; the Empress Eugenie, who spoke for them, persuaded Napoleon to dismiss

[1] There has been prolonged controversy among German historians whether Bismarck was 'sincere' in his offers of friendship to Austria. On the one side, it has been held that he aimed at war with Austria from the beginning; on the other, that he would have preferred a conservative partnership with Austria against 'the revolution' (that is against Napoleon III, against united Italy, and against German liberalism). The controversy is really without meaning. All Prussian statesmen were determined on equality with Austria; and by equality they meant hegemony over Germany at least north of the Main. This was true even of the kings—Frederick William IV and William I. (Just at this time William defined his minimum terms to the British minister as command of all German armed forces and representation of all Germany abroad by Prussia Buchanan to Russell, 29 Jan. 1863. *Auswärtige Politik Preußens 1858–1871*, iii, no. 152.) The Prussians hoped that Austria's difficulties in Italy and the Near East would compel her to agree to these terms without a war in Germany; events ever since 1848 proved that these hopes were empty. The basic principle of Austrian policy was never to yield anything except after defeat.

Bismarck, like Manteuffel before him, had a nostalgic regret for the days of Metternich and the Holy Alliance; this regret made him postpone the conflict with Austria probably more than Bernstorff would have done. But it could not make him give up the defence of Prussian interests. In short, once Schwarzenberg had made the first bid for mastery in Germany, Bismarck was bound to make the second. As in any other sort of auction, the two parties could not leave the auction-room until the prize had been knocked down to one of them. In such circumstances 'sincerity' or 'aggression' are irrelevant phrases.

[2] Talleyrand (Berlin) to Drouyn de Lhuys, 21 Dec. 1862. *Auswärtige Politik Preußens 1858–1871*, iii, no. 82.

Thouvenel and in October to recall Drouyn de Lhuys. It was the most disastrous step in the history of the Second Empire. French foreign policy fell into confusion just when the fortunes of Europe were being decided. Napoleon, though enfeebled, remained on the side of adventure—ready to speculate on the aggrandizement of Prussia. Drouyn, the man of tradition and conservatism, wanted the alliance with Austria which he had failed to win during the Crimean war. There had been a similar, though weaker, division between Napoleon and Walewski in the days before the Italian war of 1859; but it had been of lesser moment. Then Napoleon had been strong enough to get his own way; besides, even blunders in Italy could not ruin France's position in Europe. Now it was different: between 1863 and 1866 France frittered away her hegemony of Europe for ever.

Drouyn's first act was to break off the negotiations with Italy which Thouvenel had been conducting. His next was to brush aside Bismarck's approach. In case of conflict in Germany, he replied, France 'will seek guarantees for her security and for the peace of Europe'.[1] This reply was useless to Bismarck. However, without any effort on his part, the great German conflict once more blew over. When the Austrian proposal for a conference of delegates to discuss reform was put to the diet on 22 January 1863 it was defeated by nine votes to seven. Two days later these German disputes were eclipsed by the explosion of the Polish question, dreaded by every Great Power. The Russian authorities had been living in fear of a rising since the autumn. They tried to anticipate it by drafting revolutionary young Poles into the army. The stroke miscarried; and on 23 January the radical Poles answered by proclaiming a general insurrection. Though the rising was confined to Russian Poland, it drew much support from Posnania, Prussia's share of the partitions, and from Galicia, Austria's share; as well, the Poles counted on the sympathy of western Europe, particularly of France. The Russians hoped to keep the rising a matter of domestic concern, which should not disturb their international relations, especially the entente with France. This suited Napoleon, who had drawn much profit from the entente and who, besides, shrank from the European upheaval which intervention in aid of the Poles must involve. The Austrians, too, tried to ignore the rising. Before

---

[1] Drouyn de Lhuys to Talleyrand, 25 Dec. 1862. *Auswärtige Politik Preußens 1858–1871*, iii, no. 88.

1848 they had been the principal oppressors of the Poles; now, with an Empire full of strife, they did not wish to have a further discontented nationality on their hands. Moreover, while they naturally shrank from a war with Russia for the sake of the Poles, they were even more reluctant to offend England and France by joining in suppressing them. The wisest course for everybody seemed to be to pretend that nothing was happening. This general desire to hush up the Polish question was ruined by Bismarck. Alvensleben, a Prussian general, was sent to St. Petersburg; and there on 8 February concluded a convention, providing for the co-operation of the Russian and Prussian military authorities in the frontier districts against the rebels. Later in life Bismarck claimed the convention as a great stroke of policy: it had substituted Prussia for France in the affections of the tsar. The claim has little foundation. The Franco-Russian entente had been directed against Austria, never against Prussia; indeed there had always been an unspoken condition that France must not attack Prussia on the Rhine. The Polish question certainly produced an estrangement between France and Russia, but this was in no sense a consequence of the Alvensleben convention. There is more in Bismarck's other claim that by making the convention he helped to defeat the advocates of a conciliatory policy towards Poland at the Russian court. Such a party certainly existed: Gorchakov and even the tsar sympathized with it. Bismarck himself took the danger of a Russian withdrawal from Poland seriously and spoke openly of Prussia's occupying Poland should Russia give it up.[1] Here again the decision came from later events—from the inter-ference of the western Powers and the intransigence of the Poles —not from the convention. In fact, Gorchakov and the tsar were much offended at Bismarck's importunity, humiliatingly reminiscent of Russia's aid to Austria in 1849; they would have preferred him to hold aloof, as Austria was doing. The simplest explanation is, as usual, likely to be the true one. Bismarck, always furiously anti-Polish,[2] feared that the revolt would spread

---

[1] This was the occasion of a celebrated conversation with Buchanan, the British minister, who objected that Europe would never allow it. Bismarck replied: 'who is Europe?' and Buchanan answered: 'several great nations'. Memorandum by Bismarck, 11 Feb. 1863. *Auswärtige Politik Preußens 1858–1871*, iii, no. 174.

[2] In 1861 Bismarck wrote: 'I am full of sympathy for the Poles, but if we are to exist we can do nothing except root them out; the wolf cannot help having been created by God as he is, but we shoot him all the same when we can.'

to Prussian Poland and proposed military co-operation without thinking of the international consequences; these, when they came, were highly unwelcome to him.

Bismarck tried to represent the Alvensleben convention as 'a simple measure of police'. To everyone else it appeared as intervention against the Poles; and it made it difficult for the other Powers to hold to their line of non-intervention. Above all, it made it difficult for Napoleon III to continue the procrastination which now more than ever was his first response to the challenge of events. The entente with Russia was dear to Napoleon's heart: it flattered him to be on good terms with the tsar and, more than that, he believed that the Russian entente would enable him to remodel western Europe according to his will. Moreover, he had always intended that Prussia, uniting the 'lesser Germany', should make a third in the entente, thus completing the reconstruction of Europe which had started with the unification of Italy. The alternative of the 'Crimean coalition' with Austria and Great Britain was distasteful to him; it was a drab affair, defensive, with no prospect of adventure. But Napoleon could not hold out against the enthusiasm for Poland, which for once united all factions at the imperial court. The radicals, led by Prince Jerome, wished to defend the principle of nationality; the clericals, led by the empress, were on the side of the only Roman Catholic people in eastern Europe. Drouyn, in the interest of peace, had at first shared Napoleon's policy of averting his eyes from events in Poland; the Alvensleben convention made him change course. French indignation over Poland could now be turned against Prussia. In this way Drouyn hoped to silence Napoleon's sympathy with 'revolutionary' Prussia and to win him back to the conservative alliance with Austria. Besides, this policy met the practical objection that France could not strike at Russia, however much she sympathized with Poland; for Prussia was certainly accessible to French arms.

Regretfully Napoleon acquiesced in this plan. On 20 February he said to the Prussian minister: 'If it was Austria who had signed the convention, I should not waste a word . . . she is a Power in whom I am uninterested and it is therefore indifferent to me that her government makes mistakes.'[1] On 21 February Drouyn

---

[1] Goltz (Paris) to William I, 20 Feb. 1863. *Auswärtige Politik Preußens 1858–1871*, iii, no. 206.

proposed to Great Britain and Austria a joint note of protest in Berlin. On the same day the Empress Eugenie threw herself into international politics for the first time. She was in full cry for an alliance with Austria; and she tried to make it attractive to Napoleon by decking it out as a wholesale plan for the revision of the map of Europe—Venetia for Italy, Galicia for Poland, Austria to be compensated in the Balkans, Silesia, and southern Germany, France to take the left bank of the Rhine,[1] in short, all the shadowy projects which had been aired times without number. It was, of course, absurd, to offer Austria a 'conservative' alliance on condition that she first gave up the provinces which she was intent on conserving; but the alliance could be made attractive to Napoleon only if it got him out of his difficulties in Poland and Italy. He himself urged the alliance on Richard Metternich, though in vaguer terms: 'till now I had mistresses, I am looking for a wife',[2] and 'I shall belong to the Power who will aid me'.

The news from Paris threw Bismarck into high alarm. He had meant to strengthen his hold in St. Petersburg, not to expose Prussia to a French attack. He tried to make out in Paris that the convention had been a Russian idea; when this did not work, he had to ask Gorchakov to rescue him—either Russia must promise to defend Prussia against France, or the convention must be withdrawn. Gorchakov was delighted to repay the humiliation which Bismarck had inflicted on him: 'Russia never withdraws . . . it would have the air of yielding to pressure.' Gorchakov would only say that, if Prussia wished to withdraw, the tsar would have no objection; and Bismarck had to make out that, as the revolt had moved away from the borders of Prussia, the convention was now a dead letter. As a means of winning Russia's favour, the convention had certainly miscarried. But the plans of Drouyn for diverting the hostility of the French friends of Poland away from Russia and on to Prussia instead miscarried also. The British government were still dominated by the suspicion that had been aroused in them

[1] Metternich (Paris) to Rechberg, 22 Feb. 1863. Oncken, *Die Rheinpolitik Kaiser Napoleons III*, i, no. 1. It is an exaggeration to see in this chimerical proposal any serious and persistent intention by Napoleon to acquire the left bank of the Rhine.

[2] This is a slightly later version. According to Metternich's contemporary account, Napoleon varied the metaphor: his *marriage of reason* with England did not prevent an intimate and passionate affair with Austria. Metternich to Rechberg, 26 Feb. 1863. Oncken, *Die Rheinpolitik Kaiser Napoleons III*, i, no. 2.

by the annexation of Savoy. When they were invited to act against Prussia they concluded that France was looking for an excuse 'to occupy the Rhineland'; and they insisted that any protest over Poland should be made at St. Petersburg, not at Berlin. The Austrian government were not tempted by the offer of a French alliance. Rechberg said, 'the risk was certain and the advantages problematic'. But he shrank from leaving the Polish question in the hands of the western Powers. Moreover he feared that, if French feeling did not find an outlet against Prussia, it might seek an alternative distraction by turning against Austria in Venetia. As in the Crimean war, the Austrians estranged Russia for the sake of their Italian possessions. Great Britain and Austria would have liked to keep quiet about Poland; but they had to insist on some gesture against Russia in order to prevent, as they thought, a French move against Prussia. The French were caught by their own ingenuity: by proposing action against Prussia, they put the Polish question on the international field and had to commit themselves against Russia.

The Crimean coalition was now ostensibly in being; and from this moment all the confusions of the Crimean war were repeated or, rather, outdone. There was one great difference. The British were distracted by the American civil war; their navy was in decay; and they were unshakably suspicious of Napoleon III. Throughout they were resolved not to go to war. Though sympathy with Poland was strong in England, the government co-operated with Napoleon solely in order to tie him down— and of course to make an end of the Franco-Russian entente. The Austrians simply followed the Crimean course which had brought them such disasters: they appeased France with diplomatic gestures which they assured the Russians meant nothing, and so offended both sides. Venetia lay open to France, Galicia to Russia; and the Austrians could never decide which was the more endangered. Still, estrangement between Russia and Austria existed already; and, since the Austro-French alliance always proved a will o' the wisp, failure to achieve this was not decisive either. The crucial outcome of the Polish crisis was the breach between Russia and France. This was unwelcome to the Russians, who still hoped to return to Near Eastern politics once Poland was subdued. When Austria, Great Britain, and France delivered their first note of protest at St. Petersburg on

17 April, Gorchakov went out of his way to be more conciliatory to France than to the two others; and at the beginning of May he even assured the French that he would not object to discussing the Polish question at a European congress provided that every other European question (including, no doubt, the Near East) was discussed also. This was not enough for French public feeling: something had to be done for Poland before any other question could be discussed. The three Powers therefore returned to the attack on 17 June with a further note, demanding an armistice in Poland and the establishment of an autonomous Polish state.[1] These proposals were sharply brushed aside by Gorchakov.

Now, if ever, was the moment for action; and the French aired the project of a landing in the Baltic, perhaps with Swedish help. Palmerston held that a French army was less dangerous in the Baltic than on the Rhine, and promised British neutrality; but, as the opening of the Crimean war had shown, Napoleon could be dragged into these distant expeditions only by active British support, and the idea of war was abandoned. Even now the French might have saved their entente with Russia, if they had been willing to confess their helplessness in eastern Europe and had accepted a diplomatic defeat. Drouyn, however, insisted on a further Note, delivered early in August, condemning Russian policy and declaring that since Russia had taken no notice of the three Powers, 'France too resumed full freedom of judgement and action'. It was the formal denunciation of the Franco-Russian entente.

This entente had become the foundation of Russian policy when the Holy Alliance broke down; now a resurrection of this Alliance seemed possible, particularly as common hostility to Poland had always been its strongest tie. But, as on previous occasions, it again appeared that the Holy Alliance could not be built on hostility to Poland alone; each Power had other interests, though Prussia had fewer distractions than Austria or Russia. This had already been shown over the Alvensleben convention when Russia had refused to protect Prussia against

---

[1] The six conditions, which were to be taken as the basis for a conference on Poland, were a general amnesty; a Polish national assembly according to the constitution of 1815; autonomous administration through officials of Polish nationality; removal of the limitations on the Roman Catholic Church; exclusive use of Polish in administration, justice, and education; and a system of military service laid down by law.

France. It was shown again in May. Bismarck, alarmed at the last splutter of the Franco-Russian entente, proposed to the Austrians that they should join to resist any interference in their respective Polish possessions—'we would offer you bayonets for bayonets, the guarantee of Galicia for the guarantee of Posen.'[1] Rechberg replied that any alliance must also involve a Prussian guarantee of Venetia against France. A fortnight later it was Russia's turn to invoke the ghost of the Holy Alliance. On 1 June Alexander II wrote to William I, asking for his active co-operation and speaking regretfully of the old partnership with Austria. Many years later Bismarck was to claim that the Russian approach had implied war against Austria and that he would not settle the German conflict 'with foreign help'; this was certainly far-fetched. But it is equally far-fetched to imply that Bismarck missed a serious chance of reviving the Holy Alliance; this had broken down. Russia and Austria were in conflict in the Near East and neither Russia nor Prussia would guarantee Austria's possessions in Italy. William's reply on 17 June asked whether Alexander II had changed his mind on these issues: had he abandoned his entente with France (that is, his hope of revision in the Near East)? would he guarantee Venetia? It was useless for Alexander II to reply in his turn that Venetia was irrelevant to the question of Poland: neither Prussia nor Austria would commit themselves to Russia, unless Russia commited herself against France in exchange.[2]

There remained the alternative which Prussia had urged on Austria during the Crimean war and which Austria had then intermittently adopted: German solidarity against both France and Russia. Here too there was a decisive obstacle: the conflict between Austria and Prussia for hegemony in Germany. During the Crimean war Prussia had guaranteed all Austria's possessions without demanding any advantage in Germany in return; it was a policy to which Bismarck had been violently opposed, and it had not been repeated during the Italian war of 1859. Certainly Bismarck would not renew it in 1863. If Russia had guaranteed Venetia, then the risk for Prussia would have been slight and Bismarck would have joined in; without Russia, a

---

[1] Károlyi to Rechberg, 16 May 1863. *Auswärtige Politik Preußens 1858–1871*, iii, no. 508.

[2] Alexander II to William I, 1 June; William I to Alexander II, 17 June Alexander II to William I, 12 July 1863. *Auswärtige Politik Preußens 1858–1871*, iii, nos. 533, 557, 583.

guarantee of Venetia might provoke war on the Rhine, and Bismarck would not invite this for anything less than the mastery of Germany. The Austrians, or at any rate one group at the foreign ministry, had always dreamt that there was another way of achieving German solidarity: that is, by 'mediatizing' Prussia, compelling her to accept Austria's lead in Germany by the votes of the other German states. The climax of this policy came in August 1863 when the German princes met at Frankfurt under the presidency of Francis Joseph to discuss the reform of the confederation—or rather to endorse an Austrian plan of reform. Though the princes followed Austria's lead, her policy miscarried in its great objective. William I was prevented by Bismarck from coming to Frankfurt, and the princes would not acquiesce in any scheme from which Prussia was excluded. Despite the fine words of Frankfurt, the Austrian project ran to nothing when it was attempted to translate it into practical terms at Nuremberg in November. Once more Austria had failed to carry German feeling with her.

The Frankfurt meeting, with its clear threat against Prussia, enabled Bismarck to turn the tables on the Russians. In June Alexander II had asked for Prussian support against the west; in September Bismarck asked for Russian support against Austria. He talked of launching a war 'in the fashion of Frederick the Great'; declared that, if he could not get Russian support, he would go elsewhere 'even if he had to go to the Devil'; and spoke of buying French support with concessions on the Rhine. The Russians returned an evasive answer: they were still too busy in Poland to promise more than sympathy against Austria.[1] It is difficult to suppose that Bismarck, even with all the rashness and impatience which he often showed at the beginning of his career, seriously intended war with Austria in September 1863. Probably he merely wished to emphasize to the Russians how loyally and at what risks Prussia had acted as their buffer against the west. This effect he certainly achieved. In the German conflicts of the following years Russian policy never wavered: instead of insisting on the union of the two German Powers, as they had at the time of Olomouc, the Russians tolerated first disputes and then a Prussian victory. They saw in Prussia only

[1] Oubril (Berlin) to Gorchakov, 3 Sept., 15 Sept.; Loën (St. Petersburg) to Bismarck, 21 Sept. 1863. *Auswärtige Politik Preußens 1858–1871*, iii, nos. 678, 693, 705.

the decisive buffer between Poland and the west; and therefore
supposed that they were bound to gain from her aggrandizement, though they did not actively desire it. On the other hand,
they actively desired the weakening of Austria, for the sake of
the Near East—a desire now reinforced by the Polish affair. All
they asked of Prussia was neutrality, either in Poland or the
Near East; and in return they were willing enough to be
benevolently neutral in Germany. Bismarck was ready to hold
to this bargain until it had served its turn.

In the autumn of 1863 the Polish question disappeared from
international affairs for more than fifty years. The revolt, without aid from abroad, died away; henceforth Russia ruled Poland
by military power alone. Napoleon III made a last, grandiose
attempt to restore his shattered prestige. On 4 November he
launched the project that had been in his mind ever since he
reached power: a European congress to discuss every question
in dispute and to revise the map of Europe. 'The treaties of
1815 have ceased to exist', and a new order must be created,
based 'on the common interests of rulers and people'. The
rulers of Europe, however, received the proposal with common
consternation; they could all have exclaimed with Alexander
II, 'this is really too much'. All, even Austria, had the sense to
give a temporizing answer. It was left to Russell, the champion
of European liberties, to denounce the congress in the name of
treaty rights and the *status quo*. For, though the British government looked with favour on many a national cause, they were
not prepared to improve the condition of Europe at the risk of
seeing France in the Rhineland or Russia supreme in the Black
Sea; indeed, they were ready to put up with instability in Europe
so long as there was stability in the Near East.[1] Russell therefore
answered that a discussion of every European question would
increase tension, not lessen it; and the British government would
refuse to attend the congress. It was the end of Napoleon's
Utopian dream of peaceful revision; the end of his hegemony in
Europe; and the end, too, of the British alliance on which French
security had been based.

[1] Palmerston to Russell, 8 Nov. 1863: 'If the Congress gave Moldo-Wallachia
to Austria, and Venetia and Rome to Italy, incorporated Sleswig with Denmark
and separated Poland of 1815 from Russia and made it an independent state, not
touching the question of the Rhine as a French frontier or the relieving Russia
from what was imposed upon her by the Treaty of Paris, such a Congress would be
a well doer by Europe.'

VIII

BISMARCK'S WARS: THE DEFEAT OF AUSTRIA

1864–6

THE question of Sleswick and Holstein had been simmering ever since the treaty of London in 1852: disputed succession on the one side, Danish resolve to incorporate Sleswick in a unitary monarchy on the other. In November 1863 both disputes exploded at once. King Frederick VII died on 15 November; his successor, Christian IX, signed the unitary constitution on 18 November. This was a challenge to German national opinion; it could be sustained only if the Great Powers were as united against this sentiment as they had been in 1852. Instead, the crisis found the relations of the Great Powers in full disarray. Napoleon's persistence over Poland had shattered the Franco-Russian entente; the rough British rejection of Napoleon's plan for a congress had ended the Anglo-French alliance; Austria had missed alliance with France, offended Russia, failed to carry Germany. In fact the only stable relationship in Europe was the solidarity of Russia and Prussia against Poland. Even this was of a negative character; neither would take part in a coalition against the other. But Bismarck had refused to promise Russia support against a French expedition to the Baltic in favour of Poland; and neutrality was all that the Russians would offer in January 1864 in case of a French attack on the Rhine.[1]

The confusion of 1863 completed the disintegration which had been in process ever since 1848. The Concert of Europe had made a poor showing at the time of the Crimean war; only England and France had gone to the help of Turkey. In 1859 Napoleon had got his way in Italy without any interference from the Great Powers; in 1863 Russia had had a free hand in Poland. Localized wars, not a general conflict, were already the habit. All the same, it was a startling achievement to conjure a

[1] Oubril to Gorchakov, 20 Jan. 1864. *Auswärtige Politik Preußens 1858–1871*, iv, no. 350.

treaty out of existence within twelve years of its signature by all the Powers, the first of many achievements which were to make Bismarck the undisputed master of the diplomatic art. Later on, Bismarck was to claim that the whole campaign was in his head from the beginning; that he had already planned the annexation of the duchies (and for that matter the wars with Austria and France) when he took office in 1862. It is more likely that he merely planned to succeed: to keep himself in office; to keep William I on the throne; to make Prussia more powerful in Germany. The great player in diplomacy, as in chess, does not lose himself in speculation as to the remote consequences of his act: he asks only, 'does this move improve my position?' and then makes it.

In the first crisis over the duchies between 1848 and 1850, Prussia had first estranged the Great Powers by acting on behalf of German national feeling; and had then estranged this feeling by taking fright at the protests of the Great Powers. In 1863 Bismarck claimed to be acting on the basis of treaty rights, not of nationalism. German sentiment repudiated the treaty of London; it demanded the recognition of the rival claimant, the duke of Augustenburg, and the incorporation of both Sleswick and Holstein in Germany. Bismarck, on the other hand, proposed to recognize Christian IX and then to demand from him the autonomy promised to the duchies by the treaty of London. Ostensibly, he would be acting on behalf of international law, not against it; this knocked the strongest argument out of the hands of foreign powers. Bismarck would be protecting the Germans in the two duchies without an alliance with 'the revolution'; he had found, in fact, the 'respectable' cause which had always escaped Cavour in Italy. This policy certainly offended German opinion; in view of Bismarck's conflict with the Prussian parliament, this was no new matter. It was more serious that the king would have preferred to take the national line; and Bismarck could keep him in step only by arguing that this line involved a revolutionary alliance with Napoleon III. William's reluctance was an asset when it came to dealing with Austria; Bismarck could claim, with truth, that unless the Austrians co-operated with him, they would soon be faced with a liberal ministry in Prussia, aiming at leadership in Germany.

As usual, the Austrian government wanted to have things both ways. They were ripe for a return to conservative dualism.

Miles

20 10 0 20 40

NORTH SEA

SWEDEN

Aalborg

Stor Aa

Guden Aa

JUTLAND

DENMARK

Copenhagen

ZEALAND

Great Belt

FÜNEN

SLESWICK

Little Belt

LAALAND

BALTIC SEA

R. Eider

Kiel

Canal

HOLSTEIN

MECKLENBURG

LAUENBURG

R. Elbe

HANOVER

Hamburg

SLESWICK-HOLSTEIN

Francis Joseph was disillusioned with liberalism after the failure of the Frankfurt meeting in August; Rechberg held that 'there was no difference between the demand to incorporate Sleswick in Germany and the French striving for the Rhine frontier'.[1] Arguing against the liberal policy of repudiating Christian IX, Rechberg said to the council of ministers: 'If Austria accepts this policy, she will lose all her foreign allies. France will seize the welcome opportunity to attack Germany and Austria, and will set the revolution ablaze in Italy, Hungary, and Galicia. The existence of the Empire will be in danger!'[2] On the other hand, the Austrians dared not stand aside and leave Prussia to act alone; this, they believed, would lose them the leadership of Germany. In accepting Bismarck's proposal of an alliance to enforce the treaty of London, they imagined that they were taking Prussia prisoner for the conservative cause. As a matter of fact the alliance, concluded on 16 January 1864,[3] did not contain any such precise commitment. The Austrians had wished to stipulate that the two Powers should not depart from the conditions of the treaty of London except by mutual agreement. Bismarck objected that the king would not swallow a new reference to the hated treaty of 1852; and the Austrians had to be content with a vaguer promise that the future of the duchies should be settled by mutual agreement. This was not such a decisive score for Bismarck as was later made out; he would still have to buy Austria's consent to a change of programme. This clause was certainly the technical cause of the war of 1866; strangely enough from Austria's action, not Prussia's. In June 1866 Austria broke her bargain of 16 January 1864, by asking the diet to settle the future fate of the duchies; this gave Bismarck the excuse for war both against Austria and against the German states which supported her. At the time it was more important that the alliance contained no reference to the two problems which had ruined all previous attempts—no Prussian guarantee of Venetia, no Austrian recognition of Prussian military leadership in Germany. Since the federal forces were being ignored, or rather pushed aside, there was no point in stipulating who

[1] Rechberg to Prince Alexander of Hesse, 4 Jan. 1864. Stern, *Geschichte Europas*, ix. 348.

[2] Protocol of Austrian Council of Ministers, 10 Jan. 1864. *Quellen zur deutschen Politik Österreichs*, iii, no. 1410.

[3] Though actually signed (at Berlin) in the early afternoon of 17 Jan., it is conventionally dated 16 Jan.

should lead them; since this was a conservative alliance, Austria hoped that it would automatically extend to Venetia. Still, Bismarck knew that he had made the better bargain. When the Italian minister said, 'you will not need us now that you have another comrade in arms', Bismarck replied gaily: 'Oh, we have hired him.'—'Gratis?'—'Il travaille pour le roi de Prusse.'[1]

The technical question, fought out at the diet, was between Execution or Occupation of the duchies. Execution implied that Christian IX was their legal ruler; occupation that they were ownerless. On 7 December 1863 the diet agreed, with much reluctance, to a federal execution in Holstein; and this was carried out without resistance from the Danes. When, however, Austria and Prussia proposed to occupy Sleswick as a material pledge for the fulfilment of the treaty of London, German feeling could be no longer restrained; and the diet rejected the Austro-Prussian proposal on 14 January 1864. The two Great Powers then declared that they would act alone; and on 1 February their forces crossed the frontier into Sleswick.

While Austria and Prussia came together for war, the other Great Powers failed to come together for peace. Great Britain was deeply committed to Denmark. As late as 24 July 1863 Palmerston had declared that those who attempted to over-throw the rights and interfere with the independence of Den-mark would find that it would not be Denmark alone with which they would have to contend. This was the usual phrase with which Palmerston had been evoking European coalitions for the last thirty years; and in fact he supposed that he was threatening Germany with France—'in the present state of the Prussian army . . . the first serious encounter between it and the French would be little less disastrous to Prussia than the Battle of Jena'.[2] Apart from the navy, the British themselves could only provide an army of some 20,000 men. It was the essence of their policy that they could always count on a continental ally—the eastern Powers to restrain France, France to restrain Russia, France and Russia to restrain Prussia and Austria. Now the continental ally eluded them. Russia was deeply offended by British interference

---

[1] Talleyrand (Berlin) to Drouyn de Lhuys, 31 Jan. 1864. *Origines diplomatiques de la guerre de 1870–71*, i, no. 152. Bismarck was so pleased with his remark that he repeated it to the French minister himself.

[2] Minute by Palmerston, 27 June 1863. Quoted in L. D. Steefel, *The Schleswig-Holstein Question*, p. 61.

in the affairs of Poland; Napoleon by their offhand rejection of his proposal for a European congress. Moreover, the immediate issue at stake made it difficult to organize any joint action. The Danes had put themselves in the wrong by carrying the November constitution; and it was impossible for the Russians, or even the British, to resist Austria and Prussia when they were claiming to enforce the treaty of London. On the other hand, the war, despite its legal pretext, was in essence one of national liberation; impossible for Napoleon to go against it. Besides, he still believed that in case of any European turmoil he would be the ultimate gainer. In December 1863, after the failure of his congress plan, he had proposed a 'limited conference' in Paris, at which Russia, Prussia, and Italy should revise the map of Europe at Austria's expense.[1] Though Bismarck had evaded this proposal and had especially warned Napoleon off Poland, he had thrown in the assurance that the alliance with Austria did not cover Venetia; hence, all through the crisis, Napoleon was mainly concerned not to push Prussia further on to the Austrian side. Drouyn de Lhuys, on the other hand, welcomed the alliance for the exactly opposite reason: by strengthening the forces of conservatism, it would put temptation out of Napoleon's reach.

In the period between the accession of Christian IX and the outbreak of war, the British government made some feeble attempts to avert the crisis by persuading the Danes to give way. They could not undo the effect of their own rash statements earlier, nor could they convince the Danes that France would not support them. Besides they could not assure the Danes that, if they gave way on this issue, they would then be secure. In the last resort the Danes brought on their own defeat by ignoring Gorchakov's advice not to be as unyielding as Russia was over Poland: 'You are not seventy millions as we are.'[2] When the crisis approached, the British began to beat about for allies. They met with no response from Gorchakov. The Russians were still obsessed with Poland; they would do nothing to disturb the

---

[1] Goltz (Paris) to William I, 11 Dec. 1863. *Auswärtige Politik Preußens 1858–1871*, iv, no. 202.

[2] Gorchakov on 5 Aug. 1863. Steefel, *The Schleswig-Holstein Question*, p. 252. Palmerston took the same view (to Russell, 19 Jan. 1864): 'Great Powers like Russia may persevere in wrongdoing, and other States may not like to make the Effort necessary for compelling it to take the right Course. But no such Impunity in wrong is possessed by a small and weak State like Denmark.'

conservative partnership between Prussia and Austria, which seemed to be rebuilding a firm barrier between Poland and France. Besides, though the Russians were concerned for the control of the Sound,[1] they did not object to its passing from Denmark into the hands of Prussia. They believed that the strengthening of Prussia could do them no harm; this is the key to their policy in the twenty years after the treaty of Paris. It would have been a different matter if the threat to Denmark had come from 'national' Germany. The Russians were equally alarmed at the proposal for a Scandinavian union, with Sweden coming to the help of Denmark. Though this was the most sensible of many British suggestions, it only recalled to the Russians the alliance of Great Britain and France with Sweden at the end of the Crimean war. The Russians regretted the Sleswick affair; the fact remained that for them the aggrandizement of Prussia was the least objectionable of alternatives.

The British government were therefore forced back to France. Here too their appeals met with no response. Napoleon was not likely to go to war for a treaty, even for one not connected in any way with 1815. Drouyn referred bitterly to the British failure to act over Poland and said: 'we must avoid a conflict which would spread to the whole continent and the burden of which would fall on our shoulders'.[2] Once the war had started, both Drouyn and Napoleon began to throw out hints that France must be somehow rewarded; they pointed vaguely to 'the little Rhine'.[3] These remarks were not more than the rambling speculations in which Napoleon always liked to indulge. There was one moment when a crisis seemed to be blowing up. On 19 February the Austrian and Prussian forces, having driven the Danes out of Sleswick, crossed the frontier of Denmark itself. The rights and wrongs of the Sleswick question were pushed into the background; the existence of Denmark seemed to be at stake. On 21 February the British cabinet called home the Channel fleet. Russell, without consulting the cabinet, appealed

---

[1] Gorchakov said: 'Russia will never allow the Sound to become a second Bosphorus.' Pirch to Bismarck, 11 May 1864. *Auswärtige Politik Preußens 1858–1871*, v, no. 49.

[2] Drouyn de Lhuys to La Tour d'Auvergne (London), 14 Jan., 26 Jan. 1864. *Origines diplomatiques*, i, nos. 78, 126.

[3] Goltz to William I, 9 Feb. 1864. Oncken, *Die Rheinpolitik Kaiser Napoleons III*, i, nos. 12, 13. In the diplomatic jargon of the time, 'the great Rhine' meant the entire Rhineland, 'the little Rhine' the district of the Saar which France had retained by the first treaty of Paris (1814) and lost by the second (1815).

to Russia and France for naval support. Gorchakov dodged the invitation with the admirable excuse that the Russian fleet was frozen up until May. The French were more forthcoming. The opponents of Drouyn's cautious policy—some of them pro-British, some of them simply in favour of adventure—thought that the moment had come to launch a war for the Rhine with British backing. They stirred Napoleon to action. Drouyn, to keep his place, had to speak in a threatening tone to the Prussian minister, and talked to Cowley of enforcing the treaty of London. The change of policy did not last twenty-four hours. Drouyn and Metternich, the Austrian ambassador, enlisted the empress; and together they won Napoleon back to doing nothing. By 22 February Drouyn was declaring himself satisfied with the explanations from Berlin and Vienna. Almost simultaneously, the British cabinet repudiated Russell's initiative; and on their insistence he had to inform Russia and France that there was no question of sending the British fleet to Danish waters.

A myth became established in later years that Napoleon missed the moment of French destiny when he failed to respond to the British approach of 21 February. In truth there was no British approach—merely an impatient gesture by Russell (one among many), which was revoked by the cabinet as soon as they learnt of it. Apart from this, the time had long passed (if it had ever existed) when England and France could by themselves impose their will on central Europe. Even with Russia it would have been a speculative affair; as a result of the Polish crisis, Russia would be at best neutral, and possibly hostile. The British could have fought a limited naval war; the French would have had to fight a war for existence. Drouyn said that France could not undertake a war with a nation of forty-five millions merely for the sake of the treaty of 1852;[1] and he made out that France would have been willing to act if the British had promised her the Rhineland—'compensations equal to our sacrifices'.[2] These were mere excuses to cloak (no doubt even to himself) the reality that France was no longer strong enough to dominate Europe. French policy could be successful only so long as Germany was divided, in particular only so long as Austria could be played off against Prussia; and war for the

[1] Drouyn de Lhuys to La Tour d'Auvergne, 23 Feb. 1864. *Origines diplomatiques*, ii, no. 245.
[2] Drouyn de Lhuys to La Tour d'Auvergne, 10 June 1864. Ibid., iii, no. 640.

Elbe duchies would have united the two German Powers in
Venetia as on the Rhine. Napoleon and his ministers counted,
rightly as it turned out, that the duchies would ultimately cause
a conflict between Austria and Prussia. The moment of French
destiny came in 1866, when the two were at war, not in 1864,
when they were united.

The decline in French power was not fully sensed even by the
rulers of France. It was not appreciated at all in the other states
of Europe. What Bismarck had learnt in Paris—the card on
which he staked everything between 1864 and 1866—was not
French weakness, but the division in French policy. Napoleon
would never follow sincerely the path of conservatism and treaty
rights, yet he would be restrained by his advisers and his own
lethargy from a ruthless policy of adventure. Bismarck modelled
himself on Cavour and improved on the example. Though
Cavour exploited Napoleon for Italy's benefit, he had to pay a
real price with Savoy and Nice; Bismarck paid in shadows. It
is a useless speculation to debate whether he ever genuinely
considered the surrender of territory on the Rhine to France.
Certainly he boasted that he had rescued Prussia from the
mediatisation which fear for the Rhine provinces had previously
imposed upon her;[1] certainly he talked of striking a bargain
with France—'Paris is nearer Berlin than London';[2] 'who gives
the Rhine provinces to France will possess her'.[3] But there was a
fundamental difference between the Rhine provinces and Savoy.
Savoy was not Italian; the Rhineland was German. Bismarck
could never have united Germany under Prussia if he had given
German territory to Napoleon. This may prove only that in
1864 he was not yet contemplating the unification of Germany;
or it may prove that he always intended to deceive Napoleon.
More probably, it proves that Bismarck dealt with the future
only when it arrived.

What is undoubted is that Bismarck did not fear French
intervention over the duchies. This enabled him to disregard
British threats, Russian warnings, and to drag Austria along
with him. The advance into Jutland involved a new convention
with Austria in March; and the Austrians once more asked for a

---

[1] Lefebvre de Béhaine (Berlin) to Drouyn de Lhuys, 19 June 1865. *Origines
diplomatiques*, vi, no. 1433.
[2] Oubril to Gorchakov, 9 Mar. 1864. *Auswärtige Politik Preußens 1858–1871*, iv,
no. 527.
[3] Gramont to Drouyn de Lhuys, 28 Aug. 1864. *Origines diplomatiques*, iv, no. 814.

guarantee of Venetia, if they were to run the risk of a general war for the duchies. Bismarck silenced them with the argument that they should provide against the danger from France only if it arose. In any case, France, far from being a danger, soon came to his aid. Thanks to British efforts, a conference was at last arranged to consider the affair of the duchies. It finally met on 25 April.[1] The British would have liked to tie the conference to the treaty of London; and Clarendon was sent over to Paris to win Napoleon for this programme. Napoleon refused: 'He could not lay himself open to the charge of pursuing one policy on the Eider and a totally different one on the Po.' This was not a roundabout way of asking for the Rhine frontier; it sprang from Napoleon's deep conviction that every triumph of the national principle was inevitably a triumph for France and for himself. Therefore he launched the rival proposal of a division of the duchies on the national line. Though this idea had been put forward by Palmerston even in 1848 and though Russell himself had taken up the national principle in Italy with vigour, it was now met in London with shocked surprise. Russell said the idea was 'too new in Europe' and that 'the Great Powers had not the habit of consulting populations when questions affecting the Balance of Power had to be settled'.[2] Bismarck, on the other hand, encouraged the idea from the start. Napoleon then went further: he suggested that Prussia and France should work together to secure the incorporation of the duchies into Prussia and asked only for a 'genuine and effective co-operation' in other fields. He was in effect inviting the Prussians to cheat him as he had cheated the Russians in the Italian question: real gains on the one side, fine words on the other. It was an invitation which Bismarck had long decided to accept.

The London conference turned out to be nothing more than a meeting to bury the treaties of 1852. Austria and Prussia regarded themselves as freed from these treaties by the act of war with Denmark; they made a formal announcement of this on 12 May. They proposed instead personal union between the duchies and the Danish crown; this was rejected by the Danes.

---

[1] The conference has a curious interest as the only international gathering at which the German Confederation was represented. The German representative was Bismarck's enemy Beust, at that time prime minister of Saxony, later the last Austrian chancellor.

[2] La Tour d'Auvergne to Drouyn de Lhuys, 24 Mar. 1864. *Origines diplomatiques*, ii, no. 368.

Inevitably Austria and Prussia had to demand the cession of the duchies; but to whom should they be ceded? Bismarck threw out the suggestion to Austria that they should go to Prussia: 'this would be the beginning of a policy of mutual compensation'. The Austrians at once took fright: they thought that they were being tricked by Bismarck and, to repay him, took up the claims of the duke of Augustenburg on 25 May; this was the first step to the war of 1866. Bismarck ostensibly followed them;[1] and the two Powers formally proposed the cession of the two duchies on 28 May. This was the moment for the French to propose the division of the duchies on the national line; and the proposal was supported by the other Powers *faute de mieux*. For the first time an international conference broke away from treaty rights and tried to apply the doctrine of self-determination. Not surprisingly it encountered all the difficulties which have haunted international gatherings from that day to this—how could nationality be determined? should the Powers arbitrarily draw a line or should the inhabitants be consulted? If so, how— by plebiscites, as Napoleon wished, or by a meeting of their diets? These questions would have baffled the conference, even if the Danes had wished it to succeed; and they were determined it should fail. Even if they got no support from without, they preferred—like Francis Joseph in 1859—to lose the duchies by conquest rather than by agreement; in this way they supposed there would be some hope of recovering them in the future.[2] The conference broke down on 25 June; and the war was renewed.

Two attempts were made in the early part of June to rescue the Danes from complete defeat. On the one side Gorchakov urged compromise on Prussia and Austria in order not to drive the British into the arms of France; on the other the British made a last effort to win French support. Both attempts failed. Bismarck argued that he had to liberate the duchies in order to prevent revolution in Germany; besides, in the unlikely event of a French attack, Russia would have to support the German

---

[1] It is a point of dispute in German history, rather than in international relations, whether Bismarck had any serious purpose in his negotiations with the duke of Augustenburg. There can be no doubt that he would have supported the duke's claim only if the duchies were made dependent on Prussia.

[2] See the Danish opinion of 1 Aug. 1864 in Steefel, *The Schleswig-Holstein Question*, p. 251: 'Much rather a peace that is recognised by everyone to rest upon no principle at all. . . . I hope for a third act in the drama.'

Powers to avoid having French troops 'in Posen and Cracow'.[1] This was a sharp enough reminder to Gorchakov that the Holy Alliance had a serious purpose only in Poland; and no doubt Gorchakov himself was not deeply concerned with it elsewhere. By the end of July he was saying to the French representative: 'It was I who at Vienna destroyed the Holy Alliance; do you think I would pick up the fragments?'[2] This too was in the mind of Napoleon—why should he revive the Holy Alliance for the sake of a country which had refused to apply the national principle? There seems to have been some discussion and even some doubts in Paris between 8 June and 10 June; this time Drouyn was more for action—on a conservative basis—Napoleon and the adventurers naturally more against. In the end the French offered a promise of neutrality in case Great Britain went to the aid of Denmark.[3]

But the British had already decided to do nothing. On 25 June the cabinet resolved, by eight votes to six, not to go to war for the sake of the duchies; they added, with a last splutter of pride, 'if the existence of Denmark as an independent kingdom or the safety of Copenhagen was threatened, a new decision would have to be made'. Drouyn commented: 'the British do nothing by halves; they are now retreating vigorously';[4] and the decision of 25 June 1864 has usually been regarded as a catastrophic blow to British prestige. But quite apart from the obstinacy of the Danes, which put them technically in the wrong both in January and June, it is difficult to see what other course British policy could have taken. Russian backing could have been bought, if at all, only by giving up the Black Sea clauses in the treaty of 1856; and the Baltic was less important to the British than the Black Sea. Co-operation with France, even if possible, was too dangerous; here again, the Baltic was less important than Belgium and the Rhineland. Palmerston held that the aggrandizement of Prussia, however improperly attained, was not against British interests; France and Russia, not the central Powers, were the disturbing element on the Continent

---

[1] Foreign Office memorandum, 13 June; Bismarck to Werther, 14 June 1864. *Auswärtige Politik Preußens 1858–1871*, iv, nos. 136, 148.

[2] Massignac (St. Petersburg) to Drouyn de Lhuys, 28 July 1864. *Origines diplomatiques*, iii, no. 756.

[3] Drouyn de Lhuys to La Tour d'Auvergne, 27 June 1864. Ibid., no. 700.

[4] Goltz to Bismarck, 30 June 1864. *Auswärtige Politik Preußens 1858–1871*, v, no. 190.

and, as well, imperial rivals to Great Britain outside Europe. No doubt this judgement would have been modified by the unexpectedly decisive Prussian victories in 1866 and 1871. Still, the Balance of Power survived Bismarck's three wars. As for Great Britain's imperial interests, the new European balance after 1871 actually made it easier to check Russia in the Near East and, later, to defeat France on the Nile. Nothing that the British did in 1864 could have checked the industrial expansion of Germany in the last third of the nineteenth century or their own relative decline; if mistakes were made, it was rather in the twentieth century than in the last days of Palmerston.

The Danes, left to themselves, were again defeated. On 20 July they agreed to an armistice; on 1 August they signed a preliminary peace, surrendering the duchies to Austria and Prussia jointly. Three weeks later Bismarck and Rechberg, with their two royal masters, met at Schönbrunn in an effort to settle the future of the duchies. Bismarck wanted Austria to hand them over to Prussia in exchange for a vague prospect of support elsewhere—the undefined conservative partnership, in fact, which he, and every other Prussian, had rejected when Austria had tried to apply it in relation to Italy or the Danube. Now it was the Austrians who demanded a concrete advantage. Bismarck next proposed that the two Powers should retain the duchies jointly until the chance of a war against Italy; then Prussia would not merely defend Venetia, she would help Austria to recover Lombardy, and would receive the duchies as reward. The scheme was wrecked by the resistance of the two rulers. William would face a war for Italy for no less a price than hegemony over Germany; Francis Joseph would not surrender his share of the duchies except for a compensation in German territory—he named part of the Silesian lands which Frederick the Great had seized in 1740. In any case, the plan involved war with France as well as with Italy; and it is difficult to believe that Bismarck would have faced this merely for the duchies which were half his already. The abortive treaty of Schönbrunn was probably little more than a device by Bismarck to postpone the full acquisition of the duchies by Prussia to a more favourable opportunity; at best it merely confirmed what had been shown over and over again since 1859—that Austria could maintain herself in Italy only at the price of surrendering the headship of Germany to Prussia, and this price Francis Joseph would never pay without defeat in war.[1]

Faced with this deadlock, Rechberg and Bismarck could only agree to perpetuate the joint ownership of the duchies; and this was put into the final treaty with Denmark in October. Rechberg made one great concession: he agreed not to raise the question of the duchies at the diet—thus, to adhere to the Prussian alliance instead of mobilizing German feeling against her. Francis Joseph was now full of doubts in regard to this policy. Biegeleben, Rechberg's assistant, argued that it should be abandoned in favour of an alliance with France. The chance for this had, in fact, passed. Napoleon III was slowly shaking himself free of Drouyn's restraint and moving towards a new burst of activity in the Italian question. On 15 September France and Italy concluded a convention over Rome. The French troops were to be withdrawn from Rome within two years; Italy promised not to attack Rome and to move the capital from Turin to Florence. Ostensibly Italy renounced Rome; in reality she merely postponed its acquisition in order to save Napoleon's face. This was the very policy for which Thouvenel had lost office two years before. Drouyn recognized his defeat and said to Nigra: 'naturally the outcome will be that you will finally go to Rome'. The convention restored good relations between France and Italy, hence was a gesture against Austria; more, by postponing the Roman question, it turned Italian eyes—and Napoleon's as well—towards Venetia. It was a further sign of the swing away from Drouyn that one of Thouvenel's supporters, Benedetti, who had been out of favour since 1862, was now sent as French ambassador to Berlin; Napoleon told him that his task was to prevent any close association between Austria and Prussia.[2]

This task was made easy by the new course of Austrian policy. In October Rechberg failed to secure from Prussia a promise that Austria might be admitted to the Zollverein at some time in the future; though the promise would have been meaningless, its

---

[1] Rechberg and Bismarck in old age both gave confused and misleading accounts of the Schönbrunn conversations. It was for long held that no formal agreement had been drawn up. Some years ago the draft was discovered by Srbik and published by him in the *Historische Zeitschrift*, vol. 153. It is reproduced in *Quellen zur deutschen Politik Österreichs*, iv, no. 1768.

[2] Benedetti to Drouyn de Lhuys, 30 Apr., 1865. *Origines diplomatiques*, vi, no. 1376.

refusal was not. It was the final stroke against Rechberg, and he left office on 27 October. Mensdorff, who took his place, was a cavalry general with little political experience. The real director of policy, Maurice Esterházy, was a despairing conservative, who believed that Austria was doomed and should therefore perish honourably. Hence no concessions to Italy; no alliance with France; yet no yielding to Prussia in the duchies. All that Esterházy was prepared to offer Prussia was the privilege of co-operating in a war against 'the revolution'; and even this only on condition that Prussia made no gains for herself. Austria was thus to maintain her claims on every front, yet seek for allies on none. The Austrians did not even attempt to conciliate Russia, the remaining Great Power who might have counted for something in the balance of central Europe. Instead they opposed Russia as obstinately as ever in Rumania, when affairs there fell once more into a turmoil. Bismarck got an easy credit by promising to support any Russian proposals that did not lead to a quarrel with France;[1] in the words of the French ambassador at St. Petersburg, Prussia stood above par in politics as on the bourse.[2] It would be a mistake to exaggerate the importance of Russia's favourable disposition towards Prussia. The Polish revolt, coming on top of the Crimean war, had exhausted Russian strength and had made any action on a grand scale impossible. Still, in the period before a war breaks out, influence counts for much, even when not backed by arms. If Alexander II had pressed for a reconciliation between the two German Powers as persistently as Nicholas I had done before Olomouc, this would soon have shaken the king of Prussia's resolve—it hardly stood proof against expostulations by Victoria. As it was there came from St. Petersburg much sympathy with Prussia, and no murmur of condemnation.

This was, no doubt, a minor factor. Both Russia and Great Britain had virtually eliminated themselves from the European balance; this gave the years between 1864 and 1866 a character unique in recent history. The struggle for mastery in Germany was fought out on a stage limited to western Europe; and Napoleon had to speak for Europe without any assistance from the other two non-German Powers. Not surprisingly, the re-

[1] Napier (St. Petersburg) to Russell, 2 Jan.; Oubril to Gorchakov, 14 Dec. 1865. *Auswärtige Politik Preußens 1858–1871*, v, no. 423; vi, no. 387.
[2] Talleyrand to Drouyn de Lhuys, 18 Jan. 1865. *Origines diplomatiques*, v, no. 1201.

sponsibility was too much for him. The German struggle came in two bouts—a false start, or possibly a rehearsal, in the summer of 1865; the real thing in the spring of 1866. Ostensibly a conflict over the duchies, the real question, as usual in international affairs, was—in Humpty Dumpty's words—'who's to be master, that's all'. In the autumn of 1864 the Austrian government, at a loss to know what to do with the duchies, began to push the claims of the duke of Augustenburg. Bismarck answered on 22 February 1865 by defining the conditions on which Prussia would recognize Augustenburg; they were conditions of total dependence. Biegeleben commented that he would sooner plant potatoes than be ruler of the duchies under such terms. On 6 April Austria stirred up the diet to back Augustenburg—a clear gesture against the alliance with Prussia. On 29 May Prussian policy was debated in a crown council. Bismarck said: 'if war against Austria in alliance with France is struck out of the vocabulary of diplomacy, no Prussian policy is possible any longer'.[1] Despite this, the council did not resolve on war—and Bismarck probably did not intend it to; it merely decided to reaffirm the February conditions and to see what would happen. Tension continued to mount; it reached its height in August, when William I and Bismarck were both on Austrian soil at Gastein—in those civilized days it was possible for a ruler to take a holiday in the country with which he might be at war in a fortnight. At the last minute the Austrian government lost their nerve. Overwhelmed with financial difficulties and faced with a constitutional crisis in Hungary, they decided on 5 August to buy time by a compromise. They offered, and Bismarck accepted, a 'provisional' division of the duchies, Sleswick to Prussia, Holstein to Austria. Agreement on this was signed at Gastein on 14 August.

The treaty of Gastein, like the treaty of Schönbrunn before it (and the Gablenz proposals of May 1866 after it), has been a subject of endless controversy. Some have seen in it simply a calculated step by Bismarck on the path towards an inevitable war; others have found in it the proof of his desire to re-establish the conservative German partnership of Metternich's days. Maybe it was neither.[2] Bismarck was a diplomatic genius,

---

[1] This remark is not in the official record, but in Moltke's note of the meeting, hence less decisive. *Auswärtige Politik Preußens 1858–1871*, vi, no. 101.

[2] One interpretation is certainly wrong. There is no evidence that the Prussians

inexperienced in war and disliking its risks. He may well have
hoped to manœuvre Austria out of the duchies, perhaps even
out of the headship of Germany, by diplomatic strokes; marvels
of this sort were not beyond him in later life. His diplomacy in
this period seems rather calculated to frighten Austria than to
prepare for war. The only bait he held out to France was that,
if Prussia got the duchies, she would apply 'the national principle' by restoring northern Sleswick to Denmark; all he asked
in return was benevolent neutrality.[1] His approach to Italy was
equally tentative—and telegrams sent through the Austrian
post-office were surely meant to have an effect mainly at Vienna.
Both the French and the Italians suspected that Bismarck was
manœuvring them for his own ends. La Marmora, the Italian
prime minister, though eager to conquer Venetia, doubted
whether Bismarck intended 'war on a grand scale'.[2] Napoleon
kept out of the way deliberately during the crisis, and left French
policy to be defined by Eugenie and Drouyn, both of them ex-
ponents of the conservative line; Drouyn's only effective action
was to warn Italy against relying on French help against
Austria.[3]

There is one strong argument against this more or less pacific
interpretation of Bismarck's policy; he was no sooner back in
Berlin than he began to drum around for French support. Not
content with declaring that he wanted France to expand 'where-
ever French was spoken in the world',[4] he went off himself to
see Napoleon at Biarritz in October. Yet the meeting at Biarritz
was far from being a repetition of Cavour's visit to Plombières
in 1858. Cavour was resolved on war with Austria; and Napoleon

were doubtful of their ability to defeat Austria; therefore no ground for supposing that they postponed the war until they could get an alliance with Italy. The
compromise came from Austria, not from Prussia; and Bismarck accepted a
compromise simply because one was offered him. Even the Austrian decision
was made from political motives, not after military calculation. In fact it is extraordinary how little each side (and indeed anyone else) weighed the military
chances.
    [1] Benedetti to Drouyn de Lhuys, 7 May 1865. *Origines diplomatiques*, vi, no. 1387.
Admittedly Bismarck said that he would seek the alliance of France in case of
defeat and that he knew he would have to pay a price for it; but he did not at this
time specify the price.
    [2] Usedom (Florence) to Bismarck, 27 July 1865. *Auswärtige Politik Preußens
1858–1871*, vi, no. 206.
    [3] Drouyn de Lhuys to Gramont, 1 Aug.; to Lefebvre de Béhaine, 15 Aug. 1865.
Origines diplomatiques, vi, nos. 1470, 1493.
    [4] Lefebvre de Béhaine to Drouyn de Lhuys, 27 Sept. 1865. Ibid., vii, no. 1590.

intended to fight it with him. Each was concerned to tie the other down—Cavour to get a binding promise of support, Napoleon to secure Savoy and Nice. Now Bismarck and Napoleon were both anxious to avoid commitment, to keep the future open. Bismarck wanted to prevent a French alliance with Austria, not to get one for himself; to ensure, in short, that Napoleon, not Drouyn, determined French policy. Drouyn had denounced the treaty of Gastein as an act of immoral force; he would have liked to see an Austrian alliance with the smaller German states for the humiliation of Prussia—a return to the policy of Olomouc. Napoleon disliked any agreement between Prussia and Austria, whether on the basis of Olomouc or of Gastein; behind any such agreement he suspected, as always, a Prussian guarantee of Venetia. Bismarck told him that no such guarantee had been given; in exchange Napoleon insisted that a French alliance with Austria was impossible—'he would not go and stand beside a target'. Though they also discussed 'advantages which might offer themselves unsought'[1]—northern Germany for Prussia; Belgium or Luxembourg for France—these were vague speculations of the usual Napoleonic kind. The essential bargain of Biarritz was that both kept clear of commitment to Austria, Bismarck for the sake of Germany, Napoleon for the sake of Venetia.

It was indeed Venetia which henceforth determined the shape of diplomatic events. Napoleon was obsessed with it. With patient, sullen obstinacy, he was determined to achieve the unfinished programme of 1859,[2] and believed that if he died with Venetia still in Austrian hands 'his son would have a volcano as a throne'.[3] The prospect of acquiring territory towards the Rhine was of secondary interest to him (as even Savoy and Nice had been in 1859); these were demands that he made to satisfy French public opinion, in order to keep himself popular.[4] Of course he supposed that any conflict between Prussia and Austria would improve the European balance in his favour; the practical use to which he would turn this would depend upon

---

[1] Bismarck to William I, 5 Oct. 1865. *Auswärtige Politik Preußens 1858–1871*, vi, no. 313.

[2] 'My only interest is to be finished with the Italian question by the cession of Venice.' Metternich to Mensdorff, 21 May 1866. *Rheinpolitik Napoleons III*, i, no. 116.   [3] His phrase to Cowley.

[4] 'The eyes of all France are turned *towards* the Rhine.' Goltz to Bismarck, 8 May 1866. *Rheinpolitik*, i, no. 87.

events. These were shadowy prospects; Venetia was concrete and immediate. If the Austrians had found some honourable way of giving Venetia to Italy, Drouyn and his conservative line of policy would have been immensely strengthened; Napoleon would have let things slide, and the anti-Prussian coalition, sought later in vain, might have come into existence. So long as Venetia was in Austrian hands, Napoleon could not be won for a pro-Austrian, or even for a pacific, policy; though more procrastinating than ever, he remained an adventurer.

The decisive lurch towards war was given, oddly enough, by the attempt to find a peaceful solution of the Venetian question; and Venetia in the last resort gave Prussia the hegemony of Germany. In the autumn of 1865 a conservative Italian nobleman, Malaguzzi, tried to persuade the Austrian government to sell Venetia to Italy and to console themselves by gains in Germany; negotiations went on until February 1866, and then broke down. Just at this moment a more attractive alternative presented itself. On 23 February 1866 Nicholas Cuza, the prince of Rumania, was overthrown and compelled to abdicate. It occurred to Nigra, the Italian representative in Paris, that Austria might acquire Rumania in exchange for Venetia; and Napoleon acquiesced in the idea—it was one of the elaborate combinations that he always loved. But he believed that the Austrians would never give up Venetia unless driven to it by fear; therefore he advised the Italians to prod Austria into surrender by simultaneously negotiating with Prussia for a war-alliance. The advice came at exactly the right time. On 28 February a Prussian crown council had decided to challenge Austria even at the risk of war; and, as a first step, to conciliate Napoleon by seeking an alliance with Italy. Bismarck approached La Marmora, the Italian prime minister, just when La Marmora had decided to approach Bismarck. An Italian general was sent to Berlin, ostensibly to negotiate, really to alarm the Austrians. They took alarm, but not in the right direction. They saw in the proposed gain of Rumania only a device to bring down on them the hostility of Russia;[1] and refused the bargain outright in the middle of March.

[1] Bismarck did this for them in any case. He told the Russians that Austria had favoured the idea and that Napoleon had opposed it for the sake of Rumanian nationalism. Oubril to Gorchakov, 25 Feb. 1866. *Auswärtige Politik Preußens 1858–1871*, vi, no. 493. Alexander II said the scheme was 'inadmissible jusqu'à la guerre'; and Gorchakov 'if I had the nature *of a sheep*, I should revolt at the very

The Italians, and their patron Napoleon, were thus left with the Prussian negotiations on their hands; what they had begun as bluff, they now had to pursue in earnest. Though Bismarck agreed that, if there were a war, the Italians should get Venetia, he would not commit himself to go to war for its sake; he demanded that the Italians should bind themselves for three months to go to war against Austria in case Prussia did so, while he kept his hands free. Even this was a gain for the Italians: though it did not guarantee them a war, it guaranteed them Venetia in the event of war. The same argument was decisive with Napoleon: he advised the Italians, though 'as a friend, without assuming any responsibility', to accept Bismarck's offer, and even promised to protect them from an Austrian attack in case Prussia left them in the lurch. The treaty between Prussia and Italy, signed on 8 April, was the decisive step in Napoleon's policy. Henceforth, for three months, he could not offer Italian neutrality to the Austrians, even if they were willing to surrender Venetia; nor could he effectively threaten Prussia, even if the Austrians offered him the Rhineland and Bismarck did not. It is often said that Bismarck launched the Austro-Prussian war without making any concrete promise to Napoleon. This is not the case. Bismarck won the diplomatic campaign by being the first to pay the only price for which Napoleon cared; that price was Venetia. Once the treaty of 8 April was signed Bismarck listened, no doubt, to Napoleon's vague talk of compensation on the Rhine—'if only you had a Savoy'[1]—and had to face more practical demands from Drouyn;[2] the essential price had been paid, and there was no serious chance of Napoleon's forbidding Bismarck to go to war if he were determined to do so.

The treaty of 8 April turned the diplomatic situation upside down. Until then the question had been whether war could be made; thereafter, whether it could be avoided. Attempts were made from three sides—by Austria, by Bismarck, finally by Napoleon; all three broke on the problem of Venetia. The Austrians were in the embarrassing difficulty that their

idea' (Talleyrand to Drouyn de Lhuys, 21 Mar. 1866. *Origines diplomatiques*, viii, no. 1927). It certainly completed the estrangement between Russia and Austria, if this were necessary.

[1] Goltz to William I, 25 Apr. 1866. *Rheinpolitik*, i, no. 71.

[2] Drouyn said: 'we have enough prestige; we shall not fight for an idea any more. If others gain, we must.' Goltz to Bismarck, 1 May 1866. Ibid., no. 75.

unwieldy army needed seven or eight weeks to mobilize; the
Prussian only three. If the race to war started, it was they who
would have to start it. The only escape from this situation was to
promise not to start the race on condition Prussia would do the
same; if Bismarck refused, he, not the Austrians, would have
given the signal for war. This initiative was made on 7 April;
Bismarck had no effective answer with which to satisfy the king,
and by 21 April he was unwillingly driven into promising to
follow Austria on the path of disarmament. The same day the
Austrian ministers were alarmed by exaggerated reports of preparations for war in Italy. Since they had never recognized the
kingdom of Italy, they could not approach the Italians for a
promise such as they had received from Prussia; moreover, they
knew that even if they overcame this technical obstacle, the
Italians would answer by a demand for the cession of Venetia.
They therefore decided to mobilize against Italy alone. This
was enough for Bismarck; he could convince William I that the
Austrians were deceiving him. And indeed, the Austrians found
that partial mobilization was an impossible compromise; on 27
April their northern army in Bohemia began to mobilize as well.
Thus Austrian fears for Venetia enabled Bismarck to escape the
responsibility of starting the race to war.

Bismarck's own initiative may have been designed only to
remove the king's last scruples against war; it may have been a
last bid to secure German dualism by peaceful means. No one is
ever likely to penetrate Bismarck's motives. The intermediary
was Anton von Gablenz—a figure characteristic of dualism,
himself a Prussian, his brother Austrian governor of Holstein.
The Gablenz 'compromise' had two conditions: the duchies to
go to a Prussian prince, but never to be united to Prussia; the
military headship of Germany to be divided between Austria and
Prussia. The Austrians might have agreed to the condition about
the duchies; they were weary of this affair, and the Gablenz
proposal saved their honour. The second condition was more
serious. Hegemony of northern Germany was what the Prussians
had demanded in 1849, during the war of 1859, and in the
negotiations of 1860–1 after the meeting at Teplitz; it had been
the decisive demand which the Austrians had always refused.
Now, in their harassed position, they might have agreed to it, if
they could have received a Prussian guarantee of Venetia in
return. It was beyond even Bismarck's ingenuity to satisfy this

condition. He was, in fact, proposing that since Austria had got herself into difficulties by refusing to give up either Venetia or hegemony in Germany she should now lose both. This was indeed the outcome of the war of 1866; but the Austrians would not accept the consequences of defeat before the war started.[1] On 28 May the Gablenz negotiation broke down. Once more Venetia had prevented agreement.

As a matter of fact the Austrians had decided, too late, to win French friendship and Italian neutrality by surrendering Venetia after all. But they would not surrender it directly to Italy; at the beginning of May they offered to surrender it to France in exchange for Italian neutrality—they would themselves win compensation in Germany by war against Prussia. Napoleon would have liked to accept the offer. Having planned a war, he now shrank from it, just as he tried to hold Cavour back in the early days of 1859. Besides, he was being harassed by his own supporters, Drouyn and Persigny, and still more by a speech from Thiers on 3 May that support for Prussia was the wrong line: instead of building up a united Germany, he ought to restore the balance of 1815. French opinion cared nothing for Venetia; what it wanted was to turn the left bank of the Rhine into a buffer-state under French protection,[2] and since this must include Prussian territory, Austria, not Prussia, was the better partner for France. Rather half-heartedly Napoleon asked the Italians whether they would accept the Austrian offer. They refused. Their formal justification was the treaty with Prussia, which bound them until 8 July; their real condition was that the national principle should be satisfied by the surrender of Venetia after a plebiscite—a condition which it was impossible for the Austrians to accept. At heart Napoleon did not regret the refusal: he needed the Italian pressure on Austria. Besides, the criticism from Thiers had driven him into the open. On 6 May, without warning his ministers, he declared at Auxerre: 'I detest those treaties of 1815 which nowadays people want to make the sole basis of our policy.'

Napoleon still thought that there was a peaceful way out:

[1] Later in life Bismarck made out that he had offered to join Austria in war against France and to give Alsace to Austria. This was obviously untrue. There was no question of Alsace in 1866; and Bismarck evoked it later in order to cloak the fact that he could not guarantee Venetia.

[2] The clearest expression of this was from Persigny in the French council of ministers on 18 May.

the congress of which he had always dreamt to discuss every European question. This had indeed been suggested to him by the Italians as a way of buying time until their alliance with Prussia ran out on 8 July. The two neutral Powers, England and Russia, were ready to make an empty gesture in favour of peace; but both insisted on ruling out the Eastern question, the only topic that concerned them—England so that Russia should not raise the neutralization of the Black Sea, Russia to prevent the acquisition of Rumania by Austria. What remained in the programme was Venetia, which would go to Italy; the Elbe duchies, which would go to Prussia; a neutral state on the Rhine, for the benefit of France. Austria was offered a vague 'compensation'. The Austrians would have been satisfied only with Silesia, which they knew that Prussia would never surrender without a war. Bismarck himself warned the French that, if they proposed the cession of Silesia, Prussia would appeal to German national feeling by proclaiming the Frankfurt constitution of 1849 and would fight alone on a revolutionary basis.[1] The French in fact intended to cheat the Austrians: if the congress had ever met, Drouyn would have proposed to satisfy Austria with Bosnia, which Prussia and Italy were to buy from Turkey.[2] This was the very proposal that Austria should give up her hegemony in Germany and Italy and shift her centre of gravity to Hungary which the Austrians had strenuously resisted since 1862 or even 1848; it was impossible for Austria, with her dozen nationalities, voluntarily to recognize the national principle in both Germany and Italy. Besides, the cession of Bosnia would have been resisted by Great Britain and by Russia, to say nothing of being refused by Turkey; and Austria would have ended up with the whole congress against her. The Austrians suspected something of this, though they did not know the French plan; therefore they made their acceptance of the congress on 1 June conditional on the exclusion of any territorial aggrandizement or increase of power by any state taking part in it. This ruled out the cession of Venetia; hence made the congress useless to Napoleon. His only alternative was to push Austria into war. The Austrians, too, wanted to bring the war on; it seemed the only means of

[1] Benedetti to Drouyn de Lhuys, 19 May 1866. *Origines diplomatiques*, ix, no. 2382.
[2] Draft speech for opening of congress, 29 May 1866. Ibid., no. 2479. The idea of satisfying Austria with Bosnia seems to have originated with Metternich, though without the approval of his government. Drouyn de Lhuys to Gramont, 20 Apr. 1866. Ibid., viii, no. 2095.

carrying out the exchange of Silesia for Venetia which they had now come to regard as the solution of all difficulties. Thus, in the last resort, Austria and France themselves promoted the war which was to destroy their traditional grandeur in Europe; and for both Venetia was the deciding factor.

France and Austria had still to strike a bargain, though one far removed from the pacific partnership of which conservatives in both countries had dreamt. Napoleon had a binding promise of Venetia from Prussia; therefore, throughout May he did nothing to discourage her, despite the failure of his tentative effort to get some concrete offer of territory on the Rhine. Probably indeed he did not press Bismarck on this point so as not to frighten him off the war which alone could bring Venetia to Italy; it never occurred to him that he would need security against a decisive Prussian victory. Napoleon's overriding concern was to get a binding promise of Venetia from Austria; in return he was ready to promise French neutrality. He said to Metternich: 'give me guarantees in Italy in case you win and I will leave you free in Germany. . . . If not, I should be *forced to arm in my turn and eventually to intervene*.'[1] The Austrians decided that they must buy French neutrality, despite a doubt by Ester-házy 'whether Napoleon's pistol was really loaded'. On 12 June France and Austria signed a secret treaty in Vienna. France promised to stay neutral and to try to keep Italy neutral also; Austria promised to cede Venetia to France if she were victorious;[2] in addition, she would have no objection to the creation of 'a new independent German state' on the Rhine. Napoleon had secured everything he wanted: both Venetia and the Rhenish buffer-state. But the Austrians did not think that they had come away empty-handed. If they won, they would annex Silesia with French approval; and French neutrality, they supposed, gave them a chance of winning. Gramont was not alone in his illusions when he wrote to Mensdorff: 'Our *friendly* neutrality assures your victory.'[3] Later on, it came to be argued that France would have remained neutral in any case; this was to

---

[1] Metternich to Mensdorff, 23 May, 6 June 1866. *Rheinpolitik*. i, nos. 120, 132.

[2] If Austria lost she would lose Venetia in any case. The Austrians tried to stipulate that they should cede Venetia only if they got 'equivalent territorial compensation' in Germany, i.e. Silesia. Though the French refused this they agreed to sanction 'any territorial gain conquered by Austria' which would not upset the European Balance of Power.

[3] Gramont to Mensdorff, 10 June 1866. *Origines diplomatiques*, x, no. 2629.

be wise after the event. Even Bismarck took French intervention seriously in the fortnight after Sadova; if Bismarck was wrong, the Austrians may be excused for not being right. Of course, since the loss of Venetia was inevitable, the Austrians would have done better to cede it months or even years earlier; but it is not in the nature of states, least of all in the nature of a traditional Great Power, to cede territory unless faced with defeat in war.

Even now there was some technical difficulty in getting the war started. On 1 June Austria placed the question of the duchies in the hands of the federal diet; this was the formal breach of her alliance with Prussia. Bismarck retaliated by occupying Holstein; to his annoyance, the Austrian troops withdrew before a shot could be fired. On 12 June Austria broke off diplomatic relations with Prussia; on 14 June her motion for federal mobilization against Prussia was carried in the diet. Prussia declared the German confederation at an end; and on 15 June invaded Saxony. There was no formal declaration of war. When the Prussian troops reached the Austrian frontier on 21 June, the crown prince, who was in command, notified the nearest Austrian officer that a 'state of war' existed, and began the invasion. The Italians did a little better: La Marmora sent a declaration of war to Archduke Albrecht, the Austrian commander-in-chief on the southern front, before taking the offensive. These technical hesitations had the same cause as those of 1859: both Italy and Prussia were committed to programmes which could not be justified by international law. Since they were both hostile to the *status quo*, they were bound to appear as aggressors if they put their claims on paper. Yet they would have been hard put to it to start the war if Austria had not done the job for them. The war of 1866, like the war of 1859 before it and the wars of 1870 and 1914 after it, was launched by the conservative Power, the Power standing on the defensive, which, baited beyond endurance, broke out on its tormentors. Every war between Great Powers with which this book deals started as a preventive war, not as a war of conquest. The Crimean war succeeded reasonably well in its purpose; the others brought disaster on their originators. This may prove that it is a mistake to launch preventive wars; perhaps it is only a mistake to launch them without being sure of success.

The war of 1866 was astonishingly brief in its course. The

Italians were defeated on 24 June at Custoza, scene of their earlier defeat in 1848. This did not help the Austrians. On 3 July their main army was routed at Sadova[1] in Bohemia. They had already offered, the day before, to cede Venetia to Napoleon, if he would obtain for them an armistice from Italy and thus free their southern army for use against Prussia. Napoleon could not fulfil this condition: the Italians were committed to Prussia and, besides, they wanted to conquer Venetia for themselves. On 4 July, with the news of Sadova, Napoleon announced —quite incorrectly—that Austria had ceded Venetia to him and that in return he had agreed to mediate between the belligerents. This was very different from helping the Austrians by securing an armistice from Italy. Prussia and, more grudgingly, Italy accepted French mediation; but both insisted on continuing hostilities until terms were agreed. Drouyn imagined that the decision of 4 July meant the success of his policy: France would seek to impose moderate terms on the victors and, when these were refused, she would ally herself with Austria against them.[2] In this way Drouyn would secure at last the Austrian alliance which he had been seeking ever since 1853. It was inconceivable that his policy should be adopted. Though Napoleon was more procrastinating than ever, he would always come down on the side of the national principle when it came to the point. He had held out against alliance with Austria before the war; he was not likely to tie himself to 'the Austrian corpse' in the moment of defeat. Moreover, the policy of adventure was now, strangely enough, the policy of inaction: Napoleon had only to do nothing for the national principle to triumph. He himself was ill, almost incapable of decision, let alone of action; and the French army was not ready for a serious war. This was not the determining factor, though no doubt it should have been: the discussion turned on policy, not on French strength. Besides, the French army was quite up to a show of force on the Rhine, which would have tipped the Balance of Power in Germany.[3]

[1] German name: Königgrätz.

[2] It is not clear what use Drouyn would have made of the alliance except to check Prussia. Though he talked vaguely of occupying the left bank of the Rhine, he did not advocate its annexation: this would have been the policy of 'compensations', implicit in agreement with Prussia, not in war against her.

[3] Bismarck alleged that, in case of a French threat, he would have made peace with Austria and have turned the forces of united Germany against Napoleon. This was a typical Bismarckian brag. He could not have deserted Italy. In any case the Austrians, after Sadova, preferred a French to a Prussian alliance.

Bismarck made it easy for Napoleon to hold out against Drouyn, even fortified by the support of Eugenie. Not only did he accept French mediation. He put forward moderate terms: dissolution of the German confederation; exclusion of Austria from German affairs; and a Prussian military hegemony of Germany north of the Main. How could Napoleon oppose terms which he had favoured for years? The only thing to which he objected was the complete exclusion of Austria, as tilting the German balance too much on Prussia's side. Bismarck satisfied him by agreeing that the German states south of the Main should have 'an international independent existence'.[1] Napoleon would obtain the destruction of the German settlement of 1815; the gratitude of German national sentiment; and buffer states, independent of both Austria and Prussia, for the protection of his Rhine frontier; to say nothing of Venetia for Italy.[2] Napoleon learnt Bismarck's terms on 8 July. Two days later he reached decision: Drouyn's policy, 'the policy of July 4', had been mistaken, and France must seek agreement with Prussia.[3] Any other decision would have run counter to the inmost nature of the Second Empire.

The decision of 10 July settled the outcome. On 14 July Napoleon and Goltz drafted the terms which France would recommend; and these were presented at Vienna on 18 July. The Austrian ministers cared little or nothing for Austria's 'German mission', though much for her prestige. Once convinced that they could not reverse the military defeat, they insisted only on the integrity of Saxony, their one loyal ally; and a preliminary peace was concluded at Nikolsburg on 26 July.

[1] As further inducement Bismarck agreed to a plebiscite in north Sleswick. This was duly stipulated (article V) in the treaty of Prague. It was put off by one excuse after another. In 1878 Austria agreed to the scrapping of article V; and the plebiscite was held only after the allied victory in 1919.

[2] It is often overlooked that Drouyn's policy implied war against Italy as well as against Prussia (indeed even more so, since the Italians were obstinate and intransigent). Nothing could be more fantastical than to suppose that Napoleon would ever go to war against his own creation.

[3] I have omitted the dramatic version of events in Paris, according to which mobilization was decided on some time during 4 July or 5 July and then countermanded by Napoleon overnight. Even if this happened (and it seems doubtful), the decision to agree with Prussia was only made on 10 July. Between 4 and 10 July there was a discussion which drifted to and fro—Metternich, Drouyn, and Eugenie on the one side; Rouher, Prince Jerome, and at heart Napoleon himself on the other. The friends of Austria naturally exaggerated Napoleon's feebleness and lack of will; he appeared quite competent and resolute when negotiating with Goltz. In fact, like many sick men, he was most sick when it suited him.

This became the definitive peace of Prague a month later (23 Aug.). The Italians had stood aside from the negotiations: they hoped to seize south Tyrol while the Austrians were busy elsewhere. But Bismarck had fulfilled his bargain once Venetia was assured to the Italians. He made peace without them; and the full strength of the Austrian army was freed to impose terms on the Italians on 10 August. They received Venetia, and nothing more.

Austria was excluded from both Germany and Italy; she remained a Great Power. Bismarck's moderation after victory has been much praised; and it certainly showed a cool head to remain so nearly satisfied with terms that he had proposed before the war. Yet even Bismarck put up his terms: he excluded Austria from Germany, instead of dividing it with her at the line of the Main. Moreover, the alternative to Bismarck's policy was not the dismemberment of the Austrian empire; this would have horrified William I and the Prussian generals, who grumbled at Bismarck's moderation. The alternative was merely the annexation of some Austrian territory in Silesia, which would have left her still a Great Power, though a disgruntled one. As it was, she remained disgruntled enough. In October 1866 Beust— formerly prime minister of Saxony and Bismarck's principal opponent in Germany—became Austrian foreign minister. Despite his protestations of peace, the appointment had no sense except as prelude to revenge, either by war or at least by policy. The decision not to seek revenge was taken in 1870, not in 1866; and it was taken for reasons which in 1866 could not have been foreseen.

The first two years of the German question, from the opening of the Sleswick affair until the defeat of Austria, were essentially of a negative character. Bismarck's great achievement in these years was to defeat the programme of 'Greater Germany', a programme which could have been carried only under Habsburg leadership. Prussian policy had always been more limited, if not more modest, in aim; it was to establish a Prussian hegemony north of the Main. Austrian power, the greatest obstacle to this, had been removed; but Bismarck had still to overcome the resistance of the other Great Powers. Moreover, Prussia's victory had created a new and complicating factor in her policy. German national sentiment would not be stopped at the Main; and Prussia, whether she liked it or not, had become the

'German' Power. Between 1864 and 1866 Bismarck had ignored public opinion both in Prussia and in the wider Germany; and the war of 1866 was the last 'cabinet war', made purely by diplomacy. After 1866 Bismarck was, to some extent, the prisoner of his own success; he could not turn his back on the German question, even if he wanted to do so. France and Russia, the neighbouring Great Powers, were equally affected. Until 1866 both had imagined that the only question at stake was an altera-tion of the Balance of Power in Germany; and both had sup-posed that they would benefit if it was altered in favour of Prussia. After 1866 they came gradually to realize that they were faced with German unification, and not merely with a greater Prussia. France learnt this to her cost in 1870, and Russia in 1878.

IX

THE ISOLATION OF FRANCE

1866–70

As with Italy in 1859, the defeat of Austria merely cleared the way for the German problem, and did not itself solve it. Bismarck had still to reorder Germany without the interference of the Great Powers, as Cavour had united Italy in 1860. British policy was firmly committed to the line of non-intervention; so far as it had a positive outlook, it welcomed anything which strengthened central Europe against the two Powers on the circumference. It is the more surprising that these two Powers should have allowed the unification of Germany to take place. The process began when the defeat of Austria was still under weigh. After all, Prussia had to make peace with the German states who had fought against her as well as with Austria. The states south of the Main emerged unscathed; indeed with an 'international independent existence' more formal than before.[1] Bismarck himself would have been satisfied with control of the armed forces in the states north of the Main; William I wanted an increase of Prussian territory—in fact, the annexation of all the states north of the Main which had fought, however ineffectually, against Prussia. It did not at first occur to Bismarck that he could carry through this programme without some compensation to France; and he repeatedly pressed the French to state their terms before the negotiations with Austria were concluded—even throwing out the phrase that Belgium should become 'the rampart of France'.[2]

[1] It is often said that Bismarck broke this provision by signing defensive treaties with these states before the peace of Prague was concluded. But, in the circumstances of 1866, the treaties were a guarantee against Austria; and there is no reason to suppose that Napoleon III would have objected, if he had known of their existence. He made no complaint in 1867, when they were made public. Even in 1870 his policy was to protect the independence of the south German states as much against Austria as against Prussia.

[2] Benedetti to Drouyn de Lhuys, 15 July; Lefebvre de Béhaine to Drouyn de Lhuys, 25 July 1866 (recording conversation of 16 July). *Origines diplomatiques*, xi, nos. 3000, 3143.

THE RHINE FRONTIER

This was not at all Napoleon's intention. His concern had been to gain Venetia for Italy; in addition, he supposed that he had created a 'third Germany' south of the Main and so changed the German balance in France's favour. His deep belief was in the national principle, not in natural frontiers. Certainly he wished to destroy the settlement of 1815, but this had been achieved with the dissolution of the German Confederation. Though he had taken Savoy and Nice in 1860, this had been mainly as a sop to French feeling; and he had not demanded compensation when Cavour gained the whole of southern Italy. Now his heart was never in the demand for acquiring territory inhabited by Germans. What he wanted was a satisfied and grateful Prussia; and he calculated that a liberal Prussia, on a national basis, would be estranged from Russia. Far from Bismarck making demands which Napoleon refused, it was Napoleon who pressed German territory on Bismarck. In his own words when he repudiated Drouyn a little later: 'the true interest of France is not to obtain some insignificant increase of territory, but to help Germany to establish herself in the most favourable way for her interests and those of Europe'.[1] Napoleon sometimes doubted whether he should have made things easy for Prussia and cleared the way for the unification of Germany at all;[2] once the decision had been made, the only sensible course was to let it go through without demanding anything for France, as Napoleon had tolerated the success of Garibaldi in southern Italy without demanding Genoa or Sardinia. On 22 July Napoleon committed himself. He told Goltz that he would agree to the acquisition by Prussia of four million new subjects; and he asked nothing for himself.

Unfortunately Napoleon was weak as well as wise. No sooner had he made a sensible decision on 22 July than he allowed Drouyn to undo it on 23 July. If Drouyn could not have war against Prussia he was determined to gain territory; his motive was the traditional doctrine of 'compensation', according to the old school of diplomacy in which he had been brought up.

---

[1] Napoleon to La Valette, 12 Aug. 1866. *Origines diplomatiques*, xii, no. 3383. The text in *Origines*, obviously a rough draft, has the revealing variant: 'In the most favourable way for *our* interests.'

[2] Napoleon had doubts even about Italy. He said to Metternich just before the war: 'I was perhaps wrong to let the revolution triumph in Italy.' Metternich to Mensdorff, 29 May 1866. *Rheinpolitik*, i, no. 125.

Benedetti was instructed to demand the frontiers of 1814 and the territory of Bavaria and Hesse on the left bank of the Rhine under threat of 'a lasting estrangement'. Bismarck answered by refusing to surrender 'a single German village'. Napoleon swung back in alarm, put all the blame on Drouyn and repudiated him on 12 August. Drouyn left office, this time for good; and control of affairs passed temporarily to Rouher, Napoleon's general man of business. Rouher was concerned with French opinion, not with the Balance of Power. He wanted some striking success to stem the rising discontent against the authoritarian empire and thought to get it by speculating on the Prussian boom. Like many men who have come to the top in domestic politics, he supposed that foreign policy too could be run on goodwill and soft words. Drouyn had tried to threaten Bismarck; Rouher set out to cajole him. He dropped the demand for German territory and asked instead that Prussia should look on approvingly while France gained Luxembourg[1] and Belgium; in return he offered an alliance of the two Powers with a mutual guarantee of their territorial integrity. But against whom did Prussia need French protection? Prussia was not Italy: she could maintain herself alone against defeated Austria. She had no cause for quarrel with either Russia or Great Britain—unless indeed she made the French alliance. Then she would be dragged into conflict with the British over Belgium; she would be dragged into the Polish question against her interest and into the Eastern question where she had no interest. France in fact was the only Power whom Prussia had reason to fear; and the offer of an alliance, as Benedetti observed,[2] was in reality a

[1] Luxembourg had been a member of the German Confederation, though under the sovereignty of the king of the Netherlands; as a federal fortress, it was garrisoned by Prussian troops. It remained neutral in the war of 1866 and therefore could not be annexed to Prussia nor included in the new north German federation; it remained, however, a member of the German Zollverein until 1918 (when it made a customs-union with Belgium). The Prussian garrison was also there until Sept. 1867; and Prussia would therefore have to take the active step of withdrawal, in case of French annexation, whereas with Belgium she would have only to acquiesce. Luxembourg was traditionally a fortress of great strength—'the Gibraltar of the north': and it was also developing rapidly as a centre of the steel industry. Nevertheless, the French demand for it was primarily a question of prestige; they wanted a success and, as well, a precedent for the annexation of Belgium. The inhabitants of Luxembourg spoke a German dialect, though they were spiritually more akin to the Alsatians or the German-speaking Swiss than to national Germany.

[2] Benedetti to Rouher, 30 Aug. 1866. *Origines diplomatiques*, xii, no. 3527.

roundabout way of renouncing the Rhine frontier. Alliances are not made on such terms.

It would have been very different if Russia had taken alarm at Prussia's success. Throughout the war the Russians had clung to their principle: 'better a strong Prussia than a strong Austria.'[1] All the same, they had found their exclusion from European affairs hard to bear; and on 27 July Gorchakov formally proposed a congress to settle the future of Germany. As ever, the magic word congress covered the Russian hope of revising the settlement of 1856. It would, in any case, have ruined Bismarck's plan of reordering Germany without foreign interference. He replied with the two weapons which had always served Prussia well: threats in Poland, promises in the Near East. If Russia interfered in Germany, he would advise William I 'to unleash the full national strength of Germany and of the neighbouring countries'[2]; on the other hand, 'we have no interest in continuing the limitations on Russia in the Black Sea'.[3] Most of all, he invoked the family ties between William I and the tsar. Probably the Russian proposal for a congress was no more than a gesture of monarchical irritation; though the Russians wished to assert themselves, they never feared the consequences of a Prussian victory. Besides, in the last resort, Bismarck could offer them a surer road to revision than a congress: he could pin France down to western Europe. On 21 August he telegraphed to St. Petersburg: would Russia keep Austria neutral in case of a war between Prussia and France?[4] Manteuffel, the special envoy who had been sent to mollify the tsar, replied on 24 August: 'though Gorchakov did not positively commit himself, Your Excellency can take a firm line against France'.[5] No doubt Bismarck's question sprang from genuine anxiety; its effect on the Russians was calculated all the same. The lines were being already drawn for the diplomatic structure of 1870: the Russians would tolerate a war between France and Prussia when they saw in it the prospect of a free hand for themselves against Austria.

[1] Talleyrand to Drouyn de Lhuys, 13 July 1866. *Origines diplomatiques*, xi, no. 225.
[2] Bismarck to Goltz, 31 July 1866, enclosing telegram to Schweinitz (St. Petersburg). Bismarck, *Gesammelte Werke*, vi, no. 515.
[3] Bismarck to Manteuffel (special envoy to Alexander II), 9 Aug. 1866. Ibid., no. 543.
[4] Bismarck to Manteuffel, 21 Aug. 1866. Ibid., no. 582.
[5] Manteuffel to Bismarck, 24 Aug. 1866. *Auswärtige Politik Preußens 1858–1871*, viii, no. 3.

Bismarck's move was premature: the danger of war with France had passed with the fall of Drouyn. Benedetti brought back to Berlin the project of an alliance, not the threat of war. But though France offered an alliance, she was really asking to be paid for her neutrality in the war that was over: the acquisition of Luxembourg, not Prussia's alliance, was the important thing. This was an impossible bargain: no one pays for services already rendered. Bismarck had paid the price which Napoleon had demanded when he had made possible the winning of Venetia by Italy; it was too late for Napoleon to repent of this bargain. Bismarck tried to turn the alliance towards the future: he offered the French a free hand in Belgium if Prussia could lay her hands on southern Germany. This too was impossible: the independence of southern Germany was regarded by the French as the vital condition for accepting Prussia's gains north of the Main. The negotiations ran away to deadlock; and left only the trace of a draft treaty which Bismarck used to the discredit of France in 1870. This is not to say that Bismarck decided on a breach with France in September 1866. Like Napoleon III, he was a procrastinator and did not take decisions until he had to. The decision still rested with the French. If they would not turn the alliance with Prussia towards the future, their only pacific course was to accept what had happened without reserve or complaint. This was throughout Napoleon's own policy. He had always disliked the demand for compensation; his dearest wish was to appear as the disinterested patron of Italy and Germany. On 16 September he repudiated Rouher, as a month before he had repudiated Drouyn. The Holy Alliance, he announced, was dissolved; Italy and Germany liberated with French approval; the peoples of Europe were drawing together into great states which could alone hold the balance against the two giants of the future, Russia and the United States. 'The Emperor does not believe that the greatness of a country depends on the weakness of its neighbours; he sees a true balance only in the satisfied wishes of the nations of Europe.'[1]

Though Napoleon used the methods of a conspirator, he combined with them the vision of a statesman. The only security for France was to bind both national Germany and national Italy together for the common cause of western Europe. His

---

[1] Circular by La Valette (acting foreign minister), 16 Sept. 1866. *Origines diplomatiques*, xii, no. 3598.

Italian policy succeeded, apart from the fatal flaw of Rome; his German policy might have succeeded if his followers had allowed him to apply it. Against this stands the question: could Bismarck, 'the mad Junker', have been won sincerely for a western course of policy? could he have made the concessions to Polish feeling which a policy friendly to France must have implied, even if France and Russia had remained on good terms? It seems unlikely. In the twentieth century even a German republican government would not consolidate relations with France by recognizing the frontiers of Poland; how much less could Bismarck have done so. Nevertheless, the decisive breach of 1867 came from the French, not from Bismarck.

In the autumn of 1866 Napoleon was again taken prisoner by the need for Imperial prestige, and this time for good. His will and physical strength were failing. His most intimate supporters —Rouher, La Valette, and others—insisted that French opinion resented the aggrandizement of Prussia and must be given some material satisfaction.[1] For the first time foreign policy did not merely play up to public opinion; it was dictated by public opinion. The French ministers were hypnotized by the prospect of acquiring Luxembourg. This alone could silence the critics and justify Napoleon's neutrality in 1866. Prestige was their sole motive. They did not understand how much the balance of strength had shifted against France; therefore did not seek Luxembourg on grounds of security. So far as they had a serious purpose, it was to commit Bismarck to their plans, hence to make Prussia their accomplice. In Benedetti's words: 'once in Luxembourg we are on the road leading to Belgium and we shall get there the more certainly with Prussian neutrality'.[2] It never occurred to them that Bismarck might oppose their plans; at most they feared that he might not actively support them.

This seems the key to Bismarck's attitude in the negotiations with France which dragged on from November 1866 until February 1867. He would probably have acquiesced in the French gaining Luxembourg, if this could have been done

[1] Talleyrand told Gorchakov: 'The Emperor tried to bring France to his opinion of events in Germany; he has not succeeded and the country is not satisfied.' Talleyrand to Moustier, 3 Apr. 1867. *Origines diplomatiques*, xv, no. 4572. Cf. Goltz to Bismarck, 28 Dec. 1866 and 11 Jan. 1867. *Auswärtige Politik Preußens 1858–1871*, viii, nos. 156 and 178.

[2] Benedetti to Moustier, 26 Jan. 1867. *Origines diplomatiques*, xiv, no. 4115.

without compromising him in the eyes either of German opinion
or of the Great Powers; he would not do their work for them.
His constant refrain was: 'commit yourselves. Present Europe
and the King of Prussia with a fait accompli.'[1] Perhaps this was
a trap for France; but there was no other line which Bismarck
could have taken even if he had been sincere. Or rather there
was no other line which Bismarck could take in western Europe.[2]
But Germany and the Rhine were no longer the sole focus of
international attention. The Eastern question was again astir for
the first time since 1856. The symbol and excuse for this was the
insurrection of Crete against Turkish rule which began in the
summer of 1866. The deeper cause was the recovery of Russia.
With Poland fully subdued, Russia could return to the ranks of
the Great Powers. Moreover, with the development of Panslav
sentiment in Russia, Alexander II and Gorchakov could no
longer ignore affairs in Turkey, whatever their personal indifference. Bismarck's diplomacy had been shaped in its first
four years by the absence of the Eastern question. This situation
was now changed. If the wheel of events had spun a little
differently, the great Eastern crisis of 1875 to 1878 might have
preceded the Franco-Prussian war instead of following it. The
diplomatic consequences are incalculable—perhaps a Franco-
Russian entente to partition the Turkish empire, more probably
a revival of 'the Crimean coalition'; in any case some ally for
France. As it was, the Eastern question stirred enough to cause
a new breach between Russia and France, then died away before
it had brought France and Austria together. Poland had enabled
Bismarck to defeat Austria; Crete, not Poland, enabled him to
defeat France.

Bismarck tried to turn the Eastern question to good account.
In January 1867 he threw out the suggestion that France should
be made 'contented and pacific' by a system of compensations
in the Near East;[3] and he asked Benedetti: 'why do you try so

---

[1] Benedetti to Moustier, 20 Dec. 1866. *Origines diplomatiques*, xiii, no. 3949.

[2] In the autumn of 1866 the French hit on another idea by which their public
opinion might be reconciled to Prussia's victory: Prussia should join with France
in guaranteeing the temporal power of the papacy. Prussia was thus to take on a
gratuitous burden and to become estranged from Italy solely in order to gain
French favour which she did not need or to avert the danger from France that
she did not fear. It was a further illustration of the basic blunder in French diplomacy: once Austria had been defeated, Prussia neither feared France nor needed her.

[3] Bismarck to Goltz, 30 Jan. 1867. *Auswärtige Politik Preußens 1858–1871*, viii,
no. 213.

hard to put out the fire in the Near East? We could both get warm there.'[1] He hoped for a revival of the Franco-Russian entente which had been broken in 1863. This would silence the Polish question; and in any case was far less dangerous to Prussia than an alliance between France and Austria or even between France and Great Britain.[2] Bismarck was not alone in his offers. Beust, who had just become foreign minister in Austria, dreamt of restoring Habsburg prestige by gains in the Balkans and hit on the illusion that Austria could tolerate Russian gains if she herself acquired Bosnia and Hercegovina. If Russia would respect Rumania as a buffer state, Beust was prepared to scrap the neutralization of the Black Sea; it was a mistake, he said, for Austria to attach herself to such dying causes as the legitimate Italian princes, the German confederation, or the integrity of the Turkish empire.[3] This ignored the fact that the Habsburg monarchy was itself 'a dying cause'. The stumbling-block in both Bismarck's and Beust's projects was their failure to offer any real inducement to France in return for the destruction of the victory of 1856. Bismarck spoke vaguely of compensations; Beust specified Egypt.[4] With the Suez canal in its first flush of success as a French enterprise, this proposal had more sense than before or since; but even then it was hopeless. As Napoleon said: 'Unfortunately England is always in my way.' In truth France could find her compensations for the Near East only in western Europe; and raising the Eastern question, far from silencing French interest on the Rhine, made it more acute. On 1 March 1867 Moustier dismissed the Prussian offer of friendship in the Near East without concessions in the west: 'you offer us spinach without salt, Luxembourg is the salt.'[5]

As negotiations with Prussia drifted towards deadlock, the French turned to Russia; and their negotiations for an entente in the first months of 1867 were the most serious effort between the Stuttgart meeting in 1857 and the visit to Kronstadt in 1891. As always, there was a fundamental divergence of views. The French wanted Russian backing against Prussia in the west;

[1] Benedetti to Moustier, 26 Jan. 1867. *Origines diplomatiques*, xiv, no. 4115.
[2] Bismarck to Goltz, 15 Feb. 1867. *Auswärtige Politik Preußens 1858–1871*, viii, no. 242.
[3] Werther to Bismarck, 10 Dec. 1866. Ibid., no. 126.
[4] Metternich to Beust, 7 Jan. 1867. *Rheinpolitik*, ii, no. 328.
[5] Goltz to Bismarck, Mar. 1867. *Auswärtige Politik Preußens 1858–1871*, viii, no. 266.

the Russians wanted France and Prussia to be on good terms so that both could back Russia in the Near East. Each was a conservative Power, in favour of the *status quo* so far as the ambitions of the other were concerned, yet each dreamt of making gains without paying a price. The French hoped to acquire Belgium and Luxembourg without sacrificing the integrity of the Turkish empire; the Russians hoped to remodel the Near East without altering the balance in western Europe. The Russians were prepared to renew the promise which they had made in 1857 and to which they adhered even in 1870: they would not enter a coalition directed against France—after all they had refused to support Prussia against France even at the height of the Polish crisis. This had been all very well so long as France, unlike Italy, 'could do it herself'. Now the French needed active support, yet dared not say so. Moustier actually invited the Russians to name the price which they would pay: 'it is easier for the Tsar to define the limits of his good will than for us to admit prematurely plans which are not yet formulated'.[1] Gorchakov evaded commitment; in reality he would agree to anything in western Europe to which Prussia would agree also. In the Near East the position was reversed. The French were prepared to favour the annexation of Crete, and even of territory on the mainland, by Greece; but only on condition that the Russians would support the integrity of the Turkish empire that remained. The Russians cared little enough for Crete, or for the Greeks generally; they were interested only in establishing a precedent—if the national claims of the Greeks were admitted, those of the Slav peoples would follow. The French supported the Greek claims because they did not imply the disruption of the Turkish empire; the Russians because they did. Moreover, the French thought that they could advocate the annexation of Crete to Greece without estranging either Austria or Great Britain; the Russians were mainly concerned to destroy 'the Crimean coalition'. Nothing had been achieved between Russia and France when the Luxembourg crisis exploded at the beginning of April 1867.

The French had taken Bismarck's advice: they had committed themselves. They secretly negotiated the cession of Luxembourg with the king of Holland, its owner. The ostensible inducement was a French guarantee of Holland against Prussia; the real

[1] Moustier to Talleyrand, 18 Feb. 1867. *Origines diplomatiques*, xiv, no. 4180.

argument lay in the bribes which the French paid to the king's mistress. At the last moment the king of Holland lost his nerve: he refused to conclude the treaty with France until he had informed the Prussian government. An explosion of patriotic feeling followed in the north German parliament: Luxembourg, it was claimed, was an old German land which could not be surrendered to France. Bismarck always made out that he would have acquiesced in the annexation of Luxembourg by France, if it could have been done without arousing German opinion; against this must be set the fact that he himself arranged with Bennigsen the interpellation that aroused the feeling. If he really allowed patriotic sentiment to change his policy, it was for the first, and perhaps for the last, time; yet it is difficult to find any other explanation for his course. If he was setting a trap for the French, why did he not spring the trap once they were inside it and launch a war? The French were as ill prepared for war as in 1866; the Austrians in no condition to aid them. Yet Bismarck did everything to secure a peaceful outcome. He clearly cared nothing for Luxembourg and, at the end, joined with the British government in a swindle on the German public. He accepted from them a 'collective guarantee', which they— and he—knew meant nothing; yet made out to the German people that it meant a great deal. Perhaps for once he really had drifted: in the strain of the war of 1866 he had talked loosely to the French and now got out as best he could.

The crisis lasted for something like a month, until the early days of May. While it lasted both sides beat about for possible allies. Gorchakov said maliciously of the French challenge to the treaty of 1839, which had settled the status of Luxembourg: 'Say all the old treaties exist no more and I shall be the first to rejoice . . . but why two weights and two measures?'[1] He was prepared to offer France 'a sheet of completely white paper' in Luxembourg, so far as Russia was concerned;[2] this was very far from offering her an alliance against Prussia. The French tried also for an alliance with Austria, though only when the crisis was reaching its term. Towards the end of April they proposed an offensive and defensive alliance, by which France should gain the left bank of the Rhine, while Austria gained Silesia and supremacy over southern Germany. Beust at once replied

---

[1] Talleyrand to Moustier, 3 Apr. 1867. *Origines diplomatiques*, xv, no. 4572.
[2] Talleyrand to Moustier, 18 Apr. 1867. Ibid., no. 4736.

that the ten million Germans in Austria made an alliance limited to Germany impossible: he could tolerate French ambitions on the Rhine only if they arose from a war in the Near East.[1]

Bismarck came away equally empty-handed. At the opening of the crisis the Russians thought for a moment that their opportunity had arrived: they offered to prevent an alliance between Austria and France by putting an army corps on the Austrian frontier; in return Bismarck should agree to the ending of the neutralization of the Black Sea and should guarantee that Bosnia and Hercegovina would never go to Austria.[2] Bismarck had never been interested in the Black Sea, but he would not commit himself on Russia's side against Austria.[3] Instead he launched again the combination which had been dead since 1853, yet which lay at the heart of his political thought: nothing less than the Holy Alliance, the union of 'the three Northern Courts'. Implicitly this would guarantee Russia against Austrian plans; explicitly Prussia and Russia should guarantee Austria against South Slav disruption for three years and Prussia should guarantee Austria's 'German provinces'[4] for good.[5] The proposal defined the central problem of Bismarck's policy for the next twenty years. Certainly he did not want to add German-Austria to the Germany under Prussian domination that he was creating; equally certainly he did not want to commit Prussia to war for the integrity of the Habsburg monarchy. The Holy Alliance, or League of the Three Emperors as it came to be called, would give Prussia absolute security, but only on condition that Russia renounced her Balkan ambitions and Austria her suspicions—and neither would do so. Beust replied contemptuously that in case of war between Prussia and France he would expect concessions in Germany; Bismarck could not expect him to be content 'with a specially-bound copy of the Treaty of Prague on parchment'.[6] Gorchakov refused to guaran-

[1] Beust to Metternich, 27 Apr. 1867. *Rheinpolitik*, ii, no. 450.
[2] Reuss (St. Petersburg) to Bismarck, 1 Apr. 1867. *Auswärtige Politik Preußens 1858-1871*, viii, no. 380.
[3] Bismarck to Reuss, 6 Apr. 1867. Ibid., no. 436.
[4] In contemporary conception these, of course, included Bohemia.
[5] Bismarck to Reuss, 15 Apr. 1867. Ibid., no. 488. The proposal arose from a Bavarian attempt to bring Prussia and Austria together. Tauffkirchen to Ludwig II, 13 Apr. 1867. Ibid., no. 474.
[6] Tauffkirchen to Ludwig II, 16 Apr.; Werther to Bismarck, 18 Apr. 1867. Ibid., nos. 498 and 507.

tee Austrian integrity[1] or even to approve a defensive alliance between Austria and Prussia. What he wanted was an alliance between Russia and Prussia which should include France;[2] this, he imagined, was the only combination which would bring Russia gains in the Near East.

Thus, once more, the prospective crisis in the Near East and the Balkans settled the outcome in the west. France would not give Russia a free hand against Turkey; Prussia would not give her a free hand against Austria. Yet neither would break with Russia and commit themselves to the side of Austria. Therefore both botched up the Luxembourg question as best they could. On 11 May a conference of the Powers at London agreed on a solution. France dropped her treaty of annexation; the Prussian garrison was withdrawn; and Luxembourg, with its fortifications dismantled, was rather imperfectly neutralized. There was in this some slight satisfaction for French opinion, but not enough. The Luxembourg affair, though trivial in itself, marked the end of an epoch in international relations. It was the last attempt to discover something which would reconcile French opinion to Prussian aggrandizement; and the attempt had been unsuccessful. Until May 1867 Napoleon III had hoped that Germany would be united without France being humiliated; now he ceased to hope and became an instrument in the hands of his ministers. The dream of Franco-German amity was shattered for ever: it could not be revived by Jules Ferry in 1884, nor at Locarno, nor at Montoire. Jealousy on the one side, suspicion on the other; these became the fixed rule on the frontier of the Rhine. This completed the rigidity which had begun with the estrangement between Austria and Russia at the opening of the Crimean war.

The Russians did not understand what had happened. They thought that they had restored good relations between France and Prussia, as often before; and when Gorchakov came to Paris with the tsar at the beginning of June he supposed, in his complacent way, that he was going to collect the reward in the Near East for having acted as the angel of peace in the west. He announced at the frontier: 'I have brought a chancellery with me to do business.' No business was done. Gorchakov waved

---

[1] Reuss to Bismarck, 17 Apr. 1867. *Auswärtige Politik Preußens 1858–1871*, viii, no. 502.

[2] Reuss to Bismarck, 22 Apr. 1867. Ibid., no. 521.

away any apprehensions as to 'the aspirations of Prussia'. Though he made out that he was not interested in the freeing of the Black Sea ('the treaty of 1856? We remember something of that name, but so many liberties have been taken with it that we do not know what remains of it'), he also made it clear that Russia was deeply concerned with the Christians of the Turkish empire. Moustier answered by insisting that reforms must extend to all the inhabitants of the empire—that is, they must be designed to strengthen, not to disrupt it.[1] Things went badly in another way. The tsar was greeted with cries of 'Long live Poland',[2] and a Polish exile tried to assassinate him. The Franco-Russian entente was shaken, not restored, by the Paris visit. The cause did not lie in the flutter of French sentiment over Poland; it was to be found rather in what Gorchakov later called 'the mystification over the question of Crete'.[3]

The support of Russia had brought France no gains in the west; therefore the French were increasingly reluctant to second an active Russian policy in the Near East. Though Gorchakov repudiated plans for a great South Slav state, Ignatiev, the Russian ambassador at Constantinople, made no secret of his conviction that an inquiry into the state of Crete—which France and Russia were now advocating—was simply the prelude to its cession to Greece and that this cession was a prelude to cession elsewhere on a grander scale. The French told all and sundry that they were co-operating with Russia solely 'to circumscribe and moderate her initiative';[4] and the effect of Franco-Russian pressure at Constantinople was further weakened when the Sultan of Turkey was given a cordial welcome in Paris and London—the first visit ever paid by a ruler of Turkey to any Christian countries. Early in July 1867 the Turks rejected the demand for a European inquiry in Crete. Gorchakov said plaintively: 'When two countries like ours have made their voices heard, their dignity demands that they arrive at the result which they have set out to reach'.[5] The French, however, were deter-

---

[1] Note by Montebello (former ambassador to St. Petersburg), 4 June; Moustier to Talleyrand, 7 June, 9 July 1867. *Origines diplomatiques*, xvii, nos. 5226, 5238, 5380.

[2] Floquet, one of the lawyers who raised this cry at the Palace of Justice, was prime minister when the Franco-Russian entente was in the making twenty years later.

[3] Fleury (St. Petersburg) to Gramont, 31 May 1870. *Origines diplomatiques*, xxvii, no. 8178.   [4] Moustier to La Tour, 3 July 1867. Ibid., no. 5360.

[5] Talleyrand to Moustier, 22 July 1867. Ibid., no. 5461.

mined not to be drawn further on the course of threatening Turkey. They swung off on to a different path. Since they were drifting away from Russia in any case, they attempted to make Austria pay a price for their estrangement. This was the motive for the meeting of Francis Joseph and Napoleon III at Salzburg in the middle of August.

The Salzburg meeting was intended to inaugurate a policy of conservatism. Hitherto France had encouraged Prussian expansion in Germany and Russian activity in the Near East in the hope of making gains of her own in the west; now she would join with Austria in resisting the plans of Prussia and Russia. But there was a fundamental difference of emphasis. The French, for the sake of their public opinion, wanted to have some immediate gains to show in Germany; in fact the so-called policy of resistance really involved undoing the treaty of Prague. Gramont, the French ambassador, even produced the draft of a treaty for an immediate war against Prussia.[1] On the other hand Beust, the Austrian chancellor, was also the prisoner of public opinion in the Habsburg monarchy. He came to Salzburg fresh from the triumph of concluding the Compromise with Hungary;[2] by it the Hungarians had become partners with the emperor, and the Germans temporarily in the ascendant in the Lesser 'Austria'. The Hungarians, though resolutely anti-Russian, had no reason to regret the rise of Prussia; the German-Austrians admired Bismarck's success, though it had been at their expense. Both would tolerate an alliance against Prussia only if the Franco-Austrian entente first proved its worth against Russia in the Near East.[3] The French pretended to be satisfied with this conclusion. In reality they would not break openly with Russia unless assured of Austro-Hungarian backing against Prussia in Germany.[4] Francis Joseph might say: 'I hope that one day we shall march together.'[5] The day seemed to be drawing no nearer.

Oddly enough, Alexander II's visit to Paris and Napoleon

[1] French draft of a Franco-Austrian Treaty, Aug. 1867. *Rheinpolitik*, ii, no. 510A.
[2] Hence, from this moment, the Austrian empire becomes Austria-Hungary.
[3] Memorandum by Beust, and draft agreement by him, Aug. 1867. Ibid., nos. 506 and 510B.
[4] Beust had written that the two governments should approach 'the British government as well as that of St. Petersburg'. Napoleon amended this that they should first settle policy with the Russians and only then consult the British.
[5] Ducrot, *Memoirs*, ii. 185.

III's visit to Salzburg both led the French to the same conclusion. They had hoped that the simmering crisis in the Near East would provide them with some ally against Prussia—whether Russia or Austria-Hungary; instead it was threatening to distract them from the affairs of western Europe. All they wanted was to wind up the Cretan affair in some way which would offend neither Russia nor Austria-Hungary. They therefore grasped eagerly at a suggestion from Gorchakov that, as the Porte had rejected the advice to allow an inquiry in Crete, the Powers should wash their hands of Turkish affairs. By this, the Russians meant that they would allow insurrection to blaze in Crete and elsewhere; the French, however, made out that it implied freedom for the Turks to crush rebellion. Beust was not taken in; the proposal, he declared, was 'the complete success of Russian foreign policy',[1] and when the Franco-Russian note was presented to the Porte on 29 October it was supported only by Prussia and Italy—Great Britain and Austria-Hungary ostentatiously abstained. This was, in reality, the dying flutter of the old 'revolutionary' alliance. Though France would not commit herself to the support of Turkey,[2] she had gone over to the side of conservatism in the Near East; and soon Prussia, too, was abstaining in the Eastern question so as not to be left in isolation with Russia.[3] Bismarck even threw out the suggestion that Prussia and Austria-Hungary should escape from their embarrassments by coming together against France and Russia; the proposal was perhaps not meant very seriously and, in any case, was weighted against France—the Austrians, if they contemplated it at all, wanted it the other way round.[4]

---

[1] Gramont to Moustier, 15 Oct. 1867. *Origines diplomatiques*, xviii, no. 5795.

[2] The Porte offered to give Crete autonomy if France and Austria-Hungary would approve it beforehand—that is, if they would guarantee Turkey against its cession. The French refused: 'the Porte has asked to walk alone; let it march'. They wanted the Porte to present Russia with the *fait accompli* of autonomy, which would end the Cretan affair without Russia being able to put the blame on France. Bourée (Constantinople) to Moustier, 3 Dec. 1867. Ibid., xix, no. 6172.

[3] Brassier de St. Simon (Constantinople) to Bismarck, 18 Nov. 1867. *Auswärtige Politik Preußens 1858–1871*, ix, no. 336.

[4] Bismarck said to the Austrian representative: 'We want nothing more from Austria, we are completely satisfied . . . Austria can be threatened only from two sides, from France or from Russia. If Prussia and Austria are allied, the possible dangers from France cease of themselves; and as for the dangers which could threaten Austria from Russia, it would then be our task to keep the latter quiet.' Wimpffen to Beust, 12 Oct. 1867. Ibid., no. 205.

The French had a more pressing reason for turning their backs on the Near East. In the autumn of 1867 the Roman question exploded once more. Italian opinion had been whetted, not satisfied, by the acquisition of Venetia. Rattazzi, the king's favourite who had become prime minister in April 1867, thought to wield the bow of Cavour and to repeat the feat of 1860 in Naples; he would allow Garibaldi to stir up revolution in the papal states and then, sending in troops to restore order, would himself annex them. The plan miscarried. Garibaldi and his supporters failed to defeat the papal army; and Napoleon III, no longer the revolutionary of 1860, was committed in Rome as he had not been in Naples. On 26 October the French troops, who had been withdrawn in 1866, returned to the papal states; on 3 November Garibaldi's forces were routed at Mentana. Napoleon III had hoped to escape from the Roman question by the convention of September 1864; and certainly this had left him free to support Prussia and Italy against Austria in 1866. Now he was once more a prisoner. In desperation he turned to his old remedy of a European congress and invited the Powers to solve the Roman question for him. The manœuvre was futile. Only Austria-Hungary favoured the cause of the pope; and even she shrank from gratuitously estranging Italy. Both Great Britain and Prussia refused to attend the meeting unless a programme was agreed in advance; and if a programme was agreed there was no need for the meeting.[1] It was not the least irony of the Second Empire that the European congress, so often advocated by Napoleon in order to revise the map of Europe, should now be proposed in order to prop up the temporal power of the pope.

Mentana completed the pattern which had been drawn by the affairs of Luxembourg and Crete. Once France had been the standard-bearer of 'revisionism'; now she was committed to 'resistance'—in the Near East, in southern Germany, and in Rome. She defended legitimacy and treaty-rights—the treaties of Paris and of Prague. The logical consequence should have been alliance with Austria-Hungary, the other conservative Power; but the time for this had been before Austria was

---

[1] The French further offended Bismarck by inviting the lesser German states instead of confining the proposed congress to the Great Powers; their object was to pack the congress with a Roman Catholic majority against the three non-Catholic Great Powers—Russia, Prussia, and Great Britain.

expelled from Germany and Italy. Now Austria-Hungary would only offer an alliance confined to the Near East. This was the rhythm of the negotiations which ran on, almost without interruption, from the beginning of 1868 until the breach between France and Prussia in 1870.

The first move came from Austria-Hungary in January 1868. With the miscarriage of Russian plans in Crete, Beust wanted to go over to the offensive; he proposed that France should join with Great Britain and Austria-Hungary in devising a solution for Crete and that the three Powers should then impose it on the Cretan rebels, or even on Russia, 'arms in hand'.[1] There was not much sense in this suggestion. The British would not be drawn into action. Stanley, the foreign secretary, had carried isolationism to its highest point; he was 'very much interested' in Beust's proposal[2]—and offered nothing. The French, too, were not going to expose their Rhine frontier for the sake of Crete; they insisted that Prussia must be brought into the coalition of 'pacific Powers'.[3] Bismarck, of course, did not intend to join any coalition, pacific or otherwise, until this suited Prussia's needs. Benedetti, indeed, believed that Bismarck might support France in the Near East in exchange for a guarantee of Prussia's position in Germany.[4] This was the old misunderstanding which Benedetti had shown in 1866—the belief that Prussia needed a guarantee from France or from anyone else. Underlying it was the deeper misunderstanding which had haunted the western Powers during the Crimean war. Prussia's stake in Poland made it impossible for her to break with Russia for the sake of the Near East. Certainly Bismarck did not want a conflict with France. But in the last resort a war with France offered him gains—in southern Germany and, as it turned out, beyond the Rhine; a war with Russia offered him nothing but losses.

On the other hand, Bismarck had no more intention of com-

---

[1] Memorandum by Vitzthum, Jan. 1868. *Rheinpolitik*, ii, no. 537.

[2] Vitzthum to Beust, 1 Feb. 1868. *Origines diplomatiques*, xx, no. 6415.

[3] Metternich to Beust, 16 Jan. 1868. *Rheinpolitik*, ii, no. 538. Moustier to Gramont, 18 Jan.; to Benedetti, 26 Jan. 1868. *Origines diplomatiques*, xx, nos. 6354 and 6390.

[4] Benedetti to Moustier, 3 Mar. 1868. Ibid., xxi, no. 6540. Benedetti repeatedly insisted at this time that Bismarck's object was to unite south Germany with Prussia without a conflict with France: 'No one on this side of the Rhine has designs hostile to France.' Benedetti to Moustier, 5 Jan. and 4 Feb. 1868. Ibid., xx, nos. 6297, 6431, 6432.

mitting himself to Russia than to France. When rumours of a
Prussian *rapprochement* with France and Austria-Hungary reached
St. Petersburg, Bismarck at once denied them.[1] Alexander II
tried to improve the occasion. If France attacked Prussia, he
said, he would keep Austria-Hungary quiet by placing 100,000
men on her frontier; and he counted on Prussia's doing the same
in case of a conflict in the Near East.[2] Bismarck tried to evade
the invitation by emphasizing the family ties which bound together William I and the tsar:[3] monarchical solidarity in those
days, like democratic principles in ours, was a good way of
escaping treaty commitments. The Russians were not taken in;
and in March 1868 Bismarck was faced with a direct demand
for a Russo-Prussian alliance against Austria-Hungary. Bismarck
used, for the first time, a phrase that was to become the basis of
his later policy: 'of course neither Power could afford to allow
the destruction of the other'. Just as Russia would keep Austria-
Hungary neutral in a war between Prussia and France, so he
was prepared to keep France neutral in case of a war in the
Near East.[4] This was far from the alliance against Austria-
Hungary which the Russians wanted; and the Russians, on their
side, were no more inclined to an alliance against France than
Bismarck was to an alliance against Austria-Hungary. Indeed it
was now the turn of the Russians to stifle talk of an alliance and
to make out that they were satisfied with personal friendship
between the two rulers.[5] In these discussions all the diplomatic
history of the next twenty-five years was already germina-
ting.

Russia could not count on the firm support of Prussia;
Austria-Hungary could not count on that of France and England.
Therefore the incipient Eastern crisis once more died away at
the end of March 1868. The only remaining point of danger
seemed to be southern Germany, where Prussia and, more
feebly, Austria-Hungary were competing for the favours of
liberal opinion. The French tried to turn the tables on Beust.
He had asked what they would do if Russia moved in the Near

[1] Bismarck to Reuss, 1 Feb. 1868. *Auswärtige Politik Preußens 1858–1871*, ix,
no. 550.
[2] Reuss to Bismarck, 5 Feb. 1868. Ibid., no. 560.
[3] Bismarck to Reuss, 16 Feb. 1868. Bismarck, *Gesammelte Werke*, vi a, no. 1064.
[4] Bismarck to Reuss, 22 Mar. 1868. Ibid., no. 1108.
[5] Reuss to Bismarck, 27 Mar. 1868. *Auswärtige Politik Preußens 1858–1871*, ix,
no. 690.

East; now they asked what he would do if Prussia moved in southern Germany. Beust refused to be drawn: if France resisted Prussia 'we shall perhaps begin by a benevolent neutrality, but later we shall do our duty as a *good ally*'.[1] Though Beust dreamt of competing with Bismarck for German sentiment, he could do so only by keeping clear of any commitment to France: he had to be able to say that any Austro-French entente was confined to the Near East, yet pretended to the French that, by confining it there, he was preparing the way for a general alliance.[2] This deadlock persisted throughout 1868: it could have been broken only if southern Germany and the Near East had exploded simultaneously—and it is not in the nature of things to happen so conveniently. There was some desultory discussion of an Austro-French alliance in the summer of 1868. This was important only in revealing the illusions in the mind of Gramont, French ambassador at Vienna;[3] and these illusions were still to dominate him as foreign minister in the crisis of July 1870.

There was more reality in the final flare-up of the Eastern question towards the end of the year. The Cretan revolt was still smouldering; and a new element was added in Rumania, where a nationalist ministry under Bratianu tolerated or perhaps encouraged irredentist agitation against Hungary. Beust thought his chance had come: Turkey should be urged to discipline Rumania with the backing of the 'Crimean coalition'. Russia, excluded from this scheme, would be isolated and humiliated, or alternatively, Prussia would be forced to commit herself to the Russian side for an unpopular cause. Bismarck was not caught so easily.[4] It was not only his relations with

---

[1] Metternich to Beust, 9 Apr. 1868. *Rheinpolitik*, ii, no. 578. Gramont to Moustier, 12 Apr. 1868. *Origines diplomatiques*, xxi, no. 6642. Beust to Metternich, 14 Apr. 1868. *Rheinpolitik*, ii, no. 579.

[2] 'The more the entente shows itself in the Near East the more public opinion in Austria and Germany will get used to it and to the consequences which might follow from it in future eventualities.' Beust to Metternich, 12 May 1868. *Rheinpolitik*, ii, no. 598. Yet the French wrote optimistically: 'The Emperor considers it as understood that Austria has the initiative in every German question.' Moustier to Gramont, 11 May 1868. *Origines diplomatiques*, xxi, no. 6710.

[3] e.g. Gramont to Moustier, 23 July and 8 Aug. 1868. Ibid., no. 6815 and xxii, no. 6842. 'Austria will act with France as the best of allies . . . alliances will be formed and they will be loyal etc. etc.'

[4] Bismarck wrote on 6 Jan. 1869 (*Gesammelte Werke*, vi a, no. 1273): in case the Crimean coalition is re-formed, Prussia would have the alternative 'either to defend Russia and so to become involved in a struggle unpopular in Germany and with

Russia that were at stake; the Rumanian agitation threatened Hungary; and a Great Hungary, dominating the Habsburg monarchy, was—as Bismarck well knew—essential to Prussia's victory in Germany. When Andrássy, the Hungarian prime minister, gave warning that he would have to turn to Vienna and Paris for support against Rumania, Bismarck acted.[1] The prince of Rumania was a Hohenzollern; and urgent family advice persuaded him to dismiss Bratianu on 28 November. It was Bismarck's first incursion into the politics of the Near East; and it was a precedent for the rest. Prussia had no interests of her own in the Near East; and Bismarck's only concern was to prevent a crisis between Russia and Austria-Hungary—to avoid, that is, the necessity of having to take sides.

The Rumanian alarm had an aftermath. The Porte, baulked of its conflict with Rumania, turned against Greece instead and attempted to end the Cretan revolt by an ultimatum to Athens in December. This, too, suited Beust's book, but his alone. Though Russia would be humiliated if Greece had to give way, France and Great Britain—the other patrons of Greece—would be humiliated also. Besides, the Russians only cared about Greece as a preliminary; with the boom in Panslavism their interest was concentrated on the Slav peoples of the Balkans, and they were glad enough to be finished with the revolt in Crete if it could be done without loss of prestige. Therefore, despite Beust's insistence that now was the time to defeat Russia,[2] Bismarck had an easy task when he acted as 'honest broker'. On his proposal a conference met at Paris and compelled the Greeks to drop their support of the Cretan rebels (18 Feb. 1869). The revolt, left unaided, fizzled out. The Eastern question was not to raise its head again until 1876.

The alarm served, however, to revive the discussions for an alliance between France and Austria-Hungary. At the beginning of December the French accepted Beust's conditions, or so they thought. They agreed that Austria-Hungary should enter

the appearance of an aggressive Cabinet-war or to leave Russia in the lurch and be herself exposed to the danger of being faced in isolation with a similar coalition without being able to count on Russian support'.

[1] A curious and significant point: the warning was given to the Italian minister, and his government passed it on to Bismarck. Hungary, Italy, and Prussia represented the revolutionary, anti-Habsburg *bloc* of 1848; only Poland was absent. It was because Prussia was anti-Polish that Bismarck had ultimately to reconcile Italy and Hungary with the Habsburg monarchy.

[2] Gramont to La Valette, 24 Dec. 1868. *Origines diplomatiques*, xxiii, no. 7116.

a war on the Rhine only if Russia joined Prussia; similarly they would enter a war in the Near East if Prussia joined Russia.[1] This did not suit Beust in the least: he wanted an entente confined to the Near East and displaying an immediate activity there.[2] After all, France, he argued, had also a stake in the Near East; and, if the two Powers joined to defend the treaty of Paris, it would be easier later on to defend the treaty of Prague.[3] It was a striking illustration how far Austria-Hungary and France had slipped down the ladder of power that, though the treaty of Prague had been made at their expense, they should now talk in terms of defending it. They would be satisfied if they could maintain the independence of southern Germany; though, no doubt, they hoped that a war begun in the name of the *status quo* would end in the dismemberment of Prussia. This unspoken equivocation was indeed the deepest bar to any real co-operation between France and Austria-Hungary. Neither the Hungarians nor the German-Austrians could take Napoleon III and Beust seriously as defenders of the treaty of Prague, and therefore forbade an alliance.

The deadlock was as firm as ever; it seemed to be broken by the incursion of a third Power, Italy. Agreement between Austria and France had been the greatest dread of Italian policy throughout the century, as indeed it had been the doom of Sardinian ambitions in preceding times. Italy had no quarrel with Prussia and not much with Russia, apart from being a rather half-hearted member of the derelict 'Crimean coalition'; on the other hand, the Italians dared not be left out of a victorious Austro-French entente, and, in view of their previous experiences, they naturally expected such an entente to be victorious. In addition, Victor Emanuel hoped to prop up his shaky throne against republican agitation by making national gains on a conservative basis; that is, he would gain Tyrol from Austria-Hungary, and Rome, perhaps even Nice, from France by an alliance with the two emperors Francis Joseph and Napoleon, instead of by a revolutionary war against them. Italy could profit only at the expense of her two partners; the Italians were to use the same basis effectively for the Triple Alliance and indeed on many later occasions. In return they claimed to

[1] Metternich to Beust, 2 Dec. 1868. *Rheinpolitik*, iii, no. 648.
[2] Beust to Metternich, 8 Dec. 1868. Ibid., no. 651.
[3] Beust to Metternich, 3 Feb. 1869. Ibid., no. 663.

offer an army of 200,000 men; this, on practical examination, turned out to be no more than 60,000,[1] and the limited railway connexions with France and Austria-Hungary made it difficult to put even these to practical use. The real Italian offer was a neutrality which would secure Austria-Hungary on her south-west frontier and so free her from the war on two fronts which had proved disastrous in 1866; this was worth something, though not so much as the Italians imagined.

In December 1868 an Italian emissary approached Beust with the proposal that Italy should receive south Tyrol in exchange for her neutrality in a war between France and Prussia or between Austria-Hungary and Russia.[2] Beust thought the price high and that France, too, ought to contribute; he there-fore passed the emissary on to Napoleon. Here was a combination after Napoleon's heart—a dream-project for which everyone except himself would pay solid money. An alliance of the three countries would guarantee the peace of Europe; England would be drawn in; a congress of European sovereigns would call Halt to Russia and Prussia; and—the important practical considera-tion—south Tyrol would distract Italian interest from Rome.[3] The French ministers thought in more concrete terms: they wanted an anti-Prussian bloc, and they did not mind whether Italy or Austria-Hungary paid the price for it. Including Italy had this great advantage. Since she was involved with both France and Austria-Hungary, a triple alliance could be made; and this would obscure the sharp line between the Eastern question and the affairs of southern Germany, which Beust was trying to maintain. Thirty years later Italy was to play the same role in the Mediterranean agreements of obscuring the diver-gent interests of Austria-Hungary and Great Britain.

On 1 March 1869 after much wrangling, the French ministers, Rouher in especial, produced a draft-treaty, intended to commit the Austrians against Prussia without their noticing it. Under the guise of a union to preserve the peace of Europe, this was in

---

[1] In Aug. 1870 the Italians said they could offer France only 60,000 men and these only after three weeks' delay. Malaret (Florence) to Gramont, 8 Aug. 1870. *Origines diplomatiques*, xxix, no. 8937.

[2] Oddly enough, the emissary was a Hungarian general—one of the refugees of 1849—who had entered Italian service. Türr to Beust, 22 Dec. 1868; project of Austro-Italian agreement, Dec. 1868. Ibid., xxiii, nos. 7099 and 7100.

[3] Türr to Beust, 6 Jan. 1869. Ibid., no. 7165. Ollivier, *Empire libéral*, xi. 205.

reality a triple alliance against Russia and Prussia. In case Austria-Hungary was involved in war with Russia, France would put an observation corps on the Rhine and would enter the war if Prussia joined Russia; similarly, in case of a war between France and Prussia, Austria-Hungary would put an observation corps in Bohemia and would enter the war if Russia joined Prussia. In either case, Italy would contribute an army of 200,000 men. She would receive south Tyrol; and as well her two allies would help her to find a *modus vivendi* with the pope— whatever that might mean.[1] Beust was not taken in. He wrote to Metternich on 10 April: 'We know very well that the moment we have to place an observation-corps on our frontier as the result of a conflict between France and Prussia we can soon be driven to give up the neutrality we have so carefully proclaimed.'[2] It was now the French turn to protest. La Valette, the foreign minister, said to Metternich: 'How can you expect me ever to defend before the Chambers a treaty which seems made for the *exclusive* profit of Austria?'[3] Rouher, the calculating business man, took a more cautious line. Recognizing that Austria-Hungary could not be caught, he was afraid that Italy might slip through his fingers also; if the Austrians were allowed to stipulate neutrality, Italy would do the same. Therefore he proposed that the three Powers should merely bind themselves to conclude an offensive and defensive treaty in case of a European war, the conditions to be settled then.[4] The Austrians should be told secretly that they could remain neutral in the event of a Franco-Prussian war; the Italians should not—and thus they would be caught. France would have their army of 200,000 men.

This bargain suited the Austrians. They would secure an anti-Russian bloc in the Near East; yet they would keep their hands free as regards Prussia and need not estrange German sentiment inside the Habsburg monarchy. But the Italians, too, were not easily caught. So long as a Franco-Austrian alliance was in the offing, they had been anxious to make a third in it; now the alliance had clearly misfired, and there remained only the obligation on the Italians to produce 200,000 men whenever

[1] French note of 1 Mar. 1869, with four draft treaties. *Rheinpolitik*, iii, no. 671.
[2] Beust to Metternich, 10 Apr. 1869. Ibid., no. 684.
[3] Metternich to Beust, 18 Apr. 1869. Ibid., no. 685.
[4] French draft of 10 May. Metternich to Beust, 20 May 1869. Ibid., no. 698. *Origines diplomatiques*, xxiv, appendix no. 6.

it suited the whim of France or Austria-Hungary to go to war. They therefore demanded a payment on account; probably, indeed, they had been waiting for this moment all along. They decided, early in June, that they would sign the Triple Alliance when the French troops were withdrawn from Rome, and not before. Beust, a Protestant and, in his way, a liberal, thought this a reasonable condition, despite the traditional Habsburg protection of the papacy; besides, it distracted the Italians from south Tyrol. It was an impossible condition for Napoleon to satisfy: the Second Empire was drifting into increasing difficulties at home, and the favour of clericalist opinion in France was more important for Napoleon than any diplomatic combination. He fell back on the last resort of the diplomat who has failed: he pretended that he had succeeded in the hope that others would be taken in. He told the Austrians repeatedly that he regarded the alliance as 'morally signed',[1] and on 24 September 1869 wrote to Francis Joseph that if Austria-Hungary 'were menaced by any aggression, I shall not hesitate an instant to put all the forces of France at her side'; further, he would not start any negotiation with a foreign Power without previous agreement with the Austrian empire.[2] Francis Joseph again eluded the trap: he would not, he replied, make an alliance without warning Napoleon, but he made no reference to what Beust later called 'the engagement voluntarily undertaken by France'.[3] Victor Emanuel was even more reserved: he merely expressed a wish that the alliance be concluded, once the Convention of September 1864 was again in force—the French troops, that is, withdrawn from Rome.[4]

Thus the great project for a Triple Alliance against Russia and Prussia came to nothing. Though the final breakdown came on the Roman question, the negotiations of May and June 1869 were no more than an epilogue. The real conflict of outlook was

[1] Vitzthum to Beust, 7 Oct. 1869. *Rheinpolitik*, iii, no. 741. Earlier Napoleon had said: 'I shall regard this treaty as if it were signed.' Beust to Vitzthum, 26 Aug. 1869. Ibid., no. 723. Rouher said: 'The alliance is concluded and the engagements taken in the letters between the Emperors will have the same force as an international treaty.' Vitzthum to Beust, 10 Dec. 1869. Ibid., no. 756.
[2] Napoleon III to Francis Joseph, 24 Sept. 1869. *Origines diplomatiques*, xxv, no. 7674.
[3] The letter from Francis Joseph to Napoleon III is one of the few diplomatic documents to have vanished without trace. Beust described its contents (no doubt inaccurately) to Vitzthum on 20 July 1870. *Rheinpolitik*, iii, no. 911, note.
[4] Victor Emanuel to Napoleon III, about 25 Sept. 1869. Ibid., no. 733.

between Austria-Hungary and France. Despite sighs for a lost greatness, Habsburg policy was turning away from Germany and concentrating, as Bismarck had advised, on the Balkans. Francis Joseph might still regard himself as 'a German prince';[1] Beust might still hope to outshine Bismarck; neither could go against Hungarian and German opinion inside the empire. Austria-Hungary would make no attempt to undo the treaty of Prague or even to confine Prussia within its limits. In fact the only Austrian interest in the alliance so far as Germany was concerned was as insurance against a French victory: they wanted to make sure of their share if France defeated Prussia. As Francis Joseph put it rather piously: 'If the Emperor Napoleon entered southern Germany not as enemy but as liberator, I should be forced to make common cause with him.'[2] The Austrians, including Beust, wanted an entente confined to the Near East, an entente that would thwart Russia in Rumania and would stifle Pan-slavism throughout the Balkans. Though the French wanted to preserve the Turkish empire, they would not do it at the risk of forcing Russia into Prussia's arms. Gorchakov had said in 1868: 'The Emperor Alexander II will never enter a coalition directed against France. Take care that Beust does not give the impression of your having entered a coalition against us.'[3] The French wanted an ally against Prussia; the Austrians against Russia—and the two wishes could not be combined. Bismarck had wrecked the scheme in advance when he refused to commit himself to the Russian side against Austria-Hungary; this was as decisive as his earlier refusal to commit himself to the side of the western Powers against Russia. In September 1869 Beust and Gorchakov met in Switzerland. They agreed to keep things quiet in the Near East and to leave France and Prussia to fight things out in the west; Gorchakov also made it clear that Russia would repudiate the neutralization of the Black Sea as soon as she got the chance, and Beust made no objection—it was the one aspect of the Eastern question with which Austria-Hungary had no concern.[4]

The French were not ready to accept their isolation. Napoleon III had never found the Austrian alliance to his taste. Tilsit, not

[1] His objection to being crowned king of Croatia in 1868.
[2] Interview of 14 June 1870. Lebrun, *Souvenirs militaires*, p. 146.
[3] Talleyrand to Moustier, 17 Jan. 1868. *Origines diplomatiques*, xx, no. 6351.
[4] Hohenlohe, *Memoirs*, ii. 41. Gramont to La Tour, 29 Sept. 1869. *Origines diplomatiques*, xxv, no. 7692.

the marriage with Marie Louise, had been his model; the Stuttgart meeting with Alexander II in 1857, not the Salzburg meeting with Francis Joseph in 1867, the triumph of his reign. In the
autumn of 1869 he decided to make another effort for the
alliance with Russia—the only one which offered him the grandiose reconstruction of Europe of which he still occasionally
dreamt. General Fleury, a personal associate of his, was sent as
ambassador to St. Petersburg. He received secret instructions
from his master to stir up Russian suspicions against 'the
Germanic idea' and in exchange to hold out the prospect of
vague discussions concerning the future of the Near East 'after
a general upheaval'.[1] The Russians made the most of the opportunity. Gorchakov had always prided himself on the entente
with France, which he regarded as 'the finest page in his history';[2] he was delighted to renew it, though he made in his mind
the old condition—that it should be directed against Austria-
Hungary, not against Prussia. Alexander II went further; he
was jealous of the success of his uncle, William I, whom he
found 'a little too ambitious',[3] and agreed to remind him that
Prussia was committed to a plebiscite in north Sleswick. Of
course the Russians meant to ask for a service in return: it was
characteristically bizarre that they should seek to enforce the
treaty of Prague as a preliminary to revising the treaty of Paris.
Alexander's letter of 23 November had little effect in Berlin.
Bismarck at first thought of answering it by evoking once more
the memory of the Polish crisis, which had ruined Franco-
Russian relations; then decided there was no serious shift in
Russian policy and merely thanked the tsar for his advice.[4]
Benedetti much disliked Fleury's amateurish diplomacy: if
France tried to bid against Prussia for Russia's friendship,
Prussia would enter the bidding in the Near East and would
bid higher.[5]

[1] Napoleon III to Fleury, Nov. 1869. Fleury, *La France et la Russie en 1870*,
pp. 4–6.

[2] Fleury to Daru, 21 Mar. 1870. *Origines diplomatiques*, xxvii, no. 8024. Gorchakov
maliciously agreed that Austria should be encouraged 'to think of southern Germany instead of the Near East' (Fleury to La Tour, 30 Nov. 1869. Ibid., xxvi,
no. 7781), but this was more to get her away from Turkey than to embarrass
Prussia.

[3] Fleury to La Tour, 13 Nov. 1869. Ibid., xxv, no. 7751.

[4] William I to Alexander II, discarded draft, 3 Dec.; 12 Dec. 1869. Bismarck,
Gesammelte Werke, vi b, nos. 1458 and 1461.

[5] Benedetti to La Tour, 30 Nov. 1869. *Origines diplomatiques*, xxvi, no. 7776.

Fleury greatly exaggerated his achievement; he thought that he had begun to turn Russia from Prussia and preened himself when Gorchakov said: 'We are no longer in an epoch where family ties can lead to such great results as those of an alliance'.[1] But he was soon pulled up from Paris. On 2 January 1870 Napoleon launched 'the liberal empire'. Daru, the new foreign minister, disliked the policy of entente with Russia, associated with the worst advocates of personal rule from Morny onwards. Like most liberal Frenchmen, he held that friendship with Russia was possible only if she gave up all plans for revision or conquest in the Near East; moreover he shared the common French delusion that Russian was awake to the German danger, 'a truly vital interest draws us together'.[2] At most Daru was prepared to discuss the Near East in case of war in the west: then France might use it to buy Russian approval of the successes she was sure to make.[3] This was mostly humbug. Daru was more concerned not to provoke Prussia by evoking the treaty of Prague; and, above all, not to offend the British by giving Gorchakov any excuse for raising the revision of the treaty of Paris. Fleury was told abruptly to drop the question of north Sleswick and to steer clear of the treaty of 1856.[4] He appealed secretly to Napoleon, but in vain; and was left grumbling that Napoleon was being led to ruin by his ministers, as Louis Philippe had been.

Daru had no constructive German policy; his hope was fixed on better relations with Great Britain. The two countries had drifted increasingly apart since 1864. British suspicions had been stirred by the schemes of French aggrandizement in 1866; and, during the Luxembourg crisis of 1867, where Russian policy had sought to satisfy France, British policy had been concerned to thwart her. Relations reached their worst at the opening of 1869, when a French company acquired control of an important Belgian railway. The British and Belgian governments suspected, though wrongly, that this was a first step in a deliberate plan of annexation. The Belgians passed a law forbidding the transaction; the British threatened to join Russia and Prussia in alliance against France.[5] The French climbed down; and the crisis died

[1] Fleury to Daru, 23 Mar. 1870. *Origines diplomatiques*, xxvii, no. 8028.
[2] Daru to Fleury, 29 Mar. 1870. Ibid. no. 8046.
[3] Daru to Fleury, 31 Jan. 1870. Ibid. xxvi, no. 7905.
[4] Daru to Fleury, 6 Jan. 1870. Ibid. no. 7854.
[5] Much to Bismarck's annoyance: he was determined not to commit himself

away, leaving France and Great Britain on cool terms. Now in January 1870, Daru proposed to win British favour by show-ing the moral superiority of France over Prussia. Though the manœuvre had little success on this, its first, appearance, it was to carry the Anglo-French entente to triumph a generation later. His chosen method was to propose disarmament, always dear to British sentiment: France and Prussia should each re-duce their annual intake of recruits. If Bismarck agreed, liberal-ism would be strengthened in Germany; if he refused, he would be discredited in British eyes.[1] Though Clarendon, the British foreign secretary, had no illusions as to the French motives, he made the proposal at Berlin, as of his own initiative. Bismarck had no difficulty in answering it. He asked the British: 'If we disarm, will you guarantee the position that we have won?'[2] and, more impertinently, whether they would welcome a similar proposal for naval disarmament.[3] Even Bismarck, however, showed the tongue in his cheek a little too much when he suggested that Prussia had to remain heavily armed in order to face a future danger from Russia.[4]

These arguments were to be the stock-in-trade of disarma-ment conferences for the next eighty years, and they were strong enough to shake Clarendon. In April 1870 he held out to the French a different prospect of co-operation. He professed to be alarmed at Russian designs in the Near East. Austria 'was in full decomposition'; British forces were absorbed in protecting Canada from the United States; France 'could not be distracted from her essentially moderating task in central Europe'.[5] The moral was clear. France should somehow get on better terms with Prussia and thus free her hands for the Near East. Daru could think of no effective reply. The exchange illustrated again the central problem of French policy. Neither Russia, Great Britain, nor Austria-Hungary cared about south Germany. Though none of the three wanted a war between Prussia and

until the British did so. Bismarck to Bernstorff, 4 May 1869. Bismarck, *Gesammelte Werke*, vi b, no. 1383.

[1] Daru to La Valette, 1 Feb. 1870. *Origines diplomatiques*, xxvi, no. 7907.

[2] La Valette to Daru, 23 Feb. 1870. Ibid., no. 7956.

[3] Bismarck to Bernstorff, 9 Feb. and 25 Mar. 1870. Bismarck, *Gesammelte Werke*, vi b, nos. 1495, 1496, and 1541.

[4] Daru took this reply seriously and solemnly inquired of Fleury whether Russia and Prussia were on bad terms. Daru to Fleury, 25 Feb.; Fleury to Daru, 5 Mar., 10 Mar. 1870. *Origines diplomatiques*, xxvii, nos. 7967, 7993, and 8004.

[5] La Valette to Ollivier (acting foreign minister), 21 Apr. 1870. Ibid., no. 8104.

France, none of them feared it or supposed that it would disturb the Balance of Power in Europe; none of the three would support either side. If the French could hold their own against Prussia, they had no cause to worry; if they needed allies, these could only be found in the Near East and on conflicting terms. The British wished to maintain the neutralization of the Black Sea, the Russians to overthrow it; the Austrians would oppose Russia in Rumania and the Balkans, but not in the Black Sea. For the French all these policies distracted attention from Prussia and were therefore equally abhorrent. By 1870 the Second Empire had indeed returned to the 'idea' with which it started—that the security and greatness of France rested on good relations with England and Russia. But the French had discovered no means of attaining these relations, still less of reconciling the two Powers with each other.

X

THE END OF FRENCH PRIMACY

1870-5

THOUGH victory over France in 1870 certainly united Germany, the war lacked the deliberation of the war against Austria. Between 1862 and 1866 Bismarck steadily screwed up the pressure, despite occasional and perhaps genuine scruples; unless the Austrians accepted his terms, the repeated crises were bound to end in war. There was no such steady march to war between 1866 and 1870; indeed no alarm disturbed Franco-Prussian relations between the Luxembourg affair in 1867 and the outbreak of war more than three years later. Nor did Bismarck suffer in these years from the nightmare of coalitions which dominated him later. He dismissed the rumours of French alliance with Austria-Hungary and Italy as 'conjectural rubbish',[1] which indeed they turned out to be. He was not perturbed by good relations between France and Russia; since these must be based on the abandonment by France of her Polish sympathies, Prussia could always make a third in the partnership. His own policy was more passive than at any time before or afterwards. Though he kept the solid basis of friendship with Russia, this was confined to a common hostility towards Poland; and he never allowed the Russians to draw him into supporting them in the Near East. Ultimately he hoped for a conservative alliance with Russia and Austria-Hungary;[2] like all alliances based on principle, this had the advantage of providing security without having to pay a price for it. But he knew that he would have to wait until Habsburg resentment at the defeat of 1866 had died away.

In truth Bismarck's energies were consumed in building up

[1] Bismarck to Reuss, 13 Feb. 1869. *Auswärtige Politik Preußens 1858–1871*, x, no. 517.

[2] He told Andrássy this in Jan. 1870 and Archduke Albrecht in July. Bismarck to Schweinitz (Vienna), 12 Jan.; 10 July 1870. Bismarck, *Gesammelte Werke*, vi b, nos. 1474 and 1589.

the new German state; like Cavour, he aimed to satisfy the liberals without surrendering to them. This policy affected international relations only in so far as the German states south of the Main were concerned. Bismarck's problem was not to bring them into a united Germany; that was inevitable in any case. His problem was to secure that they should be brought in on the basis of loyalty to the Hohenzollern dynasty and not on that of popular enthusiasm—unification from above, and not from below. One of the plans for increasing dynastic prestige, which he played with at the beginning of 1870 and then abandoned, was to proclaim William I German emperor. The same dynastic motive lay behind his encouragement of the idea that the Spanish throne—vacant since the revolution against Queen Isabella in 1868—should be offered to a member of the Hohenzollern family.[1] Bismarck knew that there would be some French opposition; this is very far from saying that he expected it to provoke the French to war. His calculation seems to have been the opposite: by making the French anxious on their Spanish frontier, it would make them less ready to go to war for the sake of south Germany.[2] Benedetti, a good judge of German affairs, was convinced till the end that Bismarck and William I would not take the initiative in crossing the Main; they would wait for south Germany to come to them.[3] There is even better evidence. Alexander II met William I and Bismarck at Ems from 1 June to 4 June 1870. Bismarck's main concern was to persuade Alexander II that the south German princes would make a better bargain with William I than if they waited to be swept away by a democratic wave under his more liberal successor. There was some talk of affairs in Rumania; and common disapproval of the pro-Polish line that the Habsburg monarchy was taking in Galicia. War against France was not mentioned: no assurances asked for, and none given. In fact the meeting was slightly anti-Austrian, not at all anti-French.

[1] This was Leopold, of the Sigmaringen branch. Formerly the senior branch, it had subordinated itself to the Prussian royal house in 1848. Leopold's younger brother was prince of Rumania.

[2] This topic is so overlaid with later controversy and passion that it is impossible to arrive at a detached verdict. I can only say that I have tried to judge according to the contemporary evidence and to resist the later myths, whether created by French resentment or by Bismarck himself. He later boasted that he had manufactured the war with France; this is evidence of what he thought in 1892, not in 1870.

[3] Benedetti to Daru, 25 Feb. 1870. *Origines diplomatiques*, xxvi, no. 7970.

Change of policy, so far as it occurred, was in France, not in Prussia. If the 'liberal empire' had been fully maintained, Bismarck's expectation of absorbing south Germany without war might have been fulfilled. But in April Napoleon quarrelled with Daru over the attitude to be taken towards the council which the pope had summoned in Rome;[1] and in May he staged a plebiscite which was really a demonstration against his liberal ministers. Against Ollivier's wish, he appointed Gramont, ambassador at Vienna, to succeed Daru as foreign minister. Gramont was not only a fierce clerical; he was also violently anti-Prussian. Though he had not been told of the secret negotiations with Austria-Hungary, he now made them his own after a pretence of constitutional reluctance: 'The engagements taken would have no significance if I did not accept them, but I accept them.'[2] Thus Gramont arrived in Paris at the beginning of June, believing that an Austro-French alliance existed and resolved to humiliate Prussia at the first opportunity. This suited the need for prestige on which Napoleon's personal supporters were insisting. A French general, Lebrun, was sent to Vienna to translate the alliance into practical terms; and though he achieved nothing practical, he returned convinced that Austria-Hungary would at once mobilize and tie down a large part of the Prussian army, if France invaded southern Germany.[3]

An unforeseeable accident exploded the crisis. On 19 June Prince Leopold accepted the Spanish throne. The Spanish delegate telegraphed to Madrid that he would return by 26 June; and the Prince could be elected by the Cortes, which was to remain in session until 1 July. France and the world would be presented with a king of Spain before a word of warning had been said. But the blunder of a cipher-clerk made the Spanish government imagine that their representative would return only on 9 July; this was too long to keep the Cortes in session, and it was prorogued on 23 June until November. When Salazar,

---

[1] Daru had wished to insist that the council should not interfere in secular affairs. Napoleon III and Ollivier were anxious not to offend clericalist opinion in France.

[2] Beust to Metternich, 31 May 1870. *Rheinpolitik*, iii, no. 822. Daru had never learnt of the alliance negotiations; and even Gramont was informed of them only on Beust's insistence.

[3] Lebrun, *Souvenirs militaires*, pp. 83, 146. Archduke Albrecht had visited Paris for military talks in March; he had received a bad impression of the state of the French army.

the Spaniard, arrived in Madrid, he found it deserted. To justify the recall of the Cortes, he had to reveal what was afoot; and on 3 July the news reached Paris. In these cases, the wise rule is to threaten the weak state, not the strong one. But the French were more concerned to humiliate Prussia than to prevent a Hohenzollern king of Spain. Gramont told the Council of Ministers that Austria had promised to put an observation-corps on her frontier;[1] on Napoleon's suggestion, the tsar was informed that the Hohenzollern candidature 'means war' and, since Russia had always disliked the prospect of a war between Prussia and France, it was supposed that her influence would be exerted at Berlin.[2] Thus the French counted both on Austria's alliance and Russia's support. They were wrong, but they had other and unexpected assistance. Prince Leopold, his father Prince Antony, and, for that matter, William I, had disliked the Spanish affair all along; they had been pushed into it by Bismarck and now hastened to get out of it. On 12 July Leopold's father renounced the Spanish throne on his son's behalf[3] and with William I's approval. He wrote to his wife: 'a stone is removed from my heart.'

If the French government had really been concerned with Spain or even with scoring a diplomatic success, the crisis would have been over. But the fatal theme of Bonapartist prestige had been launched and could not be silenced. Gramont was driven on by Napoleon; and Napoleon in turn was driven on by his supporters at any sign of compromise. The great mass of the French people were pacific or apathetic; what counted was the Imperialist majority in the packed Chamber and Napoleon's clique of adventurers. The Second Empire had always lived on illusion; and it now committed suicide in the illusion that it could somehow destroy Prussia without serious effort. There was no policy in the drive to war, no vision of a reconstruction of Europe on lines more favourable to France, not even a clear plan for acquiring territory on the Rhine. To arrest the unification of Germany, still more to dismember Prussia, went against every canon of Napoleonic policy, if such a thing still existed; that did not matter in the explosion of irritation and impatience.

---

[1] Metternich to Beust, 8 July 1870. *Rheinpolitik*, iii, no. 851.

[2] Gramont to Fleury, 6 July 1870. *Origines diplomatiques*, xxvii, no. 8173.

[3] The crisis was so unexpected that Leopold was on a walking-tour in the Austrian Alps, and out of reach.

Like the Austrians in 1859 and 1866, though with less justification, Napoleon and his associates wanted war for its own sake,
without thought of the outcome.

The decisive step to war was taken on 12 July when Gramont
instructed Benedetti to demand that William I should endorse
Leopold's withdrawal and should guarantee that his candidature
be never renewed;[1] this demand was made with the deliberate
intention of provoking war or else of inflicting on Prussia a
humiliation equivalent to a military defeat. It was only at this
point that Bismarck entered the field. For the first few days of
the crisis he had been conscious of having overreached himself,
and his only concern had been to dissociate himself from Leopold's candidature as much as possible. Now he saw that war
could be brought about on a question of national honour, not of
the Spanish throne, and the problem of south Germany solved
at a stroke. His one fear was that William I, ashamed of the whole
affair, might satisfy the French demand. He did not need to
worry: William I refused it on 13 July, though in polite terms.
Bismarck's only contribution to the whole affair was to make
out that the king's refusal had been rather less polite than it
was in reality. The 'Ems telegram', which Bismarck issued in
abbreviated form, was meant to provoke France.[2] This was

[1] The demand was stiffened on Napoleon's instruction. Napoleon III to Gramont, 12 July 1870. *Origines diplomatiques*, xxviii, no. 8436.

[2] Bismarck in later life was anxious to get the credit for having made the war
and therefore built up a legend that he provoked it by editing the telegram which
William I sent from Ems. But Bismarck always had two irons in the fire. When he
kept out of the way at Varzin until 11 July, this certainly helped the French to go
from one provocative muddle to another; but it also left him free to blame William I
for any humiliation that might follow. On 12 July he planned to summon the
Reichstag and to present France with an ultimatum. This would certainly have
brought on a war; equally it would have given him an excuse to resign if William I
had rejected his advice. His behaviour throughout was improvised and is only
consistent with the explanation that the crisis took him by surprise. Thereafter
he was quite prepared to work for war with France in order to save his own prestige.
His alternative solution of putting the blame on William I was equally characteristic and equally discreditable. But all this goes against the theory that the
Spanish candidature was a deep-laid mine or, as Bucher called it, 'a trap for
France'. Rather it was a blunder, from which Bismarck escaped by rapid improvisation.

The editing of the Ems telegram certainly showed that Bismarck was willing
to provoke war with France in order to save his reputation. But it did not cause
the war. Napoleon III had to make increasingly impossible demands in order to
satisfy the extreme Bonapartists; and the Ems telegram merely gave him the
occasion for which he, or his supporters, had been seeking. Of course, if Bismarck
had desperately wished to avoid war, his genius might have found a means of doing

unnecessary. The French government were bent on war and seized the nearest excuse. They accepted their responsibility 'with light hearts' and committed themselves to war on 15 July[1] without waiting to learn from Benedetti what had really happened at Ems.

The French were deluded as to their military strength and even more as to their diplomatic position. They supposed that Great Britain and Russia would look on with favour, if not with support; that Austria-Hungary and Italy would enter the war as their allies; and that south Germany would remain neutral. They were wrong on all counts. Though the British and Russian governments had both laboured to resolve the crisis for opposite reasons, both blamed France for their failure. The British withdrew into anxiety for Belgium; they were additionally alarmed when Bismarck published Benedetti's draft treaty of 1866 in *The Times* on 25 July, and they negotiated with both combatants new treaties guaranteeing the neutrality of Belgium for the duration of the war—treaties which Bismarck accepted with a good grace, and Gramont with a bad one (30 July). The British government were much blamed in later years for having stood idly by, while Bismarck established German power in Europe. But the whole course of British policy for the preceding fifty years had been against just such a French campaign on the Rhine as was now being launched. The Anglo-French partnership had been confined to the Near East; and even here France had been latterly an unsatisfactory opponent of Russia. Prussia, it is true, had been still less co-operative in the Near East; but the British were tempted to believe that she would be more forthcoming if she were once freed from anxiety on the Rhine. Things would have been different if Great Britain and Russia had come together to impose peace on both sides; and they might have done it in an earlier generation. Now they were irrevocably divided by the legacy of the Crimean war, to say nothing of endless petty disputes in central Asia. British policy in Europe postulated a continental ally. She had no ally; therefore could have no policy.

Russia's principal motive was fear for Poland, not ambition

so. He alone was capable of mastering the situation. In this sense he must bear the responsibility not only for the war of 1870, but for the subsequent course of German history.

[1] The actual declaration of war was delivered in Berlin on 19 July.

in the Near East; failure to understand this was one of the gravest blunders in French policy.[1] The Russians expected a French victory and would tolerate it; what they dreaded was a French victory in co-operation with Austria-Hungary. With Prussia out of the way, this alliance would inevitably raise the Polish question, and would raise it more successfully than in 1863. The Russians aimed to 'localize' the war: to keep Austria-Hungary neutral, not for Prussia's sake, but for their own. Gorchakov happened to be in Berlin on 13 July.[2] He refused to give Bismarck any binding promise of support against Austria-Hungary, merely saying that he 'doubted whether it would be possible for Austria to fling herself into such adventures'; and in fact there was no formal agreement between Russia and Prussia at any time of the war. Though the Russians welcomed rumours of their military preparations, in reality they made none.[3] All they did was to make their neutrality conditional on that of Austria-Hungary; and this condition suited Beust's policy.[4] On 23 July Alexander II told the Austro-Hungarian ambassador that he would stay neutral so long as Austria-Hungary did not mobilize or stir up trouble in Poland; moreover he guaranteed Austria's frontiers in the name of the king of Prussia.[5] Russia had always treated Prussia with offhand patronage; and Alexander gave this guarantee without consulting William I. Bismarck at once confirmed it: 'we have no interest in seeing the Austrian monarchy collapse and in involving ourselves in the insoluble question, what should take its place'.[6] All

---

[1] Even during the crisis Fleury supposed that Russian support could be won by revision of the treaty of Paris (to Gramont, 10 July 1870. *Origines diplomatiques*, xxix, no. 8650). He did not understand that the Black Sea was a luxury in Russian policy; Poland was the reality. Of course, the Russians had also learnt from repeated disappointments that Napoleon III would never make any serious inroad into the settlement of 1856.

[2] His reports to the tsar are in *Journal of Modern History*, vol. xiv. As a further precaution against being committed, Gorchakov remained on holiday in Germany until the end of July.

[3] Bismarck used the story that Russia had placed 300,000 men in Galicia in order to frighten Austria-Hungary and the south German states; it had no solid foundation, not even of a Russian promise. Bismarck to Werthern (Munich), 16 July 1870. Bismarck, *Gesammelte Werke*, vi*b*, no. 1652.

[4] Of course both countries would have changed their tune in case of a French victory; they would then have competed for French favour, and it is by no means axiomatic that Austria-Hungary would have won the competition.

[5] Chotek to Beust, 23 July 1870. *Origines diplomatiques*, xxix, no. 8734.

[6] Bismarck to Reuss, 26 July 1870. Bismarck also sent a message to Andrássy: 'The inclusion of the so-called German-Austria with its Czechs and Slovenes in

the same, he doubtless resolved not to be patronized much longer. The French were enraged by Russia's attitude, though they tried to console themselves with the pretence that Russian hostility would bring them other allies.[1] In reality the Russians had been consistent to the end. Though they certainly did nothing to arrest Prussia, equally, as Alexander II had so often said, they would not join a coalition against France; and there is no ground for supposing that they would have entered the war if Prussia had been defeated.

It did not need the threat from Russia to keep Austria-Hungary neutral; she remained neutral from calculation. Beust insisted from the first that the crisis had nothing to do with Austria-Hungary. The French had started it without consulting him; they were provoking German opinion instead of isolating Prussia from Germany as he had always advised; they would not even tell him their military plans. He complained to Metternich: 'When I look at what is happening I ask myself whether I have become an imbecile'.[2] Like the Russians, Beust expected a French victory; but he intended to exploit this French victory, not to aid it. He would enter the war only when the decisive battle had been fought; and he would then restore the Habsburg protectorate over south Germany (which the tsar had also offered to recognize) as much against France as against Prussia. His immediate object was to keep French favour without committing himself to their side; hence he would have liked to avoid issuing a declaration of neutrality—by keeping Prussia in uncertainty, he would do something to aid France.[3] Austro-Hungarian policy was debated in a Crown Council on 18 July. Andrássy later made out that he had prevented Beust from going to war on the French side; and the story has been generally accepted. It is remote from the truth.[4] Beust proposed

the North German federation would be synonymous with its dissolution.' Bismarck to Schweinitz, 23 July 1870. Bismarck, *Gesammelte Werke*, vi b, nos. 1709 and 1701.

[1] Gramont to La Tour, 23 July 1870. *Origines diplomatiques*, xxix, no. 8724.

[2] Beust to Metternich, 11 July 1870. *Rheinpolitik*, iii, no. 871. Beust, *Memoirs*, ii. 340–2. Beust also suggested that the French should allow Leopold to sail for Spain and should kidnap him on the way. Since Bismarck had always made out that Leopold's candidature was a private affair which had nothing to do with Prussia, he would not be able to object.

[3] De Cazaux (Vienna) to Gramont, 17 July 1870. *Origines diplomatiques*, xxix, no. 8621.

[4] Austro-Hungarian policy in 1870, and especially the council of 18 July, has at last been clarified by Srbik, *Aus Österreichs Vergangenheit*, pp. 67–98.

to mobilize in readiness for intervention and meanwhile to satisfy the French with harmless gestures of sympathy. Andrássy, too, favoured some measure of mobilization; and in the radical spirit of 1848 hoped for a French victory as well as expecting it. Only he wished to enlist Prussia as well as France in the coming struggle against Russia which, like Beust, he anticipated; therefore he insisted on a declaration of neutrality, so as to secure Prussian favour also. This was done on 20 July. Otherwise Beust's policy was followed. On 20 July he wrote privately to Metternich in order 'to gild the pill of neutrality' for Napoleon;[1] and Francis Joseph followed this up with a high-sounding letter of good wishes that meant nothing.[2]

Beust attempted to perform one service for the French, or at least seemed to do so: he tried to clear the way for their alliance with Italy. After all, it could do no harm if the Italians assisted France; and in case of a Prussian victory, Austria-Hungary might even repeat Custoza instead of revenging Sadova. The Italians were not attracted by this proposal. They wanted an alliance with Austria-Hungary, leaving their allies to make the first step against Prussia, but giving them immediate possession of Rome. These negotiations ran on until 10 August; they were pointless. The French would never withdraw from Rome until they were beaten on the Rhine; and then no one would want to make an alliance with them. The negotiations between Austria-Hungary and Italy were simply an attempt at insurance against the expected French victory; and they were brought to an abrupt end as soon as the news of French defeats began to come in. The Italians were then free to occupy Rome without troubling about the Convention of 1864; and they did so on 20 September. As to Austria-Hungary, Andrássy was able to make out that he had always favoured Prussia and ultimately gained for her the only backing against Russia that remained—alliance with Bismarck's Germany; he was thus rewarded for a foresight that he did not possess. Neither Beust nor Andrássy determined Austro-Hungarian neutrality; it was not even dictated by any threat from Russia. Gorchakov said correctly: 'Russia did not paralyse a support which had no chance of being realised'.[3] Habsburg policy waited on events, and these

[1] Beust to Metternich, 20 July 1870. *Rheinpolitik*, iii, no. 911.
[2] Francis Joseph to Napoleon III, 25 July 1870. Ibid., no. 920.
[3] Fleury to Gramont, 9 Aug. 1870. *Origines diplomatiques*, xxix, no. 8948.

produced the decision. On 22 August Francis Joseph defined his aim as 'averting from us' the Prussian victories; and the aim was achieved. Like Napoleon III in 1866, the Austrians had miscalculated the outcome of the war; unlike Napoleon, they managed to extricate themselves in time from the consequences of their blunder.

Thus the French were left to fight alone against a united Germany. The unanimous enthusiasm with which the southern German states joined Prussia did not throw much weight into the military balance; but it made nonsense of the French political programme, so far as they had one. The liberation of southern Germany could certainly not be taken seriously as a war-aim. The record of French defeat began on 4 August; it reached its climax on 2 September, when the principal French army and Napoleon III himself surrendered at Sedan. Sedan marked the end of an epoch in European history; it was the moment when the myth of *la grande nation*, dominating Europe, was shattered for ever. The Balance of Power was startlingly altered. Before 1866 the French had counted on a balance between Austria and Prussia in central Europe; therefore it was they who had been beaten at Sadova. Similarly, Great Britain and Russia had always counted on a Balance of Power on the Rhine; and it was they—Russia rather more than Great Britain—who were beaten at Sedan. On the other hand, Sadova cleared the way for Prussia's domination of Germany; Sedan merely confirmed that it had happened. The Prussian gains which followed Sadova were real gains: Prussia could never have become the greatest Power in Europe without the dissolution of the German Confederation and the annexations of 1866. The gains which followed Sedan were symbolic: Alsace and Lorraine, which France surrendered in 1871, were not essential to German greatness—they were indeed a source of weakness. When France regained them in 1919, this did not materially alter German preponderance; it would have been very different if Austria-Hungary had been able, at some time, to reverse the verdict of the treaty of Prague.

European diplomacy took on a new character after the battle of Sedan. Until 2 September 1870, the object of French policy (so far as it had one) was to undo the earlier Prussian victories and to establish French influence on the Rhine; after 2 September the French accepted the fact of German unity and were only concerned to defend the integrity of their national territory. Everything turned on the German demand for Alsace and Lorraine. Bismarck made out in later years that this demand had been imposed on him by the German generals, thinking only in terms of military security. There is no evidence of this;[1] on the contrary, Bismarck preached annexation from the outbreak of war. He wanted some concrete achievement on which to focus German enthusiasm; also, in view of the old ties of sympathy between France and the south German states, he may well have welcomed a cause of lasting estrangement between the public opinion of the two countries. His foreign policy was always shaped by 'Junker' needs, and it was vital for these that Tsarist Russia, not liberal France, should be the godfather of German unity. No doubt Bismarck miscalculated the depth of French resentment. He supposed that the French would become reconciled to the loss of Alsace and Lorraine as Francis Joseph had become reconciled to the loss of Lombardy and Venetia. A hereditary monarch can lose provinces; a people cannot so easily abandon its national territory. Sedan caused the overthrow of the Napoleonic empire; henceforth the French people were alone sovereign.[2] After 2 September the Franco-German war became the first war of nations;[3] the rules of civilized warfare broke down, and the pattern of twentieth-century warfare was created.

The liberals and radicals who set up the provisional government in Paris at first supposed that history would repeat itself in foreign affairs, as they were trying to repeat it at home: just as the allies had left France intact in 1815 after Waterloo, so Bismarck would make a generous peace after Sedan. This dream was shattered when Jules Favre, the new foreign minister, met Bismarck at Ferrières on 18 September. Bismarck claimed to be indifferent to the form of government in France; in reality, he would have preferred a restoration of the empire, believing it to

[1] There is also no evidence that Alsace and Lorraine were demanded for their iron ore and phosphates, which were in any case largely unknown.

[2] Bismarck himself recognized this when he insisted that the peace terms be accepted by a national assembly, which should include the representatives of Alsace and Lorraine.

[3] The so-called national risings against Napoleon I were a fiction, partly invented by Napoleon himself as an excuse for his defeat, partly elaborated by German historians under the inspiration of the war of 1870. The Spanish and, to a lesser extent, the Russian war against Napoleon I had a national character; but both were on the periphery of European civilization.

be the weakest and therefore the most dependent on German favour. Favre answered Bismarck's demand with the grandilo-quent phrase: 'not an inch of our territory or a stone of our fortresses'. But how was this phrase to be enforced? Tradition pointed to the way of Jacobinism, the *levée en masse* and the terror of 1793; this was the way of Gambetta, who escaped from Paris in October and raised new armies on the Loire. Though these new armies fought well enough to restore French honour, they could not defeat the Prussians. The last and greatest of illusions was broken.

The alternative way was to seek the support of the Great Powers, evoking their mediation, if not their alliance. The neutrals had been kept out of the wars of 1859 and 1866 only by the rapid conclusion of peace; it was reasonable to hope that they might be drawn in if the French prolonged the war. Thiers, the historian of Napoleon and once the protagonist of war on the Rhine, now toured Europe for support; and his tour drew the lines on which French policy would henceforth develop. Previously the French had turned to Vienna when they wanted an ally against Prussia; now Austria-Hungary ceased to count in French policy. In the autumn of 1870 the men at Vienna, despite their sympathies with France, made their peace with reality; they came to recognize that Austria-Hungary could exist only with German favour. On 1 October Francis Joseph congratulated Schweinitz on the Prussian victories. He added frankly: 'You cannot expect me to be pleased about the thing itself. . . . I shall not interfere at all, I shall let anything happen.'[1] Schweinitz defined the new situation when he said to the Russian ambassador: 'If you ask me what we have promised Austria in return for her friendship, I should answer "life". She owes her preservation solely to our good will, for we are interested in maintaining her integrity, which in our view is even more necessary to the European balance than that of the Ottoman Empire.'[2] Andrássy, with Hungarian arrogance, still wanted to treat Bismarck as an equal, and insisted that Prussia must quarrel with Russia for the sake of Hungary.[3] Beust was more sensible: now that the struggle for Germany had been lost, he saw

[1] Schweinitz, *Denkwürdigkeiten*, p. 277.
[2] Goriainov, *Le Bosphore et les Dardanelles*, p. 304.
[3] Bismarck wrote angrily to Schweinitz on 3 Oct. (Bismarck, *Gesammelte Werke*, vi *b*, no. 1844) that Hungary and Italy owed everything to Prussia, yet were the most hostile to her; if Hungary wanted German sympathy, she must win it.

that the only resource was to try to make a third in the Russo-Prussian friendship and prepared the way for the League of the Three Emperors.[1] Thiers heard nothing in Vienna except Beust's pseudo-Metternichian lament: 'I do not see Europe any more.'

His visit to London was equally vain. Accustomed for centuries to French supremacy, the British were inclined to believe that the Balance of Power had been improved by Prussia's victory; certainly Belgium, the practical concern of their policy, was more secure than it had been in the days of Napoleon's restless scheming. Englishmen of both parties were already beginning to hope that Germany would take Austria's place as their 'natural ally', holding France and Russia in check while the British built up prosperity and empire overseas; an ally, too, more liberal and congenial than had been Metternich's police-state. The British were therefore hard engaged in organizing a 'league of neutrals', not as a preparation for intervention, but to prevent the intervention of others. Gladstone, the prime minister, was out of sympathy with this policy of abstention, though on high moral grounds, not from any consideration of the Balance of Power. He regarded the transfer of Alsace and Lorraine without consulting the inhabitants as a crime[2] and wished to evoke 'the conscience of Europe'; he did not yet see that, in practical terms, this appeal to conscience involved co-operation with Russia, and that the Russians were not likely to co-operate without a price which it was far beyond British ability to pay.

St. Petersburg was therefore the decisive point for Thiers's mission. If the Russians had co-operated with Austria-Hungary and England, a European mediation would have followed; so long as they seemed ready to support Prussia, Bismarck could keep France in isolation. There was no defined bargain between Russia and Prussia; and the Russians did not like to stand idly by. As early as 7 August Gorchakov said: 'It is impossible that the other Great Powers be excluded from the future negotiations for

[1] Beust and Metternich, the two Germans from the *Reich*, were the least hostile to Russia of all those who directed Habsburg foreign policy. For the others—whether Hungarians like Andrássy or grandees like Schwarzenberg—hostility to Russia was the overriding principle.

[2] All the changes of territory in Italy, including the transfer of Savoy and Nice to France, had been sanctioned, or at least condoned by plebiscites; none of Bismarck's annexations was accompanied by a plebiscite, though he was pledged to hold one in north Sleswick.

peace, even if they do not take part in the war.'[1] Determination
not to be ignored in Europe, not to be treated as a merely
Asiatic power, was always a deep motive in Russian policy.
Nothing, for instance, had done Napoleon III more good in the
tsar's eyes than the treaty of 3 March 1859: it kept up at any
rate the appearance that Russia had a say in the affairs of Italy.
Against this emotional resentment, Bismarck played the equally
emotional 'solidarity of the monarchical-conservative elements
in Europe',[2] a solidarity which was now to include Austria-
Hungary. This refurbished Holy Alliance represented Bismarck's
own political outlook, especially in regard to Poland; all the
same its practical purpose, like that of the original Holy Alliance,
was to keep Russia quiet.

Events in France strengthened Bismarck's hand. Though the
Prussian victories alarmed the Russians, the overthrow of
Napoleon III and the establishment of a more or less revolutionary government in Paris alarmed the tsar still more; the
alarm was complete when Polish exiles supported the provisional
French government. In more concrete terms, the Russians
tolerated the aggrandizement of Germany for the sake of their
Polish possessions. Yet even now this was not an 'option' for
Germany against France; it was an option for neutrality as
against action.[3] In a rather vague way the Russians hoped to
play France off against Germany at some later date; and they
were already calculating that fear of a resentful France would
keep Germany quiet while they themselves settled with Austria-
Hungary. Gorchakov said to Thiers: 'We shall occupy ourselves later with uniting France to Russia', and Alexander II
added: 'I should much like to gain an alliance like that of
France, an alliance of peace, and not of war and conquest.'[4]
These words, uttered on 29 September 1870, defined the Franco-

[1] Reuss to Bismarck, 7 Aug. 1870. Rheindorff, *Die Schwarz-Meer (Pontus) Frage*,
p. 78.
[2] Bismarck to Reuss, 12 Sept. 1870. Bismarck, *Gesammelte Werke*, vi *b*, no. 1793.
Eyck (*Bismarck*, ii. 525) calls this proposal 'the decisive change in Bismarck's
foreign policy'; but, of course, Bismarck had always wanted the Holy Alliance if
he could get it on his terms, i.e. no Habsburg ambitions in Germany and no
Russian ambitions in the Near East.
[3] This has always been the central problem in Franco-Russian relations, at any
rate since Sedan. A Franco-Russian alliance, being based on interest, must be
active; a Russo-German partnership, based on sentiment, can be passive. Hence
in 1939 as in 1870, the French demanded action; the Germans were content with
neutrality.
[4] F. Charles-Roux, *Alexandre II, Gortchakoff et Napoléon III*, pp. 501, 503.

Russian alliance as it was achieved twenty years later; they were of no use to Thiers in the circumstances of the moment. He returned to Paris empty-handed; and the French had to try to reverse the Prussian victories by their own efforts. In November the new armies which Gambetta had organized achieved a temporary success. It could not be sustained. Paris was besieged and could not be relieved; and in January 1871 the French had to sue for peace on the German terms.

Since the Russians had abdicated in western Europe, they sought a consolation prize. They found it in their denunciation of the neutralization of the Black Sea, resolved on 7 September, and announced to the Powers on 31 October. They could not regard the Black Sea as compensation for their exclusion from the affairs of western Europe; the action was at best a sop to their pride, freeing Russia from a humiliation. Hence the irrelevance of Bismarck's advice that they should build warships in the Black Sea and wait for others to complain.[1] The Russians wanted the other Powers to recognize their right to keep warships there, not actually to have them. They had no plans for action in the Near East, and in fact the war with Turkey in 1877 found them still without a Black Sea fleet—had it been otherwise, the war would soon have been over, with immeasurable consequences for the history of Europe. The denunciation was a symbolic gesture. The British answer was symbolic also. Gladstone had been opposed to the neutralization of the Black Sea even in 1856;[2] but he wished to assert the principle that treaties could be changed only by international agreement, and this time he got his way. Hostility to Russia, combined with a high moral tone, overcame even the most isolationist cabinet; and the British government began to beat about for support. Odo Russell, the British representative at Prussian headquarters, told Bismarck that Great Britain would go to war for the sanctity of treaties with or without allies; this was an exaggeration. What Granville, British foreign secretary, really had in mind was that, as France was now useless in the Near East, Prussia should jump at the chance of becoming England's 'natural ally' and should

[1] Busch, Bismarck: some secret pages of his History, i. 313.
[2] Gladstone had also held in 1856 that the national independence of Rumania was the most effective barrier against Russia; thus he was already on his way to the policy of supporting Balkan nationalism which he preached in 1878 and which, as 'Wilsonianism', triumphed on a larger scale in 1919, at the expense of Russia and the Habsburg monarchy as well as of Turkey.

join the Tripartite guarantee to Turkey of 15 April 1856. In his own words: 'it would rather weaken than strengthen the obligations of England, and would act as a powerful check against Russia trying to put them in force'.[1] Prussia was to join with the Power that she had just defeated and the Power with whom she was still at war in order to check her only friend in Europe; and this for the sake of the Near East where she had no concern. The pattern was being set for the following thirty years, in which Germany was repeatedly offered the privilege of defending British interests against Russia without other reward than a grudging patronage.

Bismarck did not respond to this offer. On the other hand he recognized, as those who came after him did not, that an Anglo-Russian conflict in the Near East would be dangerous to Prussia, even if she kept out of it. He was ready to act as honest broker and proposed a conference to revise the settlement of the Black Sea. This suited the British: recognition of the international principle was all that mattered to them. It also suited the Russians; they wanted theoretical revision, not a practical right, and could get it only at a conference. They neither wanted nor expected a serious crisis. As one Russian diplomatist wrote: 'One does not go to war for a declaration. Gorchakov foresaw a war of words, no more.'[2] The circular of 31 October was ostensibly withdrawn on the tacit understanding that the Powers would agree to the Russian proposal if it was put in more respectable form. The conference which met in London from January to March 1871 seemed a tawdry affair, merely saving appearances; but it had consequences of great value. Though it certainly freed Russia in the Black Sea, it extracted from her the decisive concession that international treaties could not be changed by unilateral action. For this reason, Russia was willing seven years later to submit the treaty of San Stefano to international examination at the congress of Berlin; and the peaceful outcome of the great Eastern crisis of 1878 was thus due in part to the despised London conference.

The conference had more immediate advantage for Bismarck. Both Great Britain and Russia were eager for it to succeed; they

[1] Granville to Gladstone, 10 Dec. 1870.
[2] Jomini to Brunnow, 22 May 1871. Goriainov, *Le Bosphore et les Dardanelles*, p. 161. Ignatiev at Constantinople wished to ignore the Powers and to make a direct deal with the Turks—an interesting anticipation of the policy that he advocated during the great Eastern crisis of 1875–8.

therefore agreed to his condition that France should not be allowed to raise the question of peace with Germany.[1] The French were therefore left in isolation and had to accept Bismarck's terms. An armistice was concluded on 28 January in order to permit the election of a National Assembly;[2] and the preliminary peace was signed on 26 February. This became the formal treaty of Frankfurt on 10 May. Bismarck's problem was different from what it had been with Austria in 1866. That war had been fought for a specific object—supremacy in Germany. Once Austria agreed to abandon the German Confederation and to withdraw from Germany, Bismarck had no desire either to weaken or to humiliate her. The war of 1870 was quite other. It had no specific object; it was a trial of strength between Germany and France. Though the victories of 1870 and the conditions of 1871—the cession of Alsace and Lorraine, and the indemnity of five milliard francs—certainly proved German superiority, they could not perpetuate it.[3] Great Britain and France had tried in 1856 to make the fruits of victory everlasting; the London conference was evidence of the futility of such attempt. The treaty of Frankfurt neither limited the French army nor forbade her to conclude alliances. It is often said that French resentment was kept alive by the annexation of Alsace and Lorraine. Bismarck was nearer the truth: 'French bitterness will exist in the same degree if they come out of the war without cession of territory. . . . Even our victory at Sadova roused bitterness in France; how much more will our victory over themselves.'[4] In the years to come, the French were hostile to Germany when they saw some chance of defeating her, and

[1] The German empire was constituted at Versailles on 18 Jan. 1871. Prussia disappeared, henceforth merged into Germany, or vice versa.

[2] The overthrow of Napoleon III raised the novel problem of discovering a recognized authority with whom to conclude a valid peace. Bismarck played with the idea of concluding peace with Napoleon III on the ground that he would thus be a German puppet; but Napoleon would accept this invidious position only if he received terms markedly more favourable than those offered to the provisional government, and Bismarck would not pay this price. He had therefore to insist on a national assembly in order to conclude peace with 'the ultimate sovereign', the French people—a curious position for a conservative Junker to take up.

[3] Bismarck calculated (wrongly) that the indemnity would cripple France for many years or even that the French would be unable to pay it, so that the German army would remain in occupation of French territory. This was, therefore, to some extent an attempt to bind the future.

[4] Bismarck to Bernstorff (London), 21 Aug. 1870. Bismarck, *Gesammelte Werke*, vi *b*, no. 1755.

were resigned to German superiority, if not reconciled to it, so long as they felt themselves too weak to overthrow it. If they had not lost Alsace and Lorraine their resentment would not have been less in periods of hostility; their will to reconciliation might have been greater in periods when tension was relaxed. The two lost provinces were a symbol of lost greatness; hence their recovery in 1919 did not end French hostility towards Germany, since it did not bring back the greatness which had vanished for ever at Sedan.

In 1871 neither party supposed that the treaty of Frankfurt would survive for more than forty years; until 1875, at any rate, the prospect of French recovery was the dynamic factor in European politics. The French, consolidating themselves under the leadership of Thiers, tried to break through the isolation which had been their ruin in 1870; Bismarck worked to consolidate Europe against them. The most secure combination for Germany was the union of 'the three Northern Courts', which had been weakened by the events of 1848 and destroyed by the Crimean war; once called the Holy Alliance, it was now to re-emerge as the League of the Three Emperors. The decisive change was in the policy of the Habsburg monarchy. After Sedan, Francis Joseph gave up all hope of an alliance with France and, with it, that of recovering hegemony in Germany. The way was open for reconciliation with Berlin. But on what basis? Beust, disillusioned by five years of failure, thought that the Habsburg monarchy would do very well to keep going at all and was ready for a conservative partnership of the three emperors, when he met Bismarck at Gastein in August 1871. But Beust no longer counted for much at Vienna. Francis Joseph had employed this Protestant stranger solely to prepare revenge against Prussia; now that this policy had failed, he was glad to be rid of him, and Beust was dismissed in November. Andrássy, Beust's successor, was of very different stuff: a self-confident Magyar aristocrat who was ready to make policy on a grand scale. Though he too wanted alliance with Germany, it was to be on the revolutionary programme of 1848—directed against Russia and with Great Britain as a third partner;[1] in his first

---

[1] Andrássy approached the British for an alliance in Dec. 1871, as soon as he came into office. The British government would not make 'prospective understandings to meet contingencies' which might not occur. Temperley and Penson, *Foundations of British Foreign Policy*, p. 345.

approach to Bismarck he even proposed the resurrection of Poland as a barrier against Russia. In his view, if Austria-Hungary renounced alliance with France, Germany should renounce alliance with Russia. Bismarck was not to be caught for this combination: in part because he believed that Great Britain would never make a reliable ally, more because good relations with Russia were essential to his conservative system and to German security against France. Grudgingly and with suspicion, Andrássy had to acquiesce in the friendship of the three emperors.

In September 1872 Francis Joseph, completing his recognition of the victor of 1866, visited Berlin; Alexander II, anxious to prevent an anti-Russian demonstration, proposed himself also at the last minute. It was the first time that the three emperors had come together since the abortive Warsaw meeting in 1860; they were never to meet again.[1] No written agreement was made; and the meeting was presented as a demonstration against 'the revolution'. This was window-dressing to conceal the fact that the three emperors could agree on little else. The Marxist International, against which they were supposed to be combining, was on its last legs; and it is difficult to think of a time when Europe was more remote from revolution than between 1871 and 1875. In practice, conservative solidarity meant only that Austria-Hungary would not stir up Poland and Russia would not stir up the Slavs of the Balkans.

The emperors did a little better in 1873. William I visited St. Petersburg in May; Alexander II visited Vienna in June.[2] Each visit produced a pact of a sort. At St. Petersburg, Moltke, now chief of the German general staff, concluded with the Russian Field Marshal Berg a military convention by which each Power would send 200,000 men to the aid of the other if attacked (6 May 1873). At Vienna Alexander II and Francis Joseph made a political agreement (which William I subsequently approved) promising to consult together if any question threatened to divide them (6 June 1873). Bismarck refused to endorse the military pact between Moltke and Berg; and it was never

---

[1] Alexander III met the other two emperors at Skierniwice in 1884.

[2] The round was completed by a visit of William I to Vienna in October; and of Francis Joseph to St. Petersburg in February 1874—his first act was to lay a wreath on the tomb of Nicholas I.

invoked later. In any case, against whom could it operate? The Russians had perhaps a confused notion that Germany needed protection against an attack from France; and that she would in return support them against England. The offer might have had its attraction for Prussia some time before 1848; now the Russians were a generation out of date. Besides they were not even serious in their offer. Alexander II told the French ambassador that he would join in nothing directed against France;[1] and Gorchakov repeated: 'Europe needs a *strong France*.'[2] The Russians made out that they were merely renewing the armed co-operation against the revolution which had supposedly existed in the days of Metternich and Nicholas I;[3] in reality they were hoping that this co-operation would somehow commit Germany against Austria-Hungary—another Russian dream-project which Bismarck had always resisted. There was a deep equivocation between Germany and Russia. Bismarck held that the Russians had been paid for their friendly neutrality in 1870 by the freeing of the Black Sea; the Russians regarded this as a relatively small gain, which they had obtained, in any case, by their own efforts, and still intended to call on Germany for payment at some time in the future.

That payment could be found only in action against Austria-Hungary. Suspicion between Vienna and St. Petersburg was the essential flaw in the League of the Three Emperors. Andrássy might tell Gorchakov that Austria was 'a defensive state', Hungary in particular so overloaded with rights and privileges 'that the Hungarian ship would immediately sink at the least addition, whether of gold or mud'; Gorchakov might reply that Russia advocated a policy of non-intervention in the Near East.[4] Both shrank from stirring up the Near East, both were convinced that they would quarrel if it exploded. The agreement of 6 June 1873 was evidence how far they were from a settlement. Though the Near East was not named, the first clause of the agreement expressed the pious wish that, when the two empires fell out, they might do so without damaging the sacred cause of

---

[1] Gontaut-Biron (Berlin) to Rémusat, 8 Sept. 1872. *Documents diplomatiques fran-çais (1871–1914)*, first series, i, no. 152.

[2] Gontaut-Biron to Rémusat, 14 Sept. 1872. Ibid., no. 156.

[3] Reuss to Bismarck, 10 Feb. 1873. *Große Politik der europäischen Kabinette 1871–1914*, i, no. 126.

[4] Gorchakov to Alexander II, 9 Sept. 1872. Goriainov, *La question d'Orient à la veille du traité de Berlin*, p. 44.

monarchical solidarity.[1] Thus Russia and Germany had a military convention of disputed validity and no political agreement;[2] Russia and Austria-Hungary a political agreement and no military convention. Both were unworkable in action. Russian reserves made the League useless against France; Russian and Austro-Hungarian suspicions made it useless in the Near East. Though the three emperors talked of their conservative principles, none of them would make any sacrifices for these principles. The League was supposed to keep Europe at peace; in reality it could exist only so long as Europe remained pacific. It was a fair-weather system as the Holy Alliance had been before it. A new conflict between France and Germany, a new twist of the Eastern question, would destroy it.

The first alarm came from the side of France. The French did not intend to start a new war; they sought all the same to restore their military strength and to break out of their diplomatic isolation. Thiers had already laid down the lines of French policy when he travelled across Europe in September 1870. France sought allies, no longer to remake the map of Europe but to offset the power of Germany. Yet, paradoxically enough, just when France became conservative, the alliance of the most conservative Power passed out of reach: once Austria-Hungary accepted the new order in Germany she found security in alliance with Germany, not against her. Russia and Great Britain remained. Though both welcomed French friendship and wanted a strong France, neither feared Germany: they wished to use France as an ally only in the Near East—and against each other. In 1870 France could have won Russian favour by supporting the freeing of the Black Sea; or she could have won British favour by opposing it. Neither would have been of any use to her against Prussia. The French were determined not to repeat the policy of the Crimean war; on the other hand, they had important financial interests bound up with the maintenance of the Turkish empire and therefore had to hope

[1] The text read: 'Their Majesties promise each other, even when the interests of their States lead to disputes over special questions, to negotiate so that these disputes may not overshadow the considerations of a higher order which they have at heart.'

[2] The agreement of 6 June 1873, to which Germany adhered, was concerned solely with questions between Austria-Hungary and Russia; it was irrelevant to Russo-German relations, and German adherence was no more than a pious blessing.

that England would go to the defence of Turkey, though they would not do so themselves. To win Great Britain without losing Russia; to win Russia without losing Great Britain; and not to lose Turkey to either—this was the central problem of French diplomacy, and it proved insoluble for more than a generation, as, for that matter, it had proved insoluble for Napoleon III.

There was a complicating factor. Alliance with Russia was, on the whole, favoured by the Right; alliance with Great Britain, on the whole, by the Left. Apart from the obvious motive of political taste, this reflected the different attitudes of the two groups towards the decline of France. Though the Left, inspired by Gambetta, had wanted to continue the war in 1871, they voiced thereafter the dislike of the great majority in France for new wars or adventures; hence they wanted an ally whose outlook was as pacific as their own. The Right had owed their electoral victory in February 1871 to their readiness to make peace; yet they dreamt regretfully of past greatness and imagined that the alliance with Russia would somehow bring revision without war. The difference was of emphasis, not a clear-cut choice. It is the essence of diplomacy to avoid decisive commitments until war makes them necessary; and French diplomacy of both schools tried to avoid the option between Russia and Great Britain just as much as Bismarck refused to 'opt' between them or even between Russia and Austria-Hungary. Of course, French diplomacy was more limited than it had been before 1870: they could manœuvre only between Russia and Great Britain. The Austrians would no longer opt for them and they would not opt for Germany. Even on this point there was a cleavage. The Right thought in terms of an early stroke against Germany; the Left acquiesced in the German victory. Bismarck held that a republic in France was Germany's best guarantee of peace on the Rhine. He justified this by the absurd argument that kings and emperors (meaning in particular the tsar) would shrink from alliance with a republic—as though he himself were the only monarchist statesman to disregard his principles when it suited his national interest. The real justification—divined by Bismarck's intuition, though not by his reason—was that a republic, based on the popular will, represented the people's hostility to war. But there was also a profound error in Bismarck's calculation. Though the Left, and the small people whom they represented, were more pacific than the French upper classes, they were at bottom also more resentful against the principle which Germany stood for in Europe—the principle of military power. Gambetta defined this attitude once and for all when he said: 'think of it always; speak of it never.' He meant not simply the loss of Alsace and Lorraine considered as two provinces, but much more the destruction of national unity and the denial of self-determination. Bismarck and his successors assumed that, since the French Left were pacific, they were also craven; this blunder was to prove Germany's ruin.

Thiers, as president, tried to straddle between Left and Right. A conservative republican, he was pacific, yet anxious to restore the greatness of France and perhaps underrated the difficulties of his task. In 1870 he had hoped more from St. Petersburg than from London; and after the war was over he continued to believe that the Russian alliance was 'the most probable in the future'.[1] He took British friendship as a second best, displayed as a balance against the League of the Three Emperors, not as any real support for France, and he looked sardonically at a flamboyant visit of courtesy which the British channel fleet paid to him at Le Havre in 1872 just when the emperors were meeting in Berlin. The liberal entente, once favoured by Palmerston and even by Louis Philippe (though not when Thiers was his minister), could not be revived in the old terms of hostility to the Holy Alliance. In any case, Thiers was more concerned to improve relations with Germany than to build up alliances against her. His great aim was to free French soil; this was accomplished in 1873 when the indemnity was paid off and the last German troops left on 16 September. Had Thiers still been in office a long period of 'fulfilment' would have followed. But he had been turned out, for purely domestic reasons, on 24 May and the new government of the Right, with Decazes as foreign minister, wanted to score quick successes in foreign policy in order to clear the way for a Restoration. Decazes, in fact, did everthing to justify the suspicions which Bismarck had always expressed for the French monarchists; and there was renewed, though rather artificial, tension between the two countries. What made the tension a little more real was Bismarck's home policy. By 1873 he was deep in conflict with the Roman church, and the conflict was proving more difficult than he expected.

---

[1] Thiers to Le Flô (St. Petersburg) 26 Sept. 1872. *Documents diplomatiques français*, first series, i, no. 157.

Always inclined to blame others for his own mistakes, Bismarck detected an international clericalist conspiracy, directed by France; and he snatched at any excuse for substantiating his grievance.

Decazes was quite prepared to play the part for which Bismarck had cast him. With aristocratic frivolity, he wanted to goad Bismarck into some indiscreet violence which would set Europe against Germany; and he did not trouble to speculate whether a showy diplomatic success would be worth the price that France might have to pay. 'The revolution' had proved a false ally; now France played off clericalism against the national states which she had mistakenly called into existence. Decazes and his associates thought that they were repeating the diplomacy of Richelieu after 1815 and dreamt of another congress of Aix-la-Chapelle, which should restore the equality of France in the ranks of the Great Powers. For this they needed another Metternich and imagined that one was still to be found in Vienna.[1] In January 1874 Decazes raised the alarm that Bismarck was threatening to attack France.[2] The result was not rewarding: words of sympathy from both Austria-Hungary and Russia, but no action. In their competition for German friendship, both had to profess their belief in Bismarck's moderation. The only detached state in Europe, however, responded without any French prompting: on 10 February Queen Victoria wrote to William I, urging him 'to be *magnanimous*'.[3]

This was a preliminary skirmish. In the course of 1874 the French improved their position, or so Decazes imagined. The new conservative government in England was very ready to be suspicious of Russian designs in central Asia and therefore almost as ready to suspect Germany, Russia's associate, of designs against France. Moreover, Decazes had the sense to see that French patronage of the pope was pushing Italy into the arms of Germany; and in October 1874 the French ship which had been put at the pope's service was withdrawn from Italian waters. The fatal heritage of Napoleon III was at last liquidated.

[1] In 1874 even Gambetta, the republican leader, shared this illusion in the Austrian alliance. Deschanel, *Gambetta*, p. 220.

[2] Decazes to d'Harcourt (Vienna), 22 Jan. 1874. *Documents diplomatiques français*, first series, i, no. 271.

[3] Victoria to William I, 10 Feb. 1874. *Letters of Queen Victoria*, second series, ii. 313.

The French felt themselves to be returning to the arena of European politics; and though they played with skill, every step increased their anxiety that Bismarck would answer their baiting. Their fears were not imaginary. Bismarck was undoubtedly irritated by the clericalist agitation in Germany and by the sympathy shown for it in France; he was surprised at the extent of French military recovery and even perhaps a little alarmed by it. If he could have silenced the French clericals or arrested French armaments by a few angry words, he would no doubt have done so; it is less likely that he seriously envisaged a preventive war. On the other hand, while the French wanted to exasperate Bismarck, they were certainly in no position to go to war.

The prelude to crisis sounded in February 1875 when Radowitz, one of Bismarck's confidential agents, went on special mission to St. Petersburg. He seems only to have been concerned to sort out some Balkan disputes; but the French got it into their heads that he had offered German backing in the Near East, if Russia would tolerate a new war against France.[1] Thus the French were primed for a German ultimatum. In March Bismarck forbade the export of horses from Germany—always a routine signal of alarm. In April he inspired a press-campaign with the slogan, 'Is war in sight?'[2] In all probability, he wanted to score off France in order to conceal his own mounting failure in the *Kulturkampf*. He may even have intended to follow up these threats by the offer of an entente with France, just as he had been reconciled with Austria-Hungary five years after the war of 1866; like other Germans, Bismarck regarded bullying as the best preliminary to friendship.[3] The French did not: they wished to heighten the alarm in order to stir up the other Powers. Their first appeals met with no response from London or St. Petersburg. Alexander II said only: 'If, which I do not think, you were one day in danger, you will soon learn of it . . . you will learn of it from me.'[4] On 21 April the French had a stroke of luck. Radowitz, always inclined to be indiscreet after dinner,

---

[1] Faverney to Decazes, 25 Mar. 1875. *Documents diplomatiques français*, first series, i, no. 373.

[2] It would be naïve to accept Bismarck's statement that he knew nothing of the articles until they appeared.

[3] Bülow to Hohenlohe (Paris), 30 Apr. 1875. *Große Politik*, i, no. 168. Decazes to Gontaut-Biron, 6 May 1875. *Documents diplomatiques français*, first series, i, no. 402.

[4] Le Flô to Decazes, 20 Apr. 1875. Ibid., no. 393.

was carried away in conversation with Gontaut, the French ambassador, and defended the doctrine of a preventive war.[1] Decazes sent Gontaut's account round the courts of Europe and revealed it to *The Times* as well—a trick as effective as Bismarck's revelation of Benedetti's draft-treaty over Belgium in 1870.

The British and Russians both took alarm. They expostulated with Bismarck—Derby, the foreign secretary, by normal diplomatic methods; Gorchakov by word of mouth, when he visited Berlin on 10 May. Moreover, they co-ordinated their action. Gorchakov sent formal assurance to London that the Russian expansion in central Asia, which was offending the British, would be arrested; and Odo Russell in Berlin was instructed to support the Russian pressure.[2] Derby also tried to draw in Austria-Hungary and Italy, but without effect. Andrássy was delighted at the prospect of an estrangement between Russia and Germany. He made three hand-stands on the table that had once been Metternich's (a practice of his), and exclaimed: 'Bismarck will never forgive it.'[3] The crisis blew over as suddenly as it had started. Bismarck insisted that it was a false alarm, and everyone professed himself satisfied. False or not, the 'war-in-sight' crisis first displayed the alignment of the Powers which was the consequence of Bismarck's two great wars. In the Luxembourg crisis of 1867—an affair of rather similar nature—only Austria had taken the side of France; Russia and Great Britain, though keeping ostentatiously aloof from each other, had assumed that peace was to be maintained by moderating France and by sympathizing with Germany. Napoleon III had been manœuvred into isolation; Bismarck had seemed the aggrieved party, 'protected' by Gorchakov and Stanley. In 1875 Austria-Hungary kept silent, apparently indifferent even to the destruction of France as a Great Power. Russia and Great Britain—still represented by Gorchakov and Stanley (now Lord Derby)—both warned Germany; in doing so, they acted together for the first time since the days of the Sleswick question in 1850. Apprehension of Germany had for once smoothed away the memories of the Crimean war.

[1] Gontaut-Biron to Decazes, 21 Apr. 1875. *Documents diplomatiques français*, first series, i, no. 395. Radowitz tried to explain his remarks away. Memorandum, 12 May 1875. *Große Politik*, i, no. 177.

[2] Derby to Russell, 8 May 1875. *Foundations of British Foreign Policy*, no. 137.

[3] Wertheimer, *Graf Julius Andrássy*, ii. 243.

Though this was a victory for France, it was a victory of a limited kind. The Anglo-Russian action humiliated Bismarck; but it humiliated him only by asserting the settlement of 1871, which was his work. Neither Russia nor Great Britain had the slightest interest in restoring France to the position which she held before 1870 or even in helping her to recover the lost provinces. Indeed they preferred things as they were. The British were relieved that they no longer had to worry their heads about Napoleon III's designs on Belgium; Gorchakov welcomed the position which Bismarck satirically offered him as an inscription for a medal: 'Gorchakov protects France.' If the crisis gave France some assurance against a German attack, it also gave Bismarck assurance that France would not find allies for a war of revenge. The Russians and the British wanted neither German nor French supremacy in western Europe; they wanted a Balance of Power, and Bismarck was ready to give it to them. He was even wise enough not to show resentment at their action or at any rate not to appear to do so: in reality he retained a bitter hostility to Gorchakov, which was to play its part in the next few years.

Essentially the French move, however adroit, was a blunder; Decazes had learnt nothing from either the success or the failure of Napoleon III. The diplomatic history of the Second Empire ought to have taught him that France could get freedom of action on the Rhine only when the Near East was ablaze. The Crimean war had been the origin of all Napoleon's success; and he ran into failure when he refused to support Russia's schemes of revision in the Near East. If Decazes had been more patient, events would have done his work for him. The Near East exploded in July 1875, only two months after the war-in-sight crisis. In May Russia and Great Britain had dropped their Asiatic rivalries in order to protect France. The crisis had convinced them that France was secure; and they could fling themselves into the Eastern question without giving France any chance of revising the settlement of 1871.

XI

THE GREAT EASTERN CRISIS

1875–8

IN July 1875 the Slav peasants of Hercegovina revolted against
Turkish rule; those of Bosnia soon followed. This opened the
great Eastern crisis which everyone had been expecting since
the end of the Crimean war. That war had been strictly a conflict between the Great Powers; the subject peoples, Slav, Greek,
or Rumanian, counted for nothing in it. When the Greeks tried
to take advantage of the war, they were brought to order by
an Anglo-French occupation; and Rumania emerged as an
afterthought, created by the rivalry of the Powers, and not for
the good of the Rumanians.[1] In 1875 the interests of the Powers
were still in conflict. The Russians still felt humiliated by the
closure of the Straits; yet, without a Black Sea fleet, would be
in a worse position if the Straits were opened. The Austrians
still depended on free navigation of the Danube as their main
economic link with the rest of the world.[2] The British still
needed the Ottoman empire as a great neutral buffer to secure
the eastern Mediterranean and the Near East—needed it more
than ever since the opening of the Suez canal in 1869. The
French were still the principal financiers of Turkey, with the
British in the second place.[3] None of them wished to raise the
Eastern question. They would all have agreed with Gorchakov
when he said to Odo Russell: 'There were two ways of dealing
with the Eastern question. 1st a complete reconstruction or 2nd
a mere replastering which would keep matters together for
another term of years. No one could possibly wish for a com-

---

[1] A judgement slightly unfair to Napoleon III. He had genuine interest in
liberating a nationality, particularly of Latin stock; and the Rumanians repaid
him by making Bucarest the Paris of eastern Europe.

[2] Trieste, and the railway to it, gave Austria-Hungary direct access to the
Mediterranean; but it never carried as much traffic as the Danube.

[3] The French held 40 per cent. of Turkish bonds, the British 30 per cent. The
Austro-Hungarian holding was negligible, the Russian non-existent.

plete settlement—everyone must wish to put it off as long as possible.'[1] Germany alone of the Powers favoured 'a complete settlement', and that for a paradoxical reason. Since Germany had no interest in the Near East, Bismarck dreaded being drawn into a conflict from which he could gain nothing and therefore dreamt of some impossible partition which would settle the question once and for all.

These negations were eclipsed when another party entered upon the scene. The Balkan Slavs alone launched the crisis of 1875; and pacific declarations by the Great Powers could not obliterate their determination to endure Turkish rule no longer. The Holy Places had merely provided the occasion for the Crimean war; the Bulgarian horrors were the core of the Eastern crisis twenty years later. The great issues of strategy and power remained; the new issue of national struggle cut across them, at once a new incentive and a new danger. Once the Balkan Slavs were astir, the Russian government dared not let them fail; Austria-Hungary dared not let them succeed. This is a long-term generalization which needed forty years to come into full effect; but it was already strong enough to shape the Eastern crisis of 1875 to 1878. Russian policy was deeply affected by Panslavism which had swept Russian thought in the previous twenty years. This mixture of western nationalism and Orthodox mysticism varied in practice from vague Slav sympathy to grandiose plans for a united Slav empire under tsarist rule; the sentiment, not the programme, was the important thing about it. Though the tsars were despots, they were always sensitive to the limited public opinion within their empire. Constitutional governments can weather unpopularity; autocrats dread it, and this is peculiarly so when they feel at their back the sanction of political assassination.[2] Even Nicholas I had been driven on by Russian opinion at the time of the Crimean war; Alexander II, himself a weaker man, was in no position to stand out against Panslav sentiment. Some of his advisers, and in particular Ignatiev, ambassador at Constantinople, were themselves inclined to Panslavism and eager at any rate to exploit it; a few at the other extreme, such as

---

[1] Russell to Derby, 1 Dec. 1875. Harris, *A Diplomatic History of the Balkan Crisis of 1875–1878: the First Year*, p. 165.

[2] Alexander II's grandfather, Paul, was murdered in 1800; he himself assassinated in 1881; his grandson overthrown by revolution in 1917 and then killed. Only Nicholas I and Alexander III died indisputably in their beds.

Shuvalov, ambassador at London, would have ignored it altogether and held on a strictly conservative course. Gorchakov stood in between and determined the oscillations of Russian policy: though he did not promote Panslavism, he knew its force and, when he gave way to it, hoped to turn it to practical advantage.

There were cross-currents, too, in Austria-Hungary. Metternich had believed half a century before that the Turkish empire was essential to Habsburg security; and Gentz, his political adviser, wrote as early as 1815: 'The end of the Turkish monarchy could be survived by the Austrian for but a short time.' Andrássy held the same view; in his case Habsburg fear of national states was reinforced by Magyar determination to be the only free nation in the Danube valley. He defined his outlook at a Crown council on 29 January 1875, before the revolts broke out:

Turkey possesses a utility almost providential for Austria-Hungary. For Turkey maintains the status quo of the small Balkan states and impedes their [nationalistic] aspirations. If it were not for Turkey, all these aspirations would fall down on our heads . . . if Bosnia-Hercegovina should go to Serbia or Montenegro, or if a new state should be formed there which we cannot prevent, then we should be ruined and should ourselves assume the role of the 'Sick Man'.[1]

This fear of national states was reinforced by an economic consideration. The German capitalists of Vienna were projecting railways in the Balkans; and these plans assumed a peninsula under a single authority, not its partition. On the other hand, the military men, who carried weight with Francis Joseph, still belonged mentally to an age in which neither nationalities nor railways counted for anything. They welcomed any chance of acquiring new territory to make up for the Italian lands that had been lost and did not concern themselves with problems of nationality.[2] Many of them would have partitioned the Balkans with Russia; some of them would even have given her a free hand in the Balkans in exchange for alliance against Germany —Archduke Albrecht, their leader, told the tsar that he would not die happy unless he could once beat the Prussians in the

---

[1] G. H. Rupp, *A Wavering Friendship: Russia and Austria 1876–1878*, p. 39.
[2] The Slav question seemed particularly unimportant to those general officers, always a large number in the Habsburg army, who were themselves Croats.

field.[1] The Austrian soldiers had set their minds on Bosnia and Hercegovina as early as 1867; and Beust, ignoring the national issue, did not discourage them. Andrássy, however, intended to preserve the integrity of the Ottoman empire; only if he failed would he take the two provinces, and this not as a signal for partition, but to deny them to the existing Slav states, Serbia and Montenegro. Though Andrássy was not supreme at Vienna, he usually got his way against the soldiers. Public opinion, so far as it existed, was German and Magyar, and therefore supported him; and Francis Joseph had learnt by failure to prefer the cautious line. There were fewer oscillations at Vienna than at St. Petersburg; but they were there. The military were strong enough to prevent Andrássy's taking a consistent line of opposition to Russia; the reverse of the situation in St. Petersburg, where Gorchakov had to hold back the Panslav military from breaking with Austria-Hungary.

The new national emphasis in the Eastern question transformed the structure of international relations. So long as the Eastern question turned principally on the Straits, Great Britain and France were pushed into the front rank against Russia; and, with the mouth of the Danube reasonably secure, Austria could remain neutral, as she had done during the Crimean war. The national issue thrust Austria-Hungary forward and left her no escape. Great Britain and France gradually lost interest in the Straits—not completely, but enough to let them be dwarfed by other issues. In 1878 the British still had priority in resistance to Russia; thereafter they began to retreat, and within twenty years, Austria-Hungary remained alone. This in turn imposed the Eastern question upon Germany. In 1854 the problem for Prussian diplomacy was to prevent Austria going to the aid of Great Britain and France; in 1876 and the following years it was to ensure that Great Britain should go to the aid of Austria-Hungary; by the first decade of the twentieth century it was solely a question of time when Germany would have to go to the aid of Austria-Hungary herself. This revolution in international affairs was the work of the Balkan Slavs; though Bismarck dismissed them as 'the sheep-stealers', in the long run they imposed policy upon him and his successors.

The Southern Slav movement was a true national revival, a

[1] Rupp, *A Wavering Friendship*, p. 91.

translation into Balkan terms of the spirit which had brought
Italy and Germany into being. It could no more be 'made' by
Panslav agitators than Italian nationalism could be 'made' by
Cavour or German nationalism by Bismarck. Statesmen exploit
popular emotion; they do not create it. Some Russian diplomats,
headed by Ignatiev, certainly encouraged this Slav movement.
The ministry in St. Petersburg was unable to control them; and
this helplessness made other governments doubt Russian good
faith. The revolt in Hercegovina was, however, touched off by
Austria-Hungary, the Power that had most to lose from Balkan
disturbance. In May 1875 Francis Joseph, prompted by his
military advisers, made a prolonged tour of Dalmatia and acted
ostentatiously as protector of Turkey's western Slavs. When the
revolt broke out, Andrássy reasserted himself and imposed a
policy of abstention on the Austrian authorities in Dalmatia.
More, he set himself to damp down the revolt—the replastering
which Gorchakov favoured. He first proposed that Austria-
Hungary, Germany, and Russia should instruct their consuls to
try to settle the revolt on the spot. This was turning the League
of the Three Emperors to good use: the Russian would be
pinioned to a safe conservative course with a German on one
side of him and an Austrian on the other. The scheme was
destroyed by French expostulations at St. Petersburg. Decazes
wished to assert the prestige of France as a Great Power. The
Russians, on their side, wanted to be free to play off the French
against Germany; besides, they feared that, if they rebuffed
Decazes, he would turn to England and recreate the alliance of
the Crimean war. On 14 August therefore the French were
invited to join the consular mission. This involved inviting also
the two remaining Great Powers, Great Britain and Italy. The
Italians were even more eager than the French to be treated
as a Great Power; they would tail along with anyone who would
recognize them as such.

The British attitude was a different matter. Derby was the
most isolationist foreign secretary that Great Britain has known.
He hated action. Besides, 'one can trust none of these Governments'.[1] Disraeli, the prime minister, wanted to pull off some
great stroke of policy, though he did not know what. He prided
himself on his knowledge of the Near East, based on a visit to
Palestine forty years before. Like Metternich, whom he once

[1] Derby to Lyons (Paris), 7 Jan. 1876. Newton, *Lord Lyons*, ii. 95.

acknowledged as his master, he hoped that the Balkan troubles would 'burn themselves out beyond the pale of civilization'; and he dismissed all stories of Turkish misrule and atrocities as 'coffee-house babble'. Any attempt to improve the condition of the Balkan Slavs made him fear the example nearer home; he complained in October, 'autonomy for Ireland would be less absurd'.[1] Yet, though ostensibly a pupil of Metternich's, his only practical aim was somehow to disrupt the League of the Three Emperors, which he regarded as an affront to British prestige. The British government would have preferred to reject the Russian invitation. They joined the mission of the consuls, only on Turkish prompting; and their sole object was to protect Turkish interests.[2] Already, by August 1875, the League of the Three Emperors had been watered down; but the Concert of Europe was not taking its place.

The mission of the consuls was a failure. Their mediation was rejected; the revolt continued. Ignatiev at Constantinople tried to revolt also—against his own government. He advocated a European mediation, led by himself, to wrest autonomy for the provinces in revolt from the Turks; this would be a preliminary to independent national states. Alternatively, he proposed offering the Turks a Russian alliance on the model of the treaty of Unkiar Skelessi in 1833. Russia would keep the Ottoman empire in being as a buffer state until prepared to eat up the whole. Alexander II and Gorchakov rejected all these projects. Though they expected the break-up of Turkey, they were determined to avoid the isolation of the Crimean war and therefore clung to the friendship of Austria-Hungary. Andrássy had another chance to lead Europe, if he had any idea where to go. The result was the Andrássy Note of 30 December 1875, a programme of reforms which the Powers were to recommend to Turkey. The pattern of the previous August was repeated. Andrássy wished to limit action to the Three Emperors; the tsar insisted on bringing in France; and the British came in to see that Turkey came to no harm. Nor did she come to good. Though the Turks accepted the Andrássy Note when it was put up to them at the end of January, they did not apply its pro-

---

[1] Disraeli to Lady Bradford, 1 Oct. 1875. Buckle, *Life of Disraeli*, vi. 13.

[2] Derby to Eliot (Constantinople), 24 Aug. 1875. Harris, *The First Year*, p. 88. 'Her Majesty's Government consent to this step with reluctance. . . . Since however the Porte has begged Your Excellency not to stand aloof, Her Majesty's Government feel that they have no alternative.'

posals; and the rebels ignored the talk of reforms which were in any case inadequate.

Nevertheless, the decay of the League of the Three Emperors pushed Bismarck forward. He had been content to make a benevolent third so long as Russia and Austria-Hungary were working together; the tsar's insistence on France alarmed him. On 2 January 1876 he told Odo Russell that Great Britain and Germany should co-operate in the Near East and threw out the idea of a partition, with Egypt as the British share.[1] On 5 January he aired the same ideas to Oubril, the Russian ambassador.[2] Gorchakov sheered off at once: it reminded him of the great tempter on the mountain, to say nothing of Bismarck and Napoleon III at Biarritz. The British took longer to formulate their negative; but in the end Derby, as usual, found decisive reasons against any sort of action. Bismarck's step has been treated by some as an effort at partition on a grand scale. This overlooks its origin and motive. It was a precautionary measure against Franco-Russian friendship. One of the few indisputable truths about the Eastern question is that the Ottoman empire could not be partitioned to the satisfaction of all the Great Powers involved. It was plausible (though in fact mistaken) to suppose that Great Britain would be content with Egypt, especially after the British purchase of Suez canal shares in November 1875;[3] it was inconceivable that France would be content with Syria or that, even if she were, Great Britain would allow her to take it. If Bismarck brought Russia and Great Britain together, France would be estranged from Russia; alternatively, if the Russians stuck to France, the British would be forced to side with Austria-Hungary. Either alternative would lessen the pressure on Germany; it was this, not the settlement of the Eastern question, which dominated Bismarck's mind.

[1] Russell to Derby, 2 Jan. 1876, in Harris, 'Bismarck's Advance to England, 1876' (*Journal of Modern History*, vol. iii); Bülow to Munster, 4 Jan. 1876. *Große Politik*, i, no. 227.

[2] Oubril to Gorchakov, 5 Jan. 1876. Goriainov, *Le Bosphore et les Dardanelles*, p. 314.

[3] This, Disraeli's first great stroke, should not be exaggerated. It gave the British government some say (not much, since it did not control a majority of the shares) in the *financial* conduct of the canal, e.g. freight-rates, maintenance, &c.; it did not bring *political* or *strategical* control which remained with the Egyptian government. It was important for the future only in that it led British public opinion to tolerate for the sake of its investment an intervention which it would have rejected if made on grounds of high policy.

The British had some inkling that the longer they delayed committing themselves the more others would be forced to accept responsibilities; this was a partial justification of Derby's negatives. The Russians, on the other hand, exaggerated the hold that they had over Bismarck. In April 1876 Gorchakov still believed that, in case of a quarrel with Austria-Hungary, 'we shall have a German army at our disposal'.[1] Hence he let things drift, waiting for the failure of the Andrássy Note, and then, *alors comme alors*: either Austria-Hungary would continue to work with Russia, or a Russo-German alliance would bring her to heel. These expectations were not borne out when Gorchakov, Bismarck, and Andrássy met in Berlin on 11 May for another attempt at settling the Eastern turmoil. Gorchakov produced a scheme for an intervention of the six Great Powers at Constantinople in order to impose reforms; at the back of his mind he expected autonomous states to be the outcome. Bismarck, who had vainly tried to win Andrássy for a partition, would support only what had been agreed by his two allies, and once more Gorchakov gave way. Andrássy drafted a new project of reforms; and Gorchakov added only a 'tail' that, if these failed, there would have to be 'the sanction of an understanding with a view to effective measures'. This memorandum was passed on to the representatives of the other three Powers—Italy, France, and Great Britain—with an invitation to adhere to it on 13 May.

This time the pattern changed decisively. Italy and France accepted the Berlin memorandum as they had previously accepted the Andrássy Note. The British government turned it down out of hand. Disraeli said to Shuvalov: 'England has been treated as though we were Montenegro or Bosnia'[2]—the offence was all the greater in that the message from Berlin broke into the calm of the British ministers' week-end. The British resented the 'insolent dictation' of the three emperors and suspected quite wrongly that their League was a combine under Russian direction for the 'disintegration of Turkey'. Disraeli suggested a conference 'based upon the territorial *status quo*'.[3] The cabinet merely endorsed his various negations. The real British answer to the Berlin memorandum was to send the fleet to Besika Bay

[1] Gorchakov to Oubril, 1 Apr. 1876. Goriainov, *La question d'Orient*, p. 68.
[2] Shuvalov (London) to Gorchakov, 19 May 1876. *Slavonic Review*, iii. 666.
[3] Memorandum by Disraeli, 16 May 1876. Buckle, *Disraeli*, vi. 24–26.

just outside the Dardanelles—the move that had ushered in the Crimean war. Disraeli was delighted with his work. The League of the Three Emperors, he thought, was 'virtually extinct, as extinct as the Roman triumvirate'.[1] A week or two later he grew more anxious. At any rate he approached Shuvalov and suggested that Great Britain and Russia should settle the Eastern question together, to the exclusion of Austria-Hungary. Discussions for a common programme ran on throughout June; in the end it turned out that Disraeli wanted the Russians to drop their sympathy for the Balkan Slavs and to allow the Turks to crush the rebellion without interference. Probably he had no further purpose than to complete the severance between Russia and Austria-Hungary which he thought that he had begun by rejecting the Berlin memorandum.

The Russian government was still anxious to keep on good terms with the other European Powers: hence their response even to Disraeli's meagre offer. At the beginning of June Gorchakov tried to persuade the French to send their fleet to Turkish waters; his object, no doubt, was to play the French off against the British.[2] But Decazes would not be moved from the line that Bismarck adopted in similar circumstances: he would co-operate in the Near East only when Russia and Great Britain were in agreement.[3] This was the only serious Russian attempt to secure an entente with France during the three years of crisis; and it came to nothing—under the shadow of Germany, France would not take sides between the two Powers who protected her. Gorchakov was thus forced back on to agreement with Austria-Hungary, if he were to escape isolation. The situation in Turkey was getting worse. On 29 May the sultan was forced to abdicate; in the provinces the revolt spread to Bulgaria; both Montenegro and Serbia declared war on Turkey at the end of June. The dissolution of the Ottoman empire seemed to be at hand. It was in these circumstances that Gorchakov and Andrássy met at Zakupy on 8 July.[4] The two of them agreed, or so they thought, on the principle of non-intervention, at any rate for the time being. If Turkey won, she was not to be

---

[1] Disraeli to Victoria, 7 June 1876. *Letters of Queen Victoria*, second series, ii. 457.

[2] Gontaut-Biron (at Ems) to Decazes, 2 June 1876. *Documents diplomatiques français*, first series, ii, no. 59.

[3] Decazes to Gontaut-Biron, 5 June, 9 June 1876. Ibid., nos. 61, 65.

[4] German name: Reichstadt.

allowed to benefit from her victory; if she were defeated, Russia would recover the part of Bessarabia which had been taken from her in 1856 and Austria-Hungary would acquire some or all of Bosnia;[1] finally, if the Ottoman empire collapsed, Constantinople was to become a free city, and Bulgaria, Rumelia, and perhaps Albania, would become autonomous or independent. There was nothing new in this programme. Gorchakov was still obsessed with the 'humiliation' of 1856—hence the demand for Bessarabia; in return for this he had always been willing to let Austria-Hungary have a slice of Bosnia. The Reichstadt agreement was not the prelude to a Panslav policy, it did not even try to apply the policy of partition which Bismarck recommended. It was rather an effort to carry out the Austro-Russian promise made in June 1873—that if differences arose, they would settle them amicably. By its means Andrássy and Gorchakov still hoped to turn their backs on the Eastern question, not to involve themselves in it. The agreement was, in fact, the last splutter of the Austro-Russian entente, and not the prelude to the Russo-Turkish war.

This was its fatal flaw: it did not allow Russia to participate in the Balkan conflicts or to go to war against Turkey. Hitherto the Russians had put the European Powers first; and the Balkans second. In the autumn of 1876 this was reversed. Alexander II decided that he could no longer endure the 'humiliation' of Turkish misrule over Slav Christians. Many factors contributed to this fundamental change. A practical factor: Serbia and Montenegro had been defeated, and the Turkish victory had to be arrested. A personal factor: Alexander was in the Crimea, surrounded by Panslav advisers and relatives and far away from the European atmosphere of St. Petersburg.[2] There was jealousy of the proud independence with which Great Britain had rejected the Berlin memorandum and desire to take a similar independent line. There was the calculation, which proved correct, that the atrocities in Bulgaria with

---

[1] No agreed record was made of the Reichstadt discussions. The Russians thought that they had conceded to Austria-Hungary only a part of Bosnia; Andrássy was later to claim all Bosnia, and Hercegovina as well. Gorchakov was always vague on geographical detail, and Andrássy probably spoke loosely of Bosnia, without any precise idea of what he wanted. After all, the important thing at Reichstadt was the Austro-Russian agreement, not the territorial hypotheses which were thrown in to sweeten it.

[2] In the same way, Napoleon III was at his most fantastic at Biarritz, when remote from the restraining influences of Paris.

which the Turks had accomplished their victory would make it impossible for the British to go to the aid of Turkey. Most of all, there was the uncanny sensitivity to the swell of Russian feeling which her despotic rulers have often shown. The change was announced to all the world on 11 November, when Alexander II, against all precedent, made a public speech at Moscow on his way back to St. Petersburg and concluded with the words: 'May God help us to fulfil our sacred mission.'

Gorchakov and the official diplomats now had a new task. Previously they had devised excuses for avoiding the Eastern question; now they had to arrange things so that Russia could intervene in the Balkans without having all Europe against her. The Russians would have had an easy time of it if they could have counted on unconditional German support; and Alexander's first step, after making his great decision, was to demand that Germany should repay the backing that she had received in 1866 and 1870. Germany should keep Austria-Hungary neutral by threat of war, while Russia got her way against the Turks. Bismarck refused to take sides. He wanted Russia to have her way in the Near East,[1] but this must be in agreement with Austria-Hungary, not by means of war against her, especially not by a war which would destroy the Habsburg monarchy. 'We could certainly tolerate our friends losing or winning battles against each other, but not that one of them should be so severely wounded and injured that its position as an independent Great Power, with a voice in Europe, should be endangered.'[2] Later on, Bismarck built up the story that he would

---

[1] Bismarck always maintained that Germany had everything to gain from a partition of the Ottoman empire among the other Great Powers. Obviously partition was better than a war in which Germany might be involved without possibility of gain. But did Bismarck really believe that partition made for lasting peace between the partitioning Powers? It is impossible to say. The partition of Poland perhaps drew Russia, Prussia, and Austria together, though not always. Other examples—such as the partition of Persia between Russia and Great Britain in 1907; of the Levant between Great Britain and France after 1919; or of Poland and the Near East between Russia and Germany in 1939—are less encouraging. It is not an unreasonable generalization that the Anglo-Saxons and perhaps the French believe in buffer states and the Germans and perhaps the Russians believe in partition as the best way to peace between the Great Powers.

[2] Bismarck, *Gedanken und Erinnerungen*, ii. 214. His contemporary formulation was rather less elegant, but more precise: 'It cannot correspond to our interests to see the position of Russia seriously and permanently injured by a coalition of the rest of Europe, if fortune is unfavourable to the Russian arms; but it would affect the interests of Germany just as deeply, if the Austrian monarchy was so endangered in its position as European power or in its independence, that one of the factors

have gone with Russia 'through thick and thin', if he could have had in exchange a Russian guarantee of Alsace and Lorraine. This was no more than an adroit excuse, and one which Bismarck was fond of making—he used the same device against the British in January 1877,[1] and on many later occasions. Even if some impossible way could have been found to bind the future and Bismarck had been assured that Russia would never again support France, he would still have opposed the dismemberment of Austria-Hungary. The Habsburg monarchy was essential to the limited Germany which Bismarck had created; and this in its turn was essential to the Balance of Power, in which Bismarck believed as the only means of preserving the peace of Europe. The Balance of Power determined everything for Bismarck; and he sacrificed to it even German national ambitions —how much more then the ambitions of others. Bismarck's answer to the tsar in October 1876 was not, however, an 'option' for Austria-Hungary—he gave a similar answer in reverse to Münch, a special emissary from Andrássy, at exactly the same time. Bismarck certainly thought Austria-Hungary the weaker of the two and therefore put his weight more on her side. Nevertheless, balance between them, not the victory of either, was always his object, as for that matter he had fought the two wars of 1866 and 1870 in order to restore a balance in Europe. Bismarck was a great 'projector' outside Europe, especially in the Near East; but he had learnt from the failure of Napoleon III not to make projects which disturbed the balance between the Great Powers in Europe. This is the reason why Europe had a generation of peace once Bismarck established his ascendancy.

Failing German support, the Russians tried half-heartedly for support from France. They were again disappointed. Even the great France of Napoleon III had refused to opt between Russia and Great Britain once the Crimean war was over; how much more a defeated France, which needed the patronage of both Powers against Germany. It was fortunate for the French that the Eastern crisis came when it did: soon enough after the war of 1870 for them to plead weakness, yet after the 'war-in-sight' affair had given them security. The French were able to sham

with which we have to reckon in the European balance of Power, threatened to fall out for the future.' Bülow to Schweinitz, 23 Oct. 1876. *Große Politik*, ii, no. 251.
[1] He allegedly offered to support Great Britain against Russia, in exchange for an Anglo-German alliance against France. The news reached both the Russians and the French; and perhaps was meant to.

dead and yet be treated with respect in the hope that they were coming to life. The Eastern crisis was sheer gain to France for the future. It was bound to disrupt the League of the Three Emperors, perhaps even to estrange Russia from Germany; yet there was no danger of estranging Russia from France. The principle of 'the dog in the night', observed by Sherlock Holmes, applies also in the relations of the Great Powers. The French did nothing between 1875 and 1878; and did it very well.

Though Alexander II was determined on war with Turkey, he was equally determined not to repeat the mistake of the Crimean war—determined, that is, not to fight Turkey with all Europe against him. Two resources therefore remained for Russian diplomacy: to revive the Concert of the Great Powers or to strike an isolated bargain with Austria-Hungary. Gorchakov did not altogether fail in the first task; he succeeded in the second. In November 1876 Derby proposed a European conference at Constantinople to impose reforms on the Turks. This proposal was made against Beaconsfield's wish;[1] he acquiesced in it only when he had failed to get an alliance with Austria-Hungary against Russia. Salisbury, the British delegate to the conference, was far removed from Beaconsfield's line; he believed that the break-up of Turkey was both imminent and desirable, and he worked closely with Ignatiev when he got to Constantinople. As a result, the conference agreed on sweeping reforms, the principal of which was to be an autonomous 'Bulgaria',[2] divided into two parts by a north–south (vertical) line. The Turks at once rejected these reforms, by the simple device of proclaiming an imperial constitution and then insisting that all changes must be referred to a constituent assembly which never met. They counted undoubtedly on British

---

[1] Disraeli became Lord Beaconsfield in July 1876.

[2] Ironically enough, 'Bulgaria' was an invention of the Turks, and one of their most successful. Until 1870 the Slav inhabitants of European Turkey were under the religious and, so far as the Porte was concerned, the political direction of the Greek Patriarch of Constantinople. On the other hand, incipient nationalist teaching regarded all the Balkan Slavs—Bulgarians, Serbs, Macedonians, Bosnians, Croats, Slovenes—as members of a single South Slav nation, differing only in dialect and provincial assignment. In 1870 the Turks created an Exarch, as independent head of the Bulgarian church. Though this was primarily designed to divide the Bulgarians from the Greeks, it also split them from the Serbs and thus inaugurated the disunity between the South Slavs which has persisted from that day to this. Yet on the basis of religion and political background, Bulgarians and Serbs were far more akin than Serbs, Croats, and Slovenes, between whom union has been successfully accomplished.

support, assuming that, as in 1853, the British would put up with any Turkish obstinacy for the sake of Constantinople. But Beaconsfield was tied down by Gladstone's campaign against the Bulgarian atrocities and by the divisions in his cabinet; Salisbury, especially, had cheated him of his war by supporting Ignatiev at Constantinople. In March 1877 Ignatiev toured Europe to get renewed backing for a reform programme; and the British government acquiesced in his proposals (the London protocol), though it refused to agree to their being imposed on the Turks. Even so, the Russians had got what they wanted. Though they had not secured a mandate from Europe to act against the Turks, they had made it certain that a European mandate would not be exercised against them. Not even Beaconsfield could condemn the Russians for going to war in order to execute a programme which the British government had helped to draft.

The negotiations with Austria-Hungary were still more decisive. In 1854 the Russians had been compelled to withdraw from the Danubian principalities by threat of an Austrian intervention; now they wished to pass through this same Rumanian bottleneck in order to fight a war in the Balkans and were more dependent than ever on Austro-Hungarian favour, since they had no fleet in the Black Sea. Andrássy drove a hard bargain. Austria-Hungary was in no condition to fight Russia, as a British observer had just discovered;[1] the Austrian generals wished to fight with Russia against Turkey, so far as they wished to fight at all; and Andrássy was determined to avoid a war which might restore Habsburg prestige and so endanger the privileges of Hungary in the Dual monarchy. All this was ignored by the Russians in their anxiety to secure Austro-Hungarian neutrality. Andrássy insisted on acquiring the whole of Bosnia and Hercegovina, according to his own questionable version of the Reichstadt agreement; Serbia and Montenegro were to form a neutral buffer between the Russian and Austro-Hungarian armies; there was to be 'no great compact state Slav or other' if Turkey fell to pieces.[2] In return Austria-

[1] In October 1876 Major Gonne reported that Austria-Hungary could only fight a defensive war against Russia and could render 'little or no help to an ally in want of battalions'. In November Archduke Albrecht and Beck, chief-of-staff, declared: 'A war against Russia dare not be taken on one's shoulders or even desired.' Rupp, *A Wavering Friendship*, p. 234.

[2] It is not clear that this excluded a great Bulgaria, such as was made by the

Hungary would observe benevolent neutrality in a Russo-Turkish war and would not respond to appeals to operate the Triple guarantee of 15 April 1856. Such were the Budapest conventions.[1] The Reichstadt agreement was developed in a form unfavourable to Russia; and the Russians had to accept as the outcome of their own victory in war a programme which had been devised in the previous July as the outcome of a natural dissolution of the Turkish empire.

All the same, the Russians could regard the Budapest conventions as a success. It is true that they abandoned the Serbs to Habsburg patronage; they did this without a qualm. They had long regarded the Serbs as half-westernized, a people trying to emancipate themselves without Russian support; and their dislike had been heightened by the Serb failure against Turkey in the previous year. Alexander II had even commented on this failure during his sensational speech of 11 November. It is also true that the Russians were pledged not to set up a great Slav state in the Balkans; but this was according to their own wish—or at any rate according to the wish of those Russian diplomats who were not Panslav enthusiasts. In any case, there was no knowing what the future of the Balkans would be once the Russians had destroyed the Turkish armies and had reached Constantinople. The Budapest conventions made this possible. The Crimean coalition was irrevocably dissolved; the Russians could be certain of the neutrality of Austria-Hungary, though not of her support. Gorchakov had managed things as well as Napoleon III in 1859 or Bismarck in 1866. The Russians were free to destroy the Turkish empire without interference if they were strong enough to do so and did it quickly.

The Russians declared war on Turkey on 24 April. They were confident of victory, though in fact the Turks were better armed and had control of the Black Sea. The British, too, expected the Russians to win; they therefore tried to limit the effects of Russian victory, and they were seconded by Shuvalov, who cared nothing for the Panslav programme. He and Gorchakov extracted from Alexander II proposals for 'a little peace'; the principal concession was that Bulgaria should be

treaty of San Stefano. At this time neither Russia nor Austria-Hungary had defined views about the future of Bulgaria.

[1] The military convention was signed at Budapest on 15 Jan. 1877; the political convention, on which this depended, was signed only on 17 Mar. but was antedated to 15 Jan.

autonomous only north of the Balkan mountains. In return, Great Britain was to remain neutral and to promise not to occupy Constantinople and the Straits.[1] This offer was unattractive to the British, especially as Alexander refused to bind himself against a temporary military occupation of Constantinople on his side. In any case, it was almost immediately withdrawn. At the beginning of June Alexander went to headquarters in Rumania and was at once persuaded by Grand Duke Nicholas, the commander-in-chief, to abandon 'the little peace'. Nicholas stormed against Gorchakov: 'Horrible fellow! horrible fellow! Pigwash! Pigwash!' On 14 June Shuvalov was instructed to cancel the offer to limit Bulgaria. The British government answered by sending the fleet once more to Besika bay;[2] and on 17 July Derby warned the Russians that they could not count on British neutrality if there was an occupation of Constantinople 'even though temporary in duration and dictated by military requirements'.[3]

While Derby had been trying half-heartedly for agreement with Russia, Beaconsfield had been pursuing more energetically an anti-Russian alliance with Austria-Hungary; he was equally unsuccessful. He supposed that Austria-Hungary was only waiting for an adequate subsidy, as in the old days, and asked on 1 May: 'How much money do you want?'[4] Money was the least of Andrássy's problems. He was pledged to benevolent neutrality so long as the Russians observed the Budapest conventions; yet needed to keep the door open for co-operation with the British in case they did not.[5] He had great doubts whether the British meant to fight Russia and was certainly not going to do their fighting for them. Hence he was ready to agree with Beaconsfield on the limits which Great Britain and Austria-Hungary should impose on Russia; but he would not promise to impose them. Negotiations ran on in this vein until August. Then the two Powers merely informed each other what they

[1] Gorchakov to Shuvalov, 30 May 1877. *Slavonic Review*, vi, no. 228.
[2] It had been withdrawn, as usual, during the autumn storms.
[3] Derby to Shuvalov, 17 July 1877. Temperley and Penson, *Foundations of British Foreign Policy*, no. 140.
[4] Montgelas to Beust, 1 May 1877. Stojanovic, *The Great Powers and the Balkans*, p. 165.
[5] He said at the time of negotiating the conventions: 'If the Russians do not keep the treaty, Russia will stand with its weakened army in the Balkans where we can cut them off from their base while England with her fleet will order them to stop at Constantinople.' Wertheimer, *Andrássy*, ii. 394.

would object to in the Near East; there was no suggestion how these objections were to be enforced. Beaconsfield was not pleased with this 'moral understanding'.[1] He would have been even less pleased, had he known that Francis Joseph had just written to Alexander II: 'Whatever happens and whatever turn the war may take—nothing can induce me to recede from my given word. England has been informed in a decisive manner that she cannot count, in any event, on an alliance with Austria.'[2]

Great Britain would therefore have to act alone if she acted at all. Beaconsfield tried repeatedly to commit the cabinet to supporting Turkey or, at any rate, to imposing 'the little peace' which Alexander had rejected in June; he was always overruled. The British cabinet was torn by dissensions, but it clung to a basic principle of British policy: Great Britain could not act effectively against a great land Power without a continental ally. There was another reason for British hesitation: the Turks did much better than expected. In June it looked as though the Russians would conquer the whole of Turkey-in-Europe within a month; then they ran against the hitherto unknown fortress of Plevna, barring their road south, and failed to take it until 11 December. Most battles confirm the way that things are going already; Plevna is one of the few engagements which changed the course of history. It is difficult to see how the Ottoman empire could have survived in Europe, in however reduced a form, if the Russians had reached Constantinople in July; probably it would have collapsed in Asia as well. Plevna not merely gave the Ottoman empire another forty years of life. In the second half of the twentieth century the Turks still control the Straits, and Russia is still 'imprisoned' in the Black Sea; this was all the doing of Osman Pasha, defender of Plevna.

The four months outside Plevna had both political and military consequences. In England they obliterated the Bulgarian horrors and transformed the Turks into heroes, gallantly resisting a Great Power; the war-fever which swept Great Britain in February 1878 would not have been possible in July 1877. Moreover, though the Turkish army was in collapse by the end of the year, the Russian was little better. It managed to stagger to the gates of Constantinople by the end of January

---

[1] Beust (London) to Andrássy, 13 July 1877. Ibid., iii. 39.
[2] Rupp, *A Wavering Friendship*, p. 405.

1878. Then an armistice was concluded, and the momentum once lost could never be recaptured. This was an essential factor in the crisis of the following months: the Russians were hardly in a condition to renew the war with Turkey, let alone take on any of the Great Powers. It was difficult, as much for the Russians as for others, to realize that a victorious army was at the end of its tether; and when the Russians met with a diplomatic setback, they sought for anything but its true cause —that they were too weak to fight another war. It was easier to blame the mistakes of some diplomatist—whether Ignatiev or Shuvalov—or the malice of Bismarck than to appreciate the Turkish achievement at Plevna. Yet wars make the decisions; diplomacy merely records them.

The Russians had started the war with no defined aims beyond the recovery of Bessarabia. War is often expected to provide a policy; but, since the Ottoman empire had not collapsed, this war had failed to do so. The Russians had hastily to botch up terms which would both confirm their victory and do something to emancipate the Balkan Christians. A revision of the rule of the Straits would do the first; autonomy for Bulgaria would do the second. Both featured in the programme which the Russians drafted in December. They soon had second thoughts about the Straits. Gorchakov insisted successfully that the Straits depended on a European agreement. Moreover, since the Russians had no Black Sea fleet, opening the Straits— though a satisfaction to their pride—would, in fact, be of advantage only to others. The question of the Straits was therefore dropped and Bulgaria had to serve both purposes: Russian aggrandizement and Christian emancipation. This was quite unpremeditated. The Russians demanded a 'Big Bulgaria', that is, Bulgaria as defined by the conference at Constantinople twelve months before. This had no Machiavellian intent; a Bulgarian national state seemed the only alternative to Turkish rule. The frontier which they drew corresponded to the best ethnographical knowledge of the time. The territory of which Bulgaria was deprived by the congress of Berlin was called 'Macedonia' simply as a matter of administrative convenience. It had no national character of its own, though it developed one in the following half-century. Now there is a Macedonian nationality; historically a Macedonian is simply a Bulgarian who was put back under Turkish rule in 1878. There was one unnecessary and provocative blunder in the Russian peace terms. Ignatiev had been kept out of the way in St. Petersburg during the war; in February 1878 he came racing down to enjoy his triumph and to negotiate the treaty of peace. He had only just learnt of the Budapest conventions and, after the Russian military effort, decided to ignore them. Moreover, the Russians felt a little ashamed at doing so little for Serbia, except for securing her technical independence of Turkey. The treaty therefore said nothing of the Austro-Hungarian claim to Bosnia and Hercegovina. This gave Andrássy his excuse for breaking away from the Russian entente.

Ignatiev had an easy time with the Turks. They had no hope of reversing their defeat unless they were backed by Austria-Hungary and Great Britain, and acquiesced in the Russian terms so as to shift the responsibility on to others. The treaty of San Stefano, which was signed on 3 March, therefore satisfied all the Russian demands. This only opened the European crisis. There had been a first alarm in January, before the armistice had been signed, when the British had feared that the Russians would actually enter Constantinople. The British fleet had been ordered to pass the Straits; then the order had been counter-manded; finally, on 8 February, the order had been sent again on a mistaken alarm that the Russians were not observing the armistice terms. Though the fleet arrived successfully in the Sea of Marmora on 13 February, it had no landing-force; and the British were still in search of an ally. They proposed alliance to Austria-Hungary in vain. To every request Andrássy answered that the British must be 'one length forward'; they must declare their readiness for an alliance and promise him a subsidy, yet expect no promise in return. It is possible that Andrássy himself would have welcomed war against Russia; after all he was not an old Magyar revolutionary for nothing. At the meetings of the Austro-Hungarian crown council he pointed longingly to the Rumanian bottleneck which put the Russian armies in the Balkans at his mercy. But Francis Joseph and the generals were always opposed to war unless it was forced on them; and besides, as Bismarck repeatedly pointed out, if England and Austria-Hungary fought Russia, this would end in the partition of the Ottoman empire, not in saving it—a result by no means to Andrássy's taste. The only effective line for Andrássy was to do nothing. He could not bind himself to the British; at the same time he would not promise neutrality to the Russians and therefore kept them in nervous uncertainty.

This was brought out in March. Ignatiev had imposed the treaty of San Stefano on the Turks without giving a thought either to the European Powers or, for that matter, to the foreign ministry in St. Petersburg. On his return there he was cold-shouldered by Gorchakov and abruptly told that, since he had made the treaty, he must carry it through by himself. At the end of March he went to Vienna with a vague hope of getting a promise of neutrality from Andrássy and so isolating Great Britain. His visit failed completely. Andrássy quoted the Buda-pest conventions and demanded the dismemberment of the Big Bulgaria; instead Austria-Hungary must be preponderant in the western Balkans. This was a passing improvisation on Andrássy's part. Partition of Turkey-in-Europe was almost as abhorrent to him as its domination by Russia; and he was simply playing for time in the hope, not altogether disappointed, that the Ottoman empire would get on its feet again. Ignatiev might have swallowed partition despite his Panslav enthusi-asm;[1] but every time he made proposals, Andrássy eluded him. It was the end of the Austro-Russian entente. Moreover, Bis-marck refused to force a compromise on Andrássy, despite his own preference for partition; and, with Russia afraid of an Anglo-Austrian coalition, his neutrality was in essence a de-cisively anti-Russian act. The friendship between Russia and Prussia, which had been the most stable element in European politics for more than a hundred years, was shaken for the first time. Bismarck was beginning to pay the price for the great decision he made in 1866. He had kept the Habsburg monarchy in being for the sake of his domestic policy; now he could not allow it to be weakened. This was not the sole cause of his diffi-culty. Russia, as well as Austria-Hungary, was weaker than at the time of the Crimean war. Then Nicholas I had been content with Prussia's neutrality; now Alexander II needed Germany's support, even though France was no longer a member of the anti-Russian coalition. Turkey, Austria-Hungary, and Russia were all three, in their different ways, 'ramshackle empires', competing for first place on the road to ruin.

---

[1] Ignatiev even offered an autonomous 'Macedonia' under the Austrian general Rodič. Since Rodič was a Croat and a 'Great Austrian', the idea was without attractions for Andrássy. Schweinitz to Bülow, 4 Apr. 1878. *Große Politik*, ii, no. 380.

Ignatiev failed in Vienna; Shuvalov succeeded in London. His task was the easier in that he hated the Panslavism of San Stefano and was glad to repudiate it—'the greatest act of stupidity that we could have committed'.[1] Moreover, the British government at last took a decided line. Derby had continued in office until the end of March with the sole object of thwarting Beaconsfield's drive to war; and foreign policy had been largely conducted behind his back by a committee of three—Beaconsfield, Salisbury, and Cairns. On 27 March Beaconsfield carried the day in the cabinet: the reserves were called out, and Derby resigned. This was not a victory for the integrity of the Ottoman empire. Salisbury, who became foreign secretary, was 'not a believer in the possibility of setting the Turkish Government on its legs again, as a genuine reliable Power'.[2] He wanted to keep the Russians away from Constantinople and to prop up some sort of Turkish state in Asia Minor—much the arrangement, in fact, which still exists in the middle of the twentieth century. Just as the Russians had found it difficult to devise terms which would show that they had won, so now Salisbury was puzzled how to define that they had failed. Bulgaria was again the symbol. He insisted that it be divided by a line running from east to west along the line of the Balkan mountains. This was supposed to give the Turks military security for the defence of Constantinople. It had no practical effect: the Turkish armies never reoccupied 'East Roumelia'. This did not matter. The important thing was to show that Russia did not dominate the Balkans; and there was nothing absurd in Salisbury's welcoming the unification of Bulgaria in 1885, once the Bulgarians had proved their independence of Russia.

The Russians were not in a state to fight another war; this was the decisive factor which Salisbury exploited to the full. In case of a war with Great Britain, they would have had to withdraw from the Balkans and so to abandon the gains of San Stefano, even if Austria-Hungary had remained neutral. Add to this that most of those in responsible positions at St. Petersburg disliked Ignatiev's success, and it is not surprising that Shuvalov got his way. The Russians agreed to give up 'Big Bulgaria'; and an Anglo-Russian agreement to this end was signed on 30 May.

---

[1] Corti, *Alexander von Battenberg*, p. 43.
[2] Salisbury to Beaconsfield, 21 Mar. 1878. Gwendolen Cecil, *Life of Salisbury*, ii. 213.

Salisbury concluded two other secret agreements. When he took office on 1 April, he had tried again for an alliance with Austria-Hungary; this failed like all the previous attempts, and Salisbury turned instead to direct agreement with Russia. Once this was made, he had no further need of Austria-Hungary. Andrássy, adroit for so long, grew alarmed at his isolation, and appealed to Bismarck. Salisbury, though now indifferent to Austria-Hungary, valued Germany's even-handed neutrality; and, to please Bismarck rather than Andrássy, made an agreement with Austria-Hungary on 6 June. He would support her claim to Bosnia, and she would support the partition of Bulgaria. In effect, Andrássy concluded an alliance with Great Britain exactly a week after all need for it had passed; and, since the alliance was without risk, it also did nothing to earn British gratitude. Salisbury attached much more importance to the agreement of 4 June which he made with the Turks or, to be more exact, imposed upon them. By this Great Britain guaranteed Asiatic Turkey against a Russian attack, and received Cyprus in return as a *place d'armes*.

The British success seemed complete, the triumph of a policy of resolution. Russia had been checked; Austria-Hungary won as an ally; Turkey restored and guaranteed. Yet it was a misleading success. Russia's armies were exhausted, and her policy in confusion. Great Britain won a bloodless victory with a music-hall song, a navy of museum pieces, and no land forces at all, except the 7,000 Indian troops sent demonstratively to Malta. Moreover, she won without a reliable continental ally: only airy phrases from Austria-Hungary and the impractical project of equipping the Turks from non-existent British resources. The resounding achievement of 1878 weakened the effectiveness of British policy in the long run; for it led the British public to believe that they could play a great role without expense or exertion—without reforming their navy, without creating an army, without finding an ally. Great Britain acquired a capital of prestige which lasted for exactly twenty years; then she tried to draw on a capital which was no longer there.

The congress of Berlin, which met on 13 June, did not have an easy passage, despite the secret agreements which had preceded it. The Russians displayed a characteristic ingenuity in trying to evade the consequences of the convention which they had signed with Salisbury on 30 May. They tried to exclude Turkish troops from eastern Roumelia, or even to dodge partition altogether. They were defeated only after a more or less open crisis, with Beaconsfield ostentatiously ordering his special train to be ready to leave—the first time that this weapon was added to the technique of diplomacy.[1] In the end Big Bulgaria was dissolved into three—an autonomous principality; the semi-autonomous province of eastern Roumelia; and 'Macedonia', which remained an integral part of the Ottoman empire. Austria-Hungary was to occupy Bosnia and Hercegovina and also to garrison the Sanjak of Novibazar, the strip of Turkish territory which separated Serbia and Montenegro. Andrássy could have annexed the two provinces if he had wished; but he clung to the pretence that the Ottoman empire was not being partitioned and even talked of handing the provinces back to the sultan after a generation or so.

The Russians recovered the Bessarabian territory which they had lost in 1856; more important, they acquired Batum at the eastern end of the Black Sea. Salisbury had promised in the agreement of 30 May not to oppose this; but he was being harassed by British outcry that too much had been conceded to Russia. He had to do something to restore the naval balance in the Black Sea which had been allegedly upset by the Russians establishing themselves at Batum. His first idea was to propose an agreement with the Turks, by which they would allow the British fleet to pass the Straits whenever 'England should be of opinion that the presence of a naval force in the Black Sea is expedient'.[2] The Turks shrank from this open provocation of Russia; but Salisbury got much the same result by other means. He declared at the meeting of 11 July that henceforward Great Britain would only regard herself as bound to respect 'the independent determinations' of the sultan in regard to the closing of the Straits. In future the sultan would either allow the British to pass the Straits or he could be disregarded as no longer independent. For all practical purposes the British repudiated the obligations of 1841 and 1856 and claimed to be free to pass the Straits whenever it suited them. Behind this

---

[1] Beaconsfield also established a precedent by addressing the congress in English. This was the first breach in the French monopoly and a sign that the old aristocratic cosmopolitanism was fading fast.

[2] Salisbury to Layard (Constantinople), 16 June 1878. Temperley and Penson; *Foundations of British Foreign Policy*, no. 147.

theoretical freedom lay a technical assumption, on which the British had acted in February 1878—that their fleet was strong enough to pass the Straits and to maintain itself in the Black Sea without anxiety as to its communications with the Mediterranean. There was also a political assumption—that Russia would continue to menace Turkey. Both assumptions turned out to be false in the following years.

The Berlin settlement was obviously a defeat for Russia. Though the Russians got all and more than all that they had wanted before they went to war, more indeed than 'the little peace' which Alexander II had grudgingly offered in June 1877, they had been compelled to surrender all the gains of victory. Yet it was a defeat of a peculiar kind. Russia had gone to war for reasons of national pride and of Panslav sentiment, not to achieve any practical aim;[1] and the congress was a blow to her prestige rather than a setback to her policy. In fact, if Russia was less secure after 1878 than before, this was because she had succeeded, not because she had failed. Turkey had ceased to be an effective Great Power, a neutral barrier between Russia and Great Britain. The British fleet could enter the Black Sea at will—or so both the British and the Russians supposed; yet this weakening of Turkey was all Russia's doing. It is not surprising that Russian policy after the congress was a mixture of fear and resentment. They feared the consequences of their own acts; and resented their own folly. Alexander III passed the best verdict many years later: 'Our misfortune in 1876 and 1877 was that we went with the peoples instead of with the governments. An emperor of Russia ought always to go only with the governments.'[2]

If the congress was a defeat for Russia, it was not a complete success for Austria-Hungary or even for Great Britain. Andrássy had meant to preserve the integrity of the Ottoman empire; but it was beyond preserving. Great Turkey was over; and a Turkish national state had not yet taken its place. Macedonia and Bosnia, the two great achievements of the congress, both contained the seeds of future disaster. The Macedonian question haunted European diplomacy for a generation and then caused the Balkan war of 1912. Bosnia first provoked the crisis of 1908

---

[1] The recovery of Bessarabia was a practical aim, but it did not cause the war and could have been achieved without it.

[2] Bülow to Bismarck, 10 Aug. 1886. *Große Politik*, v, no. 980.

and then exploded the World war in 1914, a war which brought down the Habsburg monarchy. If the treaty of San Stefano had been maintained, both the Ottoman empire and Austria-Hungary might have survived to the present day. The British, except for Beaconsfield in his wilder moments, had expected less and were therefore less disappointed. Salisbury wrote at the end of 1878: 'We shall set up a rickety sort of Turkish rule again south of the Balkans. But it is a mere respite. There is no vitality left in them.'[1] The future was shaped not by the treaty settlement, but by the actions that had preceded it: the Turkish defence of Plevna and the sending of the British fleet to Constantinople. The Turks had shown that they could still put up military resistance; the British had dominated the eastern Mediterranean and the Straits. The Turkish army has continued to exist, except between 1918 and 1921; the British have continued to control the eastern Mediterranean; they were unable to keep their hold on the Straits. All the history of the Eastern question since 1878 is in these three sentences.

The congress of Berlin marked an epoch in where it met, not in what it did. In 1856 Prussia had entered the congress of Paris late and under humiliating conditions; now Germany attained full stature as a European Power—and, with it, full responsibility. She could no longer turn her back on the Eastern question, or exploit it; instead, the Powers involved in the question could exploit her. Bismarck had done his best to ward off this outcome. He tried to pass the part of 'honest broker' to the French,[2] but there was no escaping the consequences of his victories. He needed the Habsburg monarchy as barrier against a democratic Greater Germany; yet he dared not allow a revival of 'the Crimean coalition', which might have resisted Russia without involving Germany. An Austro-French partnership which began in the Near East would go on to challenge the treaty of Frankfurt, or even the treaty of Prague. A Russo-German combination against this might have been victorious; but Bismarck dreaded further victory almost as much as defeat. He wished to preserve both Austria-Hungary and France as they were, still Great Powers though somewhat humbled. A continent

[1] Minute by Salisbury, 29 Dec. 1878. Sumner, *Russia and the Balkans*, p. 565.
[2] He first suggested that the congress should meet in Paris and, when this failed, that the French should preside. Throughout the congress he tried to cast Waddington, the French delegate, as chief mediator.

dominated by Germany was abhorrent to him—not from any deep principle of respect for others, but simply because he believed that it would mark the end of the conservative order that he valued. Hence, though against his will, he had to enforce the Balance of Power, much as Metternich had done. He redirected Andrássy's requests for support from Berlin to London and asserted a formal neutrality towards Russia; but he refused to back Russia against Austria-Hungary or even to tolerate an attack upon her. Yet he needed Russia, too, as a Great Power: partnership against the resurrection of Poland was just as important to him as the prevention of Greater Germany.

He might have tolerated a war confined to Russia and Great Britain; though even this would have been unwelcome to him if it had ended in the defeat of Russia—the Polish spectre would at once have raised its head. But he doubted whether a future Anglo-Russian war could be 'localized', as the Crimean war had been. Austria-Hungary would be drawn in, dragging Germany along with her; and then France would seek to reverse the verdict of 1870. Napoleon III had refused to buy Russian backing by surrender of French interests in the Near East; sooner or later, the French republic would pay this price. The treaty of Frankfurt made a reconciliation between France and Germany impossible; therefore a war in the Near East would become general. It was this general war from which all the Powers shrank in 1878. The congress of Berlin demonstrated that a new Balance of Power, centred on Germany, had come into existence. None of the statesmen at Berlin expected the settlement to last long, and they would have been astonished to learn that the congress would be followed by thirty-six years of European peace. But they would have been still more astonished if they could have foreseen that the next great European assembly, forty years later, would meet at Paris and that none of 'the three Northern Courts' would be represented.

XII

BISMARCK'S ALLIANCES

1879-82

THE congress of Berlin made a watershed in the history of Europe. It had been preceded by thirty years of conflict and upheaval; it was followed by thirty-four years of peace. No European frontier was changed until 1913; not a shot was fired in Europe until 1912, except in two trivial wars that miscarried.[1] It would not do to attribute this great achievement solely, or even principally, to the skill of European statesmen. The decisive cause was, no doubt, economic. The secret that had made Great Britain great was a secret no longer. Coal and steel offered prosperity to all Europe and remade European civilization. The dream of Cobden seemed to have come true. Men were too busy growing rich to have time for war. Though protective tariffs remained everywhere except in Great Britain,[2] international trade was otherwise free. There was no governmental interference, no danger of debts being repudiated. The gold standard was universal. Passports disappeared, except in Russia and Turkey. If a man in London decided at nine o'clock in the morning to go to Rome or Vienna, he could leave at ten a.m. without either passport or travellers' cheques—merely with a purse of sovereigns in his pocket. Europe had never known such peace and unity since the age of the Antonines. The times of Metternich were nothing in comparison. Then men had lived in well-founded apprehension of war and revolution; now they came to believe that peace and security were 'normal', and anything else an accident and an aberration. For centuries

---

[1] The war between Serbia and Bulgaria in 1885, and the war between Turkey and Greece in 1897.

[2] The contrast between Great Britain and other capitalist countries in tariff matters is often exaggerated. In the first decade of the twentieth century, British duties were 5·7 per cent. of the total value of imports. The German figure was 8·4 per cent., the French 8·2 per cent. The only truly protectionist countries were Russia (35 per cent.) and the United States (18·5 per cent.).

to come men will look back at that age of bliss and will puzzle over the effortless ease with which it was accomplished. They are not likely to discover the secret; they will certainly not be able to imitate it.

National passions and the rivalries of states still existed. Statesmen in fact spoke with a greater arrogance and to a wider public. Swords were rattled more as the belief grew that they would never be used. All the Great Powers except Austria-Hungary found a safe channel for their exuberance in expansion outside Europe. They stumbled on this solution by chance, without foresight.[1] The 'age of imperialism' was inaugurated oddly enough by Leopold II, king of the Belgians, and not by the ruler of any Great Power; and the empires were built up by private adventurers rather than by state action. This, too, seemed evidence that statesmen counted for little—funny little men, as H. G. Wells depicted them, making irrelevant comments on the margin of events. The work of diplomacy still went on, and the diplomatists still took themselves seriously. In 1879 Bismarck began a manufacture of alliances that was soon to involve every Great Power in Europe, and most of the small ones. The general staffs prepared war plans of increasing complexity and talked gravely of the conflict that would break out 'when the snow melted on the Balkan mountains'. Navies were built and rebuilt; millions of men were trained for war. Nothing happened. Each year the snows melted; spring turned into summer, summer into autumn; and new snow fell. In retrospect it is difficult to believe that there was ever a serious danger of war in Europe on a great scale at any time between 1878 and 1913; and the complex diplomacy of the period was perhaps no more than a gigantic game—a system of out-relief, as Bright had called it, to keep the aristocracies of Europe gainfully employed. In the preceding thirty years diplomacy had been vital; it had shaped men's destinies. If Cavour, Napoleon III, or Bismarck had followed a different policy, there would have been no united Italy or united Germany. But would it have made any difference in the generation after 1878, if there had been no Austro-German or Franco-Russian alliance? A work of diplomatic history has to take diplomacy seriously;

---

[1] The accidental, unforeseen nature of imperialism is shown in the studies of Ferry, Crispi, Chamberlain, and Leopold II, edited by C. A. Julien, *Les politiques d'expansion impérialiste*.

and perhaps it is enough to say that diplomacy helped men to remain at peace, so long as they wished to do so.

The 'relations of the Great Powers' counted for less. Bismarck shaped them so far as they counted at all. This had not been the situation in the years before the congress of Berlin, or even during the congress. Bismarck had occasionally tried to lessen the tension between the Great Powers or to act as 'honest broker'; he had not dominated the European scene. It was the British who had both caused the crisis of 1878 by determining to resist Russia and ended it peacefully by extracting from Russia satisfactory concessions. Turkey and Austria-Hungary had, in their different ways, trailed at Great Britain's heels. After the congress the British still took the lead. They controlled the commissions which were to apply the terms of the treaty and, seconded by Austria-Hungary and France, pressed on the negotiations which led to the withdrawal of Russian forces from the Balkans in July 1879. Nor were they satisfied to get the Russians out of Turkey; they were intent to get themselves in. Salisbury, the British foreign secretary, had no faith that the Ottoman empire could be restored as a Great Power. He thought rather of a system of veiled protectorates: Austria-Hungary, through her occupation of Bosnia and Hercegovina, should make herself responsible for the western Balkans; Great Britain should reform and guard Asia Minor, as provided in the Cyprus convention; perhaps, in encouraging France to take Tunis, he cast her for a similar role in North Africa. There was a flaw in this system. Constantinople was the capital of an empire which still existed; and Salisbury's projects did nothing to secure it. A British alliance with Austria-Hungary would have been the simplest solution. It had been unattainable even when the Russian armies were at the gates of Constantinople; and it continued to prove illusory in the following months. Besides, Salisbury had not much more faith at this time in Austria-Hungary than in the Ottoman empire. He preferred to do things alone; and his declaration at the congress about the rule of the Straits seemed to point the way. The British were free to pass the Straits whenever they chose to do so. In 1878, with the Russians already outside Constantinople, the British navy could have done little to save it. But once the Russian forces were withdrawn, the British could protect Constantinople by passing the Straits and attacking Russia in the Black Sea.

This was the assumption behind British policy between the congress of Berlin and the fall of the conservative government in April 1880. The policy was no doubt defensive; but, if need arose, it would defend Turkey by striking at the Ukraine, the richest and most vulnerable part of the Russian empire.

The British assumption was clear to the Russians. Indeed fear of attack in the Black Sea was the prime motive of Russia's Near Eastern policy for the next eighteen years. The Russians had done nothing to restore the Black Sea fleet which had been destroyed during the Crimean war. Therefore they needed some international combination to replace the convention of London of 1841 which had been shot to pieces by Salisbury's declaration at Berlin. A Mediterranean ally would have done something to hamper the British fleet. The Russians tried to win over Italy; but though the Italians, who had received nothing at the congress, were resentful and discontented, they dared not go against England. Some extreme Panslavs talked of alliance with France. This idea, too, was barren. The old 'liberal alliance' of the western Powers had been largely restored; and France, as well as Austria-Hungary, supported the British on the Balkan committees. In fact, whereas the congress of Paris had destroyed 'the Crimean coalition', the congress of Berlin almost re-created it. Russia's last card, as always, was the traditional friendship with Prussia, a friendship cemented by the common hostility to Poland. Since Germany had no Balkan interests, she should —the Russians argued—support Russia in the Balkans and at the Straits. Moreover, the Russians had not abandoned the old dream that Germany could somehow be used to force Austria-Hungary on to a pro-Russian path. The Russians still thought of Germany as a grateful dependent; and they supposed that they could force her into alliance by a display of bad temper. This was indeed the only method they knew.

It was this situation which forced Bismarck into action. An alliance with Russia against the Crimean coalition had been repeatedly rejected by Prussian statesmen; an alliance against Russia was equally abhorrent. During the Crimean war Prussia had evaded commitment to either side and had cheerfully paid the price of being almost ignored as a Great Power. Bismarck's activity as 'honest broker' had been a last attempt to maintain this attitude. Now he entangled himself in the European alliances, and even in the Eastern question. No doubt his motive was in part personal: the impatience of a master at the diplomatic blunders of others. More deeply, it was the moment when Germany accepted the full responsibilities of a Great Power. Bismarck had made the new Europe; now he had to preserve it. He ceased to be Cavour and became Metternich. Henceforth he, too, was 'a rock of order'.

It was the same in his home policy, which also changed decisively in 1879. Bismarck broke with the national liberals and came to rely exclusively on the conservative parties. The revolution had gone far enough; now it had to be ended. Yet, at the same time, the alliance that he made with Austria-Hungary was a sop to the liberals whom he was deserting in home affairs. Though he did not give them 'greater Germany', he gave them a union of the two German powers, based on national sentiment. But his object transcended German politics. He wanted to preserve the Balance of Power in Europe and, still more, the monarchical order. His conservatism, rooted in his own class-interest, embraced both the Habsburg monarchy and Russian tsardom. In fact, he wished to restore the Holy Alliance of Metternich's day. The old condition for that had been Russian restraint in the Near East. This certainly existed after 1878. The new obstacle was the ambition of Austria-Hungary or rather her unshakeable suspicion of Russian designs in the Balkans. Bismarck never got rid of this obstacle, and it ultimately ruined his 'system'.

It had always been something of a conjuring trick to prevent an Austro-Russian conflict. Metternich had done it by raising the spectre of 'the revolution' before the eyes of the tsar; Bismarck's method was more elaborate. He set out to detach Austria-Hungary from 'the Crimean coalition' by offering her the security of alliance with Germany; once she was caught, he made it the condition of this alliance that she be reconciled to Russia. His real fear was of Austro-Hungarian restlessness, not of Russian aggression; but he could not avow this until the Austro-German alliance was made. Such subtleties were beyond the grasp of William I. The emperor, when prince of Prussia, had once been the advocate of liberal alliance with Great Britain; now, in old age, he was devoted to family union with the Russian court. He could be bustled into alliance with Austria-Hungary only by being persuaded that Germany was in imminent danger of attack from Russia. It is unnecessary to suppose that Bismarck believed this version—though, like most men, he often swallowed a legend of his own making, so long as it suited his purpose. Only a very old and very simple-minded ruler could have believed that Germany was threatened by war or even by encirclement; but Bismarck had never had a high opinion of his master's ability and used crude arguments to influence him. After all, it had been just as easy to convince him in 1866 that he was threatened by Austria. Nor is it only absolute rulers who have to be impelled into a policy of security by imaginary dangers drawn on the wall; public opinion in democratic countries gets the same treatment. Bismarck had a second motive. He wished to convince the French that an Austro-German alliance would be directed solely against Russia, not against them, and, no doubt, to hint also that Russia had no attractions as an ally.[1] In 1879 the French were still ready to accept this line of argument; it is not necessary for the historian to do so.

Bismarck began his elaborate campaign of conjuring up the danger from Russia in the spring of 1879. The first open sign was on 4 February, when he published an agreement with Austria-Hungary, releasing Germany from the obligation to hold a plebiscite in north Sleswick, which she had incurred by the treaty of Prague.[2] This was a challenge to Alexander II, who had repeatedly asked that the plebiscite should be held. Endless small provocations, ranging from tariff restrictions to offensive remarks about the Russian character, followed. In August the Russians were provoked into hostility. Grumbling complaints from Alexander II to the German ambassador gave Bismarck pretext enough;[3] and he was already on his way to meet Andrássy at Gastein when Alexander completed the picture by writing directly to William I.[4] The two rulers supposed that there had been some misunderstanding and thought to put things right by a meeting, which took place at Alexanderovo on 3 September. It served no purpose. Bismarck had cast tsar and emperor for a quarrel, and they had to quarrel to their

[1] Saint-Vallier (Berlin) to Waddington, 7 Apr., 27 June 1879. *Documents diplomatiques français*, first series, ii, nos. 406, 440.

[2] The agreement had actually been made on 13 Apr. 1878, during the Eastern crisis. Then Bismarck had been anxious not to offend the Russians, and it was kept secret. Now he was anxious to provoke them.

[3] Schweinitz to Bismarck, 8 Aug. 1879. *Große Politik*, iii, no. 443.

[4] Alexander II to William I, 15 Aug. 1879. Ibid., no. 446.

mutual bewilderment, until the alliance with Austria-Hungary was safely concluded. No doubt their meeting made it more difficult for Bismarck to convince William I. It seemed obvious to the old gentleman that, since Germany was in no danger from Russia, alliance with Austria-Hungary was unnecessary. Bismarck was relentless and impatient. As usual, when he was forcing a distasteful policy on William I, he kept away and carried on a long-distance correspondence of extreme violence. Finally, the Prussian ministers threatened to resign in a body, and William I was forced to surrender. The treaty of alliance between Austria-Hungary and Germany was signed on 7 October 1879. It was the first thread in a network of alliances which was soon to cover all Europe. The treaty was a simple defensive alliance against a Russian attack; in case of war with any other Power, the other ally was pledged only to benevolent neutrality. Though this seemed an unfair bargain to William I, Bismarck made no serious effort to get Austro-Hungarian support against France. Indeed his effort was directed solely to forcing German backing on Austria-Hungary.

His own explanations were curiously elaborate and misleading. The alliance certainly did not increase German security against Russia. On the contrary it endangered Germany for the first time: apart from Austria-Hungary the two countries had no cause of conflict. The coalitions against which Bismarck was guarding were also imaginary. There was no immediate chance in 1879 of an alliance between France and Russia; the Austro-German alliance increased what chance there was. Bismarck professed to fear a reconciliation of Russia and Austria-Hungary at Germany's expense, or even 'the Kaunitz coalition' of her three great neighbours. Neither was remotely probable. Men's actions are, of course, to be explained by their past, not by their future; and the alliance certainly ruled out the combination which Bismarck had dreaded most in the past—the coalition of France and Austria-Hungary, as projected by Talleyrand or even by Beust. It was hardly worth making an alliance in order to avoid this: the Franco-Austrian coalition had vanished at Sedan. The French republic and the Habsburg monarchy would never come together in order to destroy national Germany with its two associates—national Italy and great Hungary. No doubt it was something that the Habsburg monarchy should openly acknowledge Bismarck's settlement of Europe; but this acknowledgement had been there even since 1871. It was Bismarck who had held out then against an alliance, not Andrássy or Francis Joseph.

The alliance did not turn Austria-Hungary back from a foreign power into a German state; instead it set the precedent for other alliances with states indisputably foreign. On the other hand, it committed Germany to Austria-Hungary much more precisely than the old Confederation had done. In fact, it was nothing other than Manteuffel's alliance with Austria of 20 April 1854 when Bismarck had complained so bitterly against tying the trim Prussian frigate to the worm-eaten Austrian galleon. Now the frigate was more trim than ever, the galleon more worm-eaten by twenty years; yet Bismarck tied them together for good, Manteuffel only for three years.[1] Great men in high office often follow the policy which they attacked when in opposition; and Bismarck was following the path of Manteuffel and Schleinitz rather as the elder Pitt confessed late in life his admiration for Walpole. Bismarck himself, during the negotiations, drew the parallel with the Austro-Prussian alliance which had been abortively sketched at Teplitz in 1860;[2] and it could be argued that the war of 1866 had compelled Austria to accept the condition of parity with Prussia which she had rejected in 1861. Yet Bismarck's policy was more than traditional; it was old-fashioned. The dangers which gave him nightmares were those of a previous generation, and often no longer real. In domestic politics he was always warding off the revolution of 1848, and so treated the social democrats as dangerous conspirators long after they had become respectable parliamentarians. It was the same in foreign affairs. When Manteuffel made his alliance with Austria the Crimean war was actually raging, at any rate in a technical sense. Only Bismarck could imagine a Crimean war in 1879. He underrated Russian weakness and perhaps exaggerated the decline of Austria-Hungary.

The only serious possibility in 1879 was further humiliation for Russia; and this Bismarck was most anxious to avoid. German conservatism, which Bismarck represented, needed despotism in Russia; and Bismarck aimed to protect Russian prestige, even when he seemed to provoke her. The alliance of

---

[1] Bismarck's alliance was to last theoretically for five years, with automatic renewal if not denounced. Manteuffel's alliance was wider in that it acknowledged the Danubian principalities as vital to Austria's defensive position; but Bismarck also acknowledged this when he extended the alliance to cover Rumania in 1883.

[2] Bismarck to Reuss, 12 Sept. 1879. *Große Politik*, iii, no. 467.

1879, just like the alliance of 1854, was designed to keep Austria from war on the side of 'the liberal alliance'. In Bismarck's own words, 'I wanted to dig a ditch between her and the western Powers'.[1] He argued repeatedly to William I that the alliance was the only way of preventing 'the Crimean coalition' and that it would restore good relations between Austria-Hungary and Russia.[2] This version was never accepted by the Austrians. They used the alliance to oppose Russia more resolutely, not to get on better terms with her; and Bismarck's strongest weapon with Austria-Hungary was to threaten to repudiate his alliance —a curious reason for making it.

Of course the German problem never changed in the deepest sense. Occupying the centre of the continent, she was bound to bear the brunt of any war between Russia and the west whichever side she chose; and, short of a war for European domination, her only solution was neutrality—a neutrality which had to extend to Austria-Hungary. If there was a neutral barrier extending from the Baltic to the Black Sea, then Russia and the western Powers could fight at the extremities of the Eurasian continent without destroying European civilization— or even each other. There was, too, a specific Prussian problem —the Junker reluctance, which Bismarck constantly voiced, against sacrificing the bones of a Pomeranian grenadier for the sake of interests in the Balkans or the Mediterranean. Bismarck made out that these interests were Austrian, not German; and he insisted that the alliance was limited to the preservation of the Habsburg monarchy. His successors are often blamed for giving up this limitation. Bismarck himself was not free from reproach. Not only did he extend the alliance to cover Rumania in 1883, he often spoke of Austria-Hungary as part of Germany; he described Trieste, for instance, as 'Germany's only port on the southern seas'.[3] Once he had given Austria-Hungary a guarantee of existence, he was always in danger of being drawn into her quarrels. He wished to keep her in being without supporting her Balkan plans. Yet an Austro-Russian war which started in the Balkans would threaten the existence of the Habsburg monarchy as much as a war which started on any other terms; and the alliance began a tug-of-war between

[1] J. Y. Simpson, *The Saburov Memoirs*, p. 74.
[2] Bismarck to William I, 31 Aug. 1879. *Große Politik*, iii, no. 455.
[3] Saint-Vallier to Barthélemy Saint-Hilaire, 29 Nov. 1880. *Documents diplomatiques français*, first series, iii, no. 307.

Vienna and Berlin which ended only when Vienna pulled
Germany into the war of 1914.

Bismarck gave the Austrians their strongest card when, instead
of a casual promise, he concluded a formal alliance—the
first permanent arrangement in peace-time between two Great
Powers since the end of the *ancien régime*. Probably even Bismarck did not fully realize the decisive nature of the step that
he had taken. He imagined, perhaps mistakenly, that a new
crisis was approaching—a crisis in which Russia would be
threatened by 'the Crimean coalition'; and he warded it off
without troubling about the means. After all, he often referred to
the Triple Alliance, which was equally formal, as 'a temporary
arrangement' when this suited his purpose; and, out of office at
the end of his life, warned his successors against taking the
Austro-German alliance too seriously. Treaties of alliance became for him the sort of conjuring trick that battles had been
for Napoleon I—they would get him out of every difficulty.
This would have been all very well if international relations
had still been an affair of courts. They had become an affair of
peoples. The war of 1866 was the last cabinet war in history;
and even it tried to exploit popular passion. In the old days
Austria-Hungary might have been satisfied with a meeting of
the two emperors and a private promise of support from
William I. Now it was necessary to bind together the peoples
of Germany and Austria-Hungary; this could be done only by
formal agreement. Treaties bound governments to their own
people as well as to each other. Alliances were engines of publicity even when their terms were secret. Bismarck himself
publicized the fact of the Austro-German alliance and would
have liked to publish its terms. He made out that it revived 'the
organic link' between Austria and the rest of Germany which
he had himself destroyed in 1866.

Bismarck had aimed to do in Germany what Cavour had
done in Italy: to exploit 'the revolution' without being taken
prisoner by it. He turned German nationalism to the service of
Prussia's aggrandizement and gave it just enough satisfaction
to tame it. In 1879 he tried to call a halt. The alliance with
Austria-Hungary was meant to pull her over to the conservative
side and to stabilize the European order; yet even it had to
be justified by arguments of nationalist sentiment. Certainly,
it strengthened the peace of Europe for many years; equally

certainly, it involved Germany, and all Europe, in the First
World War. The German nationalism which Bismarck had
tricked and restrained took his successors prisoner; and that
made them also the prisoners of the statesmen in Vienna.

The tug-of-war between Vienna and Berlin started even
before the alliance was signed. The Austrians thought of it as
supplementing the Anglo-Austrian front against Russia, which
Bismarck wanted to make unnecessary. While he was still
negotiating with Andrássy, he inquired of the British what they
would do if Germany ran into conflict with Russia through her
backing of Great Britain and Austria-Hungary in the Balkans.
Beaconsfield replied: 'We will in that case keep France quiet.'[1]
This was a reasonable answer. Germany and Austria-Hungary,
once assured of French neutrality, would have made short work
of Russia. If Bismarck had wanted an anti-Russian union, imposing the will of Europe in the Balkans, the British answer was
adequate. Instead he grumbled: 'Is that all?'[2] What more could
the British have offered? Bismarck was not impressed by the
British fleet; and the British were not a great land-power. If
they had been, the Austro-German alliance would have been
unnecessary: Austria-Hungary could have been preserved by
British backing, or even have remained neutral. Bismarck was
really protesting against the inescapable fact that in any war
against Russia Germany would carry the greatest burden. This
fact barred an Anglo-German alliance in 1879 and on every
subsequent occasion; but a man of Bismarck's grasp did not
need to launch an elaborate inquiry in order to discover this—
it was basic in European relations. Perhaps he wanted to prove
to Andrássy that an alliance with Great Britain would be un-
rewarding; and possibly he had an eye on objections from
Crown Prince Frederick, who was notoriously pro-British, just
as he certainly thought of the effect on William I in his dealings
with Russia. But he did not pass on the story to these two, nor
indeed to anyone else. It is not extravagant to suggest that, in
turning away from the liberal west and towards despotic Russia,
Bismarck had twinges of conscience and had to satisfy himself,
every now and then, that nothing could be made out of the
western alliance.

[1] Beaconsfield to Victoria, 27 Sept. 1879. *Disraeli*, vi. 386. Münster to Bismarck,
27 Sept. 1879. *Große Politik*, iv, no. 712.
[2] Bismarck's minute on Münster to Bismarck, 27 Sept. 1879. Ibid., no. 712.

The vague negotiation of September 1879 was one of those many 'lost opportunities' in Anglo-German relations where there was, in fact, nothing to lose. The British certainly did not appreciate that they had lost anything. Salisbury greeted the news of the Austro-German alliance[1] as 'good tidings of great joy'. Bismarck professed great irritation at this indiscretion; he was really angered at the consequence of his own act. Hitherto, the British had had to take the lead in opposing Russia in the Balkans; now they could resign their place to Austria-Hungary, confident that, in the last resort, Germany would have to support her. It is not surprising that Salisbury rejoiced: Germany would henceforth be fighting England's battles instead of the other way round. All Bismarck's diplomacy from October 1879 until his fall was devoted to staving off the inevitable outcome of the Austro-German alliance.

This attempt, too, began before the alliance was signed. On 27 September an influential Russian diplomat, Saburov, appeared in Berlin. Saburov was of the same school as Shuvalov: contemptuous of Panslavism and the advocate of a defensive policy based on alliance with Germany. He wrote to the tsar: 'A friendly Prussia places us in the privileged position of being the only Power in Europe which need fear no attack and which can reduce its budget without risk, as our August Master did after the Crimean War'.[2] Saburov proposed an agreement for mutual security: Germany to remain neutral in a war between Russia and England; Russia to remain neutral, and to keep others so, in a war between Germany and France. Moreover, Russia would respect the integrity of Austria-Hungary, on condition that she did not extend her sphere of interest in the Balkans.[3] If Bismarck had really feared Russia, this offer gave him everything he wanted. But Bismarck's real anxiety was the Austro-Hungarian desire to follow a 'western' policy, and Russian aggressiveness was his excuse, not his motive. He tried to make out that there had been a change of heart on the part of the Russians: they had been meditating an attack on Germany, but had been warned off by his negotiations with Andrássy. This was untrue: Russian policy had been defensive

---

[1] Much nonsense is talked about the 'secrecy' of the various alliances. The existence of the Austro-German alliance was made known at once, though its terms were not revealed until 1888.

[2] Simpson, *Saburov Memoirs*, p. 60.

[3] Ibid., p. 83.

all along, and Saburov had in fact first made his offer to Bismarck in July. As always, Bismarck rode off on a personal grievance. In 1876, he alleged, he would have been ready to go with Russia 'through thick and thin', in exchange for a guarantee of Alsace and Lorraine. Now it was too late: he had had to seek security elsewhere. Yet Saburov offered Germany security against France as effectively as the Austro-German alliance did. To judge Bismarck by these remarks, European diplomacy was often shaped by his bad temper. The Russians were used to it—they had often used the same method themselves. Saburov meekly accepted Bismarck's arguments and complaints. The Russians would pay a high price—even that of a German alliance with Austria-Hungary—if they could have security against 'the Crimean coalition'.[1]

If matters had depended on Russia alone, the League of the Three Emperors would have been revived at the end of 1879. Saburov, now ambassador at Berlin, proposed it formally to Bismarck in January 1880. The difficulty came from Austria-Hungary. Andrássy's last act as foreign minister was to advise Francis Joseph that he could not recommend a deal with Russia 'either as a minister or as a gentleman'.[2] Bismarck had made out to William I that Andrássy was the only pro-German at Vienna and that the alliance must be pushed on in order to forestall an Austro-Hungarian foreign minister who might join with Russia. Events turned out otherwise. Certainly Francis Joseph broke with the German liberals in the Austrian parliament and established a ministry which rested on clerical and Slav votes. But this, far from making Austro-Hungarian policy more friendly to Russia, made it more adventurous and ambitious in the Balkans. After all it was the liberals who had voted against the occupation of Bosnia and Hercegovina at the delegations. Haymerle, the new foreign minister, outdid Andrássy in his suspicion of Russia. Moreover, as a professional servant of the dynasty instead of a Magyar aristocrat, he had nothing against increasing dynastic prestige. Haymerle was more eager than Andrássy had been for a full-blown alliance with England: Austria-Hungary dominant in Turkey-in-

---

[1] Saburov's only gesture of independence was to decline to write down the draft treaty at Bismarck's dictation. This unwillingness to play the part of Benedetti was, no doubt, not lost on the great man.

[2] Andrássy to Francis Joseph, 1 Oct. 1879. Leidner, *Die Außenpolitik Österreich-Ungarns*, p. 113.

Europe, England dominant in Turkey-in-Asia, the position of both underwritten by Germany, and Russia nowhere. This was certainly a more attractive prospect for Habsburg militarists than to play third fiddle in a conservative League of Emperors. In February 1880 Haymerle told Bismarck that his object was 'the permanent blocking of Russia' with British assistance.[1] Haymerle was counting on a consistent energy in British policy; instead it was abruptly reversed.

The British general election of April 1880 was the only one ever fought on issues of foreign policy until the election of 1935.[2] It is a sad comment on democratic control of foreign affairs that the policy which followed the liberal victory of 1880 was unsurpassed in feebleness until that which followed the conservative victory of 1935. Gladstone's triumph came from the merging of two separate currents of opinion. Ostensibly it was a victory for the ideas which he had preached since he had emerged from retirement to attack Disraeli in 1876: a victory for moral principles in foreign affairs, for the Concert of Europe instead of the Balance of Power, and for trusting Christian Russia instead of bolstering up Turkey. In reality, however, it expressed the usual British distaste for an active foreign policy after the crisis had passed. There was an exact parallel in the opposition which drove Castlereagh to suicide in 1822 and in that which overthrew Lloyd George in favour of the do-nothing conservative government of 1922. Gladstone wanted a more virtuous foreign policy; the electorate, and especially the liberal party, were opposed to having any foreign policy. Gladstone believed that the Concert of Europe would do good; the electorate thought that it would save money. Though Gladstone did not share the illusions of the electorate, he pandered to them by his insistence on the expensiveness of Disraeli's policy. As a result he succeeded only in negation. He abandoned Salisbury's Turkish policy; withdrew the military consuls from Asia Minor (though he did not return Cyprus which had been leased by the Turks in exchange for a British guarantee of their Asiatic lands); and compelled Turkey to fulfil the promises of territorial concessions made to Greece and Montenegro at the congress of

---

[1] Pribram, *Secret Treaties of Austria-Hungary*, ii. 5–6.
[2] Though the general election of 1857 was provoked by an issue in foreign policy (Palmerston's treatment of China), it was fought on the question of confidence in Palmerston as an individual, not of approval for a particular policy.

Berlin. There his policy ended. It could only have been carried further if there had been an Anglo-Russian agreement, possibly with France as a third party, to dismember the Turkish empire. No one wanted this. Both Queen Victoria and Granville, the foreign secretary, opposed any exclusive deal with Russia. The tsar distrusted Gladstone and was estranged from the French by their refusal to arrest Hartmann, a revolutionary accused of planning to blow up the tsar's train. Besides, the party which favoured a forward policy in central Asia had now carried the day at St. Petersburg. This involved conflict with Great Britain, whatever her government; and the Russians needed security at the Straits against a British attack. By the autumn of 1880 they were again eager for an agreement with the central Powers.

Haymerle was still reluctant, though the British change of policy had cut the ground from under his feet. In September 1880 he tried to extract from Bismarck an extension of the Austro-German alliance to cover Rumania in exchange for tolerating a deal with Russia. Bismarck refused; instead he brought Russia and Austria-Hungary together by cheating them both. To Haymerle he made out that the agreement was designed to control the extremists at St. Petersburg. When asked by Haymerle whether he had faith in Russia's intentions, he replied: 'At any rate more with a treaty than without.'[1] To Saburov he said the opposite: 'the only Power which would be inclined not to keep an engagement is Austria. That is why, with her, a triple alliance is better than an alliance between two;'[2] and he even suggested that, with Russia as partner, the Austro-German alliance would be virtually undone. Saburov wrote to Giers, who was now in charge of Russian foreign policy: 'It seems to me that we have there the most eloquent funeral oration on what was done at Vienna last year!'[3] The basis of agreement was the Austrian belief that Germany would automatically support her and the Russian belief that she would not. In March 1881 Haymerle finally gave way. A new delay followed. On 13 March Alexander II was assassinated. His son, Alexander III, was a narrower man, overbearing and autocratic, and with none of his father's emotional attachment to

---

[1] Bismarck to Reuss, 22 Dec. 1880. *Große Politik*, iii, no. 521.
[2] Simpson, *Saburov Memoirs*, pp. 144-7.
[3] Ibid., p. 156.

Germany. Family ties with William I meant little to him, and monarchical solidarity still less; almost for the first time since Peter the Great, Russia had a ruler who was Russian and nothing more. But for the moment the Russian government was in confusion and unready to strike out on a new line. The negotiations were at last brought to a conclusion; and the League of the Three Emperors was signed on 18 June 1881.

The new League had little in common with the League of 1873. That had been a last gesture of conservative resistance. But Metternichian fear of upheaval was no longer enough to bring rulers together. After all, it was ninety years since the execution of Louis XVI, more than sixty since the defeat of Napoleon. The memories of 1848 were fading—they counted for something with William I and Francis Joseph, for nothing with Alexander III. Even Marx's International, fear of which had played some part in the League of 1873, was dissolved. There was social and political unrest in plenty; but its consequences were different. Both Napoleon III and Bismarck had used foreign war to distract attention from domestic opposition. Formerly only a strong government could risk war; soon there would come a time when only a secure government could remain resolutely at peace. Bismarck regarded the League of the Three Emperors as a triumph for conservatism, but he was alone in this view; for the Russians and Austrians alike it was a move in foreign policy. Metternich had been able to tide over the differences between Austria and Russia for more than thirty years merely by playing on the fear of revolution; Bismarck had to offer them both concrete advantages.

The treaty of 1881 was therefore a practical agreement about the Near East, without even a monarchical flourish. Its only general principle was a pact of neutrality if one of the three empires was involved in war with a fourth Power. Since there was no immediate likelihood of a war between Germany and France, this was straight gain for Russia: it was a promise that Germany and, still more, Austria-Hungary would not join England. The only limitation was in regard to Turkey: there neutrality would apply only if there had been agreement beforehand. This was an unnecessary precaution: the Russians had no intention of going to war with Turkey. Further, the three Powers recognized 'the European and mutually obligatory character' of the rule of the Straits and would insist that

Turkey enforce it. This was the essential security against a British expedition to the Black Sea which the Russians had been seeking all along; it was the one thing that mattered to them. Since a Russian garrison at the Straits was impossible, this was the next best thing. The Russians gained still more. The Austrians promised not to oppose the union of the two Bulgarias and thus cut themselves off from England, for whom division of Bulgaria had been the essential achievement of 1878. In return the Russians recognized Austria-Hungary's right to annexe Bosnia and Hercegovina, a concession that they had been ready to make ever since 1876.

The League was a victory for the Russians and perhaps for Bismarck. Germany was freed from having to choose between Russia and Austria-Hungary in the Balkans. Russia got security in the Black Sea in exchange for a promise of peaceful behaviour which her internal weakness compelled her to keep in any case. It was not so easy to see the advantage for Austria-Hungary, as Haymerle insisted. By supporting the Russian interpretation of the rule of the Straits, she committed herself to an eventual breach with England; yet she owed her Balkan position to the co-operation with England in 1878. She got in exchange merely Russian promises which she regarded as worthless. Andrássy and Haymerle had made the alliance with Bismarck in order to secure German backing against the Russians; instead Bismarck had used the alliance to force Haymerle into an unwelcome agreement with them. He was indeed hard put to it to discover practical arguments with which to persuade Haymerle; and a curious result followed. To justify the League, Bismarck had to invent Italy as a Great Power; and then had to take his own pretence seriously. In February 1880 when Haymerle had argued that England should be brought into the Austro-German alliance in order to keep Italy quiet, Bismarck had answered that Italy was of no importance.[1] A year later he was arguing that the great use of the League of the Three Emperors was to prevent an alliance between Italy and Russia.[2] When the League had been made, Haymerle continued to press for greater security against Russia; Bismarck would not give this. As a substitute, he had to offer Austria-Hungary security on her Italian frontier; this theoretically would free

---

[1] Pribram, *Secret Treaties of Austria-Hungary,* ii. 5–6.
[2] Bismarck to Reuss, 17 Jan. 1881. *Große Politik,* iii, no. 524.

Austrian troops for the defence of Galicia.[1] Thus the League of the Three Emperors, which was a pact of friendship with Russia, led in a roundabout way to the Triple Alliance, which was implicitly a pact against her.

There was, of course, a deeper element. The association between Italy and central Europe was the oldest in European history. It shaped the middle ages, when every ruler of Germany called himself Roman emperor and many took the title seriously; it provided the double basis for the empire of Napoleon. National Italy had been essential to the victory of national Germany. The Italian alliance had been decisive in the war of 1866; and, but for Italy, France and Austria-Hungary might have united against Bismarck in 1870. Even later it would have suited the two Powers to come together in order to dismember Italy—Austria-Hungary for the sake of the pope, France in favour of a federation of republics. Still this was a remote and speculative danger. It was more to the purpose that Bismarck was now engaged in building a conservative system, like Metternich before him; and, just as he himself had tamed the national revolution in Germany, so he wanted the Italian monarchy to become respectable. But he took a long time to arrive at this position. At the congress of Berlin the claims of Italy had been ignored, and she had been treated on the same level as Greece or Turkey. Austria-Hungary acquired Bosnia and Hercegovina; Great Britain acquired Cyprus; the French were encouraged by everybody to take Tunis. Only the Italian representatives returned from the congress with their hands clean—and empty.

In 1878 Bismarck had wished to keep France contented and pacific; Salisbury had wished to associate her with his Near Eastern policy. Therefore both had pointed to Tunis[2] as the most suitable object of French ambition. It was often alleged later that Bismarck at any rate had encouraged France in order to estrange her from Italy; but this, if it existed at all, was certainly a secondary motive. His overriding concern was that France should act as a Great Power in regions where she would not run against Germany: 'I want to turn your eyes away from Metz and Strasbourg by helping you to find satisfaction else-

---

[1] The gain was only theoretical. The Austro-Hungarian military machine was too cumbrous to adjust itself to the consequences of policy.

[2] Tunis, theoretically a Turkish dependency, was a small Mohammedan state ruled by a bey; and the immediate neighbour of Algeria.

where.'[1] Imperialism, in fact, was a means of enjoying the sensation of greatness without the trouble and expense which this usually involved. The French hesitated a good deal even over the small trouble and expense involved in acquiring Tunis. They disregarded the advice of Bismarck and Salisbury, and were concerned rather that Tunis should not go to anyone else than that they should acquire it for themselves. Unfortunately the Italians did not accept this self-denying ordinance. There were already Italian settlers in Tunis—20,000 or so against 200 Frenchmen; and Italian capitalists played railway politics there. The French were determined to have no European power established in the neighbourhood of Algiers; and the Italian rivalry pushed them reluctantly into action. A French force occupied the country; and on 12 May 1881 the bey signed the treaty of Bardo, accepting a French protectorate. The Italians were helpless. Bismarck gave France the 'benevolent neutrality' which he had always promised;[2] and though the liberal government in England at first thought of issuing one of the high-sounding protests which were its sole diplomatic weapon, even this was abandoned when Gladstone insisted that they could not object to the French taking Tunis while themselves retaining Cyprus. Besides, as he added with characteristic ingenuity: 'I do not see that it[3] neutralizes Malta more than it is neutralized by Malta.'[4]

Italian dreams of empire were harshly dispelled. The violence which had found an outlet in clamour for Tunis now turned to republicanism and, what was worse, to agitation against the pope, an agitation which threatened to discredit the monarchy in the eyes of the European Powers. The pope indeed seriously contemplated leaving Rome if he could not get his temporal power restored. Long ago, in 1825, Charles Albert had flirted ambitiously with radicalism and then, himself endangered, had been glad to accept Metternich's protection; now the Italian monarchy, which had been ready enough to ally itself with the

---

[1] Saint-Vallier to Barthélemy Saint-Hilaire, 29 Nov. 1880. *Documents diplomatiques français*, first series, iii, no. 307.

[2] Saint-Vallier to Courcel, 12 Nov. 1880. Ibid., no. 294. Bismarck offered 'even diplomatic support if we asked for it'.

[3] i.e. Bizerta, the principal port in Tunis and potentially therefore a French naval base, as it subsequently became.

[4] Gladstone to Granville, 22 Apr. 1881. Temperley and Penson. *Foundations of British Foreign Policy*, no. 161.

revolutionaries for its own aggrandizement, belatedly discovered its monarchist principles. In October 1881 Humbert,
king of Italy, paid a begging visit to Vienna; a long road had
been travelled since the proud days of Cavour. The Italians
proposed to Austria-Hungary a mutual guarantee. They made
out that they were threatened with attack by France; the real
object of the guarantee was, however, internal—to secure the
monarchy from republican upheaval or from the intervention
of foreign Powers to restore the temporal power of the pope.
The Austrians certainly wished to prop up the Italian monarchy;
and they welcomed Italian neutrality in case of war with Russia.
But a guarantor needs assets, and Italy had none. It was clear
against whom the Austrians would guarantee Italy; but against
whom could Italy guarantee Austria-Hungary? Humbert left
Vienna once more empty-handed.

Haymerle had died suddenly just before Humbert's visit.
Kálnoky, his successor, was a stronger character. As a high
conservative, he was reluctant to abandon the pope; and,
though firmly anti-Russian, counted on holding the Russians
in check without assistance. The Italian pleadings therefore
went unnoticed in Vienna. In February 1882 Bismarck suddenly brought the negotiations to life again. As so often, his
policy was reshaped overnight by an abrupt alarm—this time
the alarm that he might not be able to keep Russia on a pacific
course despite the League of the Three Emperors. In November
1881 Gambetta, the great radical patriot, had become prime
minister in France for the first and last time. He hoped ultimately for alliance with Russia and England and, rather less
remotely, for reconciliation with Italy. These, he intended,
should end the preponderance of Germany and make possible
a negotiated settlement of Alsace and Lorraine. Bismarck was
not alarmed by this prospect; he himself looked forward, in an
obscure way, to reconciliation with France. But the advent of
Gambetta had a marked effect on Russian politics. Panslavs and
conservatives were fighting for the favour of the new tsar; Gorchakov, still theoretically chancellor, was dying, and Ignatiev
hoped to succeed him. An alliance with France was the Panslavs' strongest card. In January 1882 General Skobelev, pic-
turesque hero of the Russo-Turkish war and himself a Panslav,
went to Paris on a mission of display. The visit achieved nothing.
Gambetta had already fallen before Skobelev arrived and, in

any case, did not respond to his rhetoric. Moreover, on the way home Skobelev stopped at Warsaw and extended his Panslav appeals to the Poles. This outraged Alexander III; and Skobelev fell into disgrace, carrying the Panslavs down with him. In April 1882 Giers, a conservative of German origin, became Russian foreign minister; in June Ignatiev disappeared from public life.

All the same, the Skobelev affair shook Bismarck's faith in the Russian conservatives; it caused him an alarm perhaps more genuine than that of August 1879. On 17 February Skobelev delivered his most violent speech in Paris; on 28 February Bismarck urged Kálnoky to revive the negotiations with Italy.[1] These negotiations were conducted on a curious basis. Austria-Hungary would alone benefit from Italian neutrality; yet Germany had to pay the price for it, and the treaty was very much of Bismarck's making. The Triple Alliance was concluded on 20 May 1882. Austria-Hungary and Germany promised to assist Italy against a French attack; Italy, but not Austria-Hungary, made the same promise to Germany. Each of the three would assist the others if one or both became involved in war with two Great Powers and would remain neutral in case of war with one. In practical terms Italy promised to remain neutral in a war between Austria-Hungary and Russia, and to fight in a war between the central Powers and a Franco-Russian alliance. The reward for Italy lay in the preamble. This declared that the object of the treaty was 'to increase the guarantees of general peace, to strengthen the monarchical principle, and by that to assure the maintenance of social and political order in their respective states'. Finally there was a separate declaration that the treaty was not directed against England—a watered-down version of the original Italian proposal that England should be brought into the alliance.

The Triple Alliance looked formidable and elaborate; its real aims were modest. Ostensibly it welded central Europe together and re-created the Holy Roman empire at its most grandiose so far as foreign affairs were concerned. In practice it merely propped up the Italian monarchy and secured Italian neutrality in an Austro-Hungarian war against Russia. The Austrians paid little in return. Kálnoky would not allow the Italians any say in the Balkans and therefore did not ask their aid against Russia. The sole price for Austria-Hungary was a vague approval of the

[1] Busch to Reuss, 28 Feb. 1882. *Große Politik*, iii, no. 548.

Italian monarchy and therewith an indirect repudiation of that support for the papacy which had been traditional to the house of Habsburg. The price was paid by Germany: she promised to defend Italy against France and, since Italian assistance was worthless, got nothing in return. In plain terms, Bismarck undertook to defend Italy in order to meet the Austro-Hungarian complaints against the League of the Three Emperors; even this was better in his eyes than pledging support to Austria-Hungary in the Balkans. Besides, he knew that the French were not intending to attack Italy, and therefore he did not regard the obligation as onerous. The Italians knew this also; recognition as a Great Power, not protection from France, was their real need. The Triple Alliance gave them this; it bolstered up the myth of Italian greatness, and therefore staved off internal discontent for almost a generation. There was one striking omission in the original Alliance. Though humiliation over Tunis played only a secondary part in driving Italy over to the central Powers, the Italian politicians certainly wanted backing for their imperialist designs in the Mediterranean. In 1882 they did not get it. But just as the Austrians thought that the Austro-German alliance would gradually draw Germany into supporting their Balkan plans, so the Italians counted that the Triple Alliance would gradually involve Germany in their Mediterranean schemes. So long as Russia was peaceful and Italian neutrality therefore of academic interest, their hopes were thwarted; once the peace of the Balkans was disturbed, Italy had something of value to sell and then Germany had to pay a real price.

Two other alliances completed Bismarck's 'system'. In June 1881 Austria-Hungary made a secret treaty with Serbia, virtually establishing an economic and political protectorate. The Serbian prime minister complained that 'Serbia would stand in the same relation to Austria-Hungary as Tunis to France'—or, one might add, as the Boer republics to Great Britain; and Milan, the Serbian ruler, smuggled the agreement through only by assuring his prime minister that it did not mean what it said, while assuring Haymerle 'on my honour and in my quality as Prince of Serbia' that it did. Milan was only concerned to collect Austrian money and the title of king, which he assumed with Austrian approval in 1882; and Serbia became a Habsburg dependency until the end of his reign. Though the treaty with

Serbia was hardly in keeping with the spirit of the League of the Three Emperors, it was not a direct breach of faith with the Russians. They had treated Serbia coldly in 1878 and were ready all along to recognize Austro-Hungarian preponderance in the western Balkans in return for their own preponderance in Bulgaria.

Rumania was a different matter. The independence of Rumania had been the great achievement of the Crimean war. In 1877 Rumania had been dragged into war on the side of Russia; her only reward (for a part of the Dobrudja cannot rank as such) had been the loss of Bessarabia. Certainly the Rumanians wanted support against a new Russian expedition to the Balkans; and the Austrians were anxious to supply it. But the Rumanians were prouder and stronger than the Serbs; besides they were already alive to the Hungarian oppression of the Rumanians in Transylvania. They insisted that Germany should be a party to any alliance between themselves and Austria-Hungary. Bismarck accepted the condition and himself promoted the alliance which was concluded on 30 October 1883. Austria-Hungary and Germany undertook to defend Rumania; Rumania undertook to fight if Habsburg territory adjacent to Rumania was attacked—a cumbersome definition of attack by Russia. This was a clear defensive alliance against Russia, impossible to reconcile with Bismarck's repeated assurances to the Russians that he was committed only to the defence of Austria-Hungary; and the pledge to Rumania was the most telling argument used in 1890 by the opponents of the Reinsurance treaty between Germany and Russia. Bismarck had now completed his repetition of the policy followed by Manteuffel in 1854, and he could justify himself in the same way: it was less dangerous to promise support for Austria-Hungary than to allow her to fall into the arms of the western Powers. Still, fear of 'the Crimean coalition' had carried him into strange courses. As things turned out, the alliance with Rumania caused no trouble. Russia's route to Bulgaria and Constantinople was most wisely a route by sea, as the failure of 1878 had shown; and it suited the Russians, too, to treat Rumania as a neutral area, at any rate until the mounting tension of 1914. Bismarck himself used a simpler argument. He believed that great wars occur only between Great Powers and, so long as he could maintain a peaceful balance among the

Great, his extensive promises to the smaller Powers, such as Italy and Rumania, did not trouble him.

All the same, Bismarck's 'system' was something of a conjuring trick, a piece of conscious virtuosity. Once started on the path of alliances, Bismarck treated them as the solution for every problem. He scattered promises so as not to carry them out. He promised to fight on the side of Austria-Hungary in order to make her friendly to Russia; and on the side of Italy in order to secure her neutrality. Perhaps the only promise he took seriously was that of diplomatic support for Russia against England at the Straits. His two great creations, the League of the Three Emperors and the Triple Alliance, were in direct contradiction. The League was based on Austro-Russian co-operation, the Alliance was in preparation for an Austro-Russian war. The League was an anti-British combination, its most practical clause designed to close the Straits against the British by common diplomatic action; the Alliance was specifically not directed against Great Britain, and both Austria-Hungary and Italy hoped eventually for her support. There can be no doubt where Bismarck's own sympathy lay: the League was an affair of the heart, the Alliance of calculation. His deepest attachment was to the old Russo-Prussian friendship, founded on the partition of Poland. He disliked the Austrians from his days at Frankfurt until his death, and he thought that the British were only concerned 'to get others to pull their chestnuts out of the fire'. For that matter he preferred the sensible politicians of the French republic (especially Gambetta, and, after him, Ferry) to the restless, scheming Italians. Obviously tsardom was a more conservative force than the Dual monarchy, and the Third republic than the unstable kingdom of Italy; his diplomacy was an insurance against the subversive forces in Russia and France, not against their official governments—against Panslavism in the one, and the advocates of revenge in the other. His references to the French nationalists are well known, and he said much the same about Russia. 'The Emperor is himself well-intentioned. His ministers are prudent and inclined to a conservative policy. But will they have the strength to resist the pressure of popular passions, if they are once unchained? The party of war is stronger in Russia than elsewhere.'[1]

---

[1] Courcel (Berlin) to Ferry, 14 Dec. 1883. *Documents diplomatiques français*, first series, v, no. 168.

The result was paradoxical. Bismarck claimed to be the apostle of stability, and presented his system as 'a league of peace'. In fact, by the Triple Alliance, he associated Germany with the restless Powers and, implicitly, against the conservative ones. So far as Europe was concerned (and that is all that mattered to Bismarck), Russia and France asked only to be left alone. The Russians had no ambitions in the Near East after the congress of Berlin; their only interest was security. The Balkans were economically a matter of indifference to them. They wanted the Straits closed against British warships, and they needed free passage for their grain trade. Though the best way to secure this would have been to control the Straits themselves, they knew that this was impossible, and therefore accepted gratefully the diplomatic combination which Bismarck offered them. The strategic threat in these years came from England, not from Russia; Salisbury's declaration at the congress was not repudiated even by Gladstone. The economic challenge from Austria-Hungary was even graver. The Austrians would not limit their economic sphere. They pursued a 'civilizing mission' of economic imperialism, a programme that could not be stopped by any political division. Above all, they pushed on the Orient Line, until it reached Constantinople. As Kálnoky said to a Belgian inquirer: 'We do dream of conquests . . . the conquests to be made by our manufactures, our commerce, our civilization. . . . When a Pullman car will take you comfortably from Paris to Constantinople in three days, I venture to believe that you will not be dissatisfied with our activity. It is for you Westerners that we are working.'[1] This programme, however attractive to a Belgian economist, was bound to alarm the Russians, especially when it threatened the national development of the Balkan peoples in whom they were sentimentally interested.

The same situation was true for France and Italy on a lower plane. The French asked only not to be invaded again by Germany. The Italians were the disturbing element in the Mediterranean, as the Tunis affair had shown: without their political interference and their railway politics there, the French would not have moved. For that matter the Italian agitation for Trieste was a more serious and a more practical threat to German interests than the French resentment over the loss of

[1] Laveleye, *La péninsule des Balkans*, i. 40.

Alsace and Lorraine. Bismarck's choice of Austria-Hungary and Italy against Russia and France was, in large part, the repetition of the choice that he had made earlier in German affairs. Then he allied himself with the German revolution in order to tame it; now he made foreign alliances in order to take his allies prisoner. He controlled his allies; he did not co-operate with them. There indeed was the deepest element. In international affairs, as in domestic politics, Bismarck disliked equals; he sought for satellites. Though both Russia and France wanted to turn their backs on Europe, they both remained independent Great Powers, fish too big for Bismarck's net. His system was a tyranny; and it did not console others that it was a tyranny imposed for their good, in favour of peace and the social order. An international order needs common principles and a common moral outlook, as well as treaty obligations, if it is to be effective. Metternich's 'system' had been based on a political conservatism that was still a genuine force. The monarchical solidarity to which Bismarck appealed counted for little even among crowned heads; and he himself had done most to prevent the rise of any democratic substitute. In the autumn of 1879, when Bismarck was taking the first steps in his system of alliances, Gladstone was conducting his campaign in Midlothian; and Bismarck's aims could have been achieved only if he had accepted the principles of national freedom and equality which Gladstone preached.

XIII

THE BREAKDOWN OF 'THE LIBERAL ALLIANCE' AND ITS CONSEQUENCES

1882-5

THE congress of Berlin represented a settlement of Europe, as the congress of Vienna did before it; Metternich and Bismarck both achieved 'systems', and both systems faced the same dangers—a Balkan war between Russia and Austria on the one hand, a French attempt to reverse defeat on the other. But these dangers had changed their order of importance. Metternich's system looked west: it was directed primarily against a revolutionary upheaval inspired by France, and fear of this revolution restrained even Russia in the Near East for nearly forty years. Bismarck's system looked east: French revenge was not a serious danger unless there was an Austro-Russian war. Waterloo came after twenty-five years of French victory; Sedan confirmed half a century of decline, which many Frenchmen had obscurely sensed. The majority of French-men realized after 1871, as they had not realized after 1815, that the greatness of France lay in the past—a greatness to be preserved, not to be advanced. They were determined to achieve in the Third republic what they had wanted ever since the end of the Terror in 1794—'to enjoy the fruits of the Revolu-tion'. With a stable population, a rich and fertile land, an egalitarian society, and a great past, France asked only for a quiet life. The Third republic rested on a partnership between the peasants and the professional middle class, both devoted to the rights of property and therefore seeking security. The peasants, once the mainstay of the empire, had learnt that the empire meant war; now they let the town-lawyers run the state and grow rich on the proceeds, so long as they kept clear of war or social upheaval. The town-workers had perhaps wanted both in 1871, at the time of the commune; but within twenty years they, too, made a limited peace with society and became the enemies of an adventurous policy.

Like the Habsburg monarchy after 1866, the French wanted security; but, unlike Francis Joseph, they would not obtain it at the price of putting themselves under German protection. The lost provinces, Alsace and Lorraine, were no doubt the principal stumbling-block; and Bismarck himself, with rather primitive cunning, often lamented the 'mistake' that he had made in 1871.[1] The real resentment went deeper. Though the French had no hope of defeating Germany in a new war, they would not admit German supremacy. They accepted defeat; they would not accept its consequences. As a result, any French politician who seemed to be heading for war with Germany was ruined; but so, though more slowly, was any politician who aimed at reconciliation with Germany. It would be wrong to exaggerate the decline of France. In 1871 her population was still as great as that of Germany; and her industrial resources not far behind. Bismarck's precautions against France were more justified than those of his successors; they were also more skilful. Far from trying to isolate France, he worked to draw her out of the isolation which she had imposed upon herself. He said to Courcel, the French ambassador, in 1882: 'I want appeasement, I would like to be reconciled. We have no sensible motive for seeking to do you harm; we are rather in the position of owing you reparation.'[2] He made much of the French at the congress of Berlin, accepting without demur the conditions they laid down for attending; and after it, he assured them, with perfect truth, that the object of his system of alliances was to prevent a war between Austria-Hungary and Russia rather than to guard against French revenge.[3] He offered the French more positive consolation: he would support them everywhere except on the Rhine, a policy he applied when they took Tunis.

Bismarck's patronage was perhaps too blatant. Every Frenchman realized that Germany stood to gain if France turned her ambitions from the Rhine to the Mediterranean. Yet it is a

[1] The element of truth in this is that, whereas Bismarck always meant to take Strasbourg, he had doubts about Metz. As he said to Courcel (to Ferry, 25 Apr. 1884. *Documents diplomatiques français*, first series, v, no. 249): 'I would not have taken Metz; for me, the determining principle in drawing the frontier was the language.' But Strasbourg, not Metz, was the principal symbol of French grief.

[2] Courcel to Freycinet, 16 June 1882. Ibid., iv, no. 392.

[3] Bismarck, always inclined to exaggerate in conversation, overdid things, when he said that the bases of his policy were 'the Austrian alliance and good relations with France'. Saint-Vallier to Courcel, 12 Nov. 1880. Ibid., iii, no. 294.

wrong emphasis to suggest that overseas expansion was checked principally by the advocates of revenge. Those who preached a new war against Germany were even more unpopular than the colonizers: Déroulède, the ablest of them, was persecuted, hunted, and ultimately exiled. Colonial enterprise was tolerated only so long as it involved little effort. Gambetta said: 'In Africa France will make the first faltering steps of the convalescent'; and colonial policy had to be kept on that level. As soon as serious trouble arose, the colonial enthusiast was driven from office. Ferry, the greatest figure of the Third republic between Gambetta and Clemenceau, had his career ruined with the terrible epithet, the 'tonkinois', the man who had involved France in expense for the sake of Indo-China, pearl of imperial possessions. French colonial expansion was, in fact, the result of weakness, not evidence of strength.

There was a more practical danger for the French in pursuing a colonial policy: it brought them into conflict with other Powers, and this, apart from weakening them against Germany, was unwelcome in itself. Bismarck repeatedly told the French, no doubt in all sincerity, that, when he encouraged them in Tunis, he was not thinking of winning Italy over to his side; she came over all the same, and it was small consolation to the French to be told, 'as to Italy, *she does not count*'.[1] The effect on French relations with Great Britain was infinitely more serious. Though Napoleon III never wholly lost British sympathies, the 'liberal alliance' wore threadbare in the last years of the Second Empire. It revived after 1871, and especially after the consolidation of the republic in 1877—revived, that is, as a matter of sentiment based on similar institutions and similar principles. There was no longer any attempt to offset the coalition of the three Northern Courts. The French were resolved not to act against Russia, their only friend on the Continent; and the British had lost interest in the Balance of Power. Most English-

---

[1] Saint-Vallier to Barthélemy Saint-Hilaire, 2 May 1881. *Documents diplomatiques français*, first series, iii, no. 495. Later Bismarck excused the Triple Alliance with simple lies. Waddington, when passing through Berlin, had this conversation with him: 'You authorise me to tell my Minister that you do not have with Italy an alliance as with Austria?—Yes. May I say that your arrangements with Italy have been made in view of a temporary situation?—Yes. Am I authorised to say that there is nothing written between you?—Goodbye. You will say that what you call the Triple Alliance is the completion of the policy of reparation which I follow towards Austria since Sadowa.' Waddington to Challemel-Lacour, 14 May 1883. Ibid., v, no. 35.

men had by now accepted Cobden's doctrine that events on the Continent were not their business; whatever happened, Great Britain and her trade would not be endangered. The few Englishmen who still thought of the Continent at all regarded the Balance of Power as something that worked itself without British intervention. In previous generations the doctrine of the Balance of Power had been a spur to action: the Balance had to be maintained by throwing British weight first in one scale, then in the other. Now it justified inaction. Since Germany and France, Austria-Hungary and Russia would always cancel each other out, there was no need for the British to do anything. Palmerston, the last exponent of the Balance of Power,[1] had welcomed the aggrandizement of Germany just before his death 'in order to control those Two ambitious and aggressive Powers, France and Russia';[2] and his expectation seemed to have been fulfilled. The British could turn their backs on Europe as never before or since. Between 1864 and 1906 no British statesman had to contemplate, however remotely, the problem of sending an expeditionary force to the Continent.[3]

British policy was conditioned solely by extra-European interests. Someone has said that nine English traditions out of ten date from the last third of the nineteenth century; and this is certainly true of foreign affairs. It was only in these years that Russia and France came to be regarded as the traditional, the eternal enemies of Great Britain. Though there was a long-standing rivalry with Russia in the Near East, popular hostility to Austria was deeper and more consistent—as Gladstone, ever old-fashioned, bore witness in his rash, though true, remark during the election campaign of 1880.[4] With France, friendship had been the rule ever since 1815, hostility the exception: France was the only Power with whom, during this period, the British made an effective written alliance. It is true that France

---

[1] Disraeli had claimed to be acting in favour of the Balance of Power when he disrupted the League of the Three Emperors by rejecting the Berlin memorandum in 1876. This was not much more than *gaminerie*. Though he perhaps disrupted the League, he made no serious effort to put anything in its place.

[2] Palmerston to Russell, 13 Sept. 1865. Temperley and Penson, *Foundations of British Foreign Policy*, no. 97.

[3] The treaties concluded with France and Prussia in 1870 for the protection of Belgian neutrality theoretically implied a possible British intervention; but no steps were taken to prepare it.

[4] 'There is not an instance—there is not a spot upon the whole map where you can lay your finger and say: "There Austria did good".'

and England were still the only colonial Powers. This did not necessarily make them enemies; it often made them partners. The disputes over Pacific islands in the time of Guizot were dwarfed by the co-operation between Napoleon III and the British in Syria, China, and Mexico. For most of the nineteenth century England and France represented Europe to the outer world except in remote central Asia; and this gave them a common mission. The two countries drew together whenever France was pacific and contented in Europe; they were estranged when France threatened to renew her dreams of European hegemony. After 1875 France was certainly pacific, though not contented; and friendship with England followed. The 'liberal alliance' expressed the sentiment both of the Gladstonian liberals and of Gambetta and his followers, who dominated politics in France. Though conflicts arose outside Europe, conflicts aggravated by blunders on both sides, there was enough common sentiment to ensure that these would be settled finally by negotiation, not by war. This was not understood by continental diplomatists, whether German or Russian, who were thus led into blunders even more fatal.

England and France had been more often allies than rivals during the nineteenth century even in the Mediterranean: Greece, Turkey, and Italy bore witness to it. The Egyptian crisis of 1840 had been the only serious exception. But there was here an approaching conflict of outlook. The British, established at Malta and Gibraltar, judged the Mediterranean solely in terms of sea-power. They wanted to see it ringed with independent states, not to add to their own possessions there;[1] they wanted to keep other Great Powers out, not to get themselves in. Though the French shared this outlook on the European side of the Mediterranean and were indeed the most consistent supporters of Turkish integrity, they saw things differently in Africa. There they hoped to take up the tradition of Bonaparte's expedition to Egypt in 1798 and to found a new 'Roman' empire, which would console them for the loss of their empire in Europe. Already the rulers of Algeria, they regarded themselves as the ultimate heirs of the other derelict Mohammedan states in North Africa—Tunis, Morocco, and Egypt. They were cautious, even procrastinating, in applying this policy; and

---

[1] The policy of the Cyprus convention, in any case not inconsistent with this attitude, was an aberration, which the British jettisoned in 1880.

worked cheerfully with the British so long as it was a question of keeping others out. They began to jib only when the British tried to reform these North African states and thus to make them genuinely independent—a parallel, though on a smaller scale, to the conflict between Russian and British policies at Constantinople. The cleavage was first shown in 1880, when a conference at Madrid, summoned on British initiative for the reform of Morocco, was wrecked by French opposition.[1] Still this was not a decisive issue. The British were content if Morocco remained independent, though unreformed; and the French were content so long as it remained unreformed, though independent.

A more decisive issue followed. Egypt was vital to both countries—vital to the British government for reasons of imperial strategy, vital to the French because of tradition and prestige. The Egyptian question had been created by Bonaparte when he led his expedition there in 1798. The British had answered by expelling him without establishing themselves. The pattern

[1] The Madrid conference was also of interest as the first display by Bismarck of his policy of supporting France everywhere except in Alsace and Lorraine. The British were anxious to preserve Morocco as the African counterpart of Spain—two neutral zones which gave security to Gibraltar; the French intended ultimately to add it to their African empire. Drummond Hay, British minister at Tangier for more than forty years, had had an easy time of it while Napoleon III was taken up with Europe; now he wished to round off his career by ending the system of 'protégés', which enabled Moors to put themselves under the authority of foreign diplomats and thus escape the control of their own government. When direct negotiations with the French minister at Tangier failed, Drummond Hay proposed to call in 'Europe', on the assumption that only France wished to keep Morocco weak and anarchic. The conference was, however, a warning (which the Germans might well have heeded in 1905) against supposing that the Great Powers could ever judge a question on its merits without thinking of their general relations. Only the Spaniards, who had great ambitions in Morocco themselves but were too weak to pursue them, supported the British proposals. All the other Powers joined to wreck the conference. The Italians followed the jackal principle that the more trouble there was in the Mediterranean the more chance for them somewhere; the Russians hoped to be rewarded by French support at Constantinople; the Germans, who had backed Drummond Hay in 1879, changed round and carried Austria-Hungary along with them. Once reform had been prevented, the French were content to wait. Drummond Hay (who retired in 1885) continued to preach the co-operation of the Powers. Occasionally he despaired, as when he wrote, shortly before his retirement: 'If we can take no steps to check the aim of France to become the mistress of the Straits, and if it be found that Germany would be ready to confront France in her Algerine possessions by taking possession of the country, I should say that it would be far better that she should occupy the highway of the East and of India than France, which Power never ceases in all parts of the world to be the jealous and worst enemy of England.' E. F. Cruickshank, *Morocco at the Parting of the Ways*, p. 196.

had been repeated in 1840, when the French had treated Egypt as their protégé; the British had defeated the protégé, but had again left Egypt independent.[1] The Second Empire took a more cautious, though more effective line—that of financial penetration. Egypt was fertilized with French money; and the geography of world-power was revolutionized by the Suez canal, Napoleon III's most lasting memorial. Though the British had steadily opposed the canal for obvious strategical reasons, they became the principal users of it as soon as it was open: in 1882 80 per cent. of the ships passing through the canal were British. Here was a stake in Egypt which it was impossible to repudiate, a stake increased when Disraeli acquired the khedive's shares in the canal in 1875. Still, the British declined Bismarck's repeated promptings to 'take Egypt' in exchange for a Russian control of Constantinople; they saw well enough the offence this would give to France and, besides, did not relish the turmoil that a general partition of the Turkish empire would cause. So long as their navy dominated the Mediterranean, they were content with a stable Egyptian government, giving security to the canal. Egypt, however, did not oblige them. In April 1876 the khedive could no longer pay the inflated interest on his loans; Egypt was bankrupt.[2] The French government was determined to protect the bondholders; the British wished to keep an eye on the French for the sake of the canal. In Salisbury's words: 'You may renounce—or monopolize—or share. Renouncing would have been to place the French across our road to India. Monopolizing would have been very near the risk of war. So we resolved to share.'[3] An Anglo-French financial control was therefore established; and Egypt tottered on for some three years.

In April 1879 Khedive Ismail attempted to escape from this control. The British might not have objected—they would have been satisfied to get the French out of Egypt even if they went out themselves. But Bismarck organized a protest by the other European Powers. Unless he was simply concerned to protect

[1] Or almost so. In theory the Turkish sultan was still overlord of Egypt and both the British and the French tried to exploit his suzerainty at different times.

[2] The total debt was some £90,000,000. This trivial sum, now given away as largesse by a single Great Power in a day, determined the relations of the two western Powers for twenty years.

[3] Salisbury to Northcote, 16 Sept. 1881. Gwendolen Cecil, *Life of Salisbury*, ii. 331–2.

the interests of his private banker Bleichroeder (an explanation by no means unlikely), he can only have wished to keep Egypt going as a topic of possible conflict between England and France. The two countries were forced into further action. They induced the sultan, as theoretical overlord of Turkey, to depose Ismail; and the control was re-established on a firmer basis. Opposition inside Egypt shifted from the khedive to the army officers and a few Mohammedan intellectuals, who launched the first nationalist movement; and by 1881 this movement conquered the country. Anglo-French policy fell once more into confusion. Gladstone, now in power in England, had preached the doctrine of national freedom elsewhere; on the other hand, he was outraged by financial irregularity, just as he had been turned against Turkey by the bankruptcy of 1875, which he called 'the greatest of *political* crimes'. Granville, the foreign secretary, feeble and evasive as ever, would have liked to persuade the Turks to restore order in Egypt. This was the one thing that the French would not stomach: they had to resist a precedent which might be applied to Tunis, and still dreamt that if Egypt fell to pieces it might pass to them, not to Turkey. In January 1882 Gambetta, during his brief ministry, tried to launch a bold policy of Anglo-French intervention, much to Granville's discomfort. The scheme was again wrecked by Bismarck: though he may have wanted friendship between the two countries, he certainly feared a creative alliance under French leadership. In any case, Gambetta fell at the end of January. Freycinet, the new prime minister, agreed with Granville that a European conference should meet at Constantinople to discover some means of dealing with the Egyptian question. None was found. The French would not have the Turks; the other Powers would not have anyone else.

Meanwhile, the nationalist movement in Egypt began to turn against Europeans there and even to threaten the security of the canal. In May the British and French governments agreed to stage a demonstration by sending naval squadrons to Alexandria; but, since they had neither a common programme nor a mandate from the Powers, the ships were not to do anything. The French began grudgingly to admit that a Turkish intervention might be the least of evils; but they would not agree to this until they got a satisfactory pledge that the Turkish troops would be withdrawn again. In July, with nothing settled at

Constantinople and nationalist riots increasing at Alexandria, the British admiral lost patience. He bombarded the forts, and the French ships withdrew in protest. Freycinet now at last acquiesced in an Anglo-French occupation of the canal zone; but when he proposed this to the chamber he was defeated by a striking majority on 31 July. As so often, French public opinion would tolerate the defence of imperial interests only so long as it involved neither expense nor the diversion of forces from Europe. The British continued to negotiate ineffectively for a Turkish force; but before agreement could be reached, a British army under Wolseley had landed in Egypt and defeated the nationalist forces at Tel-el-Kebir on 13 September. The Turks were told that their assistance was no longer needed.[1]

The British had become masters of Egypt. They had acquired their share of the partition of the Turkish empire, while Russia was as far off Constantinople as ever and the French without the shadowy compensation envisaged in 1878. This was an extraordinary outcome, arrived at without plan or deliberation. The British had never intended to occupy Egypt and now assured the Powers that they would leave as soon as order was restored. Gladstone said on 10 August 1882, that an indefinite occupation 'would be absolutely at variance with all the principles and views of Her Majesty's Government, and the pledges they have given to Europe, and with the views, I may say, of Europe itself'; Granville promised withdrawal in a circular to the Powers; and this promise was repeated sixty-six times between 1882 and 1922. But the condition was the restoration of order; and this condition was never fulfilled to British satisfaction. There was soon a complicating factor. The British had to take over the financial control which had broken down; and their representative, of the financial house of Baring (later Lord Cromer), took a pride in the work for its own sake. Hence there grew up the myth of Egypt as a British venture in imperialism. Absurdly enough, Cromer devoted himself—even at the sacrifice of British interests—to the interests of bondholders and investors who were mainly French.

Yet the occupation of Egypt destroyed the liberal alliance for more than twenty years. Though the French welcomed the

---

[1] It is possible that Dufferin, the British representative at Constantinople, deliberately put off settling with the Turks so that Wolseley could win his battle without them. Turkish procrastination, however, needed no encouragement from Dufferin or from anyone else.

defeat of the nationalist forces,[1] they were humiliated by their failure to take up Bonaparte's legacy—a legacy which, in reality, he had himself lost. At the outset the British would have accepted a joint occupation; and the French, by rejecting this, had caused their own humiliation. This made them the more bitter against the British; and the Egyptian question dwarfed everything else in French policy. All the same, it is wrong to speak, as so many do, of an Anglo-French conflict over Egypt, as though both parties aimed at the same prize. The French did not imagine that they could acquire Egypt for themselves. The battle of the Nile had settled that for good. The height of their ambition was that the British should fulfil their promises and withdraw. Failing this, they wanted compensation—something to show that they had had rights in Egypt and should be paid for surrendering them. The dispute was legalistic, not a struggle for a real prize. The British navy controlled the Mediterranean, and their army controlled Egypt. They had the prize and they could not be deprived of it, unless the prickings of conscience induced them to give it up. This was their weak spot. Their strategical position was strong; their moral position was shaky, and this counted for much with the British public, and even with British politicians. The British have always been anxious to show that, in defending their own interests, they are serving the interests of everyone else. Besides, they had to deny that Egypt was theirs, so as to give no excuse for the partition of the Ottoman empire elsewhere; and, on a more technical plane, they needed the consent of the Powers, on behalf of the foreign bondholders, if Cromer was to reform Egyptian finances. The British government had to pose as the mandatory of Europe, though France opposed the occupation and Russia opposed its policy everywhere. The goodwill of Germany and her allies was decisive; and Great Britain became dependent on the Triple Alliance. But the dependence was of a limited kind. The British needed votes on a commission, not armed backing; and though they would have been morally embarrassed if all the continental Powers had voted against them, no doubt they would have stayed in Egypt just the same.

Still, the disruption of the 'liberal alliance' created a new

---

[1] President Grévy said: 'I consider it of the highest importance that there should be no doubt, even for a moment, that Mussulman or Arab troops cannot resist Europeans in the field.'

situation in Europe, even though it was not followed by a war between England and France. Bismarck might dislike an effective alliance between them, recovering the leadership of Europe for the west, but their good understanding had suited him well enough: the British had ensured that the partnership would not be anti-German, the French that it would not be anti-Russian.[1] Now the conflict over Egypt threatened to reopen the Eastern question. The Austrians were quick to calculate that the British, needing their votes in Egypt, would be more forthcoming in opposing Russia in the Balkans; France, on the other hand, freed from British restraint, seemed on offer as the ally of Russia. There was a preliminary alarm in the summer of 1883, when Bulgaria broke away from Russian tutelage. Even the pacific Giers felt 'the blood mount to his head' and thought of intervention, which must have provoked an Anglo-Austrian resistance in its turn. But the Russians could not contemplate a general war: they swallowed their humiliation and let events in Bulgaria run on for another two years. Bismarck took his precautions during the crisis. He extended his alliance-system to Rumania in order to content the Austrians; and he put himself out to appease the French. He exaggerated the danger of war to them and, more remarkable still, held out the prospect of restoring an independent Poland in case of war with Russia.[2] This was a startling echo of old themes—the last time, incidentally, that the Polish question was mentioned in discussions between the Great Powers until after the outbreak of the First World War.

Poland would have been an impossibly high price to pay for French friendship; but Bismarck soon came to believe that it could be got for less. Though he had certainly counted on French resentment after 1871, he had also expected it to die away; and his hopes were not proved altogether false. Since the French politicians did not want a new war with Germany, they inclined towards good relations if only on a temporary basis; and some thought of making them permanent. Gambetta, at one moment the advocate of alliance with England and Russia, at others believed in Franco-German reconciliation; the question of Alsace and Lorraine would, he thought, lose its bitterness with the passage of time and be solved in a way to satisfy both

[1] Saint-Vallier to Waddington, 14 Nov. 1879. *Documents diplomatiques français*, first series, ii, no. 476.

[2] Courcel to Ferry, 13, 14, 16, 31 Dec. 1883. Ibid., v, nos. 166, 168, 170, 180.

countries. He, and Ferry after him, seriously considered meeting
Bismarck; and such a meeting would have been a clear symbol
that what Bismarck called 'the good days before 1866' had been
restored. Since 1877 there had been hardly a breath of ill temper
between Germany and France. But good relations were not
enough. Bismarck needed co-operation—an entente, if not an
alliance—in order to keep France away from Russian temptation; and co-operation in international affairs is best achieved
at the expense of someone else. Egypt seemed to give this opportunity. Germany and France could co-operate against England.
France would be forced into dependence on Germany, as
Austria-Hungary had been forced by fear of Russia in the
Balkans; and Bismarck would be free to work off his long-
standing resentment against the British. The analogy with
Austria-Hungary was not on all-fours. The Austrians believed,
with justice, that the existence of their empire was threatened
by the Russian plans in the Balkans (if these ever came off); the
French were exasperated, but not threatened, by the British
occupation of Egypt. The Austrians faced war with Russia
under certain circumstances; all their policy after 1878 assumed
this, and therefore they had to be on good terms with Germany.
A war over Egypt was never a serious possibility. Certainly the
British would fight in order to stay in Egypt; but the French—
and still less the Germans—would not fight to get them out. Ir
the French ever fought a war, it would be for Alsace and
Lorraine, not for Egypt. They were prepared to offer Germany
good relations; they would only use Franco-German co-operation in order to get on better terms with England.

Still, the co-operation of 1884 and 1885 was seriously meant
and seriously conducted on both sides. The French were glad
enough to embarrass the British on a diplomatic plane.
More than this, Jules Ferry—premier and foreign minister—
was the greatest colonizer of the Third republic. Though he
stumbled on colonial policy by accident, he then took it up as a
means of reviving French energy and giving her a new imperial
pride. In his first ministry he had led France to Tunis; in his
second he brought her Indo-China and equatorial Africa. Bismarck, too, wanted a conflict with the British for reasons of
domestic policy. He disliked their parliamentary democracy
and, especially, Gladstonian liberalism; he disliked, still more,
the admirers of England in Germany. Moreover, in 1884, the

Reichstag elections were approaching; and on every such occasion Bismarck sought to win a docile house by raising the cry, 'the Reich in danger!'—sometimes from Russia, sometimes from France, sometimes from the social democrats. He was already playing the card of the social peril for more than it was worth; and in 1884 his foreign policy forbade him to simulate danger from either France or Russia. Only England remained; a harmless colonial conflict with her might help Bismarck towards winning the election. There was an even more pressing consideration. Bismarck had long been taking precautions against the death of William I and the 'Gladstone cabinet' which, he alleged, the new emperor would appoint. It would cripple Frederick William's feeble liberalism if Germany was on bad terms with England when he came to the throne. Herbert Bismarck, the bullying chancellor's bullying son revealed this to Schweinitz in 1890: 'When we started colonial policy, we had to face a long reign by the Crown Prince, during which English influence would predominate. In order to forestall this, we had to launch colonial policy, which is popular and can produce conflicts with England at any moment.'[1]

Though domestic needs pushed Bismarck towards colonial ambitions, this is far from saying that they were imposed upon him by public opinion. Of course there were Germans who desired colonies—romantic historians who wanted the Reich to be an empire, and not merely a national state; trading-houses in Hamburg and Bremen who wanted imperial backing for their African trade; adventurers who hoped to obscure their shady past by appearing as the founders of empire; all those who sought a substitute for the traditions which Germany lacked by aping the traditions of others. In a parliamentary state these various currents might have diverted the trend of German policy. But Bismarck's Germany was a managed autocracy, not a parliamentary state. Bismarck took up the colonial impulses in 1884 and exploited them, pulling a wry face and making out that they were driving him on; he threw them over without difficulty the moment that they had served his turn, and after 1885 colonial considerations played no more part in his policy than they had done before he had acquired colonies at all. If it is absurd to suppose that Bismarck allowed a few colonial enthusiasts to divert and injure his foreign policy, it is even more

[1] Schweinitz, *Briefwechsel*, p. 193.

absurd to believe that Bismarck, who refused to condone German ambitions in Europe, himself succumbed to ambitions overseas. Of course Bismarck, like every Junker, had an insatiable hunger for land on the cheap; but it had to be very cheap indeed, and any price which weakened Germany in Europe made it too dear. France and Germany were essentially continental Powers; colonial ventures were for them a diversion of energy, as the French turned to colonies only when they could do nothing else. With Russia and England it was the other way round. Both adjoined Europe rather than belonging to it; both asked nothing of Europe except to be left alone.[1] Hence concentration on world policy was with them a sign of strength and security. Bismarck saw things very differently. He said: 'My map of Africa lies in Europe. Here lies Russia and here lies France, and we are in the middle. That is my map of Africa.' This sentence defined the greatest difference between Bismarck and his successors in the reign of William II. He thought solely in continental terms; they imagined that Germany could go over to 'world-policy' before she had secured the mastery of Europe. Hence, in the end, they failed in both. Bismarck was never distracted by colonial issues. His colonial gains of 1884 were a move in his European policy. He was seeking a reconciliation with France; and to prove his bona fides needed a dispute with England.

Strictly speaking, the great 'scramble for Africa' was not launched by any of the Great Powers. Leopold II, king of the Belgians, touched it off with his International Association of the Congo, founded (under a slightly different name) in 1876—a capitalist venture in piratical style. De Brazza, the great French explorer, entered the competition on the north bank of the Congo. The British, anxious to keep an open door to the Congo basin, answered with a characteristic venture in imperialism on the cheap. In February 1884 they recognized a Portuguese claim, dead for centuries, to control the mouth of the Congo; this, they supposed, would enable them to thwart both Leopold II and de Brazza. Here was a fine topic of Anglo-French discord; and Bismarck welcomed the chance to take part in it. His hands were free elsewhere. He had had a slight alarm in

---

[1] This is true even of Russia's interest in the Balkans. Her only interest was in security of passage at the Straits, that is, that they should not be controlled by any other Great Power.

the autumn of 1883 that the Russians might raise their price for renewing the League of the Three Emperors (due to expire in June 1884); but this turned out to be no more than a domestic intrigue—Saburov in Berlin trying to overcall Giers, his St. Petersburg chief. Saburov was disavowed; and the League was renewed on 27 March 1884 without alteration. On 24 April Bismarck proposed to Courcel the establishment of a League of Neutrals against England, on the model of the Armed Neutrality of 1780;[1] on the same day, the German consul at Capetown announced that a concession in south-west Africa was under German protection.[2] A confused negotiation with Great Britain followed. The British had no idea that Bismarck wished to enter the colonial business; and, since German tariffs were lower than the French, they preferred German colonies to French if Africa was to be partitioned at all. Bismarck wanted a grievance, not colonies; hence he had put forward a claim on the doorstep of Cape Colony, and he never supposed that the British would give way. Moreover, he put forward his claim in a provocative and offensive way; and, to strengthen his grievance for the future, warned the British against opposing German colonial ambitions in a dispatch which was never communicated to the British government.[3]

The British, however, did not provide Bismarck with the quarrel that he sought. Weighed down with their Egyptian troubles, they were in retreat elsewhere. On 21 June they recognized the German settlement in south-west Africa; on 26 June they abandoned their treaty with Portugal. They even promised the French to evacuate Egypt by 1888, if it was by

[1] Courcel to Ferry, 24, 25 Apr. 1884. *Documents diplomatiques français*, first series, v, nos. 246, 247, 249.

[2] This settlement, at first known as Angra Pequena, grew into German South-West Africa during the summer.

[3] Bismarck to Münster, 5 May 1884. *Große Politik*, iv, no. 738. In the following year Bismarck quoted this dispatch in the Reichstag as proof that the British government had ignored his warning. When the British answered that they had never seen the dispatch, Bismarck put the blame, quite unjustifiably, on Münster, his ambassador at London. This shady manœuvre left a lasting resentment in the British foreign office. In 1907 Eyre Crowe wrote bitterly of 'the bogy document' and of 'the deliberate deception practised on the Reichstag and the German public by the publication of pretended communications to Lord Granville which were never made'. Eyre Crowe, Memorandum on the Present State of British Relations with France and Germany, 1 Jan. 1907. *British Documents*, iii, appendix A. Crowe seems to have believed that the dispatch was published by Bismarck in a German White Paper. In fact, it was not published, but Bismarck referred to it in a speech in the Reichstag.

then orderly and if an international conference could settle its finances. This conference met on 28 June. The French refused to sacrifice the interests of the bondholders. Though Bismarck made out that he intended to support the French, he really thought that Egypt was too dangerous a topic for conflict with the British, and left the French to wreck the conference single-handed.[1] It broke up without result on 2 August. Bismarck at once trumped up new grievances in south-west Africa[2] and renewed his invitation to the French to join a coalition against the British. As he told Schweinitz, he hoped to revive the continental system of Napoleon I[3]—though, of course, this time the Berlin decrees would have a different significance. This continental league reached its highest point in September. The three emperors met at Skierniewice from 15 to 17 September—the last display in history of the Holy Alliance and, incidentally, the last time that the rulers of central and eastern Europe saw each other face-to-face until the conquerors of Germany met at Potsdam in 1945. The Skierniwice meeting was primarily a demonstration of conservative principle; the only practical topic discussed was the extradition of political offenders. Still, since Bismarck emphasized that it was not directed against France, it could only be directed against England, so far as it had an international character at all. On 21 September Bismarck again aired to Courcel the idea of a maritime league against England: 'she must get used to the idea that a Franco-German alliance is not an impossibility.'[4]

It is sometimes suggested that Bismarck raised this ghost in order to extract colonial concessions from the British; but, since they were ready to give him everything he wanted, this explanation does not work. It is more likely that he was playing genuinely for agreement with France. A maritime league was not so absurd as it seems in retrospect. The British navy in 1884 had prestige and not much else; it had made little attempt to

[1] After the conference was over, Bismarck rebuked his ambassador in London for failing to support the French. Bismarck to Münster, 12 Aug. 1884. *Große Politik*, iv, no. 749. There is, however, no evidence of a previous instruction.

[2] In June the British had only recognized the concession granted to Luderitz, a German trader. In August Bismarck demanded recognition of all the territory between the boundary of Cape Colony and Portuguese West Africa on no ground except greed.   [3] Schweinitz, *Denkwürdigkeiten*, ii. 283, 28 July 1884.

[4] Courcel to Ferry, 21, 23 Sept. 1884. *Documents diplomatiques français*, first series, v, nos. 404, 405, 407; and further in Bourgeois and Pagès, *Origines de la grande guerre*, p. 385.

keep up with technical advance, from the ironclad to the tor-
pedo, and a combined Franco-German fleet would have out-
numbered it. On paper British sea-power was more precarious
than at any time since the mutiny at the Nore in 1797; and a
naval scare, blowing up in the summer of 1884, began the first
timid step towards building a new fleet which was to revolu-
tionize the maritime Balance of Power in the next ten or fifteen
years. In 1884 British security depended on the French reluctance to follow Bismarck's promptings, rather than on naval
strength. Ferry noted in October: 'Bismarck's manifest tendency is to push us forward, promising to follow us; our policy
is to wait and not to take any step without the support of
Europe.'[1] The French exploited German backing in order to
wreck new schemes of financial reform in Egypt which the
British put forward in the autumn of 1884; but they evaded
Bismarck's suggestion of a conference at Paris on Egyptian
affairs which should dictate terms to England—how much more
then would they have evaded a war, even with Bismarck's moral
support. Bismarck might say to Courcel: 'I want you to forgive
Sedan, as after 1815 you came to forgive Waterloo.'[2] Lyons, the
British ambassador at Paris, made the sensible comment: 'The
patronage of Bismarck overthrew the Freycinet cabinet; it is
not strengthening Jules Ferry.'[3]

The most practical demonstration of the Franco-German
entente was a conference which met at Berlin in November to
settle the affairs of the Congo Basin. Though this was designed
by Bismarck as an anti-British gesture, it failed of its purpose
and even threatened to bring Great Britain and Germany together. The British, far from wishing to monopolize the outer
world as Bismarck imagined, wanted only fair competition and
low tariffs; the French were the real monopolizers. When the
conference recognized the International Association as a neutral,
free-trade zone, the British had obtained all that they wanted;
it was the French who had been defeated. This did not deter
Bismarck from staging another colonial conflict with England
over the partition of New Guinea, a conflict which ran from
January until March 1885. The topic of dispute was, no doubt,
chosen in order to exasperate the British colonists in Australia,

[1] Ferry, note of conversation with Herbert Bismarck, 6 Oct. 1884. *Documents
diplomatiques français*, first series, v, no. 421.
[2] Courcel to Ferry, 27, 28, 29 Nov. 1884. Ibid., nos. 468, 469, 471.
[3] Lyons to Granville, 25 Nov. 1884.

as Angra Pequena had been chosen for its effect on those at Cape Colony; and, since a new Reichstag had been elected in the autumn, Bismarck's policy can no longer be explained by his domestic anxieties. It was rather the effect on France that Bismarck had again in mind. But at the end of March Ferry, and with him Franco-German co-operation, ran into disaster. Ferry's real concern had been the completion of the French empire in Indo-China, and not Egypt or West Africa. This had involved him in war with China; and French forces were defeated at Lang-Son. The defeat was exaggerated by his enemies in the chamber; and he was overthrown on 30 March, just when he was within sight of peace with China. Though he had called on German mediation, this was not known at the time. Later Ferry's fall came to be regarded as a display of French distrust of Germany; in reality it was simply the result of a lost battle—much as the death of Gordon shook the Gladstone government in England.

Certainly Bismarck did not at once draw the moral that Franco-German co-operation had failed. He assured Freycinet, Ferry's successor, that German policy had not changed; and on 10 May again spoke to Courcel of his plans for a maritime league.[1] Meanwhile the continental league against Great Britain had really been displayed in a new and more menacing way. On 30 March, the very day of Ferry's fall, a Russian army defeated the Afgans at Pendjeh, and therewith threatened Afganistan, which the British regarded as India's essential buffer-state; the dreaded crisis in central Asia seemed to have opened. Russian power there had long been expanding. Apart from the inevitable tendency to encroach on remote, derelict neighbours, the Russians were seeking a weapon to use against England in case of a new crisis in the Near East. As Giers put it, they wanted to secure 'a defensive position against the hostility displayed by the English government towards us since the Crimean war';[2] and the only defensive position they knew was a threat elsewhere. It is not clear whether Bismarck had encouraged the Russian advance. Later he assured William I that he had done nothing 'to increase the chances of war'.[3] On the

[1] Courcel to Freycinet, 10 May 1885. *Documents diplomatiques français*, first series, vi, no. 23.

[2] Giers to Staal (London), 5 July 1884. Meyendorff, *Correspondance diplomatique de M. de Staal*, i. 40.

[3] Bismarck to William I, 27 May 1885. *Große Politik*, iv, no. 777.

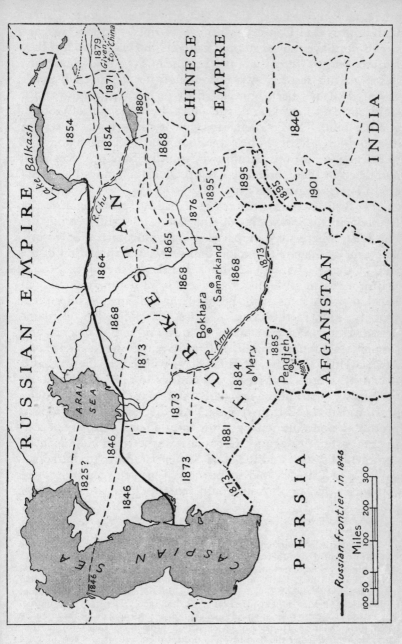

RUSSIAN ADVANCES IN CENTRAL ASIA

other hand, he knew of the Russian plans and spoke of them with approval to Courcel;[1] and it is obvious that the Russians would not have moved so provocatively in central Asia, if they had not had the security of the League of the Three Emperors. But even this security was not enough for them. Gladstone's government had been humiliated by its colonial disputes with Germany and France and, still more, by the death of Gordon at Khartoum. The Pendjeh crisis gave it a last chance to restore its crumbling prestige. The expedition which had been designed to rescue Gordon was withdrawn from the Sudan; forces were mobilized in India, and on 21 April Gladstone moved a vote of credit for eleven million pounds.

The British could not strike a decisive blow against the Russians in the mountains of Afganistan nor, still less, in the Far East, where they prepared to move against Vladivostok. The time had come to exploit Salisbury's interpretation of the rule of the Straits and to attack Russia in the Black Sea. A British invasion of the Black Sea had been the main anxiety in Russian policy since 1878. Bismarck had claimed to offer them security; and, in this crisis, justified his claim. He overcame Austro-Hungarian reluctance to quarrel with England and brought in France as well. All the Great Powers—Germany, Austria-Hungary, Italy, and France—warned the Turks that it would be a breach of treaty obligations to open the Straits to the British. The Turks were glad of the excuse to escape trouble, and evaded the British request.[2] All the same, the European protest at Constantinople was the most effective display of continental solidarity against Great Britain between Napoleon I's continental system and the Nazi-Soviet pact in 1939. Paradoxically enough, it defeated its purpose. Once the Russians were convinced that the Straits would remain closed and the Black

---

[1] Courcel to Ferry, 11 Mar. 1885. *Documents diplomatiques français*, first series, v, no. 622.

[2] The Turks tried to improve the occasion by demanding concessions from the British in Egypt. Later, they alleged that they had succeeded. They claimed that the British had offered to allow Turkey the occupation of Egypt and the Suez canal and a free hand in Bulgaria, in return for the opening of the Straits, and had threatened to sever Egypt from the Ottoman empire if she refused (Memorandum by Kiderlen, 20 May 1890. *Große Politik*, vii, no. 1376). The story was untrue. The British refused to offer any price in Egypt for the opening of the Straits; they based their claim on Turkey's need for British protection against Russia. The Turks doubted whether the British would protect them and, in any case, did not fear Russia, while she was involved in central Asia.

Sea secure, they lost interest in being able to threaten the British in Afganistan. They were willing to compromise there; they agreed to arbitration on 4 May, and the two countries settled the broad principles of a Russo-Afgan line on 10 September. Great Britain and Russia did not oblige Bismarck by engaging in a fundamental conflict far from Europe.

The Franco-German entente ran on longer. In May 1885 Bismarck trumped up a new dispute with the British in order to please the French, this time in East Africa. This was a more sensitive spot for the British, since East Africa might open a back-door to the valley of the upper Nile, which they had just left in the hands of the Mahdi. Freycinet, new to office and warned by Ferry's failure, hesitated to be pushed forward against the British; and Bismarck professed to be disillusioned. On 1 June he told the Prussian ministers: 'The French will never become even dependable defensive allies for us.'[1] Still, Bismarck had often drawn back before; and at almost the same time, he said to Courcel: 'Let us keep quiet until the autumn. Then we shall see.'[2] But the European situation changed profoundly in the following months. In June Salisbury succeeded Gladstone, and at once expressed his anxiety to co-operate with Germany.[3] In France, the elections, due in October, produced a flamboyant nationalist propaganda, which tied Freycinet's hands. The decisive event was neither in France nor in England; it was in Philippopolis. On 18 September there was a revolution in eastern Roumelia; on 19 September Prince Alexander of Bulgaria proclaimed the union of eastern Roumelia with Bulgaria. The Eastern question was reopened. The Austrians needed British backing. Bismarck could no longer afford to estrange them, and as early as 28 September he was belittling the colonial disputes as window-dressing for an abortive entente with the French.[4] The continental league vanished almost before it had begun.

It had been a serious essay in European politics all the same. The policy which Bismarck followed between 1882 and 1885 rested on two assumptions: that the continental Powers had no

---

[1] Lucius Ballhausen, *Erinnerungen an Bismarck*, p. 316.
[2] Courcel to Freycinet, 24 May 1885. *Documents diplomatiques français*, first series, vi, no. 27.
[3] Salisbury to Bismarck, 2 July 1885. *Große Politik*, iv, no. 782.
[4] Currie, memorandum of conversation with Bismarck, 28 Sept. 1885. Cecil, *Salisbury*, iii. 257

serious conflicts with each other and that both France and
Russia had conflicts with Great Britain so fundamental that in
order to win them they would put themselves under German
protection. Both assumptions were false. The Balkan rivalry
between Russia and Austria-Hungary was postponed, not
solved. Even the pacific Giers came away from Skiernewice
convinced that the Austrians meant to cheat Russia of her
preponderance in Bulgaria: 'about that there can be no illusions.'[1] Giers was right. Kálnoky told Bismarck that Austria-
Hungary could not agree to a partition of the Balkans, because
of her railway interests; and Bismarck could only comment:
'Hic haeret.'[2] Though the Russians were glad enough to make
gains in central Asia on the cheap, their overriding anxiety
was still for the security of Crimea and the Ukraine. And if
prestige was to be considered, what were Merv and Pendjeh,
villages of Afganistan, compared to Constantinople—Tsargrad,
the city of the tsars? Later on, the Russian position changed.
As they pushed on with the Trans-Siberian railway, they saw
at the end of it an imperial city, Pekin, which could be a real
substitute for Constantinople; and then they became anxious
for a continental league. This was not true in Bismarck's time.

As for the French, even Bismarck could not have believed that
they would be consoled by a few kind words. He complained
that they would not play *le grand jeu* in Egypt.[3] The only great
game for the French would have been to reverse the verdict of
1870; since this was beyond them, they would play no other.
Courcel, repeating Gambetta's phrase, defined their policy:
'Be pacific in the present; reserve the future.'[4]

The British had no inkling of what was afoot. They supposed
that they had really given Bismarck cause for offence. Queen
Victoria wrote: 'Mr. Gladstone has alienated all other countries
from us, by his very changeable and unreliable policy—un-
intentionally no doubt;'[5] and this explanation seemed to be
confirmed when the change in Bismarck's policy happened to
coincide with Salisbury's advent to the foreign office. Moreover,
colonial questions were a serious matter for the British; there-

[1] Bülow to Bismarck, 23 Sept. 1884. *Große Politik*, iii, no. 647.
[2] Reuss to Bismarck, 2 July 1884. Ibid., no. 639.
[3] Courcel to Freycinet, 27 May 1885. *Documents diplomatiques français*, first series,
vi, no. 28.   [4] Courcel to Ferry, 3 Dec. 1884. Ibid., v, no. 475.
[5] Queen Victoria to Granville, 28 Apr. 1885. *Letters of Queen Victoria*, second
series, iii. 643.

fore they, and Anglo-Saxon historians after them, supposed that
they were serious for Bismarck also. They even came to believe
that they had treated him badly. Sanderson, for many years the
leading figure at the foreign office, wrote in retrospect: 'We
countermanded some projects, but in other places we had
already gone too far and could not go back.'[1] In fact the British
drew back everywhere and Bismarck secured everything that
he had claimed. In the course of 1884 the Germans acquired
south-west Africa, the Cameroons, and East Africa. The British
took only St. Lucia bay—a keypoint indeed, since it cut off the
Boer republics from the sea. But the Germans could hardly
complain of this, unless they intended to take the Boers under
their protection and so to challenge the British empire in South
Africa, its most vital point. Some British statesmen had more
sense than to believe that Bismarck had quarrelled with them
for the sake of African deserts. Salisbury, and after him Eyre
Crowe, thought that Bismarck was trying to force Great Britain
into the Triple Alliance. This may have been true later. It
was not true in the days of the League of the Three Emperors
and of Franco-German reconciliation. At that time the purpose
of the Triple Alliance was to persuade Austria-Hungary and
Italy to do without British friendship. More, it was actually
used to support Russia at Constantinople and France in Egypt.
It was a weapon, though an auxiliary one, in Bismarck's continental coalition.

British security rested on two factors which they had come
to regard as axiomatic and self-operating: naval supremacy,
and the Balance of Power in Europe. Both were perhaps shakier
in the early eighties than the British imagined; all the same,
they turned out to be good enough. The British themselves
began slowly to improve their fleet. France and Russia steered
clear of the continental league. Egypt and central Asia were not
enough to make them accept German hegemony in Europe.
The struggle for mastery in Europe was postponed, not abandoned; this alone was the meaning of 'the age of imperialism'.
The continent of Europe would unite against Great Britain only
after it had been conquered by one of the Great Powers—
whether Germany or another; and the British could have said
to Germany what King Charles II said to his brother James,
duke of York: 'They will never kill me to make you king.'

<hr>

[1] Sanderson, observations, 2 Feb. 1907. *British Documents*, iii. 422.

XIV

THE TRIUMPH OF DIPLOMACY:
THE BULGARIAN CRISIS

1885-7

THE League of the Three Emperors, like the Holy Alliance before it, was a fair-weather system. Though designed to prevent an Austro-Russian conflict in the Balkans, in fact it worked only so long as there was no conflict. It gave Europe an impressive semblance of stability between 1881 and 1885; and was perhaps even of some real use to Russia during the dispute with Great Britain over Pendjeh. But it could not survive the strain of new Balkan troubles. These troubles came on the Great Powers unawares. Neither Austria-Hungary nor Russia had even the vague ambitions with which they speculated in the Near East ten years before. The Austrians looked forward to the opening of the Orient line (completed only in 1888) and hoped that the remnants of Turkey-in-Europe would somehow gain economic strength. The Russians had only the practical anxiety to keep the Straits securely closed. For understandable reasons of prestige they desired to maintain the political influence in Bulgaria which they had gained in 1878 and which indeed the League of the Three Emperors accorded to them. If their ingenuity had been able to make Bulgaria as subservient to them as Serbia became to Austria-Hungary, no one in the early eighteen-eighties would have objected; but the task was beyond them. Their only concept of 'liberation' was that Bulgaria should be ruled by a Russian general. Moreover, the rivalry at St. Petersburg between the foreign ministry and the war ministry was extended to Bulgaria, where the Russian diplomatists backed the conservatives and the military backed the liberals. The two parties played off their patrons against each other and gained for the tiny 'congress' Bulgaria a surprising independence. Russian resentment was concentrated against Alexander of Battenberg, the prince of Bulgaria whom they had themselves nominated; and when eastern Roumelia proclaimed its union with Bulgaria in September 1885 the Russians announced themselves as the leading advocates of the *status quo ante*, that is, of the congress settlement which had in 1878 enshrined their defeat.

The Austro-Hungarian government at first took the same line; and Bismarck was ready to support whatever was agreed to by his two imperial partners. In October 1885 it looked as though the League of the Three Emperors would have its way and would authorize the Turks to reconquer eastern Roumelia. This scheme was wrecked by British opposition. Salisbury would have welcomed a Turkish intervention in Bulgaria to restore the Berlin settlement. When, instead, the Turks appealed to the Powers, he drew the conclusion that Turkish strength was no longer to be counted on. A Turkish intervention would have been a blow against Russia; an Austro-Russian intervention would bring on a new eastern crisis and shake the Ottoman empire. Moreover, he was facing the first general election under household suffrage and feared that intervention by the reactionary Powers would offend what Bismarck (with characteristic exaggeration) called 'the communist-radical electorate'.[1] He said to Waddington, the French ambassador: 'It is the policy of the Congress of Verona, but we occidentals, who are Governments of public opinion, cannot associate ourselves with the crushing of the young Christian races in the Balkans;'[2] and to please the French he offered Turkey an agreement envisaging eventual British withdrawal from Egypt. Old themes were stirred: the Holy Alliance on the one side, 'the liberal alliance' on the other. Both combinations were too shaky to last. The French would not be pushed forward against Russia. The Austrians were increasingly tempted to side with England and to bid against Russia for control of the Balkans. In November Serbia, Austria-Hungary's satellite, demanded 'compensation' for the unification of Bulgaria and followed this up by going to war. She was defeated by the Bulgarians within a fortnight. Kálnoky, the Austro-Hungarian foreign minister, ordered the Bulgarian army to halt. He was much pressed in Vienna to

---

[1] Bismarck to Hatzfeldt (London), 9 Dec. 1885, *Große Politik*, iv, no. 789.

[2] Waddington to Freycinet, 16 Oct. 1885. *Documents diplomatiques français*, first series, vi, no. 94.

console Prince Alexander for this humiliation by supporting him at home against the Russians. On the other hand Bismarck insisted that Austria-Hungary should do nothing unless the British were first committed: 'when in doubt abstain'.[1] A compromise followed, first proposed by Salisbury, now supported by Kálnoky and finally accepted by the Russians in April 1886 —'personal union' of eastern Roumelia and Bulgaria. It was much the same compromise as had heralded the unification of Rumania twenty-five years before.

The compromise made Bulgaria; it could not save the League of the Three Emperors. The Russians would not swallow Prince Alexander. In August 1886 he was kidnapped by officers under Russian instruction. When he returned to Bulgaria in September, the tsar ordered him to abdicate; and he disappeared from history, causing a brief stir only in 1888 by proposing to marry the sister of William II.[2] A Russian general, Kaulbars, was sent to take over Bulgaria; but the politicians proved even more obstinate than their former prince, and in November Russian relations with Bulgaria were broken off. It seemed the prelude to invasion. Kálnoky had long repudiated any partition of the Balkans such as Bismarck had advocated; and he was being harassed by a campaign in Hungary, under Andrássy's leadership, for war against Russia. To avoid anything worse, he had to pledge himself to resist a Russian protectorate of Bulgaria. The Austrians had little confidence that they could fight Russia alone. They turned to Bismarck for support. Bismarck refused it. He had always insisted that the Austro-German alliance was purely defensive and that Germany had no interests in the Balkans. If Austria-Hungary wished to oppose Russia, she should obtain British backing. This was the core of the diplomatic situation. Bismarck was committed to preserving Austria-Hungary as a Great Power. Salisbury, who had returned to office in July 1886 after a shortlived Gladstone government, was determined to keep the Russians out of Constantinople. Though he may have lost faith in its strategic value, he felt committed for the sake of public opinion. A government that acquiesced in a Russian occupation of Constantinople would, he thought,

[1] Bismarck to Reuss, 13 Dec. 1885. *Große Politik*, v, no. 972.
[2] He ultimately made a morganatic marriage with an actress. It is curious to reflect that, while Romanov and Hohenzollern have vanished, the kin (though not the direct descendants) of Prince Alexander have provided the last viceroy of India and a consort for the queen of England.

'share the fate of Lord North's party'; it would be 'the ruin of our party and a heavy blow to the country'.[1]

Both Bismarck and Salisbury had an irrefutable case. If the Germans declared their support for Austria-Hungary, Russia would not attack her; if the British fleet entered the Black Sea, Russia would not invade Bulgaria. But equally whichever moved first would draw on herself Russian hostility and resentment. Germany would be threatened on her eastern frontier; the British would be threatened in India. Randolph Churchill, chancellor of the exchequer, asked: 'Who will support us against Russia in Asia, if we have secured peace in the Near East and so directed the enmity of Russia solely against ourselves?'[2] Each therefore began to make excuse. Salisbury argued that, though the fleet could protect Constantinople it could not help the Austro-Hungarian army in Galicia. 'We are fish.' Moreover, the fleet needed security at the Straits if it were to enter the Black Sea; in other words Germany must repudiate the diplomatic support for the closing of the Straits which she had given so emphatically in April 1885. This, too, Bismarck refused. He intended to support the Russians' interpretation of the rule of the Straits in order to console them for his refusal to promise neutrality in a war between Russia and Austria-Hungary. The most that he could offer the British was that Germany would keep France neutral. This offer did not interest Salisbury. He had not yet accepted the inevitability of French hostility, still less of a Franco-Russian entente; and indeed in November 1886 the French held out to him the prospect of their support in Bulgaria if only he would end the British occupation of Egypt.[3] Drummond Wolff was sent to Constantinople to negotiate with the Turks for this very purpose.

The British tried to turn Bismarck's manœuvre against himself: they in their turn offered to protect Germany against France. Bismarck, however, made France his excuse for inaction. The patriotic revival in France which had begun during the general election of 1885 reached its height in the summer of 1886. It centred round the inadequate symbol of General Boulanger, a soldier distinguished only for his management of

---

[1] Salisbury to Randolph Churchill, 28 Sept., 1 Oct. 1886. W. Churchill, *Lord Randolph Churchill* (popular edition), p. 519.

[2] Hatzfeldt to Bismarck, 6 Dec. 1886. *Große Politik*, iv, no. 875.

[3] Waddington to Freycinet, 3, 24 Nov. 1886. *Documents diplomatiques français*, first series, v.i, nos. 342, 358.

a black circus-horse. Boulanger had no political sense, and Boulangism no political programme; in practice it could only offer France certain defeat at the hands of Germany. The cautious, middle-class civilians who ruled France meant to avoid this disaster; yet they were to some extent the prisoners of nationalist agitation. They certainly could not revive Ferry's policy of co-operation with Germany; it was even difficult for them to compromise with England over Egypt, except on very favourable terms. The advocates of *revanche* pushed them towards Russia; yet the last thing they wanted was the dismemberment of the Turkish empire and the Russians at Constantinople. On the other side, the breakdown of the League of the Three Emperors pushed the tsar towards France; yet, though he wanted French backing at Constantinople, he did not want to quarrel with Germany. Besides, just as Alexander II had always urged Napoleon III to be 'respectable', Alexander III welcomed the nationalism of Boulangism, but found its demagogy 'very regrettable'.[1] Boulangism exactly served Bismarck's purpose. It retarded alliance between France and Russia; yet enabled him to argue that Germany must conserve all her strength to ward off a French attack. He made also a domestic calculation. The three-year term of the Reichstag would run out in 1887; and he needed to raise once more the cry of the Fatherland in danger, preferably in such a way as to use it against the Catholic Centre and the parties of the Left.

On 25 November 1886 Bismarck introduced a new military law in the Reichstag. He defended it solely with the argument of the danger from France; and, when it was rejected in January, dissolved the Reichstag. The general election gave a majority to the *cartel*, the coalition of conservative landowners and national liberal capitalists, which supported Bismarck; and the military law was safely passed in March 1887. It had already served its turn. Bismarck's parliamentary opponents did him many services, but never a greater than when they threw out the military law and so gave him the excuse to withstand British pressure until the spring of 1887. It would have been a disaster for his foreign policy if the law had gone through in November 1886. In his own words: 'I couldn't invent Boulanger, but he happened very conveniently for me.'[2] It would be

---

[1] Laboulaye (St. Petersburg) to Freycinet, 26 Nov. 1886. *Documents diplomatiques français*, first series, vi, no. 362.   [2] Philipp, *Gespräche*, p. 85, 14 Apr. 1887.

foolish to speculate whether Bismarck took the danger from France seriously; probably he always took a danger seriously so long as it suited the needs of his policy. On the other hand he instructed his ambassador in Paris to send alarmist reports until the election was over, and rebuked him when he failed to do so. Moreover, though he spoke in public of 'bleeding France white' in case of war, he confessed in private that Germany needed France for the sake of a future maritime balance against England and that he would offer her generous terms after the first victory.[1] The German war plan, at this time, projected an offensive against Russia, while standing on the defensive against France; and Bismarck stressed the danger from France largely to conceal the fact that the real German preparations were directed against Russia.

The French had some inkling of this. Herbette, French ambassador in Berlin, wrote in December 1886: 'I think that Bismarck really wants peace',[2] and urged that France should stay neutral in case of a war in the Balkans.[3] The French even offered to renew Ferry's entente with Germany, if Bismarck would help them against England in Egypt—then they would not need Russian support. Though Bismarck dared not estrange England, because of Austria-Hungary, he offered to mediate between the two countries. 'A combination analogous to the Crimean war would reduce the tenseness of the situation. . . . Reconciliation between England and France is the only way to make Russia respect the treaties.'[4] This was a far cry from 1879, when he had justified the Austro-German alliance as a means of warding off 'the Crimean coalition'. Bismarck's offer was refused by the British. They had already reached the position over Egypt to which they always adhered: they would settle with France, but without the aid or interference of any other Power. For, though French opposition was often an embarrassment to them, they knew that no other Power would support France if it came to a conflict. The French were thus left in isolation and could look only to Russia for protection if Bismarck ever put his threats into action. But they did their best to conceal this from the Russians, so as not to be called on in the

---

[1] Bismarck to Schweinitz, 25 Feb. 1887. *Große Politik*, vi, no. 1253.
[2] Herbette to Flourens, 19 Dec. 1886. *Documents diplomatiques français*, first series, vi, no. 378.
[3] Herbette to Flourens, 7 Feb. 1887. Ibid., no. 428.
[4] Bismarck, memorandum, 19 Nov. 1886. *Große Politik*, iv, no. 806.

Bulgarian question; and when Laboulaye, the ambassador at St. Petersburg, asked Giers whether Russia would protect France from a German attack, he was severely rebuked by the French foreign minister.[1] The French dared not oppose Russia, for fear of losing this protection; equally they dared not support her, for fear of being destroyed by a coalition of England and the central Powers—quite apart from the fact that the Russian programme in the Near East ran counter to their own interests. They therefore followed the line of measuring their Balkan attitude exactly on that of Germany; then no one could blame them. 'We have separated ourselves, it is true, from England, Italy, and Austria, but it is to follow the path on which Germany was the first to advance and where we desire to follow, not precede her.'[2] This certainly turned the tables on Bismarck. He had hoped to drive France into the arms of Russia. This would both force the British on to the Austro-Hungarian side and free him from embarrassing Russian requests. Instead, French abstention—a more active abstention than in the previous Eastern crisis, but abstention all the same—compelled Bismarck to play the leading part; it dictated, in fact, the diplomacy of 1887.

Both Bismarck and Salisbury held back until the opening of 1887, each still hoping to place the burden of Austria-Hungary on the other's shoulders. With the New Year each began to weaken, not, however, directly towards Austria-Hungary. As in the negotiations for a Triple Alliance in 1882, Italy offered a safer ground for concessions: any commitment would be against France, not against Russia, and neither Bismarck nor Salisbury took the danger from France seriously. The Italians were in a strong position for a bargain. The British needed diplomatic support against the French both in Egypt and Morocco, and they got it whole-heartedly only from the Italians; moreover, Bismarck was publicly preaching the danger from France, and the Italians could quote him to good purpose—he could not call their bluff without exposing his own. All the same, he would not have agreed to their demands unless the British had moved first. On 17 January Salisbury told the Italian ambassador that he would like to make relations 'more intimate and useful'. The Italians at once replied by proposing a formal

[1] Flourens to Laboulaye, 29 Jan. 1887. *Documents diplomatiques français*, first series, vi, no. 414.   [2] Flourens to Herbette, 23 Jan. 1887. Ibid., no. 406.

alliance against France. This was more than Salisbury intended. He was ready to give the Italians the same sort of help in Tripoli (their object of Mediterranean ambition) as they gave him in Egypt; and further to promise support 'in general and to the extent that circumstances shall permit', but not to enter an alliance. The Anglo-Italian agreement, made on 12 February, was as casual and informal as Salisbury could make it. The Italian note wanted a precise agreement to maintain the *status quo* in the Mediterranean. Salisbury merely gave a general blessing to the idea of co-operation and added the deliberately ambiguous sentence: 'the character of that co-operation must be decided by them, when the occasion for it arises, according to the circumstances of the case.'[1] To Salisbury 'by them', meant the British, to the Italians both governments. Still Salisbury was not intending to mislead the Italians. The vague phrases were designed to meet the qualms of the British cabinet and to avoid disclosures which might threaten his weak government in the House of Commons. He wrote to Victoria: 'It is as close an alliance as the Parliamentary character of our institutions will permit.'[2]

Bismarck, too, could cheerfully commit himself to the Italians once he knew that Salisbury was in train. The Italians had two complaints against the existing Triple Alliance which was due to run out in May 1887: it gave them no say in the Balkans, and it did not secure them against a French advance in Tripoli. Bismarck was ready to satisfy these complaints; Kálnoky was not. He did not want Italian interference in the Balkans; he was determined not to join any anti-French combination; and at bottom he would have been glad to see the Triple Alliance break down, so that Germany would then have less excuse not to support Austria-Hungary. Bismarck therefore had to do all the work and to make all the sacrifices. To meet Kálnoky's

---

[1] Corti to Salisbury, Salisbury to Corti, 12 Feb. 1887. *British Documents on the Origins of the War 1898–1914*, viii. 1–2. The Italians proposed: (i) maintenance of the *status quo* in the Mediterranean, Adriatic, Aegean, and Black Seas, and resistance to any annexion, occupation, or protectorate there; (ii) no change whatever in these regions without the previous agreement of the two Powers; (iii) Italian support for Great Britain in Egypt, and British support for Italy in North Africa, especially in Tripoli and Cyrenaica, against 'invasions' by a third Power; (iv) general mutual support in the Mediterranean. This was much more a pact against France or even, so far as the Adriatic was concerned, against Austria-Hungary than against Russia.

[2] Salisbury to Victoria, 10 Feb. 1887. *Letters of Queen Victoria*, third series, i. 272.

objections, the original treaty of the Triple Alliance was renewed without change on 20 February 1887—a week after the Anglo-Italian agreement was safely concluded. Austria-Hungary and Germany also made new separate treaties with Italy. The Austro-Italian treaty merely accepted the principle of 'reciprocal compensations' in case the *status quo* in the Balkans was upset. The Austrians meant at most to recognize some Italian claim in Albania; the Italians, however, had their eye on Tyrol. Austria-Hungary made no new commitment against France; and Italy made none against Russia. The Italo-German treaty was a very different affair. Germany promised to go to Italy's assistance if France attempted 'to extend her occupation or even her protectorate or her sovereignty' in either Tripoli or Morocco and if Italy then herself acted in North Africa or even attacked France in Europe. Moreover, in case of war with France, Germany would help Italy to acquire 'territorial guarantees for the security of her frontiers and her maritime position'—meaning thereby Corsica, Tunis, and Nice. This was not much like the 'League of Peace', Bismarck's rhetorical description of the original Triple Alliance; and it was far removed from his repeated promise to support France everywhere except in Alsace-Lorraine. In practice it did not mean much more than that Germany would help Italy to lay her hands on Tripoli if the French took Morocco; and Morocco would have been cheap at the price. Bismarck's underlying motive, as nearly always, was his determination not to commit himself against Russia. France was his lightning-conductor: the more he was committed against her, the more he could plead that the task of opposing Russia must be performed by others. Besides those who directed Italian policy could not wield the bow of Cavour. They might exploit the conflicts of others; they would hardly launch a war themselves. Above all, the responsibility of supporting Italy was shared with England; and unless the British acted, Bismarck also would find some excuse.

The British and German agreements with Italy secured the Mediterranean *status quo* against France; they did not affect the danger from Russia. Here, too, Salisbury was ready to make some concession; perhaps the cabinet, having been drawn into one agreement, had now less distrust of another. On 19 February he proposed that Austria-Hungary should 'accede' to the Anglo-Italian agreement as it stood. This was by no means an attractive

idea to Kálnoky: it would commit him against France in regard
to Egypt and Tripoli without providing any assistance against
Russia in Bulgaria. Moreover, Bismarck had insisted again and
again, in the days when he was trying to save the League of the
Three Emperors, that British promises were worthless unless
they involved a binding pledge of military co-operation; yet
Kálnoky knew that Bismarck would have a strong argument
against any assistance to Austria-Hungary, once the vaguest
phrases had been exchanged with Salisbury. But apparently the
excuse of the French bogy which Bismarck had raised did the
trick: better a vague backing against Russia from England than
no backing from anyone. On the essential point Salisbury got
his way. Though the notes exchanged between the British and
Austro-Hungarian governments on 24 March 1887 spoke of
maintaining the *status quo* particularly in the Aegean and Black
Seas, they did not contain the specific reference to the Balkans
on which Kálnoky had at first insisted.[1] Moreover, like the
notes exchanged with Italy, they spoke only of diplomatic co-
operation: there was no 'pledge'.

The notes of February and March 1887 created a Triple
Entente which protected British interests in Egypt, Italian
interests in Tripoli, and the interest of all three at Constantinople.[2] It was designed to stiffen the will of the two continental
partners rather than to deter their possible enemies. The existence of the Austro-German alliance had been known to the
Russians from the beginning. The French learnt of the Triple
Alliance at least by the spring of 1883; and they were given a
precise account of its renewal by the Italians in April 1887.[3]
But neither the French nor the Russians had any notion that
there was a written 'Mediterranean agreement', though the fact
of diplomatic co-operation was plain to see. On the other hand
the Italians had often threatened to make a bargain with the
French; and Salisbury, though not Bismarck, often feared
that the Austrians might strike a bargain with Russia. In fact

---

[1] Draft Austro-Hungarian note, 17 Mar.; Austro-Hungarian and British notes
24 Mar. 1887. *British Documents*, viii. 6, 3.

[2] The Italian and Spanish governments also exchanged notes on 4 May 1887
to preserve the *status quo* in Morocco. To this agreement the German and Austro-
Hungarian governments gave a vague, and the British government a still vaguer,
blessing.

[3] Moüy (Rome) to Flourens, 24 Apr. 1887. *Documents diplomatiques français*, first
series, vi, no. 507.

Salisbury justified the Mediterranean agreement to Victoria as the best means of warding off a continental league, which would seek to divide up the British empire.[1] These were far-fetched fears. Salisbury's practical object was to secure the diplomatic support of the central Powers in the Egyptian question; and, since he could not have a direct agreement with Germany, he had to be content with an approach through her two partners. Diplomatic co-operation, without any pledge on the action that might follow it, was a great score for British policy. There was a solid majority against the French in Egypt; and, except for the French, the 'Crimean coalition' had been re-created at Constantinople. But it was the Crimean coalition with a difference. That had followed the outbreak of war; this was designed to prevent it. Salisbury's real concern was to improve his bargaining position with the French and perhaps even with the Russians.

Though Bismarck and Salisbury had run over with professions of mutual friendship, each had a fundamental reservation. Bismarck did not mean to quarrel with Russia, Salisbury wanted a reconciliation with France; and the moment the Mediterranean agreement was concluded, each set out to improve relations with the supposedly bellicose Powers. Salisbury was unsuccessful. On 22 May Drummond Wolff at last concluded a convention with the Turks in regard to Egypt. Though this provided for the withdrawal of the British troops within three years, it also laid down that the withdrawal could be postponed or that the troops could return 'if order and security in the interior were disturbed'. In France the Boulangist movement was at its height; and the French civilians dared not compromise in the Egyptian question. Backed by Russia, they bullied the sultan into rejecting the draft convention, with the threat that otherwise France would occupy Syria, and Russia Armenia. On 15 July Drummond Wolff left Constantinople. Immediately the French repented of their success and offered to help England in negotiating a new convention.[2] It was too late. The Bulgarian crisis, too, was reaching its crisis, and Salisbury had to decide one way or the other. He decided for the central Powers. The failure of the Drummond Wolff convention

[1] Salisbury to Victoria, 10 Feb. 1887. *Letters of Queen Victoria*, third series, i. 272.
[2] Flourens to Waddington, 18 July; Herbette to Flourens, 26 July 1887. *Documents diplomatiques français*, first series, vi *bis*, nos. 51, 52.

was the decisive factor in sending the French along the road to alliance with Russia. Once the Anglo-French entente broke down they had no alternative. But they turned to Russia in order to force an agreement over Egypt on Great Britain, not to go to war with her. The Anglo-French disputes, though fierce, were famil⸺ ⸺ two nations with a common ⸺ralism; they were conducted ⸺ within the limits, of a parlia- ⸺liticians were resolved not to ⸺ership with the continental ⸺h he thwarted French plans, ⸺public of pals', and preferred ⸺se. Still a true revival of 'the ⸺ years as the deadlock over ⸺ July 1887.

Bismarck improved his position more successfully. With France this was not difficult. Once he ceased to be alarmed at an imaginary danger which he had himself created, there was no obstacle to friendly relations. A frontier incident in April 1887 gave him an opening. Schnaebele, a French frontier official, was illegally arrested by the Germans.[1] The French government imagined that Bismarck was provoking them to war; and Boulanger thought that his hour had come. On the contrary, Bismarck released Schnaebele with the nearest that he could manage to an apology; and Boulanger was excluded from the next French government that was made at the end of May. If there had ever been a Boulangist crisis, it was now over. A serious entente with France was, however, ruled out by Bismarck's needs elsewhere; he could not support her over Egypt from fear of losing British backing for Austria-Hungary. In this sense Salisbury had been right to argue that the Mediterranean agreement prevented a continental coalition. Bismarck's relations with Russia were more important, indeed the vital point in his policy. There had always been two parties at the Russian court: the conservative diplomatists, who advocated close relations with Germany; and the aggressive nationalists, who wanted to keep a free hand in order to exploit the Franco-German war which they, like many others, supposed to be imminent.

---

[1] Schnaebele had been invited on to German soil on official business; this was not disputed. In addition, he may have escaped on to French soil, while trying to evade the German police.

Alexander III, though conservative enough, disliked being dependent on German goodwill and hoped more from threats than from conciliation. Therefore the problem for the Russian conservatives was to get Bismarck to outbid Alexander's own inclinations. Peter Shuvalov, who had made the agreement with Salisbury in 1878, came to Berlin at the beginning of January 1887. He offered Russia's 'friendly neutrality' in a Franco-German war; in return Germany was to recognize Russia's exclusive right to influence in Bulgaria and to promise friendly neutrality if Russia were to seize the Straits.[1] The bargain suited Bismarck. He had always refused to commit himself against Russia in the Near East; and he would be rewarded by an assurance of Russian neutrality such as he had never had before, not even in 1870. But the bargain did not suit Alexander III. He would not give up the French card: Russia, he believed, could gain only by playing off France against Germany, not by backing one against the other. Shuvalov's approach was not followed up; and this silence from St. Petersburg was the decisive factor which led Bismarck both to renew the Triple Alliance and to promote the Mediterranean agreement.

The rejection of temptation brought Alexander III no reward from France. The French failed to make the clear appeal for Russian protection which would have justified his demanding support in the Balkans in exchange. On the contrary, French policy grew increasingly cautious, as was shown especially by the dismissal of Boulanger in May. Alexander came round grudgingly to the line advocated by Giers, the foreign minister: better some agreement with Germany than no agreement with anyone. The Russians tried to turn the tables on Bismarck. They offered to give up France if he would give up Austria-Hungary: each should promise neutrality if the other were involved in war 'with a third great power'. Bismarck refused this offer; indeed he read to the Russian ambassador (Paul Shuvalov, Peter's brother) the text of the Austro-German alliance. Instead he tried once more to bribe the Russians with the offer of Constantinople: 'Germany would have no objection to seeing you masters of the Straits, possessors of the entrance to the Bos-

[1] Germany was to promise friendly neutrality 'if care for the interests of Russia obliged His Majesty the Emperor of Russia to assure the closing of the straits and thus to keep in his hands the key of the Black Sea.' Draft of a Russo-German agreement by Peter Shuvalov and Herbert Bismarck, 10 Jan. 1887. *Große Politik*, v, no. 1063.

phorus, and of Constantinople itself.' This offer had no value
for the Russians. They might perhaps have abandoned France
if they could have had a firm prospect of Constantinople; but
this was impossible unless they had also a free hand against
Austria-Hungary. In any case, Russia's preoccupations were
defensive and negative: to avoid a European coalition; to prevent the whole of the Balkans falling under Austro-Hungarian
control; and to keep the Straits closed.[1] The agreement (commonly called the Reinsurance treaty), which Bismarck and
Shuvalov signed on 18 June, satisfied these negative aims. The
two parties promised neutrality of a meaningless kind: Russia
to remain neutral unless Germany attacked France, Germany
to remain neutral unless Russia attacked Austria-Hungary.
Germany renewed the promises of diplomatic support for
Russia in Bulgaria and at the Straits which she had made in
1881 at the time of the League of the Three Emperors; she
added new promises against Alexander of Battenberg and of
moral support in case Russia seized the Straits herself.

In later years the Reinsurance treaty acquired an exaggerated
importance, a process begun by Bismarck in 1896 in order to
discredit his successors. In reality it did not amount to much.
Perhaps it put Alexander III in a better temper with Germany;
and, as Bismarck noted, 'Our relations with Russia depend
exclusively on the personal feelings of the Tsar Alexander III.'[2]
But the Reinsurance treaty did not prevent a Franco-Russian
alliance, which indeed, as later concluded, was technically
compatible with its terms. The Franco-Russian alliance was
retarded, though not finally prevented, solely by the French
reluctance to give Russia a free hand in the Near East; and
Russia announced her intention of supporting France in 1887,
not in 1891. The Reinsurance treaty demonstrated the approaching failure of Bismarck's policy. In January he had hoped
that the prospect of Constantinople would make the Russians
abandon France. Now, in the Reinsurance treaty, he offered them
Constantinople, yet had to acquiesce in an implicit Franco-
Russian alliance. Again, he had always refused to support
Austria-Hungary in the Balkans and had hoped that this would
be enough to preserve Russo-German friendship. The Russians

[1] Instructions to Shuvalov, May 1887. Goriainov, 'The End of the Alliance
of the Emperors' (*American Historical Review*, xxiii. 334).
[2] Memorandum by Bismarck, 28 July 1887. *Große Politik*, v, no. 1099.

now showed that they would be satisfied with nothing short of German neutrality in an Austro-Russian war; and, failing this, they kept themselves free to support France. In fact, the treaty set it down in black and white that Germany would one day face war on two fronts, unless she abandoned the Habsburg monarchy. The Austro-German alliance imprisoned Germany; and Bismarck continued to dream that he might some time make Germany more secure by escaping from it.[1] No doubt this alliance was a lesser evil in Bismarck's eyes than the demagogic Greater Germany that must have been the alternative. All the same, the Reinsurance treaty was, at best, an expedient for postponing the catastrophe of war on two fronts which Bismarck's diplomacy had made inevitable. It is becoming fashionable to argue that estrangement with Russia was forced on Bismarck by economic developments. The Prussian landowners, once the pillars of Russo-German friendship, now wanted tariffs against the cheap Russian grain; and no doubt there was something in this change of sentiment. All the same, the friendship would have continued if Bismarck had been able to promise neutrality in an Austro-Russian war: this political conflict eased the path for economic hostility, not the other way round.

Much has been made of Bismarck's dishonesty in making the Reinsurance treaty. There was certainly no dishonesty towards the Austrians. He had always insisted that he could not support them in Bulgaria nor at the Straits. He had taken the same line with the British. When he opened negotiations with the Russians he took the added precaution of trumping up a colonial dispute with England so as to have a further excuse for not backing them at Constantinople;[2] but this was a triviality, and he did not support them even though his colonial 'grievances' were redressed. The British accepted Bismarck's argument that Germany's forces were locked away in defence against France; all the same, they would have been shocked to learn that he had given Russia promise of definite diplomatic support. But the Russians would have been more shocked had they known that, immediately before concluding the Reinsurance treaty, he had

[1] Opposing the proposal that the Austro-German alliance be made permanent, Bismarck wrote: 'A situation which implies that we cannot preserve peace for generations would endanger its preservation and strengthen the hopes of our opponents.' Bismarck to Reuss, 15 May 1887. *Große Politik*, v, no. 1103.

[2] Bismarck to Plessen (London), 27 Apr.; Herbert Bismarck to Plessen, 28 Apr.; Bismarck to Plessen, 29 Apr. 1887. Ibid., iv, nos. 812, 813, 815.

engineered the Mediterranean coalition against them or that Moltke was constantly advising the Austrians, with Bismarck's encouragement, how to improve their striking power in Galicia. The Reinsurance treaty was a fraud on the Russians; or, more exactly, it was a fraud on Alexander III, in which Giers and the Shuvalovs took part with their eyes open. Napoleon III had played the same sort of fraud a generation earlier. Alexander II had been easy-going and soft-hearted; it was probably a mistake to play tricks on Alexander III.

The Reinsurance treaty had hardly been made when affairs in Bulgaria entered their most acute stage. On 7 July the Bulgarian assembly elected Ferdinand of Coburg as prince, in defiance of Russian wishes; and the moment for Russian intervention seemed to have arrived. The pattern of the previous autumn was repeated: Bismarck and Salisbury each tried to shift the burden of supporting Austria-Hungary on to the other. On 3 August Salisbury had with Hatzfeldt, the German ambassador, the first of his many rambling discussions on world affairs, from which both the Germans and posterity found it difficult to deduce a settled policy. The Turkish empire, he insisted, was beyond saving, and England would have to partition it with Russia, unless Germany would support her.[1] Bismarck, unlike his successors, did not lose his head: he replied that he would be delighted to promote an Anglo-Russian understanding.[2] Salisbury beat a retreat: he could not, he said, desert Italy, and an Anglo-Russian agreement was, in any case, impossible[3]—the only point which Bismarck had wished to establish.

The running was now taken up by the ambassadors of the three 'entente' Powers at Constantinople. In the usual way of men on the spot, they exaggerated the surrounding dangers and were convinced that Turkey would give way to the first Russian threat, unless assured of entente support. They worked out 'a basis of ideas' 'to give Turkey a power of resistance—at least a moral one'; and proposed to communicate these ideas to the Turks. This proposal was enthusiastically adopted by the Italian government. Crispi, who had just become prime minister, was the ablest, or at least the most energetic, man to rule

---

[1] Hatzfeldt to Bismarck, 3 Aug. 1887. *Große Politik*, iv, no. 907.
[2] Bismarck to Hatzfeldt, 8 Aug. 1887. Ibid., no. 908.
[3] Hatzfeldt to foreign ministry, 12 Aug. 1887. Ibid., no. 910.

Italy between the death of Cavour and the rise of Mussolini. Acutely aware of the weakness and disunion of Italy, he proposed to remedy these by 'activism', to make Italy run in the hope that this would teach her to walk. He therefore seized any chance to thrust Italy forward as a Great Power and, in particular, was eager to win British backing for his aggressive colonial policy. Crispi was seconded, though less urgently, by Kálnoky, who had always wanted more precise British commitments in the Near East and would even pay the price of Italian participation in order to get them. Bismarck doubted whether it could be done, even with German prompting—'still we must try'.[1] Salisbury, however, accepted his rebuff of August; he had been outmanœuvred by Bismarck and wrote, 'a thorough understanding with Austria and Italy is so important to us that I do not like the idea of breaking it up on account of risks which *may* turn out to be imaginary'.[2] All he asked was that the agreement should cover Asia Minor as well as Bulgaria and the Straits—a request easily met by the other two Powers.

The British cabinet was not so yielding. They were being asked to take the unprecedented step of committing themselves in peace-time, and could not see why Germany, the head of the Triple Alliance, should be allowed to keep out of her allies' troubles. Salisbury had to ask Bismarck to meet the objections of the cabinet by giving his 'moral approbation'.[3] Bismarck was always generous with this; what he would not give was a promise of practical support. He therefore laid a false trail. He sent Salisbury the text of the Austro-German alliance and followed this up with a letter, which concluded: 'German policy will always be obliged to enter the line of battle if the independence of Austria-Hungary were to be menaced by Russian aggression, or if England or Italy were to be exposed to invasion by French armies.'[4] Salisbury in reply claimed to be convinced that 'under no circumstances could the existence of Austria be imperilled by a resistance to illegal Russian enterprises';[5] a skilful perversion of Bismarck's words. Of course he was not taken in. The exchange of letters was designed to satisfy the

---

[1] Minute by Bismarck on memorandum by Herbert Bismarck, 20 Oct. 1887. *Große Politik*, iv, no. 918.
[2] Salisbury to White (Constantinople), 2 Nov. 1887. Cecil, *Life of Salisbury*, iv. 70.
[3] Hatzfeldt to foreign ministry, 11 Nov. 1887. *Große Politik*, iv, no. 925.
[4] Bismarck to Salisbury, 22 Nov. 1887. Ibid., no. 930.
[5] Salisbury to Bismarck, 30 Nov. 1887. Ibid., no. 936.

British cabinet, not to bind German policy; and Bismarck and Salisbury combined to mislead the cabinet as, twenty years before, Bismarck and Stanley had combined to mislead German opinion over the guarantee to Luxembourg.

Once the British cabinet were satisfied, the agreement with Italy and Austria-Hungary could be made on 12 December. The three Powers united to maintain peace and the *status quo* in the Near East and, more particularly, the freedom of the Straits, Turkish authority in Asia Minor, and her suzerainty in Bulgaria. If Turkey resisted any 'illegal enterprises', the three Powers would 'immediately come to an agreement as to the measures to be taken' in order to defend her; while if she connived at any such illegal enterprise, the three Powers 'would consider themselves justified' in occupying such points of Turkish territory 'as they may agree to consider it necessary to occupy'. These were the original points as drafted at Constantinople. In the excitement of achieving them, Kálnoky and Crispi did not notice that Salisbury had added another; the agreement was not to be revealed to Turkey, and this addition defeated the original purpose of stiffening Turkish nerves.[1] Still, even so weakened, the agreement was more nearly an alliance with a group of Great Powers than any Great Britain had ever made in time of peace and more formal than any agreement made with France or Russia twenty years later. Salisbury might still insist that Austria-Hungary had *le beau rôle*—'you lead, we follow you'.[2] In fact he had made an alliance with Austria-Hungary and Italy for the defence of Bulgaria and Asia Minor.

Though often called the second Mediterranean agreement, it had little to do with the Mediterranean. The first agreement had aimed at diplomatic co-operation, principally against France; hence it had specified Egypt and Tripoli. The new agreement was a preliminary to a possible military action, directed solely against Russia. Indeed it could only work so long as France stood aside; and Salisbury at once assured the French that he had not entered into any agreement directed against them.[3] The British assumed, as the basis of their policy, that

---

[1] *British Documents*, viii. 12.

[2] Károlyi (London) to Kálnoky, 7 Dec. 1887. Temperley and Penson, *Foundations of British Foreign Policy*, p. 458.

[3] Waddington to Flourens, 17 Dec. 1887. *Documents diplomatiques français*, first series, vi *bis*, no. 68; Salisbury to Egerton, 14, 19 Dec. 1887. Temperley and Penson, *Foundations of British Foreign Policy*, p. 462.

their fleet could pass the Straits at any time and so threaten Russia in the Black Sea. Though they did not yet realize that the fleet was obsolete (that awakening was to come in 1889), they knew that it could enter the Straits only if it was secure from a French attack in the rear. The deadlock between England and France over Egypt was not yet palpably final—indeed they had reached a rather futile agreement on the neutralization of the Suez canal in October; and it was therefore reasonable to suppose that the French would welcome the checking of Russia, even though their Egyptian grievance debarred them from assisting it. Salisbury's attitude to France was the reverse of what it had been during the abortive negotiations for an alliance with Germany in 1879. Then he had offered Germany alliance against France, in the belief that this would enable Germany to support Austria-Hungary against Russia. Now he had shouldered the burden of supporting Austria-Hungary, but on the assumption that France would remain neutral. Of course Salisbury's commitment was even now as cautious as it could be. The second Mediterranean agreement, like the first, remained secret. Its object was to steady Austrian nerves and to secure the co-operation of the Italian with the British fleet, rather than to frighten or even to deter France and Russia.

The first Mediterranean agreement had been followed by the Reinsurance treaty; new German gestures of friendship towards Russia followed the second. In December 1887 Bismarck was much pressed both by the Austrians and by his own military men to agree to a preventive war against Russia. The Austrians wanted to count with certainty on German support. The German generals, believing the narrow frontier of the Vosges to be impregnable on either side, planned to stand on the defensive against France; therefore the only way of using their mass army and of avoiding a long war on two fronts, was to knock Russia out at once. Bismarck would have nothing of this reasoning. Though he had no theoretical love of peace, he did not intend to relieve England of the burden of Austria-Hungary: 'So long as I am minister, I shall not give my consent to a prophylactic attack upon Russia, and I am far from advising Austria to make such an attack, so long as she is not absolutely certain of English co-operation.'[1] The Hungarian parliament, in particular, clamoured for war; and Bismarck, to prove that the Austro-

[1] Bismarck to Reuss, 15 Dec. 1887. *Große Politik*, vi, no. 1163.

German alliance was purely defensive, published its text on 3 February 1888.[1] Three days later, he made his last great speech in the Reichstag, approving Russian policy in Bulgaria and declaring his trust in the good faith of the tsar.

Thus encouraged, the Russians made a harmless move against Ferdinand of Coburg. On 13 February they asked the Turks to declare his election as prince of Bulgaria illegal. Bismarck supported this demand. The French had, for a moment, dreamt of reconciling Russia and England. But by February 1888 they had come to realize that the British were committed to Italy, if not to Austria-Hungary;[2] and they were determined not to bear the brunt of this combination. On the other hand, they would not let Germany outbid them for Russia's friendship. They, too, therefore supported the Russian demand, but in close step with Germany. It was opposed by Austria-Hungary, prodded on by Italy and Great Britain. The sultan was, however, delighted to assert his theoretical suzerainty over Bulgaria; on 4 March he declared Ferdinand's election illegal. The declaration harmed no one. Ferdinand remained prince of Bulgaria; Russian pride was satisfied. The great Bulgarian crisis had come to a tame conclusion.

It will not do to give Bismarck all the credit for this peaceful outcome. The French statesmen contributed as much; and Salisbury contributed something. There was a deeper cause still. The Russians regarded the Balkans with indifference or even dislike; their ambition turned towards central Asia and the Far East. They wanted security at the Straits; and they resented the offence to their prestige in Bulgaria. But they would make no serious move, unless assured of German neutrality. German goodwill was not enough; they needed a firm threat to Germany from France, and they did not get it. They could only console themselves that Boulangism made France unfit to be anybody's ally. Giers wrote sullenly: 'an alliance with France at this moment is a complete absurdity, not only for Russia, but for any other country'.[3] On the other side, the Austrians

---

[1] The Austrians exacted a price. The final clause, limiting the duration of the alliance to five years, was not made public. Bismarck thus had to take an unwilling step towards acknowledging its permanence.

[2] Waddington to Flourens, 3 Apr. 1888. *Documents diplomatiques français*, first series, vii, no. 89.

[3] Giers to Shuvalov, 15 June 1888. Meyendorff, *Correspondance de M. de Staal*, i, 427.

dared not take the offensive without German backing, nor perhaps even with it; certainly the tepid British support was not enough for them. Italy was the only restless element. Bismarck tried to satisfy the Italians by elaborate staff talks, arranging for military assistance which he knew to be worthless; it gave them the sensation of their own importance. Both Salisbury and Kálnoky were irritated at Crispi's colonial demands and repeatedly told the French that they would not support them.[1] Crispi went on boasting of the military support he would receive from Germany and of the naval support from England; he lived in a world of illusions and was leading Italy to disaster. But Italy could not dictate policy to Europe. Capitalist investment brought a generation of peace. Industrial expansion made all the Great Powers pacific, as it had made England pacific ever since 1815. So far as they had ambitions, their eyes were turned to the outer world. The days of European upheaval were over; they would not come again until one of the Powers felt itself strong enough to challenge the balance which had been established at the congress of Berlin.

That Power could only be Germany. Ever since 1871 Bismarck had followed a policy of restraint. His motive was always fear, not conquest. The new Germany was conscious only of its strength; it saw no dangers, recognized no obstacles. German explorers, scientists, and capitalists spread over the world. Germans were everywhere—in the Balkans, in Morocco, in central Africa, in China; and where they were not, they wished to be. So long as William I lived, Bismarck could keep a hold on the reins. His system was doomed, once an emperor representative of the new Germany was on the throne. Bismarck in office had been to the Great Powers a guarantee of peace, even though a peace organized by Germany. Now the Powers had to seek other guarantees, and ultimately guarantees against Germany herself.

[1] Waddington to Flourens, 6 Mar.; to Goblet, 12 July; Jusserand to Goblet, 19 Oct.; Decrais (Vienna) to Goblet, 28 Oct. 1888. *Documents diplomatiques français*, first series, vii, nos. 69, 164, 247, 260.

XV

THE MAKING OF THE
FRANCO-RUSSIAN ALLIANCE

1888–94

THE balance which Bismarck had created at the beginning of 1888 was a curious one. Russia received diplomatic support at Constantinople from France and Germany, and was opposed there by the three Powers of the Mediterranean entente; on the other hand, Salisbury, not Bismarck, restrained this entente from turning against France. The outcome was more curious still. The French, much against their will, were driven to support Russia more closely; Germany, much against Bismarck's will, ceased to support Russia at all. The French recognized that support for Russia contradicted their traditional policy in the Near East and threatened their investments in the Ottoman empire; they would have preferred to resurrect the Crimean coalition with England and Italy— 'the only rational and fruitful policy'. Egypt stood in the way, and here Salisbury refused the slightest concession.[1] The French tried to approach England, as Austria-Hungary had done, through the Italian back-door; but instead of seeking to cajole Italy they chose the method of threats—patronage of the pope and the launching of a tariff war—weapons which made Crispi more hostile than ever. Their only practical result was to stimulate Anglo-Italian naval co-operation, culminating in a demonstrative visit to Genoa by the British fleet. The French were driven back to Russia. In Paul Cambon's words, 'if you cannot have what you like you must like what you have and to-day our sole resource is the hope of Russia's support and the anxiety which this simple hope causes Bismarck'.[2] In October 1888 the

[1] Waddington to Spuller, 1 July 1889. *Documents diplomatiques français*, first series, vii, no. 409.

[2] Paul Cambon (Madrid) to Spuller, 11 Mar. 1889. Paul Cambon, *Correspondance 1870–1924*, i. 331. Spuller, the foreign minister, seems to have asked Cambon for his advice on the general course of French policy.

first Russian loan was floated on the French market; and in January 1889 the Russians placed a large order for French rifles, after giving a definite promise that these would never be used against France. Alliance was already in the offing.

Bismarck's difficulties sprang from a single cause: the accession of William II in July 1888. The young emperor had once been an enthusiastic advocate of the Russian alliance; and even in 1887 Salisbury had feared that his accession would swing Germany away from Austria-Hungary. Now he was much in the hands of the military men, particularly of Waldersee, the new chief-of-staff, men who thought exclusively of a war on two fronts and wished to plan a campaign against Russia in Galicia in co-operation with Austria-Hungary. The corollary of this was close alliance with England. Besides, William II wanted to be both modern and popular: hence he favoured nationalist co-operation with the Germanic Austria-Hungary, democratic association with liberal England, and a breach of the conservative partnership with Russia. In the past Bismarck had often played a demagogic card against the old emperor; now the new emperor played demagogic cards against him. Bismarck's only resource was in diplomatic devices. Just before William II came to the throne, Bismarck argued to him that, if he wanted war, it would be better to attack France than Russia;[1] he was trying, in fact, to divert the storm on to a more harmless object. In January 1889 Bismarck proposed to Salisbury a formal secret alliance against France. It is difficult to believe that he took this proposal seriously. He had no fear of France. Indeed, at exactly the same time as he made this proposal to Salisbury, he assured Herbette that his faith in the stability of the French republic had been restored by the collapse of Boulangism and that, if Germany made colonial concessions to England, these would be because of the worthlessness of the German colonies, not from love of England.[2] On the other side, British strategy in the Mediterranean certainly counted on French neutrality; but Salisbury intended to secure this, if necessary, by some friendly gesture, not by an alliance with Germany, which would drive France over to the Russian side. Besides, the British had at last taken the decisive step of strengthening their navy. The Naval

---

[1] Bismarck to Crown Prince William, 9 May 1888. *Große Politik*, vi, no. 1341.
[2] Herbette to Goblet, 25, 26 Jan. 1889. *Documents diplomatiques français*, first series, vii, nos. 304, 305.

Defence Act, passed in March 1889, revolutionized British naval policy; it looked forward to a time when the two-power standard would be a reality and when Great Britain could shake herself free even of the continental attachments which she still had. This was hardly the time for her to make new commitments. Salisbury returned a polite negative to Bismarck's proposal, and even used this rejection as a means of winning French confidence.[1] Bismarck's tactics succeeded for the moment with William II. He was persuaded that the British had rejected an alliance; and he even refrained from proposing a bargain on colonial questions when he visited England in August 1889.

These devices could only postpone the conflict. Later in August Francis Joseph visited Berlin, and William II told him that, whatever the reason for Austrian mobilization, whether the Bulgarian question or anything else, German mobilization would follow the same day.[2] The Austrians had often been told this by Waldersee; it was a different matter to hear it from the German emperor. In October Alexander III also came to Berlin. He was sulky to his German hosts; friendly only to Herbette, to whom he said that the French army should be stronger; and gave general offence by proposing William II's health in French.[3] Worse things followed. In November William II visited Constantinople—the first (and last) Christian sovereign to seek out the Ottoman sultan.[4] This was hard to reconcile with the promise of diplomatic support for Russia in the Near East. The conservative party at St. Petersburg, with Giers at their head, were convinced that only Bismarck stood between them and the French alliance that they dreaded. Alexander III might have let the Reinsurance treaty lapse in silent resentment; Giers alone was anxious to rescue it. On 17 March 1890 Paul Shuvalov formally proposed the renewal of the treaty for six years, with the possibility of its becoming permanent.[5] He was too late. Bismarck's conflict with William II

---

[1] Waddington to Spuller, 23 Mar. 1889. *Documents diplomatiques français*, first series, vii, no. 313.

[2] Glaise-Horstenau, *Franz Josephs Weggefährte*, p. 337.

[3] Herbette to Spuller, 12, 13 Oct. 1889. *Documents diplomatiques français*, first series, vii, nos. 479, 482.

[4] William II took with him a Krupp rifle which he proposed to present to the sultan. Abdul Hamid objected that it might go off during the audience. A symbolical story.

[5] Herbert Bismarck to William II, 20 Mar. 1890. *Große Politik*, vii, no. 1366.

had exploded, and he had already resigned. The conflict was primarily on a domestic issue—whether to repudiate the imperial constitution and crush the social democrats by military force. But since it was a choice between conservative dictatorship and demagogy, it was also a choice between friendship with Russia and support for the 'German' cause in the Near East, in alliance with England.

Caprivi, Bismarck's successor as chancellor, knew nothing of foreign affairs; Marschall, the new secretary of state, not much more. Both relied on Holstein, one of the permanent officials at the foreign ministry, who now established a control over Germany's policy which lasted until 1906. There was nothing mysterious in his position. He was the one-eyed man in the country of the blind. He had great industry and experience, even great resolution; his weakness was one he shared with Bismarck—he tried to conduct foreign policy on a secretive basis, when in fact public opinion had to be increasingly considered. In 1906 this was his ruin. Holstein had close links with the general staff. He accepted their judgements on foreign policy and had for years been urging the Austrians to resist Russia, despite Bismarck's instructions to the contrary.[1] Like the generals, he had no sympathy with overseas expansion or plans for a great German navy. Caprivi had the same outlook, though he had once been at the admiralty. He said on taking office: 'In naval policy I did not ask how big the navy should be, but how small. There must be a battle and the great war, which hangs over Germany's head, must be fought, before we can build as many ships as Germany and especially the Emperor, who is very keen on the development of the navy, want.'[2] The 'new course' aimed at alliance with England, at any rate until the Continent had been conquered; and its protagonists rejected the Reinsurance treaty for fear that it might be revealed to England. The British would, they thought, be particularly offended by the German promise to maintain the closing of the Straits.[3] Caprivi added: 'we have to consider public opinion much more than in Prince Bismarck's time'.[4] The Russians were therefore told that, though German policy

---

[1] See Krausnick, *Holsteins Geheimpolitik in der Ära Bismarck 1886–1890*, passim.

[2] Hallgarten, *Imperialismus vor 1914*, i. 270.

[3] Memorandum by Holstein, 20 May 1890. *Große Politik*, vii, no. 1374.

[4] Memorandum by Raschdau with minute by Caprivi, 18 July 1890. Ibid., no. 1609.

had not changed, the treaty could not be renewed. Giers was in despair. He offered to accept a treaty without any specific promise of diplomatic support in the Near East, and sought only some 'fixing' of Germany's friendship with Russia.[1] It was useless: the Germans feared the effect of even the most harmless clause on the British government. Alexander III took the failure lightly and perhaps enjoyed Giers's discomfiture. Nor was the lack of a signed document decisive in itself. What weighed with Alexander III was the disappearance of Bismarck in Germany and of Boulanger in France; and Giers could not have saved his policy by extracting a scrap of paper from the Germans.

The 'new course' seemed to have erased the entire Bismarckian period and reverted to the foreign policy of the shortlived 'liberal era' between 1858 and 1862. In August 1890 Caprivi agreed with Kálnoky that a Russian solution of the Straits question was 'absolutely impossible' and that no changes could be allowed in the Near East without a previous agreement between Germany and Austria-Hungary.[2] The Germans had as yet no interest of their own to defend in the Near East; they were simply carrying the policy of the 'quadruple alliance' to its logical conclusion. They believed that they had solved the problem which had defeated Bismarck: by associating themselves wholeheartedly with Austria-Hungary they would secure British support for her also, and were therefore running no risks. Certainly Anglo-German relations reached their high-water mark of intimacy in the summer of 1890. On 1 July 1890 the two countries signed an agreement, by which Germany gave up her rights at Zanzibar, limited her claims in East Africa, and received in exchange the island of Heligoland.[3] The agreement

---

[1] Memorandum by Caprivi, 8 Sept. 1890. *Große Politik*, vii, no. 1612.

[2] Marschall to Bethmann Hollweg, 4 Dec. 1911. Ibid., xxx (i), no. 10987. Marschall's recollection was confirmed by William II.

[3] Salisbury's mind was dominated by Egypt and particularly by the upper Nile. The fleet could protect Egypt on the Mediterranean side, but a rival Power could break in from the south so long as the Sudan was in the hands of the dervishes. Though England was supposed to be in the hey-day of imperialism, no British government could raise a penny for the reconquest of the Sudan; hence Salisbury tried to close the back-door of Egypt by diplomacy, seeking self-denying ordinances from the other Powers. The Germans had previously wanted a blackmailing weapon against England and had therefore refused to define the frontier of German East Africa inland; now they agreed to a line which cut them off from the headwaters of the Nile, and they acknowledged the Nile valley as a British sphere of interest 'as far as the confines of Egypt' (whatever these might be). In addition they recognized the British protectorate at Zanzibar which they had always

had the rare quality of satisfying both parties. The British strengthened their position on the Nile and in the Red Sea: the Germans acquired Heligoland and were convinced that alliance with Great Britain was as good as won. Nor were they alone in this belief. Staal, the Russian ambassador, wrote from London: 'the entente with Germany has been virtually accomplished';[1] and Shuvalov told Herbette that henceforth Great Britain and Germany would co-operate in Egypt and the Balkans.[2] Coalition against a Franco-Russian alliance seemed to have come into existence even before the alliance was made. France and Russia were being forced together, whether they liked it or not.

The Russians failed to detach Germany from the 'quadruple alliance' during William II's visit to Peterhof in August 1890. French attempts with Great Britain were equally unsuccessful. The French, too, had claims at Zanzibar, dating back to 1862; they tried to sell them at too high a price. Salisbury would only offer to recognize the French protectorate of Madagascar.[3] The French asked to be freed from fiscal restrictions in Tunis; but this would estrange the Italians, and Salisbury would agree to it only if he received fiscal freedom in Egypt. In other words, he needed the support of the Italian navy until France acquiesced in British control of Egypt; and this was still far out of sight. The Anglo-French deadlock remained unbroken. All the same, Salisbury had agreement always at the back of his mind and gave no encouragement to the Italians. Crispi had taken alarm at the rumour of French action in Tunis and wished to seize Tripoli. Salisbury resisted this precedent for breaking up the Ottoman empire. He was ready to assure Crispi that 'the

previously disputed. Salisbury also tried to obtain a corridor of British territory running from north to south between German East Africa and the Congo Free State; the Germans, with their European obsession of 'encirclement', refused this, and in any case Salisbury attached little importance to it.

Heligoland, once Danish, had been retained by the British in 1815 as a potential smuggling-base against a future continental system; it had no value to them once the danger of a revived French empire disappeared. It certainly never occurred to them that they might one day need it as a naval station against Germany. For that matter the Germans had no idea of using it as a naval station themselves. They welcomed it solely as a display of national prestige. It reinforced the principle that territory inhabited by Germans should be acquired by Germany and not, say, restored to Denmark.

[1] Staal to Giers, 1 July 1890, Meyendorff, *Correspondance de M. de Staal*, ii. 89.

[2] Herbette to Ribot, 17 June 1890. *Documents diplomatiques français*, first series, viii, no. 83.

[3] This, together with a frontier agreement in West Africa, was the agreement ultimately made.

political interests of Great Britain as well as those of Italy do not allow of Tripoli having a fate similar to that of Tunis', but 'as long as the plans of France have not taken shape', nothing must be done to offend Turkey.[1] The British connexion with the Triple Alliance was in fact a form of reinsurance; nothing more.

With the same motive, the French moved slowly along the path towards agreement with Russia. On 30 May fourteen Russian nihilists were arrested in Paris to the great delight of Alexander III; it was a striking repudiation of the traditional protection which France had given to Russian, and particularly Polish, revolutionaries. In August Boisdeffre, assistant chief of the French general staff, visited Russia. His conversations were discouraging. The Russians would mobilize if Germany attacked France, but they rejected his offer of a military convention: 'two opposed camps will be formed, one of which will try to destroy the other.' The Russian plan was to attack Austria-Hungary, even at the cost of sacrificing Russian Poland to the Germans; and they urged Boisdeffre also to follow a defensive strategy. Then France could hold out indefinitely—implicitly without Russian support. The French army, in fact, was to act as a substitute for the Reinsurance treaty and to keep Germany busy while the Russians destroyed Austria-Hungary.[2] The French saw the logical outcome of the Russian plan. If France were defeated by Germany, she could then pay for the gains which Russia would make in eastern Europe. The French, however, did not feel that a Russian occupation of Budapest or even of Vienna would be any consolation for a German occupation of Paris. They waited in the hope of getting better terms.

Failing anything else, the French renewed their attempts to detach Italy from the Triple Alliance. Good relations between France and Italy would cripple the British naval position in the Mediterranean. Then the French could either enforce a settlement of the Egyptian question or sell their friendship to Russia on better terms. As with Russia, the French used the weapon of finance, but in the reverse way. They gave loans to Russia in order to sweeten her for an alliance; they refused loans to Italy unless she moved away from England and Germany. The Italians dared not accept this French bait. They were not free

[1] Salisbury to Crispi, 4 Aug. 1890. Crispi, *Memoirs*, iii. 468.
[2] Boisdeffre (at St. Petersburg) to Freycinet, 27 Aug. 1890. *Documents diplomatiques français*, first series, viii, no. 165.

agents so long as Germany and England were on the same side; and their fears increased when the French republic made up its long-standing quarrel with the pope. It would be a poor bargain if, in exchange for French money, they got British hostility in Tripoli, were excluded from the Eastern question, and were threatened as well with clericalist agitation at home. The pressure from France made Crispi wilder than ever, and he made repeated attempts to get a firmer backing from England and Germany for his ambitions in Tripoli. He achieved nothing. At the end of January 1891 he fell from office over a domestic issue. Rudinì, the new prime minister, hoped to strengthen his shaky parliamentary position by performing the miracle that had evaded Crispi; and he supposed that the British would be more easily caught if the Germans were committed first. He therefore proposed that the Triple Alliance, which ran out in 1892, should be renewed at once and he added a new clause, whereby the Germans were to support Italy if it ever suited her to take Tripoli.[1] Caprivi, with his continental outlook, disliked this proposal; for him Italy was only useful as a link with England.[2] However, the Italians insisted that, once assured of German backing, they could get England as well; and the new Triple Alliance, which was signed on 6 May 1891, contained a protocol that the parties would seek to involve England in the clauses about North Africa, and threw in Morocco also.

Rudinì's manœuvre did not work. He drafted an agreement by which England would promise to support Italy and Germany against France in exchange for diplomatic support in Egypt.[3] The Germans realized that this was bidding too high; the British would certainly not commit themselves to a continental war. They persuaded Rudinì to substitute a declaration in favour of the *status quo* in North Africa, analogous to the agreement of December 1887 about the Turkish empire.[4] Even this was too much for Salisbury. Though he regarded the friendship of the central Powers of Europe as 'essential', he did not intend to pay for it; and he recognized that the existence of Germany

---

[1] If the maintenance of the *status quo* in North Africa proved impossible, Germany promised 'after a formal and previous agreement, to support Italy in any action under the form of occupation or other taking of guarantee that she might undertake there in the interest of balance or legitimate compensation'.

[2] Memorandum by Caprivi, 23 Apr. 1891. *Große Politik*, vii, no. 1412.

[3] Solms (Rome) to Caprivi, 25 May 1891. Ibid., viii, no. 1714.

[4] Solms to Caprivi, 27 May 1891. Ibid., no. 1715.

was enough in itself to restrain France without any alliance. As he told Chamberlain: 'As long as France was afraid of Germany she could do nothing to injure us.'[1] It suited his policy better to balance between Italy and France rather than to tie himself to either. Besides, he suspected that in Italian eyes the *status quo* in North Africa meant the French expelled from Tunis and themselves established in Tripoli. He therefore expressed polite approval of the Italian proposal and waited for an excuse to evade it. Rudinì soon provided this. To prop up his government in the chamber he boasted that Great Britain had joined the Triple Alliance. There were questions in the house of commons from radical members who objected to associating with the Triple Alliance—or indeed with any European Powers; and Salisbury said that negotiations would have to wait until Parliament had quietened down. This never happened. The Italians did not get their agreement—only a visit of the British fleet to Venice.[2] It was small consolation to announce publicly on 28 June the renewal of the Triple Alliance.

Though the Italian move had failed, it alarmed the French. They did not appreciate Salisbury's hints that Tunis also was part of the *status quo* or that he had worked with Crispi only in order 'to keep him within bounds'.[3] They believed that a hostile coalition was being formed against them. Moreover, they attached exaggerated importance to the erratic personality of William II and genuinely feared that he might attack them for failing to respond to his violent gestures of amity.[4] Their only hope seemed to be to force on an agreement with Russia. Alexander III, too, resented the flirtation of England with the Triple Alliance, and favoured co-operation with France. The French gave the final push when they got the Paris house of Rothschild to refuse to float a new Russian loan, ostensibly because of Russian ill treatment

---

[1] Joseph Chamberlain, *A Political Memoir*, p. 296. Chamberlain was acting as intermediary for a proposal from Clemenceau that Great Britain and France should make an alliance against Italy, as an alternative to French alliance with Russia.

[2] Salisbury also held out against joining the agreement to maintain the *status quo* in Morocco which Spain and Italy renewed on 4 May 1891.

[3] Waddington to Ribot, 25 June 1891. *Documents diplomatiques français*, first series, viii, no. 390.

[4] The most absurd of these was sending his mother, the widow of Emperor Frederick, on a visit to Paris. The empress offended the French by visiting Versailles and other scenes of French humiliation in 1871; after public outcry, she had to be smuggled out of France.

of the Jews. The Russians were threatened with a disastrous harvest; they had to have French money on any terms. They yielded towards the Jews; what was more important, they yielded in foreign policy. The Russian chief-of-staff told Boisdeffre that he favoured a military convention providing for simultaneous mobilization if either were attacked by any member of the Triple Alliance;[1] and a French squadron visited Kronstadt in the last week of July, where it was received with tremendous enthusiasm.

Giers saw his conservative policy crumbling away. Lamsdorff, his assistant, noted: 'at bottom this whole rapprochement with France does not enjoy the sympathy of M. Giers.' But Giers could never stand against the autocratic will of Alexander III. He doubted his own judgement and used to send Lamsdorff off to pray in the nearest chapel, before he made any decision. Besides, unlike his predecessors, he had no private fortune and therefore could not threaten to resign. His only resource was to be dilatory. To prevent anything worse, he himself took the initiative towards France. On 17 July he told Laboulaye that they ought 'to take a further step on the path of the entente'. When Laboulaye proposed a military convention, Giers answered by proposing an agreement between the two governments;[2] this, no doubt, would be more harmless. Ribot, the French foreign minister, at once produced a precise draft: simultaneous mobilization against a threat from any member of the Triple Alliance and agreement 'on all questions which might threaten the peace of Europe'.[3] This was not at all to Giers's taste. He wanted a vague entente extending over the whole world—China, Egypt, and so on; what he really had in mind, but dared not mention, was the Near East. Moreover, he rejected simultaneous mobilization and would agree only that the two Powers should consult in case of danger.[4] The French realized that Giers was aiming at an anti-English entente which would not be directed against Germany; but they hoped that, if they once got a political agreement, a military convention against Germany would follow.[5] Alexander III did not want an

[1] Boisdeffre to Miribel, 16 July 1891. *Documents diplomatiques français*, first series, viii, no. 424.

[2] Laboulaye to Ribot, 20 July 1891. Ibid., no. 430.

[3] Ribot, note for Russian government, 23 July 1891. Ibid., no. 434.

[4] Laboulaye to Ribot, 5 Aug. 1891. Ibid., no. 457.

[5] Freycinet (prime minister) to Ribot, 9 Aug.; Ribot to Freycinet, 11 Aug. 1891. Ibid., nos. 480, 485.

open quarrel with Giers. Instead he decided to consult Mohrenheim, his ambassador in Paris—a typically Russian manœuvre.
Mohrenheim, who lived the dissolute life then characteristic of
ambassadors,[1] was probably in the pay of French armament
interests; he was certainly a warm advocate of the French cause.
While he was in St. Petersburg, the British came unconsciously
to the assistance of the French. Salisbury invited the French
fleet to visit Portsmouth on its way back from Kronstadt to show
them that 'England has no antipathy to France, or any partisan-
ship against her'.[2] This was a sharp reminder that France had
other ways of escaping from isolation. Alexander III and
Mohrenheim compelled Giers to swallow the entente; and
it was embodied in a letter to the French government on
27 August.[3]

The French got two concessions. If peace were threatened,
the two Powers would not merely consult; they 'agreed to agree
on measures'—feeble enough, but still something. Further,
Mohrenheim added that this was merely a beginning and that
there must be 'ulterior developments'. These two points were
the loopholes through which the French, within a year, inserted
their interpretation of Franco-Russian relations. Otherwise the
entente was a victory for Russia. The French were committed
to diplomatic action against England, particularly at Constantinople; the Russians were not committed to military action
against Germany. The entente was the last link in a long chain
of exaggerated fears. The Germans had feared a Russian initiative in Bulgaria and had therefore paraded their support for

---

[1] Khevenhüller, the Austro-Hungarian ambassador, was known as 'M. l'am-
brassadeur'. Private information.
[2] Salisbury to Victoria, 22 Aug. 1871. *Letters of Queen Victoria*, third series, ii. 65.
[3] Note from Mohrenheim, 27 Aug. 1891. *Documents diplomatiques français*, first
series, viii, no. 514. Ribot to Mohrenheim, 27 Aug. 1891. Ibid., no. 517. The
notes exchanged revealed, in subtle form, the difference in the outlook of the two
governments. Giers justified the entente by 'the manifest renewal of the Triple
Alliance and the more or less probable adherence of Great Britain to the
political objects pursued by that alliance'. Ribot referred only to the renewal
of the Triple Alliance and suppressed the reference to Great Britain. Further,
Giers described France and Russia as 'remaining outside any alliance, but not
the less sincerely desiring to surround the maintenance of peace with the most
effective guarantees'. In Ribot's letter the two Powers appeared as 'equally desiring
to give to the maintenance of peace the guarantees which spring from the balance
between the forces of Europe'. Giers stressed Great Britain and Russia's own
detachment from alliances; Ribot stressed the Triple Alliance and the Balance of
Power.

Austria-Hungary; the Italians had perhaps feared a French initiative in the Mediterranean and had therefore boasted of their alliance with England. As a result, both France and Russia had feared that they would be isolated in face of a hostile coalition; and this fear drove them together. But each Power was still looking over its shoulder. The Russians hoped that the entente would lead Germany to renew the Reinsurance treaty, the French that it would lead Great Britain to compromise in the Egyptian question. In the Russian vision of the future Germany and France would both patronize Russian expansion in the Near and Far East; in the French vision both Great Britain and Russia would sustain France against Germany. The French would certainly not fight to give Constantinople to Russia; the Russians just as certainly not to recover Alsace and Lorraine for France. In fact, the entente could become an explosive combination only if Germany became Russia's principal rival in the Near East; and that was twenty years off. Still, the entente was a turning-point in the history of Europe. With all its reserves and contradictions it was yet a declaration that Russia and France intended to avoid the dependence on Germany into which Austria-Hungary had fallen. Both made a sacrifice of their principles and traditions. The autocrat of all the Russias stood to attention for the Marseillaise; and that hymn of revolutionary nationalism was played in honour of the oppressor of the Poles.

The August entente was a defeat for Giers's conservative policy of cautious abstention; but he did his best to make it a little one. In the autumn he visited Paris and Berlin, and assured each government of the pacific intentions of the other—a dying echo of the days when Russia had claimed to protect first Prussia and then France.[1] The Germans did not take the Franco-Russian entente very seriously: they had come to assume French hostility, and did not suppose that Russia was more hostile than before. In fact, the entente might improve their position by forcing Great Britain into the Triple Alliance. With the Egyptian question always simmering, it looked indeed as though the entente might be tried out at Constantinople. Paul

---

[1] Notes by Ribot, 20, 21 Nov. 1891; *Documents diplomatiques français*, first series, ix, nos. 74, 76; notes by Caprivi and Marschall, 25 Nov. 1891. *Große Politik*, vii, nos. 1514, 1515. In both capitals Giers was more concerned with new Russian loans than with the Balance of Power.

Cambon, who had just gone there as French ambassador, regarded the entente as a mistaken abandonment of traditional
policy, for which he blamed 'the hotheads of Paris';[1] since it had
been made, he wanted to put it to practical use. Russia and
France should encourage the sultan to resist British proposals
in regard to Egypt; this would soon enforce an acceptable compromise.[2] These ideas did not meet with Ribot's approval. He
knew that the Russians would only give 'moral support' in the
Egyptian question; and their price in regard to Bulgaria was
one which the French could not pay. More serious still, French
opinion was not in the mood to accept any compromise, however reasonable, in the Egyptian question. It was useless for
Cambon to argue that the great opportunity had been lost for
ever in 1882. In Egypt even more than in Alsace and Lorraine
French policy was condemned to sterile resentment. The French
politicians had to demand concessions which they knew the
British would not give and with which, in any case, the French
public would not be satisfied.[3]

All the same Ribot and his colleagues were determined that
the entente should not take on a purely anti-British character; the only way of preventing this was to carry through
the military convention which they had always regarded as the
complement to political agreement. Or even more than the
complement, a way of superseding it. Essentially the French
did not want a political agreement with the Russians in view of
its awkward consequences in the Near East; they wanted a
military convention, guaranteeing that a certain proportion
of the Russian army be turned against Germany. Equally, this
was the essential point which Giers wished to avoid. He was
overruled by Alexander III. The tsar hated the shackles which
German policy had imposed upon him; he wanted to feel truly
independent and liked the prospect of Germany being destroyed,
at any rate in imagination. He said to Giers: 'In case of war
between France and Germany we must immediately hurl ourselves upon the Germans. . . . We must correct the mistakes of
the past and crush Germany at the first opportunity.'[4] Of course
Alexander III, with true Russian procrastination, liked drawing

[1] Cambon to Bompard, 1 July 1891. *Correspondance*, i. 343.
[2] Cambon to Ribot, 16 Nov. 1891; 25 Jan., 18 Feb. 1892. *Documents diplomatiques
français*, first series, ix, nos. 69, 175, 209.
[3] Ribot to Cambon, 6 Dec. 1891; 30 Jan. 1892. Ibid., nos. 180, 191.
[4] Lamsdorff, *Dnievnik*, p. 299: 25 Feb. 1892.

out negotiation for its own sake; but, in the last resort, he was the ally of France against his Germanic foreign minister.

To justify their demand for a military convention, the French had to make out that they were in imminent danger of attack from Germany; this was a façade. Ribot himself admitted that the convention was 'more political than military';[1] its object was to commit Russia to an anti-German course. Curiously enough, the French demand for a Russian offensive was technically ill founded when it was made. The plans of the German general staff, as devised by Moltke, envisaged an offensive against Russia, not against France; and the best answer to this was to withdraw into the heart of Russia, as the Russians intended to do. But the Germans justified the French demand *post facto* when they changed their strategic plans in 1892. As in other cases, the French alliance with Russia, which was a precaution against Germany, itself caused that danger—or at any rate aggravated it. If it had not been for the alliance German strategy against France might have remained defensive for years. Ribot wanted the Russians to concentrate at least half their forces against Germany;[2] and when Boisdeffre again went to Russia in August 1892 he took with him a draft convention providing that Russia should take the offensive even if France were attacked by Germany alone, whereas France would do nothing in case Austria-Hungary fought by herself. The Russian generals jibbed at these proposals, but finally they compromised. The French were promised support even against Germany alone; and, in any case, roughly a third of the Russian army would act against Germany. In return, the French agreed to mobilize (though not necessarily to go to war) even if Austria-Hungary mobilized in isolation.[3] Ribot thought this contingency so unlikely that it was worth taking the risk.[4] The convention was to last as long as the Triple Alliance—a curious arrangement, in that neither France nor Russia knew the latter's terms. The convention of August 1892 was as great a victory for the French version of their relations with Russia as the entente of August 1891 had been for the Russian. The first had been a diplomatic entente against England; the second was a potential

---

[1] Ribot to Montebello (St. Petersburg), 22 July 1892. *Documents diplomatiques français*, first series, ix, no. 415.
[2] Ribot to Montebello, 4 Feb. 1892. Ibid., no. 182.
[3] Boisdeffre to Freycinet, 10 Aug. 1892. Ibid., no. 447.
[4] Ribot to Freycinet, 12 Aug. 1892. Ibid., no. 449.

military coalition against Germany. The second version did not supersede the first; the two competed for many years, each side acting on its own version and disregarding the other. In political matters, the French refused to be pushed forward against England and never helped Russia at Constantinople. In military affairs the Russians neglected their preparations against Germany and used the money lent by France for almost any purpose other than strategic railways in Russian Poland. Still, the great step had been taken: the Franco-Russian alliance was made.

The statement is not technically accurate. The convention was only a draft agreed by Boisdeffre and the Russian generals; it still needed the approval of Alexander III and of the French government. Ribot and Freycinet hoped still to alter the text, at any rate so far as to escape being involved in a Balkan war; but when they visited Giers at Aix-les-Bains, he told them that he was too ill to read their proposals, though not too ill to hold forth on the virtues of a pacific policy.[1] They returned to Paris baffled. Alexander III had probably made up his mind to approve the convention in December; as Montebello wrote, he proceeded with 'an almost mathematical regularity'.[2] But in the autumn of 1892 the Panama scandal exploded in France; the moderate politicians were discredited, Ribot and Freycinet turned out of office. Alexander III welcomed the excuse for further procrastination; and the convention remained not approved. All the same, the system by which Germany directed the affairs of Europe came to an end in August 1892.

The Germans themselves drew this conclusion. They had only the Kronstadt visit and the French press, not the secret negotiations, to go on. In the summer of 1892 Waldersee, chief of the general staff, played politics once too often, and was dismissed on Caprivi's complaint. Schlieffen, his successor, was a strict technician, as well as being an abler man; yet, though he

---

[1] Ribot to Montebello, 7 Sept. 1892. *Documents diplomatiques français*, first series, x, no. 19.

[2] Montebello to Ribot, 5 Sept. 1892. Ibid., no. 17. Langer, *Diplomacy of Imperialism*, i. 59, raises unnecessary difficulties by suggesting that the tsar's final approval, rather than his delays, need explanation. He does not seem to appreciate that the tsar agreed throughout with the French case, though too Russian to admit it. The reader of Langer, however admiring of his learning, cannot but suspect that there would have been fewer strictures on Alexander III's 'heartless, irresponsible way' if he had made a pact with Germany, instead of with France.

never claimed to dictate policy, he took a great technical decision which determined.German policy ever afterwards. Even more than his predecessors he accepted a two-front war as inevitable; Germany's only answer, he thought, was to knock out one enemy before the other was ready. Russia was the weaker opponent; hence Moltke had always planned to take the offensive on the eastern front. But the geography of Russia, her very size, made a rapid victory impossible, even if her army were brought to battle; there would still be an eastern front when the German armies were needed in the west. France, however, could be knocked out at a blow, if the blow were great enough; hitherto the Germans had not thought themselves able to make it. Schlieffen now proposed so to increase the strength of the German army that it could reach a quick decision in the west.[1] Great political consequences followed. Previously the Germans had hoped to localize a Balkan war, with themselves and the French standing neutral; even if they went to war with Russia, they would only increase their garrisons on the western frontier. Henceforth they could not settle with Russia until they had defeated France; therefore they had to attack France at once, even if the war originated in the Balkans. In short, though the prospect of war on two fronts produced Schlieffen's plan of campaign, this plan first made a war on two fronts inevitable.[2]

There was a more immediate political consequence. Caprivi had to introduce a new military law in November 1892 in order to give Schlieffen the larger army that his strategy demanded. Bismarck's army-law of 1887 had been directed against the Russians; yet, since he depended on the votes of the Right, he justified it by the danger from France. Caprivi's army-law was directed against France; but, depending on the votes of the Left, he had to emphasize the danger from Russia. Not only Progressives, but the Polish deputies in the Reichstag, voted for Caprivi's bill in the final division of July 1893; and even the social democrats gave it grudging approval, in phrases reminiscent of the radicalism of 1848. Caprivi also won votes from the

---

[1] His plan of campaign, devised in 1894, was to attack France in the Vosges. He decided only ten years later that the French fortifications made a repetition of Moltke's success in 1870 impossible and that they could only be turned by an advance through Belgium.

[2] This makes nonsense of the theory that the 'alliances' caused the First World War. With or without alliances, an Austro-Russian war had to involve the west, once Schlieffen's plan was adopted.

agrarian right by rejecting the Russian approaches for a new commercial treaty. Yet just when the Germans were planning for a war on two fronts, policy might have made these plans unnecessary. The Panama scandal gave the Germans a last chance to postpone, perhaps to avert, the Franco-Russian alliance. Giers seemed to have been justified in his doubts; Alexander III refused to see the French ambassador and sent his son on a visit to Berlin. But though William II talked of a league of monarchs,[1] facts were more important than sentiments. Agrarian rivalry and the Polish votes for Caprivi soon silenced this last splutter of the Holy Alliance.

While good relations with Russia were not renewed, the intimacy with Great Britain, which had been the keystone of the 'new course', was fading. In August 1892 a general election brought Gladstone back to power with an uneasy majority. Gladstone himself distrusted the Triple Alliance, Austria-Hungary above all, and regarded reconciliation with France as 'a righteous cause';[2] the bulk of his cabinet had no foreign policy beyond isolation. Rosebery, the foreign secretary, meant to maintain 'the continuity of foreign policy'—a doctrine which he had himself invented. His main task was thus to deceive both his chief and his colleagues, a task which he discharged conscientiously, but only at the cost of aggravating his naturally nervous temperament to the point of insanity. Salisbury left behind him a defence of his policy for Rosebery's instruction: 'the key of the present situation in Europe is our position towards Italy, and through Italy to the Triple Alliance'.[3] Though Rosebery agreed with this policy, he refused even to read the Mediterranean agreements, so as to be able to deny their existence if questioned;[4] all he would do was to express the 'personal view' that Great Britain would aid Italy 'in the event of France groundlessly attacking her'.[5] In May 1893 he allowed the retiring British ambassador at Vienna to describe Austria-

[1] Marschall to Werder (St. Petersburg), 30 Jan. 1893. *Große Politik*, vii, no. 1527.
[2] Waddington to Develle, 31 Jan. 1893. *Documents diplomatiques français*, first series, x, no. 153.
[3] Salisbury to Currie, 18 Aug. 1892. Cecil, *Life of Salisbury*, iv. 404.
[4] He evidently gave the denial. Gladstone told Waddington: 'He had enquired at the Foreign Office concerning relations with Italy, and he could affirm categorically to me that there was no written agreement between England and Italy.' Waddington to Ribot, 9 Dec. 1892. *Documents diplomatiques français*, first series, x. no. 64.
[5] Note by Rosebery, 5 Sept. 1892. *British Documents*, viii. 4.

Hungary as 'the natural ally' of Great Britain; but this well-worn phrase had its old meaning—it was to be the substitute for agreement, not the prelude to it.[1] Whatever the Germans had achieved with Salisbury was certainly undone in the first year of the liberal government; and there was mounting irritation at Berlin that the assumptions of the 'new course' had failed to work.

This might not have mattered to the British had they managed to restore good relations with France; but Gladstone's influence was without practical result, and Rosebery was probably the most anti-French of all foreign secretaries. When Waddington tried to achieve something in regard to Egypt by appealing to Gladstone over Rosebery's head, all he achieved was his own recall on Rosebery's complaint.[2] For that matter, the French feared an agreement over Egypt even with Gladstone; the most he could offer them was an international conference, where no Power would have given them serious support.[3] In fact they had no idea what they wanted in Egypt; it was a grievance without a solution.[4] The foreign ministry wanted to force an Egyptian negotiation on the British, though they did not know on what terms; the colonial ministry wished to launch a more direct challenge by sending an expedition from West Africa to the upper Nile and joining hands with the Abyssinians. This, too, was at bottom a diplomatic manœuvre, for the colonial ministry had no idea what their expedition would do on the upper Nile when it got there. They played with the project of damming the Nile, more as a means of frightening the British than as a serious project in engineering. It would make the question of Egypt 'fluid' in a metaphorical sense; for the French object, from start to last, was to reach an agreement with the British, not to destroy the British empire. On 3 May 1893 President Carnot told the explorer Monteil: 'we must *occupy* Fashoda'.[5] Nothing came of this grandiose resolution for the time being; but equally the French avoided negotiating with Great Britain until the situation had changed in their favour.

[1] Deym (London) to Kálnoky, 14, 28 June 1893. Temperley and Penson, *Foundations of British Foreign Policy*, nos. 186 and 187.
[2] Waddington to Ribot, 2 Nov. 1892. *Documents diplomatiques français*, first series, x, no. 37.   [3] Waddington to Develle, 5 May 1893. Ibid., no. 224.
[4] Minute on Reverseaux (Cairo) to Develle, 8 Nov. 1893. Ibid., no. 421.
[5] Monteil to Lebon (Minister of Colonies), 7 Mar. 1894. Ibid., xi, no. 65.

In this uneasy situation—the French not yet certain of Russia, Great Britain holding aloof from the Triple Alliance, and the Egyptian question in suspense—there came a sudden alarm. The French were completing the work of Ferry in Indo-China by rounding off its western frontier, and this brought them into conflict with Siam, last neutral buffer between them and the British empire in India and Burma. The British and French foreign offices had, in fact, agreed to maintain this buffer; and agreement would already have been signed had it not been for opposition from the government of India. But on 30 July 1893 a report reached London that the French had ordered British warships to withdraw from Siamese waters. Rosebery believed that war was imminent and lost his nerve. William II happened to be in England, and Rosebery appealed to him for German backing.[1] Before he could make up his mind what to answer, the report from Bangkok turned out to be false, and the alarm passed. The French stuck to their previous bargain; Rosebery overrode the government of India; and Siam survived as a buffer-state. The crisis, however, had a profound effect on the Germans. They thought they could at last tie Great Britain to the Triple Alliance. Hitherto Austria-Hungary and Italy had needed British backing in the Near East more than the British needed them; and therefore they had never been able to get a binding promise of support. But no one except the British cared for Siam; and the Germans determined to hold them up for ransom: there would be no German backing against France unless the British committed themselves in the Near East. Caprivi wrote: 'For us the best opening of the next great war is for the first shot to be fired from a British ship. Then we can be certain of expanding the triple into a quadruple alliance.'[2]

This blackmail became the basis of German policy. It rested on false assumptions. Even if the British bound themselves to Austria-Hungary, Germany would still have no interests in Siam or the valley of the Nile; and it would still have been

---

[1] The Germans were much impressed by the anxiety of Ponsonby, the queen's secretary, through whom the appeal was made. They thought that he was afraid of war and that this fear was typical of the British governing class. What Ponsonby feared was a cabinet crisis and the political turmoil that it would involve for him. The prospect of having to act as intermediary between Victoria and the radicals turned him pale—and no wonder. War with France was child's play in comparison.

[2] Minute by Caprivi on Hatzfeldt to Foreign Office, 31 July 1893. *Große Politik*, viii, no. 1753.

senseless to fight a great war in Europe for their sake (which is
what Germany must have done). Things might have been different if the existence of the British empire had been in danger, but
it was not. These were frontier disputes with the French or—as
on the Pamir mountains—with Russia, nothing more. If the
Germans had looked more closely, they would have seen that
even in Siam the British, though behaving ingloriously, secured
their essential demand of a neutral buffer. After all, the French
turned to colonial advance as a substitute for a great war in
Europe; and such a war in Asia or Africa would have been even
more unwelcome to them. The Germans did not grasp this;
hence they came to believe that the Franco-Russian alliance,
by weakening the British position, was strengthening their own.

That alliance was now to be completed. In the summer of
1893 the coolness between France and Russia which had been
caused by the Panama scandal blew over. Earlier in the year
Alexander III had made President Carnot apologize in writing
for the charge (no doubt well founded) that Mohrenheim had
been involved in the scandal. Now the tsar felt that he had
carried the humiliation of France too far; and he agreed that
a Russian squadron should visit Toulon.[1] The visit took place in
the middle of October. This was a more serious affair than the
French visit to Kronstadt two years before. The French public
were enthusiastic and welcomed the visit as the real end of
'isolation'. Moreover, it seemed to be a real strategical gesture.
There could be no sense in Franco-Russian naval co-operation
in the Baltic—therefore the French visit to Kronstadt meant
nothing; now the Russians talked of establishing a permanent
Mediterranean squadron, which would join the French in
challenging British naval supremacy. It was a feeble answer for
the British to stage an Anglo-Italian naval meeting at Taranto.
Apart from everything else, the British knew that the Italian
fleet was no good. A British officer wrote: 'If I had a heavy job
on hand here, I would rather, even if I had a very inferior force
of my own, attempt it without than with Italian help.'[2]

The Toulon visit was an assertion of the Russian version of
Franco-Russian relations: it was purely anti-British, not at all

---

[1] Montebello to Develle, 2, 11 June 1893. *Documents diplomatiques français*, first
series, x, nos. 255 and 264. It is not true that Alexander III was led to agree to the
Toulon visit either by the Siam crisis or the German military law.

[2] Marder, *British Naval Policy*, p. 172.

anti-German—nothing could be more remote from the Germans than the Mediterranean. Yet the assertion was not so complete as it seemed. No convention for naval co-operation followed. Instead the French took up again the draft military convention of the previous year and insisted that they could not commit themselves to Russia unless they had security against Germany. This time they got their way. We do not know what brought Alexander III to his final decision. Perhaps it was an unconscious sense of timing—that he had kept the French waiting long enough; perhaps his growing conviction that they would not drag him into a war of revenge. On 16 December he said to Montebello, the French ambassador: 'You would not be good patriots, you would not be Frenchmen, if you did not hold to the thought that the day will come when you can recover possession of your lost provinces; but there is a great distance between this natural feeling and the idea of provocation to realize it, of *revenge* in a word; and you have often shown that you want peace above everything and that you know how to wait with dignity.'[1] In other words, no French war against Germany, but no reconciliation either. On 27 December Giers informed Montebello that Alexander III had approved the military convention; on 4 January 1894, the French government gave their approval in reply. The alliance, though still secret, was thus formally in existence. Its serious intention, so far as it had one, was to keep Germany neutral while the two partners pursued their several objects elsewhere. All the same, it was a weapon loaded only against Germany, whatever the reservations of the two partners.

[1] Montebello to Casimir-Périer, 17 Dec. 1893. *Documents diplomatiques français,* first series, x, no. 475.

XVI

THE ABORTIVE CONTINENTAL LEAGUE

1894-7

Iᴛ is customary to speak of the last twenty or thirty years of
the nineteenth century as the period of 'splendid isolation'[1]
in British foreign policy; but this is true only in a limited
sense. The British certainly ceased to concern themselves with
the Balance of Power in Europe; they supposed that it was self-
adjusting. But they maintained close connexion with the continental Powers for the sake of affairs outside Europe, particularly in the Near East. The Mediterranean entente was a firmer
combination against Russia than anything they had entered
into earlier in the century; and until the autumn of 1893 they
supposed that they still had 'the liberal alliance' with France
up their sleeve if they ever really needed it. The Toulon visit
destroyed these easy assumptions; the Third republic had done
what Napoleon III had always refused to do—it had committed
itself to Russia without being, at the same time, on good terms
with England. Moreover, the Balance of Power in Europe, which
had been the pride of British policy, now worked against Great
Britain. The Balance certainly secured the peace of Europe;
indeed many Frenchmen rightly complained that the Russian
alliance implicitly accepted the treaty of Frankfurt as the *status
quo*. But this balance would be upset, not strengthened, if Great
Britain found a continental ally. Previously the British had made
alliances in order to maintain the peace of Europe; now alliances
escaped them for the same reason—a European Power which
made an alliance with Great Britain would be nearer war than
before, not farther away, for it would be involved in the burdens
of the British empire. In these circumstances the British had
two resources. They tried, rather half-heartedly, to get German

---

[1] Ironically enough, Salisbury, who coined the phrase, used it to describe a
position which it was impossible for Great Britain to achieve: only if the British
lived in 'splendid isolation' could they base their policy on moral principles.

backing; at first indirectly through Austria-Hungary, later, when the storm-centre moved from the Near to the Far East, by a direct bargain. They also set out so to strengthen their navy that they could defend all their imperial interests without an ally. This second course succeeded.

There was another reason for British success. The continental Powers differed widely in the use to which they would put their new security. The French had throughout an overriding object: they meant to settle the Egyptian question on terms acceptable to their public opinion and so to restore 'the liberal alliance'. The Russians had also an object, to which everything else was subordinated. They were building the Trans-Siberian railway with the money from French loans; and the prize they saw at the end of it was their domination of the Chinese empire. Sea power had saved Constantinople; it could not protect Pekin. Their interest in the Near East was purely defensive. They had accepted their humiliation in Bulgaria; and it was not all that decisive—by 1894 Bulgaria had a government friendly to Russia. The only Russian concern in the Near East was that the British should not counter their threat to China by an attack in the Black Sea, as they had proposed to counter the threat to Afganistan in 1885. Since the Russians had lost faith in 'the rule of the Straits', they thought vaguely of controlling the Straits themselves; and this provoked a Near Eastern crisis of a sort until they gave it up in despair. As to the Germans, they did not know what use to make of their secure position. Certainly it left them free to pursue imperial ambitions—in Africa, Turkey, and the Far East; but this was not grand policy. Sometimes they thought of forcing Great Britain into an alliance, sometimes of organizing 'a continental league' against her. The one was too dangerous, the other offered more rewards to France and Russia, especially Russia, than to themselves. Hence they accepted the inevitable and made a merit of 'the free hand'. Finally, both Austria-Hungary and Italy were left high and dry by the new situation: the one exposed to Russia, the other to France. Since Russia, too, became pacific in the Near East, Austria-Hungary had a breathing-space; but Italy came to disaster.

In the winter of 1893–4 the British began to face seriously the problem of the Franco-Russian alliance. Hitherto they had assumed that they could pass the Straits in case of war with Russia; and a squadron had been kept more or less permanently in the Aegean. Leaving it there after the Toulon visit was simply what Rosebery called 'a policy of honour'. It could never risk an action.[1] The full resources of both the Mediterranean and Channel fleets would be needed to deal with the French; and it was disputed whether they could do even this. Chamberlain, always given to exaggeration, said, 'the British navy in the Mediterranean would have to cut and run—if it could run'.[2] In addition, the Russian fleet was now supposed to be formidable; and the Russians would, it was thought, be able to reach Constantinople by sea, avoiding the long land-route which put them at the mercy of Austria-Hungary. The immediate answer was a new programme of naval building, called after Spencer, the first lord of the admiralty. Gladstone resisted it: 'Bedlam ought to be enlarged at once,' he said, 'it is the Admirals that have got their knife into me.'[3] He was not supported even by his more radical colleagues; and resigned on 1 March 1894. Rosebery, becoming prime minister, was freer than before to follow the imperialist policy in which he believed.

Though the increased navy might solve the problem for Great Britain, it would not be ready for years; Rosebery needed an immediate ally. Previously he had held out against Austro-Hungarian importunity; now it was his turn to be importunate. On 31 January 1894 he told Deym, the Austro-Hungarian ambassador, that he was prepared to fight for the Straits: 'I should not shrink from the danger of involving England in a war with Russia.' But this was possible only if France remained neutral; therefore he needed 'the assistance of the Triple Alliance to hold France in check'.[4] Of course talk of the Triple Alliance was pretence; the only member of it that could threaten France into neutrality was Germany. The proposal would have been eagerly accepted in the great days of 'the new course'; Bismarck, for that matter, had offered it in 1889. Now times had changed; since the Franco-Russian alliance, Germany could not threaten France without being in danger of war with Russia also. Besides, a different wind was blowing in German home politics. The Left coalition that supported Caprivi was breaking up. Many former liberals now regarded Great Britain as their

[1] Memorandum by first sea lord, 15 Apr. 1894. Marder, *British Naval Policy*, p. 221.
[2] Debate in house of commons, 19 Dec. 1893. *Hansard*, 4, xix. 1771–86.
[3] Algernon West, *Diaries*, p. 262.
[4] Deym to Kálnoky, 7 Feb. 1894. *Foundations of British Foreign Policy*, no. 189.

colonial rival. On the other side, the heavy industrialists who coveted the Russian market silenced agrarian protests, and William II agreed with them. 'I have no desire to wage war with Russia on account of a hundred crazy Junkers.'[1] A new commercial treaty with Russia passed through the Reichstag in March 1894. The 'German cause' in the Balkans and the liberal alliance with England were at a discount. William II had wearied of his demagogic role and favoured Bismarckianism, if not Bismarck. As early as September 1893 he told Kálnoky that Germany would not fight for Constantinople; if the Russians took it, Austria-Hungary should take Salonica.[2] This was the old line for which Bismarck had been dismissed. Caprivi had to follow it if he were to keep office. Therefore he could only offer to Kálnoky Bismarck's old answer: Great Britain must commit herself to Austria-Hungary without relying on Germany. Of course he made out that the British would get German support, once they had made a formal treaty; in reality he meant to conclude a new Reinsurance treaty with Russia, or something like it, as soon as the British were caught.[3]

Kálnoky did not relish this answer. He was afraid that he would be in difficulties himself, before the storm blew for the British. The Germans, nagged at ceaselessly from Vienna, would not cajole the British; instead they tried to threaten them. They would oppose Great Britain in colonial matters, and thus force her into alliance with Austria-Hungary. Hatzfeldt assured them that a little unpleasantness would soon drive Rosebery to brave the cabinet—after all he was now prime minister and could no longer shelter behind Gladstone's opposition.[4] The Germans seized the opportunity of an agreement which Rosebery had made on 12 May with the Congo Free State, designed to bar the French from the valley of the Nile.[5] Not only did they protest

[1] Waldersee, *Denkwürdigkeiten*, ii. 306.
[2] Minute by William II on Eulenberg (Vienna) to Caprivi, 20 Dec. 1893. *Große Politik*, ix, no. 2138.
[3] Memoranda by Caprivi, 8 Mar. 23 Apr.; Marschall to Hatzfeldt, 28 Mar. 1894. Ibid., nos. 2152, 2155, 2153.
[4] Hatzfeldt to Caprivi, 1 June 1894. Ibid., viii, no. 2039.
[5] The treaty was in fact concluded on 12 April. It was postdated in order to conceal the fact that Leopold II, king of the Belgians and owner of the Congo Free State, had already committed himself to the British before negotiating with the French on the same subject between 16 and 23 April. The object of the treaty was the same as that of the Heligoland-Zanzibar treaty of 1890—to seal off the

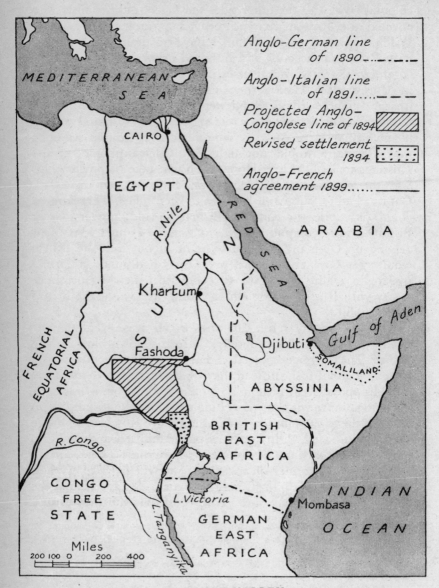

THE NILE VALLEY

against the treaty; they offered to co-operate with the French in resisting it. Thus some gain was bound to follow: either Rose-bery would make an alliance with Austria-Hungary to appease Germany, or the French, appreciating the value of Franco-German co-operation, would forget about Alsace and Lorraine. The policy miscarried on both counts. Instead of taking fright, Rosebery threatened to break with the Triple Alliance alto-gether 'if Germany continues to place herself on the side of France in Colonial questions'.[1] When Kálnoky took alarm at Rosebery's anger the Germans hastily changed course. They made out that they had never intended to co-operate with the French[2] and professed themselves satisfied with a trivial British

valley of the upper Nile by diplomacy. It was closed from the east by the 1890 treaty and by an Anglo-Italian agreement made in 1891, except by way of Abyssi-nia: hence the British encouragement of the Italian ambitions there and the French patronage of the Abyssinians. In November 1893 the Germans also renounced entry from the west by agreeing with the British to place the eastern limit of the Cameroons at the Nile watershed. The British hoped that the Germans would extend their claims as far as the watershed and so bar the way against the French; instead the Germans made an agreement with the French in March 1894, which left the route from the French Congo to the Nile still open. A new barrier had to be created. Previously the British had also tried to exclude the Belgians of the Congo Free State; now they agreed to lease to Leopold II the Bahr-el-Ghazal —the critical buffer-area which the Germans had just declined. In return Leopold II leased to the British a strip of Congolese territory from north to south—the very proposal which the Germans had struck out of the Heligoland treaty in 1890. This gave them the excuse to complain that they were being 'encircled'—in darkest Africa! They would have objected in any case, on the ground that the Congo Free State, being set up as a neutral territory by the Berlin act of 1885, was not entitled to acquire land outside the conventional basin of the Congo.

The French objections were more serious. Unlike the Germans they had never recognized the upper Nile as a British 'sphere of influence'. They insisted that it was either under Ottoman sovereignty or ownerless. If it was still Turkish, then the British as well as the French should leave it alone; and in addition the British should leave Egypt, to which Ottoman sovereignty also applied. In any case the British had no right to lease Ottoman (or Egyptian) territory to Leopold II, or to anyone else. If it was ownerless, then the French had as much right to penetrate into it as anyone else and could not be debarred from it by a fictitious transaction between the British and Leopold II; it could only be claimed, like other parts of Africa, by whoever got there first. The British had no answer to these objections. The only answer would have been the right of possession; and that the British gained only in 1898.

[1] Deym to Kálnoky, 13, 14 June 1894. *Foundations of British Foreign Policy*, no. 192.

[2] Langer (*Diplomacy of Imperialism*, i. 139) seeks to show (*a*) that there was no German offer of co-operation, (*b*) that the French did not resent the German with-drawal from the question. He is wrong on both counts. On 13 June 1894 Marschall proposed to Herbette that France and Germany should 'take as the common basis for the negotiations with England the maintenance of the *status quo* as established by the Berlin act' (*Große Politik*, viii, no. 2049). The same day Rosebery complained to Deym; on 15 June Kálnoky passed this complaint on to the Germans (Ibid.,

concession. Though they did not wreck the Anglo-Congolese treaty (the French did that without assistance), they certainly wrecked any chance of British support for Austria-Hungary. On 9 July Deym gave Rosebery a long apology for German abstention in the Near East.[1] Rosebery was no longer interested. He had despaired of the Triple Alliance and proposed to lessen British difficulties by improving relations with France and Russia. 9 July 1894 was a historic date. It marked the end of Anglo-Austrian co-operation against Russia: a policy which the British had begun at the congress of Vienna (or perhaps even in 1792), failed to achieve during the Crimean war, and on which they had staked much in 1878 and everything in 1887. In fact, it was the day on which British 'isolation' began.

British agreement with France was not achieved, though the French would have welcomed it. They were under no illusion that any other Power would support them in the question of the upper Nile. When the Germans proposed co-operation they answered by asking whether this would extend to the Egyptian question;[2] they were not surprised by the negative answer, nor when the Germans withdrew from the affair altogether. Russia was no better. Hanotaux, the French foreign minister, attempted to invoke the Franco-Russian alliance.[3] Giers replied, after three weeks of silence: 'The tsar entirely approves the attitude taken by the government of the Republic.'[4] No action followed, not even a harmless expression of opinion in London; in fact, the Russians were blessing the quarrel, not its cause. The French did not much regret these refusals. Though Hanotaux later

---

no. 2054). On 17 June Marschall eluded further co-operation with the French and professed himself satisfied (Ibid., no. 2061). This was before the British concession to Germany which was only made on 18 June. Hence the Germans changed course because of Austro-Hungarian anxiety, not because they had got what they wanted.

On 19 June Hanotaux, French foreign minister, expostulated to the German ambassador against making a separate agreement with England (*Documents diplomatiques français*, first series, xi, no. 161); he repeated his complaint on 22 June (no. 172). Herbette in Berlin expostulated to Marschall on 19 June (no. 162) and 25 June (no. 175). Marschall then went on holiday into the country in order to escape further complaints. He was rightly ashamed of his actions. The shame was not shared by the editors of the *Große Politik* (who suppressed the evidence of French complaints).

[1] Deym to Kálnoky, 9 July 1894. Langer, *The Franco-Russian Alliance*, p. 200.

[2] Herbette to Hanotaux, 17, 24 June; Hanotaux to Herbette, 18 June 1894. *Documents diplomatiques français*, xi, nos. 154, 174, 157.

[3] Hanotaux to Montebello, 1 June 1894. Ibid., no. 122.

[4] Montebello to Hanotaux, 21 June 1894. Ibid., no. 169.

acquired the reputation of a colonial zealot, his object was to be reconciled with Great Britain, not to humiliate or even to defeat her. But in his eyes reconciliation was only possible if the British withdrew from Egypt; whereas the British expected France to acknowledge their occupation of Egypt, and even its perman- ence, before they would talk of reconciliation. Hanotaux at least tried to keep the question open. He offered to discuss the upper Nile and even to recognize the British 'sphere of influence' there—at a price (unnamed and indeed beyond discovery)— if the British would scrap the treaty with Leopold II. The British wanted things the other way round; they would nego- tiate only if the French acknowledged the treaty and therewith their defeat. Deadlock followed once more. Hanotaux broke it by threatening not the British, but Leopold II. The Congo Free State was already unpopular enough in Belgium; and Leopold's ministers would not support him in a quarrel with France. Nor, for that matter, would the British. They had sought a buffer against France, not a liability. If there was to be a quarrel, they preferred to fight for their own interests. On 14 August Leopold II agreed with France not to take up the lease which barred their way to the upper Nile.[1]

The French still tried for agreement with England. The ex- pedition that was preparing was told that it must not penetrate into the Nile valley;[2] and in October Hanotaux proposed that England, too, should become a party to this 'self-denying ordinance'.[3] The British negotiator in Paris thought this a good compromise; he was overruled from London. Negotiations broke down. It was the nearest that Great Britain and France came to agreement between the occupation of Egypt in 1882 and the successful entente of 1904. The stumbling-block was simple. The British were determined to stay in Egypt; they would not be content with a French promise not to step into their empty shoes. If the French could not eject the British from Egypt— and they could not—then they must devise some price which would reconcile French public opinion to the occupation. This

---

[1] Curiously enough, the French success turned finally to British advantage. Leopold II would have been much more difficult to eject from Fashoda than Marchand, since he had a title which the British at any rate would have had to recognize.

[2] Delcassé (colonial minister) to Monteil (with minute by Hanotaux), 13 July 1894. *Documents diplomatiques français*, first series, xi, no. 191.

[3] See my article, 'Prelude to Fashoda', in *English Historical Review*, vol. lxv.

price eluded them. Paul Cambon wrote from Constantinople a little later: 'If we can give the English the impression . . . that our Government, pushed on by public opinion, would be capable of occupying Port-Said, the demonstration will have a certain effect. But . . . we must know what we want and say it frankly, cordially, but clearly. We have stood too much on our rights and not taken enough account of the facts.'[1] This logic was too ruthless. The French continued to hope that they might improve their bargaining position without provoking a serious conflict. On 17 November their expedition was instructed to reach the upper Nile as soon as it could.[2] Even this was a move in diplomacy, not preparation for a real conflict. The British would become more reasonable once the French were on the upper Nile. Marchand, who commanded the expedition, wrote before his departure: 'The object, in the last analysis, is to put England by pacific, but certain means, in the necessity of accepting, if not herself proposing the meeting of a European conference. . . . May we not hope that the question of the evacuation of Egypt will follow naturally from that of the Egyptian Sudan?'[3]. The British had no answer to these preparations. They therefore fell back on the threadbare resource of diplomacy by threats. On 28 March 1895 Grey, the undersecretary of foreign affairs, said in the house of commons that a French expedition to the upper Nile would be 'an unfriendly act'.[4] It was a delayed declaration of war, and certainly far from the reconciliation with France which Rosebery had hoped to diplay to the Germans.

Rosebery was equally unsuccessful with Russia, despite some flickers of good feeling. He made an agreement with the Russians defining their frontiers on the Pamir mountains; and on 9 November 1894 declared at the lord mayor's banquet that relations with Russia had never been 'more hearty'. In the Near East a new bout of Turkish atrocities, this time against the Armenians, gave him the chance to stage a flamboyant co-operation with France and Russia. It soon came to nothing.

[1] Paul Cambon to Bourgeois, 31 Mar. 1896. *Documents diplomatiques français*, first series, xii, no. 362.

[2] Note by Hanotaux, undated (17 Nov. 1894), Ibid. xi, no. 285.

[3] Marchand, Note, 10 Nov. 1895. Ibid. xii, no. 192.

[4] This is the 'Grey declaration', of which Grey was later so ashamed that he made out he had meant to use strong language about the Niger and transferred it to the Nile by mistake. Grey, *Twenty-Five Years* i. 18.

While the British government was driven on by a storm of public indignation, the French joined only to see that no harm came to Turkey, and the Russians, themselves the oppressors of many Armenians, only to see that no good came to the Armenians. The Russians regarded these British approaches with contemptuous complacency. Nor could Rosebery fall back on the Triple Alliance, though he tried to do so in December. Kálnoky was delighted by the Armenian atrocities, which carried the storm-centre away from the Balkans:[1] and in Germany the resignation of Caprivi in November formally terminated 'the new course'. Hohenlohe, the new chancellor, was the nearest thing to Bismarck short of being Bismarck himself. He rested on the old cartel of industrialists and agrarians, but with a new enemy. Projects to renew the persecution of the social democrats fell through; therefore Hohenlohe had to rely for enthusiasm on 'world policy'—the drive for expansion overseas and for a great navy which was directed against England. Earlier, Germany had often been indifferent to Great Britain; soon she would become hostile.

British isolation was displayed to all the world in the spring of 1895 when the Far East first thrust itself to the front of the world stage. Hitherto the British had been content to patronize and to bully the derelict Chinese empire, while virtually monopolizing its trade. Their control of sea power had enabled them to check any attempts at partition; and in particular they had twice thwarted those by Russia, in 1861 and in 1885. Now the Trans-Siberian railway was being built; and Russian forces would soon arrive in China by land. But the European Powers were not alone with China. By a unique feat, Japan had transformed herself from a decaying oriental kingdom into a modern industrialized state, determined to play its part as a Great Power. The Japanese foresaw the Russian concentration on the Far East which would follow the completion of the Trans-Siberian railway; and they resolved to protect themselves by establishing Korea as a buffer-state, independent of Chinese influence. In September 1894 they went to war with China— the first Korean war. The British, as patrons of China, tried to organize a combined intervention of the European Powers in her favour. The attempt failed. The Chinese were defeated. In April 1895 they made peace at Shimonoseki. They recognized

---

[1] Eulenberg to Hohenlohe, 4, 14 Dec. 1894. *Große Politik*, ix, nos. 2168, 2170.

the independence of Korea and surrendered to Japan Port Arthur and the Liaotung peninsula—the keys of Manchuria and indeed of all northern China.

These events threw Russian policy into disarray. Sixty years before, in 1829, they had planned to dominate the Ottoman empire by peaceful penetration. Hardly had this scheme got under weigh than Turkey had been threatened by Mehemet Ali; and to defeat him the Russians had to call other European Powers into the Eastern question. Now once more the Russian plans for a political monopoly at Pekin would be barred at conception if the Japanese kept Port Arthur. The Russian foreign ministry, which had just passed to Lobanov, learnt wisdom from the old disappointment. This time Russia should strike a bargain with her immediate rival and exclude all other Powers from the Far East. After all, Russia's practical need was for a zone of influence in northern Manchuria, linking up Siberia and the Maritime Province; and this could be gained by agreement with Japan. Such a cautious policy did not suit Witte, the minister of finance; he was projecting the economic and political domination of all northern China and wanted no partner. The new tsar, Nicholas II, who had succeeded in November 1894, prided himself on his knowledge of the Far East (he had actually been there) and was all for resistance. Thus Russian diplomacy was pushed into a policy of adventure in the Far East as in 1877 it had been pushed into a Panslav adventure in the Balkans. Lobanov hit on a device to lessen the danger. Russia should organize a joint protest by the European Powers and, keeping in the background herself, should emerge later as the protector of Japan.

The French joined in at once. Though their own interests in Indo-China would best be served by dismembering the Chinese empire, they welcomed an opportunity of demonstrating the Franco-Russian alliance anywhere—except of course at Constantinople. Besides, they assumed that the British, who had already proposed joint action in the autumn of 1894, would again co-operate also. Instead, to the great dismay of the French, the British stayed out and the Germans came in. The Germans had originally thought of joining the Japanese in a partition of China. They switched round in order to prevent the Franco-Russian alliance from having its 'baptism of fire'. William II even supposed that his working with Russia would somehow be a demonstration that she had deserted France and joined the

Triple Alliance; in any case Russian action in the Far East meant security for Germany's eastern frontier in Europe.[1]

British abstention sprang from no such elaborate calculations. Nine years later, when Japan defeated Russia and so preserved British commercial greatness in China at any rate for a time, the British seemed to have been amazingly far-sighted. In fact they had no policy in the Far East and not much anywhere else. They were losing faith in the capacity of the oriental empires to reform themselves—Turkey in the first place, but also China, Persia, Morocco; and they had no substitute. Partition seemed as objectionable as preservation was impossible. It never occurred to them that Japan could thwart the Russian designs on China; nor indeed did they yet realize that a great Russian encroachment was imminent. Abstention was merely the last negative of a liberal cabinet in full dissolution. All the active forces in government—the queen, Rosebery (the prime minister), Kimberley (the foreign secretary)—wished to co-operate with the European Powers; the cabinet was resolute for inaction. They had always disliked Rosebery's 'imperialist' policies, and this time they defeated him. Moreover they resented the cynicism with which Russia and France had emptied the 'Armenian entente' of its idealism in the autumn of 1894 and were determined not to be caught again. The British were elbowed aside in the Far East, long their private preserve, by the three continental Powers.

More truly, they were elbowed aside by Russia alone. Neither France nor Germany derived any benefit from the 'Far Eastern entente'. Their united protest compelled the Japanese to hand their gains on the mainland back to China, and the keys to the Far East thus remained for Russia to grasp. The Chinese indemnity to Japan was met by a loan, for which the French put up the money and from which the Russians got the political advantage; the Germans were excluded from the loan, despite their protests, and accepted their exclusion rather than quarrel with Russia. In fact France and Germany were competing for Russia's friendship; both encouraged her in the Far East so as to turn her eyes from Constantinople. The French were much embarrassed by this development; they had meant the Franco-Russian alliance to protect them from Germany, not to force

[1] Minute by William II on Eulenburg to Hohenlohe, 7 Apr. 1895. *Große Politik*, ix, no. 2313.

them on to good terms with her. As Hanotaux said, in case of action in the Far East 'we shall be compelled to discuss in public what has been done against Germany with Russia at the moment when we shall be asking to go *with* Germany to Russia's help. It is a perfect mess.'[1] There was no help for it. In June 1895 the Kiel canal was opened; this was the humiliating symbol of Napoleon III's first setback in the Sleswick affair. The French meant to boycott the international celebrations.[2] Nicholas II abruptly ordered them to attend: 'It seems to me that the French government is wrong in hesitating to reply to the German invitation. Once all the powers have accepted, the participation of France, along with ours, is indispensable.'[3] The only consolation for the French was that they were allowed for the first time to refer publicly to 'the alliance'.

What seemed important, however, in the summer of 1895 was not the Franco-Russian alliance, but the approach to 'the continental league'. The Russians imagined that it would work in the Near East as it had done in China; Germany and France, competing for Russia's friendship, would back her every demand. The Russians had no ambitions in the Near East; they had only anxieties. They wanted to turn the key in the lock of the Black Sea and so be free to concentrate on China without fear of a British attack on Crimea or the Ukraine. In July 1895 a Russian council decided: 'We need the Bosphorus and the entrance to the Black Sea. Free passage through the Dardanelles can be got later by diplomacy.'[4] The second sentence revealed the flaw in Russian policy. Security was no longer enough. Once the French loans started, iron-rails and machinery came in, and grain had to go out—both through the Straits. Moreover, the Trans-Siberian railway was not completed; and even when ready, it would only be single-track. Russia depended on the sea-routes even in the Far East; and this meant free passage through the Suez canal as well as through the Straits. The military men and the more old-fashioned diplomatists would have been content with a partition of the Ottoman empire, leaving Egypt and perhaps even the Dardanelles to England. The more far-sighted statesmen,

[1] Hanotaux to Montebello, 25 Apr. 1895. *Documents diplomatiques français*, first series, xi, no. 483.
[2] Hanotaux to Montebello, 27 Feb. 1895. Ibid., no. 382.
[3] Montebello to Hanotaux, 2 Mar. 1895. Ibid., no. 384.
[4] Khostov, *Istorik Markzist*, xx. 108.

led by Witte, recognized that this would no longer do: they had to keep the Ottoman empire in existence and work for the neutralization of the Suez canal *faute de mieux*. Lobanov at first favoured partition; but he saw that it would only be tolerable if the Egyptian question, and therewith the control of the Suez canal, were settled at the same time. He therefore encouraged the French to go ahead with the expedition to the upper Nile;[1] and the final decision to launch Marchand was in fact made in November 1895. Lobanov also supposed that the French would swallow a Russian control of Constantinople if they got their way over Egypt; therein he was much mistaken. Rather the French hurried on the Marchand expedition in order to get Egypt settled before the Eastern question blew up.[2]

The Russians were not alone in considering a partition of the Turkish empire. In June 1895 Salisbury returned to power in England. He had never had much faith in the ability of the Turkish empire to reform itself; now he had none. Besides, the campaign in England against the Armenian atrocities would have made it impossible for him to support Turkey even if he had wished to do so—and he did not. He told Courcel, the French ambassador: 'it is impossible to keep things as they are . . . Turkey is dying slowly'.[3] Moreover, he was disillusioned with his former associates of the Mediterranean league. Austria-Hungary seemed weak; Italy was a liability instead of an asset; and Germany was shifty. England had 'backed the wrong horse'. He wanted a deal with Russia. He said to Courcel: 'I am an old Tory and have no prejudice against the Russian government.' He harked back with regret again and again to the proposals for partition which Nicholas I had made in 1853. 'If we had only listened to the Emperor Nicholas when he spoke to Sir Hamilton Seymour, what a much pleasanter outlook would meet us when we contemplate the continent of Europe.'[4] At the end of July he told Hatzfeldt that he was ready to let the Russians have Constantinople *avec tout ce qui s'ensuit*.[5] These

---

[1] Paul Cambon later attributed the Marchand expedition to Lobanov's prompting of Hanotaux in the autumn of 1895. Paul Cambon to Henri Cambon, 10 June, 6 Sept. 1904. *Correspondance*, ii, pp. 143, 159.

[2] Herbette to Berthelot, 2 June, 1896. *Documents diplomatiques français*, first series, xii, no. 264.

[3] Courcel to Hanotaux, 12, 29 July 1895. Ibid., nos. 88 and 144.

[4] Salisbury to Iwan-Muller, 31 Aug. 1896. *British Documents*, vi, appendix iv.

[5] Hatzfeldt to Holstein, 30, 31 July, 5 Aug. 1895. *Große Politik*, x, no. 2371, 2372, 2381.

proposals threw the Germans into a panic. They suspected, no doubt with some justification, that Salisbury was trying to repeat his manœuvre of 1887: he was declaring his lack of interest in the Turkish empire in order to saddle them with sole responsibility for Austria-Hungary. They, on their side, tried to repeat the manœuvre of the Reinsurance treaty. William II told Lobanov in October that he would like to revive the League of the Three Emperors (against the United States!) and 'was not indisposed to give Russia moral support in the Near East'. According to Lobanov he even asked: 'Why do you not take Constantinople? I should have no objection.'[1] But Lobanov may have been exaggerating in order to frighten the French.

In any case, the German manœuvre did not last long. There was no escaping the burden of Austria-Hungary. Kálnoky had fallen earlier in the year when he had tried to arrest the anti-clerical legislation of the Hungarian government.[2] His successor Goluchowski was a Pole and was therefore even more anti-Russian; the last thing he wanted was the partition of the Ottoman empire or a League of the Three Emperors. He insisted that England would take a stand against Russia if only she were promised the military backing of the Triple Alliance.[3] German policy was abruptly reversed. On 14 November the Austrians were told that if their vital interests were endangered—and of this they were to be the sole judge—they could count on German support.[4] The Italians were equally insistent that Germany should help to revive the Mediterranean agreements.[5] They had worries of their own quite apart from Turkey. Ten years before they had been encouraged by the British to establish themselves in the Red Sea in order to thwart French plans for an advance to the Nile from the east. Now Italian plans there were going badly: the Italians had the ambition, but not the strength, of a Great Power. They had run up against Abyssinia; and the Abyssinians, with French assistance, were more than a match

[1] Memorandum by Eulenburg, 13 Oct. 1895. *Große Politik*, ix, no. 2323. Lobanov to Hanotaux, 24 Oct. 1895. *Documents diplomatiques français*, first series, xii, no. 182.

[2] When Kálnoky lost British support, he decided that his only resource was an alliance with the Vatican—a desperate remedy.

[3] Eulenburg to Hohenlohe, 8 Nov. 1895. *Große Politik*, x, no. 2497.

[4] Hohenlohe to Eulenburg, 14 Nov. 1895. Ibid., no. 2542.

[5] Bülow to Hohenlohe, 8 Nov. 1895. Ibid., no. 2538.

for them. The Italians needed British help desperately.[1] It was not forthcoming. Salisbury wanted to detach France from the Russian side, not to estrange her further. Like Rosebery with Leopold II in 1894, if he had to quarrel with the French over the upper Nile, it would be for his own profit, not for that of the Italians. The only hope for the Italians, and it was a thin one, was that they might be paid in Abyssinia for the services which they could render Salisbury at the Straits.

Austria-Hungary and Italy therefore took the lead. Goluchowski proposed on 1 November that the fleets of the six Great Powers should force the Straits and virtually take over authority at Constantinople; nothing more abhorrent to the Russians could be imagined. Both Russia and France at once rejected the proposal. Even more striking, the British refused to act. In the autumn of 1895 Salisbury had decided that, since the Russians showed no interest in his plans for partition, he would thwart their supposed aggressive designs on Constantinople by sending his own fleet there. Some time in November this plan was vetoed by his naval advisers. The fleet could not be sent through the Straits without a cast-iron guarantee of French neutrality; and even then they would only agree to an occupation of the Dardanelles, which must be primarily a military, not a naval, operation.[2] On 4 November, the British fleet was abruptly withdrawn from the Aegean. The Russians, of course, did not appreciate this revolution in British policy. They thought that the British would be at Constantinople at any moment and decided to seize the Bosphorus themselves first. In fact the plans of both sides, which appeared aggressive to the other, were alike based on fear and had a purely defensive motive. This did not make them any less alarming to others. The French tried, successfully, to put a brake on the Russians; the Germans tried, unsuccessfully, to push the British forward.

Previously the French had avoided discussing the Near East with the Russians so as not to disrupt their fragile alliance; now

---

[1] The Italians wished to send troops through Zeila in British Somaliland. Salisbury made this conditional on French assent, which was refused.

[2] According to one account, Richards, the first sea lord, when consulted by the cabinet, refused to have anything to do with the project of sending the fleet to Constantinople and abruptly left the room; according to another, opposition came from Goschen, first lord of the admiralty, and Salisbury said that, if British ships were made of porcelain, he would have to change his policy. Marder, *British Naval Policy*, p. 244.

they had to state their terms. The Russians offered the French support in Egypt in exchange for their backing at Constantinople; this was not enough. Not even Egypt would make the French forget Alsace and Lorraine. If there was a peaceful partition of the Ottoman empire by agreement among all the Great Powers, the French would be content with the British evacuation of Egypt, neutralization of the Suez canal, and 'privileges in Syria' for themselves; since these terms would never be accepted by the British, they were obviously a futile speculation. If the Near East was reordered by 'the continental league', that is, by Germany and France backing Russia, then the principle of settling the question of Alsace and Lorraine must first be formally accepted by all three partners. Finally, if Russia acted alone against either Austria-Hungary or England, 'only a great national interest such as a new settlement of the question which since 1870 so profoundly divides Germany and France, would be enough to justify a military action in the eyes of the French people'. In short, Alsace and Lorraine were not merely *desirable*, but *absolutely necessary*.[1] But the basic assumption of Russian policy was good relations with Germany; therefore the French answer was a bare and absolute negative. The French would never allow the Russian alliance to become actively anti-British unless they first recovered Alsace and Lorraine. In consequence, the Russians made no move. They were no doubt assisted towards inaction by the discovery that the Black Sea fleet was not ready and that the troops that it was supposed to transport to the Bosphorus did not exist. As usual, Russian strength rested on boasts and grandiose projects, not on reality.

Meanwhile, the Germans had launched their plan for forcing the British into supporting Austria-Hungary and Italy. On 24 October William II told the British military attaché: 'It is not in the interest of my country to follow every whim of British policy. Such behaviour is forcing me formally to make common cause with France and Russia;'[2] and again on 20 December: 'England's plan to play off the continental powers will not succeed; instead she will find the continent against her as a solid block.'[3] Marschall had the same idea; 'We shall use the next

[1] Berthelot to Montebello, 20 Dec. 1895; 17, 31 Jan. 1896. *Documents diplomatiques français*, first series, xii, nos. 241, 275, 292.

[2] William II to Marschall, 25 Oct. 1895. *Große Politik*, xi, no. 2579.

[3] William II to Hohenlohe, 20 Dec. 1895. Ibid., x, no. 2572.

opportunity, where a plus or minus of co-operation on our side towards England was concerned, to show the English that in politics, as elsewhere in life, unpleasantness can be mutual.'[1] Holstein, ever a 'projector', worked out an elaborate scheme for a continental league. France could be offered the Congo Free State, and Russia Korea; Italy would be freed from French opposition in Abyssinia, and Austria-Hungary could be promised something in the Balkans. Germany would pretend that she wanted nothing, but—once the other Powers were engaged— she would take a coaling-station in China. India, Egypt, and Persia would not be included in the bargain; and England would be forced to seek the help of the Triple Alliance in order to defend them.[2] It only remained to discover some ground for conflict with England so as to convince France and Russia (or rather to delude them) that Germany had a real quarrel with the British and was not using the continental league as blackmail. The ground soon presented itself. On 31 December news reached Berlin that Dr. Jameson, an agent of Cecil Rhodes, had launched a filibustering raid to overthrow the Transvaal republic.[3] The Germans decided to thrust themselves forward as defenders of Boer independence.

[1] Marschall to Bülow, 28 Dec. 1895. *Große Politik*, xi, no. 2759.

[2] Holstein, memorandum, 30 Dec. 1895. Ibid., no. 2640.

[3] The essential British problem in South Africa was strategical and political, not economic. The gold-mines in the Transvaal were developing on a great scale, despite Boer reluctance and despite their dynamite-monopoly, from the proceeds of which they acquired the arms to fight the war of 1899. But the British needed a united white South Africa in order to have strategic security at the Cape—the lynch-pin of the British empire. The Boer republics hampered this; and there was an even greater danger—the 'Uitlanders' who owned the mines might stage a revolution against the Boers and set up a republic of their own. The solution, first devised in 1894, seemed to be to assist an Uitlander revolution, but to make sure that it was followed by the assertion of British authority. A force under Dr. Jameson was therefore stationed on the borders of the Transvaal ready to march on Johannesburg as soon as the Uitlander revolution took place there. There can be no doubt that both Sir Hercules Robinson, the British high commissioner, and Chamberlain, the colonial secretary, knew all about the plans for a revolution and were also vaguely aware of the force that Jameson had collected. They kept in the background in order to be able to appear as the restorers of authority when Boer power had obviously broken down. Instead the Uitlanders lost their nerve, refused to stage a revolution, and Jameson, without consulting anyone, decided to make a dash for Johannesburg on his own. Not even Jameson knew that there was going to be a 'raid' until he started; and Chamberlain therefore was able to avow his innocence with a plausible case, if not a clear conscience—not that the lack of this ever worried him. But there can be no doubt that he had welcomed and encouraged the preparations which made the raid possible nor that he would have taken full advantage of it, had it succeeded. Two pieces of evidence are decisive. The

Attempts have been made to show that the German government was dragged into the Transvaal affair by capitalist interests; economic imperialism is supposed to have disturbed the even course of foreign policy. It is, of course, true that some Germans had investments in the Boer gold-fields; it is also true that German propagandists had made much of the Teutonic origin of the Boers and had cast covetous eyes on the derelict Portuguese colony at Delagoa bay—the maritime gateway of the Transvaal. But there is no evidence of capitalist pressure on the imperial government; and Holstein, the man most in touch with capitalist circles, was also the one most opposed to patronizing the Boers. German interests in the Transvaal, in any case small, were as irrelevant as their interests in Morocco ten years later. In both cases their policy was a move in the European Balance of Power—the one taken for its effect on England, the second for its effect on France. The Transvaal was not an important issue for the Germans; it was unimportant. That is why they chose it. More, they thought that it was unimportant also for the British, at any rate in comparison to Egypt or the Straits. This was their fundamental mistake. The British could manage without the Mediterranean route to the East, if the worst came to the worst—they did so between 1940 and 1943. The naval station at the Cape was however fundamental to them; without it the British empire could not exist.

The Germans did not, of course, mean to claim the Transvaal for themselves; they intended to protect its independence, as they presented themselves as the defenders of Moorish independence ten years later. Since the Boers had acknowledged British control of their external affairs by the treaty of 1884, this was a speculative line. In any case, how was it to be done? The Germans thought vaguely of an international conference. William II, ever the irresponsible schoolboy who parodies the activities of his elders, proposed to send a detachment of marines to the Transvaal and there to fight a limited war with the

parliamentary commission of inquiry condemned Bower, Robinson's secretary, for his knowledge of the preparations that Jameson was making. Bower's papers show that any knowledge he had was shared by Robinson and by Chamberlain; and Bower was, in fact, persuaded to sacrifice himself for the sake of his superiors. Being a former naval officer he foolishly agreed. Secondly, the attorney-general, himself a member of the Unionist government, said of one of the telegrams that were sent to the Cape on Chamberlain's instructions that it 'could not be explained away'. This telegram was suppressed at the inquiry and also by Garvin, Chamberlain's biographer. (Jean van der Poel, *The Jameson Raid*, p. 174.)

British, whose navy would be pledged not to intervene. The practical outcome was a telegram sent to Kruger, President of the Transvaal, on 3 January 1896 congratulating him on having preserved the independence of his country 'without appealing to the help of friendly powers'. The Russians were invited to join in upholding the sanctity of treaties;[1] and the French urged to co-operate in defending their interests in the gold-mines. But, of course, the co-operation would not extend to Egypt. At the same time, the British were told that they would be faced with a continental league unless they made a secret alliance with Germany 'binding England to go to war under certain conditions'.[2]

The grotesque miscalculation of the Germans was at once revealed. The Russians had enough quarrels with the British; they did not want more. Besides, they did not like the independence of small countries. Lobanov replied brusquely that the British had a protectorate over the Transvaal.[3] Herbette emphasized the exclusion of Egypt and said: 'I do not see the advantage for us.'[4] The British, instead of being frightened, invoked their naval power. They organized a 'flying squadron' ready to be sent to any part of the world; this made it ridiculous for the Germans to claim that they could defend the Transvaal. They had to make out that the telegram to Kruger should not be taken seriously. On 10 January, only a week after the telegram, Holstein wrote: 'Let us be glad if the affair ends as it seems to be doing: with a little diplomatic success for Germany and a little political lesson for England.'[5] The Kruger telegram was not laughed off so easily. The diplomatic results were the least of its consequences. The telegram touched off a violent reaction of public opinion in both England and Germany. Sparks cause a fire only when there is something to burn; but this time the fuel was ready, and the telegram gave the predestined spark. Most Englishmen were isolationist at the end of the century, whether from pacific or imperialist sentiment. A mere diplomatic challenge would have left them cold, particularly when associated with the Near East. The telegram seemed to threaten their imperial

[1] William II to Nicholas II, 2 Jan. 1896. *Willy–Nicky Letters*, p. 29.
[2] Salisbury to Victoria, 15 Jan. 1896. *Letters of Queen Victoria*, third series, iii. 22.
[3] Radolin to Hohenlohe, 8 Jan. 1896. *Große Politik*, xi, no. 2624.
[4] Herbette to Berthelot, 1 Jan. 1896. *Documents diplomatiques français*, first series, xii, no. 254.
[5] Holstein to Hatzfeldt, 10 Jan. 1896. *Große Politik*, xi, no. 2629.

concerns. In addition, there had long been simmering an unconscious resentment of German economic rivalry. Joseph Chamberlain, for example, shared the contempt of John Bright, his predecessor at Birmingham, for the Balance of Power and the affairs of Europe; it was a very different matter when markets and South Africa were involved. On the other side, the great majority of Germans were indifferent to Bismarck's elaborate calculations or even to 'the continental league': they could be stirred only by 'world policy'. Germany could do nothing to help the Boers, and the telegram was therefore a senseless act. But it seemed somehow glorious, dramatic, a demonstration that Germany had become a Power of the first rank. The later German excursions into world policy were all implicit in the telegram—Morocco, China, the Bagdad railway. Plans for a great German navy were already being worked out; after the telegram they proved irresistible. In itself the telegram, a routine diplomatic move, no more marked the beginning of a new policy than had Bismarck's colonial venture in 1884. But Bismarck had been able to turn colonial enthusiasm off as artificially as he had turned it on. After 1896 the rulers of Germany could no longer keep popular ambitions within bounds, and often did not try to do so. Even official policy showed the change. When Bismarck organized a 'continental league' in 1885 he asked nothing for himself and offered much to others: he was prepared to back France in Egypt, and Russia at Constantinople. Holstein's continental league was offered to the French and Russians on condition that they made only trivial gains. Holstein and Marschall were the last survivors of 'the new course'. Their real interest was continental, and they still hoped to enlist British backing in order to hold France and Russia in check. It is not surprising that the two countries showed no interest in a continental league which aimed ultimately at weakening them and making Germany supreme not only in Europe, but outside it.

Salisbury appreciated this. Though he made no serious approach to Russia, he put out some feelers for a reconciliation with France. By chance an agreement with France over Siam was published on 15 January;[1] and on 19 February he even mentioned Egypt to Courcel—the first attempt at a discussion of the

---

[1] The agreement had, in fact, been reached before Christmas. It was not therefore, as the Germans imagined, an answer to the Kruger telegram. Courcel to Berthelot, 15 Jan. 1896. *Documents diplomatiques français*, first series, xii, no. 272.

subject since Waddington's failure in 1892.[1] A catastrophe to
Italy, not altogether unexpected, interrupted this attempt at
agreement. On 1 March the Italian forces in Abyssinia met
disaster at the battle of Adowa. The Italians appealed for
British assistance. Salisbury had no intention of assisting them.
On the other hand, the Italian failure seemed to leave the way
open for a French advance to the Nile from the east as well as
from the west. Diplomacy had failed; military action alone remained. On 13 March the British government decided to
reconquer the Sudan, ostensibly to aid the Italians, really to
forestall the French. The Italian disaster ended what remained
of the continental league. The Germans had to conciliate the
British for Italy's sake. Salisbury still tried to avoid estranging
the French. He offered to declare that the Sudan expedition
'would not affect the conditions or duration of the presence of
the British in Egypt', and asked in return to be allowed to spend
Egyptian money on the expedition.[2] The French refused this
demand; Salisbury made his declaration all the same.[3] It was
not enough. On 7 May Courcel said to him: 'You have made
your choice',[4] and was unmoved by the suggestion that France
should take Syria.[5]

The British expedition to the Sudan completed the revolution
in Mediterranean politics. Previously the British had intended
to oppose Russia at the Straits and therefore sought to keep
France neutral. The collapse of Italy gave the final blow to this
policy. The Italian fleet was useless: the Italians would need
help instead of giving it. A naval intelligence officer noted:
'Unless the security of her coastline is guaranteed, Italy, as a
factor in a European war, may be practically neglected.'[6] Since
the British could not pass the Straits, they decided to stay in
Egypt permanently and to defend the Suez canal by the armed
forces stationed there. The director of naval intelligence wrote
in October 1896: 'do not imagine that any lasting check can be

---

[1] Courcel to Berthelot, 19 Feb. 1896. *Documents diplomatiques français*, first series,
xii, no. 306. There is no evidence that Courcel said, as the Germans alleged: 'We
have one enemy—Germany.' But it was true.

[2] Courcel to Berthelot, 22 Mar. 1896. Ibid., no. 346.

[3] The Russians complained even of this limited agreement, but there is no evidence that they tried to forbid it or insisted on Berthelot's dismissal. Montebello
to Berthelot, 27 Mar. 1896. Ibid., no. 355.

[4] Courcel to Hanotaux, 7 May 1896. Ibid., no. 383.

[5] Courcel to Hanotaux, 20 June 1896, Ibid., no. 410.

[6] Marder, *British Naval Policy*, p. 271.

put upon Russia by action connected with the Dardanelles . . .
the only way is by holding Egypt against all comers and making
Alexandria a naval base'.[1] This was an ironic outcome. The
French had made their alliance with Russia partly in order to
strengthen their bargaining-position with Great Britain in regard to Egypt; instead the alliance made it impossible for the
British to act at the Straits and so pushed them deeper into
Egypt. The advance into the Sudan made an Anglo-French
conflict certain; by the same token the British lost interest in the
Straits as their position in Egypt became stronger. Where the
British had once aimed to keep France neutral while they opposed Russia at the Straits, they now hoped to keep Russia
neutral while they defeated France on the Nile. The French
were the architects of their own failure; the road ran straight
from Toulon to Fashoda.[2] The French appreciated that the
advantages of the alliance had been reversed. On 1 July
Hanotaux, once more foreign minister, wrote to Paul Cambon[3]
that England was planning to take Egypt, Crete, and Tangier
and that France must work more closely with Russia. But, of
course, the Russians had no interest in co-operating with France
in the Mediterranean once they felt secure at the Straits; and
soon they could reverse the answer which Berthelot had given
them in December 1895—only a great national interest such as
Constantinople would justify Russia becoming involved in a
great war.

The Eastern question had been nearest to crisis in December
1895; now the British were turning away to Egypt, and the
Russians to the Far East. There was a last splutter of alarm in the
autumn of 1896. Renewed massacres of Armenians revived the
talk of international action. When Nicholas II visited the two
western countries in September, both Salisbury and Hanotaux
proposed to him some form of intervention at Constantinople.
Salisbury threw in the opening of the Straits to warships of all

[1] D.N.I. memorandum on naval policy, 28 Oct. 1896. Marder, *British Naval
Policy*, p. 578.

[2] Of course the alliance also made it more difficult for the Russians to seize the
Straits; and in this sense they too organized their own failure. But their funda-
mental concern was to strengthen their security at the Straits, not to seize them;
and this was certainly achieved by the alliance. There can be little doubt that
British ships would have passed the Straits in 1895 if the 'liberal alliance' or the
Crimean coalition had been in existence.

[3] Hanotaux to Paul Cambon, 1 July 1896. *Documents diplomatiques français*, first
series, xii, no. 418.

nations—the best alternative for the British once they had lost faith that the ruler of the Straits would keep them closed to Russia. Naturally Nicholas II was not interested: 'we want the Straits kept closed'.[1] International action was also repugnant to the Russians: better the Turk in Constantinople than the fleets of the Great Powers. On 5 December a Russian crown council decided to anticipate any more of the Concert by seizing the Bosphorus; this was the 'plan' which Nelidov, ambassador at Constantinople, had been advocating for years. The Nelidov plan might well have succeeded. The Turkish fortifications had been neglected; the Turkish fleet had not left its moorings since 1878; the British had just decided that even a landing at the Dardanelles was impracticable. But the Russians did not know this. They needed French backing, and it was again refused. Hanotaux would not sacrifice the Ottoman empire even for the sake of Egypt. He told the Russian ambassador on 30 December 1896: 'France would not regard herself as at all committed in a conflict which sprang from the question of the Black Sea and the Straits'; and when Muraviev, the new Russian foreign minister, visited Paris, Hanotaux said: 'you can have no illusions respecting our military assistance'. Certainly the Germans offered Russia a rather vague support; but Witte, the finance minister, was insistent that nothing must be done without French approval. He needed French money for his grandiose plans in the Far East and was ready in exchange to accept the *status quo* at the Straits. After all, the Russians had planned to seize the Bosphorus in order to be secure in the Far East; now they dropped their plans for the same reason.

The Russians did not turn away from the Near East empty-handed. In the autumn of 1896 Goluchowski had made desperate efforts to build up an anti-Russian coalition. He even urged the Germans to give autonomy to Alsace and Lorraine so as to enlist the support of France.[2] The Germans did not respond to these suggestions. On 20 January 1897 Salisbury finally rejected the idea of reviving the Mediterranean entente: the defence of Constantinople was 'an antiquated standpoint'.[3] The Austrians had no alternative but to make an agreement

---

[1] Note by Hanotaux, 12 Oct. 1896. *Documents diplomatiques français*, first series, xii, no. 472.

[2] Holstein to Eulenburg, 22 Jan. 1897. *Große Politik*, xii (i), no. 3116.

[3] Salisbury to Rumbold, 20 Jan. 1897. *British Documents*, ix (i), p. 775. Hatzfeldt to Hohenlohe, 10 Dec. 1896. *Große Politik*, xii (i), no. 2029.

with Russia on the best terms they could. Francis Joseph and Goluchowski visited St. Petersburg at the end of April 1897. They found to their surprise that the Russians were anxious to maintain the *status quo* in the Near East; even the existing rule of the Straits gave Russia 'full and entire satisfaction'. The Austrians talked vaguely of a future partition, in which they would annexe Bosnia and Hercegovina; the Russians did not respond to these suggestions, and the agreement between the two countries, which was concluded on 5 May 1897, was purely negative. Neither country would disturb the Balkans; nor would they allow anyone else to do so. The Austro-Russian agreement put the Near East 'on ice' for the next ten years.[1]

Both Germany and France were greatly relieved at this outcome and both hastened to demonstrate their friendship with Russia. In August William II, Hohenlohe, and the new foreign secretary, Bülow, visited St. Petersburg to confirm that Russo-German relations were 'not only friendly and cordial, but truly intimate'.[2] Finally it was the turn of President Faure and Hanotaux. They had the satisfaction of hearing Nicholas II describe their two countries as 'friends and allies'—the first time a tsar had used the latter word in public. But he added: 'both resolved to maintain the peace of the world'. In other words, no Russian move at Constantinople, but also no Russian support for France in Alsace and Lorraine nor, what was of more practical importance, in the Sudan. A continental league of a sort had come into existence. Every great European question had been put 'on ice'. Austria-Hungary had a breathing-space in which to attempt (unsuccessfully) to solve her internal problems; still, she emerged in 1908 with more appearance of a Great Power than she had had in 1897. Turkey and Italy also had a breathing-space, which the Italians used to effect a revolution in their diplomatic position, the Turks to no purpose at all. The rest had a 'free hand'. The French were free to go forward to defeat at Fashoda, the Russians to disaster in the Far East, the Germans to concentrate on 'world policy'. The British were isolated and seemed in great danger. This was in large part an illusion. For, though they were isolated, so also were their rivals. Constantinople had provided a point on which all the Powers could focus. Certainly it had brought England the

---

[1] Pribram, *Secret Treaties of Austria-Hungary*, i, pp. 185-95.
[2] Bülow to Eulenburg, 20 Aug. 1897. *Große Politik*, xiii, no. 3444.

friendship of Austria-Hungary and Italy; but there had also been a distant prospect that France and Russia might meet there. Of course the two could only really join hands at 'Tilsit', that is, after the complete military destruction of Germany; but failing that, they might achieve some real co-operation in the Mediterranean. The Toulon visit had been the symbol of this, though a trivial one. The Russian squadron in the Mediterranean never amounted to anything; and the berths at Bizerta which the French prepared for the Russian fleet remained unused until the 'white' Russian ships took refuge there in 1920.[1] The continental league of 1897 rested on mutual jealousy, not on common sympathy; it was an agreement to differ, not to co-operate. The only continental league really dangerous to the British was one dominated by a single Power—the empire of Napoleon or of Hitler. Though they sought in vain for allies, no alliance was formed against them. Still, the next few years were to show that it was awkward for the British empire when the Powers of Europe were on even reasonably friendly terms with each other.

[1] The ships are rotting at their moorings still.

XVII

THE ERA OF 'WORLD POLICY'

1897–1902

THE Austro-Russian agreement of May 1897 put not only the Balkans but all European tensions 'on ice'. The Balkan antagonism between Russia and Austria-Hungary had been the most disturbing element in European politics since 1815; and since the Franco-German war the only one—France could not hope to challenge her existing position in Europe without a conflict in the Near East. Now the Balkans were ignored; and no events there—revolt in Crete, war between Greece and Turkey, troubles in Macedonia—could ruffle the calm. Of course nothing in history is simple cause and nothing simple effect; and the Great Powers would not have made themselves free to pursue ambitions in the outer world unless they had already had ambitions which they were eager to pursue. This was clear enough for Russia in regard to the Far East and for France in regard to Africa. The great new development of 1897 was that Germany, too, turned to 'world policy'. Her ambitions burst the Bismarckian bounds. Most Germans had a sensation of limitless strength and desired a world policy without reserves; those who realized the existence of other Powers believed that their rivalry, and especially the rivalry between England and Russia, would always prevent their combining against Germany. William II would be *arbiter mundi*.[1] The clearsighted and cynical promoted world policy in order to divert attention from difficulties at home—from the emperor's eccentricity, from the conflict between industrial and agrarian interests, from the rising strength of the social democrats. World policy was the demagogic price which the Prussian landowners paid for survival: they abandoned Bismarck's foreign policy in order to retain the position which he had created for them at home. Every conflicting interest was bought off. A great navy

[1] Bülow to William II, 24 Aug. 1898. *Große Politik*, xiv (i), no. 3867.

was built, on capitalist prompting, to safeguard Germany's
food supplies from overseas; at the same time high tariffs made
Germany self-sufficient in foodstuffs to please the agrarians. The
Junkers courted Russia for the sake of Poland and in order to
avoid a war on two fronts; the capitalists challenged Russia by
their search for concessions in Asia Minor and the Far East.

Bülow, who became secretary of state in July 1897 and chancellor at the end of 1900, was the symbol of world policy.
Bismarck, and even Caprivi, had posed alternatives: Germany
must follow one line or the other. Bülow chose both. In home
affairs it was his task to reconcile opposites—'to satisfy Germany
without injuring the Emperor'; and he played the two roles of
democratic statesman and Byzantine sycophant. So his diplomatic task was to provide the grease (his own phrase—'pomadig') by means of which Germany should slide past her rivals to
world power. In regard to the great navy, for example—plans
for which were made in 1897 and which was launched in 1900—
he and his advisers recognized that there was a 'danger-zone',
an imaginary period when the British might suspect German
designs and destroy her navy before it could hold its own. This
'danger-zone' existed in every other department of German
policy—in the plans for the Bagdad railway for instance. But it
was Bülow's underlying assumption that the danger-zone would
be passed and Germany reach a point where she would be too
strong to be attacked by any Power or even group of Powers.
Until then it was his diplomatic object to keep his hands free,
to remain on good terms with both Russia and Great Britain
without committing himself to either side. For it was also confidently assumed that an Anglo-Russian conflict was inevitable;
this made the policy of 'the free hand' both safe and profitable.

All the German incursions into world policy were unexpected;
none more so than her appearance in the Far East. At the beginning of 1897 Witte supposed that he had the Chinese empire
within his grasp. Its finances were dominated by his Russo-
Chinese Bank; in May 1896 he concluded with China a defensive alliance against Japan—it was the story of Unkiar Skelessi
over again. As Witte put it: 'My motto is, trade and industry
always in the front, the army always in the rear.' This was the
combination with which he hoped to beat the British. Instead
his plans were upset by the Germans: in November 1897 they
seized the Chinese port of Kiao-Chow. The occasion was the

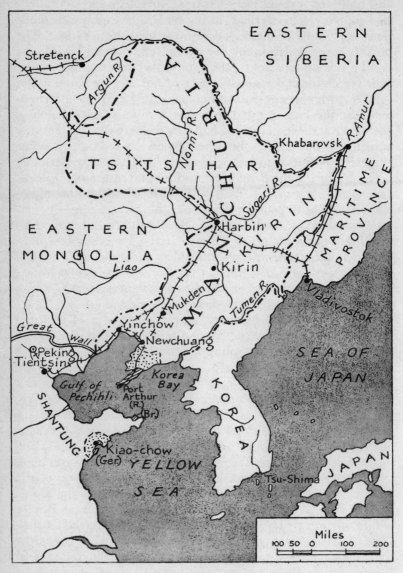

THE FAR EAST

murder of two missionaries (hence the Roman Catholic Centre for once supported an imperialist venture) ; the ostensible motive was that Germany needed a coaling-station for her non-existent fleet—and thereafter a fleet to protect her coaling-station. In reality Kiao-Chow was the first demonstration of 'world policy'; Germany should thrust herself forward wherever Great Britain and Russia occupied the front of the stage. Witte wanted to pose as the defender of Chinese integrity and to support China against the German demands. Muraviev and the military men overruled him. Russian diplomacy and strategy in the Far East both assumed a secure frontier in Europe; it was not worth endangering this for the sake of Kiao-Chow. Besides, the generals had no faith in Witte's weapons of finance and railways; they were eager to follow the German example and to seize Port Arthur, the key to the Yellow Sea. In January 1898 Witte, as a last resort tried to set up an anti-German coalition with the British.[1] They had not objected to the German intervention in China; indeed, they were busy negotiating an Anglo-German loan to China, as a check to Russia's preponderance at Pekin. On the other hand they were quite prepared to play off Russia against Germany, much as Palmerston had played off Russia against France in the great Eastern crisis of 1840. Salisbury offered Russia 'no partition of territory, but only a partition of preponderance';[2] each side would have first claim on railway concessions and other capitalist undertakings in its own zone, and both would join no doubt to exclude any third party. This was much the bargain made over Persia nine years later; in 1898 the Russians were in no mood to share China (or Turkey, which was also included in the offer) with anyone. They were only concerned to squeeze out Germany; the British, on the other hand, wanted to arrest Russia's advance and pushed on simultaneously with the Anglo-German loan. This was agreed to by the Chinese government on 3 March. The Russians held that it was for them, not for the British, to play with both sides. They broke off the negotiations with Salisbury and, a fortnight later, formally demanded the lease of Port Arthur.[3]

---

[1] Salisbury to O'Conor (St. Petersburg), 17 Jan. 1898. *British Documents*, i, no. 5. This telegram clearly implies that the initiative came from Witte.

[2] Salisbury to O'Conor, 25 Jan. 1898. Ibid., no. 9.

[3] Previously powers had annexed territory in the Far East, as the British did at Hong-Kong and the French in Indo-China. Now both Kiao-Chow and Port Arthur were 'leased'—an empty gesture of righteousness which was to lead, after

British commercial interests, long accustomed to regard the Chinese market as their secure possession, demanded some drastic answer. Their outcry would have been ignored, if policy had rested solely with Salisbury. He described the Chinese question a little later as 'a sort of diplomatic cracker that has produced a great many detonations, but I think the smoke of it has now drifted into the distance': and he guessed, with great accuracy, that the Far Eastern question would not become of world importance for another fifty years. But Salisbury did not rule alone. In the unionist cabinet, Joseph Chamberlain regarded himself almost as co-premier; arrogant, self-confident, and impatient, he insisted on action of some kind. The cabinet considered expelling the Russians from Port Arthur; and ships of the China squadron were sent north for this purpose. But once more the Franco-Russian alliance stood in the way: action in the north China seas was too risky with a French squadron in Indo-China. Salisbury wrote: ' "the public" will demand some territorial or cartographic consolation in China. It will not be useful, and will be expensive; but as a matter of pure sentiment, we shall have to do it.'[1] On 25 March the cabinet decided to demand from China the lease of Wei-hai-wei.[2] The partition of China seemed to have begun.

Chamberlain was not prepared to watch this idly. He drummed around for allies to resist any further Russian advance. First he tried the Americans; generous of phrases, they did nothing except carry off the Philippines from helpless Spain in the course of the summer. He tried the Japanese. They had already attempted to start the partition of China in 1895; now they were intent to strike a bargain with Russia over Korea and would do nothing to offend her. Chamberlain's principal effort was with the Germans; he bombarded them with proposals for an alliance in secret negotiations and public speeches. His only concern was with the Far East: 'We might say to Russia—"You have got all you say you want. We are ready to recognise your position, but you must go no further. The rest of China is under our joint protection." '[3] William II gave the

the First World War, to the high-flown system of 'mandates'. Imperialism had to devise ever more elaborate fig-leaves.

[1] Salisbury to Chamberlain, 30 Dec. 1897. Garvin, *Chamberla n*, iii. 249.

[2] Wei-hai-wei turned out to be useless as a naval base. It provided only a bathing beach for the ratings of the China squadron.

[3] Chamberlain memorandum, 1 Apr. 1898. *Chamberlain*, iii. 263.

decisive answer: 'Chamberlain must not forget that in East Prussia I have one Prussian army-corps against 3 Russian armies and 9 cavalry divisions, from which no Chinese wall divides me and which no English ironclads hold at arm's length.'[1] This argument was unanswerable even though the statistics on which it rested were inaccurate. Like Chamberlain's own, they were for purposes of illustration. Elaborate attempts have been made to discover deep 'sociological' grounds for the failure to make an Anglo-German alliance in 1898—British dislike of German trade rivalry on the one side; Junker hostility to democracy and capitalist aggressiveness on the other. These speculations are unnecessary. The British would have jumped at alliance with Germany if it had been offered. As Salisbury wrote to Chamberlain: 'I quite agree with you that under the circumstances a closer relation with Germany would be very desirable; but can we get it?'[2] And, for that matter, the German people would have accepted alliance with Great Britain, as they had accepted the alliances with Austria-Hungary and Italy, if they had been told that it was necessary for their security or for the success of 'world policy'. But nothing the British offered (and they offered little) could make it worth while for Germany to fight a major war in Europe against both France and Russia for the sake of British investments in China. Naturally the rulers of Germany did not admit the impossibility of alliance to the British. They needed British favour in the outer world as much as they needed Russian friendship in Europe; and if the British were once convinced that they could not avert Russia's imperial expansion, they might—as a consolation—arrest Germany's. Moreover, the Germans did not admit the impossibility of alliance even to themselves. They invented imaginary difficulties, such as the instability of British governments; and counted that the British would pay a high price for alliance as their difficulties increased. But alliances are not made by purchase; they spring from a community of vital interests. Austria-Hungary had had interests at Constantinople even more vital than those of the British; therefore the Mediterranean entente had been possible. Germany had no such vital interests in China; therefore all talk of alliance was vain.

[1] Minute by William II on Hatzfeldt to Hohenlohe, 7 Apr. 1898. *Große Politik,* xiv (i), no. 3789.
[2] Salisbury to Chamberlain, 2 May 1898. *Chamberlain,* iii. 279.

The impossibility of an alliance did not mean estrangement between Great Britain and Germany. Though Chamberlain described his offers as '*le bonheur qui passe*,[1] in fact he continued to importune the Germans for years afterwards; and Salisbury worked for co-operation with Germany, though in a less dramatic form. Moreover, the German policy of 'the free hand' rested on good relations with Great Britain as well as with Russia; and they sought for some means of pleasing the one without offending the other. As William II said: 'he would view with the greatest pleasure a thoroughly good understanding with England, but it must be clearly understood that Germany did not intend to go to war with Russia for the purpose of driving her out of China.'[2] The Germans soon found something to serve their turn. At the end of 1895 they had used the Transvaal as the symbol of conflict with England; in June 1898 they used it as a symbol of reconciliation. The British government was now heading straight for a conflict with the Boer republics; the only hope of winning this conflict without war was to cut the Boers off from the outer world, and the key to this was the railway which ran from the Transvaal through Portuguese territory to Delagoa bay. Milner, Chamberlain's agent in South Africa, wrote on 6 July: 'I look on the possession of Delagoa Bay as the best chance we have of winning the great game between ourselves and the Transvaal for the mastery in South Africa without a war.'[3] Portugal was in grave financial difficulties; and the British planned to close the Delagoa bay railway by means of a well-placed loan to the Portuguese government. The Germans thought of raising difficulties, and even sounded France and Russia for a revival of the continental league. These approaches, in any case not meant seriously, came to nothing. Muraviev said: 'all that leaves me absolutely cold'.[4] The French had at last settled their frontiers in West Africa with the British on 15 June and were expecting their expedition to the upper Nile to explode at any moment; until then their policy towards Great Britain was conciliation, not quarrel. The Germans were therefore free to 'sell out' of the Transvaal; they had indeed no other resource. On the other side, though the British still disputed the

[1] Chamberlain memorandum, 25 Apr. 1898. *Chamberlain*, iii. 273.
[2] Lascelles to Salisbury, 26 May 1898. *British Documents*, i, no. 53.
[3] Milner to Chamberlain, 7 July 1898. *Milner Papers*, i. 267.
[4] Tschirschky to foreign ministry, 23 June 1898. *Große Politik*, xiv (i), no. 382.

German claim to interfere in South Africa, it was simpler to pay a hypothetical price than to quarrel. The two countries reached agreement on 30 August 1898. The Germans renounced all interest in Delagoa bay and so implicitly in the Boer republics; the British agreed to share any future loan to Portugal with the Germans and to allow them the security of the rest of the Portuguese empire.

This, the first Anglo-German colonial agreement, has aroused even greater, and less deserved, interest than the discussions for an alliance in the spring. It was merely a move in the British campaign to reduce the Boer republics without war; when this campaign failed, the British closed Delagoa bay by direct agreement with Portugal.[1] Nor did the British need to buy off Germany, once war became certain. The Germans could give the Boers no military assistance; they could blackmail the British only so long as the South African affair remained a question of diplomacy. The Germans had less concern in the dispute between Great Britain and the Transvaal than the British had in the dispute between the German Reich and the dethroned house of Hanover; to save trouble, the British bought the Germans off with a cheque that 'bounced'. There was no Anglo-German loan to Portugal and therefore no partition of the Portuguese empire. Still, the Germans were not aggrieved, except in distant retrospect. The hypothetical promise of the Portuguese colonies gave them a sensation of 'world policy'; only in 1912, when the question was taken up again, did they notice that it had not given them the Portuguese colonies. To say that 'a real reconciliation between England and Germany was a high fence to ride at'[2] is to transfer to 1898 the circumstances of 1912. In 1898 this fence was not high: Germany and Great Britain were, in fact, reconciled. The fence of 1898 was an alliance; that was not surmounted by the colonial bargain. The British wished to prevent a new Kruger telegram; the Germans wished to avoid the embarrassment of sending one. That alone was the reality of the colonial pact. The Germans were no more ready than before to support England against Russia, or even against France.

Much to everyone's surprise, except that of Salisbury, the

---

[1] Anglo-Portuguese Secret Declaration, 14 Oct. 1899. *British Documents*, i, no. 118.

[2] Langer, *Diplomacy of Imperialism*, ii. 532.

British turned out not to need support from anyone so far as France was concerned. On 2 September 1898 Kitchener destroyed the dervish armies of the Sudan at Omdurman; four days later he learnt that a French expedition under Marchand had occupied Fashoda, higher up the Nile. The Anglo-French conflict over the valley of the Nile reached its decisive point. It was not a conflict of equals. The British had control of Egypt and meant to keep it; the French wanted only some compensation for renouncing the legacy that Bonaparte had failed to bequeath to them. Their policy in the upper Nile was a face-saving affair from first to last. Every French politician of any sense knew that Egypt had been lost for good in 1882; all they asked for was some sop which would make this loss palatable to the French public. Their ultimate object throughout was to restore 'the liberal alliance' with Great Britain. Until March 1896, when the British decided to reconquer the Sudan, French policy had been reasonable enough: even a token occupation of the upper Nile would have strengthened their diplomatic position. And, until the Italian defeat at Adowa, they could hope for co-operation from Abyssinia.[1] Once the British put the question of the upper Nile on a military basis, diplomacy had no standing; and the French were bound to lose, unless they too were prepared to face a war. In 1898 this was beyond them. Their navy had been neglected; the Dreyfus case was tearing home politics asunder; and, in any case, war over Egypt had been ruled out by the French ever since 1840.

In June there had been a change of government in France. Delcassé, who then became foreign minister, was to remain in office until 1905—the longest single span in the history of the Third republic. At the outset, no great difference of principle seemed to divide him from his predecessor, Hanotaux. Delcassé had helped to launch Marchand's expedition; and Hanotaux had tried, on occasion, for an agreement with Great Britain. Delcassé was a disciple of Gambetta; and though his master had often preached a triple entente with Great Britain and Russia, he had also talked sometimes of reconciliation with Germany. In June 1898 Delcassé had no clear-cut plan except to improve France's diplomatic position. Experience soon taught him that Germany would do nothing to win French friendship;

[1] Thereafter the Abyssinians did not need French help against Italy, and so did not themselves give help against the British.

and from then on it became his aim to reconcile Great Britain
and Russia, with France as the vital link between them. By a
happy chance, he was again foreign minister on 5 September
1914, when the formal alliance between the three Powers was at
last signed. But this alliance was much more the result of German
policy than the work of Delcassé or of any other French statesman.

In September 1898 such calculations were remote. The Fashoda crisis caught Delcassé unprepared. He knew that France
could not go to war; and his only hope was to put the question
back on a basis of diplomacy. On the one hand, he offered 'the
liberal alliance' to the British, if they would give him some
reasonable compensation; on the other, he sought diplomatic
backing from Russia and even from Germany. Both policies
failed. The British refused to return to diplomatic and legalistic
wranglings. Salisbury said: 'We claim the Sudan by right of
conquest because that is the simplest and most effective.' The
British arguments were the Mediterranean fleet and Kitchener's
army; their terms were Marchand's unconditional withdrawal.
No one supported the French. Though the Russians welcomed
Anglo-French conflict they would no more take part in it than
they had supported Germany over the Transvaal. Muraviev
happened to pass through Paris in October. He gave Delcassé
cold comfort: vague assurances of loyalty to the Franco-Russian
alliance and an even vaguer hope that Russia might find a
chance to reopen the question of Egypt at some time in the
future—no doubt when she needed to distract the British from
the Far East.

The Germans were even more aloof. Delcassé hinted that he
might ask for their support if they would first give autonomy to
Alsace and Lorraine; the Germans would not have responded
even without the barrier of this condition. They had excluded
the question of Egypt from their scheme for a continental league
in 1896; they were not likely to offend the British for its sake
now, when they needed all their diplomatic agility to steer
between Great Britain and Russia in the Far East. They, too,
calculated that they had everything to gain from French
humiliation and resentment. The more France was driven into
the Russian alliance, the more the Germans would have a
'free hand' between the continental league on the one side and
alliance with the British on the other—a free hand, that is, to

refuse both. The Germans often hesitated between Great Britain and Russia; they never hesitated seriously between Great Britain and France. Though bouts of Franco-German cordiality were still possible even after 1871, alliance between them was never practical politics, except on terms of such dependence and humiliation as could only follow catastrophic defeat—of France in 1940, of Germany in 1945; and even then the alliance was sham.

Delcassé had no alternative but to surrender. In November 1898 Marchand left Fashoda; on 21 March 1899 Great Britain and France made an agreement, by which France was excluded from the valley of the Nile. This agreement did not settle the Egyptian question. The French attitude towards the British occupation remained unchanged: they continued to protest and to hamper Cromer's schemes of financial reorganization. The agreement merely knocked from the hands of the French their most promising diplomatic counter; only in this sense did it bring a general settlement nearer. Fashoda and its aftermath was for the French a crisis in political psychology, for the British not even that. They carried the day with their normal peace-time strength: the extra cost of Fashoda to the British admiralty was £13,600. This economy was, of course, illusory. The true 'battle for Egypt' had been fought in 1798; and the French never meant to renew it. Fashoda was a triumph for 'splendid isolation'. The British had become indifferent to the continent of Europe and the Balance of Power (or so they thought); therefore they could build an invincible navy and dominate the Mediterranean. Fashoda, moreover, made 'splendid isolation' more secure. The British did not need the diplomatic support of other Powers in the Egyptian question, once they put it on a military basis; and with their troops close to the Suez canal they worried less than ever about a Russian occupation of Constantinople. At any time after 1898 the British could say of the opening of the Straits what the Committee of Imperial Defence said in 1903: 'it would not fundamentally alter the present strategic position in the Mediterranean'.[1] Fashoda finished off what remained of the Mediterranean entente. Great Britain needed neither Italy nor Austria-Hungary. Italy, deprived of British protection, had to seek reconciliation with

[1] Report of Committee of Imperial Defence, 13 Feb. 1903. *British Documents*, iv. 59.

France.[1] Austria-Hungary enjoyed an illusory security so long as Russian attention was concentrated on the Far East; once Russia turned back to the Balkans, Germany could no longer find a third party on whom to shoulder off the defence of Austria-Hungary, and a Russo-German conflict became well-nigh inevitable.

Fashoda alone was not responsible for this. At the very moment when the British withdrew from the Eastern question, the Germans pushed themselves in. In October 1898, while Marchand was still at Fashoda, William II paid his second visit to the Ottoman empire. He called on Abdul Hamid at Constantinople, and declared at Damascus that the 300 million Mohammedans in the world could count him as their friend. More practical interest in the Near East followed. A German firm had started railway building in Asia Minor in 1893; in the spring of 1899 it sought a more grandiose concession from the Sea of Marmora to the Persian gulf. Since Germany was the only Power which had not bullied Turkey at some time in the preceding years, Abdul Hamid regarded 'the Bagdad railway' with favour. The British were glad to see German railway projects diverted from Delagoa bay to Asia Minor—hence the enthusiasm of Cecil Rhodes for Germany's 'mission' there. The French not merely welcomed this new associate in maintaining the independence of Turkey; they wished to share the profits and offered to put up 40 per cent. of the capital. The German foreign ministry, Bülow and Holstein, made out that the railway was a commercial venture without political significance.[2] Marschall, now ambassador at Constantinople, was franker: if Germany continued to expand economically in the Near East, he foresaw the moment 'when the famous remark that the whole Near East is not worth the bones of a Pomeranian grenadier will be an interesting historical reminiscence but will no longer correspond to reality'.[3] The Russians also foresaw this moment and sought to guard against it. Though they had no desire to bring on the collapse of the Ottoman empire, they were opposed to anything that might make it stronger or more independent; failing a 'Chinese

[1] The Italians feared that the Anglo-French agreement of 21 Mar. 1899 involved the abandonment of Tripoli to France. Though Salisbury refused to give them any assurance to the contrary, Delcassé is said to have made a verbal declaration of disinterestedness in regard to Tripoli.

[2] Bülow to Radolin, 24 Mar. 1899. *Große Politik*, xiv (ii), no. 4015.

[3] Helfferich, *Georg von Siemens*, iii. 90.

wall' round their empire, they wanted weak neighbours. They would have liked to forbid the Bagdad railway. Since this was beyond their strength, they proposed an 'arrangement', by which Germany in return for their consent would promise them control of the Straits.[1] The Germans, in fact, were to renounce in advance the political interest which must inevitably follow from their economic success.

The Russian offer was firmly refused at Berlin. The Germans knew that the Russians could not prevent the Bagdad railway; their consent was therefore not worth buying. Besides, though the Germans had refused to support Great Britain against Russia at the Straits, equally they would not commit themselves to supporting Russia against Great Britain. They counted on an Anglo-Russian conflict and therefore held confidently to 'the free hand'. Still there was a price at which, so they said, they would be prepared to offer Russia the Straits: let Russia guarantee Alsace and Lorraine to them or at least promise neutrality in a Franco-German war, and they themselves would then risk a conflict with England.[2] This was an impossible condition for the Russians to fulfil. Though they certainly held France back from a war of revenge against Germany they needed alliance with France in order to preserve their own independence. If they renounced this alliance, they would not in fact get the Straits. Either France would be reconciled to Germany, and in this case there would follow a German coalition with Austria-Hungary and France, powerful enough to exclude both Russia and Great Britain from the Near East. Or, more likely, France would turn to Great Britain; and Russia would be faced with 'the Crimean coalition'. In short, the security of both Russia and Great Britain rested on France's estrangement from Germany; both, in the long run, had to support—though not to encourage—her. The negotiations over the Bagdad railway died away. The Germans got their concession in November 1899. The Russians made the best of a bad job, by concluding an agreement with Turkey in April 1900, which prevented the building of railways in the Black Sea districts of Asia Minor except with their consent. No practical effect followed. The

---

[1] Memoranda by Bülow, 18, 26 Apr., 5 May 1899. *Große Politik*, xiv (ii), nos. 4017, 4018, 4020.

[2] Memorandum by Holstein, 17 Apr.; Hatzfeldt to foreign ministry, 1 May 1899. Ibid., nos. 4016, 4019.

Bagdad railway took much longer to build than either the Russians or the Germans had expected in 1899—it was only a fragment when war broke out in 1914. Still, the time had been foreshadowed when the Russians would have in Germany a new and more formidable rival at Constantinople.

Though the Russians would not abandon France to Germany, they continued to dream of a continental league in which both countries would support them against Great Britain, though remaining hostile to each other. And, on the other side, Germany and France continued to compete for Russia's friendship, at any price short of backing her against the British. In August 1899 Delcassé visited St. Petersburg, no doubt to make the alliance more satisfactory than it had been at the time of Fashoda. There was an odd outcome. The text of both political entente and military convention was changed. The alliance was 'to maintain the balance of power in Europe' as well as to maintain peace; the military convention was no longer to come to an end with the dissolution of the Triple Alliance. Wild accusations were made against Delcassé when these changes became known many years later: he had committed France, it was said, to supporting Russia's aggressive plans in the Balkans and so indeed involved her in the war of 1914. This is an absurd exaggeration. The Schlieffen plan, not the Franco-Russian alliance in its original or modified form, brought war to France: after 1894 the Germans had to knock out France first in case of war with Russia, and the French would have no choice except between defence and surrender—neutrality was not on offer. In any case, the clauses of 1899 had only a temporary significance. Between 1896 and 1899 Austria was passing through a constitutional crisis which almost brought the Habsburg monarchy to the ground; and it was no unreasonable speculation that it would, at any rate, dissolve on the death of Francis Joseph. Then Russia and Germany might partition Austria-Hungary; all Delcassé did was to ensure that, in that case, France could invoke the Balance of Power and so, perhaps, recover Alsace and Lorraine. The Russians often talked of this project; and Delcassé claimed to be aiming at a peaceful partition of central Europe and the Balkans, linked up with Alsace and Lorraine, as late as November 1904.[1] The scheme was, no doubt, grotesque. The Germans had no intention of sharing either Austria-

---

[1] So he told Paléologue in conversation. Paléologue, *The Turning Point*, p. 158.

SOUTH AFRICA

Hungary or the Balkans with Russia, let alone of parting with Alsace and Lorraine. In any case, no opportunity arose to operate it. Francis Joseph lived on for another seventeen years; and when the Habsburg monarchy collapsed, the Franco-Russian alliance had predeceased it. In practice the modification of August 1899 amounted to little. At most it made it easier for Delcassé to resist the rather feeble Russian suggestions that he should get on better terms with Germany by renouncing Alsace and Lorraine.

If ever there was to be a continental league, October 1899 seemed the time. British plans for a peaceful settlement in South Africa were not fulfilled. The Boers refused to be cowed; and Milner, Chamberlain's agent, deliberately raised his terms in order to provoke a conflict. He was confident of easy success: 'They will collapse if we don't weaken, or rather if we go on steadily turning the screw.'[1] Salisbury made the despairing comment: 'I see before us the necessity for considerable military effort—and all for people whom we despise and for territory which will bring no power and no profit to England.'[2] On 9 October the Boers declared war; and it turned out to be a much tougher war than Milner had expected. There could never be a more favourable opportunity, in theory, for the continental Powers to exploit British difficulties. But the opportunity was indeed theoretical. The British navy decided the issue. Land power counted for something in the Near East and for more in the Far East; it counted for nothing in South Africa. Though the continental Powers could mobilize millions of men, no European soldier would ever cross the Vaal; and the British navy could have held its own against any naval coalition—it continued to dominate the Mediterranean throughout the Boer war, while controlling the sea routes to South Africa and also protecting the British Isles. Even more than Fashoda, the Boer war was a triumphant demonstration for 'splendid isolation'.

The continental Powers could have done nothing against the British even if they had been united; and they were not. This being so, their wisest course would have been to ignore the war; but even Great Powers do not always act wisely. Each had to make out that it favoured a continental league and to blame the others for failure to achieve it. The Russians, who had often

[1] Milner to Chamberlain, 16 Aug. 1899. *Milner Papers*, i. 516.
[2] Salisbury to Lansdowne, 30 Aug. 1899. Newton, *Lord Lansdowne*, p. 157.

been held up to the obloquy of Europe by the British, wished to turn the moral tables; besides it flattered their sense of grandeur to feel that the British empire was at their mercy. Nicholas II wrote: 'I do like knowing that it lies entirely with me to decide the ultimate course of the war in South Africa...all I need to do is to telegraph orders to all the troops in Turkestan to mobilize and advance to the frontier.' But, as he added with an after-thought, the railway to Tashkent was not yet completed—in fact it was not yet started and was not completed until years after the end of the Boer war.[1] Muraviev saw clearly that a conti-nental league was impossible, and isolated diplomatic action against the British too risky;[2] his only practical step was to lament the lost opportunity. In both France and Germany public opinion was strongly on the side of the Boers; since many of the best elements in Great Britain were also 'pro-Boer', this was hardly surprising. Sympathy for the Boers was reinforced in Germany by academic 'Teutonism', and in France by resent-ment against the humiliation at Fashoda. Official policy in both countries had to reckon with this feeling and, in addition, to avoid offending Russia by taking the initiative against any pro-Boer action. The French line was simple. They would take part in a mediation or any other action to which the Germans would also commit themselves. This was a safe line to take. It satisfied the Russians; it was pretty certain that Germany would refuse to take part; and, if she did, the Anglo-German estrangement that would follow was worth, for France, a certain risk.

The German position was more complicated. They had a safe diplomatic answer to make to the Russians. They could join in common action with France and Russia only if the three Powers mutually guaranteed each other's European territory[3]—hence a Russian (and French) guarantee for Alsace and Lorraine, but no German backing for Russia in the Far East. But the German rulers had also 'world policy' to consider. On the one hand, they wished to stand well with the British for the sake of their colonies and their overseas trade; on the other, they wished to exploit the pro-Boer feeling in Germany in order to carry a great Navy Law through the Reichstag. The British empire had to be pre-served as a balance against Russia; at the same time a German

---

[1] Nicholas II to his sister, 21 Oct. 1899. *Krasny Arkhiv*, lxiii. 125.
[2] Memorandum by Muraviev, 7 Feb. 1900. Ibid., xviii. 24.
[3] Bülow to Radolin, 3 Mar. 1900. *Große Politik*, xv, no. 4472.

navy was being prepared which must ultimately challenge this empire. As a result the 'free hand' was exaggerated until it turned into the gestures of a tic-tac man. At the beginning of the war the Germans were engaged in a dispute with the British over the control of Samoa, in which the United States also shared. This trivial affair had little sense, except to justify a tariff war with the Americans for the benefit of the German agrarians. Chamberlain, eager as ever for German favour, compelled Salisbury to give way in November. The British got their reward. William II and Bülow visited England—a gesture of friendship which gave open defiance to the German pro-Boers. Salisbury did not care for this performance and kept out of the way. Chamberlain bid once more for a German alliance. Previously the Germans had rejected his proposals on the ground that they had no conflicts with France or Russia. Now he attempted to supply them: he urged the Germans to push on with the Bagdad railway (so as to quarrel with Russia) and offered to partition Morocco with them (so that they might quarrel with France).[1] Bülow did not respond. He was glad to appear as the gracious protector of a needy relative in distress; he did not mean to take any practical action. Besides, he suspected that, if the worst came to the worst, Salisbury would buy off France and Russia rather than seek German backing.

But Bülow could not let well alone. Flattery was his stock-in-trade as a statesman; and he spoke condescendingly to Chamberlain of the mutual interests which Germany had with Great Britain and the United States.[2] Chamberlain took the hint seriously. On 30 November he spoke at Leicester of 'a new Triple Alliance between the Teutonic race and the two great branches of the Anglo-Saxon race' and said that 'the natural alliance is between ourselves and the great German Empire'. Bülow had to swing in the other direction for the sake both of Russia and of German public opinion. Talk of a continental league was renewed; and Bülow told the naval committee of the Reichstag: 'two years ago he could still have said that there was no danger of war with England, now he could say it no longer'.[3] When, in January 1900, the British stopped some German mail-steamers in South African waters and searched

---

[1] Memorandum by Bülow, 24 Nov. 1899. *Große Politik*, xv, no. 4398.
[2] Chamberlain to Eckardstein, 7 Dec. 1899. *Lebenserinnerungen*, ii. 107.
[3] Kehr, *Schlachtflottenbau und Parteipolitik*, p. 201.

them for contraband, Bülow, Tirpitz, and William II drank
champagne to the British naval officer who had given them such
help in promoting the second Navy Law. The Law was carried,
the continental league, of course, came to nothing.[1] Sympathy
with the Boers, envy of the British empire, altruistic dreams of
European co-operation, made interesting topics of conversation;
they could not make a continental league. With Russia absorbed in the Far East and France growing ever weaker, Germany had no reason to compensate either at the expense of the
British empire. Germany was already secure; she would only
lessen her security by co-operating against the British.

Both France and Germany had pretended to respond to
Russian promptings in order to keep up in the race for her
favour; both also sought British favour by making a virtue of
their rejection. William II at once revealed the Russian suggestions to his British relatives;[2] later Delcassé, during the
negotiations for an Anglo-French entente, tried to extract concessions from the British as a reward for having prevented a
continental league;[3] finally even Izvolski tried the same trick,
though no one took him seriously.[4] At the time, the British,
being theoretically on good terms with Germany and certainly
on bad terms with France and Russia, mostly accepted the
German version; though Salisbury always denied British dependence on German favour and was therefore sceptical of their
story.[5] Later, after the making of the ententes, the British, for the
most part, charitably accepted the version of their new friends.
Grey, however, always claimed that the ententes, far from being
anti-German, were made solely because France and Russia
were more troublesome than Germany; hence he accepted the
German version, for the more hostile France and Russia had
been, the more the ententes were justified.[6] At bottom, the
British did not concern themselves much about the continental
league one way or the other. Chamberlain might dream of
alliance with Germany; Salisbury might plan more realisti-
cally to make concessions to France in Morocco and to Russia
in Persia. Neither expedient was necessary. The British navy

[1] See note, p. 401.
[2] William II to Edward, Prince of Wales, 3 Mar. 1900. Lee, *Edward VII*, i, p. 769.
[3] *British Documents*, iii. 432.
[4] Nicolson to Grey, 31 Oct. 1908. Ibid., vi, no. 126.
[5] Salisbury to Victoria, 10 Apr. 1900. *Letters of Queen Victoria*, third series, iii. 527.
[6] Grey to Bertie (Paris), 1 Dec. 1908. *British Documents*, vi, no. 142.

controlled the oceans; and the Boer war could be won in splendid isolation.

But South Africa, like the Nile valley, was only an episode in 'the age of imperialism'. The issue which overshadowed all others was the Far East. China had taken the place of Turkey as the pre-eminent Sick Man; and between 1897 and 1905 the future of China determined the relations of the Great Powers. The crisis of March 1898 had passed over with only a preliminary partition; its recurrence was all the more certain. The Russians sought to postpone the inevitable conflict. In April 1899 they agreed to a British proposal for spheres of interest: they would not seek railway concessions in the Yangtze valley, if the British would not seek any 'north of the great wall'. This was a Far Eastern treaty of Gastein, papering over the cracks. The British seemed in a hopeless position. No one would help them against Russia. The French were estranged by Fashoda; the Germans determined not to commit themselves; the Japanese anxious to agree with the Russians before it was too late. The Americans professed to be eager for 'the open door'; but when in September 1899 the Russians answered with a negative that was hardly even evasive, the Americans pretended to be satisfied. After October 1899 British forces were locked up in South Africa. Witte thought that his policy of peaceful penetration was again within sight of success. He had silenced the Russian advocates of violence; and his position was further strengthened in June 1900 when, on the sudden death of Muraviev, the timid and conservative Lamsdorff became foreign minister.

The British were saved, paradoxically enough, by the Chinese. Resistance to foreign penetration was growing. The first sign came in March 1899 when the Chinese government refused to grant a concession to the Italians. The following year the Chinese people intervened. The Boxer rising, chaotic and spontaneous, was the greatest effort at defence against the Christian West by a non-European civilization since the Indian Mutiny in 1857. The movement had been at first pent up and was then later encouraged by the dowager empress, the real ruler of China. In June 1900 European missionaries and merchants were attacked, the legations at Pekin besieged, the German minister killed. The Boxer rising upset more than one nice policy. It upset the policy of Witte. Chinese violence provoked Russian violence in return. Kuropatkin, the minister of war, got his way and invaded Manchuria. The rising upset, too, the German policy of the 'free hand'. Whatever the dictates of wisdom, a 'world power' had to avenge the murder of its minister. William II swept aside Bülow's reserve and insisted that Germany must take the lead in an international punitive force. German soldiers, departing for China, were exhorted by William II to acquire there a reputation like that of 'the Huns a thousand years ago under the leadership of Attila'; and the other Powers were cajoled into accepting the elderly Field-Marshal Waldersee as commander of an international force. Troops of all the European Great Powers served under a single commander for the only time in history. It is often said that the world will only unite against another planet; in 1900 the Chinese served much the same purpose. Neither the British nor the Russians, the two Powers really concerned with China, cared much for the international force. The first British move was to negotiate with the Chinese viceroys in the Yangtze valley, in order to prevent the rising spreading into their 'sphere'. The Russian change to a militaristic policy actually played into British hands; for they and the Russians together relieved the legations at Pekin in August. Witte then persuaded Nicholas II that the most important thing was to get all European forces out of China as soon as possible. On 25 August the Russians announced that, as order had been restored, they were withdrawing their troops and expected others to do the same.

Waldersee had not yet left Germany; and the Russian proposal therefore offended German vanity. They had to turn to Great Britain in order to pay the Russians out. Moreover, a more important consideration, they feared—quite wrongly—that the British were planning to take the Yangtze valley for themselves. They could not co-operate with the Russians against the British to defeat these imaginary plans because of the dispute over Waldersee; therefore they had to pretend to co-operate with the British against the Russians. Since the British had no plans for partition, they could not understand what the Germans were after; but any agreement with Germany seemed bound to be pointed against Russia, and the British welcomed the opportunity. The result of these misconceptions was the China agreement between Great Britain and Germany of 16 October 1900. The two Powers agreed to maintain the open door in China and the integrity of the Chinese empire. The

Germans insisted, however, that they would do nothing against Russia and originally wished to set a geographical limit to the agreement so as to exclude Russia's sphere of interest. Though they finally agreed to uphold the open door 'for all Chinese territory as far as they can exercise influence', they never concealed that they could not exercise influence wherever they ran up against Russia. In short, the Germans bound the British to keep the door open on the Yangtze, yet did not bind themselves to hold it open against the Russians in the north. The British hoped that the Russians would be taken in and would regard the agreement as 'implying the defection of Germany to Great Britain'.[1] The China agreement seemed a great victory for Salisbury's policy of limited arrangements without a general alliance; it was the exact parallel in the Far East to the Mediterranean agreements of 1887. It was the only formal agreement for diplomatic co-operation ever made between Great Britain and Germany, and ought therefore to have heralded a period of Anglo-German intimacy. Instead, it failed to work, and this failure provoked a deeper estrangement than before. It was 16 October 1900, and not the negotiations of 1898 or of 1901, that marked the moment of decision in Anglo-German relations. Though the two countries seemed half-way to an alliance, events soon proved that alliance was impossible.

The explanation was simple: German 'world policy' was artificial, a pretence. Her map of Asia, like Bismarck's map of Africa before it, lay in Europe. When the Mediterranean agreements were made, Austria-Hungary was as vitally concerned in the Near East as Great Britain; there was no contradiction between her Near Eastern policy and her position as a European Power. But Germany had no vital interest in China. Her vital interest was security in Europe, and she could not endanger this for the sake of the China market. There was also a basic difference on the Russian side. In the Near East their concern had been defensive; and they backed away as soon as they ran against opposition. Russian policy in the Far East was aggressive and expansionist. A hostile coalition in the Near East reinforced the arguments of every influential Russian statesman; in the Far East it provoked no answering call. The Mediterranean agreements were perhaps bluff; neither Austria-Hungary

---

[1] Hardinge (St. Petersburg) to Salisbury, 26 Oct. 1900. *British Documents*, ii, no. 19.

nor Great Britain was eager to go to war. But in the Near East
the Russians were willing to be bluffed; in the Far East bluff
did not work. This was shown soon after the Anglo-German
agreement had been signed. The Russians brought on a new
crisis with China. Under Witte's prompting, they prepared,
rather unconvincingly, to evacuate Manchuria; but Kuropatkin and the generals would withdraw the troops only if the
Chinese would hand over to them political control. Witte,
furious at not getting his way, devised a draft of their demands
even more extreme than the real one and revealed it to the
Japanese. Everyone believed with some excuse—though not so
much as was thought—that the partition of China had begun in
earnest. The Japanese were confident that they could resist Russia
with success. Their problem was with France, for the French fleet
in the Far East, combined with the Russian, could cut them off
from the mainland. Great Britain must keep France neutral;
this was the request made by the Japanese in March 1901.

The British felt that they were on the edge of great decisions.
In December 1900 Salisbury had relinquished the foreign
office. Lansdowne, his successor, though technically adroit, had
none of his massive confidence. Salisbury had relied on his
great reputation to cloak the difficulties of the present; Lansdowne needed diplomatic success to atone for his failure as
secretary for war, when he had been responsible for the disasters
in South Africa. The British certainly wished to encourage
Japan, if only because they feared that the Japanese, unless
encouraged, would strike a bargain with Russia to the exclusion
of all other Powers.[1] On the other hand, conflict with France
was, for the time being, impossible. Though the British fleet was
superior to the combined fleets of Russia and France, it was
fully occupied in guarding the British Isles and the route to
South Africa. No ships could be spared for the Far East until the
Boer war was over. The British were back, more or less, at the
position in which they had been in the Mediterranean in 1894:
they needed the threat of the German army to keep France
neutral, while they (or in this case the Japanese) dealt with
Russia. On 8 March Lansdowne asked whether the Germans
would join Great Britain in imposing on France a 'localization'
of any Russo-Japanese war.[2]

---

[1] Memorandum by Bertie, 11 Mar. 1901. *British Documents*, ii, no. 54.
[2] Hatzfeldt to foreign ministry, 8 Mar. 1901. *Große Politik*, xvi, no. 4829.

This was the decisive moment for the Germans so far as the Far Eastern crisis was concerned. They were committed to upholding the integrity of China by the agreement of 16 October 1900; they were anxious to increase the tension between Russia on the one side and Great Britain and Japan on the other; they liked to imagine that Great Britain would offer something in the future which would make alliance with her worth while—more hypothetical colonies in Africa, new concessions in Asia. Holstein repeated as confidently as ever: 'We can wait. Time is working for us.'[1] But when it came to the point the inescapable fact stared them in the face: neither British offers nor their own commercial interests could ever make it worth their while to face a conflict with Russia (and so also with France) for the sake of the Far East. 'World policy' could not take first place for a Power with two hostile neighbours. The Germans tried once more to dodge this conclusion even to themselves, and still more to the British; but there was no evading it. They temporized by offering the British and the Japanese 'benevolent neutrality'; when questioned further, they explained that this meant 'strict and correct neutrality' and no more.[2] On 15 March Bülow laid all doubts; he declared in the Reichstag that the Anglo-German agreement of 16 October 1900 'was in no sense concerned with Manchuria'. This was true enough; but Bülow, by revealing it, shattered the bluff on which British policy had been based. The British had hoped that the Russians would be restrained by fear of Anglo-German co-operation; now the fear was shown to be groundless. The revelation proved decisive in Anglo-German relations, though not in the history of the Far East. The Japanese resolved to check Russia even without British or German backing. On 24 March they demanded withdrawal of the proposed agreement between Russia and China. The Russians were not ready for a conflict. They dropped their demands on China; and Lamsdorff was soon declaring that 'there never was any draft of a Manchurian Agreement, but only a programme of points to be discussed'.[3] Denied an agreement over Manchuria, the Russians stayed there without one, confident that their patience would outlast that of China or of the other Powers. The shadow of crisis deepened in the Far East.

[1] Holstein to Metternich (London), 21 Jan. 1901. *Große Politik*, xvii, no. 4984.
[2] Memorandum by Mühlberg, 14 Mar. 1901. Ibid., xvi, no. 4832.
[3] Sanderson to Satow, 12 Apr. 1901. *British Documents*, ii, no. 73.

The British statesmen could not reconcile themselves to the conclusion that there was nothing to hope for from Germany. They still supposed that German backing could be won if only they hit on the right price. This was a view common to 'high finance' in both Great Britain and Germany; it was held with particular conviction by the liberal unionists, of whom Chamberlain was the chief. In January he told Eckardstein, a member of the German embassy himself associated with the city, that he would prefer 'co-operation with Germany and adherence to the Triple Alliance'.[1] Lansdowne, pushed on by Chamberlain and Eckardstein as well as by his own anxiety, took soundings for a defensive alliance between Great Britain and Germany on 18 March.[2] This put the Germans in a hopeless difficulty. Germany was trying to be at once a European and a world Power. Her European security depended on good relations with Russia; her colonies and overseas trade rested on British favour. She had to stand well with both Powers and could not afford to estrange either. Of course Germany was not alone in this dilemma. The French were always hampered in their imperial expansion by anxiety on their eastern frontier; the British saw their empire gravely shaken, if not lost, by the two European wars that they had to fight in the course of the twentieth century; and even Russia was handicapped in the Far East by her European troubles. But Germany was the most European of the Powers and was therefore the most embarrassed of all, unless she could first establish her domination over the whole continent. This was still far out of sight in 1901. Therefore the Germans had to return a temporizing answer. They posed the condition that Great Britain must join the Triple Alliance, not seek an alliance with Germany alone. The answer was not meant seriously: its purpose was to strengthen German prestige with Austria-Hungary and Italy, not to reach any practical conclusion. What the Germans really counted on was war between Russia and Great Britain, with themselves selling their neutrality to each side at a high price. Napoleon III had had the same idea in the distant days of Austro-Prussian rivalry.

The German evasion did not lead to any change in British policy. Lansdowne continued to hope for an alliance; and in

---

[1] Hatzfeldt to foreign ministry, 18 Jan. 1901. *Große Politik*, xvii, no. 4979.
[2] Lansdowne to Lascelles, 18 Mar. 1901. *British Documents*, ii, no. 77. Eckardstein to foreign ministry, 19 Mar. 1901. *Große Politik*, xvii, no. 4994.

May actually had a formal draft of a defensive agreement prepared,[1] despite Salisbury's objection that isolation was 'a danger
in whose existence we have no historical reason for believing'.[2]
Lansdowne had come to realize that he could not expect a German alliance against Russia; instead he proposed to slide into
one by co-operating with Germany against France. Morocco
seemed to be the predestined spot for this co-operation.[3] The
sultan's authority there was fast breaking down; the British
wanted to control Tangier in order to complete the security of
Gibraltar, and they were ready to offer the Atlantic coast of
Morocco to Germany in return for co-operation against France.
Chamberlain had already made this offer at the Windsor meeting with William II in November 1899; he repeated it in January
1901; and it was made rather more formally to the Germans in
July.[4] They were not to be caught. Bülow noted: 'in this affair
we must behave like the sphinx'.[5] In Morocco, as in the Far
East, the British would receive German support only if they
joined the Triple Alliance.[6] The 'free hand' did not operate only
against the British. In June 1901 Delcassé also sought German
co-operation in Morocco. For him, too, Bülow had a ready
answer: Germany would help him only if France renounced
her claims to Alsace and Lorraine.[7] Both answers were excuses,
not meant to be attained; the free hand was in itself the German
aim, and in the summer of 1901 they were more confident than
ever that Great Britain was running into increasing difficulties
with both France and Russia.

The Russians were confident too. The Anglo-German agreement of October 1900 (which was made public at once) had
somewhat alarmed them; this alarm blew over when Bülow
emptied it of meaning in March 1901. In September Nicholas
II visited William II at Danzig and was told that he could
count on German neutrality in the Far East. Moreover, this
renewed friendship made the French bid higher. It was never
enough for them to offer the same as the Germans; they had
always to offer more. If the Germans offered neutrality, the

[1] Memorandum by Sanderson, 27 May 1901. *British Documents*, ii, no. 85.
[2] Memorandum by Salisbury, 29 May 1901. Ibid., no. 86.
[3] Hatzfeldt to foreign ministry, 19 June 1901. *Große Politik*, xvii, no. 5177.
[4] Eckardstein, *Lebenserinnerungen*, ii. 358.
[5] Minute by Bülow on Hatzfeldt to foreign ministry, 19 June 1901. *Große Politik*,
xvii, no. 5177.   [6] Bülow to foreign ministry, 9 Aug. 1901. Ibid., xvii, no. 5185.
[7] Bülow to Radolin, 19 June 1901. Ibid., xviii (ii), no. 5871.

French had to offer support. They agreed to provide money for a railway to Tashkent so that the Russians could threaten India; a convention for joint military action against Great Britain was agreed on; and plans for naval co-operation against Great Britain were begun, though never completed. It is unlikely that Delcassé ever seriously projected a Franco-Russian war against Great Britain. He intended to link the two questions of Manchuria and Morocco,[1] as Hanotaux had earlier tried to link the Straits and the Nile; and his practical object was probably to extract a British surrender of Morocco in exchange for French neutrality in the Far East. The threat of co-operation with Russia was necessary in order to make this policy work. Beyond this was the grandiose design of remodelling the continent of Europe with both British and Russian approval. In the meantime, Great Britain had to be kept isolated. Delcassé noted in July: 'We must prevent England finding in the Far East in Japan the soldier that she lacks.'[2]

British isolation hardly needed Delcassé's prompting. Since all else had failed, the British tried their last expedient of a direct deal with Russia. It came to nothing. The Russians did not trouble to moderate their ambitions; and threw in the demand for a port on the Persian gulf in addition to control of northern China. By November Lansdowne was back at the old alternative of an approach to Germany. He thought that if he offered to co-operate with them everywhere except in the Far East—in the Mediterranean, the Adriatic, the Aegean, the Black Sea, and the Persian gulf—co-operation might become a habit and they might one day slip into the habit in the Far East without noticing it.[3] On 19 December he aired this idea to Metternich, the new German ambassador. Metternich was not impressed: the British empire must make up its mind to a defensive pact with the Triple Alliance.[4] There was nothing decisive in this conversation. Both men agreed to try again when the bitter feelings caused by the Boer war and the events of the spring had blown over. The decision came from elsewhere, from the Japanese.

[1] Delcassé to Montebello, 19 Feb. 1901. *Documents diplomatiques français*, second series, i, no. 88.

[2] Note by Delcassé on Beau (Pekin) to Delcassé, 1 July 1901. Ibid., no. 310.

[3] Memoranda by Lansdowne, 22 Nov., 4 Dec. 1901. *British Documents*, ii, nos. 92 and 93.

[4] Lansdowne to Lascelles, 19 Dec. 1901. Ibid., ii, no. 94; memorandum by Metternich, 28 Dec. 1901. *Große Politik*, xvii, no. 5030.

Unlike the British, they could not wait. The British could console themselves that the maturing of Russian plans in the Far
East would take a long time; the Japanese were concerned to
establish the independence of Korea and therewith the security
of their own coast. In the autumn of 1901 they resolved to take
the plunge one way or the other. Hayashi, their ambassador in
London, was to try for a British alliance; simultaneously Ito, one
of their most distinguished statesmen, was to seek a bargain
with Russia.

Ito approached the Russians through Delcassé, who was
delighted to see his policy coming to fruition; and the Japanese
were offered the bait of a French loan if they settled with
Russia. In November 1901 Ito arrived in St. Petersburg. The
Russians were, as ever, willing to bargain; but, again as usual,
they offered nothing. Witte was prepared to give the Japanese
a free hand in Korea on the characteristic ground that the expense would ruin them; Lamsdorff insisted that the Japanese
must promise to support Russian plans elsewhere in China if
they got any concessions in Korea; and the only proposal made
by Kuropatkin and the military men was that the Japanese
should not act in Korea without Russian permission. Ito tried
to claim that something could be made of these ideas. The
government in Tokio had fewer illusions and decided on the
alternative course of an agreement with the British. Hayashi
renewed the request which he had made in the spring: Great
Britain should hold the ring for Japan in the Far East while she
settled with the Russians. This time it was easier for the British
to meet the request. The Boer war was virtually over, and the
British navy was now free to hold France in check. Moreover,
the British knew that Ito was negotiating simultaneously with
the Russians; and they might well be faced with a Russo-
Japanese combination unless they were forthcoming to the
Japanese. They therefore agreed readily to the basic principle
of mutual aid if either were attacked in the Far East by two
other Powers. Two difficulties remained. Lansdowne, or to be
more accurate, the cabinet objected to limiting the alliance to
the Far East; Japan, they claimed, ought to promise them help
in India. Moreover, they disliked recognizing Korea as a
Japanese sphere of influence; this made nonsense of their
avowed policy of maintaining the *status quo* in the Far East. The
Japanese held firm on both points. The first mattered only for

its impression on British public opinion: a Russo-French attack on India was never within the bounds of possibility. Korea, however, was vital to the Japanese; it was the cause of their quarrel with Russia, and an agreement which did not cover it had no purpose for them. The British gave way on both points, but succeeded in the essential provision. Article IV of the agreement provided that neither party would 'without consulting the other, enter into separate arrangements with another Power to the prejudice of the interests above described'.

The Anglo-Japanese agreement, signed on 30 January 1902, gave both parties what they wanted. The Japanese got recognition of their special interest in Korea, and the assurance that Great Britain would keep France neutral in case they went to war with Russia. The British prevented any Japanese combine with Russia and strengthened the barrier against any further Russian advance. The price they paid was small: now that the Boer war was over, the British could easily spare the ships to counter France in the Far East; their only sacrifice was Korea, and that was only a sacrifice of principle. The gain, however, was not so great at the time as it was made by later, unforeseen, events. No one, not even the Japanese, supposed that they were capable of sustaining a serious war against Russia; and both parties hoped to strike a bargain with Russia, not to go to war with her. Nor did the agreement threaten Russia's position in Manchuria; at most it made further Russian expansion more difficult. Again, the alliance did not mark the end of British isolation; rather it confirmed it. Isolation meant aloofness from the European Balance of Power; and this was now more possible than before. On the other hand, the alliance certainly did not imply any British estrangement from Germany. Rather the reverse. The British would no longer have to importune the Germans for help in the Far East; and therefore relations between them would be easier. The Germans had constantly suggested alliance with the Japanese to the British; and they were given advance notice of its conclusion. They believed that it would increase the tension between Great Britain and Russia, and welcomed it much as Napoleon III had welcomed the Prussian alliance with Italy in the spring of 1866. William II remarked: 'The noodles have had a lucid interval.'[1] More general

---

[1] An echo of his description of the British cabinet as 'unmitigated noodles' for failing to make an alliance with Japan in March 1901.

causes seemed to hold the two countries together. Though
many Englishmen disliked Germany, they disliked Russia and
France much more. Germany's economic rivalry had come to
be accepted; Bülow's bitter speeches—designed for the home
market—were more than offset by William II's gestures of goodwill in visiting England during the Boer war, in November 1899
and again at the death of Victoria in January 1901. Germany
still seemed to be England's only friend on the Continent—an
unsatisfactory, but now fortunately a less necessary, friend. In
April 1902 Lansdowne anticipated that Germany would 'stick
to her role of the honest broker, taking advantage, if you like, of
our difficulties in order to pursue a *politique de pourboire* at our
expense, but without pooling her ironclads with those of France
and Russia'.[1] The 'natural alliance' at its most fatuous was still,
in fact, his only glimmer of policy. He was to be jolted out of it
by events; he did not think of an alternative for himself.

Note 1, p. 390.

1. A continental league was twice proposed during the Boer war, both times
by the Germans, though on each occasion more to embarrass the British than
to please the Russians, still less to help the Boers. In October 1899 the Germans
were quarrelling with the British over Samoa. On 10 October the German
under-secretary told the French representative that there ought to be 'colonial
co-operation' between them.[2] On 18 October Bülow repeated the suggestion,
'except for the little triangle' of the Anglo-German agreement over the Portuguese colonies.[3] On 29 October William lamented to the French ambassador
that the other Powers had not responded to his proposals at the beginning
of 1896; now the British fleet was too strong.[4] As Muraviev was expected in
Germany, these vague remarks seem intended to provoke a French refusal,
which could be used to discredit them with the Russians. Delcassé, however,
replied by asking how the two countries could best co-operate. On 6 November Bülow answered that he must think it over,[5] but never returned to the
subject. Muraviev did not propose a continental league to the Germans;
and they snubbed him by publishing their agreement with the British over
Samoa on 8 November, the day on which he arrived in Potsdam.

The discussions between January and March 1900 were more serious.
They were provoked by the British seizure of the German mail-steamers.

---

[1] Lansdowne to Lascelles, 22 Apr. 1902. Newton, *Lansdowne*, p. 247.
[2] Memorandum by Derenthall, 10 Oct. 1899. *Große Politik*, xiii, no. 3584.
[3] Noailles (Berlin) to Delcassé, 18 Oct. 1899. Bourgeois and Pagès, *Origines de
la grande guerre*, p. 281.
[4] William II to Bülow, 29 Oct. 1899. *Große Politik*, xv, no. 4394.
[5] Delcassé to Bihourd (Berlin), 13 Jan. 1905. *Documents diplomatiques français*
second series, vi, no. 24.

On 6 January Bülow[1] and on 7 January Holstein[2] threatened the British
with a continental league—it could be concluded 'within a few days'. On
11 January Bülow told the Russian ambassador that he would like to act
against Great Britain, but 'what was the French attitude? What guarantee
did France offer?'[3] Though the Russians had no hope of success, Muraviev
asked Delcassé whether he would join a mediation with Russia and Germany. Delcassé agreed on condition that Germany took the initiative.[4] On
3 March Muraviev proposed 'a friendly pressure' of the three Powers on
England to end the war.[5] Bülow replied that this would be possible only
if the three Powers 'mutually guaranteed their European possessions for a
long period of years'. Negotiations then ended. In short, while the Russians
—urged on by France—certainly took the initiative on 3 March, this was
provoked by the German initiative of 11 January.

[1] Bülow to Hatzfeldt, 6 Jan. 1900. *Große Politik*, xv, no. 4425.
[2] Holstein to Hatzfeldt, 7 Jan. 1900. Ibid., no. 4429.
[3] Memorandum by Bülow, 12 Jan. 1900. Ibid., no. 4463.
[4] Bourgeois and Pagès, *Origines de la grande guerre*, p. 286.
[5] Bülow to Radolin, 3 Mar. 1900. *Große Politik*, xv, no. 4472.

XVIII

THE LAST YEARS OF BRITISH ISOLATION: THE MAKING OF THE ANGLO-FRENCH ENTENTE

1902–5

THE Anglo-Japanese agreement was a challenge to Russia, despite its cautious phrases: it ended her monopoly in the Far East. The Russians sought to answer it by a demonstration of 'the continental league', the partnership with France and Germany which had arrested Japan in 1895. Lamsdorff proposed a joint declaration by the three Powers which, while ostensibly accepting the principle of Chinese integrity, should in fact assert a protectorate against all others—a triple alliance against Great Britain and Japan. France and Germany were to take on the British navy, while Russia ate up northern China at her leisure. The Germans turned down Lamsdorff's proposal out of hand. They gave their stock excuse: they could not support Russia so long as France refused to renounce her lost provinces.[1] Besides, German interests in the Far East were not great enough to justify the risk of war. They were confident that Great Britain and Russia would come to blows, and therefore preserved their 'free hand' against Russia in 1902, as they had preserved it against Great Britain since 1898. Holstein wrote: 'It is in our interest to keep our hands free, so that His Majesty will be able to claim appropriate compensation not only for eventual support, but even for remaining neutral.'[2]

Delcassé had to take a different course. The Russians would always choose Germany, the fellow empire and joint oppressor of the Poles, if she and France offered equal advantages. France had to outbid Germany—by loans, by becoming an ally of Russia where she was merely a friend, even by appearing to

[1] Bülow to Alvensleben (St. Petersburg), 22 Feb. 1902. *Große Politik*, xviii, no. 5050.

[2] Memorandum by Holstein, 24 Mar. 1902. Ibid., xix, no. 5920.

support Russia in the Far East. Delcassé tried to take the sting out of Lamsdorff's proposal, but in vain. On 20 March 1902 the Franco-Russian declaration was published. While ostensibly welcoming the Anglo-Japanese agreement, it really announced a Franco-Russian protectorate of China. 'In case the aggressive actions of third Powers or new troubles in China, endangering the integrity and free development of this Power, became a threat to their interests, the two allied Governments would consult on means for safeguarding them.'[1] Delcassé got an empty reward. A Russian squadron joined the French fleet in a visit to Tangier in April. This was a gesture without substance, last fleeting glimpse of a policy that had failed. Delcassé had planned to play off Great Britain and Russia; instead France was in danger of being caught between them. The alignment of France and Russia versus Great Britain and Japan had somehow to be undone. France needed the Russian alliance to preserve her continental independence; hence she could not desert Russia. But equally she could not risk war with Great Britain. Two alternatives remained. Either France must reconcile Russia and Japan and so prevent a war in the Far East; or she must herself be reconciled to the British, so as to tempt them away from Japan's side—enough at any rate to prevent their giving Japan active assistance. The Anglo-Japanese alliance, by forcing France into an open declaration of hostility to Great Britain, became in fact the inevitable prelude to the Anglo-French entente.

The field of reconciliation was to be Morocco. With the Egyptian question stagnant, this was not only the sharpest issue between the two countries; a settlement there would erase Fashoda and win over the French advocates of colonial expansion, who were the core of hostility to Great Britain. In theory agreement did not seem difficult. The British were only interested in the security of Gibraltar and hence in neutralizing the Mediterranean coastline of Morocco;[2] the French wanted

---

[1] Franco-Russian declaration, 20 Mar. 1902. *Documents diplomatiques français*, second series, ii, no. 145. Austria-Hungary also gave a platonic adherence to the declaration, as a harmless demonstration of the Austro-Russian entente. Italy did not, as an equally harmless gesture towards Great Britain. Both really showed by their opposite actions that they were not world Powers.

[2] The British had the largest share of Moorish trade and therefore any political concession to France had to be sweetened to public opinion, especially to the Liverpool trading interests, by political gains elsewhere and, if possible, by securing

to add the missing piece to their North African empire. What kept them apart was suspicion—the fear that neither side would respect a line of partition if one were drawn. There was no reason for haste so far as the general international situation was concerned. Faced with the Anglo-Japanese alliance the Russians drew back, and in April 1902 made an agreement with China to withdraw from Manchuria by annual stages; the Far Eastern crisis was again postponed. But conditions in Morocco pushed Delcassé on. While both Great Britain and France assumed that Morocco would one day fall to pieces, both also assumed that this might be indefinitely postponed. By 1902 this assumption was proving shaky. Muley Hassan, the last strong ruler of Morocco, had died in 1894; and the authority of Abdul Aziz, his feeble successor, was visibly crumbling. Things could not stand still. Either Morocco would be 'reformed' under British tutelage, as Nicolson, the British representative, still planned, or else France would take it over. To defeat the British plans, Delcassé pushed French financiers into investing money in Morocco, in the hope that its loss would give him an excuse for intervention;[1] this, too, pushed on diplomacy, for his object was settlement with Great Britain, not a conflict.

Delcassé's diplomatic plan was to deprive the British of allies so far as Morocco was concerned and then to settle with them in isolation.[2] He made repeated inquiries of Germany to ensure that she would not play any part there, and received always from Bülow the same reply: 'Germany has so to speak no interests in Morocco, they are so trifling and insignificant.'[3]

---

the open door in Morocco itself. But, of course, the British economic stake in Morocco was a fleabite compared to their general overseas trade. This, though true, was however no consolation to those firms who made their money out of trade with Morocco; and sectional interests are often stronger than the public good.

[1] French ambitions in Morocco are often ascribed to economic motives; the opposite is the case. The economic interests were the stalking-horse for strategical and political aims. The French financial houses and trading houses knew that they were likely to lose their money and were driven to build up a stake in Morocco against their will; they would have much preferred to invest in the safer speculation of the Bagdad railway.

[2] Departmental note, 15 July 1902. *Documents diplomatiques français*, second series, ii, no. 333.

[3] Bihourd to Delcassé, 13 Jan. 1903. Ibid., iii, no. 24. There was also an abortive attempt at Franco-German co-operation over Siam in the summer of 1902. After the Anglo-Japanese alliance had been made, Japanese agents appeared

The only German interest, in fact, was to keep Morocco in existence as a cause of discord between Great Britain and France. Delcassé had a more concrete success with the Italians. They had been Great Britain's one sure ally in the Mediterranean; but the Anglo-French agreement of March 1899 made them fear that Tripoli would slip through their fingers. In December 1900 Delcassé offered them a good bargain. France would not encroach in Tripoli and would allow Italy to take it, once she had herself acquired Morocco; in return the Italians abandoned Morocco to France. Italy was excluded from Morocco, yet could not cash her cheque in Tripoli until the French chose to move. In 1902 Delcassé went further: he virtually detached Italy from the Triple Alliance. He insisted that the Italians could not count on political or financial friendship with France so long as the Triple Alliance was directed against her; and he demanded that the text be changed. The Germans were equally insistent that it be renewed unaltered; and, since the Austro-Russian entente deprived the Italians of their blackmailing position, they were helpless. They therefore fell back on the resource of the weak and deceived both sides. On 28 June 1902 the Triple Alliance was renewed, together with the clauses providing for military co-operation with Ger-

in Siam. The French therefore wished to get from Siam a recognition that the part of Siam adjacent to Indo-China was a French sphere of interest (the British had had a similar agreement with Siam on the Burmese side since 1897). On 30 June the French ambassador asked for German backing, apparently without authorization from Delcassé (Richtofen to Metternich, 30 June 1902. *Große Politik*, xviii, no. 5881). On 18 Aug. the Germans replied that France could count on their 'benevolent attitude' (Mühlberg to Radolin, 18 Aug. 1902., Ibid., no. 5882). On 18 Sept. Delcassé inquired how benevolent the Germans intended to be (Delcassé to Prinet, 18 Sept. 1902. *Documents diplomatiques français*, second series, ii, no. 398); he received no reply. Meanwhile Lansdowne had made it clear that he could not oppose the French action in Siam; after all the British treaty of 1897 was 'more stringent'. In October Delcassé concluded a treaty with Siam. It was, however, defeated in the French chamber by the colonial enthusiasts, who objected to its moderation. Fortunately the Japanese were too taken up with Russia to have time for any diversion; and in 1904 the entente agreement, by dividing Siam into British and French spheres of interest, removed Siam from international politics until 1941.

It is difficult to believe that there was any serious project in Delcassé's mind for Franco-German co-operation. Probably it all originated with Noailles, the retiring French ambassador in Berlin who was inclined to be anti-British and pro-German. The discouraging German response must have given Delcassé further proof, if such were needed, that he could not count on serious German support. The Germans, on their side, had just steered clear of the question of Morocco and were therefore hardly likely to involve themselves in that of Siam.

many against France; two days later the Italian foreign minister exchanged letters with Barrère, the French ambassador, assuring him that Italy was not committed in any way to take part in a war against France.[1] This was a rash transaction. What was the good of a promise to one party to break a promise already made to another? Maybe the Triple Alliance did not count for much in practice; all the more reason not to annoy the Germans by tampering with it, especially as Delcassé's plans rested on their abstention. His Italian manœuvres first brought down on him the German hostility which was to be his ruin three years later; but few French statesmen can resist taking Italy seriously as a Great Power. At any rate, one result was certain: the Italians, caught between Germany and France, would not add to their embarrassments by supporting the British in Morocco.

There remained Spain, a Power even weaker than Italy, but in a decisive strategic position and with vast ambitions in Morocco—a legacy of her imperial past. Delcassé had to offer a high price in order to detach Spain from the British side. In November 1902 a draft treaty was ready for signature, by which all northern Morocco, including Fez, the greatest city, should pass to Spain and the rest to France.[2] At the last minute, the Spaniards drew back. They knew that in affairs of this kind all the blows fall on the weaker party. Just as the French had wrecked the Anglo-Congolese treaty of 1894 by threatening Leopold II, so the British would wreck this treaty by opposing Spain: she would not fulfil her Moorish ambitions, whatever might happen to the French. They refused to proceed with the treaty unless the British became a party to it; alternatively they asked to be admitted to the Franco-Russian alliance, so that the partition of Morocco would be underwritten by Russia. Still more, they threatened to reveal the abortive treaty to the British—and finally did so in February 1903. By this spin of the wheel, Delcassé, planning to isolate the British, was instead driven to negotiating with them.

---

[1] The Italians themselves were ashamed of this transaction. The letters were therefore given the fictitious date of 10 July and were subsequently recalled to be replaced by identical texts dated 1 Nov. 1902. In this way the act of repudiating the obligations of the Triple Alliance almost on the day of signing it was somewhat obscured.

[2] Draft Franco-Spanish treaty, 8 Nov. 1902. *Documents diplomatiques français*, second series, ii, no. 483.

There was little sign in the summer of 1902 that agreement between Great Britain and France was any nearer than it had been for the last twenty years. Salisbury ceased to be prime minister in July; this removed the closest friend of France from the government. Early in August, Paul Cambon—always inclined to outrun events—aired the idea of a 'liquidation' of Morocco to Lansdowne.[1] Professional jealousies were stirred; and someone in the British foreign office—probably Nicolson —'leaked' the French plans to the Moors. A special envoy was sent to London.[2] Lansdowne drew back in alarm. He told the Moorish envoy 'there is not the slightest chance of any one Power being given a free hand in that country', and advised him to share out loans and railway concessions between England, France, and Germany. 'This method of procedure seems well calculated to prevent rivalry between the Powers.'[3] In reality it was meant to provoke it and, as usual, to saddle Germany with the task of a policeman for Great Britain. The 'natural alliance' was still her only resource.

In the late autumn a series of factors caused this alliance to crumble. In October the admiralty suddenly realized that the German fleet, with its short cruising range, was designed solely for war against the British; they answered by projecting a naval base on the North Sea.[4] The admiralty did not yet anticipate that the German navy by itself would ever challenge British maritime supremacy; but they appreciated that it would become a formidable danger if they were at war with France and Russia. This had indeed been the basis of Tirpitz's 'risk' theory, by which he had justified his naval programme. Unfortunately for the Germans, the British admiralty did not draw the further conclusion which Tirpitz had expected. Instead of seeking to buy German friendship, they became urgent to avoid a conflict with France or Russia; as well they began to put the navy on a 'three-power' standard, with the intention of outdistancing all rivals for good and all. Naval policy, in fact, turned the British away from Germany, though as yet it turned them more

[1] Lansdowne to Monson (Paris), 6 Aug. 1902. *British Documents*, ii, no. 322; Cambon to Delcassé, 9 Aug. 1902. *Documents diplomatiques français*, second series, ii, no. 369.

[2] This envoy, Kaid Maclean, though subsequently dismissed by Lansdowne as an adventurer, was in Oct. 1902 invited to Balmoral by Edward VII and knighted.

[3] Memorandum for Kaid Maclean, 24 Oct. 1902. *British Documents*, ii no. 328.

[4] Marder, *British Naval Policy*, p. 464.

towards isolation than towards reconciliation with France and Russia.

Another old song was heard again at the close of 1902, also not in Germany's favour. This was none other than the Straits question, a dead issue since the spring of 1897. In September 1902 the Russians obtained Turkish permission to send four torpedo-boats, which they had bought in France, through the Straits into the Black Sea. The British did not mind traffic in this direction; but they feared that the Russians might send out warships as well from the Black Sea to the Far East and thus upset the Anglo-Japanese naval supremacy there. For twenty years after the congress of Berlin the British had planned to send warships to Constantinople and even into the Black Sea and therefore had interpreted the rule of the Straits in a way that virtually kept them open. Now they wished to close the Straits and so swung round to the interpretation which for twenty years had been exclusively Russian. They appealed to the other Powers for support and took out of the lumber-room the forgotten Mediterranean agreements of 1887.[1] The French, wisely, ignored the British appeal. The Germans also refused and, less wisely, justified their refusal by recapitulating all Salisbury's sins—a recapitulation which lost nothing in the telling when personally delivered by William II during a visit to England in November.[2] The old partners of the Mediterranean entente were equally cold. The Austrians would do nothing to disturb their Balkan agreement with Russia; the Italians hoped to insert themselves into it. The Russian ships passed the Straits, after a solitary British protest. The Mediterranean entente was dead; and when the British considered their position they realized that they no longer needed it. The opening of the Straits to Russia would not alter the strategic position.[3] Secure in Egypt and with their enormous naval resources at Malta and Gibraltar, the British could close the exits of the Mediterranean to the Russians, even if the French threatened to support them. Of course this had been true ever since 1898; but men go on thinking in an old pattern even when its logical

---

[1] So forgotten that Sanderson, the permanent under-secretary, had to write their history in two memoranda, July 1902 and Jan. 1903. *British Documents*, viii, nos. 1 and 2.

[2] Metternich to foreign ministry, 17 Nov. 1902. *Große Politik*, xviii, no. 5659.

[3] Opinion of committee of imperial defence, 13 Feb. 1903. *British Documents*, iv, p. 59.

foundations have been destroyed. Until February 1903 the British had the tradition of the Mediterranean entente at the back of their minds; they recollected in a muddled way that the connexion with Germany had once been of use and supposed that it would be so again. After all, a system which had satisfied Salisbury was good enough for Lansdowne.

Now they realized that this pattern was outmoded. They did not need Germany, or for that matter Italy, as a link with Austria-Hungary; they could attempt to settle their disputes outside Europe without fearing the reaction at the Straits. It is a far cry from this to supposing that they desired a conflict with Germany. They wanted her friendship, though they no longer needed her favour. At the close of 1902 they co-operated with the Germans in a debt-collecting expedition to Venezuela and backed out only when this stirred up opposition in the United States.[1] More striking still, they continued to favour the German projects for a great railway in Asia Minor.[2] They believed that

[1] As the Anglo-German action in Venezuela was one of the few practical displays of 'the natural alliance', its breakdown has attracted exaggerated importance. It is true that the Germans behaved with unnecessary violence, and that this offended British opinion. It was more important that it offended American opinion. The strongest principle of British foreign policy was to keep on good terms with the United States. The British abandoned their efforts in Venezuela at the murmur of American disapproval and accepted such terms as the United States chose to offer. This was not evidence of estrangement from Germany, but of British good sense about their relations with the United States.

[2] In 1899 the German company had received only a preliminary concession to explore the ground. In 1903 they had reached the point of a definitive concession with an obligation to start work. The Germans needed foreign participation for two reasons. They could not raise enough capital on the German market; and it would have been a stroke of good business if German firms could have supplied the steel at a high profit, while capitalists of other countries put up the money for the railway-stock at a limited rate of interest. Further, the railway was not expected to pay. The Turkish government was to guarantee so much a kilometre (hence the railway was made as devious as possible); and it could not honour this guarantee unless it raised the customs-dues, which were its principal source of income. This needed the consent of all the Powers, because of the international control of Turkish finances which had followed earlier defaults.

Obviously the Russians, who were themselves short of capital, would oppose the scheme for economic as well as for political reasons. Equally obviously, the French capitalists wished to be in the position of debenture-owners while the Germans acted as ordinary shareholders; as well, they wanted to strengthen Turkey, in which so much French money was invested. The British capitalists were afraid of being outvoted by the French and Germans; they disliked putting up the money for a railway when they did not provide the steel; most of all, they disliked the house of Morgan, through whom the deal was negotiated. Investigation, if it were possible, would probably show that the supposed swing of British opinion against Germany was, in fact, organized by the capitalist interests which

the railway would be built with or without British participation; and, in any case, they wanted it built—it would enable the Ottoman empire to stand on its own feet as a barrier against Russia. The director of military intelligence expressed the general official opinion in November 1902: 'It would be a great mistake to oppose the project, which we ought, on the contrary, to encourage to the best of our power.'[1] As always, the German projects were greater than their resources; the Bagdad railway needed foreign capital, and the British government would have been glad to see it supplied. The British steamship interests on the Euphrates, which would be ruined by the railway, engineered a revolt in the city and even decked it out with anti-German patriotism. The scheme for British participation fell through, much to the government's regret; and this failure was to supply the mythical evidence some years later of Anglo-German estrangement. At the time the Germans noticed nothing, and Bülow, still confident of a quarrel between Great Britain and Russia, made the characteristic comment: 'Meo voto we simply cannot take things "pomadig" [greasily] enough.'[2] In France the German search for money also miscarried, but for exactly the opposite reason. There the capitalists, led by Rouvier, the minister of finance, were eager to take part; Delcassé was anxious not to offend Russia and therefore opposed them. He appealed to the council of ministers and in October 1903 got his way,[3] much to the annoyance of Rouvier and his financial associates. Here, too, the motive was not hostility to Germany or to her imperialist expansion. Delcassé's overriding concern was to stand well with Russia and to outbid Germany in the competition for her friendship.

This was also the deciding factor in his relations with Great Britain. By the close of 1902, it is true, he was aware that the Spaniards were about to reveal their negotiations over Morocco to the British. Events in Morocco themselves were more important. In December 1902 there was a widespread revolt against

stood to lose by the railway. Oddly enough, in France the financial forces favoured participation, political motives were against it; and the politicians won. In England, the politicians were favourable, the financiers hostile; and the financiers won. But it would be absurd to see in this a decisive event in Anglo-German relations.

[1] Memorandum by Lansdowne, 14 Apr. 1903. *British Documents*, ii, no. 216.

[2] Bülow to foreign ministry, 3 Apr. 1903. *Große Politik*, xviii, no. 5911.

[3] Delcassé to Rouvier, 24 Oct. 1903. *Documents diplomatiques français*, second series, iv, no. 34.

Abdul Aziz; and, though it was suppressed, the authority of the sultan was broken for good. The British hope of reforming Morocco under the direction of Kaid Maclean and Sir Arthur Nicolson was shattered; and they had to negotiate with the French *faute de mieux*. Even this was not decisive. The British had always been willing to settle with France so long as they could settle on their own terms. They had been asking for security in Egypt ever since 1882 and at Gibraltar ever since Morocco began to break up; they did not now lower their demands. Hence, anyone who tries to explain the Anglo-French entente by a change in British policy, does the wrong sum. The change was solely on the French side; and its motive was the approaching crisis in the Far East. This crisis had threatened every spring since 1898, when it had led to the first abortive partition. Thereafter something had always tided things over. In 1899 there had been the temporary Anglo-Russian agreement, in 1900 the Boxer rebellion. In 1901 the Russians had been deterred by doubts concerning the Anglo-German agreement, in 1902 by the reality of the Anglo-Japanese alliance. Now the spring was here again, and there seemed to be no new device in the arsenal of diplomacy. The Russians were due to evacuate the second zone of Manchuria in April 1903, according to the agreement that they made with China the year before. When April came they put forward, as the condition of evacuation, new demands that would have made their control of Manchuria more complete than ever. Japan, Great Britain, and the United States protested. The Russians dropped their demands, but dropped also the idea of leaving Manchuria. The Far Eastern crisis was a stage nearer war.

This crisis threatened France. At some point Japan would oppose the Russians; and they would appeal for French support. Then France must either break with Russia or find herself at war with Great Britain. The only way out was an Anglo-French reconciliation, which might detach the British from Japan or at least moderate both parties in the Far East. Beyond this Delcassé had a more elaborate vision. If France won Manchuria for Russia with British, and therewith Japanese, approval, she would win also British and Russian gratitude. Then both countries would join France in reordering Europe on national lines—the old dream which Napoleon III had had in the days after the Crimean war. The Habsburg monarchy would be divided between Germany and Russia; and France would recover Alsace and Lorraine. The first essential step was the reconciliation with Great Britain. This was not difficult. The practical conflicts between the two countries had ended at Fashoda; the only problem was to remove the resentment in French public opinion. Sentimental reconciliation was achieved when Edward VII visited Paris in May 1903 and President Loubet returned the visit in July. The demonstrations in Paris effaced the bitterness of the Boer war;[1] they were a display by the radicals who now controlled the French chamber. These radicals had always disliked colonial ventures and wanted to be on good terms with Great Britain, if only the humiliation over Egypt could somehow be got out of the way. What is more, they had always disliked the alliance with autocratic Russia and the possible war against Germany that it implied. Certainly they felt, like all Frenchmen, the grievance of Alsace and Lorraine; but they echoed Gambetta's hope of recovering the lost provinces through some general softening of international relations, not by a new war. The Russians expected France to remain hostile to Germany and ready to march, if ever this suited the whims of Russian policy. The British, on the other hand, had no army on a continental scale and no basic hostility to Germany; friendship with them made *revanche* more remote. This was a point in its favour for the pacific French radicals. The British on their side, had always wanted to be friendly to France, if she would leave them alone in Egypt. They welcomed Loubet in order to give a sporting victor's cheer, in their usual way, for a gallant loser; but there was to be no doubt that France had lost. The British regarded the entente as the settlement of a tiresome irritation, not a fundamental shift in foreign policy. By ending Egypt and Morocco as topics of international conflict, it increased, not ended, their isolation.

The practical bargain between France and Great Britain took nine months to settle, from July 1903 until April 1904. Both sides agreed that the minor topics of dispute—Siam, Newfoundland, and the rest—should be got out of the way somehow. The hard core of the bargaining was Morocco. Delcassé originally aimed only at an agreement to maintain the

---

[1] As no doubt demonstrations in Berlin would have done, if an Anglo-German reconciliation had been politically necessary.

status quo. The British would drop Kaid Maclean and the other
British adventurers at the sultan's court. The French would be
free from British rivalry, and the sultan would probably welcome their support against his unruly subjects, once he realized
that he could no longer play off the British against them. Lansdowne did not need much encouragement to abandon the
bankrupt Palmerstonian policy of running Morocco as a British
puppet state. He asked for commercial equality in order to
silence the outcry of British trading interests.[1] He asked further
that Spanish interests be considered. After all, Spain had refused to settle without the British in November 1902; now the
British must refuse to settle without Spain and especially must
not give her an excuse for seeking support elsewhere—in fact,
from Germany. Most important of all, he insisted on an agreement that the Mediterranean coastline opposite Gibraltar remain unfortified. The French were ready to meet all these
conditions. Political control of Morocco was bound to give
them economic preponderance sooner or later; they had no
wish to threaten Gibraltar, and there was, in fact, no good
harbour on the Moorish coast; and they, too, wished to keep
Spain away from Germany, though, of course, they did not
intend to pay as high a price as they had offered for Spanish
co-operation against the British in November 1902.

The real difficulty lay elsewhere. Delcassé had planned to
settle only the outstanding causes of Anglo-French friction;
and in this sense Egypt was not outstanding—it had been
crossed off the agenda in 1899. The British control of Egypt
was politically secure; but Cromer, a banker by nature and by
origin, wished to carry through grandiose schemes of financial
reconstruction. The machinery of international control stood
in his way; and he insisted that the French should not merely
acquiesce in the British occupation of Egypt—they should
second it. This was a high fence for Delcassé to ride at; in Cambon's words, he would need plenty of *estomac*.[2] He had hoped
that the acquisition of Morocco would gradually lead French
opinion to forget Egypt; instead he was being asked to make
the renunciation—formal no doubt, but great all the same—
before any gain in Morocco had begun to show itself. Small
wonder that he tried to put off the Egyptian question—first

[1] In the final agreement commercial equality was to last only thirty years.
[2] Lansdowne to Monson, 5 Aug. 1903. *British Documents*, ii, no. 364.

to avoid it altogether; and then to suggest that France should withdraw *pari passu* with her advance in Morocco. Lansdowne was adamant; and from his point of view he was right—a settlement which did not contain a final French recognition of British supremacy in Egypt would be a poor affair.

The agreement, signed on 8 April 1904, therefore appeared to contain a gross inequality: the British gains in Egypt operated immediately; the French gains in Morocco depended on their future exertions.[1] The inequality was apparent, not real. The British were already established in Egypt beyond all challenge; their gain was merely a free hand for Cromer and his financial schemes—gratifying, no doubt, but irrelevant to their imperial strength. The French, on the other hand, were at liberty to add the finest part of North Africa to their empire. But in politics it is the apparent which counts. When Delcassé gave up Egypt, he renounced a cause which ranked, however mistakenly, second only to the lost provinces; when Lansdowne gave up Morocco, he wrote off a country unknown to all except a few traders and experts in strategy. Both British and French opinion believed that France had paid the higher price. Because of the sentimental weight of Egypt, the entente was on trial in

---

[1] Apart from minor agreements concerning Newfoundland, Siam, and frontier adjustments in West Africa, the agreement dealt with Egypt and Morocco. The French declared that they 'will not obstruct the action of Great Britain in Egypt by asking that a limit of time be fixed for the British occupation or in any other manner' and they assented in advance to Cromer's financial reforms. The British 'recognise that it appertains to France . . . to preserve order in Morocco, and to provide assistance for the purpose of all administrative, economic, financial, and military reforms which it may require. They declare that they will not obstruct the action taken by France for this purpose.' The open door was to be preserved in both countries for thirty years; the two governments 'agree not to permit the erection of any fortifications or strategic works' on the Mediterranean coast of Morocco; and Spanish interests in Morocco were to receive 'special consideration'. Each government was to give the other 'their diplomatic support in order to obtain the execution of the clauses of the present Declaration'. This article was inserted by the British in order to get French backing for Cromer's schemes; but a year later it landed them in supporting France against Germany after William II's visit to Tangier. There were secret clauses as well as the published articles; and it is often implied that these gave France additional advantages. This is not so. The published clauses recognized French predominance in Morocco, so long as the sultan's authority lasted. The secret clauses did not arrange for his overthrow— events would bring this about, as they did. The secret clauses merely provided that, when the sultan's authority collapsed, northern Morocco with the Mediterranean coastline should go to Spain. The clauses were therefore a limitation on France, not an advantage to her. Nothing could save the independence of Morocco. Without these clauses all Morocco would have become French (short of a war with Great Britain); by them she renounced the strategic area of Morocco in advance.

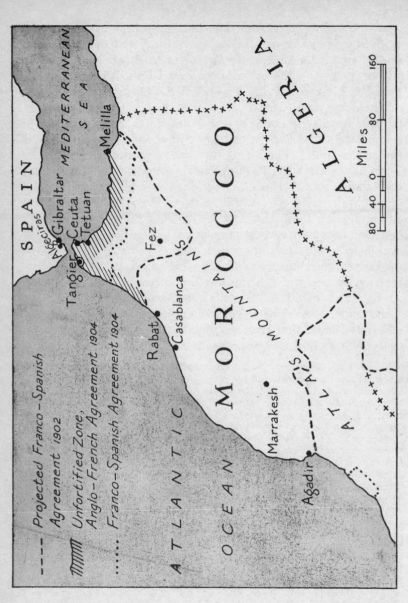

Projected Franco–Spanish
Agreement 1902
Unfortified Zone,
Anglo–French Agreement 1904
Franco–Spanish Agreement 1904

SPAIN
Algeciras
Gibraltar
MEDITERRANEAN
SEA
Melilla
Ceuta
Tetuan
Tangier
Fez
Rabat
Casablanca
M O R O C C O
Marrakesh
Agadir
A T L A S
M O U N T A I N S
ALGERIA
A T L A N T I C
O C E A N

Miles
80 40 0   80   160

THE PARTITION OF MOROCCO

France as it was not in Great Britain. The entente was essential for France; it was merely an advantage for the British. But the French had paid cash down, the British with a promissory note. Hence the French could take an independent line—could try to go back on their bargain towards Spain and could flirt with Germany. British good faith was on trial; they had to back the French up in Morocco when international difficulties arose. Yet all the entente did for the British was slightly to lessen their naval needs in the Mediterranean and to give Cromer a field-day in Egypt; for the French the situation in the Far East made it a matter of life and death.

Paul Cambon wrote on the conclusion of the entente: 'Without the war in the Transvaal, which bled Great Britain and made her wise, without the war in the Far East which made for reflection on both sides of the Channel and inspired in all a desire to limit the conflict, our agreements would not have been possible.'[1] The first explanation is doubtful. The British yielded nothing of the demands that they had made in the eighteen-nineties, before the Boer war; the only change was, perhaps, their loss of faith in the ability of independent Morocco to keep going. The great change was on the French side; and here Cambon's second explanation was decisive. The Far East, and the Far East alone, caused the Anglo-French entente; but in this vital matter Delcassé's plans miscarried. He recognized that the Russians were bent on having Manchuria. It was essential to them as providing the secure land-route to Port Arthur; hence, as Bompard, the French ambassador at St. Petersburg observed, 'organising Russian domination in Manchuria' and 'preparing for its evacuation' were merely two different formulas for the same thing.[2] Delcassé assumed that the Russians could obtain Manchuria without a war. In this he was right. The British would have recognized Russia's privileged position there, on condition that this was the limit of her expansion. The Japanese were ready to do the same and even to abandon the British alliance if they could have recognition of their own privileged position in Korea.

Here was the real problem. All the official advisers at St. Petersburg would have been content with Manchuria.

[1] Paul Cambon to Henri Cambon, 16 Apr. 1904. *Correspondance*, ii. 134.
[2] Bompard to Delcassé, 24 Apr. 1903. *Documents diplomatiques français*, second series, iii, no. 194.

Lamsdorff, always timid, favoured retreat whenever opposition showed itself; Witte relied solely on economic penetration; even Kuropatkin, the minister of war, and earlier the apostle of extremism, now wished to gain Manchuria by agreement with the Japanese and therefore would meet their wishes in regard to Korea. As for public opinion, the Russian capitalists, who had once supported Witte, were now weary of his Far Eastern dreams and were taken up with imperialist projects in Persia. But Russia was an autocracy in decay; and all the advocates of moderation were shouted down by a hare-brained schemer, Bezobrazov, and his circle of 'Koreans', who caught the ear of the tsar. The 'Koreans' admitted no limit to Russian strength. They proposed to add Korea to Russia's sphere of influence and persuaded Nicholas II to create a bogus timber concession on the Yalu river, between Korea and Manchuria, in order to smuggle in soldiers under the guise of lumbermen. In April 1903 Bezobrazov was made a secretary of state; and henceforth compromise in the Far East was impossible, though no one outside the court at St. Petersburg knew this. In August 1903—just when Delcassé was first bringing Lansdowne and the Russian ambassador together—Witte was turned out of the ministry of finance; and Alexeiev, one of the Korean 'circle', was made viceroy of the Far East, in full control of the negotiations with Japan. When Lamsdorff visited Paris in October, Delcassé said to him: 'Talk to Lord Lansdowne, probably many misunderstandings will disappear.'[1] Instead new ones appeared. Though the British might compromise over Manchuria, they wished to arrest Russian expansion in Persia; but this was the work of the more sensible capitalists in Russia, who disliked the adventure in the Far East. The British seemed intent on checking Russia everywhere; and the rival Russian groups were forced back to a common anti-British line. The extremists would not yield over Manchuria; their critics would not yield over Persia. Great Britain and Russia remained on bad terms.

Delcassé could not urge moderation on Russia; this would merely underline the German claim to be Russia's only true friend. His only resource was to ask the British to urge moderation on the Japanese. This the British refused to do. They still feared a Russo-Japanese bargain at their expense. Moreover,

[1] Departmental note, 28 Oct. 1903. *Documents diplomatiques français*, second series, iv, no. 45.

like everyone else, they believed that if it came to a war, the Japanese would be defeated. They were resolved to keep out of this war, therefore had to keep out of the negotiations. For if they once urged concessions on Japan, they would be under a moral obligation to support her, if these failed of their object.[1] By January 1904 Delcassé was driven to mediate between Japan and Russia without British assistance. The Russian foreign office was prodigal of generous offers; these bore no resemblance to the activities of 'the circle' in the Far East. By now Bezobrazov had established the principle that Korea was essential to Russia's security. The Japanese despaired of further negotiation; and on 8 February 1904 launched the war by a surprise attack on the Russian ships at Port Arthur.

In January, when it still seemed possible to avert war, Delcassé had tried to force the British into conciliation by hanging back in his negotiations with them.[2] Once the war had started, he hurried the negotiations on, in the faint hope that a British settlement with France would bring a settlement with Russia in its train. Anglo-Russian negotiations were, in fact, taken up again on Delcassé's prompting in April. They came to as little as before. The war was already going badly for Russia; and these mishaps certainly discredited Bezobrazov. But this strengthened the advocates of expansion in Persia; and it was concession here on which the British principally insisted. Delcassé's policy had miscarried. France was in danger of straddling between Russia and Great Britain, as Austria had estranged both Russia and the western Powers during the Crimean war. Paul Cambon thought that France should repudiate the Russian alliance even at the risk of a Russian *rapprochement* with Germany.[3] Though Delcassé rejected this, he had no alternative resource; he could only wait for the storm to break.

This was also the German calculation. The long-expected climax of an Anglo-Russian conflict was at last in sight. Bülow wrote triumphantly: 'Time is working against France.'[4] Equally time was working against Russia. Soon she would seek alliance with Germany. What price should the Germans then demand?

[1] Dugdale, *Life of Balfour*, i. 376–83.
[2] On 8 Jan. 1904 Delcassé even made out that the French council of ministers knew nothing of the negotiations and threatened to break off altogether. Newton, *Lord Lansdowne*, p. 288.
[3] Paul Cambon to Henri Cambon, 26 Dec. 1903. *Correspondance*, ii. 102.
[4] Bülow to Radowitz (Madrid), 22 May 1904. *Große Politik*, xx (i), no. 6484.

The moment that they made an alliance they would draw on themselves the full weight of British hostility, and perhaps of French as well; they would be 'not beside Russia, but in front of her'.[1] Hence Germany must somehow evade the Russian demand. It was exactly the same situation as that with Great Britain before and during the Boer war. On the one hand Germany must keep Russia's friendship; on the other, she must not fight Russia's battles. The free hand was still the only resource. On 13 April Bülow advised William II that they must avoid two things: 'firstly that our relations with Russia be injured because of the war . . . on the other side letting ourselves be pushed forward by Russia against Japan or still more against England.'[2] Germany and France were involved in an auction for Russia's friendship; an auction in which each wished to avoiding bidding. The one who remained passive longest would win.

Passivity was also the keynote of German policy in regard to Morocco and the Anglo-French entente. Sooner or later, the Germans still believed, Great Britain and France were bound to quarrel. On 23 March, just before the entente was concluded, Delcassé assured the Germans that France would keep the door open for trade in Morocco;[3] and since they had always insisted that trade was their only Moorish interest, there was no other assurance that they could legitimately demand. Neither France nor Great Britain had consciously planned to exclude the Germans from Morocco;[4] they had repeatedly excluded themselves. Holstein, it is true, did not like this policy of abstention; it was an affront to German greatness. He consulted Schlieffen, who replied that Russia would be unable to help France;[5] and at the same time Schlieffen prepared to make victory over France certain by planning an attack through

---

[1] Memorandum by Holstein, 16 Jan. 1904. *Große Politik*, xix (i), no. 5944.

[2] Memorandum by Bülow, 14 Feb. 1904. Ibid., no. 5961.

[3] Delcassé to Bihourd, 27 May 1904. *Documents diplomatiques français*, second series, iv, no. 368. It was later made a high count against Delcassé that he had failed to communicate to the Germans the (published) text of the Anglo-French agreement. Since the Germans had repeatedly told the British and the French that they had no political interests in Morocco and since they were not a Mediterranean power, what was there to communicate?

[4] During the negotiations, the French had often tried to extract concessions from Lansdowne by scaring him with stories of German ambitions for a Moorish port. He never responded to these hints and, so far as he feared difficulties with Germany, feared them over Egypt, not over Morocco.

[5] Schlieffen to Bülow, 20 Apr. 1904. *Große Politik*, xix (i), no. 6032.

Belgium. Holstein wrote in June: 'Germany must object to the projected absorption of Morocco not only on economic grounds, but far more to maintain her prestige.'[1] The Paris embassy urged that Germany should either renounce Morocco once and for all or should openly challenge France there.[2] Neither course was followed. The Germans did not think it necessary to win French friendship; on the other hand they waited for the bigger explosion in the Far East.[3] In the summer of 1904 Holstein fell ill; and Bülow had a free hand for his policy of the 'free hand'. He had other proof, fallacious as it turned out, that Great Britain and France were bound to quarrel. The Spaniards had been left high-and-dry by the Anglo-French agreement; they appealed to the Germans for support. Bülow was convinced that the Spaniards were acting as British agents and even proposed to Lansdowne a joint backing for Spain against France.[4] Though Lansdowne did not take up this odd idea, the Germans remained convinced that the Franco-Spanish negotiations would either come to nothing or would cause a breach between France and Great Britain. They were again disappointed. The Spaniards, deserted by the British and not supported by the Germans, had to take any price that France chose to offer. On 3 October 1904 France and Spain reached agreement. Spain received only a narrow strip of northern Morocco, as a neutral area between the French zone and Gibraltar; and she could claim her share only when it suited the French to move.[5] The

[1] Memorandum by Holstein, 3 June 1904. *Große Politik*, xx (i), no. 6521.

[2] Radolin to Bülow, 27 July 1904. Ibid., no. 6524.

[3] There were two further obstacles to German action in Morocco. For one thing, they could not make up their minds whether to pose as the defenders of the sultan's independence or to claim that his authority had broken down and blame the French for not keeping order there. As some German subjects had just been kidnapped, it was impossible to take the first line; while the second involved recognizing French preponderance. It was therefore simpler to do nothing.

The other difficulty was more serious. There had just been a ormidable native rebellion in German South-West Africa; and all colonial schemes were unpopular in Germany as a result. A deal with France which brought colonial gains to Germany (whether in Morocco or in the shape of French colonial territory as compensation) would have provoked a storm in the Reichstag and would probably have been repudiated. William II, ever the medium of German feeling, expressed this when he told the king of Spain: 'We do not want any territorial gains in Morocco' (William II to Bülow, 16 Mar. 1904. Ibid., xvii, no. 5208). This declaration was to hamper German policy considerably in the following year.

[4] Bülow to Metternich, 31 May 1904. Ibid., xx (i), no. 6488.

[5] The Spaniards also accepted the provision that the Mediterranean coastline (except for the places such as Ceuta which were Spanish already) should remain unfortified. On one point, German expectations were fulfilled. The French could

Spaniards were disgruntled and discontented. All the same, the question of Morocco was as much finished in October 1904, from the diplomatic point of view, as the question of the upper Nile had been in March 1899; only the threat of war could reopen it.

In October 1904 the Germans did not worry about Morocco. All their hopes were pinned on the conflict which they believed to be approaching between Great Britain and Russia. The war in the Far East was going badly for the Russians. The Trans-Siberian railway, single track and even that incomplete, could not compete with the Japanese advantage of sea power. The only hope for the Russians was to redress the balance in the China seas and thus cut off the Japanese armies in the mainland from their island base. They dared not send their Black Sea fleet through the Straits. For, though the British no longer cared about the closing of the Straits on their own account, they would enforce a treaty provision which was in the interest of their Japanese ally. The Baltic fleet could move without the same difficulties; its journey to the Far East caused a first-rate crisis all the same. Its incompetent officers mistook other Russian ships for the Japanese, and in their panic sank a number of British fishing-vessels off the Dogger Bank on 21 October. Here was the long-postponed Anglo-Russian conflict which the Germans had awaited with confidence, the French with dread. Both worked overtime, the Germans to entangle Russia in an alliance, the French to prevent a breach between Russia and Great Britain.

The Germans offered Russia alliance against attack 'by a European power'; the two allies would also 'combine in order to remind France of the obligations which she has assumed by the terms of Franco-Russian alliance'.[1] The Germans did not know these terms; they always assumed that it was a general

not bring themselves to renounce Tangier; and they slipped in a provision that, though apparently included in the Spanish zone, it was to retain its 'special character'. The sultan was to continue to control Tangier; and the French evidently calculated that, when they controlled him, they would control Tangier also. Tangier was excluded from the settlement of Morocco in 1912; and the outbreak of the First World war found the question still unsolved. In 1923 the British used the French difficulties in the Ruhr to impose on them a three-power control which included Spain; and Italy was brought in as a fourth in 1926. This settlement was upset by the Second World war; and at the time of writing the status of Tangier is still provisional.

[1] William II to Nicholas II, 30 Oct. 1904. *Willy–Nicky Letters*, p. 129.

defensive alliance, never dreaming that it was directed solely against themselves. Now they were projecting a continental league against Great Britain. If France came in, she would have to drop her hostility to Germany; if she refused, the Franco-Russian alliance would be disrupted. In either case, Germany would end the danger of 'war on two fronts'. At the same time, she would strengthen her hand for 'world policy'. The Russians would be pushed forward against the British in India; the French fleet would carry the brunt nearer home. Yet the Germans hoped to buy this great success for nothing: the alliance was to operate only when the Dogger Bank affair had been settled. The Russians would, no doubt, have grasped an alliance if it had helped them in their immediate difficulty. They were in no condition to fight the British on their own. They eagerly accepted the British suggestion to submit the dispute to an international inquiry, and saved their prestige only by launching the myth that the suggestion had come from the tsar. The great Anglo-Russian conflict turned out to be a damp squib, thanks to Russia's weakness. All the same, the Russians tried to make something of the German offer. Certainly they did not want a Franco-German reconciliation. The estrangement over Alsace and Lorraine gave Russia security on her western frontier, to say nothing of an endless flow of French money. The Russians wanted a return to the circumstances of 1895, when France and Germany, themselves at loggerheads, competed for Russian favour. Therefore Nicholas II proposed to 'initiate' the French into the alliance before it was signed.[1] If they agreed, all would be well; if they refused and so wrecked the project, they would at least be under a moral obligation to scare the British into being more friendly to Russia.

The negotiations reached deadlock. The Russians wished to strengthen their position in the Far East without making Germany supreme in Europe; the Germans wished to gain security in Europe without becoming involved in the Far East. It was the worst possible moment for German policy to turn against Great Britain. The British had just taken the first serious steps to build up their naval power in the North Sea, and the Germans even imagined that the British might use their power to

[1] Nicholas II to William II, 7, 23 Nov. 1904. *Große Politik*, xix (i), nos. 6124, 6126.

make a preventive attack on the growing German fleet. The only wise course for the Germans was to avoid all conflict with the British until their fleet was stronger. As Bülow wrote to William II: 'Our position is like that of the Athenians when they had to build the long walls at the Piraeus without being prevented by the stronger Spartans from completing their defences'.[1] Yet an alliance with Russia must inevitably be anti-British. It could be tolerable only if the French were made to join or, alternatively, if the Franco-Russian alliance were destroyed. The Russians wanted neither of these things. They insisted that the French must be told before the alliance was signed; the Germans were equally insistent that it must be signed before the French were told. On 28 December William II wrote to Bülow: 'A completely negative result after two months of honest work and negotiations. The first failure which I have personally experienced.'[2] Previously the Germans had boasted of the advantages of the 'free hand'; now they came to realize that the contradictory needs of 'world policy' and continental strategy imposed the free hand on them, whether they would or no.

To some extent the German approach served Russia's turn. News of it reached Delcassé almost at once.[3] He seemed to be faced, like Napoleon III, by the choice between alliance with Russia and entente with Great Britain; like Napoleon III, but with more success, he was determined not to choose. He overwhelmed Lansdowne with promptings to conciliate the Russians;[4] and these, perhaps, did something to bring about a peaceful settlement of the Dogger Bank affair. The main reason for this was, however, simpler: neither the British nor the Russians were as eager for the conflict as both French and Germans supposed. The British wished only to keep out of the

[1] Bülow to William II, 26 Dec. 1904. *Große Politik*, xix (ii), no. 6157.

[2] William II to Bülow, 28 Dec. 1904. Ibid., xix (i), no. 6146.

[3] Radolin, the German ambassador in Paris, said on 2 Nov.: 'France must choose between Russia and Germany or England.' Secret notes by Paléologue, 4 and 5 Nov. 1904. *Documents diplomatiques français*, second series, v, nos. 424, 425, 426. Since there is no reference to this in the German documents, it is impossible to tell whether Radolin was acting on instructions or on his own initiative.

[4] Paléologue, Delcassé's principal assistant, was sent to London to impress on Lansdowne that this was the greatest crisis in French policy since Sadova. Lansdowne, however, took these melodramatic remarks so lightly that he did not record them. Note by Paul Cambon, 7 Nov.; secret note by Paléologue, 8 Nov. 1904. Ibid., nos. 433, 434.

Far Eastern war; and they were confident that they could check Russia in Persia and Afganistan without serious dispute. The Russians were weary of the Far East, which had become in the last year or two merely a court folly. Bezobrazov and his 'circle' had lost all influence. The foreign office, the sensible soldiers, and the great capitalists were once more in control; and they, far from wishing to extend the Far Eastern war, were anxious to end it on any terms not blatantly humiliating. They attached little importance to alliance with Germany, and much to not being at her mercy. The experiences of Bismarck's time had bitten deep in their recollection. Yet from him they had asked only neutrality; the price of active German support would, they knew, be much higher.

The British did not consider Germany one way or the other. They did not need her support; they did not suspect her enmity. The Dogger Bank affair marked, indeed, the end of an epoch in European history—the epoch in which an Anglo-Russian conflict seemed the most likely outcome of international relations. This conflict had been expected in the Near East for fifty years, in central Asia for twenty, and in the Far East, with the greatest likelihood of all, for ten. After November 1904 the conflict was indefinitely postponed. The British had settled their differences with France; they had escaped war with Russia. Their security, and therewith their isolation from continental affairs, seemed at its height. A few journalists raised the cry that a new danger was approaching from Germany. This cry was little regarded. The tradition of 'the natural alliance' died hard. Germany and Great Britain had no quarrels; only for this reason was there no entente between them. Liberal opinion looked with admiration at German industry and local government; Chamberlain was by no means the only radical who thought that Great Britain had more in common with Germany than with any other European Power. The trade rivalry which had made some stir ten years before was now less acute; Great Britain was entering on a new period of prosperity, much of which depended on German custom. The German navy was indeed becoming a serious factor in the maritime balance, but this was more than offset by other changes. The alliance with Japan had reduced British needs in the Far East; entente with France had reduced them in the Mediterranean; the bulk of the Russian fleet had been destroyed in the Far East, and the Black Sea remnant was in mutiny. In addition, the British had been building on a scale without previous parallel. In 1898, when their isolation was first aired, they could only set twenty-nine battleships against a Franco-Russian total of twenty-eight; Germany's thirteen, though hardly up to modern war, did something to justify Tirpitz's risk theory—ironically enough, before it was applied. At the beginning of 1905 the British had forty-four battleships. The French had twelve, the Germans sixteen; the Russians did not count. In other words, the British enjoyed a naval supremacy without parallel in their history and could have taken on 'the continental league', if one had ever existed, almost without serious mobilization. Isolation, far from dwindling, reached its peak. Yet within twelve months the British would be seriously considering sending an expeditionary force to the Continent for the first time since 1864. This was not the culmination of a policy slowly evolved. It was a revolution, and one unexpected by all observers.

XIX

THE FORMATION OF THE TRIPLE ENTENTE

1905-9

IN 1905 there took place a revolution in European affairs. This was caused neither by Delcassé nor by British statesmen fearful of isolation. It was caused solely by German initiative. The Germans were not in any danger; in fact they, too, enjoyed greater security than at any time since the Crimean war and the breakdown of the Holy Alliance. The Russian army, crippled by the Far Eastern war, could not face even a defensive war in Europe; Russia herself was in revolution. Pacific radicals were in power in France; and the French generals did not believe that they could keep the Germans out of Paris for more than a month. Nevertheless, the Germans had come to count on a conflict between Great Britain and Russia; when this failed to take place, they sought a substitute, and this could only be 'the continental league'. Though they still talked of security, this preoccupation was fraudulent; their real object, not formulated even in their own minds, was to establish peacefully their predominance over the Continent and thus be free to challenge the British empire overseas. In the autumn of 1904 they had believed themselves within sight of an alliance with Russia; the Russians had refused to make it without French approval. Now, if France could be forced into dependence on Germany, Russia would have to enter the continental league or be herself excluded from European affairs. The moment seemed favourable. The French armies were in a bad state, and Russia could do nothing to help her ally. Port Arthur fell on 1 January 1905; and the Russians lost the prolonged battle of Mukden early in March. At home Russia was in chaos. Revolution broke out in January and mounted steadily until the climax of October. Russia had ceased to exist as a Great Power; and the Germans had an opportunity without parallel to change the European Balance in their favour.

It was also a gain for the Germans (though they do not seem to have appreciated it) that Rouvier became prime minister of France in January. He disliked Delcassé's foreign policy, wished to end the Moroccan affair, and instead to co-operate with Germany in the Bagdad railway.[1] The Germans had no clear idea what they meant to do when they butted into Morocco. They wished to show that Germany could not be ignored in any question in the world. More vaguely, they hoped to weaken the Anglo-French entente or perhaps to shake the Franco-Russian alliance. But essentially they speculated on some undefined success. They complained that they had not been officially informed of the Anglo-French agreement over Morocco, as though nothing could happen in the world without their permission. They therefore insisted on treating Morocco as an independent country, much as they had treated the Transvaal in 1896, and William II announced this publicly when, much against his will, he landed at Tangier on 31 March 1905. The Germans had given as little thought to the consequences of this action as they had to those of the Kruger telegram. Holstein may have consulted Schlieffen, the chief-of-staff, with whom he was well acquainted; and if he did, he must have learnt—what was indeed obvious enough—that the military position was all to Germany's advantage. But there is no scrap of contemporary evidence that he consciously planned to force France into war; and it seems more likely that, having talked so long of German power, he invoked it without any clear idea of what would happen next. After all, it was more than a generation since there had been a serious war-crisis on the continent of Europe outside the Balkans. As to Bülow, he was satisfied by the argument that the stroke would improve Germany's prestige—and his own; and William II was dragged reluctantly along, always hoping that he might win France for the continental league by some twist of conciliation.

The Tangier visit caught Delcassé unprepared. It has been

[1] According to Paul Cambon, Rouvier had a personal reason for his dislike of Delcassé, who, in hope of peace, had insisted till the last minute that there would be no war between Russia and Japan. Rouvier had speculated on a rise in Russian bonds and lost heavily when they fell. Paul Cambon to Henri Cambon, 29 Apr. 1905. Cambon, *Correspondance*, ii. 188. Delcassé, on the other hand, thought Rouvier 'the man who would sell France for a speculation on the Stock Exchange'. Paléologue, *The Turning Point*, p. 237.

made a serious charge against him, even by so detached a historian as Renouvin,[1] that his foreign policy outran France's material resources: he challenged Germany when the French army was in no state to resist her. But in 1904, when the Anglo-French entente was made, it was impossible to foresee this danger. French policy then had feared the consequences of the entente on Russia, not on Germany; and the Moroccan crisis was provoked only by the surprising developments in the Far East. Even now Delcassé was pulled two ways. He had to tolerate a 'forward' policy in Morocco in order to satisfy the French colonial enthusiasts, who would otherwise turn against the entente; at the same time he had to conciliate Germany. He offered again and again to maintain 'the open door'—the only point on which Germany might claim to be considered; if he had ever got negotiations started he might also have offered her colonial concessions elsewhere—perhaps by reviving the Anglo-German arrangement over the Portuguese colonies with French approval. These offers would have ended the crisis; the Germans therefore ignored them. Besides, they could not consider colonial gains, in view of the temporary unpopularity of colonies in Germany. They therefore demanded that the question of Morocco should be submitted to an international conference. Holstein assumed that Italy and Austria-Hungary would support Germany, Russia would do nothing to offend her, the United States would support the open door, and both Great Britain and Spain would be glad to escape from the concessions that they had promised to France. He concluded: 'It is most unlikely that a conference will give Morocco to France against the vote of Germany and America.'[2] Bülow seconded him: 'It is out of the question that the conference should result in a majority handing over Morocco to France.'[3] The conference was demanded as a demonstration of German power, not as a means of settling the Moroccan question; and once the Germans sensed their power, they largely forgot that they had appealed to it in order to get on closer terms with France. Diplomatic victory became an end in itself.

The Germans had overlooked Delcassé's preparations. The

[1] Renouvin, *La paix armée et la grande guerre*, p. 485.
[2] Memorandum by Holstein, 4 Apr. 1905. *Große Politik*, xx (ii), no. 6601.
[3] Bülow to Kühlmann (Tangier), 6 Apr. 1905. Ibid., no. 6604.

proposal for a conference, far from displaying French isolation, compelled the interested Powers to acknowledge their commitments to France. Italy, Spain, and Great Britain could not accept a conference, unless France agreed to it first; even the United States had no intention of taking sides between France and Germany. The Germans had meant to turn the French flank; instead they were forced back into intimidating her. At the end of April an unexpected door was opened to them. Delcassé had at last realized Rouvier's hostility. On 19 April he resigned, and withdrew his resignation only when he had forced from Rouvier an expression of confidence. The expression was insincere. Rouvier was a man of strong character, though ignorant of foreign affairs. Years before he had broken Boulanger in the interest of peace with Germany; now he meant to break Delcassé. He was convinced that Delcassé was leading France to war and that this would bring defeat and, even worse, social upheaval—'the Commune' over again. He was also convinced that the Germans would welcome economic collaboration with France, once Delcassé was overthrown. On 26 April he revealed his intentions to Radolin, the German ambassador.[1] Henceforth the Germans had a policy provided for them: they had only to screw up the tension, and Delcassé would fall—then France would be reconciled with Germany. Though no serious military preparations were made, war was threatened; and Delcassé's conciliatory offers were brushed aside.

The British had at first taken a negative, aloof attitude: they would give France whatever diplomatic support she needed. They thought that the affair was purely a question of Morocco; 'grand policy' and the Balance of Power did not enter into their calculations, and it never occurred to them that the independence of France was essential to British security. Their only anxiety was that the French might buy Germany off with a port on the Atlantic coast of Morocco, probably Rabat; and, since much of the British fleet was being moved to the North Sea, this would have raised an awkward strategical problem. On 22 April Lansdowne was prepared to offer 'strong opposition' to the Germans acquiring a Moorish port;[2] and on 17 May he said that the British and French governments 'should con-

---

[1] Radolin to foreign ministry, 27 Apr. 1905. *Große Politik*, xx (ii), no. 6635.
[2] Lansdowne to Bertie, 22 Apr. 1905. *British Documents*, iii, no. 90.

tinue to treat one another with the most absolute confidence, should keep one another fully informed on everything which came to their knowledge, and should, so far as possible, discuss in advance any contingencies by which they might in the course of events find themselves confronted'.[1] This was not an offer of an alliance, nor even of military support; it was a warning that France could not make any concession to Germany without British approval. Delcassé, however, exploited Lansdowne's words in the domestic conflict that he was fighting with Rouvier. He insisted that the British were offering an alliance and that, if it were rejected, they would turn to Germany—'then we shall be isolated, exposed to an attack, in danger of losing the battle in Europe, and of being in time stripped of our colonies.' Rouvier answered that the German threats were real: 'Are we in a state to make war? clearly no.'[2] Both arguments were remote from the facts. The British were not offering an alliance, nor did they mean to turn to Germany; the German army would not be equipped for war until June 1906, as the French experts recognized,[3] and, for that matter, Rouvier himself later defied German threats when it suited his purpose. As so often, men fought with misleading phrases, handled false coin. The underlying issue was real all the same—whether France should hold aloof from Germany or be reconciled to her. On 6 June the French council of ministers decided against Delcassé, and he resigned. On the same day, William II created Bülow a prince. It was the greatest German victory since Sedan.

The victory was, however, only one of prestige; it still had to be put to some practical use. Rouvier was eager to subscribe the French capital for the Bagdad railway which had been refused in 1903; and he supposed that in return the Germans would give him a free hand in Morocco. Though his policy might be compatible with the Anglo-French entente, it would certainly have disrupted the Franco-Russian alliance—a far greater score for Germany. But Germany, in the hey-day of imperialist schemes and with a new naval programme in the offing, wanted a continental league with Russia, not a combination

[1] Lansdowne to Bertie, 17 May 1905. *British Documents*, iii, no. 94.
[2] Note by Chaumié on the council of ministers, 6 June 1905. *Documents diplomatiques français*, second series, vi, annexe I.
[3] Berteaux (minister of war) to Delcassé, 27 May 1905. Ibid., no. 457.

of the western Powers against her. Besides, Bülow and Holstein were the prisoners of their own publicity. Having once
insisted on a conference over Morocco, they could not now
go back on it; though they dreamt vaguely of partitioning
Morocco at some time in the future, they had to insist on its
independence in the present. Rouvier therefore had to renew
the diplomatic struggle in a weaker position—without friends
or allies, and having announced in advance France's inability
to fight. Time and again he held out the prospect of French
friendship, if only the Germans would turn their backs on
Morocco; time and again the Germans refused. On 8 July
Rouvier gave way and agreed to the German demands: an
international conference should be held to provide for the
security and independence of Morocco. This was a grave defeat
for French diplomacy. Delcassé had worked to remove Morocco
from the field of international relations; Rouvier had had to
put it back there more formally than before. But the Germans
paid too high a price for their success: they estranged their
friends in France. Rouvier's faith in collaboration with Germany was destroyed; pacific radical finance was forced along
the anti-German path.

Tension suddenly relaxed, and for an unexpected reason.
The Russian defeat in the Far East was now complete—her
last fleet destroyed at Tsushima on 27 May. Witte shouldered
the task of making peace with Japan under American mediation. The time seemed ripe for William II to reassert himself.
Though he too wanted a continental league, he hoped to get
it by conciliating Russia, not by threatening France; besides,
the Russian revolution stirred his monarchical conscience, as
also the anxiety of German capitalists who were building the
industry of the Ukraine, and he wished to bolster up the tsar's
prestige. On 24 July he and Nicholas II met at Björkö; and
Nicholas II was cajoled into signing a defensive alliance against
attack by any European Power.[1] William II brushed aside the
difficulty from France which had been insuperable the previous

---

[1] At the last moment, William II added that mutual aid was only to be given
'in Europe'. His intention was to avoid sending German troops to India and so of
ensuring that the Russians would do all the fighting. Bülow, piqued that William II had pulled off the great stroke in his absence, used this addition as an
excuse for threatening to resign; but this was purely a personal quarrel, and the
Germans, led by Holstein, recognized that, in Europe or outside it, the alliance
was a decisive success.

autumn: the question of Morocco, he said, was settled and now 'we shall be good friends of the Gauls'.[1] Nicholas II wanted to show his resentment against the British and, although the alliance was only to come into operation when peace was made between Russia and Japan, hoped that it would somehow help him during the peace negotiations.

For a few weeks the Germans supposed that they had attained their goal: alliance with Russia was made, and the continental league would follow. There was no point in making further difficulties over Morocco; on the contrary, France should be conciliated in order to prepare her for the revelation of the Björko treaty. Holstein opposed this policy: he wished to define the programme of the coming Moroccan conference so closely as to ensure the defeat of France in advance. Bülow overruled him: 'all that matters is to get out of this muddle over Morocco so as to preserve our prestige in the world and to take account of German economic and financial interests as far as possible.'[2] Holstein went sulkily on holiday; and the programme for the conference, to which France and Germany agreed on 30 September, left the future of Morocco to be settled by the conference itself. The Germans gratuitously cleared the way for their own failure the following year. They could go from success to success so long as they negotiated with France alone; if they had pressed their advantage in July they could have imposed on France a conference which would simply have given a formal registration to the defeat of Delcassé's plans. By agreeing to a genuine conference they exposed themselves to the risk of a diplomatic coalition. Their mistake was in large part that of all those who appeal to international conferences: they imagined that somewhere there was an impartial 'world opinion', which would be voiced by the supposedly neutral powers. But their mistake was fortified by the belief, after Björko, that the continental league was as good as made and that there was in consequence no further need to break the French nerve.

Instead the treaty of Björkö and all the paper structure that followed from it crumbled away over-night. On the Russian side it had sprung from the tsar's resentment against Great Britain and a vague hope of reinsurance in case the Far Eastern war was renewed. But on 5 September Witte made peace with

[1] William II to Bülow, 25 July 1905. *Große Politik*, xix (ii), no. 6220.
[2] Bülow to foreign ministry, 8 Sept. 1905. Ibid., xx (ii), no. 6803.

the Japanese on America's mediation. The Japanese were exhausted, and the peace gave the Russians everything which their moderate men had always wanted: though the Japanese would control Korea they did not claim Manchuria. A war of revenge by Russia would have no serious purpose. Besides, such a war was ruled out by the changes made in the Anglo-Japanese alliance, when it was renewed on 12 August: the alliance was extended to cover India and henceforth it would operate against attack by one Power, instead of by two. Unconsciously, the alliance gave a decisive answer to the treaty of Björko. The German threat could no longer keep Great Britain neutral in a second Russo-Japanese war—she was pledged to intervene in any case. Nor could Russia plan to attack the British in India with German backing, for Japan in her turn was then pledged to intervene. Finally and decisively, the Russian government needed new French loans to drown the revolution and to repair the damage of the war; they dared not threaten France, still less confirm the German alliance without her. France was the rock—somewhat flaky, but a rock all the same—on which the German schemes broke. Though Rouvier had wanted good relations with Germany, he no more intended to enter a continental league against Great Britain than he had endorsed Delcassé's plans for a supposed British alliance; and, in any case, by the autumn his negotiations with Germany had made him feel that Delcassé was perhaps right after all. The Paris Bourse made a stronger appeal than monarchical solidarity; and Nicholas II had to undo his own work. He wrote on 7 October: 'I think that the coming into force of the Björkö treaty ought to be put off until we know how France will look at it;[1] and on 23 November: 'Russia has no reasons to abandon her ally nor suddenly to violate her.'[2] He tried to save appearances by proposing that the Björkö alliance should not apply in case of war with France; in reality the scheme was dead. The Russians had no interest in reconciling Germany and France, still less in making an exclusive alliance with Germany, which would inevitably provoke in its turn a 'Crimean coalition'.

Morocco returned to the centre of the stage. The Germans had no idea what to do with it. Bülow laid down: 'we could not

[1] Nicholas II to William II, 7 Oct. 1905. *Große Politik*, xix (ii), no. 6247.
[2] Nicholas II to William II, 23 Nov. 1905. Ibid., no. 6254.

tolerate a diplomatic triumph for France and would rather let
things come to a conflict',[1] but he made no military preparations. He did not even discuss Morocco with other Powers—
apparently the conference was to defeat France automatically
without any German initiative. It was twenty years since an
international dispute had been referred to a general meeting
of the Powers; and since that time men had forgotten the lesson
of the congress of Berlin that such a meeting succeeds only if
the broad lines of agreement have been settled beforehand. The
French, too, had no clear-cut plans for the conference; but at
least they had agreements over Morocco with Great Britain,
Italy, and Spain, to say nothing of their alliance with Russia.
Besides, they had recovered from their panic of June. It had
suited Rouvier to emphasize the danger from Germany so
long as he was bent on a Franco-German *rapprochement*; he
grew as confident as Delcassé, or even more so, once this ceased
to interest him.[2] And this new obstinacy against Germany,
oddly enough, turned Rouvier, the man who had never believed
in the Anglo-French entente, into the man who made it a
reality. The fall of Delcassé had shaken British faith in France;
Lansdowne declared it 'was disgusting'.[3] But he blamed
French feebleness rather than German bullying; and he drew
the moral that France was useless as a partner, not that Germany should be resisted. The ending of the Russo-Japanese
war also made the entente less necessary; and there was very
little contact between Great Britain and France in the autumn
of 1905.

The entente was revived by the third partner in the affairs
of Morocco—Spain. The Spaniards were always sharply aware
of their weakness and always fearful that France might sacrifice
their claims in Morocco to Germany for the sake of her own.
In December Alfonso XIII, the king of Spain, alleged that the
Germans were trying to win him over.[4] His real intention was,

[1] Memorandum by Mühlberg, 25 Dec. 1905. *Große Politik*, xxi (i), no. 6914.

[2] The French nerve was strengthened by one of those odd misunderstandings
which are common in diplomacy. They had supposed that William II was bellicose
and Bülow pacific. This was the reverse of the truth. William II hated the Moroccan affair and Bülow was merely being 'pomadig'. In the autumn of 1905, some
of William's pacific remarks reached the French; and they concluded, quite
wrongly, that the leading advocate of war had changed his mind.

[3] Newton, *Lord Lansdowne*, p. 341.

[4] Margerie (Madrid) to Rouvier, 14 Dec. 1905. *Documents diplomatiques francais*,
second series, viii, no. 227.

no doubt, to extract a new promise of support from the French or to be free to go over to the German side if they refused. The French always resented these Spanish importunities: Spain, they held, was England's affair, and Paul Cambon discussed the Spanish alarm with Edward VII.[1] A liberal government had just taken office in England; and Edward VII saw his opportunity to commit it to a firm foreign policy. Sir Edward Grey, the new foreign secretary, had served under Rosebery at the time of greatest tension with France and Russia. He had known well 'the very disagreeable experience' of having to rely upon Germany for a support that was rarely forthcoming. He held that it was 'a matter of interest as well as a point of honour' to preserve the entente with France.[2] Moreover, though there was no recognized difference over foreign policy between the two British parties, the unionists, being in office, had tended to accept 'the natural alliance' with Germany as a matter of day-to-day practice; and the liberals, being in opposition, had stressed the advantages of better relations with France and Russia. Grey had inherited something of Gladstone's moral earnestness; and the 'Concert of Europe' meant more to him than it had done to his predecessors. Lansdowne had regarded German roughness with a diplomat's finesse; Grey's north-country sturdiness was outraged by it.

There was a further consideration, which played a vital part in determining Grey's foreign policy. The unity of the liberal party had only just been restored after a long period of conflict and weakness. Liberal imperialists—Grey, Asquith, Haldane—had joined with radical 'pro-Boers', such as Morley and Lloyd George, under the leadership of Campbell-Bannerman to win the greatest electoral victory since the Reform Bill. Grey would do nothing to shake this unity by any step in foreign policy, unless it were absolutely necessary. On the other hand, as often happens when a party of the Left takes office, he was anxious to show that he could be as firm and realistic as any conservative; and the staff of the foreign office were soon expressing their 'agreeable surprise'. Grey evolved a satisfactory compromise, no doubt without conscious thought. He followed a resolute line—more resolute indeed than Lansdowne's; but he consulted the cabinet very little, and he in-

---

[1] Paul Cambon to Rouvier, 21 Dec. 1905. *Documents diplomatiques français*, second series, viii, no. 262.   [2] Grey, *Twenty-Five Years*, i. 104.

formed the public hardly at all. The Balance of Power was a concept alien to the mind of most liberals, and Grey himself often repudiated the phrase. Yet, in reality, he was concerned about the European Balance in a way that no British foreign secretary had been since Palmerston. He endorsed the opinion of his leading adviser: 'if France is left in the lurch an agreement or alliance between France, Germany and Russia in the near future is certain.'[1] His underlying object was to prevent 'the continental league' and the German domination that would follow from it; therefore he had to encourage France and, later, Russia, in their efforts to preserve their independence. On the other hand, he had to keep his hands free in order to keep the liberal party united. His policy was throughout determined by these two considerations. Immediately on entering office, he laid down the line that he was to follow, more or less consistently, for the next eight years: he warned Germany without committing himself to France. He told Metternich on 3 January 1906: 'the British people would not tolerate France's being involved in a war with Germany because of the Anglo-French agreement and in that case any English government, whether Conservative or Liberal, would be forced to help France.'[2]

It was more difficult to answer Cambon when he talked of the danger of German aggression. In earlier days, British governments had satisfied their friends by sending the fleet on a visit to the Straits or to some Italian port; now the fleet was of no use to France—as Rouvier had said earlier, 'it could not run on wheels'. Grey hit on a new device. On 31 January 1906 he authorized conversations between the British and French general staffs; but, as in his opinion no question of policy was involved, he did not inform the cabinet.[3] Grey held, indeed, that he had actually increased British freedom of action. It was universally believed that the decisive battle of the next war would be fought within the first month; therefore Great

---

[1] Minute by Hardinge on memorandum by Grey, 20 Feb. 1906. *British Documents*, iii, no. 299.

[2] Metternich to Bülow, 3 Jan. 1906. *Große Politik*, xxi (i), no. 6923.

[3] Grey was later ashamed of this neglect and made out that it was an accident. It was, in fact, deliberate. Grey and Campbell-Bannerman so decided, after consulting Edward VII, so as not to alarm the radicals. 'Certain ministers would be astonished at the opening of such talks . . . it was better to keep silent and continue preparations discreetly.' Paul Cambon to Rouvier, 31 Jan. 1906. *Documents diplomatiques français*, second series, ix (i), no. 106.

Britain could help France only if plans were already prepared. In Grey's own words: 'We must be free to go to the help of France as well as free to stand aside. . . . If there were no military plans made beforehand we should be unable to come to the assistance of France in time. . . . We should in effect not have preserved our freedom to help France, but have cut ourselves off from the possibility of doing so.'[1]

This was a good argument. But it would not have appealed to the radicals in the British cabinet; and that for a simple reason. However strong the technical justification, the military talks were a political act. There was no pressing danger of war in January 1906, despite the Spanish alarm; and the Moroccan affair was, in fact, fought out at Algeçiras purely with diplomatic weapons. Though the French accepted Grey's statement that 'no British government will ever commit itself on a hypothesis', the talks were the substitute for an alliance—and in some ways a more decisive one. Once the British envisaged entering a continental war, however remotely, they were bound to treat the independence of France, not the future of Morocco, as the determining factor. The European Balance of Power, which had been ignored for forty years, again dominated British foreign policy; and henceforth every German move was interpreted as a bid for continental hegemony. Whether such suspicions were justified or not, they could not easily be eradicated once they had been formed; exactly the same had been true, for instance, of the designs which the Russians had been supposed, for many years, to harbour against Turkey. No Russian assurances could remove these suspicions in the one case; no German assurances would remove them in the other. A vital change of emphasis followed. Though imperial interests still counted from Morocco to Persia, they had henceforth to be fitted into the framework of relations with the European Powers, instead of determining them, as they had done previously. In Salisbury's time, Great Britain made arrangements with European Powers in order to defend her empire; now she made concessions outside Europe in order to strengthen the Balance of Power. On the French side, the talks counted for less. The French did not take the British army seriously and assumed even till 1914 that they would have to hold the German attack on their own. They would gladly compromise with Germany if it could be done

[1] Grey, *Twenty-Five Years*, i. 75.

at any price less than the end of their independence as a
Great Power; but when this proved impossible, they were
grateful enough for British diplomatic support. If it came to a
war, Russia was their only hope; and they knew that they
would have to wait for many years before she was fit to take
on Germany—in 1906 she could not even face war against
Austria-Hungary with any confidence.[1]

The Moroccan conference met at Algeçiras on 16 January.[2]
The Germans wanted to assert the independence of Morocco;
the French to lay hold of the Moroccan bank and the police.
For six weeks there was deadlock: neither France nor the
Powers pledged to her would take the initiative in provoking
German resentment. On 3 March a vote over future procedure
revealed that only Austria-Hungary and Morocco supported
Germany. Bülow lost his nerve. He took over the conduct of
affairs from Holstein, who left office within a fortnight, and
agreed to the French demands: the agreement, signed on
31 March, gave them control of the police, with Spain as a
junior partner. On 5 April Bülow, defending his policy in the
Reichstag, had a heart-attack and was out of action for some
months—as symbolic in its way as the title of prince he had
received ten months before. Algeçiras defeated the German
plan of reducing France to subordination without a war. Holstein, indeed, made out that he would have risked even war
and complained that he had misjudged 'the leading personali-
ties': 'I ought to have realised that it would be difficult to
make Bülow, and impossible to make His Majesty, resolve on
the last resort.'[3] This was a short-sighted explanation. Holstein,
neglecting public opinion, had played at 'cabinet-diplomacy';
and Bülow saw more clearly when he recognized that 'the
German people would not understand a war for the sake of
Morocco'.[4] They had to be educated into believing that they
were 'encircled', just as everyone else had to be educated

---

[1] Moulin (St. Petersburg) to Étienne (minister of war), 27 Jan. 1906. *Documents
diplomatiques français*, second series, ix (i), no. 77.

[2] No doubt much to the satisfaction of the Spanish delegate, who owned the
principal hotel. The conference was attended by the Great Powers and by those
interested in Moorish trade (Germany, Austria-Hungary, Belgium, Spain, the
United States, France, Great Britain, Italy, Morocco, Holland, Portugal, Russia,
and Sweden).

[3] Lancken, *Meine dreißig Dienstjahre*, p. 55.

[4] Bülow to Speck von Sternburg (Washington), 19 Mar. 1906. *Große Politik*,
xxi (i), no. 7118.

into believing that Germany was threatening to dominate
them. Even Bismarck had had to prepare his wars; this was
even more necessary in the age of mass-parties and conscript
armies.

The French flattered themselves that Algeçiras had been a
demonstration of the Concert of Europe against dictation by a
single Power.[1] This, too, was an exaggeration. Though the act
of Algeçiras kept the door open for the French, they could not
enter it. Previously the Germans had no standing in Morocco,
except as a Great Power; now they could claim to be paid if
France exceeded the rights given her at Algeçiras. Nor did the
conference really demonstrate the Concert of Europe. None of
the Powers, except to some extent the British, thought in terms
of resisting German dictation. Rather they grudgingly honoured
the bargains which they had made with Delcassé;[2] and both
Italy and Spain were resentful at having been manœuvred into
taking sides in a Franco-German quarrel. Even in England
few people were convinced that the Balance of Power had been
at stake. Eyre Crowe, a member of the foreign office, wrote a
powerful memorandum towards the end of the year, in which
he argued that Germany was bidding for the mastery of Europe;
but most Englishmen regarded Morocco as an unfortunate
accident which had interrupted the even run of Anglo-German
relations. Metternich wrote in August: 'English policy is
founded on co-operation with France. . . . Only if English
policy succeeds in making a Franco-German agreement will
English friendship become politically useful for us.'[3] British
statesmen would have agreed with Metternich that only the
Franco-German dispute over Morocco estranged their two
countries.

The conflict over Morocco which ran from William II's
Tangier visit until the end of the Algeçiras conference gave a

[1] Billy, report, 1 May 1906. *Documents diplomatiques français*, second series, ix (ii),
appendix, p. 993.
[2] The Russians had to be kept firm by the French refusal to allow a loan until
the conference was successfully concluded. Grey tried to press a compromise on
the French at exactly the moment when Bülow's nerve broke. Bertie, British
ambassador at Paris, revealed this move to the French press and then quoted the
protests as proof that compromise was impossible. Grey had to insist that he was
not deserting France; and this, in its turn, led the French government to suppose
that he was urging them not to yield. At the crisis it was touch-and-go: if Holstein
had kept his hands on affairs for another week, the French would have given way.
[3] Metternich to Bülow, 23 Aug. 1906. *Große Politik*, xxi (ii), no. 7198.

first hint of things to come and foreshadowed the world war. But it was only a hint and a shadow. The threat of war was made only in discreet private conversations, whether by Bülow or Grey; no practical steps were taken towards war—no men were mobilized, no ships sent to their action-stations. Yet it was a true 'crisis', a turning-point in European history. It shattered the long Bismarckian peace. War between France and Germany was seriously, though remotely, contemplated for the first time since 1875; the Russians had to envisage for the first time honouring their engagements under the Franco-Russian alliance—and did not like the prospect; the British contemplated military intervention on the Continent for the first time since 1864. None of this reached the public ear or affected public opinion. Even the statesmen pretended that nothing had happened. Those who had opposed German policy at Algeçiras declared that they had meant no harm. The military talks between Great Britain and France died away and were forgotten. The Italians paraded their loyalty to the Triple Alliance. They agreed, for instance, to its renewal (due in 1907) prematurely, without cancelling the military convention directed against France and even without reviving the original declaration of 1882 that the Alliance could never operate against Great Britain.[1] Both the British and the Russians made gestures of friendship. Haldane, the British secretary for war, allowed himself to be trapped into visiting the German army on the anniversary of Sedan;[2] and Izvolski, the new Russian foreign minister, came to Berlin in October, while refusing to visit London.

Nevertheless, the great event in the period after Algeçiras was a further blow to Germany; it was the reconciliation between Great Britain and Russia. Hostility to Germany was not the primary motive. Grey, it is true, had argued during the conference of Algeçiras that the moment was ill chosen for resisting Germany and that they should wait until he had

---

[1] The Germans had no faith in Italy, but renewed the alliance so as not to seem dependent solely on Austria-Hungary. Bülow wrote: 'We must let the Austrians notice our relative political isolation as little as possible.' Bülow to William II, 31 May 1906. *Große Politik*, xxi (ii), no. 7154.

[2] In January 1907 Haldane told Metternich: 'He did not know whether non-committal talks between English and French soldiers had taken place or not.' Metternich to Bülow, 31 Jan. 1907. Ibid., no. 7205. Haldane had, of course, been kept fully informed by Grey.

reached agreement with Russia: 'An entente between Russia, France and ourselves would be absolutely secure. If it is necessary to check Germany it could then be done.'[1] The Russians were alarmed by the Bagdad railway and, still more, by the first signs of German penetration into Persia. They feared an Anglo-German partnership in the Middle East at their expense, and therefore decided to compromise with both countries before it was too late. The defeat in the Far East had made the Russians more moderate and sensible than usual. Izvolski, who became foreign minister in May 1906, was an abler man than his immediate predecessors; vaguely liberal in outlook, he knew something of western Europe and was not bemused either by Slav sentiment or principles of monarchical solidarity. The practical Russian need in the Middle East was to have a neutral zone in front of their Caucasus frontier; in return for this, they would tolerate the Bagdad railway and divide control of Persia with the British.[2] The Russians were, however, far from taking sides between Germany and Great Britain; rather they wished to be on good terms with both countries, as ten years before they had been intimate with France and Germany at the same time. They had no reason to fear Germany in Europe. In 1905 the German army could have overrun Russia with the greatest ease; instead of threatening, the Germans had pressed their alliance on Russia and were now helping to build up her industrial strength. The Russians had, as yet, no conceivable cause for war with Germany except a German threat to destroy France,[3] and they would have been reluctant to go to war even for that. In 1906 and 1907 much the same was true of the British.

The Anglo-Russian entente had thus little to do with Germany. The British had wanted a compromise for years and had been working actively for it since 1903. It was the Russians who had changed their mood, just as the French change of mood caused the entente of 1904. The bargain was a limited

[1] Memorandum by Grey, 20 Feb. 1906. *British Documents*, iii, no. 299.
[2] Protocol of Russian council of ministers, 14 Feb. 1907. Siebert, *Graf Benckendorffs diplomatischer Schriftwechsel* (1928), no. 1.
[3] In Apr. 1906 the Russians agreed to drop the anti-British military conventions, which they had made with France in 1900 and 1901. They also agreed that there should be 'previous concert', and not action, if Italy or Austria-Hungary mobilized alone. Bourgeois to Bompard, 25 June 1906, enclosing *procès-verbal* of 21 Apr. *Documents diplomatiques français*, second series, x, no. 119.

one, confined—for all practical purposes—to Persia. The Far Eastern war had eliminated Anglo-Russian rivalry there. Izvolski originally intended to demand British pressure on Japan as the price for yielding over Persia, but this turned out to be unnecessary. The Japanese were willing to compromise without British pressure; and a Russo-Japanese agreement, virtually establishing a joint monopoly of Manchuria, was signed on 30 July 1907, before negotiations with Great Britain were ended. At the other end of Asia, Izvolski raised the question of the Straits during the discussions. This was purely a question of prestige. Russia had no Black Sea fleet, and the closing of the Straits suited her well enough. But ultimately Izvolski hoped to get theoretical permission for theoretical Russian warships to pass the Straits, in order to show that a 'liberal' foreign minister could do better than his reactionary predecessors. There was no strategical objection on the British side, only a fear that public opinion might be offended—'there would be a storm'. Grey answered that it would be easier to meet Russian wishes over the Straits when the entente had proved its worth elsewhere. 'Good relations with Russia meant that our old policy of closing the Straits against her, and throwing our weight against her at any conference of the Powers must be abandoned.'[1] Izvolski tried to interpret this as a promise of British support at some future conference, but Grey refused to commit himself: 'If negotiations now in progress lead to a satisfactory result, the effect upon British public opinion would be such as very much to facilitate a discussion of the Straits question if it came up later on.'[2] Though Izvolski claimed to be satisfied, there was here an equivocation which was to cause trouble in the following year.

The agreement, signed on 31 August 1907, eliminated two minor problems. Tibet was made a neutral buffer-state, and the Russians renounced direct contact with Afganistan, so that India had security on the north-west frontier. The essential bargain was over Persia. The north adjacent to the Caucasus was to be Russia's sphere of interest, the south-east, adjacent to India, was to be British; the centre, including the Gulf, was to be neutral. This division was purely strategical;[3] neither side

---

[1] Memorandum by Grey, 15 Mar. 1907. *British Documents*, iv, no. 257.
[2] Grey to Nicolson, 1 May 1907. Ibid., no. 268.
[3] A characteristic Russian trait; the chief-of-staff objected to giving up the

PERSIA

Anglo-Russian agreement
of August 31st 1907

CASPIAN
SEA

•Tehran

RUSSIAN SPHERE
OF INFLUENCE

AFGANISTAN

NEUTRAL SPHERE

BRITISH
SPHERE OF
INFLUENCE

PERSIAN GULF

Gulf of Oman

Miles
80 40 0   80   160   240

THE PARTITION OF PERSIA

mentioned or considered Persia's oil, and it was quite by accident that this turned out to be easy of access to the British. The
two Powers were concerned to deprive each other of strategical
advantages; excluding Germany was a secondary consideration,
and Izvolski had taken care to secure German approval before
he made the agreement. Of course the Germans could no
longer count on an Anglo-Russian war; but this had been true
since November 1904. On one subject the agreement brought
an immediate score to the Russians. When William II visited
England in the autumn of 1907, he again offered the British a
share in the Bagdad railway; and they would have liked to
accept it, in order to control the final stretch where the railway
reached the Persian gulf. But they were anxious to prove their
good faith to the Russians and therefore replied that they
could only discuss the railway *à quatre* with France and Russia.
The prospect of being outvoted three to one did not appeal to
the Germans, and they dropped the question. In later years
both French and Russians were to be less punctilious than
Grey had been: an obligation of honour is usually more onerous
than a formal pledge.

Still, this was not the decisive side of the entente. It was
essentially a settlement of differences, not a disguised alliance.
Its two great weaknesses sprang from causes inside Great Britain
and Russia, not from any German threat. On the one side the
Russians found it difficult to moderate their ambitions for long.
They soon slipped back into assuming that Russia was the
greatest, or even the only, Power in the world; and the temptation to cheat in Persia was increased by the fact that Teheran,
the capital, was in the Russian zone. Whatever the foreign
ministry said in St. Petersburg, the Russians at Teheran constantly encroached on Persia's independence. On the British
side, the entente stirred up imperialist, and still more radical,
opposition. Radical hostility to Russia was of long standing;
but in the old days there had been nothing to choose between Russia and the central Powers, and Gladstone had even
managed to create the impression that Russia was somehow

strategical threat to India and told Nicolson so openly. Yet he had neither soldiers
with which to implement this threat nor was there a railway on which to carry
them. Quite apart from this, Russia and Great Britain were supposed to be getting on friendly terms. Of course, the British refusal the following year to allow
Russian warships to pass the Straits was equally absurd, if they took the entente
seriously.

'Christian' in a way that Austria was not. As a result, when Salisbury worked with Austria-Hungary, he had had to disguise this by the link through 'liberal' Italy. Now Russia was clearly the most reactionary Power in Europe. The revolution of 1905 had aroused much sympathy in England; and even Campbell-Bannerman, the prime minister, had publicly lamented its defeat. On the other hand, the reputation of the two Germanic Powers had gone up. Austria had just established universal suffrage; and nothing was known in England of the Magyar tyranny in Hungary. Between 1907 and 1909 there was a Left majority in the German Reichstag, and Bülow posed as the chancellor of a liberal coalition. The entente with Russia seemed an unprincipled act of 'power politics', all the more so when the Russians worked against the parliament in Persia. Radical feeling turned even against France. Her association with Russia, instead of making Russia respectable, made France, too, appear reactionary and militaristic. French ambitions in Morocco were blamed for the crisis of 1905; and Germany was presented as a pacific Power, threatened by French longings for Alsace and Lorraine and by Russian designs in the Balkans and at the Straits. If the Germans had kept quiet, the 'triple entente' might soon have dissolved; instead their actions turned it into a reality.

In August 1907, when the entente was concluded, both British and Russians supposed that they had no quarrel with Germany except in regard to France. The Russians were pledged to defend French independence; the British were committed over Morocco. Neither appeared a dangerous issue. The Germans were no longer attempting to bring France into subordination; and the French were feeling their way towards a bargain with Germany over Morocco, by which they would get political supremacy in exchange for sharing the economic advantages. Jules Cambon, who went as ambassador to Berlin in July 1907, no doubt wished to rival his elder brother's achievements as a maker of ententes, and early began the negotiations which ultimately exploded in the crisis of 1911.

Before then the Moroccan question was eclipsed by un-expected German conflicts with Great Britain and Russia. One was the naval race; the other the Bosnian crisis. In neither case were these conflicts wholly of Germany's doing. Though the growing German navy must have estranged the British sooner or later, until 1906 any serious challenge still lay in the remote future. In 1906 the British admiralty launched the *Dreadnought*, the first all-big-gun ship; this made all existing battleships, including the British, obsolete. The British had to start the naval race all over again, at much less advantage and a race more expensive than ever before. In 1907 they tried to set an example to others by reducing their building-programme; instead this increased the temptation for the Germans to catch up. In November 1907 Tirpitz introduced a supplementary naval law, projecting a large programme of Dreadnought building. The British government had to increase their naval estimates in March 1908 and, still worse, looked forward to much greater increases the following year. This naval race seemed senseless to them. They were confident that they could win it, though at great expense. On the other hand, they had no quarrel with Germany (or so they supposed), and they could not understand her reluctance to have her overseas trade and colonies dependent on British goodwill. They could find a rational explanation of this German building only in a deliberate intention to destroy British independence. In reality, there was no rational explanation. The Germans had drifted into naval expansion, partly for reasons of domestic politics, partly from a general desire for grandeur. They certainly hoped that a great navy would make the British respect, and even fear, them; they never understood that, unless they could actually outbuild Great Britain, the only effect of this naval competition would be to estrange her.

The British had no solution for breaking the deadlock. Their only suggestion was that the Germans should voluntarily cut down their rate of building. This would lessen the tension and save money for both sides.[1] This proposal was made by Lloyd George, who had just become chancellor of the exchequer, in July 1908;[2] it was repeated with less sincerity by Hardinge, the permanent under-secretary, when he went with Edward VII

---

[1] The British never understood the political difference between the two countries. In England the taxpayers were also the ruling class; economy was of immediate benefit to them. In Germany the ruling class did not pay the taxes; economy brought them no advantage, but rather (since it reduced the contracts with which they kept the Reichstag sweet) increased their political difficulties. Further, the British naval programme was settled each March; the German was laid down for years ahead.

[2] Metternich to Bülow, 16 July, 1 Aug. 1908. *Große Politik*, xxiv, nos. 8217, 8219.

to visit William II in August.[1] The Germans gave a flat negative —William II with violence, Bülow and Metternich more evasively. The only attempt at an answer was that Great Britain would not fear the German fleet if she made an alliance with Germany. Bülow speculated vaguely that Germany might make some concessions in naval building if she received political concessions in return; no attempt was made at this time to work out what these should be. In the summer of 1908 estrangement between Great Britain and Germany was clear for all the world to see.

Though both France and Russia had certainly welcomed the ending of Anglo-German collaboration years before, they were alarmed at the prospect of being caught up in an Anglo-German conflict. Clemenceau, French prime minister from 1906 to 1909, was, of all Frenchmen, the most convinced adherent of co-operation with Great Britain; but he was also convinced that Germany would treat France as a hostage in case of war with her. He urged the British to concentrate on increasing their army,[2] and, in the meantime, tried to lessen the danger by conciliating the Germans over Morocco. Here, too, there was equivocation. The French wanted to get on better terms with Germany so as to mediate between her and their friends; the Germans would make concessions to France only if she deserted her friends. Bülow had laid this down in 1907: 'the only price for giving up our position in Morocco would be an alliance with France.'[3] The Russians were even more anxious not to commit themselves to either side. In June 1908 Edward VII and Nicholas II met at Reval, bringing Izvolski and Hardinge along with them. It was no doubt a symbol of reconciliation and, for that reason, much criticized by the British radicals; but the only practical outcome was agreement on a programme of reforms in Macedonia. Hardinge urged the Russians to

[1] Hardinge was mainly concerned to be able to prove to British politicians that a large naval programme was necessary. He wrote after his meeting with William II: 'I do not think it is to be regretted that a clear exposition of the views of the Government on the subject of naval armaments has been placed before the Emperor and the German Government, since their reply offers a complete justification to Parliament and to the world at large for any counter-measures that His Majesty's Government may decide upon taking in the near future.' Memorandum by Hardinge, 15 Aug. 1908. *British Documents*, vi, no. 116.

[2] Clemenceau to Pichon, 29 Aug. 1908. *Documents diplomatiques français*, second series, xi, no. 434; Goschen to Grey, 29 Aug. 1908. *British Documents*, vi, no. 100.

[3] Bülow to William II, 27 June 1907. *Große Politik*, xxi (ii), no. 7259.

build up their army so as to act as the arbiters of peace if a
critical situation arose 'in seven or eight years' time'. Izvolski
refused to be drawn: 'it was imperative that Russia should act
with the greatest prudence towards Germany, and give the
latter Power no cause for complaint that the improvement of
the relations of Russia and England had entailed a correspond-
ing deterioration of the relations of Russia with Germany'.[1]
Soon afterwards he told Clemenceau that there could be no
question of signing 'an Anglo-Franco-Russian agreement';[2] and
the Russian general staff insisted on an agreement with the
French that a German mobilization against Great Britain
would not bring the Franco-Russian alliance into operation.[3]

   This caution reflected Russia's weakness. She needed a long
period of peace and, having made herself secure in the Middle
and Far East, she could have it. The Austro-Russian agreement
of 1897 kept the Near East on ice; and it suited Russian interests
to keep it so. But Izvolski itched for some dramatic success.
On 3 February 1908 he proposed to the council of ministers
an Anglo-Russian military action against Turkey 'which might
lead to dazzling results'. The other ministers were horrified:
Russia had no money, no navy, no arms. Stolypin, the prime
minister, declared: 'only after some years of complete quiet
can Russia speak again as in the past'.[4] Izvolski ignored the
warning. He determined to play the game on his own and
secured the approval of Nicholas II for his plan of getting the
Straits open to Russian warships. Russia had no warships;
and the only bit of sense in the plan was that it would give
more work to the dockyards at Nikolayev, which were near the
iron-fields of the Ukraine. In any case, Izvolski was not interested in sense; he wanted a score.

   Russian action was hardly necessary to get the Near East on
the move. The Ottoman empire in Europe was breaking up of
itself. Macedonia was in chronic unrest, with a full-scale revolt
in 1903; attempts at international action served, as usual,

---

[1] Memorandum by Hardinge, 12 June 1908. *British Documents*, v, no. 195.

[2] Clemenceau to Pichon, 2 Sept. 1908. *Documents diplomatiques français*, second
series, xi, no. 441. Grey, too, disliked the term 'triple entente', though for a different
reason: 'if it appeared in a parliamentary Blue Book, it would be assumed to have
some special official meaning and might provoke inconvenient comment or en-
quiry'. Hardinge to Nicolson, 30 Apr. 1909, *British Documents*, ix (i) no. 7. Izvolski
feared Germany, Grey the British radicals in the house of commons.

[3] *Procès-verbal*, 24 Sept. 1908. *Documents diplomatiques français*, second series, xi,
no. 455.   [4] Pokrovski, *Drei Konferenzen*, pp. 17-31.

only to show the jealousy of the Powers. In July 1908 a Young Turk revolution ended the precarious tyranny of Abdul Hamid. Moreover, Austria-Hungary had made good use of the ten years when her entente with Russia put the Balkans on ice. Austrian capital penetrated deeply; and it looked as though Turkey-in-Europe would become a Habsburg sphere of interest, if things were left alone. But Austro-Hungarian policy was increasingly shaped by a vital domestic problem which defied Habsburg statesmanship. The South Slavs of the monarchy were becoming restive under Magyar oppression in Hungary; and since nothing could be done to shake the Magyar monopoly of power, the only 'solution' was to break the self-confidence of Serbia, the independent state which was regarded in Vienna as 'the Piedmont of the South Slavs'. This danger was largely imaginary. The Serbs had no Cavour, and all their historic traditions estranged them from the westernized Serbs and Croats of Austria-Hungary. Indeed, far from Serb ambition stimulating South Slav discontent, it was this discontent which dragged Serbia into Habsburg affairs. Once men imagine a danger they soon turn it into a reality. So it was now with Vienna and Belgrade. Austria-Hungary set out to destroy the independence of Serbia and so gave the Serbs no choice but to challenge the existence of Austria-Hungary.

The new line was symbolized by two personal changes in the autumn of 1906. Conrad succeeded Beck as chief-of-staff; Aehrenthal succeeded Goluchowski as foreign minister. Beck had been cautious, indeed timid, as military adviser; he doubted Austria-Hungary's capacity to fight a great war. Conrad was always ready to plan beyond the monarchy's resources. He wished to break the ring which was supposed to be closing round Austria-Hungary, and favoured war against either Serbia or Italy while Russia was still weak. The actual opponent mattered less than to display the monarchy's strength in war. For Conrad war was the solution in itself. Similarly Goluchowski had been content to keep things quiet. He had trailed along at Germany's heels during the Moroccan crisis; but he had insisted on a compromise at Algeçiras when things reached a deadlock. Aehrenthal, like Conrad, wanted to restore the prestige of the monarchy by some great stroke. He was arrogant, vain, impatient, eager for action. He had observed with satisfaction Germany's isolation at Algeçiras and, still more, her estrangement from Great Britain in 1908. He meant to turn this situation to his own advantage; Germany, he believed, would have to support Austria-Hungary, whatever action she undertook in the Balkans. He prided himself also on 'knowing Russia' (a common failing among diplomatists), and imagined that he could keep her in step by vague references to the League of the Three Emperors. His great stroke[1] was to be the annexation of Bosnia and Hercegovina, which the monarchy had administered since 1878; this would end Serb dreams of adding the two provinces to their national state[2] and, more vaguely, would enable the monarchy to show how beneficently it could govern a Slav people, when free from Magyar interference. Then, in a more remote future he planned to partition Serbia with Bulgaria.

Izvolski took the words out of Aehrenthal's mouth. On 2 July he offered to support the annexation of Bosnia and Hercegovina by Austria-Hungary, if she in return would support Russian designs at the Straits.[3] The two met at Buchlov[4] on 15 September and struck their bargain. Izvolski supposed that both questions, involving as they did changes in the treaty of Berlin, would have to be submitted to a European conference; and he went leisurely off to collect the approval of the other Powers. Aehrenthal, however, proclaimed the annexation of the two provinces on 5 October. Izvolski had just arrived in Paris, with nothing accomplished. To make matters worse, he was repudiated by his own government. Stolypin cared nothing for the Straits and much for Slav sentiment; he threatened to resign, and Nicholas II had to pretend that he knew nothing of Izvolski's schemes.[5] Izvolski still hoped to save himself by gaining something at the Straits. The French did not commit themselves one way or the other,[6] but as soon as Izvolski got to

[1] To be accurate, his first stroke was the project for a railway through the Sanjak of Novibazar, which had been in the military control of Austria-Hungary since 1878. This, too, was prestige-politics. The railway was impracticable; and Aehrenthal withdrew from the Sanjak when he annexed Bosnia and Hercegovina.

[2] Until 1912 everyone, including the Serbs, assumed that most of Macedonia was inhabited by Bulgarians. Therefore Bosnia and Hercegovina appeared more important to Serbia than they became in the later Jugoslavia.

[3] Russian *aide-mémoire*, 2 July 1908. *Österreich-Ungarns Außenpolitik*, i, no. 9.

[4] Obsolete German name: Buchlau.

[5] Charykov, *Glimpses of High Politics*, p. 269.

[6] It is often suggested that France, too, opposed the opening of the Straits. This is not so. Pichon 'expressed no opinion'. Bertie to Grey, 13 Oct. 1908. *British Documents*, v, no. 368.

London he ran into difficulties. British opinion supposed that, with the Young Turk revolution, Turkey had started on a liberal course, and therefore would do nothing to weaken her. More serious still, Grey's vague phrases of 1907 had assumed that the Russians would make a good impression by behaving well in Persia; instead they were already behaving badly, and obstinacy over the Straits seemed the only way of forcing them to keep their Persian bargain. Grey insisted that, if the rule of the Straits were revised, 'there must be some sort of reciprocity', that is, others must be allowed to enter the Black Sea on the same terms as those on which Russia could come out. No proposal could have been more repugnant to Russia. In any case, it was, as Hardinge admitted, 'a shop-window ware': 'it is already a settled principle of naval warfare with us that in no case would our fleets enter the Straits.'[1] The real obstacle was the radicals, not the admiralty. Asquith and Grey, supported by Edward VII, would have liked to make some concession to Izvolski; the cabinet thought only of the effect on public opinion and overruled them. All Izvolski got was an assurance from Grey that he would like to perform a miracle: 'I positively desire to see an arrangement made, which will open the Straits on terms which would be acceptable to Russia . . . while not placing Turkey or outside Powers at an unfair disadvantage.'[2] Izvolski had to change course. On his return to St. Petersburg he demanded that the annexation of Bosnia and Hercegovina be submitted to a conference and even presented himself as champion of the Serbs, a people of whom he had previously known nothing.

This put the affair on a different footing. Aehrenthal had intended to humiliate Serbia, not Russia; his references to the League of the Three Emperors had been genuine enough, and he had even hoped by his independent action in the Balkans to escape the satellite relationship towards Germany which Goluchowski had shown at Algeçiras. He had told the Germans nothing of the Buchlov bargain; and the annexation, by offending Turkey, cut clean across German interests in the Near East. The Germans, on their side, had almost forgotten Austria-Hungary in the preceding years—for instance, it occurred to none of them that the treaty of Björkö contradicted

---

[1] Hardinge to Nicolson, 13 Oct. 1908. *British Documents*, v, no. 372.
[2] Grey to Izvolski, 15 Oct. 1908. *British Documents*, v, no. 387.

their alliance with her as much as Russia's with France. Now they determined to stand by Austria-Hungary less to keep her firmly on their side than to humiliate Russia for having made an entente with Great Britain. Bülow laid down: 'Since Russia demonstratively joined England at Reval, we could not give up Austria. The European situation was so changed that we must be more reserved to Russian wishes than we used to be.'[1] The Germans went back at a bound to the policy of the 'new course', which Caprivi and Holstein had followed in 1891:[2] they promised to support Austria-Hungary in the Balkans whatever action she took. Bülow wrote to Aehrenthal on 30 October: 'I shall regard whatever decision you come to as the appropriate one';[3] and in January 1909 the nephew of the great Moltke, who had now become chief of the German general staff, wrote to Conrad with Bülow's approval: 'the moment Russia mobilizes, Germany also will mobilize, and will unquestionably mobilize her whole army'.[4] The men of the 'new course' had supposed that they were actually threatened by Russia; Bülow and Moltke knew that Russia was incapable of war—they were out to make a diplomatic score without effort.

Hostility to Russia logically implied conciliation of Great Britain and France, as in the reverse way the attack on Delcassé in 1905 had been balanced by the treaty of Björkö. Both countries were ready to respond: they had no desire to be involved in a Balkan war and hoped that Germany would join with them in mediating between Russia and Austria-Hungary. The German intention was quite other: it was to isolate Russia so that she could be humiliated at leisure. Then, in Bülow's words, 'the ring of encirclement which has long been weak will be destroyed for good'.[5] The Germans did not have much success with the British. Bülow edged towards offering them some naval concession, but failed to shake Tirpitz and shrank from a conflict. In any case, conciliating the British was a bad political card after the interview with William II (itself an attempt at conciliation) which the *Daily Telegraph* published on 28 October and after the unprecedented explosion of public

[1] Memorandum by Bülow, 27 Oct. 1908. *Große Politik*, xxvi (i), no. 9074.
[2] Holstein was, in fact, still Bülow's adviser and, on his death-bed, nominated Kiderlen as his successor.
[3] Bülow to Aehrenthal, 30 Oct. 1908. Ibid., no. 9079.
[4] Moltke to Conrad, 21 Jan. 1909. Conrad, *Aus meiner Dienstzeit*, i. 379.
[5] Bülow to Tschirschky (Vienna), 6 Feb. 1909. *Große Politik*, xxvi (ii), no. 9372.

opinion which this provoked in the Reichstag.[1] Besides, the British were not concerned to assert the Balance of Power by supporting Russia; they were outraged by Aehrenthal's offence against the sanctity of treaties just as they had been by Russia's denunciation of the Black Sea clauses in 1870 and, once mounted on the high horse of principle, they would not have got off it even for a reduction of the German naval programme.

Bülow did better with the French. They were a good deal more alarmed than the British and less high principled. They used their advantage to strike at last the bargain over Morocco which they had been hoping for since the summer of 1907. On 9 February 1909 France and Germany signed a declaration, by which Germany recognized France's political predominance in Morocco and the French promised not to injure Germany's economic interests. The same day Edward VII arrived in Berlin, and at the end of his visit, an official statement announced rather misleadingly: 'a complete understanding exists between Great Britain and Germany.' In fact, the Germans refused all suggestions to mediate between Russia and Austria-Hungary. When this became clear, the French lost their nerve.

---

[1] This affair—more important in German domestic politics than in international relations—was the absurd climax of William II's private diplomacy. He had always prided himself on his efforts at conciliation and now dreamt of ending Anglo-German antagonism by a few kind words. Earlier in 1908 he attempted to explain away the German navy in a private letter to Lord Tweedmouth, the first lord of the admiralty. As Edward VII remarked, this was 'a new departure'. Now he explained to an English acquaintance that he was one of England's few friends in Germany: he had prevented a continental league against her during the Boer war and had provided the British generals with a successful plan of campaign; the German fleet was designed for use in the Far East—that is, against Japan. The interview was submitted before publication to Bülow, who, in turn, submitted it to the foreign ministry, where a few corrections of fact were made.

Its publication had little effect in England, except amusement. In Germany there was great indignation, the more so in that the substance of William's remarks was true. He was indeed more pro-British than most of his subjects. The German politicians blamed William both for admitting this and yet for causing Germany's isolation. Bülow made out that he had failed to read the interview; and he used the crisis in order to assert his 'constitutional responsibility' and therewith his control over William II. Some authorities have suggested that Bülow deliberately allowed the interview to be published in order to discredit William; but the storm in Germany could hardly have been foreseen. It is more likely that Bülow was, as usual, negligent and incompetent; when the crisis arose, he adroitly turned it to his political advantage. It did him no good in the long run. William II was deeply estranged; and he dismissed Bülow, when the Reichstag majority crumbled in the following year. In international affairs, the crisis served only to show that German opinion was anti-British; but this was known to all, except a few English radicals, already.

On 26 February they told the Russians that the Bosnian affair was 'a question in which the vital interests of Russia are not involved' and that 'French public opinion would be unable to comprehend that such a question could lead to a war in which the French and Russian armies would have to take part'.[1] Grey was prepared to hold out for a conference, but this was no use to Izvolski. At a conference, Aehrenthal would reveal that Izvolski had agreed to the annexation, yet Russia would not get the opening of the Straits. Izvolski wanted 'compensation' for Serbia, but here Grey would not support him. Early in March the Russian government formally decided that they would not intervene in a war between Austria-Hungary and Serbia; this had, indeed, been obvious all along.

The Austrians were thus free to conquer Serbia if they wished to do so. Instead events took a different course. For one thing Aehrenthal took fright at the consequences of his own policy. If Austria-Hungary partitioned Serbia with Bulgaria, she would be saddled with millions of discontented subjects, and the national problem would be worse than ever. Much to Conrad's anger, he decided to be content with a Serbian acknowledgement of the annexation. This did not suit the Germans. They cared little for humiliating Serbia, much for humiliating Russia. Besides, they did not want Aehrenthal to score an independent success. Kiderlen, who had just been called in to the foreign ministry, intended to repeat Holstein's success against Delcassé in 1905 and 'to press M. Izvolski to the wall'.[2] On 21 March the Germans summoned Izvolski to give 'a precise answer— yes or no' whether he would acknowledge the annexation; otherwise 'we shall draw back and let events take their course'.[3] Izvolski had no choice but to accept his humiliation; ten days later the Serbs did the same. The Bosnian crisis was over.

The Austro-German alliance had scored a great success, yet not one which made much difference. The annexation of Bosnia and Hercegovina did not solve the South Slav problem; rather it created it. Nothing was done to improve the conditions of the two provinces; Serbia was forced into hostility; and Austria-Hungary had ultimately to fight her under less favourable

[1] French embassy to Russian government, 26 Feb. 1909.

[2] Szögyény (Berlin) to Aehrenthal, 21 Mar. 1909. *Österreich-Ungarns Außenpolitik*, ii, no. 1299.

[3] Bülow to Pourtalès (St. Petersburg) (drafted by Kiderlen), 21 Mar. 1909. *Große Politik*, xxvi (ii), no. 9460.

conditions. Though the Russians had been humiliated, they no more took the course of subservience to Germany than France had done after the fall of Delcassé. On the contrary, they began in 1909 the reconstruction of their armed forces on a large scale. Moreover the Germans soon repented of what they had done. Unconditional support for Austria-Hungary went against every tradition of German foreign policy except in the brief period between 1889 and 1892. Hostility to Russia was popular only among radicals and social democrats; and the liberalism of the Bülow bloc was even more precarious than that of Caprivi's coalition. Old-style Prussians were always more worried about Poland than fearful of the competition from Russian grain. The great industrialists were developing southern Russia and hence wanted friendly relations with her; navy contracts and the search for concessions overseas made them regard Great Britain as their enemy. The professional soldiers, concerned solely with a continental war, were certainly anti-Russian and wanted good relations with Great Britain; but Tirpitz was stronger than they were, so far as politics went. In June 1909 the agrarians and the industrialists combined to force Bülow from office. When he resigned, he passed his own verdict on his greatest success. He said to William II: 'Do not repeat the Bosnian affair.'[1]

---

[1] Bülow, *Memoirs*, ii. 288. The remark may have been a later invention of Bülow's; there is no contemporary evidence for it. If he really made it, he was wiser than usual.

XX

THE YEARS OF ANGLO-GERMAN HOSTILITY

1909–12

THE Bosnian crisis first showed to Europe the shadow of a general war. The conflict over Morocco had been fought almost entirely with diplomatic weapons; even the remote threat of war, made in May 1905, had been only of German attack on an isolated France. No concrete preparations for war were made even between October 1908 and March 1909; but Austria-Hungary would have gone to war with Serbia if Aehrenthal had not backed away at the end of February. The Russians, too, interpreted Kiderlen's action of 21 March as a threat of war; though it was perhaps war between Austria-Hungary and Serbia, not between Germany and Russia, which he had in mind. Even the remote threat was enough to make all the Powers draw back and try to modify their course. Austria-Hungary slipped back into a Balkan policy of negations; Germany retreated from the promises of unconditional support to her which she had given in January 1909; and Great Britain, France, and Russia all sought better relations with Germany. The two continental Powers did so with least reserve. They regarded the Anglo-German rivalry as primary and would be glad to contract out of it, if they could do so at any price less than the loss of their independence; each had an added temptation to back away from the ententes— Russia that she might acquire all Persia, France that she might acquire all Morocco (including Spain's promised share).

Those who directed British policy—Grey, Asquith (now prime minister), the officials of the foreign office—drew a lesson from the Moroccan and Bosnian crises; Germany, they believed, was bidding for the domination of Europe and her chosen method was to isolate the independent Powers one from another. They would therefore accept reconciliation with her only so far as this did not imply any weakening of their ties

with France and Russia. This is not to say that they promoted
the 'triple entente' as a preparation for war against Germany.
On the contrary, they held that it would prevent war, and that
isolation would bring it on. Grey wrote: 'if we sacrifice the
other Powers to Germany we shall eventually be attacked.'[1]
Of course they recognized that in the ententes they had made
a good bargain, and they resented the German attempts to
shake them; but, though they would certainly support the
independence of France and Russia, it never occurred to them
to promote any aggressive designs by their two friends against
Germany, even for the sake of the gains that they had made in
Persia, Egypt, and Morocco.

Until March 1909 the official suspicion of Germany was not
shared by the British public, least of all by the British radicals.
The Germans, on their side, with the Bosnian affair still on
their hands, were anxious to conciliate the British. Tirpitz un-
intentionally provided justification for British suspicions. In
the autumn of 1908 he secretly allotted the building contracts
for two ships which were only to be authorized in 1909. It is
impossible to determine whether, as he claimed, this was merely
a move to break the contractors' 'ring' or whether he hoped
to steal a march on the British and actually to have a larger
fleet than theirs by 1911. The intention did not matter; the
consequence could not be escaped. Henceforth, the British
admiralty had to base their plans on Germany's potential ship-
building capacity, not on her published programme. Strictly,
there was nothing dishonest in Tirpitz's action, at any rate so
far as Great Britain was concerned. The German programme
was a pledge to the Reichstag, not to foreign governments; and
if Tirpitz chose to break the constitution, that was an affair
solely for the German people. Such subtleties are beyond popular understanding. The alarm of German 'acceleration' stirred
the British people as they had not been roused since the annexation of Savoy by Napoleon III in 1860. The conservative party
whipped up the agitation for their own purposes; but they
succeeded only because this agitation had a basis of fact. Previously, public opinion and official policy had been out of step.
The cry, 'we want eight and we won't wait' brought them
together, or even put public opinion ahead. Often afterwards

[1] Minute by Grey on Goschen (Berlin) to Grey, 2 Apr. 1909. *British Documents*,
vi, no. 169.

official policy would seek better relations with Germany; public opinion remained anti-German for more than a generation.[1]

The British outcry had not been expected by the Germans. Bülow and his advisers tried to turn it to good purpose. They dared not offend either William II or the Reichstag by proposing to reduce the naval programme, but they hoped to extract political concessions from the British by offering not to increase it. In April Kiderlen suggested 'a naval convention by which the two Powers should bind themselves for a fixed period (1) not to make war against each other, (2) to join in no coalition directed against either Power, (3) to observe a benevolent neutrality should either country be engaged in hostilities with any other Power or Powers'.[2] The Germans thought it reasonable that, if they were to reduce their fleet, they should receive a promise from the British not to go to war against them; and from this it was a short step to thinking it reasonable that they should receive such a promise, even though they did not reduce their fleet. The British heard only the demand for 'benevolent neutrality'; this confirmed their suspicions that Germany was seeking to divide the Entente Powers. Grey noted: 'An entente with Germany such as M. Kiderlen sketches would serve to establish German hegemony in Europe and would not last long after it had served that purpose.' On 3 June Bülow made a last effort to get some concession from Tirpitz; the only suggestion in reply was to slow down the building of ships now in order to speed it up later on.[3] Three weeks later Bülow was defeated in the Reichstag and resigned. His fall was due mainly to the distrust which his handling of the *Daily Telegraph* affair had implanted in William II. Perhaps his despair at the Anglo-German naval race, which he himself helped to start, made him the more willing to go. More

[1] The Germans, having been caught out, did not 'accelerate' again; this is not, of course, a proof that they had never intended to do so. The British public got its 'eight'—four battleships in March and four more 'contingent' ships, which were in fact authorized in July. To avoid further 'war-scares', Grey proposed to the Germans an exchange of information on building-programmes or even inspection, perhaps by neutrals, of dockyards in both countries. Negotiations for this dragged on until they were interrupted by the Agadir crisis; they were finally dropped by the Germans after the failure of the Haldane mission. Germany had nothing to lose by satisfying British opinion in this way and everything to gain; the delays and final refusal sprang from arrogance and tactlessness, not from high policy.

[2] Goschen to Grey, 16 Apr. 1909. *British Documents*, vi, no. 174.

[3] Protocol of conference, 3 June 1909. *Große Politik*, xxviii, no. 10306.

probably, 'the Eel', as Kiderlen called him, was glad to slip out of an impossible situation.

Bethmann Hollweg, the new chancellor, had no experience of foreign affairs, though much goodwill. Kiderlen characterized him also: 'the Earth-worm'. He was the first of a type common later in the century—'the good German', impotent to arrest the march of German power, deploring its consequences, yet going along with it. His attitude was revealed in a letter which he wrote to Kiderlen regarding the armament programme of 1912: 'The whole policy is of a sort that I cannot co-operate with it. But I ask myself again and again whether the situation will not develop even more dangerously if I go and then probably not alone.'[1] In the eighteen-fifties, his grandfather had been the leader of those Prussian conservatives—administrators without Junker ties—who advocated alliance with Great Britain and a breach with Russia; and Bethmann himself felt more sympathy with Great Britain than with any other Power. Though he could not hope to stand up to Tirpitz, he snatched at the hint of slowing down 'the *tempo*'; the British should be content with having to build fewer ships now, even though they would have to build more later. The British would receive a theoretical German acknowledgement of their naval supremacy; but, as they meant to keep this in any case and believed that they could do so, the offer had no attraction for them. In any case, Bethmann was really concerned to secure a political agreement in order to strengthen himself in the Reichstag. Grey was prepared to declare that 'the isolation of Germany is not our aim and our understandings with France and Russia have no such object';[2] beyond this he would not go. He would not promise to stand aside in case Germany was at war with France and Russia; he could not even make a declaration in favour of the *status quo* in Europe, since 'the French could not be a party to anything which looked like confirming the loss of Alsace and Lorraine'.[3] The British position would have been easier if they had had formal alliances with France and Russia; then they could have made

[1] Bethmann to Kiderlen, 2 Jan. 1912. Jäckh, *Kiderlen-Waechter*, ii. 174. Asquith compared Bethmann with Abraham Lincoln; and Grey, who never met him, said 'the more I hear of him the better I like him'. Mensdorff (London) to Aehrenthal, 16 Feb. 1912. *Österreich-Ungarns Außenpolitik*, iii, no. 834.

[2] Notes by Grey, 31 Aug. 1909. *British Documents*, vi, no. 193.

[3] Grey to Goschen, 1 Sept. 1909. Ibid., no. 195.

an exception for their pledges to their two allies, just as Germany did for those to Austria-Hungary. As it was, Great Britain played a sort of in-and-out game, sometimes claiming to be committed, sometimes not, as suited her purpose. Grey referred to 'the two great groups of Powers, ourselves, France and Russia on one side and the Triple Alliance on the other';[1] Hardinge, at exactly the same time, wrote: 'Great Britain owing to her insular position, and having no alliance with any Great Power in Europe, stands alone, and is the pacific advocate of a friendly grouping of the European Powers'.[2]

Negotiations dragged on intermittently from August 1909 to June 1911. Neither side changed its ground. Bethmann offered naval concessions only if the British would make a general political agreement; and then, he held, the naval concessions would be unnecessary (they were, in any case, impossible—Tirpitz was too strong for him). The British would be content only if Germany cut down her naval programme without conditions;[3] then political relations would improve without a formal agreement. This was the first time in history that reduction of armaments had been discussed between two Powers of equal rank; the only result was greatly to increase the suspicion of each for the other. The British became convinced that Germany was bent on challenging their supremacy at sea and on establishing her domination in Europe as well; the Germans became equally convinced that Great Britain was planning to 'encircle' them and would ultimately join France and Russia in war against them. Of the two, Germany was the more mistaken. The Germans could not, in fact, challenge Great Britain, so long as there were two independent Great Powers on the continent of Europe. If they had abandoned their great naval programme and concentrated on land armaments, they might have won British neutrality and would certainly have won the continental war. As it was, when war came in 1914, the German dreadnoughts remained uselessly in harbour; the

[1] Minute by Grey on Goschen to Grey, 21 Aug. 1909. *British Documents*, vi, no. 187.

[2] Memorandum by Hardinge, 25 Aug. 1909. Ibid., no. 190.

[3] The Admiralty were never asked what conditions would satisfy them. Minute by Crowe on Goschen to Grey, 9 May 1911. Ibid., no. 462. There was a further difficulty: the British could not make an agreement with Germany alone. They feared that, if they agreed to put their fleet on an agreed base of superiority to the German, Austria-Hungary would then build dreadnoughts and establish the supremacy of the Triple Alliance in the Mediterranean.

steel that had gone in to them would have given Germany the heavy artillery and mechanized transport with which to win the war on land.

The British loyalty to France and Russia was not repaid by their two associates. The Russians, in particular, had never intended to launch themselves on an anti-German course. Their alliance with France was no more than a reinsurance treaty against isolation; and, apart from that, they did not worry about German domination of Europe. The Bosnian affair had been a private venture by Izvolski; and more sensible Russians attributed the German reaction in it to his blundering. They had no pressing interest in the Near East, except that the Straits should remain under the control of an independent Turkey. In fact, they wished to turn their backs both on the Near East and on Europe. Asia was still their overriding concern: here, in China and Persia, they had both pressing anxieties and great ambitions. In China the Manchu empire was drifting to collapse; revolution dissolved it in 1910. The Russians wished to profit from the confusion and to prevent any recovery; they were seconded by the Japanese, and the French—with no great stake of their own except in the far south—tailed along for the sake of the Franco-Russian alliance. The great capitalist Powers —Germany, Great Britain, the United States—had a common interest to restore order in China and to build up her prosperity. This cut clean across Russian designs. Hence, they welcomed Anglo-German tension, which prevented a united front in China of the advanced Powers; on the other hand, they wished to avoid any tension between Germany and themselves, for fear that the Germans would take it out of them by compromising with the British. Persia reinforced the same Russian need: bad blood between Germany and Great Britain, good blood between Germany and themselves. The Persians struggled constantly to free themselves from the Russian control at Teheran. In 1909 a revolution overthrew Russia's protégé, the reactionary shah; and the liberals attempted to set up a parliamentary state, with much British sympathy. Here again the Russians counted on Anglo-German antagonism. Germany was to be given concessions, so as not to co-operate with Great Britain; and the British government was to abandon the Persian liberals, in order to keep Russia's weight in the general balance against Germany. Sazonov wrote, shortly after becoming foreign

minister: 'the English in pursuing political aims of vital importance in Europe will abandon in case of necessity certain interests in Asia simply in order to maintain the convention with us
which is so important for them'.[1]

The Russians did not get far so long as Izvolski remained
foreign minister. He could not forget his personal humiliation
in the Bosnian affair, and dragged himself complainingly over
Europe, still hankering for the opening of the Straits. In October 1909 he even struck a bargain with the Italians at Racconigi,
by which they would acquiesce in Russian designs at the Straits,
in exchange for Russia's approval of their ambitions in Tripoli.[2]
This was not much of a score: like the Italian bargain with
France in 1900 and 1902, it sprang from the Italian resolve not
to commit themselves until it was clear which side was the
winning one. In any case, Izvolski was only waiting for a rich
embassy; and in September 1910 Paris at last fell vacant. Sazonov, who had been preparing for office for some time, was a
more cautious character, indifferent to the Straits, and more
in touch with Asia. He went at once with Nicholas II to visit
William II at Potsdam, and there offered the Germans a
practical bargain: if they would respect Russia's monopoly of
railways in north Persia, she would tolerate the import of
German goods there and would drop her opposition to the
Bagdad railway. This satisfied Russia's strategic needs; it was
not a good bargain for the Germans, since they could get on
with the Bagdad railway despite Russia's disapproval. Their real
concern was to disturb the Anglo-Russian entente. Kiderlen said
Germany would not support an aggressive Austro-Hungarian
policy in the Balkans, and asked a concession in return: 'The
Russian Government declares that it is not committed [to] and
that it does not intend to support a policy hostile to Germany
which England might follow.'[3] The Germans knew that Russia
would not support such a policy; what they wanted was written
proof to show to the British, who could then be induced to
make a similar declaration in their turn. Kiderlen wrote: 'The
Russian assurance concerning relations with England is the
alpha and omega for me of the whole agreement. It must be

---

[1] Sazonov to Poklevsky (Teheran), 8 Oct. 1910. *Benckendorffs Schriftwechsel*, p. 1.
[2] Immediately after this (19 Dec. 1909) the Italians made an agreement with
Austria-Hungary, promising to communicate to each other 'any proposal by a third
Power which might conflict with the principle of non-intervention or the *status quo*'.
[3] Bethmann to Pourtalès, 15 Nov. 1910. *Große Politik*, xxvii (ii), no. 10159.

so drafted that it will compromise the Russians the day the English learn of it.'[1] The Germans were not concerned with security, still less with Persia or the Bagdad railway; they wished to divide the independent Powers, so as to be able to impose their will upon each in turn. This was clear enough to Sazonov, who had a competent diplomatic head. He refused Kiderlen's draft; the Germans would not sign the agreement on Persia and the Bagdad railway without it. All remained in suspense.

News of the alleged 'Potsdam Agreement' soon reached the British;[2] they were already resentful over Russia's behaviour in Persia and were now the more offended in that they had been holding out against an isolated bargain with Germany over the Bagdad railway throughout 1910. Grey told Benckendorff that he contemplated resigning in favour of a foreign secretary who would make an agreement with Germany on naval armaments and then combine with her to oppose Russia in Persia and Turkey.[3] The radicals in parliament were in revolt against Grey's policy in regard to Persia and to the German navy; and early in 1911 relations with Germany were put in the hands of a cabinet committee, more to control Grey than to strengthen him.[4] He had to drop his previous insistence that a reduction of naval expenditure must precede a political agreement; on 8 March he offered the Germans 'a general political formula', together with a deal over the Bagdad railway and railways in Persia.[5]

The Triple Entente seemed in process of disintegration. It was put back on its feet by a German attempt to improve relations with the third partner, France. A Franco-German reconciliation would certainly give Germany security: neither Russia nor Great Britain could do much against Germany herself without French assistance. Even the Franco-Russian alliance

---

[1] Kiderlen to Pourtalès, 4 Dec. 1910. *Große Politik*, xxvii (ii), no. 10167. Kiderlen added: 'you had better burn this letter.'

[2] The 'leak' was arranged by Tardieu, a French journalist, who was himself planning a Franco-German reconciliation and was therefore jealous of good relations between Germany and Russia. He bribed a member of the Russian embassy in Paris, perhaps with Izvolski's assistance.

[3] Benckendorff to Sazonov, 9 Feb. 1911. *Benckendorffs Schriftwechsel*, ii, no. 342.

[4] The committee was composed of Asquith, Grey, Lloyd George, Morley, Crewe, and Runciman. (Nicolson to Hardinge, 2 Mar. 1911. *British Documents*, vi, no. 440.) Asquith and Grey saw eye to eye, and were supported by Crewe; Runciman and Lloyd George were radicals, Morley an isolationist, unhappy as well about Persia.

[5] Grey to Goschen, 8 Mar. 1911. Ibid., no. 444.

and the Anglo-French entente had no dangers, unless linked by France into an anti-German coalition. On the other hand, France could offer Germany little in the realm of 'world policy'; there the Near East and the oceans were decisive. Bismarck had sought security; the new Germany wanted gains, and only old-fashioned 'Bismarckians', such as Holstein and Kiderlen, still included France in their calculations. Holstein, locked away in this study, had made the crisis of 1905; Kiderlen, who had been out of the world in Rumania for twelve years, repeated the crisis in 1911.

On the French side, there was a strong current running towards reconciliation. Radicals of the Rouvier school aspired to a Franco-German financial partnership, in which Germany would run the risks of the ordinary shareholder and France would be the holder of secure debentures; Caillaux, minister of finance, now led this party. They were reinforced by the socialists, who disliked reactionary Russia and looked admiringly at the German social democrats, the strongest and most orthodox Marxist party in Europe.[1] The agreement over Morocco of 9 February 1909 had been a victory for this school, but it had been hastily botched up so that the Germans could score a point during the Bosnian crisis, and it lacked precision. Moreover, the German government was now the prisoner of its own propaganda. In 1905 and 1906 no one in Germany had cared for Morocco—hence the failure of Holstein's policy; and there would have been little outcry if France had acquired Morocco unconditionally. Now a prolonged campaign by private interests[2] had taught the German people that Morocco

---

[1] Paul Cambon told Benckendorff: 'Jaurès was like all Socialists and extreme Radicals an opponent of the alliance with Russia and outspoken representative of the idea of reconciliation with Germany.' Benckendorff to Sazonov, 15 Jan. 1911. *Benckendorffs Schriftwechsel*, ii, no. 324.

[2] Morocco is sometimes presented as an economic conflict between French and German steel-interests. This is not so; in its last stage, it was much more a conflict between rival German firms. The great German undertakings, Thyssen and Krupp, were linked with Schneider-Creusot, the French concern, in the 'Union des Mines', which exploited what iron-ore there was in Morocco. Mannesmann brothers, an interloping German firm, sought to break the Krupp–Thyssen monopoly by inventing shady claims in Morocco and posing as the defender of German national interests. Mannesmann worked with the Pan-Germans and organized agitation in the Reichstag; they never raised any iron-ore in Morocco. In fact, they were one of the first to discover that stirring up political trouble is a more profitable activity than serious industry. The Moroccan crisis was a victory for them, and a defeat for the great steel magnates who wanted Franco-German co-operation.

represented a great economic prize. Though the German government had acknowledged French predominance they could agree to the ending of Moorish independence only if they received some concrete reward with which to still public agitation. Endless schemes were devised by ingenious French speculators.[1] All broke on the opposition of the French chamber. The Right, though capitalistic, was faithful to the Russian alliance and therefore disliked any deal with the Germans; the Left, though hostile to Russia, would not do anything to benefit the French capitalists.

Meanwhile, conditions in Morocco went from bad to worse. In May 1911 the French occupied Fez, the most important city; it was certain that a French protectorate would follow. Kiderlen feared that the French would take Morocco before they had paid a price for it to Germany; and the failure of the schemes for compensation seemed to confirm his fears. On the other hand, France, he supposed, was isolated: Great Britain and Russia were on bad terms, and both were seeking better relations with Germany. Therefore, he had only to take a firm line and France would pay; then opinion in both countries would be satisfied, and a lasting reconciliation would follow. On 21 June he told Jules Cambon that Germany must be compensated: 'bring us something back from Paris'. In the Bismarckian manner, he imagined that the French would yield only to threats. In his own words: 'It is

---

[1] The most ingenious of these schemes concerned the N'Goko Sangha company —a French undertaking which had a large rubber concession (probably illegal under the Berlin act of 1885) in the French Congo. It had never developed the concession, which had been broken into by German interlopers from the Cameroons. The N'Goko Sangha company failed to get damages in a German court; it then claimed compensation from the French government. To give its shady claim a political disguise, it proposed that the area of its concession should be ceded to Germany (as reward for Germany's withdrawal in Morocco); the company would then amalgamate with its German competitor—the Germans to contribute as their share the investment which they had made in the territory, the N'Goko Sangha to contribute the compensation which it was to receive from the French government for damage done to it by the Germans who would now be its partners! A later cloak for this scheme was the project for a Franco-German railway through the French Congo and the Cameroons. Both schemes were devised by Tardieu, who was simultaneously a government official, a big business man, and chief political writer on the *Temps*; both schemes were broken by Caillaux, the minister of finance, who—though pro-German—disliked crooked finance. When the schemes failed, Tardieu became a fire-eating patriot; the N'Goko Sangha company got its compensation from the German government in the treaty of Versailles; the Congo–Cameroons railway was never built.

necessary to thump the table. However, the only object of this is to make the French negotiate.'[1] On 1 July the German gunboat *Panther* anchored in the south Moroccan harbour of Agadir.[2]

Kiderlen's stroke was miscalculated and mistimed. On the very day that the *Panther* reached Agadir, Caillaux became prime minister of France. Though he had certainly wrecked the shady schemes for buying off Germany, he was the leading advocate of Franco-German reconciliation. His plan was the old Rouvier one: he would offer French co-operation in the Bagdad railway, if Germany would drop her interest in Morocco. Caillaux had a further idea: if France acquired Morocco with German approval, she could disregard the promises which she had given to Great Britain and Spain, and could take the whole of Morocco, without respecting the proposed Spanish zone. French public opinion would be won over; and Franco-German reconciliation would be complete. But such negotiations assumed a friendly atmosphere; it was Bismarckianism run mad for Kiderlen to suppose that Caillaux would find it easier to compromise if he was first threatened. The *Panther*'s move did not create much stir in France; but Caillaux had to give the impression that he was not frightened by it. His only hope was to wait for its effect to blow over. He never meant to resist Germany; apart from anything else, he was convinced that neither Russia nor Great Britain would support France. His

---

[1] Lancken, *Meine dreißig Dienstjahre*, p. 96.

[2] The *Panther* was supposed to protect Germans who might be 'endangered'. Agadir was a closed port, and the nearest German was at Mogador. He was instructed to go to Agadir in order to be endangered. When he arrived there on 4 July he could not attract the notice of the *Panther*, as the captain had been told to avoid trouble with the natives and therefore to keep half a mile out. On 5 July a ship's officer remarked that one of the 'natives', prancing on the beach, had his hands on his hips and was therefore perhaps a European; the endangered German was then rescued.

Kiderlen always claimed that he never meant to remain at Agadir; he took it only as a 'pledge'. All the same, there was an element of reinsurance. If all else failed, Germany could hang on to Agadir and so still the agitation in the Reichstag. Agadir was the gate to the valley of the Sus, which possessed legendary wealth; and it was also supposed to be far enough south from Gibraltar not to alarm the British. On the other hand, Kiderlen certainly dropped all ambition for Agadir, long before a German representative reported that it and its hinterland were valueless. The Germans, of course, were not to foresee that, though the minerals did not exist, Agadir would one day have the largest sardine-canning factories in the world. Even the French only hit on this during the Second World War.

plan was to continue discussions in secret and then to spirit
the tension away by a compromise satisfactory to both parties.
Jules Cambon returned to Berlin to discover what compensation Kiderlen wanted; and Caillaux, always vain of his own
diplomatic skill, negotiated with the Germans in less official
ways.

The Russians certainly lived up to the expectations of Kiderlen and Caillaux. The Russian ambassador at Berlin agreed
with Kiderlen that there was a danger of war only if France
succeeded in invoking the Triple Entente;[1] and later, in
August, Izvolski had the satisfaction of repeating word for
word the warning that France had given him in February
1909: 'Russian public opinion could not see in a colonial dispute the cause for a general conflict.'[2] The Russian general
staff insisted that their army could not be ready for war against
Germany in less than two years.[3] The Russians turned the
crisis to good use. On 19 August they finally extracted from the
Germans confirmation of the 'Potsdam agreement' over Persia
and the Bagdad railway, without the general political declaration on which the Germans had hitherto insisted—an exact
echo of the French action in signing their Moroccan agreement
with Germany in February 1909. The Russian move was even
more effective. French co-operation in the Bagdad railway was
the main concession which Caillaux offered to the Germans;
and the Russians, by dropping their own opposition to the
railway, knocked this card out of his hand.[4] In fact, each
member of the Triple Entente wished to be on good terms with
Germany, while deploring attempts at reconciliation by the
other two. On the other side, Austria-Hungary paraded her
neutrality with equal ostentation, in protest against the German
concessions to Russia;[5] but this counted for little. Germany
could defeat France without the assistance of Austria-Hungary;

[1] Osten-Sacken to Neratov, 8 July 1911. *Mezhdunarodnye otnosheniya v epokhu imperializma*, second series, xviii (i), no. 197.

[2] Izvolski to Neratov, 21 Aug. 1911. Ibid., no. 358.

[3] Military protocol, 31 Aug. 1911. Ibid., no. 384.

[4] Caillaux was an opponent of the Russian alliance, like Rouvier before him; and the Russians no doubt rubbed in their unwillingness to support him. In addition, Caillaux had attempted to promote an anti-Russian financial combination in China.

[5] Aehrenthal to Szögyény, 14 July 1911. *Österreich-Ungarns Außenpolitik*, iii, no. 277. Aehrenthal hoped to have the Paris bourse opened to him as reward for his neutrality.

France could not hold her own against Germany without the Russian army—in 1911 doubtfully even with it.[1]

The British foreign office was equally alarmed at the prospect of Franco-German reconciliation, particularly if it weakened the security of Gibraltar. On this point they outdid their own naval experts. The admiralty decided that it had no objection to the Germans acquiring Agadir;[2] Bertie, the Ambassador at Paris, rejected this opinion and told the French: 'British government would never allow it.'[3] The radicals in the cabinet, on the other hand, sympathized with the German grievance over Morocco and were determined not to be dragged into war against her; their remedy was to propose a new international conference, at which France would have to compensate everybody (including the British) for going beyond the Act of Algeçiras. Grey was pulled one way by the foreign office, the other way by the cabinet. On 1 July de Selves, the new and inexperienced French foreign minister, proposed to send a ship to Agadir to lie alongside the *Panther* or to the nearby port of Mogador; this was a routine move if France was to head towards a conflict. Caillaux forbade it; all the same de Selves —pushed on by his permanent officials—asked the British to send a ship of their own. Grey at once agreed;[4] the next day he was overruled by the cabinet.[5] They would only allow him to warn Germany: 'we could not recognise any new arrangement which was come to without us.'[6] This warning did not alarm Kiderlen. Rather the reverse: he intended to demand the French Congo, and any dispute over Morocco would then be purely between Great Britain and France. On 15 July he stated his demand to Jules Cambon; he was ready 'to proceed very forcibly'.[7] William II at once revolted. He disliked the Moroccan affair as much as he had done in 1905 and was resolved not to go to war over it. Kiderlen threatened to resign;

---

[1] Joffre told Caillaux that France had not a 70 per cent. chance of victory. Of course, generals always foretell defeat if they do not wish to go to war.

[2] Grey to Bertie, 6, 12 July, 1911. *British Documents*, vii, nos. 363, 375.

[3] Bertie to Grey, 11 July 1911. Ibid., no. 369. Bertie had to pretend that he had not received Grey's instruction of 6 July in time.

[4] Grey to Bertie, 3 July 1911. Ibid., no. 351. Grey had decided to send a ship before receiving the French request. Minute by Grey on Salis (Berlin) to Grey, 2 July 1911. Ibid., no. 343.

[5] Nicolson to Hardinge, 5 July 1911. Ibid., no. 359.

[6] Grey to Salis, 4 July 1911. Ibid., no. 356.

[7] Bethmann to William II, 15 July 1911. *Große Politik*, xxix, no. 10607.

and, though William II dropped his protest for the moment, Kiderlen was henceforth fighting with both hands tied behind his back.

This was not known to the British or French governments. The French exaggerated the German demands—de Selves and the foreign ministry in order to get British backing, Caillaux in the hope that this backing would be refused and he would then be justified in agreeing to them. The British cabinet would not pledge themselves to France.[1] The Balance of Power was still alien to them; and the majority would certainly have repudiated Grey's 'general and underlying' principle 'to give to France such support as would prevent her from falling under the virtual control of Germany and estrangement from us'.[2] What weighed with them was 'the formation of a great naval base across our trade routes'.[3] Like most isolationists, their high principles depended on maritime supremacy and, besides, their hearts sank when they contemplated the increased estimates that a German base near Gibraltar would involve.

Their apprehension was altogether unfounded. The Germans never aspired to any Moorish base north of Agadir, which the admiralty did not regard as dangerous; and even their ambition for Agadir was only a passing whim. Kiderlen had already claimed the French Congo, and if the British cabinet had known this, they would have tolerated his claim—hence, no doubt, the French silence about it. In essence, the cabinet agreed with the German case, though they did not know it. They wished to propose a conference, at which France would have the choice of yielding part of Morocco to Germany or returning to the Algeçiras Act; if Germany acquired Moorish territory, they would also claim some for themselves.[4] The French would have preferred a private deal with Germany to this, as Bertie and the foreign office recognized.[5] They did their best, therefore, to thwart the cabinet's plan, and Grey assisted them. On 21 July Lloyd George, leader of the radical group,

---

[1] They would have been indignant if they had known that Wilson, director of military operations at the war office, settled the technical details of military co-operation with the French on 20 July. It is impossible to say who authorized this. Memorandum, 21 July, 1911. *British Documents*, vii, no. 640.

[2] Conversation between Grey and C. P. Scott, 25 July 1911. Hammond, *C. P. Scott*, p. 161.

[3] Conversation between Lloyd George and Scott, 22 July 1911. Ibid., p. 155.

[4] Grey to Bertie, 20 July 1911. *British Documents*, vii, no. 405.

[5] Bertie to Grey, 21 July 1911. Ibid., nos. 407 and 408.

put forward a compromise either at the cabinet or shortly after it.[1] He would make a speech at the Mansion House that evening, declaring that Britain could not be treated as of no account 'where her interests were vitally affected'. Since he was a radical, this was decked out with a reference to British services 'to the cause of human liberty'. Yet, in essence, this was not a pledge to support France against Germany; it was a warning that Great Britain could not be left out of any new partition of Morocco. It was directed against Caillaux, not against Kiderlen.[2]

Public speeches are a dangerous diplomatic weapon: they hit someone, but usually the wrong party. The Mansion House speech was read by the German and French public, as well as by their statesmen; and in both countries it made compromise impossible. Kiderlen had to screw up his demands and to talk seriously of war; Caillaux had to retreat from the compromise that he had prepared. Jules Cambon, who had co-operated with Caillaux, was 'rather aghast at the effect which Mr. Lloyd George's speech has had on the French Colonial Chauvinists';[3] the effect on the Germans did not apparently worry him. What had been an attempt at Franco-German reconciliation turned into an Anglo-German conflict, with the French trailing along behind. The British fleet prepared for action; and, what was more important for the future, the admiralty was forced, for the first time, to subordinate its own plans to the shipping of an expeditionary force to northern France. The decision to take part in a continental war was given practical shape. In 1911 war between Great Britain and Germany stood clear on the horizon. Yet, oddly enough, war between France and Germany was never in sight. Kiderlen knew all along that William II would never tolerate war for the sake of Morocco; and he had not even Holstein's vague hope in 1905 of forcing

---

[1] According to Grey, Churchill, and Lloyd George himself, the speech was drafted by him on his own initiative after the cabinet meeting. All these are later accounts; and the memory of statesmen is notoriously bad. Mensdorff, who spent the week-end with members of the government (21 July was a Friday), was told that the speech had been settled in cabinet. Mensdorff to Aehrenthal, *Österreich-Ungarns Außenpolitik*, iii, no. 283.

[2] Grey saw Metternich on 21 July and was subsequently criticized for allowing the Mansion House speech before the Germans had time to reply. But the speech was an answer to the French requests for support, not a declaration against the Germans, and therefore could not be delayed.

[3] Goschen to Grey, 27 July 1911. *British Documents*, vii, no. 431.

the kaiser's hands. Caillaux was only concerned to shake off the unwelcome British backing and to return to private bargaining. On 25 July he opened secret negotiations, behind the backs of de Selves[1] and Jules Cambon; and these negotiations ran on through all the talk of crisis. But the great stroke had failed: though Morocco might be settled, reconciliation between France and Germany would not follow.

In September, Kiderlen—perhaps spurred on by a financial crisis in Germany—decided to cut his losses. He agreed to a French protectorate over Morocco; Germany acquired, in return, two strips of territory in the French Congo which gave her access to the Congo river.[2] This agreement was signed on 4 November.[3] Public opinion in both countries was indignant. Caillaux was attacked in France not for what he had achieved or failed to achieve, but for the underhand way in which he had done it. The Right, who disliked his enlightened financial policy, combined with Jacobin radicals, such as Clemenceau, who were hostile to Germany. Caillaux was overthrown in January 1912; and there followed a patriotic ministry under Poincaré. It was the beginning of the *réveil national*.

Bethmann and Kiderlen had an equally rough time in the Reichstag; the attacks on them were ostentatiously applauded by the crown prince—the first such demonstration since Frederick William had spoken against Bismarck's policy at Danzig in 1863. What was worse, Tirpitz rubbed his hands: 'The more we are humiliated, the more uproar there will be. The possibility of a new Naval Law comes ever nearer';[4] and in October he won the emperor's authority to go over to 'three-time'—three dreadnoughts a year instead of two. Bethmann was helpless. His only attempt at an answer was to encourage increased demands from the army, in the hope that the financial strain would be too much for the Reichstag. This tactic raised new difficulties both at home and abroad. The army certainly

---

[1] The French secret service deciphered the German telegrams, describing these negotiations; and henceforth de Selves worked solely to defeat and discredit Caillaux.

[2] Kiderlen consoled himself that Germany would one day acquire the Belgian Congo and would then have an empire stretching from the Atlantic to the Indian ocean.

[3] Caillaux tried a last anti-British stroke by claiming that Spain should, in her turn, compensate France by surrendering part of her zone of Morocco, including Tangier. Bertie defeated this attempt, not without much ill feeling.

[4] 3 Aug. 1911. Tirpitz, *Politische Dokumente*, i. 200.

had a case: the full quota of conscripts had not been called up for twenty years. But a mass-army implied a social revolution; there would not be enough Prussian Junkers to provide the officers. Ludendorff, the director of operations and the brain of the general staff under Moltke, was already a symbol of this: he was a technician, not an aristocrat. Moreover, an army which fully exploited Germany's predominance in men and industry would challenge France and Russia as much as the navy challenged Great Britain. Bethmann had wanted to lessen tension in Europe and overseas. The outcome of his policy was to increase both.

The crisis of Agadir was a more serious affair than either the first crisis over Morocco in 1905 or the Bosnian crisis in 1909. Preparations for war had been made by England, though none by the continental Powers. It was more significant still that public opinion had played a decisive part in diplomacy for the first time since 1878. In England Lloyd George had evoked public opinion by his speech at the Mansion House on 21 July and, in the following month, had ended a railway strike by pointing to the danger of war. In France outraged national feeling had defeated Caillaux's policy of conciliation. The change was more striking still in Germany. In 1905 German opinion was indifferent to Morocco, and Holstein's resolute policy was ruined by lack of public support. In 1911 Kiderlen had tried to act the strong man; but German feeling was ahead of him, and both he and Bethmann were denounced in the Reichstag for their weakness. The conflicts of 1905 and 1909 had been crises of diplomacy; in 1911 nations faced each other in a 'pre-war' spirit.

Yet Europe still seemed far from an explosion. In the autumn of 1911 Anglo-German tension alone seemed acute. The continental Powers tried to turn the situation to their advantage. Caillaux had missed reconciliation with Germany; all the same, France acquired Morocco as a by-product of this Anglo-German conflict. Aehrenthal paraded his neutrality in the Agadir crisis and claimed, as a reward, that the French bourse should be opened to Austro-Hungarian loans. More grandiloquently, he talked of 'the perfect relations' between Austria-Hungary and France, quite in the spirit of Metternich and Talleyrand.[1]

---

[1] Crozier (Vienna) to de Selves, 19 Nov. 1911. *Documents diplomatiques français*, third series, i, no. 152.

Caillaux would have liked to take up the offer, but his days were numbered; and he dared not offend against the alliance with Russia, when he was already accused of shaking the entente with Great Britain. Italy did much better. The Triple Alliance had long promised her a free hand in Tripoli; and the Russians had made the same promise at Racconigi. The French promise of 1900 was more conditional: Italy could move only when France had acquired Morocco. This time had now come. On 29 September 1911 Italy declared war on Turkey for no good reason and invaded Tripoli. All the Powers deplored the war for the same reason: all wished to keep Turkey going and to postpone the Eastern question as long as possible. But none would risk losing Italy's friendship. Conrad in Vienna was dismissed when he preached war against Italy; Marschall at Constantinople was ignored when he proposed an alliance with Turkey. Only the British were formally uncommitted; but in view of the naval rivalry with Germany they could not spare any ships for the Mediterranean. Grey wrote regretfully: 'It is most important that neither we nor France should side against Italy now;[1] and he influenced *The Times* to be more sympathetic to the Italian case.[2] Though the war, as usual with Italy, had no shadow of excuse, no Power protested against it.

The Russians thought that their opportunity had arrived also. They had a pressing motive for action. The Italians made no headway in Tripoli and were soon tempted to reach a decision by carrying the war against Turkey to the Straits. This would be intolerable to Russia: her economic life depended on the passage of the grain ships through the Straits to the western world and the flow of capital goods from the west to Russia. She must secure control of the Straits for herself; and, in view of her equivocal policy during the Agadir crisis, no Power would oppose her—Great Britain and France from fear, Germany and Austria-Hungary from hope, that she was about to desert her present partners. Sazonov was absent, ill in Switzerland; and Izvolski in Paris, Charykov in Constantinople, were free to try their hand. Nicholas II 'approved extremely'.[3] Izvolski asked for French support at the Straits in

[1] Grey to Nicolson, 19 Sept. 1911. *British Documents*, ix (i), no. 231.
[2] Minute by Grey on Rodd (Rome) to Grey, 30 Sept. 1911. Ibid., no. 256.
[3] Minute by Nicholas II on Neratov to Izvolski, 5 Oct. 1911. *Mezhdunarodnye otnosheniya*, second series, xviii (ii), no. 531.

exchange for Russia's acceptance of the French protectorate in Morocco.[1] Charykov had a more daring flight. He offered Turkey a guarantee of the *status quo* in exchange for the opening of the Straits to Russian warships; if Turkey did not object, the other Powers could hardly do so. This would not only be a guarantee against Italy. Charykov proposed, in some vague way, to promote an alliance between Turkey and the Balkan states. Then Turkey would be secure in Europe; and the great alliance would be a solid barrier against Austria-Hungary.

The 'Charykov kite' never managed to get airborne. The Turks would make an alliance with Russia, only if Great Britain was a party to it; and the British turned down the idea with soft words.[2] In any case the Turks knew quite well that neither Russia nor Great Britain would guarantee them against Italy, though they might against each other. The French repeated their policy of 1908: they sympathized with Russia's wishes, but would not commit themselves unless the British did so also. Benckendorff very reluctantly had to put the idea to Grey. He could not have chosen a worse moment. In 1908 the British had refused to balance Austria-Hungary's illegal act in Bosnia by condoning Russian ambitions at the Straits; their reaction to Italy's illegal act was the same—Turkey should be sustained, not further weakened. Moreover, radical opinion had been offended enough by the support given to France in Morocco; it would certainly not tolerate support for Russia at the Straits. Most of all, Anglo-Russian relations in Persia had gone from bad to worse during 1911. An American adviser, Shuster, had been trying to put the finances and administration in order; and though Grey was ready to co-operate in getting rid of him, he insisted that this must be done with a certain decency for the sake of British opinion. On 2 December he repeated his threat of resigning and of allowing the entente with Russia to dissolve.[3] Benckendorff thought that Russia could achieve her wishes at the Straits only if she abandoned Persia;[4] and this was too high a price for her to pay. Grey was prepared to

---

[1] Izvolski to de Selves, 4 Nov. 1911. *Documents diplomatiques français*, third series, i, no. 18.

[2] Memorandum by Grey, 2 Nov. 1911. *British Documents*, ix (i), appendix IV.

[3] Benckendorff to Neratov, 2 Dec. 1911. *Mezhdunarodnye otnosheniya*, second series, xix (i), no. 139.

[4] Benckendorff to Neratov, 11 Nov. 1911. Ibid., xviii (ii), no. 836.

repeat his offer of 1908—the opening of the Straits to all; beyond this he would not go.

This was no use to the Russians. Charykov tried to settle things at a rush and presented his terms to the Turks almost as an ultimatum. They thought that the great crisis had arrived and appealed to Marschall, the German ambassador. He had been the protagonist of an anti-Russian policy for twenty years and, latterly, the successful patron of German economic penetration in Asia Minor. He wrote on 4 December: 'the eastern policy that we have followed for twenty years is *irreconcilable* with conniving with Russia in the Straits Question';[1] and he threatened to resign unless Turkey was supported. Kiderlen insisted that Great Britain and France would do Germany's business for her;[2] and it soon turned out that he was right. On 6 December Sazonov arrived in Paris on his way home from Switzerland. He learnt of the Izvolski-Charykov intrigue for the first time and repudiated it. Charykov, he said, had no instructions and had spoken 'à titre en quelque sort personnel'.[3] Sazonov was, no doubt, offended by the initiative of his two subordinates and understood, as well, Russia's need both for peace and for British and French money. Beyond this, he had a plan of his own for the Balkans which was soon to come to unexpected fruition. For the moment the alarm at Constantinople died away.

The two decisive features of the Agadir crisis had been Anglo-German tension and the lack of solidarity in the Triple Entente. The new year saw attempts to remove both, unsuccessful in the one case, successful in the other. There were always elements in England seeking reconciliation with Germany. The radicals disliked the policy which had followed Lloyd George's Mansion House speech and pressed hard for a new British gesture. The government perhaps wished to frighten the Russians into better behaviour over Persia. The Triple Entente was far from being a perfect arrangement from the British point of view. They had to be loyal to France; yet Russia was not loyal to them. Improved relations with Germany would, it was hoped, lessen the tension between Germany and France;

[1] Marschall to Bethmann, 4 Dec. 1911. *Große Politik*, xxx (i), no. 10987.
[2] Kiderlen to Marschall, 7 Dec. 1911. Ibid., no. 10984.
[3] De Selves to Paul Cambon and Bompard, 9 Dec. 1911. *Documents diplomatiques français*, third series, i, no. 326.

at the same time, they would make it easier to oppose Russia in Persia. On the German side it was logical enough, as Marschall pointed out, to co-operate with Great Britain, if both were to oppose Russia at the Straits.[1] Bethmann had a more immediate ambition. He wanted some political concession from the British so as to resist Tirpitz's new plans for further naval expansion before they were formally introduced in the Reichstag.

The motive in both countries was in fact primarily internal, a matter of domestic politics. Bethmann wished to defeat Tirpitz, Grey to silence the radicals. This had a curious effect on the negotiations. Bethmann wanted them to succeed, yet could make no concessions for fear of Tirpitz; Grey had to offer concessions to please the radicals, yet expected the negotiations to fail. The Germans asked for a visit from Grey or Churchill, now first lord of the admiralty; the British cabinet decided to send Haldane, a liberal imperialist, though friendly to Germany.[2] He came to Berlin from 8 February to 11 February and had long talks with Bethmann and William II. Probably he talked more loosely than a trained diplomatist would have done; and some unnecessary confusion followed. But the main line of difference was clear enough. The British had abandoned their original claim that the German naval plans should be reduced without any political concession from them; they had even ceased to ask that naval limitation and a political agreement should go hand in hand. They would be content if the German programme was not further increased; and they offered in exchange colonial concessions as well as a political agreement. The Germans insisted that their new naval law, which had not yet been published, should be treated as part of their existing programme; and in exchange for a promise not to go beyond this, they wanted, not a simple declaration of friendship, but a promise of neutrality in case Germany was involved in a continental war.

The new German increases would have ruined the negotiations in any case. Even Morley said that the government would be regarded as 'idiots' if they made concessions to Germany

[1] Marschall to William II. 1 Dec. 1911. *Große Politik*, xxx (i), no. 10998.

[2] The discussions were arranged by Ballin, head of the Hamburg-Amerika line, and Cassel, an Anglo-German financier who had been a friend of Edward VII. This led to some confusion, since each government thought that the initiative had come from the other.

just when they had to increase their own naval programme.[1] Quite apart from this, political agreement was as far off as ever. Though the British were always ready to declare that 'England will make no unprovoked attack upon Germany and pursue no aggressive policy towards her',[2] they would not renounce their freedom of decision. The Germans, however, wanted to eliminate Great Britain from the Balance of Power. As Tirpitz wrote, England 'should give up her existing ententes and we should take the place of France'.[3] Yet even then Tirpitz would not have reduced his programme, since he held that only the threat of a great German navy would force Great Britain on to the German side and keep her there. Early in March Bethmann attempted to resign, perhaps in the hope of shaking Tirpitz; instead Tirpitz threatened to resign also, and William II came down on his side. On 22 March the new naval programme was published. Tirpitz had won. Bethmann withdrew his resignation, and was soon explaining that Germany needed her fleet 'for the general purposes of her greatness'.[4] The Anglo-German negotiations tailed away at the end of March, and were never renewed in this general form.

Inevitably the failure seemed to push Great Britain more on to the French side. The French government were alarmed whenever the British negotiated with Germany, and their alarm was encouraged by the permanent members of the British foreign service. Or perhaps both understood the situation well enough, but sought to improve the occasion by extracting some promise from the British government and so satisfying French public opinion. On the news of Haldane's visit to Berlin, Poincaré proposed to declare that England and France would 'co-operate, if necessary, to maintain the European balance'.[5] Grey would only express a wish 'to co-operate in maintaining European peace'.[6] This was not enough for Poincaré, and he contented himself with a general evocation of the entente. At the end of March, when the Anglo-German negotiations had already failed, Bertie, the ambassador at Paris, took alarm

---

[1] Metternich to Bethmann, 11 Mar. 1912. *Große Politik*, xxxi, no. 11398.
[2] Grey to Goschen, 14 Mar. 1912. *British Documents*, vi, no. 537.
[3] 26 Feb. 1912. Tirpitz, *Politische Dokumente*, i. 299.
[4] Granville (Berlin) to Nicolson, 18 Oct. 1912. *British Documents*, ix (ii), no. 47.
[5] Poincaré to Paul Cambon, 26 Feb. 1912. *Documents diplomatiques français*, third series, ii, no. 105.
[6] Paul Cambon to Poincaré, 28 Feb. 1912. Ibid., no. 119.

again; perhaps he was encouraged by Nicolson, now permanent under-secretary, to give things a final push. He went privately to Poincaré and urged him to protest in London. He said of Grey: 'I no longer understand his policy and I am disturbed.'[1] Poincaré followed Bertie's advice. Grey was irritated by these French complaints: 'Russia and France both deal separately with Germany and it is not reasonable that tension should be permanently greater between England and Germany than between Germany and France or Germany and Russia.'[2] Bertie, however, continued to stir up the French: '*an irreparable misunderstanding* would follow', and Poincaré should speak 'with energy'.[3] On 15 April Paul Cambon proposed to Nicolson that the British should renew the offer of an alliance, which he now genuinely supposed that Lansdowne had made in May 1905. Nicolson said that 'this radical-socialist cabinet' would not agree to it. He spoke contemptuously of the 'financiers, pacifists, faddists and others' who wanted closer relations with Germany, and concluded: 'the Cabinet will not last, it is done for', and, with the Conservatives, you will get something precise'.[4] This was curious language for a civil servant supposedly without political leanings; and it is hardly surprising that after it the French sometimes had doubts about British policy. For the time being, they had to be content with Grey's repeated assurance: 'although we cannot bind ourselves under all circumstances to go to war with France against Germany, we shall also certainly not bind ourselves to Germany not to assist France.'[5]

In practice, the increase of the German navy made it ever more difficult for the British to avoid committing themselves on the French side. In March 1912 Churchill, first lord of the Admiralty, not only announced a larger British programme: the bulk of the Mediterranean fleet was to be withdrawn from Malta to home waters and the rest concentrated at Gibraltar. The Mediterranean would have to look after

---

[1] Note by Poincaré, 27 Mar. 1912. *Documents diplomatiques français*, third series, ii, no. 266.

[2] Minute by Grey on Bertie to Grey, 3 Apr. 1912. *British Documents*, vi, no. 564.

[3] Note by Poincaré for Paléologue, 10 Apr. 1912. *Documents diplomatiques français*, third series, ii, no. 319.

[4] Paul Cambon to Poincaré, 18 Apr. 1912. Ibid., no. 363; minute by Nicolson, 15 Apr. 1912. *British Documents*, vi, no. 576. Asquith would hardly have noted: 'I entirely approve the language used by Sir A. Nicolson', if he had known everything that Nicolson had said.

[5] Grey to Nicolson, 21 Apr. 1912. Ibid., no. 580.

itself, or rather it was hoped that the French would look after it. Bertie and Nicolson thought this a good opening to press again for alliance with France; Nicolson said: 'it offers the cheapest, simplest and safest solution'.[1] Churchill, still a radical though now the advocate of a great navy, held out against this solution. He was ready to authorize naval talks with the French, but wished to insert the clause: 'these dispositions have been made independently because they are the best which the separate interest of each country suggests.'[2] This was true. The German danger overrode everything else for the British. The French navy could do nothing against the Germans, but it would be adequate against Austria-Hungary and even Italy; besides, it was vital for them to protect their communications with North Africa. The French, however, would not admit this; if they did, alliance would again escape them. Early in September the French fleet at Brest was moved to Toulon; and Cambon tried again. He asked for an agreement that 'if one or other of the two governments had reason to fear an act of aggression or threats to peace, they would discuss the situation and seek means to assure in concert the maintenance of peace and to remove any attempt at aggression'.[3] The British cabinet skilfully altered this formula so as to preserve their freedom of action;[4] and they added the preamble that 'consultation between experts is not and ought not to be regarded as an engagement that commits either Government to action in a contingency that has not arisen and may never arise'.[5] Grey and Paul

[1] Nicolson to Grey, 6 May 1912. *British Documents*, x (ii), no. 385.

[2] Admiralty draft, 23 July 1912. Ibid., p. 602.

[3] Grey to Bertie, 19 Sept. 1912. Ibid., no. 410. Poincaré devised a sharper formula which did not meet with British approval: 'The two governments, foreseeing the case where one of them would have a grave motive to apprehend, either the aggression of a third Power, or some event threatening the general peace, agree that they will immediately deliberate on the means for acting together in order to prevent aggression and safeguard peace.' Paléologue to Paul Cambon, 26 Sept. 1912. *Documents diplomatiques français*, third series, iv, no. 301, note.

[4] 'If either Government had grave reason to expect an unprovoked attack by a third Power, or something that threatened the general peace, it should immediately discuss with the other, *whether* both Governments should act together to prevent aggression and to preserve peace, and *if so* what measures they would be prepared to take in common.'

[5] Paul Cambon managed to slip in a final sentence referring to the plans of the general staffs. But even here Grey had the last word—or, to be more exact, the last silence. When he read the letter to the house of commons on 3 Aug. 1914, he omitted the final sentence. 'Perhaps I thought the last sentence unimportant.' Grey, *Twenty-Five Years*, ii. 16.

Cambon duly exchanged letters to this effect on 22 November. The French could feel satisfied that the agreement between the two countries was now on a more formal basis; on the other hand, that basis was a formal assertion that an alliance did not exist. In August 1912 Poincaré told Sazonov that there was 'a verbal agreement, by virtue of which England has declared herself ready to aid France with her military and naval forces in case of an attack by Germany'.[1] He can hardly have believed this, though it was no doubt useful to him that the Russians should do so. At any rate, the French never acted on the confident assumption that Great Britain would support them in a continental war, whatever its cause.

The period between the outbreak of the Agadir crisis and the failure of Haldane's mission certainly marked the highest point of Anglo-German tension. Then tension lessened, even though German naval building continued unabated. The party in the British cabinet friendly to Germany, now led by Lulu Harcourt, the colonial secretary, continued to work for agreement with Germany on the pattern of the French entente of 1904; they were ready to offer colonial concessions even without any naval settlement, and they got their way. The bargaining over the Bagdad railway and over the Portuguese colonies, which had once been conditional on a general agreement, now went on in isolation;[2] and the English radicals thought it a proof of Germany's goodwill that she condescended to discuss these bargains. The negotiations put the radicals in a good temper; they had no effect on the German side, except to revive the hope that Great Britain might remain neutral after all.

Oddly enough, the ending of the talks on naval limitation itself brought an easier atmosphere. The British had been angered by the German refusal to slow down their naval building; the Germans had been angered by the British request. Now both sides recovered their temper. The British found that they could outbuild the Germans, though with occasional lamentations. British naval supremacy had been least in 1911; thereafter it grew steadily. In any case, the German naval

[1] Sazonov to Nicholas II, 17 Aug. 1912. *Diplomatische Schriftwechsel Iswolskis 1911–1914*, ii, no. 401.

[2] Grey acquiesced in these negotiations rather than cause a cabinet crisis. All the same he was much embarrassed when Eyre Crowe caught him out abetting Harcourt. Minute by Crowe on colonial office to foreign office, 1 Apr. 1912. *British Documents*, x (ii), no. 285

challenge had exacerbated, not caused, the conflict with Great Britain. On the contrary, the naval threat made it easier for the British government to follow a policy that they would have followed in any event, short of a radical revolt. The fundamental motive of the changed British policy was the German threat to the independence of France, which had been shown in the two Moroccan crises. When the question of Morocco was ended and when France became more independent and self-confident under Poincaré's leadership, British anxieties grew less, and Anglo-German relations automatically improved.

The British choice between Germany and France was clear; they were never so decided between Germany and Russia. In the spring of 1912 the Russians improved their behaviour in Persia, temporarily at any rate; and in this sense British relations with them became easier. But even those who advocated co-operation with Russia were never clear why they did so. Some argued that Russia was weak and must be supported in order to maintain the European Balance. Others, Nicolson in particular, argued that she was strong and must be supported for fear of the trouble that she would otherwise cause. He wrote in October 1912: 'this understanding is more vital to us than it is to Russia, though of course it is not necessary to let them know this';[1] and again in February 1913, 'were we to split up the partnership we should be the chief sufferers'.[2] This was an extreme view. Most Englishmen would have been ready to stand up to Russia, if they could have been confident that Germany would not improve the occasion to establish her supremacy on the continent of Europe. They had little doubt that Great Britain and Russia should co-operate in order to sustain France; they were by no means so decided that Great Britain and France should co-operate in order to sustain Russia. In the autumn of 1912 the Balkans exploded; and Russia had to stand unwillingly in the front line. As a result, relations between Great Britain and Germany became better than at any time since the turn of the century, though the danger of a general war was greater than at any time since the congress of Berlin.

[1] Nicolson to Buchanan (St. Petersburg), 22 Oct. 1912. *British Documents*, ix (ii), no. 57.

[2] Nicolson to Cartwright (Vienna), 19 Feb. 1913. Ibid. x (ii), no. 632. Nicolson regarded the Anglo-Russian entente as very much his own work and was therefore not particularly scrupulous as to the arguments he used in order to justify it.

XXI

THE BALKAN WARS AND AFTER

1912–14

FOREIGN policy rarely follows a straight line. It is more often the outcome of a conflict of interests at home, which sometimes balance and sometimes provoke each other. In Great Britain, for example, the hostility towards Germany, which sprang from naval and continental anxieties, was moderated by the rivalry with Russia which still went on in Persia and China. In Germany, on the other hand, the naval and colonial advocates who looked overseas made their peace with those other imperialists whose ambitions were centred on the Ottoman empire, and the two agreed to treat the Anglo-Russian entente as an unshakeably hostile partnership. Russian policy, too, was pulled in different directions. In 1897 the Russians had consciously turned their backs on Europe in order to seek greater prizes in China and Persia; and the traditional 'empire-builders'—military adventurers and financial speculators—continued to seek these prizes even after the Japanese victory in the Far East and the entente with Great Britain over Persia. Russian policy did not swing back to concentration on Europe after 1905 or 1907; the Russians were quite capable of doing two things at a time, and China and Persia took up most of the energies of the foreign ministry until the very outbreak of the European war in 1914. Nor was the motive of Russian policy a naïve taste for 'warm-water'[1]—a sort of political sea-bathing. Ever since the Crimean war, if not before it, the Russian concern at the Straits had been defensive, though traditional motives of prestige complicated the issue. The Russians wanted a naval monopoly of the Black Sea; and they could have it cheaply so long as Turkey kept the Straits firmly closed.

By 1912 this policy was breaking down. The Ottoman empire

[1] 'The key to the foreign policy of Russia throughout the centuries is the urge towards warm water ports.' Gooch, *Before the War*, i. 287.

seemed on the point of collapse. The Young Turk revolution had brought no improvement; the war with Italy strained Turkish resources; and the Balkan states were impatient to end Turkish rule in Europe. Further, the strategical closing of the Straits no longer satisfied Russia's needs: she must also have a more certain passage for merchant-ships than Turkey could provide. This was underlined in April 1912 when the Turks closed the Straits for a fortnight against a possible Italian attack and, in so doing, produced a grave economic crisis in Russia. For she had now to send out increasing quantities of grain from Odessa to pay the interest on her foreign loans; and, as well, an industrial revolution of the first magnitude was in full swing in the Ukraine, for which she needed equipment from abroad. The Russians had accepted a Turkish control of the Straits, so long as the Turks did the job properly; they could not tolerate the domination of any Great Power there, without sealing their own death-warrant as an independent state. They had no ambitions in European Turkey nor interest in the Balkan states, except as neutral buffers against Austria-Hungary and Germany. The prizes there were trifling and hard to come by, compared to those in China or Persia. There were no Russian banks in the Balkans, no Russian-owned railways, virtually no Russian trade. Middle-class opinion counted for something in Russia after the revolution of 1905 and even after its failure; and intellectuals talked of Russia's mission to protect the Slavs or to take Constantinople much as English liberal journalists talked of the British mission to promote freedom or French professors dreamt of a frontier on the Rhine. This sentiment had little practical weight; fear of being strangled at the Straits was the dominant motive of Russian policy. Izvolski and Charykov had tried to solve the problem in the autumn of 1911; they had failed. Hartvig at Belgrade and Nekludov at Sofia did better. Acting very much on their own initiative, they helped to bring Serbia and Bulgaria on to good terms; and on 13 March 1912 the two states signed an alliance. In Russian eyes, this was simply a defensive barrier. Sazonov said when he heard of it: 'Well, this is perfect! Five hundred thousand bayonets to guard the Balkans—this would bar the road forever to German penetration, Austrian invasion.'[1]

This was not at all the idea of the two Balkan allies. Bulgaria

[1] Nekludov, *Reminiscences*, p. 45.

had no interest in a war against Austria-Hungary or even in opposing her peacefully. The Serbs certainly regarded her as their enemy. The Serbian foreign minister said: 'Ah yes, if the disintegration of Austria-Hungary could take place at the same time as the liquidation of Turkey, the solution would be greatly simplified.'[1] This was not likely to happen. Therefore the Serbs were ready to join Bulgaria in dismembering Turkey, in the hope that Bulgaria might later co-operate with them against Austria-Hungary out of gratitude, once the solidarity of the alliance had been shown in action. The alliance seemed at last to solve the competing claims of the two countries to Macedonia. The Bulgarians had regarded all Macedonia as theirs ever since the treaty of San Stefano—a view with which most ethnologists agreed. The Serbs could not claim the inhabitants of Macedonia as Serb, except in the extreme north; but they invented the theory that most of Macedonia was inhabited by neither Bulgarians nor Serbs, but by 'Macedo-Slavs'; and this invention of a nationality ultimately carried the day.[2]

The treaty of alliance allotted a strip of northern Macedonia to Serbia outright. A further area, misleadingly called 'the contested zone', was reserved to the arbitrament of the tsar, with the secret understanding that he would award all of it (except a tiny zone near Struga) to the Serbs. This was a face-saving device, to assuage Bulgarian pride. The Bulgarian motive for compromise was their belief that, once war started against Turkey, they would overrun all Thrace and even capture Constantinople. The Serbs, on their side, planned to acquire also the Turkish territory on the Adriatic. It was a matter of indifference to them that this was inhabited by Albanians, not by Serbs. Like many enthusiastic nationalists, they found it easy to ignore the national existence of others.[3] This alliance of Serbia and Bulgaria was soon joined by Greece, though without any definition of her territorial aims; she, too, hoped to gain Salonica and even Constantinople, both of which the Bulgarians had privately allotted to themselves. The Balkan League was not made by Russia. Its point against Turkey was, indeed, most

[1] Gueshov, *The Balkan League*, p. 22.

[2] The theory of the 'Macedo-Slavs' did not prevent the Serbs treating the inhabitants of Macedonia as Serbs once they had been conquered.

[3] Even the heart of Old Serbia, which was the first object of Serb ambitions and contained their most historic site of Kossovo Field, was mainly inhabited by Albanians—all the more reason to deny their existence.

unwelcome to her. But Sazonov dared not estrange the Balkan states. For that matter, he dared not estrange sentiment inside Russia. He knew from the start that the Balkan League, far from being a defensive arrangement, was a combination for the destruction of Turkey-in-Europe. Since he could not forbid this himself, he tried to get the French to forbid it for him. On 24 January 1912 Izvolski proposed that France and Russia 'should envisage together all the hypotheses which can arise in the Near East';[1] and on 15 February Sazonov asked what they should do 'in case of an armed conflict between Turkey and a Balkan Power'.[2]

At any earlier time the French would have given an easy answer: France and Russia should stand aside or forbid the war altogether. But French policy changed fundamentally at the beginning of 1912. Agadir was the turning-point. National pride revolted against the pressure from Germany and brought Poincaré to power. His predecessors from Rouvier to Caillaux had represented pacific peasants and pacific bankers, whose interests cut across Russian ambitions in China as well as in Turkey. With Poincaré, himself the legal adviser of Schneider-Creusot, heavy industry came to power. Russian arms contracts and railways became more important than Turkish loans; and France, too, had a decisive stake in the free passage of the Straits. Apart from these economic motives, Poincaré had a clear political task—to reassert the equality of France as a Great Power. Poincaré was a man of strong character, with a clear, logical mind; himself from Lorraine, he never forgot the humiliation of 1871. He certainly did not want a great European war; but, unlike any of his predecessors since 1875, he intended to show that France was no more afraid of war than Germany was. A change in French military plans which took place at the same time underlined this new attitude. Previously, French plans had been defensive; the French generals would be content if they could prevent the Germans from taking Paris. Now Joffre, the prospective commander-in-chief, believed that he could actually defeat the Germans and therefore planned a great offensive from the Vosges across the Rhine.[3]

Poincaré's new line brought with it a new French attitude

[1] Note by Poincaré, 24 Jan. 1912. *Documents diplomatiques français*, third series, i, no. 513.

[2] Louis (St. Petersburg) to Poincaré, 15 Feb. 1912. Ibid., ii, no. 43.

[3] This new strategy actually made British support less necessary for the French. So long as they planned a defensive war, they welcomed a British reinforcement on

towards the alliance with Russia. Previous French governments had regarded the alliance as a reinsurance against Germany; and they had been deeply concerned not to be dragged into Russia's Balkan ventures. Poincaré wanted Russia to be as independent of Germany as he was, though of course he tried to avoid paying the price. His attitude towards Russia was, in fact, very like the British attitude towards France: he wanted her to be firm towards Germany, while keeping a free hand himself. In the result, he did more to encourage Russia than to restrain her, much as the British had with France during the Agadir crisis. Though he expostulated when the Russians allowed the Balkan League to come into being without warning him, he expostulated a good deal more when Nicholas II met William II at Port Baltic in the middle of June. 'We are obliged to demand in advance the formal assurance that no political question either about the Near East or any other subject will be raised without us'.[1]

This was a new attitude. Previously Russia, and for that matter France, had negotiated with Germany without informing her partner—the Potsdam agreement was evidence on the one side, the discussions which preceded and accompanied the Agadir crisis evidence on the other. Poincaré was now demanding solidarity from both Russia and Great Britain. Previous French governments had held Russia back in the Near East. Though they gave public opinion as their excuse, their real motive was the clash of French and Russian interests at the Straits. This clash no longer existed, or rather Poincaré no longer emphasized it.[2] Southern Russia, not the Ottoman empire, was now the prize for French capitalism. Moreover,

their left wing. When they changed to offensive plans, they became indifferent to the projected German attack through Belgium, though it was vaguely known to them. They assumed that the Belgian army would hold the Germans up until the decisive battle had been won in Alsace. Even if the Germans broke through, this would only increase their disaster when the French reached southern Germany. Hence the French lost interest in the British expeditionary force. Ironically enough, the British gave up the idea of sending an independent force to Antwerp and agreed to co-operating with the French in northern France instead, just when this co-operation ceased to be an essential part of French strategy. Of course, the French pressed hard for British entry into the war in 1914; but the pressure came then principally from the diplomatists and the government—in 1906 and 1911 it had come from the French soldiers. Joffre believed confidently that he could beat the Germans without British assistance.

[1] Poincaré to Louis, 7 June 1912. *Documents diplomatiques français*, third series, iii, no. 72.

[2] Of course the older interests still persisted. Bompard, for instance, continued to preach distrust of Sazonov from Constantinople.

with the withdrawal of the British fleet from the Mediterranean, the French would welcome Russian co-operation there; and a naval convention was concluded in July.[1] Hence Poincaré, unlike his predecessors, would not allow Russia to put the blame on him for her own reluctance to move in the Near East. When Sazonov showed him the full text of the alliance between Serbia and Bulgaria in August, he exclaimed: 'This is an agreement for war'; and he emphasized that French opinion would not allow the government 'to decide on military action for purely Balkan questions'. But he added the vital rider: 'unless Germany intervened and of her own initiative provoked the application of the *casus foederis*'.[2] He confirmed this to Izvolski a month later: 'If conflict with Austria brought intervention by Germany, France would fulfil her obligations.'[3] To encourage Sazonov still further, he exaggerated his own confidence in Great Britain and urged that Russia, too, should make a naval agreement with her. Sazonov duly took this line when he visited England in September.

Poincaré later claimed that he had only stated a loyalty to the Russian alliance which was accepted by all French statesmen. But there was something new. The alliance provided that France would aid Russia 'if she were attacked by Germany or by Austria supported by Germany'. What happened if Russia attacked Austria-Hungary and herself provoked the attack from Germany which must follow according to the Austro-German treaty of 1879, itself public property? Previous French statesmen had evaded this question. Poincaré answered it: France would go to war. This 'extension' of the alliance was nothing like as emphatic as the assurances which the Germans gave to Austria-Hungary in 1890 and 1909 and were again to give in 1913 and 1914; and its purpose was no doubt primarily to keep Russia from dependence on Germany. Nevertheless it reflected also the new French confidence. The Russian general staff still doubted whether they could hold their own against Germany;[4] the French general staff believed that a war would liberate either Poland or Lorraine, even if the Austrians overran the Balkans in the process.[5]

[1] Project of naval convention, 16 July 1912. *Documents diplomatiques français*, third series, iii, no. 206.
[2] Sazonov to Nicholas II, 17 Aug. 1912. *Schriftwechsel Iswolskis*, ii, no. 401.
[3] Izvolski to Sazonov, 12 Sept. 1912. Ibid., no. 429.
[4] *Procès-verbal*, 13 July 1912. *Documents diplomatiques français*, third series, iii, no. 200.
[5] Note by the French general staff, 2 Sept. 1912. Ibid., no. 359.

Though Poincaré did not want to provoke a war, France was more ready to act as an independent Great Power than at any time since 1870; and, after forty years of effortless German superiority, this was provocation enough. As a result, none of the powers of the Triple Entente did anything to prevent the coming explosion in the Balkans. Poincaré would not repeat the policy of 1909 and risk being accused of deserting Russia. The British were taken up with Persia and therefore also evaded the Balkan question, so as to escape difficulties with Russia.[1] Sazonov did not want a Balkan war, yet dared not forbid it for fear of Russian opinion. He said to Nicholas II of the Balkan states: 'we have given them their independence, our task is finished'. From first to last, he and Kokovtsov, the prime minister, were determined not to go to war for any issue except the Straits: 'On the Bosphorus there can be only the Turks or ourselves.'[2] If the Balkan states won, this would strengthen the barrier against Austria-Hungary; if they lost, Russia might act at the Straits, but she would not start a European war.

The members of the Triple Alliance were almost equally passive. Italy welcomed the Balkan storm: it compelled the Turks to give way in Libya, and peace between Italy and Turkey was made on 15 October just when the Balkan war broke out.[3] The Germans were in two minds about the Balkans all along. They had patronized Turkey and were deeply committed to maintaining Austria-Hungary as a Great Power. On the other hand, Germany was the greatest of national states; and the Germans believed rightly that a victory for Balkan nationalism would bring them advantages, just as the victory of Italian nationalism had done. They never understood the Austro-Hungarian terror of nationalism and supposed, at most, that it would prevent any new display of independence in Vienna, such as Aehrenthal had shown during the Agadir crisis. In fact, their policy was much like Poincaré's towards Russia; they wanted to tie Austria-Hungary down without becoming involved in war themselves. If Austria-Hungary had taken a resolute line, they would have supported her. But this the Austrian statesmen were incapable of doing.

[1] Memoranda by Grey, 24–27 Sept. 1912. *British Documents*, ix (i), no. 803.
[2] Louis to Poincaré, 21 Dec. 1912. *Documents diplomatiques français*, third series, v, no. 105.
[3] Turkey surrendered Libya. Italy was to withdraw from the Aegean islands which she had occupied, when the Turkish troops left Libya. For one reason and another, this withdrawal never took place.

They had always held that the Habsburg monarchy could not long survive the destruction of the Ottoman empire and the rise of national states. Yet they had no Balkan policy. In 1908 Aehrenthal had planned to destroy Serbia; at the last moment he decided that the remedy was worse than the disease and drew back. He died in 1912, having accomplished nothing. His successor, Berchtold, was even more at a loss: he could only regard Balkan developments with helpless lamentation. Here again, if Germany had given a firm push into war, the Austrians would have allowed themselves to be propelled. As it was, their only decision was that the Monarchy must keep out of war.[1] Berchtold made some feeble efforts. On 13 August he proposed that the Powers should urge reform on Turkey—a last echo of Andrássy's policy in 1876, itself no great success. None of the Powers welcomed this proposal. At the last moment, the rulers of Europe revolted at being dragged into trouble by the Balkan states. There was a flurry of diplomatic activity, in which Kiderlen and Poincaré took the lead; and finally Austria-Hungary and Russia were entrusted with the task of warning the Balkan states in the name of the Powers that no change of the *status quo* would be permitted. It was a curious dying display of the Austro-Russian partnership which had once given Europe and the Balkans long years of peace.

The Austro-Russian note was presented on 8 October; the same day Montenegro declared war on Turkey. Bulgaria, Greece, and Serbia did the same within a week. By the end of the month every Turkish army in Europe had been defeated. Only Adrianople, Scutari, and Janina remained in Turkish hands. The Great Powers were bewildered. None was ready for war; yet none could turn its back on the Eastern question. The Austrians had to make up their minds to something. In 1908 they had declared, when evacuating the Sanjak, that they could not allow it to fall into Serbian hands; now they made no move to reoccupy it. Kiderlen did his best to encourage them: 'as at the time of the annexation, Austria-Hungary could count unconditionally on the support of Germany'.[2] Experience in Bosnia had taught them that it was futile to acquire more Slav subjects; besides, they could never make a rapid decision and so missed

---

[1] Protocol of ministerial conference, 14 Sept. 1912. *Österreich-Ungarns Außenpolitik*, iv, no. 3787.

[2] Szögyény to Berchtold, 10 Oct. 1912. Ibid., no. 4022.

the chance of moving into the Sanjak while the Serbs were still busy elsewhere. Austria-Hungary stood by and allowed the national reconstruction of Turkey-in-Europe. Of course this was not something that happened suddenly in October 1912. It had really been determined when Andrássy and Disraeli failed to assert the integrity of the Ottoman empire in 1878, or even earlier when Metternich had failed to prevent the establishment of an independent Greece in the eighteen-twenties. Once the Ottoman empire crumbled, national states were inevitable, unless Austria-Hungary conquered the Balkans herself; and that had been beyond her ever since the end of the Crimean war. As a logical sequel, the Austrians should have been re-conciled with Serbia and should have sought to co-operate with her. The Serbs would have welcomed it: they already foresaw a conflict with Bulgaria over Macedonia and, besides, the 'Balkan' Serbs did not really relish unification with the more cultivated Serbs within the Habsburg monarchy, still less with the sophisticated and Roman Catholic Croats. Thomas Masaryk, a Czech professor who dreamt of transforming Austria-Hungary into a democratic federation of free peoples, acted as intermediary. Berchtold thought 'that he was a *pauvre diable* who probably wanted a commission' and told him: 'we are not here to help people to earn a percentage.'[1] The 'percentage' which Masaryk ultimately earned was to be President-liberator of Czecho-slovakia.

The victory of Balkan nationalism was a disaster beyond remedy for the Habsburg monarchy. Berchtold beat about for some issue on which to reassert the monarchy's 'prestige'. At the end of October he found it: he would not allow Serbia a port on the Adriatic[2] and would insist on setting up an independent

[1] Kanner, *Katastrophenpolitik*, p. 112.

[2] Attempts were made to rationalize this decision. It was argued that Austria-Hungary would have a stranglehold over Serb trade if this had no outlet to the sea. But Durazzo and the rest were useless to Serbia except for reasons of prestige. They were cut off from Serbia by great mountains; there was no railway, and none was ever likely to be built. The Dalmatian ports, such as Split, which Jugo-slavia acquired after the world war, never served her trade to any extent. The Austro-Hungarian stranglehold was, in any case, effectively broken when Greece gave the Serbs access to Salonica. Even more absurd was the suggestion that a port on the Adriatic would become a Russian naval base. The Russians were hard enough pressed to hold their own in the Baltic and the Black Sea; they never used even the facilities at Bizerta which the French offered them. The one serious argument was that, if the Serbs were at Durazzo, this would attract the Serbs of Dalmatia farther north up the coast; but they were disaffected already.

Albania. This was a good issue on which to make a stand. Italy, jealous of both Serbia and Austria-Hungary, would back it for fear of the alternatives. Besides, the Albanians were a genuine nationality, as much entitled to freedom as anyone else. This certainly affected opinion in Great Britain and France, though it was odd for Austria-Hungary to appear as the champion of national independence. Most of all, the Russians did not care about this remote issue. From the day that it arose, Sazonov told the Serbs that Russia would not fight for the sake of a Serb port on the Adriatic.[1] The Russians had a more pressing anxiety. They were afraid that the Bulgarians would capture Constantinople. To prevent this, they were ready to go to war 'within twenty-four hours'.[2] Sazonov wrote: 'The occupation of Constantinople could compel the appearance of our whole Black Sea fleet before the Turkish capital.'[3] This, too, was an odd outcome: the only serious preparations for war made by Russia in 1912 were against a Slav national state.

War in the Balkans had been expected to produce a conflict between Russia and Austria-Hungary. Instead it seemed to be bringing them together—Russia would resist Bulgaria at Constantinople; Austria-Hungary would resist Serbia over Albania. On the other side, the Germans urged co-operation on Great Britain and France in order to keep the Russians out of Constantinople. The idea was not unwelcome to Grey, who wanted Constantinople to be made a free city if the Turkish empire fell to pieces[4]—a solution abhorrent to the Russians. Poincaré recognized that, if he took this line, the Franco-Russian alliance would fall to pieces, the Austro-German alliance would remain, and Germany would be master of Europe. At the same time, he too, wished to keep the Russians out of Constantinople. His solution was to urge the Russians to back Serbia and to promise, ever more emphatically, that France would support her. He told Izvolski on 17 November: 'If Russia goes to war, France will also, as we know that in this question Germany is behind

[1] Sazonov to Hartvig, 9 Nov. 1912. *Mezhdunarodnye otnosheniya*, second series, xii (i), no. 195.

[2] Louis to Poincaré, 28 Oct. 1912. *Documents diplomatiques français*, third series, iv, no. 258.

[3] Sazonov to Izvolski, 4 Nov. 1912. *Mezhdunarodnye otnosheniya*, second series, xxi (i), no. 157. Sazonov also opposed a Bulgarian occupation of Adrianople; Nicholas II, more Slav in sentiment, favoured it.

[4] Benckendorff to Sazonov, 7 Nov. 1912. Ibid., no. 173.

Austria'.[1] This is the sentence, which in later years brought on Poincaré the accusation of 'war-mongering'; and it was certainly much more than had been said by any previous French statesman. But it was not designed to provoke a war. It was designed to prevent either a Russian occupation of Constantinople or an Austro-Russian partnership, which must have brought a revival of the League of the Three Emperors. Poincaré was determined to preserve the Franco-Russian alliance, which alone guaranteed French independence; and a Great Power which wishes to remain independent must be ready to face war in order to do so.

In any case the alarm turned out to be premature. The Bulgarians failed to take Adrianople, let alone Constantinople; and the Russians could revive their patronage of Balkan nationalism without risk to their own interests. The Balkan states could make no further headway and on 3 December they concluded an armistice with Turkey. A peace conference met in London—the most 'neutral' of the great capitals. The Balkan states meant to collect their gains without waiting for the permission of the Great Powers. These, however, saved appearances by setting up a conference of their ambassadors in London under Grey's chairmanship to decide what changes they would tolerate.[2] The situation still seemed dangerous. Some forces had been mobilized in Austria-Hungary; and the Russians, in retaliation, did not disband the contingent of conscripts that was

---

[1] Izvolski to Sazonov, 17 Nov. 1912. *Mezhdunarodnye otnosheniya*, second series, xxi (i), no. 268. Poincaré disliked Izvolski's definition, and Izvolski modified it the next day: 'France would march in the case in which the *casus foederis* laid down by the alliance should arise, i.e. in the case in which Germany should give armed support to Austria.' Izvolski to Sazonov, 19 Nov. 1912. Ibid., no. 280. Poincaré had second thoughts even about this and on the following day he tried again: 'France would respect the treaty of alliance and would support Russia even militarily in case the *casus foederis* arose.' Poincaré to Louis, 19 Nov. 1912. *Documents diplomatiques français*, third series, iv, no. 494. These attempts to square the circle reveal Poincaré's difficulty. He wanted Russia to take an independent line and to stand up to Austria-Hungary; yet he shrank from the reproach of involving France in a war which started in the Balkans. Germany would have to intervene and the issue of the Balance of Power be clearly stated before France could go to war. Poincaré did not solve this insoluble problem; but in November 1912 the danger was that Russia would desert the French alliance, not that she would go irresponsibly to war. Therefore Poincaré had to emphasize that France would not desert Russia.

[2] Paris was originally proposed for the conference of ambassadors; but the Germans and Austrians did not want to meet under Poincaré, and everyone, including the Russians, wanted to keep Izvolski out of things.

due for release at the end of the year. But the great decision
against a general war had already been made, when Austria-
Hungary had failed to intervene against Serbia in October and
when the Russians, on their side, had refused to support the
Serb claim to a port on the Adriatic. Of course, both blamed
their allies for their timidity. The Russians tried again and again
to make Poincaré say that he would not support them if they
went to war for the sake of Serbia. Poincaré refused to be caught.
Millerand, his minister of war, said: 'we are not to be blamed;
we are prepared, and that fact must be borne in mind.'[1] This
was not an encouragement for Russia to go to war; it was an
insistence that she must make her own foreign policy. Similarly,
Germany would not be saddled with Austria-Hungary's irresolution. Francis Ferdinand, heir to the Habsburg throne, reported
after meeting William II: 'as soon as our prestige demands, we
must intervene in Serbia with vigour, and we could be sure of
his support'.[2] But war against Serbia was not at all in Francis
Ferdinand's calculations. He dreamt of solving the South Slav
question by conciliation once he was on the throne; and he told
Conrad, who became chief-of-staff again in December: 'I do
not want from Serbia a single plum-tree, a single sheep.'[3] On
his initiative a great Austrian aristocrat, Prince Hohenlohe, was
sent to St. Petersburg in February 1913 with an appeal to
dynastic solidarity. The appeal worked, and the military preparations on both sides were relaxed.

The conference of ambassadors was in appearance a striking
demonstration of the Concert of Europe. It could not undo the
results of the Balkan war—nor of its renewal in March which
deprived Turkey of Adrianople, temporarily as it turned out.
The ambassadors had to make these results palatable to Russia
and Austria-Hungary. Russia had only one urgent concern: to
keep the Bulgarians out of Constantinople. But the Turks were
strong enough to do this themselves without the assistance of
the Great Powers. Russia therefore could appear conciliatory
and reasonable. The only serious task of the conference was to
translate into practical terms the condition on which Austria-
Hungary had insisted and to which Russia had agreed—the

[1] Ignatiev to Zhilinski, 19 Dec. 1912, Adamov, *Die europäischen Mächte und der
Türkei*, i. 56.
[2] Francis Ferdinand to foreign ministry, 22 Nov. 1912. *Österreich-Ungarns Außenpolitik*, iv, no. 4571.
[3] Memorandum by Conrad, 10 Feb. 1913. Conrad, *Aus meiner Dienstzeit*, iii, 127.

establishment of an independent Albania. This marked in principle an Austro-Hungarian victory; but when it came to details, Russia could dispute about frontier villages, such as Dibra and Djakova, and it was Austria-Hungary that seemed intransigent. Grey often took her side in these disputes. As Eyre Crowe remarked with unconscious irony: 'the whole position of Great Britain in the world rests largely on the confidence she has earned that, at least with questions not touching her own vital interests, she deals strictly on their merits according to the generally accepted standards of right and wrong'.[1]

Grey wanted to make a practical demonstration that 'no hostile or aggressive policy would be pursued against Germany or her allies by France, Russia, and ourselves, jointly or separately'.[2] The Germans, on their side, forced compromise on Austria-Hungary, but with different motives. While Grey wished to show that Triple Entente and Triple Alliance could live peacefully side by side, the Germans hoped to detach Great Britain from her existing friends. This was Bethmann's own favourite idea. Kiderlen, who might have been tempted to repeat at some moment his Bosnian stroke of March 1909, died at the end of 1912; Jagow, who succeeded him as secretary of state, was a routine diplomat, incapable of any flight of policy. The way was therefore clear for Bethmann, the patrician from Frankfurt, who dreamt always of a conservative alliance with England against Russia and looked back nostalgically to the 'lost opportunity' of 1854 at the beginning of the Crimean war. Though Bethmann had failed to curb the German naval enthusiasts, he still hoped to appease the British by colonial bargaining and by a pacific line in the Balkans—for the time being. He wrote to Berchtold in February 1913: 'we may look for a new orientation of British policy if we can get through the present crisis without any quarrels. . . . I think it would be a mistake of immeasurable consequence if we attempt a solution by force . . . at a moment when there is even the remotest prospect of entering this conflict under conditions more favourable to ourselves.'[3] Similarly, Moltke wrote to Conrad that they should wait until the Balkan League broke up. But he had no

---

[1] Minute by Crowe on Bunsen (Vienna) to Grey, 12 Dec. 1912. *British Documents*, x (i), no. 100.

[2] Grey to Goschen, 30 July 1914. Ibid., xi, no. 303.

[3] Bethmann to Berchtold, 10 Feb. 1913. *Große Politik*, xxxiv (i), no. 12818.

doubt that war was approaching: 'a European war must come sooner or later in which ultimately the struggle will be one between Germanism and Slavism.'[1]

The Germans expressed their policy even more forcibly in January 1913 when they prepared a new army bill which was formally introduced by Bethmann in March. This vastly increased their armed forces and first created the mass-army; what is more, the increases were financed by a capital levy. The Lloyd George budget of 1909, which had caused a constitutional crisis in Great Britain, had only raised taxes by fifteen million pounds. Germany, a poorer country, had to provide an extra fifty million pounds within eighteen months. This was an effort that could not be repeated. In the summer of 1914, German preparations for war would be at their height; the temptation to use their superiority against France and Russia would be very great. It was the object of Bethmann's policy (so far as he had one) to increase this temptation by ensuring that, at the decisive crisis, Great Britain would not stand by France and Russia.

The success of the ambassadors' conference was therefore illusory; all the same it was, for the time being, a success. The Balkan war did not lead to a conflict between the Great Powers. The greatest score of the conference came in April, when Montenegro seized Scutari, which the Great Powers had resolved should go to Albania. They agreed on a naval demonstration against Montenegro; and the Russians implored Great Britain and France to take part in it, though characteristically evading doing so themselves. The gesture worked: the king of Montenegro gave way, after making a fortune on the stock-exchange by stirring up rumours of war. By May 1913, when the treaty of London ended the first Balkan war, Albania had an international existence, though its internal ordering remains unsettled until the present day. This was a victory, of a sort, for Austria-Hungary: Albania was evidence that the Habsburg monarchy could still impose its will as a Great Power. More important, the treaty of London brought with it the disruption of the Balkan League. While the Bulgarians had been tied down in the hard fighting outside Adrianople, the Serbs had occupied all Macedonia; and they now insisted on keeping Bulgaria's share as well as their own and 'the contested zone'.[2] Their principal concern

---

[1] Moltke to Conrad, 10 Feb. 1913. Conrad, *Aus meiner Dienstzeit*, iii. 144–7.
[2] The Serbs argued that they had sent troops to help Bulgaria at Adrianople,

was to control the railway down to Salonica, which was now in Greek hands and which, with the Adriatic denied to them, was their only outlet to the outer world. Salonica was a further Bulgarian grievance. Their troops had reached it only four hours after the Greeks; and the latter, not content with this, had extended their claims far along the Aegean coast.

The Bulgarians had done most of the fighting against Turkey; they imagined that they could take on Greece and Serbia together, and attacked them on 29 June without warning. The plan misfired disastrously. Greece and Serbia more than held their own. Rumania, who had hitherto remained neutral, entered the war against Bulgaria in order to acquire the Dobrudja. Even Turkey recaptured Adrianople. The moment was decisive, too, for Austria-Hungary. The Germans had always told Berchtold that he should wait until Serbia and Bulgaria quarrelled; and he, on his side, had always insisted that he could allow no new Serb aggrandizement. For a moment he talked big and threatened war. When it came to the point he would not risk a quarrel with Rumania. What is more, the Germans were all against war. They hoped to win the competition for Rumanian, Greek, and even Serb friendship, and rated Bulgaria very low. They had no sympathy with Austria-Hungary's national problems. Bethmann hoped that 'Vienna would not let its peace be disturbed by the *cauchemar* of a Greater Serbia'.[1] Once more Berchtold did nothing. Later on the Austrians complained that Germany had forbidden them to crush Serbia, when conditions were still favourable. Berchtold was nearer the truth when he said to Conrad concerning an attack on Serbia: 'his heart was for it but not his head'.[2]

The combatants of the second Balkan war met at Bucarest and made peace there in August. Bulgaria had to pay a price to everyone—the Dobrudja to Rumania, Adrianople to Turkey. The Serbs took the bulk of Macedonia; the Greeks took the rest

while the Bulgarians, on their side, had never offered to help them against Austria-Hungary. The Serbs further claimed that they should receive more of Macedonia to compensate them for the disappointment of their hopes on the Adriatic (which had never been specified in the Serbo-Bulgarian treaty of alliance). Their real motive was that, being in occupation of most of Macedonia, they were unwilling to withdraw from it.

[1] Zimmermann to Tschirschky (Vienna), 7 July 1913. *Große Politik*, xxxv, no. 13490.

[2] Conversation of Conrad with Berchtold, 29 Sept. 1913. Conrad, *Aus meiner Dienstzeit*, iii. 444.

and western Thrace, including Salonica. Bulgaria gained only a narrow strip of Macedonia and eastern Thrace, which gave her a position on the Aegean. In all, she acquired only 400,000 new subjects, where Serbia and Greece each gained a million and a half. The Peace of Bucarest was not submitted to the approval of the Great Powers. Berchtold wanted them to insist on concessions for Bulgaria. This idea was firmly rejected by the Germans: they were set on alliance with Rumania, Greece, and even Serbia. With their great economic stake in Asia Minor, they welcomed the strengthening of Turkey, which came from the recovery of Adrianople. William II thought Vienna 'completely crazy',[1] and recognized the Peace of Bucarest as soon as it was made. Curiously enough, the Russians had also favoured Bulgaria. They wished to atone for keeping her out of Constantinople the previous autumn; besides, they disliked Greek expansion in the Aegean, which seemed to be preparing the way for a new Byzantine empire at the Straits. But they got equally little support from Great Britain and France. Sazonov said bitterly: 'it was France who had placed at Turkey's disposal funds which had enabled her to retake Adrianople';[2] and of the Balkan states: 'they have escaped me'.[3]

This was true. The Balkan states had become truly independent; they were nobody's satellites. Though the treaty of Bucarest is often spoken of slightingly as a mere truce which settled nothing, its frontiers have remained unchanged to the present day, except that Bulgaria lost her outlet on the Aegean in 1919; the frontiers of the continental Great Powers have changed much more drastically. That old phrase, 'the Balkans for the Balkan peoples', had come true. All the Great Powers, except Austria-Hungary, accepted this outcome. Even Russia was reasonably satisfied: though the Balkan states had become independent of her, this was better than that they should be dependent on anyone else. Only the Austrians looked on with sullen resentment, just as they had refused to recognize the kingdom of Italy after 1861 or dreamt feebly of revenge on Prussia between 1866 and 1870. This was sentiment, not policy. In October 1913 Berchtold

[1] Minute by William II on Pourtalès to Bethmann, 7 Aug. 1913. *Große Politik*, xxxv, no. 13740.
[2] Buchanan (St. Petersburg) to Grey, 9 Aug. 1913. *British Documents*, ix (ii), no. 1228.
[3] Doulcet (St. Petersburg) to Pichon, 10 Sept. 1913. *Documents diplomatiques français*, third series, viii, no. 136.

Miles
40 20 0 40 80 120

R. Theiss

R. Mures

R. Drave

R. Save

BELGRADE

B O S N I A

S E R B I A

Sarajevo

R. Danube

Mostar

HERCEGOVINA

R. Morava

Nish

A D R I A T I C   S E A

MONTENEGRO

SOFIA

Skoplje

Stip

R. Vardar

R. Struma

Okhrida

G R E E C E

Boundary of 1856

Gains of 1878

Gains of 1913

"Contested zone"

SERBIA

made a last gesture of violence. The Serbs, provoked by guerrilla attacks, had crossed the provisional frontier of Albania in order to restore order. On 18 October Berchtold sent an ultimatum, demanding Serb withdrawal within a week. Conrad, as usual, hoped that this would be a prelude to action; Tisza, prime minister of Hungary and the strongest man in the monarchy, was equally insistent against anything more than a diplomatic success; Berchtold had no idea what he wanted. The Serbs were in the wrong and unready for war; they withdrew from Albania. This time Conrad was not the only one disappointed. William II had favoured the strong course, despite his former contempt for Austrian policy. He said to Berchtold: 'You can be certain I stand behind you and am ready to draw the sword whenever your action makes it necessary . . . whatever comes from Vienna is for me a command'.[1] This was perhaps no more than the impulsive violence with which William II always responded to the first news of a challenge; and it might have been followed by cautious second-thoughts, as on other occasions, if the crisis had matured. It left its mark on Berchtold all the same.

This alarm in October was the last splutter of the Balkan question in its old sense. The Balkan wars had increased the tension between the Great Powers; yet, since they had ended without a general conflict, a shift in existing arrangements seemed likely to follow. Certainly the preparations for war were everywhere increased. The Balkan wars had seen the first serious fighting in Europe since the fall of Plevna in 1877.[2] The battles had been swift and decisive; and every observer, ignoring the lessons of the Russo-Japanese war, where the battle of Mukden had dragged on for weeks, assumed that future wars between the Great Powers would follow the same pattern.[3] Hence there began a race to be ready for the first engagements, a race which the Germans started with their army-law of January 1913. The French could not call more men to the colours; with their stationary population they had no more men to call. They could only answer in August by extending the

---

[1] Memorandum by Berchtold, 28 Oct. 1913. *Österreich-Ungarns Außenpolitik*, vii, no. 8934.

[2] The Serbo-Bulgarian war of 1885 and the Greco-Turkish war of 1897 had both been abortive.

[3] If observers had looked more closely, they would have seen that even the Balkan war bogged down once the Turks reached their fortified line in front of Constantinople.

period of service to three years.[1] By 1915 or 1916, though not before, they would have a front-line army as great as the German; and they believed that even before then they could take the offensive successfully, if the German forces were divided in order to meet a threat of invasion by Russia.[2] Hence the French insisted that Russia must push on with her strategic railways to the west and increase her peace-time effectives if she were to receive a new loan.[3]

Yet, at the same time, the French backed away from the prospect of a general war. In Germany the military increases strengthened Bethmann's position in the Reichstag; in France the three-year service was opposed by the socialists and by a growing section of the radicals. Poincaré, who became president in January, and his successors at the foreign ministry, had to follow a more cautious line than that of November 1912; and they were more and more reluctant to give Russia unreserved backing. In February 1913 Benckendorff had written: 'France is the Power that would go to war with comparatively the greatest calm.'[4] At the end of the year, Kokovtzov, the Russian prime minister, reported to Nicholas II after a visit to Paris: 'All French statesmen want quiet and peace. They are ready to work with Germany and are much more peaceful than two years ago.'[5]

British policy showed the same double pattern—increased armaments on the one side, increased willingness to conciliate Germany on the other. There was no further attempt at an agreement on naval limitation, except for Churchill's proposal of 'a naval holiday', during which all building of battleships should cease. He first made this suggestion in March 1912 and repeated it in 1913 when he introduced the naval estimates; the Germans never replied, and probably only Churchill took

[1] It had been reduced to two years in 1905.

[2] The French ignored the other German step of increasing the army's equipment in machine-guns. Their larger man-power turned out to be a disaster. If their army had been smaller, they would not have undertaken the offensive in Lorraine on the outbreak of war which broke their fighting strength.

[3] De Verneuil to Pichon, 6 June, 7 July 1913. *Documents diplomatiques français*, third series, vii, nos. 134 and 309. His judgement of Russia's future is of interest: 'In the next thirty years we shall see in Russia a prodigious economic expansion which will equal if it does not surpass the colossal movement which took place in the United States during the last quarter of the nineteenth century.'

[4] Benckendorff to Sazonov, 25 Feb. 1913. *Benckendorffs Schriftwechsel*, iii, no. 896.

[5] Kokovtzov to Nicholas II, 13 Dec. 1913. *Schriftwechsel Iswolskis*, iii, no. 1169.

it seriously.[1] Some liberals tried to get the naval estimates reduced in January 1914; and Lloyd George fought for this in the cabinet.[2] But the question had lost its bitterness: the British had come to tolerate the German navy and were outstripping it without undue financial strain. Until 1912 naval limitation had been the condition for any agreements with Germany on other topics. This condition was now dropped. Harcourt, the colonial secretary, believed that the Germans had a real grievance from being denied 'a place in the sun'; and he warmed up the agreement with them over the Portuguese colonies which had been made in 1898. This was a shady transaction. Harcourt sought to conciliate Germany by giving her the colonies of an ally, not by surrendering British territory. Indeed, it was an essential part of the arrangement that Great Britain should share in the plunder—her only 'concession' was to claim rather less than she had been allotted in the original agreement.

The French were much alarmed when news of this bargain reached them. Not only did they dislike reconciliation between Great Britain and Germany: they feared that Belgium's colonies, or even their own, would be next on the list for partition—and they were not far wrong so far as Germany's plans were concerned. In much the same way, the Austrians were always afraid that a partition of the Habsburg monarchy might follow any agreement between Germany and Russia. Both Austria-Hungary and France were traditional Great Powers on the edge of decline; it would not take much to turn them into the greatest of the smaller states. Hence when France defended the interests of small states—Portugal or Belgium—it was in order to protect her own. Despite these French objections an agreement between Great Britain and Germany was reached in June 1913. An unforeseen difficulty then arose. Grey was ashamed of the transaction and wished to put the blame on his predecessors, Salisbury and Balfour, who had made the original agreement of 1898. Further, though he disliked Portuguese misrule in her

---

[1] 'It is worth a good push . . . I *do* think this is right.' Churchill to Grey, 24 Oct. 1913. *British Documents*, x (ii), no. 487.

[2] The French chargé d'affaires regarded Lloyd George's action as a bid to recover popularity, to cover up the Marconi scandal in which he had just been involved. 'We know by experience that there is no need to attach great importance to the words of a statesman who is as unstable as he is ignorant'—ungrateful words to be said of the man who made the Mansion House speech. Fleuriau to Doumergue, 2 Jan. 1914. *Documents diplomatiques français*, third series, ix, no. 5.

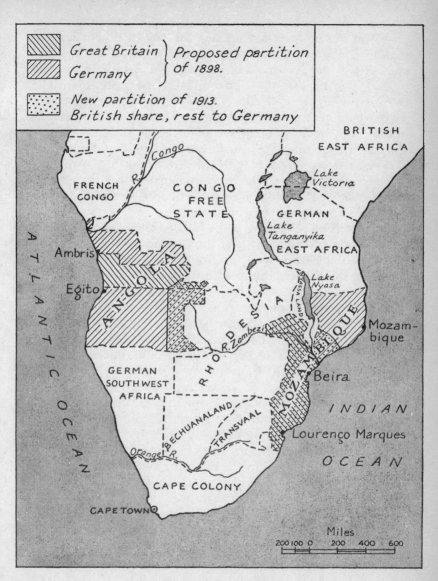

PORTUGUESE AFRICA

colonies, he wished to make it clear that she would not be deprived of her colonies against her will. He therefore insisted that, when the new agreement was signed, it must be published and, with it, the agreement of 1898 and the British declaration made to Portugal in 1899, guaranteeing her possessions. The Germans thought rightly that this would defeat their purpose. They would get neither the Portuguese colonies nor a demonstration that would estrange Great Britain from France. Lichnowsky, the German ambassador, told Grey that he seemed to assume the position of medical adviser to the Portuguese empire, 'while what Germany contemplated was rather that of being the heir'.[1] The agreement remained unsigned; still, it was a striking gesture of reconciliation.

It was still more striking when Great Britain and Germany moved towards agreement over the Bagdad railway. With the ending of the Balkan wars, the future of Turkey-in-Asia was becoming the decisive question in international relations. The Balkan prizes were very small beer; those offered in Asia seemed immense. This question cut across the existing alliances. Russia had no economic stake in Turkey—no trade with her, no share in her national debt, not a single railway concession. In fact it was her policy to prevent railways being built, in order to preserve the security of the Caucasus frontier. On the other hand she had an immense stake in the free passage of the Straits. Fifty per cent. of her export trade, and in particular 90 per cent. of her grain exports, went through them. She preferred the Ottoman empire at the Straits to any Great Power; only if it collapsed would she try to seize them for herself. Similar Russian plans had been opposed in the old days by Great Britain and France. Now the two were drifting apart. The British had lost interest in the closing of the Straits once they were established in Egypt. Though they still had the largest share of Turkish trade, this did not demand her political survival; the trade would go on, whatever the political authority. They had a small share in Turkey's debt—14 per cent. against France's 60 per cent. and Germany's 24 per cent. They had one derelict railway in Asia Minor. They were ready to write off their relatively

<hr>

[1] Grey to Goschen, 13 June 1913. *British Documents*, x (ii), no. 337. Grey told the French, somewhat disingenuously, that the agreement had been held up because of their objections. Paul Cambon to Doumergue, 19 Feb. 1914. *Documents diplomatiques français*, third series, ix, no. 333.

small stake in the Ottoman empire, if they could have security at the Persian gulf. On 29 July 1913 they concluded an agreement with Turkey, which gave them this so far as she was concerned; and they wanted the same from Germany—in return they would drop their objections to the German railway as far as Bagdad. Germany would be a more effective barrier than the decaying Ottoman empire against Russia; and the British would be free to renew their disputes with Russia in Persia—disputes which flared up again in 1914.

The French, on the other hand, were still deeply committed to the Ottoman empire. Though their old economic interests at Constantinople were somewhat dwarfed by their new interests in Russia, these still existed; and the agitation against the three-year service gave them fresh political force. As Poincaré weakened, Caillaux grew stronger: he became minister of finance in December 1913 and dreamt of being prime minister at the head of a radical-socialist coalition, which would collaborate economically with Germany. The French would not contemplate a partition of the Ottoman empire, in which they would be fobbed off (if they were lucky) with Syria. Even Paléologue, of the foreign ministry, though a wild advocate of the Russian alliance, said to Izvolski in April 1913: 'You want to exhaust Turkey; we want her to be capable of still living and even of recovering in Asia.'[1] Jules Cambon from Berlin and Bompard from Constantinople both preached co-operation with Germany against Russia.[2]

The Germans never took this idea seriously. Certainly they had a great stake in Turkey, in some ways the greatest of all the Powers. For their interests were in the heart of Turkey, at Constantinople and in Asia Minor, not on the fringes, like the British on the Persian gulf. But they did not believe that France would abandon the Russian alliance. And in this they were right. The French had managed somehow to reconcile the alliance and their Turkish interests for over thirty years, and they would not lightly abandon the effort now. Moreover, the nationalist fervour in Germany, which went along with increased armaments, provoked disturbances in Alsace, culminating

[1] Paléologue, note, 7 Apr. 1913. *Documents diplomatiques français*, third series, vi, no. 222.

[2] Jules Cambon to Pichon, 26 May, 4 June, 25 Sept., 27 Nov.; Bompard to Pichon, 4 Apr., 30 Nov. 1913. Ibid., vi, no. 621; vii, no. 31; vii, nos. 192 and 537; vi, no. 196; viii, no. 554.

in the incident at Saverne, where a German officer took the law into his own hands. Popular feeling in both countries was stronger than the solidarity of the financiers at Constantinople. Bethmann favoured instead co-operation with England: 'we can settle Asia Minor in a way favourable to ourselves only with England, just as colonial questions of the future point to co-operation with England'.[1] This, too, was an unworkable idea. The British hoped to control the Persian gulf without a general partition of Turkey-in-Asia; and the agreement with Germany over the Bagdad railway showed that they were in a fair way to do it. They would not oppose German plans in Asia Minor; on the other hand they would not support them against Russia. They might have been more forthcoming if Germany had cut down her navy and still more if she could have somehow guaranteed the security of France. This was an impossibility unless the Germans reduced their birth-rate and economic expansion, and the French increased theirs. In any case, even these factors were not decisive. In Asia the British feared Russia more than Germany; therefore they were more anxious to be on good terms with her. It would do them little harm if Germany dominated Asia Minor; it would be a disaster if Russia dominated Persia. And most disastrous of all if the two agreed to partition the Middle East. Nicolson wrote in April 1914: 'This to me is such a nightmare that I would at almost any cost keep Russia's friendship.'[2]

The British exaggerated the danger of agreement between Germany and Russia. For more than twenty years the directors of German policy had insisted that their economic interests in Turkey did not give them any political interest there; even in 1911 Kiderlen had overruled Marschall's desire to resist Russian designs on the Straits. What they had really meant by this was that Turkey would resist Russia herself without German assistance—either by her own strength or with the backing of the western Powers. Now this calculation had broken down. Great Britain and France would not resist Russia; and the Balkan wars had made Turkey too weak to do it herself.[3] The only resource left seemed to be a German protectorate at Constantinople—whether

[1] Memorandum by Bethmann, 30 Jan. 1913. *Große Politik*, xxxiv (i), no. 12763.
[2] Nicolson to Bunsen, 27 Apr. 1914. *British Documents*, x (ii), no. 540.
[3] This, too, was an exaggeration. Though the Russians boasted of being a Great Power, their Black Sea fleet was in 1914 weaker than Turkey's.

by partitioning or by maintaining the Ottoman empire did not matter. The Germans had drifted into this unconsciously. The great navy, too, had been in large part the unconscious outcome of profound economic conflicts; but it had at least the excuse of a political theory—the 'risk' which would increase Germany's bargaining power against Great Britain. There had been no political design in the Bagdad railway and all that went with it.[1] Germany had simply promoted it 'for the general purposes of her greatness'. But the result was the same. Previously Germany had been estranged from Russia only indirectly because of Austria-Hungary; now the two countries had a direct cause of conflict for the first time in their history. The economic stake in Turkey might be for the Germans, as Winston Churchill had said of their navy, 'something in the nature of a luxury'. For the Russians it was a question of existence. Sazonov wrote to Nicholas II: 'To abandon the Straits to a powerful state would be synonymous with subordinating the whole economic development of southern Russia to this state.'[2]

The Russians had no more desire than the British to 'destroy' Germany—in fact, even less, for the British had economic rivalries with Germany, while the Russians needed German as well as French capital for their industrial development. Besides, the balance between Germany and the western Powers was the foundation of Russian security. Indeed, it was more important for the Russians that Germany should threaten France and England than that they should threaten her; only so would the western Powers tolerate Russian designs in Asia Minor, Persia, and the Far East. Fear of Germany had driven France to seek the Russian alliance and had at any rate helped Great Britain to welcome the Anglo-Russian entente. If Germany ceased to exist, Russia would soon be faced again with 'the Crimean coalition', as indeed she was in 1919 and the years after. The Russians had therefore fought hard, as in the negotiations of 1899, to avoid a conflict with Germany at the Straits; the Balkan League itself had been a device for doing this—it was intended

[1] Marschall, of course, knew what he was doing, but his opinions were disregarded in Berlin. He recognized that his policy could work only on the basis of an Anglo-German alliance (such as he had tried to promote in 1890), and he went to London as ambassador in 1912 in order to accomplish this. He died in Sept. 1912 before he had discovered even the difficulties.

[2] Sazonov to Nicholas II, 8 Dec. 1913. *Schriftwechsel Iswolskis*, iii, no. 1157. Other authorities give the date as 6 Dec.

by the Russians to bar the way against Austria-Hungary, not to weaken Turkey. But once the conflict came it was inescapable, decisive; the Russians were condemned to an anti-German course.

The conflict exploded without design in November 1913. The Germans were anxious to restore the prestige of their armaments, which had been much shaken when the Greeks and Serbs had defeated the German-trained Turkish armies with French equipment. Moreover, they were always on the lookout for armament contracts for Krupps, in which William II was himself a large shareholder. They were therefore delighted when the Turks asked for a German mission which should reorganize their armed forces. In May 1913, when the request was made, the Bulgarians were at the gates of Constantinople; and even the Russians blessed the idea of strengthening Turkish resistance. Nicholas II himself approved when on a visit to Berlin.[1] By November the Russians had lost their fear of Bulgaria. They were indignant when a German general, Liman von Sanders, was put in charge of the Turkish army and, as well, given command at Constantinople. They appealed to their partners in the Triple Entente for support. Both France and Great Britain gave it with some hesitation. The French had a common interest with Germany in restoring Turkish finances and even armaments; the British were in the even more embarrassing position that a British admiral was reorganizing the Turkish navy—no doubt with an eye to ship-building contracts, but against whom if not against Russia? The Germans, on their side, shrank from the conflict which they had unwittingly provoked. In January 1914 they found a way out: Liman von Sanders was promoted to the rank of field-marshal in the Turkish army and thus became too dignified to command the troops at Constantinople.

The immediate crisis was over; the underlying conflict continued. Sazonov said to a German journalist: 'You know what interests we have at the Bosphorus, how sensitive we are at that point. All southern Russia depends upon it, and now you stick a Prussian garrison under our noses!'[2] During the alarm over the Liman von Sanders affair, the Russians examined in detail their strategic position. They decided that they were not strong

---

[1] Minute by William II on Wangenheim (Constantinople) to foreign ministry, 3 Dec. 1913. *Große Politik*, xxxviii, no. 15461.

[2] Lucius (St. Petersburg) to Bethmann, 11 Apr. 1914. Ibid., no. 15531.

enough to seize Constantinople: they had no troop-transports, and their fleet would be inferior to the Turkish until 1917. They could not even threaten the Turks by land, on the Caucasus, without denuding their western frontier. Therefore they planned in December 1913 a vast increase in their peace-time forces; but this programme, too, would not be effective until 1917. For the first time Russia needed her partners against Germany instead of their needing her. Zhilinski, the chief-of-staff, said: 'the struggle for Constantinople would hardly be possible without a general war'; and the ministers as a whole agreed: 'unless the active participation of both France and England in joint measures were assured, it does not appear possible to resort to measures of pressure such as might lead to a war with Germany.'[1]

The Russians set out to consolidate the Triple Entente as it had never been consolidated before. Further, they strove to restore the Balkan front against the central Powers which had been shattered in the second Balkan war. Bulgaria and Serbia were somehow to be reconciled; even more important, Rumania, the neutral zone which had been respected by both sides since the Crimean war, was to be won as a Black Sea Power for a policy that would be anti-Turkish and therefore now anti-German. Most striking of all, the Russians resurrected the question of Poland. On 20 January 1914 during the discussions over Liman von Sanders, Sazonov urged Nicholas II to compete with Austria-Hungary for Polish favour: 'we must create a real interest binding the Poles to the Russian state'.[2] This was a weapon which, if once loaded, would go off with devastating effect more against the traditional friendship between Romanov and Hohenzollern than against the Habsburg monarchy. The Russians did not want a war against Germany, just as the British did not want one, despite the German navy. Neither Russia nor Great Britain had anything to gain, in Europe. But Great Britain depended on the command of the seas; and Russia depended on the free passage of merchant-ships at the Straits. As Nicholas II said: 'we do not aim at Constantinople, but we need the guarantee that the Straits will not be closed to us.'[3]

---

[1] Ministerial conference, 13 Jan., 21 Feb. 1914. *Mezhdunarodnye otnosheniya*, third series, i, no. 291.

[2] Sazonov to Nicholas II, 20 Jan. 1914. Ibid., no. 52.

[3] Delcassé (St. Petersburg) to Doumergue, 29 Jan. 1914. *Documents diplomatiques rançais*, third series, ix, no. 189. Nicholas II also said: 'Our commerce will develop with the exploitation—thanks to railways—of Russia's resources and with the

If the Balkan wars had merely strengthened the national states, this would have harmed nobody except Austria-Hungary; and she no longer counted as a Great Power. But, by weakening Turkey, they gave Germany an opening to become dominant at the Straits. The temptation was irresistible and indeed, if Germany were to continue on her course as a Great Power, unavoidable. The Pomeranian grenadier was forgotten. Old Prussia had vanished; and the Greater Germany preached by the radicals of 1848 had taken the place of Bismarck's Reich. William II passed a true verdict in February 1914: 'Russo-Prussian relations are dead once and for all! We have become enemies!'[1]

increase of our population which in thirty years will exceed three hundred million.' Russian exaggeration did not come in with the Bolsheviks: forty years later Russia's population had not yet passed the two hundred million mark.

[1] Minute by William II on Pourtalès to Bethmann, 25 Feb. 1914. *Große Politik*, xxxix, no. 15841.

XXII

THE OUTBREAK OF WAR IN EUROPE

1914

THE new antagonism between Germany and Russia which had been brought out by the Liman von Sanders affair dominated European relations in the spring of 1914. Both sought to strengthen their diplomatic position. But there was a basic difference of aim. The Russians wanted to create an alliance with Great Britain and France so strong that Germany would shrink from war; the Germans wanted to challenge Russia before the opposing alliance was consolidated and while they still had a military lead. Sazonov wrote to Benckendorff on 19 February: 'The peace of the world will be secure only when the Triple Entente . . . is transformed into a defensive alliance without secret clauses. Then the danger of a German hegemony will be finally ended, and each of us can devote himself to his own affairs: the English can seek a solution of their social problems, the French can get rich, protected from any external threat, and we can consolidate ourselves and work on our economic reorganization.'[1] Benckendorff replied, 'If Grey could, he would do it to-morrow.'[2] This was an exaggeration. Though the permanent officials at the foreign office advocated an alliance with Russia—as much to keep her favour as to restrain Germany —Grey would have none of it. He sheltered behind the excuse of public opinion; and any proposal for alliance with Russia would certainly have broken up the liberal government. But the policy of keeping a free hand represented Grey's own outlook. He wished to be on good terms with Russia; and he would undoubtedly urge support of France if she were attacked by Germany. Beyond this he would not go. He could not understand an alliance as a security for peace; like most Englishmen,

[1] Sazonov to Benckendorff, 19 Feb. 1914. *Mezhdunarodnye otnosheniya*, third series, i, no. 232.
[2] Benckendorff to Sazonov, 25 Feb. 1914. Ibid., no. 328.

he regarded all alliances as a commitment to war. Besides, though he welcomed Russia's weight in the Balance of Power, he was not convinced that her interests in the Near East were a vital concern for Great Britain—perhaps it would be better if Russia and Germany fought things out there and exhausted each other. In April he accompanied George V to Paris—his first visit to the Continent as foreign secretary—and, while there, defined his attitude to the French:

If there were a really aggressive and menacing attack made by Germany upon France, it was possible that public feeling in Great Britain would justify the Government in helping France. But it was not likely that Germany would make an aggressive and menacing attack upon Russia; and, even if she did, people in Great Britain would be inclined to say that, though Germany might have successes at first, Russia's resources were so great that, in the long run, Germany would be exhausted without our helping Russia.[1]

The French did not welcome this reply. They felt themselves to be a hostage towards Germany for both Great Britain and Russia; and were more anxious to bring the two together than at any time since Delcassé first launched the project of a Trpile Entente in the days before the Russo-Japanese war.

Grey made some concession, more to please the French than the Russians: he agreed to Anglo-Russian naval talks on the model of the 1912 discussions with France.[2] This was not a serious project: the two fleets could not co-operate anywhere. As Grey wrote later, it was useful 'for the purpose of keeping Russia in good disposition, and of not offending her by refusing'.[3] The British cabinet held that they were not committed by the naval agreement with France; therefore they authorized similar talks with the Russians. These, on the other hand, exaggerated the extent to which Great Britain was committed to France; and therefore supposed that they were getting something of value. Grey exacted a price even for this concession. He repeated his old demand that Russia must behave better in Persia if she wanted the entente to become more effective; and this time the Russians did something to meet him. Sazonov tried to restrain his agents in Persia. Moreover, he offered to surrender

---

[1] Grey to Bertie, 1 May 1914. *British Documents*, x (ii), no. 541.

[2] This time Grey took the precaution of securing the approval of the cabinet from the start.

[3] Grey, *Twenty-Five Years*, i. 284.

the neutral zone to the British[1] and even to give them a guarantee of India, for what that was worth, if only the naval agreement could be settled.[2] These negotiations were still hanging fire
at the end of June: there was no Anglo-Russian alliance, nor
even any certainty that their disputes in Persia would be
smoothed over.[3]

Russia had not improved her diplomatic position against
Germany. On the contrary, the Germans learnt of the proposed
naval talks through the treachery of a member of the Russian
embassy in London, who kept them regularly supplied with
Benckendorff's correspondence; and they published the story in
a German newspaper. The outcry which followed in England
made it impossible for Grey to go on with the talks for the
moment. What is more, radical members of the government
still believed that relations with Germany were improving.
Churchill imagined that a meeting between himself and Tirpitz
'might do good, and could not possibly do any harm'.[4] Lloyd
George went further. On 23 July he spoke in the house of commons and said of Germany: 'Our relations are very much better
than they were a few years ago. . . . The two great Empires
begin to realize they can co-operate for common ends, and that
the points of co-operation are greater and more numerous and
more important than the points of possible controversy.'[5] A
general election was now approaching in Great Britain;[6] and,
though a historian should never deal in speculations about
what did not happen, it is difficult to resist the surmise that Lloyd
George was planning to fight this election as leader of a radical-
labour coalition. Reconciliation with Germany, and resistance
to Russia in Persia, must have been part of the coalition's programme. In France, too, opinion was changing. There a general
election in April returned a majority against the three-year
service; and in June Poincaré had to appoint a left-wing
government under Viviani, much against his will. Only a sordid

---

[1] Sazonov to Benckendorff, 24 June 1914. *Mezhdunarodnye otnosheniya*, third
series, iii, no. 343.

[2] Sazonov to Benckendorff, 25 June 1914. Ibid., no. 361.

[3] The last letter written by George V to Nicholas II in peace-time (16 June
1914) was an appeal to improve relations in Persia. *British Documents*, x (ii), no. 549.

[4] Memorandum by Churchill, 20 May 1914. Ibid., no. 511.

[5] *Hansard*, fifth series. lxv. 727.

[6] By the terms of the Parliament Act of 1911, a general election must have taken
place before December 1915; practice made it more likely in the autumn of 1914
or, at latest, the spring of 1915

private scandal[1] enabled him to escape Caillaux, supported by Jaurès and the socialists, with a programme of full Franco-German reconciliation. In fact, a coalition of the three advanced western Powers against the Russian colossus seemed just round the corner.

Bethmann, at least, recognized that the situation was changing in Germany's favour. He wrote on 16 June: 'Whether a European conflagration comes depends solely on the attitude of Germany and England. If we both stand together as guarantors of European peace, which is not prevented by the engagements of either the Triple Alliance or the entente, *provided we pursue this aim on a common plan from the start*, war can be avoided.'[2] Nor had the Germans any illusion about Austria-Hungary. Tschirschky, the ambassador at Vienna, wrote in May: 'How often do I consider whether it is really worth while to unite ourselves so closely to this state-structure which is cracking at every joint and to continue the laborious task of dragging her along.'[3] The Germans could have escaped this task, if security was their only object, by accepting the friendship of British and French pacific radicalism; but a genuine alliance for peace was not to their taste. The Germans were bent on going forward in the world; and Austria-Hungary was essential to them if they were to gain control of the Near East. The Austro-Hungarian ambassador at Constantinople posed the choice before the Germans with bitter satisfaction: 'Either the abandonment of the Bosphorus and of Germany's position in the Near East or marching on the side of Austria through thick and thin.'[4] As often happens, Germany's ambitions made her the captive of her weaker partner. The Germans set out to refloat Austria-Hungary as a Great Power; her ambitions had to be encouraged, her resources bolstered up for the conflict. On 12 May Conrad met Moltke at Karlsbad (Kárlovy Vary). Previously Moltke had urged Conrad to keep the peace until a more favourable opportunity. Now he declared that it was hopeless to wait for a promise of neutrality from Great Britain which she would never give: 'Any delay means a lessening of our chances; we cannot

---

[1] Caillaux's second wife killed the editor of a Paris newspaper, to prevent the publication of love-letters which her husband had written to her before their marriage. This made Caillaux impossible as prime minister for the time being.

[2] Bethmann to Lichnowsky, 16 June 1914. *Große Politik*, xxxix, no. 15883.

[3] Tschirschky to Jagow, 22 May 1914. Ibid., no. 15734.

[4] Pallavicini to Berchtold, 6 July 1914. *Österreich-Ungarns Außenpolitik*, viii, no. 10083.

compete with Russia in man-power.'[1] The conclusion was obvious: Germany and Austria-Hungary must strike before the
expansion of the Russian army got under weigh.

The two central Powers were still far from an agreed programme. The Germans had neither sympathy nor understanding for the national problems of the Habsburg monarchy.
Certainly they wanted to preserve it as a Great Power; and they
even recognized that Hungary was its core. William II said to
Tisza in March: 'a *German* Austria and a *Hungarian* Hungary
were the two firm pillars of the Monarchy.'[2] But they thought
that this was compatible with a policy which would win both
Serbia and Rumania to their side. They never considered how
this could be done with Serbia, except for vague talk 'of the
dependence of the lesser upon the greater as in the planetary
system'.[3] Rumania seemed to them to hold the key to the
Balkans: if she were loyal to her alliance of 1883 she could force
Serbia on the same course. This policy was antiquated. Rumania
had once sought security against Russia; now, as a great wheat-
exporting country, she had a common interest with her in the
free passage of the Straits. Even more decisive, her national
aspirations had been stirred by the victory of the Balkan states.
Unlike theirs, these could not be achieved against Turkey. They
could succeed only by liberating the 2,000,000 Rumanians of
Transylvania who were under Hungarian rule. This was a
more dangerous challenge to the Habsburg monarchy than even
the South Slav movement. A South Slav, or at any rate a Croat,
kingdom might have been set up if Francis Ferdinand had
come to the throne. The rulers of Hungary would never surrender Transylvania, where lay their richest estates and where
lived nearly a million Magyars.

William II preached 'a *Hungarian* Hungary'; yet he also advocated a conciliation of the Rumanians, which must have
caused a head-on struggle with the Magyars. Only Francis
Ferdinand was ready for this; and even he dared not air it to
William II. The party of the heir-apparent made some feeble
efforts to achieve their policy. In the autumn of 1913 Czernin,
one of this group, went as minister to Bucarest. He soon reported:

[1] Conrad, *Aus meiner Dienstzeit*, iii. 670.
[2] Treutler to foreign ministry, 24 Mar. 1914. *Große Politik*, xxxix, no. 15716.
[3] Memorandum by Berchtold, 28 Oct. 1913. *Österreich-Ungarns Außenpolitik*,
vii, no. 8934.

'the treaty of alliance is not worth the paper and ink with which it is written'.[1] He proposed that Berchtold should put matters right by offering Rumania and Serbia a 'guarantee'[2]—as though this would have satisfied either of them. The guarantee could have operated only against Bulgaria; and Berchtold was always dreaming of an alliance with her, so far as he had a policy at all. Czernin also urged some concessions to the Rumanians in Transylvania. Tisza, the Hungarian prime minister, brushed these aside; the German alliance should be used to force Rumania back into line.[3] The Germans wanted Hungary to make concessions to Rumania and Serbia in order to strengthen the Austro-German alliance; Tisza answered that this alliance made concessions unnecessary. He got his way. No one in Vienna could control him; and the Germans were dazzled by his resoluteness. William II found him 'a truly great statesman'.[4]

On 13 June Francis Ferdinand met William II, for the last time, at Konopischt.[5] He nerved himself to denounce Tisza as the cause of all their troubles. William II only replied that he would instruct his ambassador to repeat to Tisza: 'Lord, remember the Rumanians.'[6] The Magyars were free to continue on their intransigent course; in the last resort, they dominated the Habsburg monarchy and so Germany, and could drag both Powers along with them. On 24 June Berchtold completed a memorandum on Austro-Hungarian policy, which had originated with Tisza. It advocated alliance with Bulgaria against both Serbia and Rumania. This was nothing new—it had been urged ineffectively by Berchtold since the beginning of the Balkan wars. But the Russian spectre was now brought in to make the proposal more attractive to the Germans: 'the open endeavours of Russia to encircle the Monarchy have the ultimate aim of making it impossible for the German Empire to oppose Russia's distant aims of gaining political and economic supremacy.'[7]

[1] Czernin to Berchtold, 7 Dec. 1913. *Österreich-Ungarns Außenpolitik*, vii, no. 9062.
[2] Czernin to Berchtold, 23 Apr. 1914. Ibid., no. 9600.
[3] Memorandum by Tisza, 15 Mar. 1914. Ibid., no. 9482.
[4] Treutler to foreign ministry, 27 Mar. 1914. *Große Politik*, xxxix, no. 15720.
[5] This was the meeting at which the two were supposed to have planned a European war. In reality, they discussed only the question of Rumania. In any case, it is difficult to see how Francis Ferdinand could have planned a war which was to begin with his assassination.
[6] Treutler to Zimmermann, 15 June 1914. Ibid., no. 15736.
[7] Memorandum by Berchtold, 24 June 1914. *Österreich-Ungarns Außenpolitik*, viii, no. 9984.

The Austrians had been raising the cry for thirty years that Russia was aiming directly at their destruction. The Germans had always been able to reply that Austria-Hungary was in no danger, so long as she kept clear of aggressive action in the Balkans; and this reply was often given. It was truer now than it had ever been. The Russians had no interest in the aggrandizement of either Serbia or Rumania; they merely wanted to keep these two countries as independent barriers between Germany and the Straits. But the Austrians could now argue that the real Russian challenge was to Germany and that she must therefore support Austria-Hungary's Balkan plans for her own sake. The Germans, like the Russians, had no Balkan interests. Their route to Constantinople was predominantly by sea through the Channel to the Mediterranean. They, too, wanted to keep Serbia and Rumania independent, though, of course, they hoped to keep them friendly by concessions at Austria-Hungary's expense. Instead they were dragged into these Balkan disputes in order to keep their only reliable ally afloat. The greater includes the less, as William II said on another occasion. The Germans anticipated a struggle for the mastery of Europe and the Middle East; the Austrians merely wished to end the nationalist agitation of two Balkan states with whom Germany had no quarrel. The only point of agreement between them was in believing that both problems could be settled by war.

The Austrians were right on the question of fact: both Serbia and Rumania were lost to the central Powers. That had been obvious with Serbia for long enough; though the Austrians exaggerated the Serb danger in order to excuse their own helpless incompetence in dealing with the South Slavs. The defection of Rumania was a more dramatic blow; it symbolized the ending of the precarious balance which had existed on the lower Danube since the Crimean war. On 14 June Nicholas II and Sazonov visited the king of Rumania, at Constantsa. Sazonov, on a motor-tour, crossed the Hungarian frontier into Transylvania. This somewhat tactless sign of approval for Rumanian irredentism was rewarded by assurances of neutrality, though not of armed support, in an Austro-Russian war. Sazonov noted: 'Rumania will try to go with the side that turns out to be the stronger and can offer her the greater gains.'[1] Sazonov had no

---

[1] Sazonov to Nicholas II, 24 June 1914. *Mezhdunarodnye otnosheniya*, third series, iii, no. 339.

serious intention of offering these gains unless war actually broke out. His policy was encirclement, not aggression, so far as the Balkans were concerned; or, to use a more respectable modern term, it was containment. Exactly the same was true of Great Britain in the west. No Power of the Triple Entente wanted a European upheaval;[1] all three would have liked to turn their backs on Europe and to pursue their imperial expansion in Asia and Africa. Germany, on the other hand, had come to feel that she could expand her overseas empire only after she had destroyed the European Balance of Power; and Austria-Hungary wanted a Balkan war in order to survive at all.

Yet it would be wrong to exaggerate the rigidity of the system of alliances or to regard the European war as inevitable. No war is inevitable until it breaks out. The existing alliances were all precarious. Italy was only the extreme example—renewing the Triple Alliance and making exaggerated promises of military support to Germany on one side; seeking to negotiate a Mediterranean agreement with France and Great Britain on the other. In France the Russian alliance was increasingly unpopular; it was threatened by a coalition between Caillaux the radical and Jaurès the socialist, which in the summer of 1914 seemed inevitable. Both men were anti-Russian, or at least anti-tsarist; both were friendly to Germany. In England the crisis over Home Rule was reaching its height. If it had exploded, there must have followed either a radical government, which would have been friendly to Germany, or—less likely—a conservative government, so weak as to be debarred from having a foreign policy. Moreover, in June 1914, the British government at last reached agreement with Germany over the Bagdad railway; and the French had already done so in February. Both seemed to be taking sides with Germany against Russia in the great question of Turkey-in-Asia. The Russians had every reason to be dissatisfied with their position. The conservatives at court disliked both the estrangement from Germany and the dema-

---

[1] It is often said that the French projected war in order to recover Alsace and Lorraine. There is not a scrap of evidence for this. The French knew that they would be hard put to it to maintain their independence against Germany if it came to a war, let alone make gains. Of course they demanded Alsace and Lorraine when war broke out, just as the British demanded the destruction of the German navy and the Russians demanded Constantinople. But these demands did not cause the war; they were caused by it.

gogic patronage of Serbia. Imperialists were offended by British policy in Persia, especially its pursuit of oil-concessions.[1] They would gladly have swung on to an anti-British course, if Germany had given them security at the Straits.[2] Some Russians, more daring still, thought of an alliance with Turkey against the three western 'capitalist' Powers; and in May 1914 a Turkish delegation visited Nicholas II at Livadia. If this revival of Unkiar Skelessi had been achieved, a diplomatic revolution must certainly have followed. As it was, alliance between Russia and Turkey had to wait until 1921.

Plenty of Germans knew that the ring round them was not solid. Bethmann and the foreign ministry counted rightly that Great Britain would turn away from Russia and towards them, if France were left alone. The great capitalists were winning the mastery of Europe without war: the industries of southern Russia, the iron-fields of Lorraine and Normandy were already largely under their control. Each group in Germany had a single enemy and would have liked to make peace with the others. But Germany lacked a directing hand to insist on priorities. It was easier to acquiesce in all the aggressive impulses and to drift with events. Germany lay in the centre of Europe. She could use this position to play off her neighbours against each other, as Bismarck had done and as Hitler was to do; or she could abuse her position to unite her neighbours against her, not from policy, but by having none. Tirpitz and his capitalist supporters wanted a naval conflict with Great Britain and deplored the hostility to France and Russia; the professional soldiers and their capitalist supporters wanted a continental war, especially against France, and deplored the naval rivalry with Great Britain; the mass parties—the social democrats and the Roman Catholic Centre—were friendly to both Great Britain and France and could be won only for the old radical programme of war against Russia. It is futile to discuss whether the great navy, the Bagdad railway, or the bid for continental supremacy was the decisive factor in German policy. But the

---

[1] In the spring of 1914 the Anglo-Persian Oil company, which was controlled by the Admiralty, made a compact with German interests in order to exclude their Russian and American competitors.

[2] This was always Nicolson's fear, and also that of Buchanan, ambassador at St. Petersburg. 'Russia may strike a bargain with Germany and then resume her liberty of action in Turkey and Persia. Our position then would be a parlous one.' Buchanan to Nicolson, 26 Apr. 1914. *British Documents*, x (ii), no. 588.

bid for continental supremacy was certainly decisive in bringing on the European war. If Germany destroyed France as an independent Power, she could then pursue her imperial rivalries against Russia and Great Britain with some chance of success. Both Powers had recognized this by supporting the independence of France long before either the German navy or the Bagdad railway existed. Nevertheless, they would not have been so ready to co-operate with France, and not ready at all to co-operate with each other, if Germany had not also challenged them directly. German policy, or rather lack of it, made the Triple Entente a reality. The feeble rulers of Germany, William II and Bethmann, preferred a ring of foreign enemies to trouble at home.

It has been strongly argued that the Germans deliberately timed war for August 1914.[1] There is little evidence for this, and a decisive argument against it. Bethmann and William II were incapable of consistent policy; Moltke, the chief-of-staff, could not conduct a campaign, let alone make a war. The Germans were involved in war by Austria-Hungary, but they went with her willingly. It was easy to co-operate with her; it would have needed a statesman to refuse. On 28 June Francis Ferdinand was assassinated at Sarajevo, the capital of Bosnia, by a Bosnian Serb.[2] Berchtold was weary of being jeered at by Conrad as irresolute and feeble. Moreover, when Turkey-in-Asia took the place of the Balkans as the centre of international rivalry, Austria-Hungary was pushed aside too; and the Germans had rejected with impatience Berchtold's claim to be allotted a 'sphere' in Asia Minor. The murder at Sarajevo revived the Balkan question and enabled Austria-Hungary to reappear mis-

---

[1] For instance by R. C. K. Ensor, *England 1870–1914*, pp. 469–70, 482.

[2] Much ink has been spilled over the question whether the Serbian government knew of the plot. A certain Ljuba Jovanovich claimed to have been told of it by Pashich, the Serb prime minister, in May. It later turned out that he also claimed to have been told of the plot to assassinate King Alexander in 1903. He was evidently an accomplished crystal-gazer. The Serbian government was unprepared for war, which could not have come at a less welcome time, when the army had not been remodelled after the Balkan wars. They certainly thought that it was likely Francis Ferdinand would be assassinated, if he provoked nationalist feeling by going to Sarajevo; and they warned Bilinski, the Austro-Hungarian minister of finance who was in charge of Bosnia, against the visit early in June. But, of course, the visit was meant to provoke nationalist feeling or, rather, to challenge it. It was deliberately timed for Serbia's national day, the anniversary of Kossovo. If a British royalty had visited Dublin on St. Patrick's day at the height of the Troubles, he, too, might have expected to be shot at.

[3] Jagow to Tschirschky, 25 Jan. 1914. *Große Politik*, xxxvii (ii), no. 15100.

leadingly as a Great Power. This time she could only hold the centre of the stage if she actually provoked a war. The German talk of writing off Austria-Hungary and of somehow restoring good relations with Russia at her expense had not escaped Austrian attention: and the Habsburg monarchy brought on its mortal crisis to prove that it was still alive.

Berchtold determined to force war on Serbia, though he had no proofs of Serbian complicity and never found any.[1] Tisza, the Hungarian prime minister, opposed him. Berchtold wanted to restore the prestige of the monarchy; Tisza cared only for great Hungary. Like Kossuth before him, he looked to Germany, not to Vienna, as Hungary's ally and would not have much regretted the collapse of the Dual Monarchy, so long as great Hungary survived.[2] Berchtold turned Tisza's opposition by appealing to Germany for support; Tisza could not hold out if Berlin, not Vienna, urged war. Berchtold took out his memorandum of 24 June, which had urged alliance with Bulgaria; added a postscript blaming Serbia for the assassination; and accompanied this with a letter from Francis Joseph to William II, which managed to blame Russian Panslavism as well. The conclusion: 'Serbia must be eliminated as a political factor in the Balkans . . . friendly settlement is no longer to be thought of.' These two documents were presented to William II on 5 July.

At Berlin there was no serious consultation. William II invited the Austro-Hungarian ambassador to lunch at Potsdam. At first he said that he must wait for Bethmann's opinion; then changed his mind after lunch and committed himself. Szögyény, the Austrian ambassador, reported: 'Action against Serbia should not be delayed. . . . Even if it should come to a war between Austria and Russia, we could be convinced that Germany would stand by our side with her accustomed faithfulness as an ally.'[3] Bethmann arrived in the afternoon, went for a walk in the park with William II, and approved of what he had said. The next day he gave Szögyény official confirmation: 'Austria must judge what is to be done to clear up her relations

---

[1] This is agreed by all authorities. The later evidence of Serbian complicity, even if accepted, is therefore irrelevant to the judgement of Berchtold's policy.

[2] Tisza also disliked Francis Ferdinand personally, for his favouring the South Slavs and Rumanians. He said on the news of his death: 'The Lord God has willed it so, and we must be grateful to the Lord God for everything.'

[3] Szögyény to Berchtold, 5 July 1914. *Österreich-Ungarns Außenpolitik*, viii, no. 10058.

with Serbia; but whatever Austria's decision, she could count with certainty upon it, that Germany will stand behind her as an ally.'[1] Berchtold's plan of partitioning Serbia with Bulgaria was explained to Bethmann. He approved of it and added: 'If war must break out, better now than in one or two years' time when the Entente will be stronger.'

William II and Bethmann did more than give Austria-Hungary a free hand; they encouraged her to start a war against Serbia and to risk the greater consequences. They had grown used to Berchtold's irresolution during the Balkan wars and were determined not to be blamed for it. The most probable outcome of all the stir, they expected, would be an Austro-Hungarian alliance with Bulgaria. Further, both of them thought that Russia was not ready for war and that she would allow the humiliation of Serbia after some ineffective protest; then their position would be all the stronger to strike a bargain with Russia later. On the other hand, if it came to war, they were confident of winning it now and less confident of winning it later. They did not decide on war; but they did decide on 5 July to use their superior power either to win a war or to achieve a striking success. Bethmann had always said that Germany and Great Britain should co-operate to keep the peace. If he had wanted a peaceful solution of the present crisis, he would have approached the British at once. Instead he did nothing. He did not wish to alarm them. His aim, so far as he had one, was to keep them neutral in a continental war, not to enlist their support for a general peace.

The German reply gave Berchtold what he wanted: it enabled him to convert Tisza. He could now argue that Germany was urging them to war. On 14 July Tisza gave way: great Hungary had to keep German favour. He laid down one condition: Austria-Hungary should not acquire any Serbian territory. Though Berchtold accepted this condition, he meant to cheat Tisza, once Serbia had been crushed: her southern territories would be partitioned between Albania and Bulgaria, and the rest would become a dependency of the monarchy, even if it were not directly annexed.[2] The one chance of success for

[1] Szögyény to Berchtold, 6 July 1914. *Österreich-Ungarns Außenpolitik*, viii, no. 10076.

[2] This plan of partition, never carried out during the First World war, was put into operation by the Germans (many of them Austrian) in 1941, when Bulgaria received Macedonia, and Albania the plain of Kossovo.

Austria-Hungary would have been rapid action. Instead Berchtold dawdled, in the usual Viennese fashion. The ultimatum to Serbia was sent on 23 July, when all Europe had forgotten its first indignation at the archduke's murder. The Serbs replied on 25 July, accepting Berchtold's conditions much more nearly than had been expected. It made no difference. The Austrians were determined on war; and the Germans encouraged them to action. On 28 July Austria-Hungary declared war on Serbia. Military reasons were not the motive: the Austro-Hungarian army could not be ready even against Serbia until 12 August. But, as Berchtold said: 'the diplomatic situation will not last as long as that'. He needed a declaration of war in order to reject all attempts at mediation or a peaceful solution: they had now been 'outstripped by events'.

The Austro-Hungarian declaration of war on Serbia was the decisive act; everything else followed from it. Diplomacy had been silent between the assassination of Francis Ferdinand on 28 June and the Austro-Hungarian note of 23 July; there was nothing it could do until the Austro-Hungarian demands were known. Then the statesmen tried to avert the crisis. The Russians advised Serbia not to resist, but to trust to the Great Powers;[1] Grey offered to mediate between Serbia and Austria-Hungary. But the Russians had repeatedly declared that they would not allow Serbia to be crushed; they could do no other if they were to maintain the buffer of independent Balkan states. Poincaré and Viviani were in St. Petersburg just before the Austro-Hungarian note to Serbia was sent off. They emphasized again French loyalty to the alliance; but there is no evidence that they encouraged Russia to provoke a war, if a peaceful settlement could be found. When Austria-Hungary declared war on Serbia, the Russians attempted to mobilize against her alone, although they had no plans except for total mobilization. They were, in fact, still acting in terms of diplomacy; they were raising their bid, not preparing for war. The Germans now entered the field. They had assured the Austrians that they would keep Russia out of things, and they set out to do so. On 29 July they warned Sazonov that 'further continuation of Russian mobilization would force us to mobilize also'.[2]

---

[1] Russian council of ministers, 24 July 1914. *Mezhdunarodnye otnosheniya*, third series, v, no. 19.   [2] Bethmann to Pourtalès, 29 July 1914. *Deutsche Dokumente*, p. 342.

This time the Russians were determined not to retreat; they raised their bid still higher. On 30 July they resolved on general mobilization. This, too, was a diplomatic move; the Russian armies could not be ready for many weeks. But, in Jagow's words, 'the German asset was speed'. Their only military plan was to defeat France in six weeks and then to turn against Russia before she was fully prepared. Therefore they had to precipitate events and to force a rupture on both Russia and France. William II might still carry on a private telegraphic correspondence with Nicholas II, which was prolonged even after the declaration of war; Bethmann might still seek an impossible diplomatic success. They were both swept aside by the generals; and they had no answer to the military argument that immediate war was necessary for Germany's security. Yet even the generals did not want war; they wanted victory. When Bethmann urged caution at Vienna and Moltke at the same time urged speedier action, Berchtold exclaimed: 'What a joke! Who rules at Berlin?' The answer was: nobody. German statesmen and generals alike succumbed to the demands of technique.

On 31 July the Germans took the preliminary step towards general mobilization on their side.[1] From this moment, diplomacy ceased so far as the continental Powers were concerned. The only German concern was to get the war going as soon as possible. On 31 July they demanded from Russia the arrest of all war measures; when this was refused, a declaration of war followed on 1 August. The French were asked for a promise of neutrality in a Russo-German war; if they had agreed, they would also have been told to surrender their principal fortresses on the frontier, Toul and Verdun, as pledge of their neutrality. Viviani merely replied: 'France will act in accordance with her interests.' The Germans had no plausible excuse for war against France. They therefore trumped up some false stories of French violation of German territory; and with these decked out a declaration of war on 3 August.

Negotiations between Germany and Great Britain were more prolonged. Their object, on the German side, was to secure British neutrality, not to avert a continental war. All along, Bethmann had urged Berchtold to appear conciliatory in order to impress the British, not in order to find a compromise. On

---

[1] The Austrians also decided on general mobilization on 31 July, as the result of German prompting, and before learning of the Russian mobilization.

29 July he offered not to annexe any French territory if Great Britain remained neutral; the offer did not extend to the French colonies. As well, Germany would respect the integrity of Belgium after the war, provided that 'she did not take sides against Germany'.[1] Grey stuck to his line of policy to the end. He made repeated attempts to settle the original Austro-Serb dispute by negotiation; later he tried to assemble a conference of the Great Powers. He warned the Germans not to count on British neutrality; equally he warned the French and Russians not to count on her support.

It is sometimes said that Grey could have averted the war if he had defined his policy one way or the other. This is not so. The German general staff had long planned to invade France through Belgium and would not have been deterred by any British threat. Indeed they had always assumed that Great Britain would enter the war; they did not take her military weight seriously, and naval questions did not interest them. Bethmann had wanted a British declaration of neutrality in order to discourage France and Russia; once it was clear that they would go to war in any case, British policy ceased to interest him. Emotionally he deplored the breach with Great Britain; but he did nothing to avert it and, in any case, was impotent to influence the German generals. On the other side, France and Russia decided on war without counting firmly on British support; the French believed that they could defeat Germany, and the Russians could not risk their own diplomatic defeat. A British declaration of neutrality would not have influenced their policy. Besides, Grey was resolved that they should decide their policy without encouragement from him; war must spring from their independent resolve.

Those who urged a clear British line did so from contradictory motives. Nicolson feared that Russia and France would win a complete victory and that the British empire would then be at their mercy. Eyre Crowe, more representative of official opinion, feared that France would be defeated and that Great Britain would then be at the mercy of Germany. In any case it was impossible for Grey to make any clear declaration; public opinion would not have allowed it. If there is a criticism of Grey, it must be that he had not educated the British public enough in the previous years. No doubt he had shrunk from increasing the

[1] Goschen to Grey, 29 July 1914. *British Documents*, xi, no. 293.

tension in Europe; but, as well, the unity of the liberal party and the survival of the liberal government had ranked higher in his mind than a decisive foreign policy. It was common form to regret discussion of foreign issues. Eyre Crowe, for instance, 'deplored all public speeches on foreign affairs';[1] and Grey agreed with him. As a result, in July 1914, the cabinet overruled any commitment. On 27 July Lloyd George said: 'there could be no question of our taking part in any war in the first instance. He knew of no Minister who would be in favour of it.'[2]

Moreover, Grey supposed that British intervention would not carry much weight. He thought solely of naval action; it seemed impossible to him to send even an expeditionary force to France,[3] and he certainly never imagined military intervention on a continental scale. On 2 August the cabinet authorized him to warn the Germans that their fleet would not be allowed to attack France in the Channel. Even this condition was not decisive; the Germans would have gladly agreed to it, in exchange for British neutrality. But on 3 August they sent an ultimatum to Belgium, demanding free passage to invade France; the British answered on 4 August demanding that Belgian neutrality be respected. Here again Grey has been criticised for not acting earlier; he should, it is said, have made British neutrality conditional on respect for Belgium. It would have made no difference. The German ultimatum to Belgium was drafted on 26 July, that is, even before the Austro-Hungarian declaration of war on Serbia; invasion of Belgium was an essential, indeed the essential, part of their plans. Only a French surrender could have held them from it. If Grey had acted earlier he would have achieved nothing, except perhaps the break-up of the liberal government; if he had delayed longer he would not have saved Belgium and he would have lost the inestimable value of moral superiority.

On 4 August the long Bismarckian peace ended. It had lasted more than a generation. Men had come to regard peace as normal; when it ended, they looked for some profound cause. Yet the immediate cause was a good deal simpler than on other

---

[1] Paul Cambon to Pichon, 21 Oct. 1913. *Documents diplomatiques français*, third series, viii, no. 367.

[2] Memorandum by Scott, 27 July 1914. Hammond, *C. P. Scott*, p. 177.

[3] So he told Benckendorff on 2 Aug. (to Sazonov, 2 Aug. 1914. *Mezhdunarodnye otnosheniya*, third series, v, no. 456) and Cambon on 4 Aug. (to Doumergue, 4 Aug. 1914. *Documents diplomatiques français*, third series, xi, no. 754).

occasions. Where, for instance, lay the precise responsibility for the Crimean war, and when did that war become inevitable? In 1914 there could be no doubt. Austria-Hungary had failed to solve her national problems. She blamed Serbia for the South Slav discontent; it would be far truer to say that this discontent involved Serbia, against her will, in Habsburg affairs. In July 1914 the Habsburg statesmen took the easy course of violence against Serbia, as their predecessors had taken it (though with more justification) against Sardinia in 1859. Berchtold launched war in 1914, as consciously as Buol launched it in 1859 or Gramont in 1870. There was this difference. Buol counted on support from Prussia and Great Britain; Gramont on support from Austria-Hungary. They were wrong. Berchtold counted rightly on support from Germany; he would not have persisted in a resolute line if it had not been for the repeated encouragements which came from Berlin. The Germans did not fix on war for August 1914, but they welcomed it when the occasion offered. They could win it now; they were more doubtful later. Hence they surrendered easily to the dictates of a military time-table. Austria-Hungary was growing weaker; Germany believed herself at the height of her strength. They decided on war from opposite motives; and the two decisions together caused a general European war.

The Powers of the Triple Entente all entered the war to defend themselves. The Russians fought to preserve the free passage of the Straits, on which their economic life depended; France for the sake of the Triple Entente, which she believed, rightly, alone guaranteed her survival as a Great Power. The British fought for the independence of sovereign states and, more remotely, to prevent a German domination of the Continent. It is sometimes said that the war was caused by the system of alliances or, more vaguely, by the Balance of Power. This is a generalization without reality. None of the Powers acted according to the letter of their commitments, though no doubt they might have done so if they had not anticipated them. Germany was pledged to go to war if Russia attacked Austria-Hungary. Instead, she declared war before Russia took any action; and Austria-Hungary only broke with Russia, grudgingly enough, a week afterwards. France was pledged to attack Germany, if the latter attacked Russia. Instead she was faced with a German demand for unconditional neutrality and would have had to accept war even had there been no Franco-Russian alliance, unless she was prepared to abdicate as a Great Power. Great Britain had a moral obligation to stand by France and a rather stronger one to defend her Channel coast. But she went to war for the sake of Belgium and would have done so, even if there had been no Anglo-French entente and no exchange of letters between Grey and Cambon in November 1912. Only then, the British intervention would have been even less effective than it was.

As to the Balance of Power, it would be truer to say that the war was caused by its breakdown rather than by its existence. There had been a real European Balance in the first decade of the Franco-Russian alliance; and peace had followed from it. The Balance broke down when Russia was weakened by the war with Japan; and Germany got in the habit of trying to get her way by threats. This ended with the Agadir crisis. Russia began to recover her strength, France her nerve. Both insisted on being treated as equals, as they had been in Bismarck's time. The Germans resented this and resolved to end it by war, if they could end it no other way. They feared that the Balance was being re-created. Their fears were exaggerated. Certainly, Russia would have been a more formidable Power by 1917, if her military plans had been carried through and if she had escaped internal disturbance—two formidable hypotheses. But it is unlikely that the three-year service would have been maintained in France; and, in any case, the Russians might well have used their strength against Great Britain in Asia rather than to attack Germany, if they had been left alone. In fact, peace must have brought Germany the mastery of Europe within a few years. This was prevented by the habit of her diplomacy and, still more, by the mental outlook of her people. They had trained themselves psychologically for aggression.

The German military plans played a vital part. The other Great Powers thought in terms of defending themselves. No Frenchman thought seriously of recovering Alsace and Lorraine; and the struggle of Slav and Teuton in the Balkans was very great nonsense so far as most Russians were concerned. The German generals wanted a decisive victory for its own sake. Though they complained of 'encirclement', it was German policy that had created this encirclement. Absurdly enough, the Germans created their own problem when they annexed

Alsace and Lorraine in 1871.[1] They wanted an impregnable frontier; and they got one, as was shown in August 1914, when a small German force held its own there against the bulk of the French army. After 1871 the Germans could easily have fought Russia and stood on the defensive in the west; this was indeed the strategical plan of the elder Moltke. It was not a strategy which guaranteed final, decisive, victory; and Schlieffen therefore rejected it. In 1892 he insisted that France must be defeated first; ten years later he drew the further inevitable conclusion that the German armies must go through Belgium. If the strategy of the elder Moltke had been adhered to with all its political consequences, it would have been very difficult to persuade French and British opinion to go to the assistance of Russia; instead, it appeared in 1914 that Russia was coming to the assistance of France and even of Great Britain. Schlieffen first created the Franco-Russian alliance; and then ensured that Great Britain would enter the war as well. The Germans complained that the war could not be 'localized' in 1914; Schlieffen's strategy prevented it. He would be content with nothing less than total victory; therefore he exposed Germany to total defeat.

There is a deeper explanation still. No one in 1914 took the dangers of war seriously except on a purely military plane. Though all, except a few fighting men, abhorred its bloodshed, none expected a social catastrophe. In the days of Metternich, and even afterwards, statesmen had feared that war would produce 'revolution'—and revolutionaries had sometimes advocated it for that very reason. Now they were inclined to think that war would stave off their social and political problems. In France it produced the 'sacred union'; in Germany William II was able to say: 'I do not see parties any more; I see only Germans.' All thought that war could be fitted into the existing framework of civilization, as the wars of 1866 and 1870 had been. Indeed, these wars had been followed by stabler currencies, freer trade, and more constitutional governments. War was expected to interrupt the even tenor of civilian life only while it lasted. Grey expressed this outlook in extreme form, when he

[1] This was, of course, also true politically. Though France would have had an interest in maintaining Russia as a Great Power even if she had not lost Alsace and Lorraine, her public opinion would have been less deeply committed; and the Germans would not have assumed that France would inevitably attack them in case they were at war with Russia.

said in the house of commons on 3 August: 'if we are engaged in war, we shall suffer but little more than we shall suffer if we stand aside';[1] and by suffering he meant only the interruption of British trade with the continent of Europe. No country made serious economic preparations for war. In England the cry was raised of 'business as usual' to mitigate the unemployment which war was expected to cause. The Germans so little understood the implications of total war that they abstained from invading Holland in August 1914, so as to be able to trade freely with the rest of the world.

The Balkan wars had taught a deceptive lesson. Everyone supposed that decisive battles would be fought at once, and a dictated peace would follow. The Germans expected to take Paris; the French expected to break through in Lorraine. The Russian 'steam-roller' would reach Berlin; more important, from the Russian point of view, their armies would cross the Carpathians and take Budapest. Even the Austrians expected to 'crush' Serbia. The British expected to destroy the German fleet in an immediate naval engagement and then to establish a close blockade of the German coast; apart from that, they had no military plans, except to applaud the victories of their allies and perhaps to profit from them.

None of these things happened. The French armies failed to make headway in Lorraine and suffered enormous casualties. The Germans marched through Belgium and saw from afar the Eiffel Tower. On 6 September they were halted on the Marne and driven back in defeat. But though the French won the battle of the Marne, they could not exploit their victory; the Germans were neither destroyed nor even expelled from French soil. By November there was a line of trenches running from Switzerland to the sea. The Russians invaded east Prussia; they were catastrophically defeated at Tannenberg[2] on 27 August, and their armies in Galicia failed to reach the Carpathians. The Austrians occupied Belgrade, from which the Serbs had with-

[1] Grey, *Twenty-Five Years*, ii. 306.

[2] The Russian advance led Moltke to send two army corps to east Prussia from the western front. In this sense the Franco-Russian alliance justified itself, and the Russians helped to win the battle of the Marne. But this was only a minor cause of the German defeat: The principal causes were the blunders of German leadership and the strategical recovery of Joffre, the French commander-in-chief. Of course, Germany would have had more forces available for the western front if the Franco-Russian alliance had not existed; but in that case France and Germany would not have been at war.

drawn; they were driven out again in November, and Serbian forces entered southern Hungary. The German fleet remained in harbour; and the British fleet was similarly imprisoned in order to balance it. Everywhere siege warfare superseded decisive battles. The machine-gun and the spade changed the course of European history. Policy had been silenced by the first great clash; but in the autumn of 1914 diplomacy was renewed. All the Powers sought to consolidate their alliances; to enlist new allies; and, more feebly, to shake the opposing coalition.

XXIII

THE DIPLOMACY OF WAR

1914–18

WAR in 1914 was confined to the Great Powers. Of the smaller states, only Serbia and Belgium were involved from the beginning; even Italy marked her equivocal position on the edge of greatness by remaining neutral for the best part of a year. At the outset this suited Great Britain and France; their concern was to defeat Germany on the western front, and they had no wish to be saddled with the defence of small countries—they had more than enough to do defending Belgium. Great Britain even staved off the assistance of her oldest ally. The Portuguese were afraid that their colonies would be used as a bargaining-counter to buy the Germans out of Belgium and wished therefore to enter the war; Grey told them firmly that their intervention was unnecessary 'for the moment'. The Russians were in a different case. Though they invaded east Prussia for the sake of their French allies, they had no serious ambitions against Germany herself; their concern was to destroy Germany's link with the Near East, the Habsburg monarchy, and they would welcome any assistance for this purpose. Besides, as their arms could do little to aid Serbia, they had to rely on diplomacy. Italy had announced her neutrality on 3 August, claiming that the Triple Alliance applied only to a defensive war and that Austria-Hungary had offered her no 'compensations'. Sazonov at once repaired the deficiency: he offered Tyrol, Trieste, and Valona (in Albania) to Italy if she would attack the Austrians. This was not enough. The Italians regarded themselves as the heirs of the republic of Venice and therefore claimed 'the supremacy of the Adriatic'. Sazonov, however, hoped to bribe Bulgaria into the war by offering her part or all of Macedonia, which Serbia had carried off in 1913, and intended to give Serbia the Habsburg lands on the Adriatic in exchange. His negotiations with Italy therefore came to nothing.

Nor were his Balkan negotiations any more successful. He offered Serb and Bulgarian territory to Rumania; Rumanian, Turkish, and Serb territory to Bulgaria; and Bulgarian territory to Turkey, if any of them would enter the war. All three held back until a decisive battle had been fought. They would join Russia only when it was obvious that she had won, and then their aid would be unnecessary. It was certainly a score that Rumania, like Italy, repudiated her obligation to the Triple Alliance on 3 August. This had nothing to do with Russian diplomacy. All Rumania's national ambitions were concentrated on Transylvania; and she would do nothing to help a Habsburg victory. At the same time, the Rumanians hoped to hang back as they had done in 1913, and then to gain Transylvania without a serious struggle. Sazonov fed this hope. In his anxiety to secure the left flank of the Russian armies in Galicia, he would pay a high price for Rumania's neutrality; and on 1 October promised her Transylvania in exchange only for 'benevolent neutrality' during the war. The bargain was to cost Russia dear; henceforth the Rumanians could let others do their fighting for them.

Relations with Turkey took a more decisive and more disastrous turn. In May 1914 there was some sign that the Turks were drawing closer to Russia; but, though they perhaps hoped to play her off against Germany, they still counted on playing France and Great Britain off against her. The outbreak of war made this balancing impossible; and the Turks were convinced that the Triple Entente would partition the Ottoman empire, if it won, or even as consolation if it failed. Germany, on the other hand, offered them an alliance which would preserve the integrity of their empire, just as a similar alliance preserved that of Austria-Hungary. By a curious twist of circumstance, Germany, though drawing her own strength from revolutionary nationalism, had become the protector of the two great non-national empires; and, if things had gone a little differently, she might have been the protector of Russian tsardom as well. There was a more practical argument: the Young Turks, themselves trained in Germany, were convinced that she would win. On 2 August Turkey signed an alliance with Germany against Russia. This was a supreme blunder, which brought down the Ottoman empire. The Turks had made up for their internal weakness by a subtle diplomacy playing off one Great

Power against another; now they gratuitously involved themselves in the European conflict. Perhaps they had no choice. Liman von Sanders and his staff had a firm grip on the Turkish army; and, later in August, two German cruisers, the *Goeben* and the *Breslau*, which had escaped from the Mediterranean to the Sea of Marmora, held Constantinople under the fire of their guns.

But the Turks were willing prisoners. Whatever their relations with other Powers, their policy always revolved round Russia, with a mixture of hatred and fear. Now they supposed that the final decision had come: either they would destroy Russian power in the Black Sea or Russia would destroy them. Like the statesmen of Vienna, they abandoned the dilatoriness which had preserved them, and bid 'all or nothing'. In a confused way they overrated both German and Russian strength. They imagined that Germany might knock out Russia; yet, at the same time, they feared that Russia would knock out them. They could not believe, what was indeed the case, that Russia had nothing left over for an expedition against Turkey, so long as she was involved in the European war.

Sazonov had no such illusion. He made Turkey the most extravagant offers in exchange for her neutrality—a guarantee of her territorial integrity, Greek and Bulgarian territory on the Aegean, the German railway concessions, even the abolition of the capitulations. These offers shocked his two partners. The French disliked the precedent of surrendering European concessions. Grey, himself anxious to buy Greece into the war at Turkey's expense, said: 'Turkey's decision will not be influenced by the value of the offers made to her, but by her opinion which side will probably win and which is in a position to make the offers good.'[1] The offers were made all the same. They were of no avail. On 26 September the Turks closed the Straits to commercial traffic. On 28 October the two German cruisers entered the Black Sea and bombarded Odessa, without waiting for Turkey's permission. Three days later, the Powers of the Triple Entente broke off relations with her and declared war. 1 November was in its way as decisive a date in European history as 6 September, the day when the Germans had been stopped on the Marne. The first settled the fate of the German

[1] Benckendorff to Sazonov, 15 Aug. 1914. *Mezhdunarodnye otnosheniya*, third series, vi (i), no. 95.

military monarchy; the second that of the old Russian empire. There could be no quick victory for Germany after the Marne; therefore she would be ground down by the superior forces gradually brought against her. Russia gradually ceased to be a Great Power after the closing of the Straits. She could not nourish her armies without supplies from the west; and the route through Archangel and, later, Murmansk was no substitute for the Straits. On 18 December the Russian commander-in-chief, Grand Duke Nicholas, had to inform his allies that Russia's munitions were exhausted and that henceforth she must stand on the defensive; the most she could hope was to keep on her feet while Great Britain and France somehow won the war.

The deadlock which followed the first battles drove all the Powers to consider their war-aims. None had entered the war with any defined aim except to win. Victory was expected to provide a policy; in fact victory was the policy. Austria-Hungary came nearest to an objective: at least she wished to end the challenge of South Slav nationalism. But she had no idea how to accomplish even this except by conquest and, in any case, was dragged along by Germany in the vaster struggle for the reordering of Europe. In every country men not only assumed that the war would end with a decisive result; they were determined that it should do so. They had come to look on peace as 'normal'; therefore they would only tolerate 'a war to end war'. No concrete gains would satisfy them. For instance, in December 1914, the Germans offered tentatively to withdraw from Belgium and even to pay her an indemnity by buying the Belgian Congo at three or four times its value. The offer was no doubt fraudulent; Grey not only rejected it, he declared that England and her allies 'must have security against any future attack from Germany'.[1] There was the core of the problem. Once a treaty has been broken, it is not enough to restore it. The Germans had brushed aside the guarantees of 1839 as 'a scrap of paper'; any new promises from them would be worthless. It was the old problem which had been presented a hundred years before by revolutionary France and

[1] Memorandum by Buchanan, 15 Jan. 1915. *Mezhdunarodnye otnosheniya*, third series, vi (ii), no. 759. According to other reports, the Germans did not offer an indemnity for evacuating Belgium, but asked for one. In any case, the offer was designed to cause trouble: France had a right of first refusal to the Belgian Congo.

which was to be presented later by communist Russia. What is the good of making treaties with a country which, because of its political philosophy, regards itself as free to break them? Metternich had once given an answer: by maintaining an unassailable coalition against her. This answer did not satisfy the British. Though they had abandoned isolation in order to fight the war, they wished to return to isolation once it was over. And, for that matter, Russia and France, too, wanted to turn their backs on Europe. Therefore all three were committed to the destruction of Germany as a Great Power.

This raised a further difficulty. When past combatants had lacked a common morality and had preached a fight to the finish, the conflict between them had been genuine and fundamental; two 'ways of life' were really at war. Islam and Christianity, like the Jacobins and the old monarchies, were right to see in each other 'infidels' and 'pagans', between whom there might be truce, but never trust. The war of 1914, however, was ostensibly a conflict between sovereign states of similar character; it should have been fought for defined, practical objects. But these objects were lacking—at best glosses on the fundamental conflict, not its cause. The real cause was not far to seek: German power had increased vastly in the preceding generation, and her existing position in Europe no longer corresponded with her resources of power. But all the Great Powers of Europe were combinations for power, as their name implied. How could they condemn one state for following the rules of power on which they were all based? The simplest solution was to make out that the Germans conducted war, or governed in peace, in a peculiarly brutal manner; an argument in which there was some truth, though not much. A more refined version of this was to present William II as a world-conqueror in the mould of Attila or Napoleon—though the latter analogy was not, of course, suited to French ears. Hence it came to be supposed that the German problem would disappear if the house of Hohenzollern were overthrown and if Germany became a democratic republic. Yet the French at any rate were more tenderly disposed towards the house of Habsburg, though it was the more anachronistic survival of the two.

The German 'grievance' was the reverse of that of the Entente Powers. They complained that Germany used her power in order to extend it further; she complained that they objected to her doing so. But the Germans, too, had to find a moral basis for this grievance; hence they had to claim that they represented a superior form of culture. Once, the Germans had been anxious to demonstrate their solidarity with western civilization; now they were equally anxious to emphasize their difference. This difference certainly existed; but both sides had to make more of it than there was in reality, in order to provide a fundamental conflict.

On the Entente side, the war was essentially a war for survival as independent Great Powers. But this cause lacked emotional appeal. Hence the war had to become 'a war for democracy'. Even this wore rather thin. It was difficult to maintain the claim that there would be no international conflicts if Germany ceased to exist as a Great Power. Therefore the Entente had to assert that they would all accept a higher standard of international morality, if only Germany would allow them to do so. This was a slow process, hardly perceptible in the first year of the war. But as the struggle dragged on, the Entente Powers found themselves committed, rather against their will, to the doctrine of an international order, based upon law, instead of upon force. It is curious that the greatest conflict of power in modern times should have been increasingly conducted for the sake of repudiating 'power-politics'.

The 'war-aims' of the Entente Powers sprang therefore from a tangle of contradictory motives. Each wanted to improve its position—almost as much against its present partners as against Germany. Each came to accept the view that Germany should be destroyed as a Great Power, though each naturally emphasized that aspect of destruction which best suited its own need. And, shadowed behind this, was the vague hope that the destruction of Germany would somehow inaugurate a better world. The British insisted, from the outset, on the destruction of the German fleet; and as well, remembering that they always made colonial gains in previous wars, demanded the German colonies. The French claimed Alsace and Lorraine; though they would not have gone to war for the lost provinces, they would not make peace without them. This claim gave French policy an illusory realism: they seemed to be demanding something concrete, where the British and Russians were talking vaguely of security. In fact, the French demanded Alsace and Lorraine as the symbols of Germany's defeat; they would not have been content to receive them as the price of acquiescing in her victory. The Russians were hardest put to it to devise practical claims against Germany; in essence, they asked nothing from her except to be left alone while they destroyed Austria-Hungary. Any territory they took from Germany would be inhabited by Poles; and though they had promised on 14 August the revival of the Polish nation 'free in its religion, its language, and its internal administration', they were reluctant to put this promise into practice. Therefore they fell back on vague talk of 'destroying German militarism': Prussia must be dismembered and, as a sop to supposed English sentiment, Hanover must be restored. The British and French were at bottom just as vague: they, too, hoped that defeat would somehow settle the German problem or, at least, bring about a German 'change of heart'. As a result, the attempt to define the policy which should follow victory arrived back at its starting point: victory would provide the policy of itself.

The Germans ought to have had an easier time of it. The war would be a victory for them if they came out of it stronger than they went in. But they, too, could not accept this limited outcome; they, too, insisted on a final victory which would destroy all the forces opposing them. Before the war they had created the coalition against them by failing to go one step at a time; and now they kept the coalition in being by refusing to jettison any of their demands. Once they had missed a quick victory their only hope of success lay in a separate peace either with Russia or the western Powers. It eluded them. In the autumn of 1914 there was, no doubt, little to be done with Great Britain and France. War strengthened both the military men and the capitalists in Germany, who held that decisive victory had to be won in the west: once Germany dominated the capitalist world, she would overshadow Russia. The campaign of 1914, which left Germany in occupation of Belgium and northern France, was itself a disaster for German policy. The offer of a return to the *status quo* in the west would, at any rate, have shaken British and French opinion; but the Germans could not bring themselves to renounce Antwerp or the iron-fields of Lorraine. They were committed, without design, to a war of conquest against the western Powers.

There was all the more reason, then, to postpone the struggle in the east; and in Russia there was material on which to work. Co-operation with the west was favoured only by the liberal middle-class, which carried little weight. Sazonov and perhaps Nicholas II had the sense to see that a separate peace would only postpone the conflict to a less favourable moment; but they also knew that a long war might bring all Russian life to the ground. The non-political bureaucrats still hoped to turn their backs on Europe and to build up Russian power in Asia. Witte, their chief spokesman, always hankered after the set-up of 1895 or even of Björkö: Germany and France, balancing each other, should compete for Russia's friendship, and this revived continental league should throw all its weight against the British empire.[1] Certainly Witte wished to make peace with Germany and had no claims against her; but his essential condition was the preservation of the continental balance. The Germans, on the other hand, would make peace with Russia only in order to destroy the balance. They, too, therefore arrived at the same conclusion as the Entente. Instead of seeking a peace which would give them partial victory, they looked to a victory which would give them a final peace.

At the opening of 1915 the Entente had withstood the first shock of German arms and her feebler efforts at diplomacy. This had been done by the three Powers in isolation. On 5 September they had agreed not to make a separate peace nor to pose peace terms without previous agreement. This consolidation of the Triple Entente sprang, appropriately enough, from the initiative of Delcassé, who had become French foreign minister again on 26 August. But it had little practical effect. Despite twenty years of Franco-Russian military talks, there was no common war plan and no programme of war-aims. Joffre and Grand Duke Nicholas, the two commanders-in-chief, did not reveal their strategy to each other or attempt to combine their operations. Joffre, ignorant of Russia's shortage of materials, complained that she was not doing her share of the fighting; the Grand Duke feared that France would make peace if the Germans withdrew to the Rhine.[2] The Russian military men, in occupation of Polish

---

[1] Conversation with Paléologue, 12 Sept. 1914. Paléologue, *La Russie des Tsars*, i. 120; Carlotti (St. Petersburg) to Sonnino, 19 Jan. 1915. *Mezhdunarodnye otnosheniya*, third series, vii (i), no. 37.

[2] Sazonov to Izvolski, 17 Sept. 1914. Ibid., vi (i), no. 269.

Galicia and much disliking it,[1] urged that they had nothing to gain from defeating Germany; control of the Straits seemed to them the only prize worth fighting for. Yet they had no forces to spare for operations against Turkey. Russian headquarters urged that Sazonov must gain Constantinople by diplomacy; he was equally insistent that it could be acquired only by a military *coup de main*. Yet absurdly enough, even the Russian military did not really want Constantinople. Every expert opinion agreed that garrisoning Constantinople and the Straits would be an intolerable military burden.[2] But what was the alternative? Turkey was an enemy, no longer to be trusted; internationalization was 'the worst of all possible solutions', which would put Russia at the mercy of the other Great Powers. Besides, liberal opinion in Russia demanded Constantinople; and, with military failure, this opinion had to be conciliated by Nicholas II.

On 30 December 1914, Grand Duke Nicholas launched the Straits question with the western Powers. He told the British representative at his headquarters that the Russian armies in the Caucasus were threatened by a Turkish attack, and he appealed for assistance from the allies. This was a political move. The danger in the Caucasus was imaginary. The Grand Duke wished to distract attention from his own inability to take the offensive against Germany; more important, he wished to compel Sazonov to acquire Constantinople by diplomacy, since he could not do it himself by force of arms. The Russian appeal was welcomed in London, where many ministers dreaded the deadlock on the western front and wished to find a way round it by the use of sea-power. British official circles had long been indifferent to the question of the Straits. They had held out before the war, for the sake of British public opinion; they were now ready to yield for the sake of Russian opinion, in the belief that this would keep Russia in the war. Besides, they meant to consolidate their position in Egypt, now that Turkey was their enemy; and this removed their last objection to a Russian control of the Straits. On 13 November George V, anticipating events, had said to Benckendorff: 'As to Constantinople it is

---

[1] The Russian officers were particularly angered by the attempts at Orthodox propaganda there: 'we ask for guns and you send us priests.'

[2] Memoranda by Basili, Nemitz, Neratov, Nov., 14, 27 Dec. 1914. *Konstantinopel und die Meerengen*, ii, nos. 2, 3, 4.

clear it must be yours';[1] and on 18 November the British announced that they proposed to annexe Egypt.[2]

These developments were most unwelcome to the French. They were afraid that the Ottoman empire would be shared out between their allies, while their own strength was absorbed on the western front. Paléologue in St. Petersburg complained: 'Great Britain has given Constantinople to Russia; to-day Russia gives Egypt to England. The programme of Nicholas I has been realised';[3] and Delcassé wanted all these questions postponed to the end of the war, when France could also annexe Tunis and Morocco.[4] When in January 1915 the British proposed to satisfy the Grand Duke by attacking the Dardanelles, the French deplored this diversion from the western front. They acquiesced, not in order to please the Russians, but to steal a march on them; they hoped to keep them out of Constantinople, not to hand it over to them, and actually kept the preparations for an expedition secret from their ally. The British were not so reticent. They boasted of the coming expedition to the Russians in order to keep them in the war—an unnecessary display, as it turned out, since Witte, the principal advocate of a separate peace, died on 13 March.

Sazonov was driven into diplomatic action, whether he would or no. He had a yet more immediate spur, when the British proposed to use Greek troops for the attack on Constantinople; this raised the old ghost of a revived Byzantine empire. On 4 March he formally demanded of his two allies that the Straits and adjoining territory be included within the Russian empire.[5] The British made no difficulties. Grey agreed to the Russian demand on 12 March, after securing the approval of the leaders of the opposition;[6] in return, he asked that the neutral zone of Persia should become British and that Russia should not oppose neutral Powers, especially Greece,

---

[1] Benckendorff to Sazonov, 13 Nov. 1914. *Konstantinopel und die Meerengen*, ii, no. 25.

[2] Buchanan to Sazonov, 18 Nov. 1914. *Mezhdunarodnye otnosheniya*, third series, vi (ii), no. 533. In the outcome, the British contented themselves with a protectorate in Egypt for the duration of the war.

[3] 18 Nov. 1914. Paléologue, *La Russie des Tsars*, i. 194.

[4] Izvolski to Sazonov, 18 Nov. 1914. *Mezhdunarodnye otnosheniya*, third series, vi (ii), no. 543.

[5] Sazonov to Paléologue and Buchanan, 4 Mar. 1915. *Konstantinopel und die Meerengen*, ii, no. 53.

[6] Benckendorff to Sazonov, 14 Mar. 1915. Ibid., no. 84.

entering the war.[1] The French were more obstinate. Delcassé would only offer 'a friendly attitude' to Russia's wishes when it came to the peace conference;[2] Poincaré wrote personally to Paléologue—an unprecedented step for a French President—urging him to make no concessions.[3] The Russians answered with threats and bribes. Sazonov threatened to resign and make way for a supporter of the League of the Three Emperors.[4] Nicholas II said to Paléologue: 'Take the left bank of the Rhine; take Mainz; go further if you like.'[5] A few days later he agreed that France could have Syria, Cilicia, and Palestine.[6] We do not know why the French gave way—perhaps as much from British pressure as from any desire to please the Russians. On 10 April a grudging French note agreed to Russia's claims on condition 'that the war was carried to a victorious conclusion and that France and England achieved their aims in the Near East and elsewhere'.[7] In this way, the 'Crimean powers' at last gave a theoretical approval to Russia's ambitions at the Straits —ambitions which were, in practice, unwelcome to the Russians themselves.

The agreement over Constantinople and the Straits was the most important 'secret treaty' made between the allies during the course of the First World war. There was a great outcry when the Bolsheviks published it in 1918; the allies, it was said, were pursuing selfish imperialist aims under a smoke-screen of ethical principles. The situation was not really so simple. The agreement followed inevitably from the British expedition to the Dardanelles. It was essential to dispel the Russian suspicion that, in Grey's words, 'Britain was going to occupy Constantinople in order that when Britain and France had been enabled, by Russia's help, to win the war, Russia should not have Constantinople at the peace.'[8] Even without the expedition, something would have had to be done to revive Russian confidence, after her military losses in the campaign of 1914. Of course, it would have satisfied the Russians much more effec-

---

[1] Buchanan to Sazonov, 12 Mar. 1915. *Konstantinopel und die Meerengen*, ii, no. 81.

[2] Paléologue to Sazonov, 8 Mar. 1915. Ibid., no. 70.

[3] Poincaré to Paléologue, 9 Mar. 1915. Poincaré, *Au service de la France*, vi. 92.

[4] 3 Mar. 1915. Paléologue, *La Russie des Tsars*, i. 314.

[5] Minute by Sazonov, 5 Mar. 1915. *Mezhdunarodnye otnosheniya*, third series, vii (i), no. 312.

[6] 16 Mar. 1915. Paléologue, *La Russie des Tsars*, i. 322.

[7] Paléologue to Sazonov, 10 Apr. 1915. *Konstantinopel und die Meerengen*, ii, no. 103.　　　　　　　　　　　　[8] Grey, *Twenty-Five Years*, ii. 181.

tively, if the western allies could have defeated the German armies in northern France or could even have sent massive military supplies to Russia. Both were beyond them. Joffre could not move the Germans; England and France had not enough munitions for themselves and could not have sent them to Russia even if they had. Diplomacy had to make up for the failures of strategy and materials; and a promise for the future was the cheapest coin in which to pay.

The promise served its purpose. It removed Russia's suspicions; it perhaps helped to keep her in the war. It is more likely that she would have continued to fight in any case. Later in 1915 the Germans offered Constantinople to the Russians if they would make a separate peace. Sazonov and Nicholas II recognized that their possession of the Straits was likely to be temporary unless Germany was defeated; and they rejected her offer. In fact, the best that can be said for the 'secret treaty' is that it would have made conflict between the allies less likely if Russia had remained in the coalition to the end. All the same, it had awkward diplomatic consequences. Russia had obtained her reward in advance; Great Britain had Egypt and the neutral zone of Persia; the French had nothing, not even a firm promise of Alsace and Lorraine. They insisted on partitioning Asiatic Turkey with Great Britain; and the British had to acquiesce, though this cut across promises which they had made to the Arabs. In January 1916 Great Britain and France concluded the Sykes-Picot agreement, by which Syria was allotted to France and Mesopotamia to Great Britain. The Russians claimed a further reward for approving this agreement: they were allotted Armenia and Kurdistan (16 Sept. 1916). This bargain, too, was not as cynical as it subsequently appeared. The British had to console French feeling, if France was to carry the main burden on the western front. Besides, it was a reasonable assumption that the Ottoman empire would not survive the war; and the allies had therefore to make plans for the future. It is easy to say in retrospect that the allies should have planned for independent Arab states; but this was not a thought that came easily to the two protecting Powers of Egypt, Tunis, and Morocco.

The Russians did not get the promise of Constantinople without paying some price for it, though the price was in fact paid by Serbia, their protégé. While the British planned early in 1915 to turn Germany's flank by knocking Turkey out of the war, the French hoped to achieve the same aim by bringing Italy into it. The British acquiesced in this policy. The Italian army would be a substitute for the forces which they could not yet provide themselves; the Italian navy would strengthen the Entente in the Mediterranean; and, besides, both Great Britain and France were not sorry to introduce a fourth Power into the Eastern question as an offset against Russia. In August 1914 Russia had been the most eager to draw Italy into the war; but then Russian forces had been turned against Germany, and the Russians needed Italy in order to distract Austria-Hungary. By the beginning of 1915 the Russians, though ineffective against Germany, still hoped to hold their own against Austria-Hungary, or even to defeat her; and they had no desire to revive 'the Crimean coalition' in its full extent. On 2 March Sazonov insisted that Italian participation had lost its value and would only increase the difficulties of peace-making—there would be less to go round among the victors.[1]

The Italians were certainly not modest in their claims. The other Powers had been forced into war before they could define their aims; Italy could insist on being promised her aims before she entered the war. She hoped to achieve all her ambitions at a stroke: completion of her 'national unity' by acquiring Tyrol and Istria;[2] domination of the Adriatic; and recognition as a Great Power both in the Near East and in colonial matters. The Italians made some attempt to gain this programme by peaceful means. They offered their neutrality to the central Powers in exchange for 'compensations' for Austria-Hungary's Balkan gains, according to the terms of the Triple Alliance. The Germans were ready for this bargain; and Bülow, who prided himself on his Italian connexions, was sent to Rome to offer the Italians anything they could find in Francis Joseph's pocket. The Austrians held out; as on previous occasions, the 'state of nationalities' could make no concession to the national principle. Besides, the cession of Tyrol—with its 300,000 Germans—would offend the German-Austrians, the most stalwart supporters of the monarchy; and concessions in the Adriatic

---

[1] Sazonov to Paléologue and Buchanan, 2 Mar. 1915. *Mezhdunarodnye otnosheniya*, third series, vii (i) no. 276.

[2] The 'national' claim in these areas was mythical: neither had an Italian majority.

would drive the Croats into the arms of the Serbs. When Berchtold, as usual, showed 'weakness', he was at last dismissed, and his place taken by Burian—the first Hungarian to become foreign minister since Andrássy. The negotiations were, in any case, pointless; as in 1866, the Italians recognized that the only security for their claims was the defeat of Austria-Hungary.

On 4 March the Italians turned to the Entente; by simple coincidence it was the very day on which Russia stated her claim to Constantinople and the Straits. The Entente did not mind sacrificing to Italy the Germans of Tyrol; none of them, not even Russia, knew anything of the 600,000 Slovenes of Istria; Great Britain and France were also willing to promise to Italy the whole of Dalmatia and a protectorate over Albania,[1] particularly as the Italian claims in the colonies and the Near East were left vague. Sazonov, however, would not sacrifice the South Slavs of Dalmatia—a million of them against some 10,000 Italians. Russia had been unable to do anything to help Serbia; all the more reason not to desert her diplomatically. Moreover—a fact which the western Powers never understood—the Russians felt a genuine duty to protect Slav interests, just as much as the British government stood by people of British stock in the Dominions. There is no need to explain Sazonov's objections by far-fetched speculation about Russian ambitions to secure a naval base in the Adriatic. Of course, there were practical elements in his opposition to the Italian claims. Having estranged Bulgaria by keeping her out of Constantinople in 1913, he now hoped to win her over by the offer of Macedonia, which was in Serbian hands; and the Serbs therefore would have to be mollified by great gains on the Adriatic. More vaguely, Sazonov saw the shadow of a union between Italy, Hungary, and Rumania, which would threaten his own project of a Slav confederation in the Balkans. He was also much pressed by Supilo, a Croat leader in exile, not to sacrifice South Slav claims in their widest extent; but Sazonov had enough to do defending Serbia, without patronizing Roman Catholic Croatia as well.

Sazonov's obstinacy infuriated his western partners. Paléo-

[1] The Italians assumed that Hungary would survive the war in integrity; they did not therefore claim Fiume (Rijeka) or the short strip of Croat coast, which was a dependency of the kingdom of Hungary. This was to cause them embarrassment in 1919, when they tried to obtain all that they had been promised in the treaty of London and Fiume as well.

logue said: 'we took arms to save Serbia, not to realise the chimeras of Slavism. The sacrifice of Constantinople is quite enough!';[1] and Grey regarded the entry of Italy as the turning-point of the war—'we cannot prolong it just to get a stretch of coast for Serbia'.[2] Sazonov could not grudge Italy her claims at the very moment when he was demanding Constantinople. Moreover he had a weak spot in his own camp. Grand Duke Nicholas feared an Austro-German attack and urged that Italy be brought into the war as soon as possible.[3] Still, Sazonov would only compromise: he gave up the Croat part of Dalmatia, but demanded southern Dalmatia for Serbia. The Italians, too, had reason to compromise. On 22 March the Galician fortress of Przemysl was taken by the Russians—a deceptive sign that they might still defeat Austria-Hungary without Italy's assistance; a few days later, Sazonov frightened the Italians with talk of a peace-offer from Vienna.[4] In fact, they began to fear a Russian victory in eastern Europe, just when the Russians, more accurately, began to fear defeat. On 26 April Italy signed the treaty of London with the Entente Powers. Southern Dalmatia was to go to Serbia, though the Italians insisted that it be 'neutralized'; Italy, being a Great Power, was above any such restriction. Otherwise, the Italians received all the conditions that they had demanded; in return they promised the Entente to go to war 'against all their enemies' within a month.[5]

[1] Paléologue, *La Russie des Tsars*, i. 336. 31 Mar. 1915.

[2] Benckendorff to Sazonov, 24, 31 Mar. 1915. *Mezhdunarodnye otnosheniya*, third series, vii (ii), nos. 419, 451. Grey suggested that Serbia should be consoled with the Banat. As this was part of the projected price for buying Rumania into the war, the idea, too, cut across Sazonov's plans.

[3] Muraviev (at G.H.Q.) to Sazonov, 3 Apr. 1915. Ibid., no. 471.

[4] Minute by Sazonov, 28 Mar. 1915. Ibid., no. 441. The peace-offer, made through a Russian court-lady, Maria Vassilshikova, so far as it had any reality, came, in fact, from Germany, not from Austria-Hungary.

[5] This summary is technically a little abrupt. In Article II Italy promised to pursue the war in common with the Entente Powers 'against all their enemies'; only in conclusion did she promise to 'enter the field' (against an undefined enemy) within a month. In May 1915 she declared war only against Austria-Hungary; and not against Germany until 28 Aug. 1916. Article I provided that a military convention should 'fix the minimum of military forces which Russia must employ against Austria-Hungary in order to prevent this Power concentrating all her efforts against Italy, in case Russia decides to make her principal effort against Germany'. Thus, the Italian anxiety in regard to Russia was the exact opposite of the French.

The future Italian frontiers in Tyrol, Istria, and Dalmatia were defined with much exactness (though not always accuracy). Article IX recognized that 'Italy is interested in the maintenance of the balance in the Mediterranean' and promised

It was a close echo of the treaty of 8 April 1866 between Italy and Prussia. The diplomacy of 1866 was again echoed when the Austrians nerved themselves to concession, once more too late. On 9 May Burian, much pressed by Tisza, offered to surrender the Italian-speaking part of Tyrol and to give Trieste autonomy; he even threw in the Dalmatian islands, though not the mainland. When the Italian government failed to reply, Bülow informed the former prime minister, Giolitti, who favoured neutrality. He had the support of the majority of deputies and was able to enforce the resignation of the government. Agitation was stirred by d'Annunzio, the romantic writer, and by men of the extreme Left, such as Mussolini— once anti-militarists, now anxious to revive the legend of Garibaldi. The chamber surrendered only when the crowd broke its windows. On 20 May it voted war-credits by 407 to 73; on 23 May Italy declared war on Austria-Hungary.

Italy's war had a character of its own. The Great Powers were locked in a struggle for the mastery of Europe; Italian policy echoed the past and pursued phantoms. Even the demonstrations of May 1915 echoed the riots of March 1848 in Genoa, which drove Charles Albert into Lombardy. While the Italian agitators wanted to force their country to be great the statesmen tried to define their war-aims with Machiavellian realism. But even the war-aims were a matter of theory; they were an imitation of the policy of others, not an expression of practical needs.[1] The First World war was essentially a struggle against German power. Italy was indifferent to this struggle. She had nothing to lose from a German victory over France and Russia —indeed much to gain. France was her successful rival in the

her 'an equitable share' in Adalia. Article XIII promised Italy 'compensation in principle', notably by colonial frontier adjustment, in case Great Britain and France acquired German colonies. The Italians, in fact, were so eager to define their Adriatic claims precisely that they accepted vague, and ultimately unprofitable, phrases in regard to colonies and the Near East.

By Article XV the three Entente Powers agreed to 'support Italy's opposition to any proposal tending to introduce a representative of the Holy See in all negotiations for peace and for settling questions raised by the present war'.

The Italians were not told of the Anglo-French promise to Russia regarding Constantinople and the Straits; and the Russians insisted on the two western Powers reaffirming their promise when Italy entered the war.

[1] There was a practical aim behind the agitation for Trieste. The shipping firms of Genoa and Venice wished to cut Trieste off from its hinterland and so to divert the Mediterranean trade of central Europe to themselves. But it was hardly possible to avow the ruin of Trieste as the object of nationalist agitation.

Mediterranean, Russia a possible danger in the Balkans and the Near East. Her only immediate enemy was Austria-Hungary, as her diplomacy and strategy showed. Yet even this policy was largely out-moded. Italy's one justifiable ambition was Italian-speaking Tyrol; and this could have been achieved by peaceful negotiation. Otherwise Italy, like Hungary, the other 'revolutionary nation' of 1848, really needed the Habsburg monarchy as a barrier against Germany and still more against the Slavs. As it was, Italian policy first revived Croat loyalty to the Habsburgs and then, on their defeat, inevitably brought into being a South Slav state, which was able to deny her Dalmatia after the First World war and to deprive her of Istria and Trieste after the second.

Nor was Italy's entry into the war a gain for the Entente Powers. Their enemy was Germany; and the time came when they would have welcomed a separate peace with Austria-Hungary. Their Italian partner prevented it. Of course, the promise of Constantinople to Russia also prevented a separate peace with Turkey; and this promise, too, was out of date. But at least it did not prevent Russia putting her main weight (so far as she still had any) against Germany until her collapse in 1917. Italy's declaration of war was too late to prevent even the Austro-German offensive against Russia. On 4 May the central Powers broke through at Gorlice. By the end of June the Russians were driven out of Galicia; by the end of September they had lost Poland and Lithuania. If the Italians had entered the war a month earlier, there might have been a real 'turning-point'; as it was, Italy soon became a liability, whom Great Britain and France had to defend.

The two attempts to turn Germany's flank—on the Italo-Austrian frontier and at the Dardanelles—both failed during the summer of 1915. Frontal attacks in France failed also. On 7 October Joffre foresaw 'a long period of a defensive attitude'. Diplomacy made another effort, this time to draw Bulgaria into the war. The Bulgarians were determined to gain all that had been denied them in 1913. The Entente made them a firm offer of Turkish territory; they could promise Macedonia only if Serbia received 'equitable compensations' in Bosnia and Hercegovina and on the Adriatic. Germany offered Macedonia and, as well, Greek and Rumanian territory, if either of these states joined the Entente. On 6 September Bulgaria made an alliance with the central Powers. The Entente planned to keep Bulgaria out of the war and to drag Greece into it by an expedition to Salonica. Their preparations were too slow. Greece evaded commitment; Bulgaria entered the war on 5 October; and before the Anglo-French expeditionary force could achieve anything, Serbia had been overrun. New confusions followed. The diplomatic failure in Bulgaria discredited Delcassé; and he carried Viviani with him in his fall. Briand combined their offices, in a government that was great only in talk. The British now wished to withdraw from both Salonica and the Dardanelles; with exaggerated gloom, they feared a Turkish attack on the Suez canal. The French wished to maintain their prestige in the Balkans and still dreamt of an offensive from Salonica, which might encourage Rumania into war. On 10 December compromise, of the usual unsatisfactory kind, was achieved. The British agreed to remain in Salonica 'provisionally', but the army there was not to be reinforced. For the rest of the war, nearly a quarter of a million men remained imprisoned there to the great convenience of the central Powers; they employed only the Bulgarian army, which in any case would not have left the Balkans.

By the end of 1915 all the original expectations had been disappointed. In 1914 the Germans had aimed at decisive victory on the western front; the Entente had counted on the Russian 'steam-roller'. Both had failed. In 1915 the Entente had aimed at decisive victory over Germany, either by turning her flank or by a frontal attack; the Germans had tried to knock Russia out of the war.[1] Again both had failed. Yet Germany had achieved her essential aims. *Mitteleuropa* existed in practice. Germany and Austria-Hungary were virtually united in economic and military matters; and there was a political unity which extended from Antwerp to Bagdad. The Entente Powers, who had entered the war to defend themselves, had to destroy a German empire that was already in being. German policy, on the other hand, had only to secure recognition of the new *status quo*. This was indeed the object

---

[1] The strategy of Falkenhayn, who had succeeded the younger Moltke as German chief-of-staff, showed, however, that the elder Moltke had been right in planning to defeat Russia and Schlieffen wrong in planning a decisive victory over France. Falkenhayn was able to defeat Russia, while standing on the defensive in the west. If this strategy had been followed at the beginning of the war, Great Britain would have remained neutral and France would soon have made peace.

of Falkenhayn's strategy in 1916. He assumed that Russia, after her defeats of 1915, was no longer the principal enemy. Even in the west he did not aim at decisive victory. The French army was to be worn down, so that it would no longer be the 'instrument' of British policy on the Continent; then the British would be forced to accept a German peace by the threat of submarine warfare. The practical expression of this strategy was a persistent attack from February to June on the symbolical fortress of Verdun, where the French army was to 'bleed to death'.

This strategy was not successful. Though the French army was brought almost to exhaustion at Verdun, the German army also bled to death there and, slightly later, against the British army on the Somme. On the eastern front the Russians under Brusilov undertook an offensive in May, which carried them unexpectedly back to Galicia and the foot of the Carpathians.[1] This success brought to the Entente a diplomatic reward. They had been trying to draw Rumania into the war ever since August 1914. The Rumanians had always been eager to state their price, but unshakeably reluctant to act. Brusilov's offensive made them fear that they would be too late. Alliance with Rumania had long been a favourite device of French diplomacy; it would lessen the Slav predominance in eastern Europe which the French disliked almost as much as the Germans. The Russians would have preferred to defeat Austria-Hungary without Rumanian assistance; having failed to do so, they were ready to give Rumania her chance. On 17 August Russia and France accepted the Rumanian terms. She was to receive Transylvania, the Bukovina, and the Banat; the great allies would keep Bulgaria busy, so that Rumania could concentrate on Austria-Hungary;[2] they would continue the war until Rumania's aims were achieved and would admit her as an equal at the peace conference. These last terms were less of a score for Rumania than they seemed: on 11 August

[1] The Russians repaid in May 1916 the service which the Italians had failed to perform in May 1915. Brusilov's offensive, though designed only to relieve the French, saved the Italians (already defeated at Asiago in April) from an Austro-Hungarian attack in Tyrol.

[2] The army at Salonica was to take the offensive against the Bulgarians; and the Russians were to send 50,000 men to the Dobrudja (the Rumanians at first asked for 200,000). In the outcome neither promise was fulfilled. As the Russians themselves coveted part of the Bukovina, they did not altogether regret Rumania's defeat.

France and Russia agreed between themselves to ignore them when they came to negotiate peace.

The alliance with Rumania was the last attempt to involve a small Power in the war.[1] The statesmen of the Entente had still not learnt from events. They still thought in terms of a casual accumulation of man-power and failed to recognize that war had become a struggle solely between Great Powers. Every alliance with a small state meant an additional liability, not a gain—Serbia, Belgium, even Italy on the one side; Turkey on the other. The secret of German success, while it lasted, was that she had fewer allies and treated these as subordinates. Rumania entered the war on 28 August. Like Italy the previous year, she had waited too long. Brusilov's offensive had been checked; the battle of the Somme was nearly over. Soon the Germans had troops to spare once again for the rescue of Austria-Hungary. They took the offensive in November; and overran all Rumania by the end of the year. Rumania's wheat and oil fell into German hands;[2] *Mitteleuropa* seemed more secure than ever, though little nearer to decisive victory.

The campaign of 1916 had again failed to produce a decision. The debate between compromise peace and total victory was reopened more sharply than ever. Many civilians in high places were sceptical of military success. Bethmann had never believed in it; and his doubts were seconded by Burian. In England Lansdowne urged on the cabinet in November that a decisive victory was unlikely and that negotiations should be encouraged; in France Caillaux saw support growing in the chamber. The decline of confidence was greatest in Russia. In July Sazonov had urged concessions to the Poles. He was overthrown, and his place taken by Stürmer, who favoured a separate peace with Germany. The generals in every country, however, swung the other way, except of course in Russia, where they were incapable of formulating any decision. On the German side, Falkenhayn's failure at Verdun led to his dismissal on 27 August; he was succeeded by Hindenburg and

[1] In 1917 the Entente forced Greece into war by a *coup d'état* at Athens; but this was designed to improve the position of the allied armies at Salonica rather than to acquire the resources of the Greek army. There were also political motives. Great Britain and France wanted a further rival against Italy in the Near East; later, Greece was played by Great Britain against France.

[2] The Germans did not move fast enough to prevent the destruction of the oil-wells by British agents. They were not restored to full production until after Germany's defeat.

Ludendorff, who had previously commanded on the eastern front. Their recipe was still decisive victory, though they did not know how it should be accomplished. On the western side, Nivelle, who had defended Verdun, claimed that he possessed the secret of defeating the Germans; on 26 December he superseded Joffre in the supreme command and was given authority over the British army as well, with a programme of achieving a 'break-through' early in 1917.

Hence there began a competition between the generals and civilians which lasted almost until the end of the war, though the decisive stage was over by the spring of 1917. The civilians tried to negotiate; the generals still hoped to win. The attempts at negotiation broke on a single fact: what was compromise for the one side represented defeat to the other. The statesmen of the Entente understood by compromise a return to the *status quo* of 1914: Germany would recover her colonies and keep her fleet, but she would withdraw from Belgium and the occupied territories in France and Russia; she would perhaps even help to restore them. Bethmann understood by compromise the *status quo* of 1916: Germany would retain at least the iron-fields of Lorraine and military control over Belgium; she would receive additional colonies and perhaps part of Poland. Bethmann came a little nearer to compromise than anyone else in that he would pay a tiny price for Germany's gain—a fragment of upper Alsace to France and Italian-speaking Tyrol to Italy. But essentially his position and that of the Entente compromisers was the same: neither would accept the compromise terms proposed by the other side without military defeat, and in that case compromise was unnecessary. The decisive victory which was needed to achieve a compromise would, in fact, be followed by a dictated peace. Hence Bethmann was pushed aside by Ludendorff, and Lansdowne and Caillaux were silenced by Lloyd George and Clemenceau, the advocates of 'the knock-out blow'.

Bethmann's efforts at compromise took most practical form in the autumn of 1916. He seemed then within sight of a separate peace with Russia. Here a genuine compromise was possible. There were no great prizes for Germany in eastern Europe, and the *status quo* of 1914 would be tolerable for her there, if it freed her hands to make vital gains in the west. Ludendorff ruined Bethmann's negotiations with the Russians.

He was concerned only to raise new man-power for the decisive struggle, and in his search for it insisted on playing for Polish support. On 5 November William II and Francis Joseph issued a joint proclamation, promising the Polish people 'an independent State, with a hereditary and constitutional monarchy'. The Poles were not taken in. Only 1,400 men joined the German forces, instead of the fifteen divisions which Ludendorff had expected. But the offer to Poland, however fraudulent, ended Bethmann's negotiations with Russia. The Russian reactionaries, who favoured the restoration of the Holy Alliance, were the most offended at Germany's repudiation of the anti-Polish principle on which the Holy Alliance had been based.

Ludendorff's zest for victory soon threatened Bethmann's moderate policy even more seriously. Though Falkenhayn had already recognized that Great Britain was Germany's essential enemy and that she could be defeated only by unrestricted submarine warfare, he had planned to wear France down first and then to bring Great Britain to compromise merely by threats. Ludendorff, however, wished to launch the submarines at once; and he pressed this the more urgently because of the deadlock on land. Bethmann was as sceptical of submarine warfare as of everything else; moreover he was convinced, rightly, that it would bring the United States into the war. This was indeed to be the turning-point of European destiny. Across the Atlantic Ocean a new Great Power had come into existence—greater in material resources than any European Power, and greater in population than any Power except Russia,[1] but without interest in European rivalries and wedded to isolation by an unbroken tradition. Wilson, president since 1912 and re-elected in 1916, could not move faster than American opinion; in any case, though deeply attached to the cause of democracy, he doubted whether it was at stake. Like the English radicals before 1914, he distrusted France and Russia as much as he disliked German imperialism, and he endorsed the words of his unofficial adviser, House: 'If the Allies win, it means largely the domination of Russia on the Continent of Europe; and if Germany wins, it means the unspeakable tyranny of militarism for generations to come.'[2]

[1] In 1914 the United States had a population of 96 millions; produced 455 million tons of coal, 32 million tons of steel, and 30 million tons of pig-iron.

[2] House to Wilson, 22 Aug. 1914. *Private Papers of Colonel House*, i. 291.

Moreover Wilson, like most American academics, had deep ties with 'the other Germany' of the professors; and he hoped all along that a liberal Germany would remain the greatest of the continental Powers. There was an alternative programme to which he could be won: the three empires of eastern Europe could all be pushed aside in favour of free national states. Pilsudski, the Polish leader, expressed an outlook very similar to Wilson's, when he said: 'Germany must first defeat Russia and must then be herself defeated by the western Powers.' Great Britain and France had very little sympathy with this outlook in the first two years of the war. They needed Russia in order to divide the German armies. Moreover, a victory achieved in partnership with Russia would, they supposed, give them their practical aims. Great Britain would destroy the German fleet; France would recover Alsace and Lorraine; both would get their share of the Ottoman empire. A peace arranged by the United States would, probably, be a peace of the pre-war *status quo*; certainly it would be 'anti-imperialist'. Therefore, though they paraded their common democracy with America and listened politely to Wilson's offers of mediation,[1] their sole concern was to draw the United States into the war, not to escape a Russian victory. By the end of 1916 this seemed remote; and Great Britain, threatened by the German submarines, needed American assistance desperately. Henceforth her diplomacy aimed at bringing America into the war without paying the 'ideological' price for it.

In truth, the United States would go to war only if her own interests were challenged; and her overriding interest was 'the

[1] House, Wilson's agent, first visited the belligerent capitals in the spring of 1915; he found no opening for mediation. In the winter of 1915–16 he tried again. This time he reached an agreement of a sort with Grey on 22 Feb. 1916. America would offer mediation 'on terms not unfavourable to the Allies'; and if these were refused she would enter the war. The terms seem to have been the restoration of Belgium; the return of Alsace and Lorraine to France; and 'the acquisition by Russia of an outlet to the sea'; in return, Germany should be compensated 'by concessions to her in other places than Europe' (Grey, *Twenty-Five Years*, ii. 123). Grey did not accept this offer: he put it in cold storage for use in case of an allied defeat. House, on the other hand, proposed it in order to end the fighting. Alternatively, he hoped to lure Wilson into war without his noticing it. Wilson, however, was not taken in; he emptied the agreement of any meaning it had by inserting that America would 'probably' go to war if the terms were refused. The so-called Grey–House agreement made great stir when it was revealed; but there was nothing in it. Grey may have been deceiving House. House was certainly deceiving both Grey and Wilson. He dangled war before the one, peace before the other, and in reality achieved nothing.

freedom of the seas'. Bethmann had recognized this and had promised that Germany would not practise unrestricted submarine warfare. Now he had no means of keeping his promise; Ludendorff was too strong for him. When Bethmann appealed to the Reichstag, this resolved that 'in making his decisions, the Imperial Chancellor must rely upon the views of the High Command'. Bethmann's only resource was to start negotiations for peace before the submarine campaign was launched. On 12 December Germany announced her willingness to negotiate, but without stating any terms; since the note lauded Germany's victories, it was clear that the terms would be, at best, those of the existing *status quo*. In fact, Bethmann meant to demand guarantees from Belgium and the incorporation of the Lorraine iron-fields into Germany. Yet he imagined that the reply of the Entente 'will not be a refusal'. He was wrong. The forces which favoured compromise in the west were not strong enough to gain power, and they were fatally weakened by the German offer. Briand, still shakily in office in France, rejected the 'trap' on 19 December. In England the Asquith government had just been overthrown; and Lloyd George had come to power with a programme of total victory. He replied to the German note with a quotation from Abraham Lincoln: 'We accepted this war for an object, and a worthy object, and the war will end when that object is attained.' This undefined object was, presumably, the destruction of German militarism, in other words, 'the knock-out blow'.

Yet the Entente Powers did not escape without some political commitment. Wilson, too, saw crisis approaching; and he, too, hoped to avoid it by negotiation. On 20 December he invited the contending Powers to formulate their war-aims; perhaps 'they would not prove irreconcilable'. The Germans refused: they had conquered Belgium and Poland, and they meant to keep them by negotiation. They would not submit these terms to preliminary scrutiny or to American mediation. The Entente Powers, however, were playing for American support; they had to devise terms which would meet with her approval. On 10 January 1917 they defined their war-aims for the first time. It was easy to insist on the restoration of Belgium[1] and Serbia, and of the occupied territory in Rumania, Russia, and northern France. But restoration had never been enough; as well, some

[1] The Belgians claimed, unsuccessfully, that this be the subject of a special note.

WAR-AIMS OF THE ENTENTE

great principle was needed to arouse American emotion. This great principle could only be 'national self-determination'. The Entente therefore demanded 'the liberation of the Italians, as also of the Slavs, Rumanians, and Czechoslovaks from foreign domination' and 'the freeing of the populations subject to the bloody tyranny of the Turks'. They thus committed themselves to the dismemberment of the Habsburg and Ottoman empires. Yet this programme did not interest Great Britain and France, so far as the Habsburg empire was concerned; even Italy had put in the Czechoslovaks (an absurd reference, since they were Slavs) in order to eliminate any mention of 'the South Slavs'; and there was no promise of independence for Poland—only a reference to the promises of the tsar.[1] Most of all there was no policy in regard to Germany, only talk of 'full security . . . and international settlements such as to guarantee land and sea frontiers against unjustified attack'. Yet the German problem was alone decisive for the Great Powers. The Italians were glad to get a further blessing for their own ambitions. The British and French sought to win American favour, but secretly hoped to win the war before the United States could play a decisive role.

The French indeed still hoped to escape American patronage by recalling Russia to life. In February 1917 an allied conference was held at Petrograd to co-ordinate their strategy and resources. It was a futile formality. Milner, the British delegate, said repeatedly: 'We are wasting our time.' Doumergue, the French delegate, however, did some private business on his own. He had intended to demand Russian support for the recovery of Alsace and Lorraine in exchange for the promise of Constantinople and the Straits which Russia had received in April 1915. The Russians refused to pay again for what they had already; instead, they wanted further payment if they were to stay in the war at all. Doumergue therefore put up the terms on both sides. France should receive the coal-mines of the Saar as well as Alsace and Lorraine; and the rest of the left bank of the Rhine should become 'an autonomous and neutralised State', garrisoned by French troops. In return, Russia should be free 'to fix her western frontiers as she wished'. By this agree-

---

[1] In March 1916 Briand had proposed that the allies should 'guarantee' Russia's promises to Poland. Sazonov replied: 'Beware of Poland; it is a dangerous subject for an ambassador of France.' Paléologue, *La Russie des Tsars*, ii. 274.

ment of 14 February 1917 France made at last the sacrifice
which Napoleon III had always refused and which the Third
republic had hitherto evaded. She abandoned Poland to Russia
for the sake of the Rhine frontier.[1]

By 1917 this was no more than the echo of a dead past. The
days when France and Russia could hope to destroy Germany,
even with British assistance, were over. Germany could be
defeated only if a new world Power entered the war; and this
was achieved by German folly, not by Entente diplomacy. On
9 January the Germans resolved on unrestricted submarine
warfare. Bethmann still hoped that the United States might
remain neutral if he revealed his 'compromise' terms. The note
of 31 January, which announced the beginning of the submarine campaign, was accompanied by a secret letter to House,
containing the terms on which Germany would negotiate.
They were 'a frontier which would protect Germany and
Poland strategically against Russia'; more colonies; 'strategic
and economic changes' of the Franco-German frontier: and
'special guarantees for the safety of Germany' in Belgium. Even
these were only a beginning of what Germany would demand
if the situation changed in her favour. Wilson was outraged by
these terms: 'It is not possible!' Yet even now he waited for
further German provocation. Only when American ships were
sunk and the Germans tried to stir up Mexico against her
neighbour, did the United States declare war on 2 April. Wilson,
though resolute against German militarism, remained sceptical
of his new partners and did not mean to underwrite their war-
aims. The United States became 'an Associated Power', not an
ally; Wilson brushed aside the secret treaties when Balfour, the
British representative, attempted to show them to him; and
he wrote to House in July: 'England and France *have not the*

[1] Doumergue had apparently no instructions. He acted on his own initiative
and struck a bargain with the Russians without waiting for authorization from the
French cabinet. The exchange of letters between Paléologue and Pokrovsky, the
Russian foreign minister, on 14 Feb. 1917, dealt only with the future frontiers of
France; but on 12 Feb. Izvolski had demanded freedom for Russia to fix her
frontiers as she wished. The French council of ministers dared not reject this
demand for fear of ruining Doumergue's negotiation, the details of which were unknown to them. They therefore agreed to Izvolski's demand on 10 Mar. Doumergue
claimed that he had secured Russian backing for the Rhine frontier without
paying a price for it and was furious with Briand (who in his turn criticized
Doumergue); but it is clear that to the Russians one concession was conditional on
the other.

same views with regard to peace that we have by any means. When the war is over we can force them to our way of thinking.'[1] Still, the essential preliminary to this was the defeat of Germany. The conflict between American idealism and the realism of the Old World could be fought out only when this had been accomplished. The Germans had brought on themselves a new and irresistible enemy.

They did so just when the war changed otherwise decisively in their favour. Things went so badly for the Entente in 1917 that they would have been glad to accept a compromise peace on German terms, if it had not been for the prospect of American aid on an ever-increasing scale. In March revolution broke out in Russia: the tsar was dethroned, and a provisional government took his place. The western allies at first welcomed this development: a Russian republic would be more respectable in the eyes of the United States, as well as more efficient in fighting the war, and a free Russia would agree to a free Poland.[2] These hopes were soon disappointed. It soon became clear that the Russians had made their revolution in order to cease fighting, not to fight the war better. When Miliukov, foreign minister in the provisional government, invoked the prize of Constantinople and declared Russia's will 'to fight the world war until decisive victory', he was driven from office; and the Russian armies fought a last catastrophic battle in July. Nor was this the only military failure. Nivelle's boasted offensive also achieved nothing, except to shatter the morale of the French army; and there were serious mutinies there in the summer of 1917.

Moreover, the Russian revolution provoked, for the first time, a violent cleavage in public opinion. Hitherto, anti-war feeling had been confined to a few pacifists; and compromise peace had been advocated by men of the Right, who feared that further war would shatter the fabric of society. Now the socialist parties in Great Britain and France, and with them a large section of the industrial working-class, responded to the new programme of the Russian revolutionaries—'a peace without annexations or indemnities'. The war became 'the war of

[1] Wilson to House, 21 July 1917. R. S. Baker, *Woodrow Wilson: Life and Letters*, vii. 180.

[2] This was particularly true of the French. Balfour, foreign secretary in Lloyd George's government, regarded an independent Poland as a misfortune, since it would make Russia a less effective ally against Germany in a future war.

the Bosses', a war in which the masses had nothing to gain and much to lose. Men were ready to believe that the war was being fought for selfish 'imperialist' aims, even before the Bolsheviks published the secret treaties in December 1917. International socialism, which had disintegrated at the outbreak of war, seemed to be reviving. Previously only a few socialists of the extreme Left had met in Switzerland (at Zimmerwald and Kienthal). Now the moderate Russian socialists, themselves in the provisional government, proposed a wider meeting at Stockholm; and they were supported by 'Pro-war' socialists in Great Britain and France. In the end, the two governments forbade their attendance; and only Germans met the Russians at Stockholm. Yet even the shadow of the Stockholm meeting was enough to cause a stir; in July 1917 Ramsay MacDonald, not usually a revolutionary, looked forward to the rule of workers' and soldiers' councils in Great Britain.

Extreme answered extreme. The agitation for a People's peace could be met only by a People's war; moderate men were everywhere pushed aside. The conflict took different forms in different countries. In Germany Bethmann still tried to restrain the High Command, until he was dismissed—on its order—in July; in England Lloyd George played with the idea of being the Man who made Peace (a role he also coveted in the Second World war) before deciding to become the Man who won the War; in France Ribot, the veteran who had made the Franco-Russian alliance, tried to symbolize the will to victory, until he was superseded in November by a greater symbol, Clemenceau. In Russia Kerensky, head of the provisional government, opened the door to the Bolsheviks by attempting to revive the war. Even the Habsburg monarchy, so long moribund, tried to show a last sign of life. Francis Joseph had been content to trail hopelessly behind Germany until his death in November 1916. The new Emperor Charles saw disaster approaching. The Allied peace-terms of 10 January 1917 foreshadowed the dismemberment of the Habsburg monarchy; a German victory would mean its domination from Berlin. Charles said in May: 'a striking military success by Germany would be our ruin.' Czernin, whom he had made foreign minister, also despaired of victory; but he despaired just as much of breaking loose from Germany.

Still, the 'peace-offensive' of 1917, so far as it had any

meaning, sprang from Austria-Hungary's initiative—the last effort of a monarchy which was bound to perish in a fight to the finish. Emperor and foreign minister differed in their tactics. Charles hoped for a separate peace with the allies; Czernin hoped to persuade Germany into making peace merely by threatening to desert her. Both lines were barren: if Austria-Hungary had been strong enough to break with Germany, she would not have needed to do it. As a result, Charles and Czernin deceived both their allies and their enemies, and they also deceived each other. Charles approached the French through his brother-in-law, Prince Sixte of Bourbon-Parma. He agreed to support the French claim to Alsace and Lorraine; Serbia should receive an access to the Adriatic, but should prevent any agitation against Austria-Hungary; at a later stage he offered concessions to Italy, on condition that the Habsburg monarchy received 'adequate compensation', presumably in Albania. In other words, it was assumed that Austria-Hungary had won the lesser war in the Balkans; and that Germany had lost the greater war for the mastery of Europe. Yet the opposite was the case; and this was the only motive of Charles's action.[1]

The British and French statesmen were, at first, greatly excited by the prospect of a separate peace with Austria-Hungary. They had no reason to desire the destruction of the Habsburg monarchy. Lloyd George wished to lessen the strain on the British navy in the Mediterranean and welcomed the reputation of making peace with somebody; Poincaré would not be sorry to play off Austria-Hungary against Russia at Constantinople. In fact, the western allies had no scruple in abandoning Russia and never revealed Charles's peace-offer to her; they did not even mind abandoning the political independence of Serbia, though its defence had given the occasion

[1] This confused negotiation was further confused by the actions of Prince Sixte, who—like other amateur diplomats—misrepresented the position to both parties. He first drafted the terms which he thought the French likely to accept; submitted them to Poincaré, who did not object to them; and then communicated them to Charles as official French demands. Thus both Charles and the allies thought that they were faced with a 'peace-offer'. At a later stage, when Charles asked for an agreement which he could submit to his German ally, Sixte transformed thi: into a request for terms on which Austria-Hungary could make a separate peace Charles may have dreamt of making a separate peace, if Germany refused a sensibl peace-offer; but, in fact, the specific promise of a separate peace was made onl by Sixte, not by Charles, and Sixte repeated this myth even in the title of his bool when he revealed the negotiations in 1920.

for war. Italy was a more difficult matter. She alone was fighting Austria-Hungary and would have to agree to make peace with her. Admittedly she was almost as near collapse as the Habsburg monarchy and, in fact, suffered a great military disaster at Caporetto in November, after the negotiations were over. Her very weakness kept her in the war; her statesmen dared not make peace without a striking success, for fear of the internal disturbances that would follow. In April Lloyd George tried to sweeten them by offering Smyrna as compensation for the promised territory in the Adriatic. The Italians insisted on the treaty of London; though, in the confusion, they managed to carry off a promise of territory in Asia Minor as well.[1]

In any case, the French soon turned against the idea of a separate peace with Austria-Hungary. There was always a deep jealousy between the two 'Latin sisters'; and it would be intolerable for the French, if they were still fighting for Alsace and Lorraine when Italy had already received her *irredenta* of the Tyrol. Besides, the French suspected that, if the Italians made peace with Austria-Hungary, they would improve the

[1] This is the so-called agreement of St. Jean de Maurienne. The Italians had been promised gains in Asia Minor by the treaty of London; but the allies refused to negotiate on this until Italy declared war on Germany, which she did in September 1916. Negotiations were then opened in London; and Lloyd George and Ribot met Sonnino at St. Jean de Maurienne on 1 Apr. 1917 in order to carry them further. Though they were pledged not to reveal the negotiations with Emperor Charles, they talked vaguely of the advantages of a separate peace with Austria-Hungary. Lloyd George pointed to Smyrna as Italy's reward; Ribot tried to distract Sonnino from Smyrna by offering him Koniah. Sonnino said 'it was not opportune to open a conversation which might threaten the close union between the allies'. He agreed, however, to take both Smyrna and Koniah. Lloyd George and Ribot, not daring to confess that they were already negotiating with Charles, had to pretend that they had offered Smyrna and Koniah out of sheer goodness of heart.

The Italians then pressed for a more formal agreement; and their allies were dragged along in order to conceal their double-dealing with Austria-Hungary. Besides, the British were afraid that otherwise the Italians might join with the French in refusing them Mesopotamia; they did not mind handing over part of Asia Minor, adjacent to the French sphere. The French acquiesced, apparently to divert Italian ambitions from their colonies. Agreement was reached in August. Though made by an exchange of letters in London, it is usually called the agreement of St. Jean de Maurienne. It was conditional on Russia's approval; and this was never obtained. Hence the British and French argued later that it had no validity.

This abortive partition would have left an unworkable rump-Turkey, cut off from the sea. This is the share which would have gone to Germany, if the pre-war plans for partition of the Ottoman empire had been carried through. In the outcome, Great Britain and France got their shares more or less; Bolshevik Russia renounced hers; and, as Turkey reasserted her national existence, Italy got nothing —and there was no reason why she should.

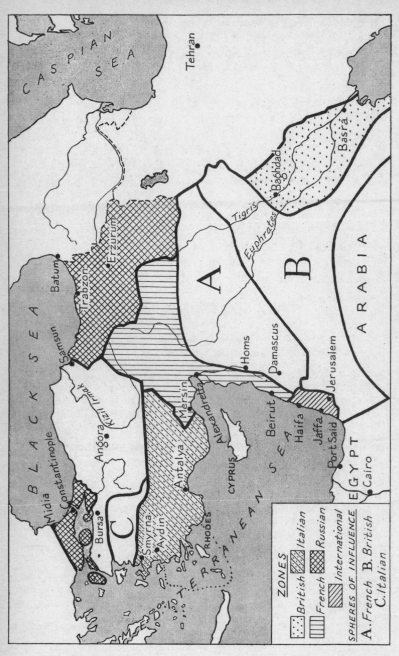

THE PARTITION OF TURKEY-IN-ASIA

ZONES
British
Italian
French
Russian
International

SPHERES OF INFLUENCE
A. French B. British
C. Italian

occasion to seize the objects of French ambition in the Near East. This was not the decisive objection. Even Lloyd George had to admit that nothing would be gained merely by making peace between Austria-Hungary and Italy; Charles must agree to impose the peace-terms on Germany. The British government even proposed to turn Austria-Hungary into an ally by offering her the part of Silesia which she had lost to Prussia in 1742. This was an impossible fantasy. Bismarck's victory of 1866 could never be undone. There could never be a south German confederation, presided over by the Habsburg emperor; nor an Austrian alliance with the western Powers against Prussia and Russia. Such projects were nearly a century out of date. Charles was Germany's prisoner; if he had attempted to turn against her, he would have been resisted by the Germans and Hungarians who dominated the Habsburg empire. The negotiations between Austria-Hungary and the Entente ran into the sand.

Czernin, meanwhile, tried his own line of winning over Bethmann. He insisted that Austria-Hungary could not face another winter of war and offered to hand over her share of Poland, if Germany would surrender Alsace and Lorraine to France.[1] Bethmann encouraged him by suggesting, *in great secret*, that he would offer to France 'something more' than the old frontier of 1914; Czernin did not understand that the price for this trivial concession was to be the iron-fields of Lorraine. In any case, Bethmann, at the very moment of discussing moderate peace-terms with Czernin, underwrote the extreme demands of the high command on 23 April—military control of Belgium, the Lorraine iron-fields, and Russian territory as far as Riga. Bethmann's own explanation of his action was characteristic: 'I have signed the minutes because my resignation over such fantastic matters would be ridiculous. But I shall not let myself be tied in any way by these minutes. If somewhere and somehow possibilities arise for peace, I shall pursue them.'[2] He planned 'somewhere and somehow' to cheat the high command; in reality, he was their prisoner.

More, the high command was soon able to get rid of Bethmann altogether. In the Reichstag the social democrats and

[1] Charles, with characteristic Habsburg appetite, did not approve of this suggestion; he favoured the 'Austro-Polish Solution', by which Poland should be reconstituted under a Habsburg archduke.

[2] Westarp, *Konservative Politik im letzten Jahrzehnt des Kaiserreichs*, ii. 85.

the centre, pushed on by popular discontent, agitated for 'a peace of understanding', and Bethmann welcomed this agitation in order to play it off against the high command. Instead, he was caught between them. At the beginning of July Erzberger, a leader of the centre party, launched a peace resolution. Hindenburg and Ludendorff accused Bethmann of weakness and threatened to resign unless he was dismissed. The Reichstag parties of the Left supported this demand in the hope of putting Bülow in Bethmann's place. But William II had never forgiven Bülow for his behaviour over the *Daily Telegraph* affair in 1908. The high command hastily nominated an unknown bureaucrat, Michaelis, as chancellor; and William II accepted him without demur. Henceforth Ludendorff was supreme in Germany. When the peace resolution was passed by the Reichstag on 19 July Michaelis endorsed it 'as I understand it'; and he understood it to include all the annexationist aims of his masters. The Peace resolution was an incident in German domestic politics, not an act of diplomacy. The Entente saw in it a sign of weakness, not a gesture of conciliation; and its only practical outcome was the fall of Bethmann, the one man who had tried, however ineffectually, to check the appetite of the German generals.

The disappearance of Bethmann really determined that the war would be fought to a finish; nothing else would break Ludendorff's ambition. Nevertheless, there was a last attempt at peace from an even older authority than the Habsburg monarchy—the papacy. The pope had long wanted to end the war and, in particular, to save the old order in Europe. Now he felt the competition of the socialist agitation for peace. As William II said to the papal representative: 'it is in the interest of the Catholic church that peace should be introduced by the Pope, not by the Social Democrats.' The pope was lured by Bethmann's usual vague conciliation: Belgium, he said, would be fully restored and, as to Alsace and Lorraine, 'peace would not fail because of this problem'.[1] Bethmann's fall hurried the pope on; he wanted to anticipate the German high command. Therefore he proposed peace to the belligerent Powers on 10 August.[2] Only Belgium was mentioned specifically; she

---

[1] Bethmann, *Betrachtungen zum Weltkriege*, ii. 212.
[2] The pope's note was dated 1 Aug., but was not issued until the middle of the month.

should be restored 'with full guarantees of her political, military and economic independence against every Power'. Otherwise there should be a return to the *status quo* of 1914. Of the western Powers, Great Britain was alone represented at the Vatican—and even she was pledged to Italy not to accept the help of the Vatican in peace negotiations. Nevertheless, Balfour, the foreign secretary, replied to the Vatican on 23 August: 'though the Central Powers have admitted their guilt in regard to Belgium, they have never definitely intimated that they intend either to restore her to her former independence or to make good the damage she has suffered.' Even this reply was too much for France and Italy. They protested; and Balfour withdrew his inquiry—it had been made, he said, by mistake.

The Vatican, however, still saw its chance of peace. If the British could be satisfied over Belgium, they might drop the French claim to Alsace and Lorraine and, even more important from the Vatican's point of view, Italy's claim to Tyrol, and insist on peace. On 30 August the Vatican asked the Germans for 'a precise declaration of their intentions concerning the full independence of Belgium'. Kühlmann, who had become secretary of state on 6 August, tried to follow Bethmann's line, though more feebly: he planned to give up Belgium if Great Britain would abandon her allies. But he meant to use Belgium as a 'pawn' to bargain with, and therefore would not commit himself to withdrawal publicly: 'Who told you that I want to sell this particular horse? He is the finest animal in my stable.' Moreover, he wished to negotiate directly with the British through the Spanish government and therefore brushed papal mediation aside.[1] But he used it to extract some concessions from the high command. On 11 September a crown council was held, ostensibly to decide on a reply to the papal inquiry. Kühlmann, and even Michaelis, urged the renunciation of Belgium. The generals, as usual, put up their terms every time they were asked to define them. Ludendorff demanded Liége and the line of the Meuse; the spokesman of the admiralty added his claim to the Flemish ports—Zeebrugge and Ostend. William II gave a contradictory verdict: the annexation of Belgium would be 'a risky operation, perhaps contrary to

[1] Kühlmann later explained that he wished to end papal mediation because he knew that the French government intended to give a negative reply to it; but there may have been also Protestant jealousy of papal intervention.

WAR-AIMS OF THE CENTRAL POWERS

Germany's true interests', but strategic and economic 'precautions' must be secured under cover of restoring Belgian independence.

The generals had won. An empty answer was given to the pope on 24 September; papal mediation came to an end. Kühlmann made some further effort to negotiate with the British through Madrid. He never came out with a clear offer to restore Belgium. In any case, the British were in no mind to desert their allies; with the Italians defeated at Caporetto and the French armies still shaken by Nivelle's failure, they were far more afraid that their allies would desert them. They would consider only a general peace; and this was the very thing that Kühlmann was determined to avoid. To silence rumours of his negotiations in Germany and to strengthen his hand, as he supposed, for a withdrawal in Belgium, he announced on 9 October that Germany would *never* surrender Alsace and Lorraine. Two days later, Lloyd George answered by making the French recovery of Alsace and Lorraine, for the first time, an essential British war-aim. All hope of a compromise peace between Germany and the western Powers had vanished.[1]

Both sides still hoped for a decisive victory. The Germans counted on the collapse of Russia; the Entente on aid from the United States. Both were right. In 1918 the Germans won the European war, only to see victory snatched from them by America before the end of the year. The Russian army had ceased to exist. In November 1917 the Bolsheviks seized power. They recognized no obligation to Russia's allies and looked to an international socialist revolution for their salvation. When the German proletariat failed them, they made some tentative approach to the Entente. Lenin said he was 'in favour of taking potatoes and ammunition from the Anglo-French imperialist robbers'.[2] This, too, failed; and on 3 March 1918 the Bolsheviks made a peace of surrender with the Germans at Brest-Litovsk. Russia lost the Baltic provinces and the Ukraine. The Germans dominated all eastern Europe; but, instead of being content with this, they regarded it only as preliminary to victory in the west. They counted on defeating the British and French before

[1] Negotiations between allied and Austro-Hungarian representatives ran on in Switzerland almost until the end of the war. All broke on the same point: the allies would make peace only in return for assistance against Germany, which Austria-Hungary could not give.

[2] E. H. Carr, *The Bolshevik Revolution 1917–23*, iii. 46.

American troops arrived; alternatively, they hoped that Great Britain would make peace from jealousy of losing the leadership of the Entente to the United States. In essence, the Germans still had no defined war-aims and expected victory to provide them.

The German hopes were disappointed. The forces of the western Powers held together; and American aid arrived in time. But with it there arrived also America's programme for reconstructing the world. Wilson was as much a Utopian as Lenin. He, too, planned to end the Balance of Power in Europe, not to restore it. As well, he was in idealistic competition with the Bolsheviks. He wished to show that America's war-aims were, like theirs, 'anti-imperialistic', and so to persuade them to continue in the war. The Fourteen Points laid down on 8 January 1918 were the outcome. Self-determination was to supersede the historic states of Europe. Belgium, of course, was to recover her independence; Alsace and Lorraine were to return to France, and all Russian territory was to be evacuated. But, as well, Poland was to be restored; the peoples of Austria-Hungary and the Balkans freed. Secret diplomacy was to be ended, and a League of Nations to take the place of the Balance of Power. The defeat of Germany was for Wilson merely a preliminary, whereas to Great Britain and France it was the essential aim. Yet they did not acquiesce in the Fourteen Points solely in order to commit the United States. They, too, had a public opinion which thought of 'a war to end war' and demanded a permanent peace, secured by some other means than the Balance of Power.

Not only had men ceased to believe in the Balance of Power. It had, in any case, ceased to exist. Though Germany's bid for the mastery of Europe was defeated, the European Balance could not be restored. Defeat could not destroy German predominance of the Continent. Only her dismemberment could have done it; and, in the age of national states, this was impossible. France was exhausted by the First World war; Great Britain, though less exhausted, was reduced no less decisively in the long run. Their victory was achieved only with American backing and could not be lasting without it. On the other side, old Russia was gone for good. The Bolsheviks refused to accept the permanence of a system of independent states; they continued to count on a universal revolution, which would make them masters of the world. When they restored Russian power they found their principal resource in international communism, not in the play of alliances. Moreover, the political and economic boycott with which the rest of the world answered them drove them, willy-nilly, further into the isolation which had always been a temptation for Russian statesmen. The tsars had often been urged to base their strength on Asia; the Bolsheviks had no choice.

In January 1918 Europe ceased to be the centre of the world. European rivalries merged into a world war, as earlier the Balkan wars had prepared the conflict of the Great Powers. All the old ambitions, from Alsace and Lorraine to colonies in Africa, became trivial and second-rate, compared to the new struggle for control of the world. Even the German aim of dominating Europe became out of date. Europe was dwarfed by two world Powers, the Soviet Union and the United States —implacable, though often unconscious rivals. This was more than a rivalry of Power; it was a rivalry of idealisms. Both dreamt of 'One World', in which the conflict of states had ceased to exist. Universal revolution on the one side and the Fourteen Points on the other presented Utopian programmes for achieving permanent peace. Ever since the defeat of the French revolution Europe had conducted its affairs merely by adjusting the claims of sovereign states against each other as they arose. In 1914 Germany had felt strong enough to challenge this system and had aimed to substitute her hegemony over the rest. Europe was to find unity as Greater Germany— the only way in which the Continent could become a world Power, capable of withstanding the other two. Though Germany was defeated by a narrow margin, the legacy of her attempt was Bolshevism and American intervention in Europe. A new Balance of Power, if it were achieved, would be worldwide; it would not be a matter of European frontiers. Europe was superseded; and in January 1918 there began a competition between communism and liberal democracy which has lasted to the present day.

BIBLIOGRAPHY

THE study of diplomatic history has its peculiar difficulties. These are different from, but no worse than, those of other forms of history. Little of the raw material of history was devised especially for the use of historians; and that little is often the least reliable. The historian of the middle ages, who looks down on the 'contemporary' historian, is inclined to forget that his prized sources are an accidental collection, which have survived the ravages of time and which the archivist allows him to see. All sources are suspect; and there is no reason why the diplomatic historian should be less critical than his colleagues. Our sources are primarily the records which foreign offices keep of their dealings with each other; and the writer who bases himself solely on the archives is likely to claim scholarly virtue. But foreign policy has to be defined as well as executed; and a great deal of our material comes from this process of preliminary discussion. No foreign minister is an autocrat. In the absolute monarchies of eastern Europe the foreign minister had to carry his king or emperor along with him; and in Great Britain the foreign secretary needed the acquiescence of the cabinet, as well as of the crown.

In the course of the seventy years with which this book deals, a new factor appeared or increased in importance. Public opinion had to be considered; the public had to be educated. Parliaments had to vote money for the purposes of foreign policy; ultimately, the people might have to fight in a war resulting from it. Foreign policy had to be justified both before and after it was made. The historian will never forget that the material thus provided was devised for purposes of advocacy, not as a contribution to pure scholarship; but he would be foolish if he rejected it as worthless. This material is of various kinds. Some of it is advocacy before the event. Speeches in parliament, or memoranda submitted to an absolute ruler, seek to justify a course of action and to define it. They will reveal something, but not all, of what was in the mind of the speaker or writer. The same is true of the volumes of memoirs, in which statesmen seek to justify themselves in the eyes of their fellow countrymen or of posterity. All politicians have selective memories; and this is most true of politicians who originally practised as historians.

The diplomatic record is itself drawn on as an engine of publicity. Here Great Britain led the way. The British government was dependent on parliament; and it presented to parliament selections from the diplomatic record in the form of Blue Books. A comparison of these selections with the archives will often bring out those aspects of policy which the government wished to stress, and those which it wished to conceal.[1] The Blue Books were fullest and most revealing in the first part of the nineteenth century. 'Open diplomacy' is a luxury which a Power can afford only when it is strong and remote enough to ignore the feelings of others. Great Britain lost this position later in the nineteenth century, as the United States has done in our own time. Professors Temperley and Penson say rightly: 'Judged by a Blue-Book test Sir Edward Grey took the public into his confidence very much less than Palmerston'; they add, with more exaggeration: 'as Parliament became more democratic its control over foreign policy declined'.[2] It would be truer to say that parliamentary interference has had to be exercised with less knowledge of the details of diplomacy. On the other side, other governments gradually followed the British example, as they, too, came to depend on public opinion. The first French White Book was published in 1861, the first Austrian Book in 1868; both synchronized with an advance towards constitutional government. Bismarck adopted the practice after the foundation of the German empire;[3] Russia only in the twentieth century. The outbreak of war in 1914 was the first international crisis which produced a coloured Book by every Great Power—and later examination has shown how selective and tendentious some of these books were.

Governments also used their archives for propaganda in a less direct way. An historian, favourable to his government though ostensibly independent, was allowed to use the archives and wrote a diplomatic narrative with their aid. Sybel did this for the unification of Germany,[4] Bianchi for the unification of Italy.[5] After the fall of the Second Empire in France, Ollivier, who had carried off many papers, wrote a long history, which was a justification of imperial policy as well as of himself. These books were source-books of history, so long as the archives remained closed. Once historians could use the archives for themselves, such books lost their value; and it would be a waste of time to analyse the partial use of archives made by historians, who themselves had only partial access to them. But no historian can examine all the archives for himself; and, where no printed collection is available, he must often rely on the excerpts made by other scholars. Again, some are more fortunate than others. The American Marder, for instance, was allowed to use Admiralty papers which are still rigorously denied to British historians.[6]

[1] A full list of these Blue Books and an examination of Blue-Book policy has been made by Temperley and Penson, *A Century of Diplomatic Blue Books 1815–1914.*

[2] Ibid., p. ix.   [3] Johann Sass, *Die deutschen Weißbücher 1870–1914.*

[4] Sybel, *Die Begründung des deutschen Reiches durch Wilhelm I.,* 7 vols.

[5] N. Bianchi, *Storia documentata della diplomazia europea in Italia dal 1814 al 1861,* 8 vols.   [6] A. J. Marder, *British Naval Policy 1880–1905.*

The great advance in diplomatic history has come with the publication of papers from the archives on a scale more extended than the Blue Books. These publications, too, have a propaganda purpose. No government pays for the production of many volumes, merely from a disinterested love of scholarship. Sometimes it seeks to justify its predecessors; sometimes, especially if a revolution has intervened, to discredit them; even, more remotely, to revive national pride by displaying the glories of the past. The historian will seek, in each case, the motive for publication; and he will examine, as well, the scholarly repute of the individual editor. Publications on more distant periods (such as the Austrian and Prussian documents on the struggle for supremacy in Germany) can be accepted with less question than those on recent and more controversial events. As against this, interest in the immediate past is greater; and publication, if made at all, is likely to be fuller. Though documents may be occasionally suppressed, there is no evidence that a document has ever been manufactured *ex post facto* in order to deceive the scholar. Governments do not take historians seriously enough for that. Historical evidence remains evidence, whatever be the motive for revealing it; and it would be foolish to dismiss this wealth of material merely because it is incomplete or to deny gratitude to editors merely because public honours have been their reward. Charles A. Beard laid down the ideal from which historians should not retreat: 'Official archives must be open to all citizens on equal terms, with special privileges for none.' But in this imperfect world, where government departments often guard their secrets as much to flatter their own importance as because they have secrets to guard, the historian must make do as best he can. If he waited until he possessed all the evidence, he would never write at all—a doctrine favoured by some scholars.

The first of the great collections seems to have been the French series on the diplomatic origins of the war of 1870. This was proposed in 1907, began publication in 1910, and was completed only in 1930, sixty years after the events to which it relates. Since this collection opened an era in scholarship, it would be agreeable to discover for it clear, dramatic motives; unfortunately this is not possible. The *Origines diplomatiques* was certainly not a stroke in foreign policy; it was not designed as an answer to Sybel or other German writers. There was perhaps an element of professional pride. The French diplomatic service resented Ollivier's criticism of their predecessors, and wished to show that the war had been caused rather by the 'secret diplomacy' of Napoleon III and his unofficial advisers. As well, the republican politicians were provoked by the suggestion, which some Bonapartist apologists still made, that the republican opponents of the empire had helped to cause the war. Diplomatists, politicians, and professors alike appealed from polemics to the evidence. In so far as the *Origines diplomatiques* had a propaganda purpose, this was in domestic politics, not in international relations.[1] Though the *Origines diplomatiques* set a model for scholarship, it was hardly noticed in other countries and has indeed been little used to this day.

The real battle of diplomatic documents opened at the end of the First World war. The Bolsheviks wished to discredit impartially the government of the tsar and its allies; standing aloof from 'imperialism', they were at first eager to reveal everything. They published the secret treaties and continued to make spasmodic revelations for many years. The Germans followed this example more systematically. The republican government was anxious to emulate the Bolsheviks in frankness, if in little else, and to emphasize the breach between it and its imperial predecessor. Besides, if war guilt could be firmly limited to 'William of Hohenzollern', the allies might accept the new Germany as a democratic equal. Karl Kautsky, the leading theoretical Marxist, was therefore given a free run to publish the record of July 1914. This was a 'muckraking' expedition, though the sensations were not as decisive as had been expected. The imperial government turned out to be more incompetent and less wicked than socialist theory had supposed. This in itself gave a hint for the next use to which the archives could be put—whitewashing instead of muckraking.

The occasion was article 231 of the treaty of Versailles—the clause which was supposed (erroneously) to contain the admission of Germany's 'war-guilt'. During the peace conference, the French attempted to fortify their thesis against Germany by an historical survey, hastily put together.[2] The Germans originally intended no more than an answer to this. Their ambition soon widened; and they challenged the 'war-guilt lie' by a collection of documents, ranging back to 1871. The editors, though conscientious historians, regarded themselves as discharging a patriotic task. They worked fast, completing their task—in fifty-four volumes—by 1926. The documents were arranged so as to win a wide circle of readers. The earlier volumes were enriched by the literary genius of Bismarck; the later volumes enlivened by the eccentric comments of William II. This is indeed the only collection of diplomatic documents which can be recommended as bedside reading to the layman.

[1] Professor Renouvin most kindly answered my queries on this point, though he was unable to find in the French archives anything which shed a clear light on the reasons for publication.

[2] E. Bourgeois and G. Pagès, *Les origines et les responsabilités de la grande guerre* (1921).

The *Große Politik* was a great political stroke. It was not the least of the factors which made possible Hitler's destruction of the Versailles system. In the decisive years when interest in the origins of the First World war was high, it held the field alone; most works of diplomatic history are still based upon it. Even after the Second World war an American historian of the highest distinction declared that the many volumes of French and British documents, subsequently published, had not led him to change the judgements which he formed from the *Große Politik* alone. Perhaps the version of European history, created by seeing everything through German eyes, will never be wholly eradicated. On the other hand, it would be a mistake to dismiss the *Große Politik* as solely a work of propaganda. English scholars dipped into the German archives here and there, while they were in this country after the Second World war. They found that, while the selection and still more the arrangement was sometimes tendentious, there was little deliberate suppression.

The British and French governments were gradually shamed into publication by the German example. The French collection, which began in 1929 and is still leisurely under weigh, was a work of detached scholarship, designed neither to justify nor to condemn French policy. The British collection, though also a work of scholarship, had an element of muckraking. One of the editors had been among Grey's radical critics before the war; and the collection was perhaps meant to substantiate, or to disprove, the charges against Grey's 'secret diplomacy'. On the other hand, Ramsay MacDonald, the prime minister who authorized the publication, though once a pacifist, was now on the move to a more 'statesmanlike' position; and the alert critic might have seen in his desire 'to displace the pamphleteering rubbish that some so-called historians palmed off upon us'[1] an early sign of that evolution which was to carry him to leadership of a National government.

Little need be said about other countries. The Serbs often promised to publish their documents, but failed to do so, perhaps from lethargy, perhaps because it would have been too compromising. The Austrian republic could afford to publish a collection only from 1908 to 1914; significantly enough, this was a whitewash of the imperial government, which the republic had succeeded rather than overthrown. The Italians maintained an unrelenting silence which, they supposed, became a Great Power; recently, they have launched the most grandiose of publications partly for the same reason. The Russians projected a publication from 1878 to 1917, indiscriminately muckraking against all 'imperialist' governments, including their

[1] *British Documents*, x (ii), facing p. viii.

own; but they later came to feel that even tsarist secrets were sacred. Publication was interrupted; and the existing volumes, so far as possible, suppressed. It is unlikely that we shall have any more great collections for this period. The origins of the First World war have lost their controversial importance; perhaps history as a whole is ceasing to be a political weapon. Who cares now whether William II and Berchtold were 'war-criminals'?

Still, we are left with an incomparable body of material. When the present projects are completed, we shall have a printed record of Prusso-German policy from 1858, of Italian from 1861, of French policy from 1863, and of British from 1898. Of course none of these records is a full reproduction of the archives; but, taken together, they enable the historian to study foreign policy comparatively, which would otherwise be physically impossible. The worst gap is the First World war, which remains blank, except for the Russian documents.[1] No doubt, diplomacy looks pretty small beer in wartime. Perhaps, as a compensating advantage, historians may be able one day to write this story directly from the archives, as M. Pingaud has done in part for French policy.[2] Ultimately, all archives will be open, unless previously civilized life comes to an end;[3] and then there will be a period of further revision.

There are those who speak slightingly of history based on these records. Mr. G. M. Young once described diplomatic history as 'what one clerk said to another clerk'; and Bismarck said that no historian would ever understand the documents, because he would not know the background of personality and unwritten influence. This is to underrate our skill. Historians have broken Bismarck's secrets and disentangled his intrigues more effectively than any contemporary statesman managed to do. The seventy years covered by this book are an ideal field for the diplomatic historian. Full records were kept, without thought that they would ever be published, except for the occasional dispatch which a British statesman composed 'for the Blue Book'. It was the great age of writing. Even close colleagues wrote to each other, sometimes two or three times a day. Bismarck did all his thinking on paper, and he was not alone. Only Napoleon III kept his secrets to himself and thwarted posterity. Now the telephone and the personal meeting leave gaps in our know-

[1] Curiously enough, the Franco-German war is also something of a blank. The Prussian documents have not reached it. The first set of French documents ends with the outbreak of war; and the second begins only at its close.

[2] Certain English historians have been allowed to examine the foreign office records for the First World war. I am not among these privileged few.

[3] Since conditions of access are still irregular, I have not thought it worth while to specify how far the archives are open. The British records are open until the end of 1902. Most others are still matter of special inquiry.

ledge which can never be filled. While diplomacy has become more formal, the real process of decision escapes us.

The secondary works on international history reflect the gradual advance in revelation. The first layer are those written almost contemporaneously, on the basis of speeches, public documents, and newspaper reports. They are not to be despised. The late G. B. Henderson once pointed out[1] that contemporary writers understood the 'feel' of the Crimean war better than did those of fifty years later. They knew, for instance, that it was a war for the Balance of Power and the liberties of Europe, not a war for the route to India. The great French historian, Sorel, wrote a masterly diplomatic history of the Franco-Prussian war immediately after its conclusion; and, in our own time, Sir Lewis Namier has shown what can be done with the 'coloured books' which accompanied the outbreak of war in 1939.[2] The second stage comes when, as already described, privileged historians are allowed to see some of the archives; these are the books which have least permanent value. In the third stage, historians write on the basis of the printed collections. And finally—a stage we are beginning to reach—the historians have free and indiscriminate access to the archives for themselves.

Of course, this diplomatic approach does not exhaust international history. Policy springs from deep social and economic sources; it is not crudely manufactured in foreign offices. The historian needs to study the psychology of absolute rulers and, in constitutional countries, the outlook of the political parties. Economic factors— the search for markets or for investments, banks, and railway-building—have been explored. The influence of strategy has been strangely neglected. While the diplomatic records have been ransacked, the military and naval archives remain largely closed. 'Public opinion', in its widest sense, has had a great fascination, though with unsatisfactory results. Historians have been unable to make up their minds whether newspapers create public opinion or express it. Those who have experience in this curious trade may doubt whether they do either. In short, diplomatic history between the fall of Metternich and the end of Europe as the centre of the world is still a field wide open to study. We must be grateful for what our predecessors did, and try to improve on them.

A bibliography of international history, to be complete, would have to include practically everything on the period. I have not attempted to list the Blue Books and other contemporary official publications. There is a full list for British publications between 1814

---

[1] G. B. Henderson, *Crimean War Diplomacy and other Essays*, p. 243.

[2] *Diplomatic Prelude*, by L. B. Namier, began as a study of coloured books, though it was swelled by later revelations.

and 1914 in Temperley and Penson, *A Century of British Blue-Books* (1938). Johann Sass, *Die deutschen Weißbücher 1870–1914* (1926) is less exhaustive and more discursive. There are also two lists by Americans: J. Meyer, *Official Publications of European Governments* (1929), and W. Gregory, *List of the Serial Publications of Foreign Governments 1815–1931* (1932).

No bibliography adequately covers the seventy years 1848 to 1918, though nearly every general book has a list of some sort and the books on special topics are usually well equipped with references. I have found some lists especially useful. L. J. Ragatz, *Bibliography of European History 1815–1939* (1942 with two supplements) is the only general list; it is strictly confined to books in English, French, and German. The bibliographies published by the *Weltkriegsbücherei* (often attributed in British catalogues indiscriminately and, I think, wrongly, to M. Gunzenhäuser) are useful, especially those on *Geschichte Österreich-Ungarns 1848–1914* (1935) and on *Die Außen- und Kolonialpolitik des deutschen Reiches 1871–1914* (1943). They, too, are restricted to works in English, French, and German, and more particularly the last. P. F. Palumbo, *Bibliografia storica internazionale 1940–47* (1950) is the most up-to-date list, with many titles which escaped attention in this country when they were published. E. Rota, *Questioni di storia del Risorgimento e dell' unità d'Italia* (1951) is a collection of articles and bibliographies which fills up some of the gaps in Italian. I am less happy about books in Russian. C. Morley, *Guide to Research in Russian History* (1951) does not claim to be exhaustive.

For the period preceding the world war, there is a reliable list of sources in A. von Wegerer, *Bibliographie zur Vorgeschichte des Weltkrieges* (1934). G. P. Gooch, *Recent Revelations of European Diplomacy* (fourth edition, 1940), is a unique combination of bibliography and commentary for the years preceding and during the World war. It, too, is confined to books in English, French, and German; the dates of publication are not given, except in odd cases.

Even with the aid of all these, the following bibliography does not claim to be complete. W. L. Langer says of the bibliography in his *Diplomacy of Imperialism*: 'I frankly do not see how this project could have been carried through without access to the rich collections of the Harvard College Library'; and he is right. No library in this country can be relied upon to have all the books even in the list I give; and many periodicals referred to by Professor Langer and others are not to be found anywhere in England. But, since the study of recent European history is regarded here as of little importance, this is not surprising. I have, however, attempted to list all the sources and most outstanding secondary books in the five great

European languages (I do not read any other); and I have not mentioned any book that I have not, at least, seen the outside of. Omission may mean that I have not come across the book; but it may also mean that I do not rate the book well enough to put it in. After all, there is no sense in listing a book except as in some way a recommendation.

I have shrunk from listing the material in periodicals; yet much of it is essential, especially among the sources. But it would have more than doubled a list which seems, as it is, too long. This material is scattered through the learned historical journals in five languages; and I have not listed even these. But I should mention three periodicals, devoted exclusively to diplomatic history and 'war-origins'. They are the *Revue d'histoire de la guerre mondiale*; *Berliner Monatshefte* (published earlier as *Die Kriegsschuldfrage*); and *Krasny Arkhiv*. All three expired at or about the outbreak of the Second World war.

The bibliography is arranged in two sections—raw material and secondary works. This arrangement is not watertight. Many original sources, particularly biography, are also works of history; and most secondary works have some original material. The sources fall into (i) official publications; (ii) papers of individuals, themselves ordered as rulers, prime and foreign ministers, ambassadors and diplomatists, and others. Each of these is presented by country, ordered—as becomes a work of diplomatic history—according to the French alphabet. That is, Germany (which includes Prussia), Austria (which includes Austria-Hungary), France, Great Britain, Italy (which includes Sardinia), Russia. The rest include the minor countries and (in the latest period) the United States. The secondary works are arranged topically in chronological order. Where a book has been translated into English I have referred only to the English version.

SOURCES

I. *Official Publications*

GERMANY (including Prussia). Prussian foreign policy can be followed in print from the time of the agreement at Olomouc. The earliest documents were published by the Bismarckian scholar, Poschinger, when he had exhausted publicity for his hero; the period of unification was revealed as a spur to national pride under the Weimar republic; and the documents of the empire were produced as answer to the 'war-guilt lie'.

Preußens auswärtige Politik 1850–1858, 3 vols. (1902), edited by H. Poschinger, gives mainly Manteuffel's dispatches. Poschinger also published Bismarck's reports from Frankfurt as *Preußen im*

Bundestag 1851–1859, 4 vols. (1882–4); this collection has been largely superseded by the volume in Bismarck's collected works.

Die auswärtige Politik Preußens 1858–1871, edited by Erich Brandenburg and others, 10 vols., with two to come (1932 et seq.), is a more ambitious affair. It has one unique feature. It includes documents from foreign, as well as from the Prussian, archives. Though this gives us a sight of unpublished British documents and of Russian documents, otherwise inaccessible, it is an unsatisfactory device, swelling the volumes to enormous size, yet giving no more than a lucky dip from the foreign archives. Another tiresome point is that Bismarck's dispatches, printed in his collected works, are not reproduced; and the student must therefore shuffle from one set to the other. The documents are arranged in chronological order, without any analysis of subject. Till the final volume appears, its place must be taken by *Origins of the War of 1870*, edited by R. H. Lord (1924).

Die große Politik der europäischen Kabinette, edited by A. Mendelssohn-Bartholdy, I. Lepsius, and F. Thimme, 40 vols. in 54 (1922–6). covers the period from the preliminary peace with France in 1871 to the opening of the pre-war crisis on 28 June 1914. With 'warguilt' always in mind, the selection is very thin for the Bismarckian period and becomes fuller only when it reaches the twentieth century. The worst feature of this great collection is its arrangement by subject, instead of in strict chronology. The connexion of one topic with another is thus concealed. For instance, E. N. Anderson created a sensation, when he showed that the treaty of Björkö (treated in volume xix) had a vital influence on the Moroccan crisis (treated in volume xxi). I myself elucidated Bismarck's colonial policy, merely by linking up his dealings with Great Britain (in volume iv) and those with France (in volume iii). It is bad enough for the unfortunate historian that he must have, say, the British, French, and German documents all open on his desk at the same time; but this becomes intolerable when he has to use three or four volumes of the German documents simultaneously. Thimme, the principal editor, expressed regret, at the end of his life, for this arrangement.

Something can be done to alleviate the burden. The summary by B. Schwertfeger, *Die diplomatischen Akte des auswärtigen Amtes. Ein Wegweiser*, 8 vols. (1924–7), is not much use in itself, but at the end of each volume the documents are sorted into chronological order. The French translation (32 vols. to date) is also arranged chronologically; unfortunately it only goes to 1908. There is an English selection in four volumes (1928–31); it is too brief to be of much use.

The Germans were first in the field with the documents for the crisis of 1914. The 'Kautsky documents' are officially called *Die deutschen Dokumente zum Kriegsausbruch*, edited by Kautsky, Montgelas, and Schücking, 4 vols. (1919, enlarged edition, 1927). There is an English translation, *The Outbreak of the World War* (1924). There are also *Bavarian Documents*, edited by P. Dirr (1922); and documents from the archives of Baden, Saxony, and Württemberg, entitled *Deutsche Gesandtschaftsberichte zum Kriegsausbruch 1914*, edited by A. Bach (1937).

After the war the national assembly and then the Reichstag inquired into its causes and why it was not ended sooner. The answers of the political and military leaders are given in *Official German Documents relating to the World War*, 2 vols. (1923). These are as valuable as can be expected of answers, given years after the event, to questions which were mainly political in motive. At least, they make interesting reading.

AUSTRIA and AUSTRIA-HUNGARY. The Austrian material is less complete than the German, though very full in the periods that it covers. *Quellen zur deutschen Politik Österreichs 1859–1866*, edited by H. Srbik, 5 vols. (1934 et seq.), has the defect of being limited to German policy and has therefore little about the Italian question, Poland, or the Near East. The documents are in chronological order without table of contents of any kind.

Die Rheinpolitik Napoleons III., edited by H. Oncken, 3 vols. (1926), is primarily a selection from the Austrian archives. Though it claims to start in 1863, it becomes valuable only in 1866; its main importance is as a source for the futile Franco-Austrian alliance. There is an aggressively anti-French introduction by the editor.

The Secret Treaties of Austria-Hungary 1879–1914 edited by A. F. Pribram, 2 vols. (1920–1), is a slight, but invaluable, collection. The first volume gives the texts of the treaties; the second summarizes the negotiations which accompanied each renewal of the Triple Alliance. The editor also threw in the texts of the Reinsurance treaty and of the Franco-Russian alliance.

Österreich-Ungarns Außenpolitik, edited by Bittner, Srbik, Pribram, and Übersberger, 9 vols. (1930), is a very full collection from the beginning of the Bosnian crisis until the outbreak of the World war. The emphasis is on the Balkans and especially on the misdeeds of Serbia. The documents are arranged chronologically without a table of contents.

FRANCE. *Les origines diplomatiques de la guerre de 1870–71*, 29 vols. (1910 et seq.), begins with Napoleon's proposal for a congress in November 1863 and goes until the outbreak of war in 1870. Though focused on Germany, it contains a good deal about Italy and the Near East. The arrangement is chronological, with a summary of the documents (also chronological) at the beginning of each volume.

This collection, and the *Große Politik*, alone have volumes of a reasonable size, which may be held in the hand without muscular exhaustion.

Documents diplomatiques français 1871–1914, 32 vols. with more to come (1929 et seq.), is the most perfect of the collections, except for the clumsiness of the volumes. The documents are arranged in chronological order, while a table at the beginning of each volume sorts them into subjects. It is difficult to understand how any subsequent editor can have strayed from this arrangement. There are two faults. The individual editor of each volume is not named; and the reader is therefore unable to allow for the editor's idiosyncrasies or special interests. Secondly, the volumes were brought out in three series, the first beginning in 1871, the second on 1 January 1901, the third on 4 November 1911. This was no doubt a wise precaution, given the leisurely publishing habits of the French foreign ministry; but it is tiresome to have to cite the series, every time a document is quoted.

GREAT BRITAIN. *Foundations of British Foreign Policy*, by H. Temperley and L. M. Penson (1938), gives a random selection of documents from 1792 to 1898. The volume also includes a few documents, erratically chosen from the Austrian archives. T. Filipowicz, *Confidential Correspondence of the British Government concerning the Insurrection in Poland 1863* (1914), supplements the Blue Books. V. Valentin, *Bismarcks Reichsgründung im Urteil englischer Diplomaten* (1938), gives reports from Germany, unfortunately in German translations.

British Documents on the Origins of the War, edited by G. P. Gooch and H. Temperley, 11 vols. in 13 (1927 et seq.), covers the years 1898 to 1914. In actual fact, the first two volumes, up to the conclusion of the Anglo-French entente in 1904, give only a thin introductory selection; while the captious might complain that there is too much on the Balkan wars. The arrangement is by subjects, on the model of the *Große Politik*; and the copy is even more cumbersome than the original. The editors seem to have adopted this arrangement without reflection. They attempted to justify it only in the foreword to volume vii; and then described it as 'the British way'—a phrase often used in this country to cloak any irrational act.[1] Volume xi, on the outbreak of war, was edited by J. W. Headlam-Morley and is arranged chronologically; it is superior to the others. The volumes contain a unique declaration by the editors 'that they would be compelled to resign if any attempt were made to insist on the omission of any document which is, in their view, vital

---

[1] The editors of *Documents on British Foreign Policy 1919–1939*, did even better. They wrote: 'the disadvantages of a chronological method . . . are too obvious to need mention', and they did not mention them.

or essential'. Though this declaration may have been unnecessary, it was well worth making for the sake of posterity and foreign scholars.

ITALY. Unlike the Germans, the Italians continued to be proud of the revolutions of 1848, even under Fascism, and there is therefore a good deal of material about the diplomacy of the revolutionary year—most of it, however, concerned with the relations of the Italian states among themselves. *La diplomazia del Regno di Sardegna*, 3 vols. to date (1949 et seq.), gives the Sardinian correspondence with Tuscany, the papal states, and the kingdom of the two Sicilies. *Sicilia e Piemonte nel 1848-49* (1940) gives the Sicilian documents. *La repubblica Veneta nel 1848-49* (1949) gives the Venetian documents. Relations between Lombardy and Sardinia are in *Carteggio del governo provvisorio di Lombardia con i suoi rappresentanti al quartier generale di Carlo Alberto* (1923) and *I rapporti fra governo Sardo e governo provvisorio di Lombardia durante la guerra del 1848* (1938).

C. Maraldi has edited *Documenti francesi sulla caduta del Regno meridionale* (1935), which should perhaps be included under France.

A grandiose collection of documents from the founding of the kingdom of Italy until the armistice of September 1943 is now projected. *I documenti diplomatici Italiani* will be 'exclusively historical and not political'. The arrangement is chronological, without a subject-table. So far only volumes for 1861 (edited by W. Maturi) and for 10 March 1896–30 April 1897 (edited by C. Maraldi) have appeared for this period.

RUSSIA. A. M. Zaionchkovski, *Vostochnaya voina*, 2 vols. (1908–12), has a valuable collection of documents on the origins of the Crimean war. The Russian material for the later period is in great confusion, owing to the Bolshevik habit of leaking out fragments in a polemical way. For some twenty years their magazine *Krasny Arkhiv* published documents spasmodically. The first thirty volumes are summarized in *A Digest of the Krasnii Arkhiv*, translated by L. S. Rubinchek, edited by L. M. Boutelle and G. W. Thayer (1947). Neither the British Museum nor the Bodleian has a copy.

The first important Russian collection was *Materialy po franko-russikh otnoshenii za 1910–14 gg* (1922). This was translated into French as *Un livre noir*, 3 vols. (1922–3). Siebert, first secretary at the Russian embassy before the war, published the documents which he had abstracted for the Germans as *Graf Benckendorffs diplomatischer Schriftwechsel*, 3 vols. (1928). There is a less complete English edition, *Entente Diplomacy and the World War* (1921). F. Stieve published *Der diplomatische Schriftwechsel Iswolskis 1910–14*, 4 vols. (1924), and a thinner collection, *Iswolski im Weltkrieg* (1927), which goes only to May 1915. He does not explain how he acquired the documents.

In *Tsarskaya Russia v mirovoy voina* (Russian, 1925; German, 1927) are documents dealing with the entry of Turkey, Bulgaria, Rumania, and Italy into the war. A more important collection, edited by E. D. Adamov, covered the Near East in the war years more fully. The volumes are *The European Powers and Greece* (Russian 1922, German 1932); *The Partition of Asiatic Turkey* (Russian 1924, German 1932); and *Constantinople and the Straits*, 4 vols. (Russian 1925–6, French 1930, German 1930–2). The last deals with the military as well as with the diplomatic problems involved.

The most ambitious Russian project was *Mezhdunarodnye otnosheniya v epokhu imperializma* (1930 et seq.). This was projected to cover the years 1878–1917. None of the first series has been published. Of the second series, vols. xviii to xxi (i) cover 1 May 1911 (o.s.) to 20 November 1912 (o.s.). The third series, vols. i to x, goes from 1 January 1914 to 31 March 1916 (o.s.). The documents are in chronological order, with an inadequate subject-index. Those already printed in *Constantinople and the Straits* are not reproduced. There is a German translation, called *Die internationalen Beziehungen im Zeitalter des Imperialismus* (1930 et seq.), edited by O. Hoetzsch, of the third series, vols. i to viii (described as first series, vols. i–v and second series, vols. vi–viii), and of the second series (described as third series, vols. i–iv (i)).[1] For the period covered, the Russian documents are invaluable. They are the only systematic source for the diplomacy of the World war. The volumes include a good deal of foreign correspondence (British, French, Italian, Rumanian) which the Russians deciphered. The volume on the outbreak of war also draws on the Russian foreign office diary, which was originally published by Schilling as *How the War Began* (1925).

OTHER COUNTRIES. During the war the Germans looted the Belgian foreign office in an attempt to justify their violation of her neutrality. *Belgische Aktenstücke* (1915) gives reports from Belgian ministers abroad; *Zur europäischen Politik 1897–1914*, 5 vols., edited by B. Schwertfeger (1919), the circular letters sent from the Belgian foreign office.

A pro-German Serb, M. Bogičević, published documents which he had carried off from the Berlin legation in *Die auswärtige Politik Serbiens 1903–14*, 3 vols. (1928–31). This is a very unsatisfactory collection.

The United States have long published an annual volume, entitled *Foreign Relations of the United States*. The World war was excluded at the time, but supplementary volumes have now been published (1928–33). Two further volumes contain the *Lansing Papers* (1939–

---

[1] The second Russian series (in German the third) is very hard to come by. I have seen vols. xviii and xix only in Russian; vol. xx not at all; and vol. xxi (i) only in the German translation. I am not sure whether it ever appeared in Russian.

40), which remained in the State Department. These volumes, which have not yet been adequately used, supersede the earlier and more polemical accounts, based only on private correspondence.

From Denmark there is A. Fries and P. Bagge, *L'Europe, le Dane-mark et le Slesvig du Nord*, 3 vols. (1939–48).

II. *Private Papers*

(a) *Rulers*

GERMANY (including PRUSSIA). Frederick William IV was a prolific and stimulating letter-writer. Though most of his letters deal with German affairs, there is in all of them material on international affairs. The most useful collection is the oldest: *Aus dem Briefwechsel Friedrich Wilhelms IV. mit Bunsen*, edited by L. von Ranke (1873). There is also *Briefwechsel mit Ludolf Camphausen*, edited by E. Branden-burg (1906); *Briefwechsel zwischen König Johann von Sachsen und Friedrich Wilhelm IV. und Wilhelm I.* (1911); *Briefwechsel zwischen Friedrich Wilhelm IV. und dem Reichsverweser Erzherzog Johann von Österreich* (1924); and *Revolutionsbriefe. Ungedrucktes aus dem Nachlaß Friedrich Wilhelms IV.*, edited by K. Haenchen (1930).

There are many collected volumes of the correspondence of William I, all uninteresting. The most substantial are his *Correspon-dence with Bismarck*, 2 vols. (1903), and *Briefe an Politiker und Staats-männer*, 2 vols. (1930).

William II supplies one collection of high importance, his *Letters to the Tsar* (1920), sometimes called 'the Willy–Nicky Letters'. A good many of these letters are not in the *Große Politik*. They were written in English, but the German translation, edited by W. Goetz (1920), is rather fuller.

AUSTRIA (including AUSTRIA-HUNGARY). The letters of Francis Joseph contain little of either personal or political interest, *Franz Joseph in seinen Briefen*, edited by O. Ernst (1924; English 1927), can be supplemented by his *Letters to his Mother* (1930) and to his mistress, Katherina Schratt (1949). His correspondence with Nicholas I before the Crimean war is reproduced in H. Schlitter, *Aus der Regierungszeit Franz Josephs I.* (1919), and in J. Redlich, *Emperor Francis Joseph of Austria* (1929).

There is not much information in the various books on Francis Ferdinand. The most useful is *Erzherzog Franz Ferdinands Wirken und Wollen* by L. von Chlumecky (1929).

Two books give material on Emperor Charles's peace-offer in 1917: one by his chef de cabinet, Polzer-Hoditz, *Kaiser Karl* (1928; Eng. 1930), the other by his secretary, K. von Werkmann, *Deutsch-lands Verbündeter* (1931). Prince Sixte, *L'Offre de paix séparée* (1920) gives some of the documents.

FRANCE. No historical figure is more elusive than Napoleon III. He wrote few letters, and fewer survived. The only published fragments are in the *Lettres inédites entre Napoléon III et le prince Napoléon*, edited by E. d'Hauterive (1925).

The French presidents were not given to the writing of memoirs. A. Combarieu, *Sept ans à l'Élysée* (1932) gives useful notes by Loubet's secretary. Poincaré is the great exception: *Au service de la France*, 10 vols. (1926–33). These run from the time when he became prime minister in 1912 until the armistice in 1918; notes for a further volume are not to be released until 1990—a flattering exaggeration of their importance. The earlier volumes on the Balkan wars are the most valuable. For the war years, there is a little on the secret treaty with Russia in 1915 and rather more on the negotiations with Emperor Charles in 1917.

GREAT BRITAIN. The papers of Prince Albert at Windsor are said to contain much valuable material; but it is not revealed in the official life by T. Martin, 5 vols. (1876–80). *The Letters of Queen Victoria*, ed. by Esher, Benson, and Buckle, are very important. They are in three series—1837–61 (1907); 1861–85 (1926); and 1886–1901 (1930–2)—of three volumes each. They improve in value as they go on. Of course, though prime ministers and foreign secretaries wrote constantly to the queen, they did not reveal all that was in their minds.

Edward VII, by Sidney Lee, 2 vols. (1925–7), has a good deal of interest, though presented in a rather polemical way. *George V*, by Harold Nicolson (1952), makes a good showing with what material there is.

ITALY. Charles Albert wrote a pathetic *Memorie inedite sul 1848*, edited by A. Lumbroso (1948); and there is a study by N. Rodolico, *Carlo Alberto negli anni 1843–49* (1942). The official life of *Vittorio Emanuele II* (1878), by Massari, has some original material. There is much of value in *Pio IX e Vittorio Emanuele II dal loro carteggio privato*, edited by P. P. Pirri, vols. i and ii (1944–51).

RUSSIA. There is some original correspondence in the last volume of T. Schiemann, *Rußland unter Kaiser Nikolaus I.* (1919). The life of *Alexandr II*, by S. S. Tatishchev, 2 vols. (1903), has a great deal of value. There is nothing on Alexander III. For Nicholas II, apart from the Willy–Nicky letters, there are his letters to his wife (1929) and to his mother (1938) and his *Journal intime* (1934). They are remarkable only for their triviality.

OTHERS. *Aus meinem Leben* by Ernst II of Saxe-Coburg-Gotha, 3 vols. (1887–8), though mainly devoted to German affairs, has some curious material on Napoleon III. Under the misleading title, *The*

Downfall of Three Dynasties (1934), E. C. Corti uses the papers of Prince Alexander of Hesse (progenitor by a morganatic marriage of the Mountbattens); they run from the Crimean war to the congress of Berlin. Corti also wrote *Alexander of Battenberg* (1920); useful for the Bulgarian crisis. For later Balkan affairs there are *The Story of My Life*, by Marie of Rumania (1923), 3 vols.; *Aus dem Leben König Karls v. Rumänien*, 4 vols. (1899–1900); and *A King's Private Letters*, by Constantine of Greece (1925).

Two American presidents had an impact on European affairs—Theodore Roosevelt during the Russo-Japanese war and the first Moroccan crisis, Wilson during the First World war. For Roosevelt, J. B. Bishop, *Theodore Roosevelt and His Times*, 2 vols. (1920); Tyler Dennett, *Roosevelt and the Russo-Japanese War* (1925); A. L. P. Dennis, *Adventures in American Diplomacy* (1928). For Wilson, R. S. Baker, *Woodrow Wilson: Life and Letters*, 8 vols. (1927 et seq.).

(b) Prime and Foreign Ministers

GERMANY (including PRUSSIA). On Radowitz (f.m. 1850), an outstanding book with some original material by F. Meinecke, *Radowitz und die deutsche Revolution* (1913); and a full collection of *Nachgelassene Briefe und Aufzeichungen 1848–53*, edited by W. Mohring (1922). Poschinger edited the *Denkwürdigkeiten*, 3 vols. (1901), of Otto Manteuffel (f.m. 1850–8), as well as the correspondence mentioned earlier. Bernstorff (f.m. 1861–2) is the subject of K. Ringhoffer, *Im Kampfe für Preußens Ehre* (1906; Eng. 1908). This has also some material about the negotiations with Austria in 1849, when Bernstorff was minister at Vienna, and about the abortive peace-move through the Empress Eugenie in autumn 1870.

The essential source for Bismarck (f.m. 1862; federal chancellor 1867; imperial chancellor 1871–90) is the collection of *Politische Schriften* in his *Gesammelte Werke*, 6 vols. in 8 (1924 et seq.). This gives virtually all his diplomatic correspondence until the end of the Franco-Prussian war, after which the *Große Politik* must be used. The many other collections of his letters are mainly concerned with internal affairs. The volumes of *Gespräche*, 3 vols. (1924–6), have a few points of interest, though the casual conversations hardly qualify as Bismarck's 'works'. *Gedanken und Erinnerungen* (1898) ranks with the most remarkable political memoirs ever written, not least for its artistic inaccuracy of detail. The edition in the *Gesammelte Werke* (1932) includes some curious fragments discarded from the published version.

There is nothing on Caprivi (chancellor 1890–4).

For Hohenlohe (chancellor 1894–1900) the *Denkwürdigkeiten der Reichskanzlerzeit* (1931). Bülow (secretary of state, 1897; chancellor,

1900–9) wrote four volumes of *Memoirs* (1931–2). The first two
cover his period in office, the third *inter alia* his mission to Italy at
the beginning of the World war. They are vain, inaccurate, and
vague, yet with an odd penetration here and there. An anthology
of criticism has been launched against them in *Front wider Bülow*
(1931), edited by F. Thimme—a sillier book than any Bülow ever
wrote.

Bethmann Hollweg (chancellor 1909–17) defended himself in
Betrachtungen zum Weltkriege, 2 vols. (1919–22; Eng. vol. i only, 1920).
The first volume discusses the outbreak of war, the second the
attempts at peace in 1916 and 1917.

The secretaries of state came late to publicity. There is nothing,
for instance, on Marschall. Schoen (secretary 1906–9) in *Erlebtes*
(1921, Eng. 1922) provides nothing of interest. E. Jäckh does better
with *Kiderlen-Waechter*, 2 vols. (1924) (secretary 1909–12), though
there is more of amusement than of information in the letters. Jagow
(secretary 1913–16) defended himself plaintively in *Ursachen und
Ausbruch des Weltkrieges* (1919) and *England und der Kriegsausbruch*
(1925). Kühlmann (secretary 1917–18) left *Erinnerungen* (1950),
which resemble Bülow's in their vanity and vagueness.

AUSTRIA (including AUSTRIA-HUNGARY). Ficquelmont, Metternich's immediate successor, gave *Aufklärungen über die Zeit vom 20.
März bis zum 4. Mai 1848* (1850). Pillersdorf, his temporary successor,
left *Handschriftlicher Nachlaß* (1863). Both are feeble. Much better is
A. von Arneth, *Johann von Wessenberg*, 2 vols. (1898). The papers of
Felix Schwarzenberg (prime minister 1848–52) were destroyed at
his death. There is nothing on Buol (f.m. 1852–9). F. Engel-Janosi,
Graf Rechberg (1927) (f.m. 1859–64), has some material from his
private papers. Beust (f.m. 1866, chancellor 1867–71) wrote his
memoirs as *Aus drei Viertel-Jahrhunderten*, 2 vols. (1887)—interesting,
though unreliable. E. Wertheimer, *Graf Julius Andrássy*, 3 vols.
(1910 et seq.) (f.m. 1871–9), is a work of great importance, despite
its length and heavy style. Thereafter there is silence until the First
World war. Even Berchtold never produced his 'eagerly awaited
memoirs', which were reported 'far-advanced' for almost a generation. Burian (f.m. 1915–16 and 1918) tells little in *Three Years* (1925);
Czernin (f.m. 1916–18) displays incorrigible subtlety in *In the World
War* (1920).

FRANCE. Lamartine (f.m. Feb.–May 1848) has some grandilo-
quent passages on foreign affairs, especially concerning Poland,
in his *Histoire de la révolution de 1848*, 2 vols. (1859). There is further
material in P. Quentin-Bauchart, *Lamartine et la politique étrangère*
(1908). Bastide (f.m. May–Dec. 1848) later defended his policy in

La République française et l'Italie en 1848 (1858). There are a few fragments on foreign affairs in the *Souvenirs* of Tocqueville (Eng. 1948)
(f.m. 1849). The most persistent, though least Bonapartist, foreign
minister of the Second Empire (f.m. 1849, 1850, 1852–5, 1863–6) is
the subject of B. d'Harcourt, *Les quatre ministères de Drouyn de Lhuys*
(1882). This is still useful for the years before 1863, when the
Origines diplomatiques begins. L. Thouvenel published large selections
from the papers of his father, E. A. Thouvenel (f.m. 1860–2); some
of them cover the period when he was French ambassador at Constantinople. *Nicholas I et Napoléon III 1852–54* (1891); *Trois années de
la question d'Orient 1856–59* (1897); *Le secret de l'empereur*, 2 vols. (1889),
correspondence of 1860–3; and *Pages de l'histoire du second empire*
(1903), a final miscellany. The recollections of Ollivier (Napoleon III's only p.m., 1870) are in the last volumes of *L'empire libéral*.
Gramont (f.m. 1870) defended himself unconvincingly in *La France
et la Prusse avant la guerre* (1872).

The foreign ministers of the Third republic were as taciturn as
its presidents. The *Souvenirs* (1913) of C. de Freycinet cover 1878–93,
but have little on foreign affairs. Nor is there much to be learnt in
Mon temps (1938 et seq.) by G. Hanotaux (f.m. 1894–5, 1896–8).
J. Caillaux (p.m. 1911–12) defended himself pugnaciously in *Agadir*
(1919); this contains confidential letters from Kiderlen which fell—
perhaps by design—into French hands. *Mes mémoires*, vol. ii (1942),
adds nothing on Agadir; vol. iii (1947), by its emphatic silence, perhaps exaggerates the peace-manœuvres of 1917. A. Ribot (f.m. 1917)
in *Lettres à un ami* (1924) and *Journal et correspondance inédite* (1936) has
some important information on the affair of the Austrian peace-offer.

GREAT BRITAIN. The private papers of Palmerston (foreign
secretary 1846–51, p.m. 1855–8, 1859–65) have not been examined
after 1841. We must make do with the few fragments in E. Ashley,
Life of Viscount Palmerston, 2 vols. (1879). Malmesbury (f.s. 1852,
1858–9) wrote *Memoirs of an Ex-Minister* (1882); they are feeble and
inaccurate. Clarendon (f.s. 1853–8, 1865–6, 1868–70) has an inadequate life by H. Maxwell, 2 vols. (1913); his papers (in the Bodleian
Library) have been turned to good use by Temperley and Henderson. Russell (p.m. 1846–52, 1865–6, f.s. 1852, 1859–65) has an
official biography by Spencer Walpole, 2 vols. (1889); his *Later
Correspondence*, ed. G. P. Gooch, 2 vols. (1930), includes everything of
value from his papers (now in the Record Office) on foreign affairs.

Granville (f.s. 1851–2, 1870–4, 1880–5) has a life by E. Fitzmaurice,
2 vols. (1905); his correspondence with Gladstone between 1868 and
1874 has been edited by A. Ramm (1952). He is hardly worthy of
so much attention. There is some material for the views of Gladstone
(p.m. 1868–74, 1880–5, 1886, 1892–4) in Guedalla, *Gladstone and*

Palmerston (1928) and *The Queen and Mr. Gladstone*, 2 vols. (1933); but, despite P. Knaplund, *Gladstone's Foreign Policy* (1935), this subject still needs exploration. There is much more material for Disraeli (p.m. 1867–8, 1874–80) in the later volumes of the life by G. E. Buckle (1920); though historians have assumed too easily that, since Disraeli depicted events in a dramatic and controversial way, they were in fact dramatic and controversial.

For Salisbury (p.m. 1885, 1886–92, 1895–1902; f.s. 1885, 1887–92, 1895–1900) the *Life* by Gwendolen Cecil, 4 vols. (1921–32), is of great value, but it goes only to 1892. *Lord Rosebery* (f.s. 1886, 1892–4; p.m. 1894–5), by Crewe, 2 vols. (1931) has little. Blanche Dugdale on *Balfour*, 2 vols. (1936) (p.m. 1902–5; f.s. 1916–19), has a little on the alliance with Japan, virtually nothing on his tenure of the foreign office. Newton, *Lord Lansdowne* (1929) (f.s. 1900–5), is admirable within its limited range.

J. A. Spender on *Campbell-Bannerman*, 2 vols. (1923) (p.m. 1905–8), is important for the first Moroccan crisis. The life of *Asquith* (p.m. 1908–16) by J. A. Spender and Cyril Asquith, 2 vols. (1932), has little; but Asquith's own books, *The Genesis of the War* (1923) and *Memories and Reflections* (1928), though pot-boilers, have important material. Grey (f.s. 1905–16) wrote his own defence in *Twenty-Five Years*, 2 vols. (1925), the most substantial contribution to history by any British foreign secretary. The life by G. M. Trevelyan (1937) adds little. The *War Memoirs*, 6 vols. (1933 et seq.) of Lloyd George (p.m. 1916–22) are extremely important, though no less unreliable; they are particularly useful for the discussion of war-aims and for the peace-negotiations of 1917.

ITALY. Italian memoirs are almost as sporadic as their official publications; but the few are of first-rate importance. The diary of Dabormida (f.m. 1850–5) is used by Chiala, *L'Alleanza di Crimea* (1879). The correspondence of Cavour (p.m. 1850–9, 1860–1) is the most important single source in any language for the diplomacy of the period. The vital volumes are the correspondence with Nigra, *Il carteggio Cavour–Nigra dal 1858 al 1861*, 4 vols. (1926–9), and with E. d'Azeglio, *Cavour e l'Inghilterra*, 2 vols. (1935). There is a certain amount on foreign policy in the papers of Cavour's successor, Ricasoli (p.m. 1861–2, 1866–7): *Lettere e documenti*, 10 vols. (1887–96), and *Carteggi*, 4 vols. to date (1939–45). Minghetti (p.m. 1863–4) revealed something of the Roman question in *La convenzione di settembre: un capitolo dei miei ricordi* (1899). La Marmora (p.m. in 1866) wrote a controversial work against Bismarck, *Un po' più di luce sugli eventi politici e militari dell' anno 1866* (1879).

The *Memoirs*, 3 vols. (1914), of Crispi (p.m. 1887–91, 1893–6), are extremely important, though unreliable. The papers of Tittoni (f.m. 1903–9) are used extensively in *L'Italia alla vigilia della guerra*, 5 vols. (1934–41), by F. Tommasini. The *Memoirs* of Giolitti (1923) (p.m. 1892–3, 1903–5, 1906–9, 1911–14) have some information on the years immediately before the war. The two volumes by Salandra (p.m. 1914–16) on *La neutralità italiana* (1928) and on *L'intervento* (1931) are the main source on Italy's entry into the war.

RUSSIA. The last two volumes of *Lettres et papiers* of Nesselrode (chancellor until 1856) have a good deal of material. There is nothing on his successor Gorchakov and virtually nothing on Giers (f.m. 1881–94). In *L'alliance franco-russe* (1936) B. Nolde made some use of the latter's papers. There is also light on Giers in the *Dnievnik, 1886–90* (1926) and *1891–92* (1934) of Lamsdorff (later f.m. 1901–6). Izvolski (f.m. 1906–9) began his *Memoirs* (1920), but only reached 1906. His *Correspondance diplomatique 1906–11* (1937) gives mainly private letters from Russian ambassadors. Sazonov (f.m. 1910–16) wrote *Fateful Years* (1928), very useful and honest. There is also a volume of criticism, *Rings um Sazonov*, ed. E. Steinitz (1928). S. Y. Vitte, *Vospominaniya*, 2 vols. (1922, Eng. 1921) is important for Russian policy in the Far East; Kokovtsov (p.m. 1911–14), *Iz moego proshlayo*, 2 vols. (1933: Eng. abbreviation 1934), for the years before the World war.

OTHER COUNTRIES. There are a few scraps from Balkan countries. Gueshov, Bulgarian prime minister, described *The Balkan League* (1915), slightly expanded in *La genèse de la guerre mondiale* (1919). B. Bareilles published *Rapport secret sur le congrès de Berlin* (1919) by Caratheodory Pasha, the chief Turkish representative. *Memories of a Turkish Statesman* (1922), by Djemal Pasha, is important for Turkey's entry into the World war.

On Spain, there is Romanones, *Las responsabilidades políticas del antiguo regimen de 1875 a 1923* (1924), important for the two Moroccan crises.

An essential source from Japan is *Prince Ito* (1937), by Kengi Hamada.

(c) Diplomats

GERMANY (including PRUSSIA). The old Prussian diplomatists did not write much for the public. Schweinitz, ambassador first at Vienna then at St. Petersburg, left important evidence for the entire Bismarck era: his *Denkwürdigkeiten*, 2 vols. (1927), are more useful than his *Briefwechsel*, 3 vols. (1927–8). The *Aufzeichnungen und Erinnerungen*, 2 vols. (1925), of J. M. von Radowitz (son of Frederick William IV's friend) cover only 1875 to 1890 and have nothing about his time at Madrid. L. Raschdau (foreign office under Bismarck) wrote in his old age *Ein sinkendes Reich* (1933)—reminiscences of Turkey—and *Unter Bismarck und Caprivi* (1938). Holstein, the mystery-man of the foreign office from 1890 to 1906, is partially revealed in *Lebensbekenntnis* (1931); a full edition of his private papers has long been promised. The *Lebenserinnerungen*, 3 vols. (1919–21), of Eckardstein made a great stir when they were published; they are the principal source for the exaggerated stories of Anglo-German negotiations between 1898 and 1901. Lichnowsky, ambassador at London from 1912 to 1914, adds little in *Heading for the Abyss* (1928). The *Memoirs* (1937) of Bernstorff, ambassador at Washington, are more useful. Pourtalès, ambassador at St. Petersburg, describes the outbreak of war in *Meine Verhandlungen in St. Petersburg Ende Juli 1914* (1927). Further light on Russo-German relations in *Die Militärbevollmächtigen Kaiser Wilhelms II. am Zarenhofe 1904–14* (1937), ed. G. Lambsdorff.

Erinnerungen und Gedanken des Botschafters Anton Graf Monts (1932) are useful for Italo-German relations in Bülow's time, as well as being very entertaining. *Aus einem diplomatischen Wanderleben*, 2 vols. (1931–2), by F. Rosen, is important for the first Moroccan crisis and for Portuguese affairs in 1913–14. The second Moroccan crisis and the peace-negotiations of 1917 are illuminated in *Meine dreißig Dienstjahre 1888–1918* (1931), by Lancken Wakenitz; not very reliable.

AUSTRIA (including AUSTRIA-HUNGARY). The two volumes of diary by Hübner, ambassador at Paris 1849–59, are very important: *Ein Jahr meines Lebens* (1891) and *Neuf ans de souvenir* (1904). There is a gap between March 1849 and the beginning of 1850. *Aus den Briefen Prokesch von Osten* (1896) has a little about Frankfurt in the early 'fifties. H. Salomon, *L'ambassade de R. de Metternich* (1931), adds nothing. After this there is little until the years of the World war. Here come Giesl, *Zwei Jahrzehnte im nahen Orient* (1927); Dumba, *Memoirs of a Diplomat* (1932), America during the war; Musulin, *Das Haus am Ballplatz* (1924), outbreak of war; Macchio, *Wahrheit! Fürst Bülow und ich in Rom 1914, 1915* (1931); Hoyos, *Der deutsch-englische Gegensatz* (1922), for 5 July 1914; Szilássy, *Der Untergang der Donaumonarchie* (1921), Russia before 1914.

FRANCE. *Souvenirs d'une mission à Berlin* (1908), by A. de Circourt, are very important for French policy towards Poland and Prussia in the early months of 1848. *Mes souvenirs*, by de Reiset, 3 vols. (1901–3), have a certain amount about Italy. *Extraits des Mémoires*, by Morny (1892), describe his embassy at St. Petersburg. The *Memoirs* of Persigny (1895) are fragmentary. Benedetti wrote a good deal in his own defence: *Ma mission en Prusse* (1871); *Ma mission à Ems* (1895); *Trois ans en Allemagne* (1900). They add little to the official collection.

Nor is there much in Fleury, *La France et la Russie en 1870* (1902). G. Rothan, a minor Bonapartist diplomat, wrote works half of reminiscence, half of history: *Souvenirs diplomatiques — L'affaire du Luxembourg* (1882); *La politique française en 1866* (1884); *L'Allemagne et l'Italie 1870–71* (1885); *La Prusse et son roi pendant la guerre de Crimée* (1888); *L'Europe et l'avènement du second empire* (1890); and *La France et sa politique extérieure en 1867* (1893).

For the Third republic, there are de Broglie, *La mission de Gontaut-Biron à Berlin* (1896); Gontaut-Biron, *Ma mission en Allemagne 1872–73* (1906); A. Dreux, *Dernières années de l'ambassade de Gontaut-Biron* (1907), mainly superseded by the official collection; Ch. de Mouy, *Souvenirs et causeries* (1909), useful for the Constantinople conference; E. M. de Vogüé, *Journal: Paris, Saint-Pétersbourg 1877–83* (1932); E. Toutain, *Alexandre III et la république française 1887–88* (1929), mainly official papers; A. Billot, *La France et l'Italie 1881–99*, 2 vols. (1905); A. Gérard, *Ma mission en Chine 1894–97* (1918) and *Mémoires* (1928); J. Laroche, *Quinze ans à Rome avec Camille Barrère* (1943), hostile to both Barrère and Italy.

For the period before the World war, Paul Cambon, *Correspondance*, 3 vols. (1940 et seq.), important; M. Bompard, *Mon ambassade en Russie 1903–08* (1937); *Les carnets de Georges Louis*, 2 vols. (1926); M. Paléologue, *La Russie des Tsars pendant la grande guerre*, 3 vols. (1921–2, Eng. 1923–5), *Un Grand Tournant de la politique mondiale (1904–06)* (1934, Eng. 1935), and *Journal 1913–14* (1947), all very dramatic and unreliable; A. Dumaine, *La dernière ambassade de France en Autriche* (1921); Saint-René Taillandier, *Les Origines du Maroc français* (1930).

GREAT BRITAIN. Many British ambassadors received biographies, most of little value. The best are S. Lane-Poole, *Life of Stratford Canning*, 2 vols. (1888); Mrs. R. Wemyss, *Sir Robert Morier*, 2 vols. (1911); Newton, *Lord Lyons*, 2 vols. (1913), France, 1868–86; H. Sutherland Edwards, *Sir William White* (1902), the Near East in Salisbury's prime; R. B. Mowat, *Lord Pauncefote* (1929), Washington under Cleveland. The *Diplomatic Reminiscences*, 4 vols. (1892–4), of Lord Augustus Loftus are fatuous. The papers of Lord Cowley (Paris, 1850–68) are used inadequately in Wellesley and Sencourt, *Conversations with Napoleon III* (1934). Odo Russell (Lord Ampthill) gets almost too much attention in W. Taffs, *Ambassador to Bismarck* (1938) and *Letters from the Berlin Embassy*, ed. P. Knaplund (1942). *Letters and Friendships of Sir Cecil Spring Rice*, 2 vols. (1929), is of more interest for Balliol College than for foreign policy. Arthur Nicolson gets brilliant and sympathetic treatment in H. Nicolson, *Lord Carnock* (1930). A. Hardinge, *A Diplomatist in Europe* (1927), has a little about Spain. G. Buchanan, *My Mission to Russia*, 2 vols. (1923), covers the war years. *The Diary 1914–18*, 2 vols. (1924), of Lord Bertie of Thame is engaging.

ITALY yields only *Carteggio . . . di Emanuele d'Azeglio* (1920) and Aldrovandi-Marescotti, *Guerra diplomatica* (1939), on the treaty of London.

RUSSIA. Russian private papers are few but important. The *Politischer und privater Briefwechsel* of Peter von Meyendorff, ed. O. Hoetzsch, 3 vols. (1923), is essential for Berlin in 1848 and for the origins of the Crimean war. A. P. Zablotsky-Desyatovsky, *Graf P. D. Kiselev*, 3 vols. (1883), has a certain amount on Franco-Russian relations after the war. J. Y. Simpson, *The Saburov Memoirs* (1929), is the principal source for the League of the Three Emperors in 1881. Meyendorff, *Correspondance diplomatique de M. de Staal 1884–1900*, 2 vols. (1929), is useful for Anglo-Russian relations. Rosen, *Forty Years of Diplomacy*, 2 vols. (1922), is mainly concerned with the Far East. Taube, *La politique russe d'avant-guerre* (1928), is an attack on Izvolski; the German edition (1937) is more emphatically pro-German. Other useful memoirs are Nekludov, *Diplomatic Reminiscences* (1920), Bulgaria; Savinsky, *Recollections of a Russian Diplomat* (1927); and Charykov, *Glimpses of High Politics* (1931).

OTHERS. *The Secret Memoirs of A. Y. Hayashi* (1915) are essential for the Anglo-Japanese alliance. American ambassadors: Allan Nevins, *Henry White* (1930), for Algeçiras; W. H. Page, *Life and Letters*, 2 vols., Great Britain during the World war; and E. M. House, *Intimate Papers*, 4 vols. (1926–8), Wilson's ambassador-at-large. Beneš, *My War Memoirs* (1928), is important for the development of war-aims.

(d) Other Witnesses

To be complete, this would include almost every public figure of the seventy years. I have cut it down to those who were primarily concerned with foreign affairs. They were mainly soldiers and journalists, with an occasional banker thrown in.

GERMANY (including PRUSSIA). The Saxon diplomatist, Vitzthum von Eckstädt, ranks as an independent observer in the years of unification: *St. Petersburg and London 1852–64*, 2 vols. (1887); *Berlin und Wien 1845–52* (1886); *London, Gastein und Sadowa* (1889). Otherwise there is nothing until the Empire. Moltke, *Die deutschen Aufmarschpläne* (1929), gives the German strategy in Bismarck's time. Waldersee, *Denkwürdigkeiten*, 3 vols. (1922–3), and *Briefwechsel* (1928) are important for the 'new course'. J. Haller, *Philip Eulenburg, The Kaiser's Friend*, 2 vols. (1931), also reveals the intrigues of the 'nineties.

Tirpitz, *My Memoirs*, 2 vols. (1919), and *Politische Dokumente*, 2 vols. (1924–6), are essential for naval policy. Liman von Sanders, *Five Years in Turkey* (1928), does not tell much.

Of business men, Helfferich, *Georg von Siemens*, 3 vols. (1923), has a good deal about German plans in Turkey. *Aus meinen Akten* (1927), by Paul von Schwabach, is the record of a banker, Bleichroeder's successor, who was a friend of both Holstein and Eyre Crowe; it is particularly important for the two Moroccan crises. The life of *Albert Ballin* (1922), by B. Huldermann, is useful for the Haldane mission. Of politicians, the Pan-German Heinrich Class, *Wider den Strom* (1932), and the half-Polish Hutten-Czapski, *Sechzig Jahre Politik und Gesellschaft*, 2 vols. (1936), deserve mention. Theodor Wolff, of the *Berliner Tageblatt*, drew on his memories in *Das Vorspiel* (1927) and *The Eve of 1914* (1935).

The books on the war years are mostly military; but there is a good deal of politics in Ludendorff, *The General Staff and Its Problems* (1920). *Erlebnisse im Weltkriege* (1920), by M. Erzberger, the Centre politician, explains the peace resolution. There is not much of importance in the *Memoirs of a Social Democrat*, by P. Scheidemann, 2 vols. (1928).

AUSTRIA (including AUSTRIA-HUNGARY). The *Tagebuch des Polizeiministers Kempen 1848–1859* (1931), edited by J. P. Mayr, has some interesting points for the period of absolutism. *Erinnerungen eines alten Oesterreichers*, 2 vols. (1911–13), by L. von Przibram, gives an account of the Austro-Hungarian press bureau in the 1870s. Two successive chiefs of the general staff supply vital evidence of very different kinds: Beck in *Franz Josephs Weggefährte*, by Glaise von Horstenau (1930), and Conrad von Hoetzendorf in *Aus meiner Dienstzeit*, 5 vols. (1921–5). H. Kanner, *Kaiserliche Katastrophenpolitik* (1922), is the work of a journalist which speaks for itself.

FRANCE. Beyens, *Le second empire vu par un diplomate belge*, 2 vols. (1924–6), is more interesting for atmosphere than for facts. Lebrun, *Souvenirs militaires* (1892), gives the Austro-French negotiations in 1869 and 1870. The *Souvenirs 1883–1933*, 3 vols. (1932–4) of C. Benoist are valuable and entertaining. C. J. Huguet, *Britain and the War* (1928), is a prime source for the military conversations. Joffre, *Personal Memoirs*, 2 vols. (1932), is mainly useful for the pre-war years. A. Messimy, *Mes souvenirs* (1937), is important for the Agadir crisis.

GREAT BRITAIN. The various volumes of Nassau Senior's conversations, too numerous to list, have scraps of information. A particularly important fragment on the 'Cowley interview' is preserved by his daughter M. C. M. Simpson, in *Many Memories* (1891). H. Drummond Wolff, *Rambling Recollections*, 2 vols. (1908), has much on the Near East in Salisbury's time. The third volume of Garvin, *Chamberlain* (1934), is essential for the Anglo-German negotiations in 1898. The *Milner Papers*, 2 vols. (1931), edited by C. Headlam, give the background of the Boer war. Haldane described his mission in *Before the War* (1920). Liberal ministers attacked Grey in Loreburn, *How the War Came* (1919) and Morley, *Memorandum on Resignation* (1928), a misleading account of the crisis in July 1914. The soldiers have not much to say on foreign affairs, except for Sir Henry Wilson, *Life and Diaries*, 2 vols. (1927), by C. E. Caldwell. Two unofficial politicians of very different kinds appear in Esher, *Journals and Letters*, 4 vols. (1934 et seq.)—court intrigue—and *Foreign Policy from a Back Bench 1904–1918* (1932), by T. P. Conwell-Evans—the radical M.P., Noel Buxton. The most important journalists are Valentine Chirol, *Fifty Years in a Changing World* (1927); Wickham Steed, *Through Thirty Years* (1924), with many stimulating speculations; and J. L. Hammond, *C. P. Scott* (1934), for radicalism between the Agadir crisis and the World war. The *History of the Times* (1936–52) has much important material, especially on Anglo-German relations. In an appendix to volume iii it explodes most of the previous studies of public opinion, based on newspapers.

ITALY. Most unofficial Italian memoirs are concerned with internal politics. A few figures transcend the Italian scene. The voluminous writings of Mazzini, for instance, present the dream of a republican Europe based on something other than the Balance of Power. There are 93 volumes of his *Scritti editi ed inediti* (1906 et seq.) and 6 vols. of appendixes (1941–3). The *Memorie* (1907) and *Scritti politici e militari* (1907) of Garibaldi have a few points of interest. More important are the writings of C. Cattaneo, the Lombard federalist of 1848, especially his *Considerazioni sulle cose d'Italia nel 1848* (1946). For a much later period, the recollections of Luigi Albertini, editor of *Il Corriere della Sera*, are of some interest: *Vent' anni di vita politica: l'esperienza democratica italiana dal 1898 al 1914*, 2 vols. (1950).

SECONDARY WORKS

GENERAL. The general histories of international relations by Debidour, 4 vols. (1891–1918), and by E. Bourgeois, 4 vols. (1906–32) are now out of date. *Istoria Diplomatii*, 3 vols. (1945), edited by V. P. Potemkin, is better, though marred by erratic Marxism. The best summary is in the volumes of *Peuples et civilisations* by Pouthas (1941), Hauser and others (new edition 1952), Baumont (1948), and Renouvin (new edition 1949); but it is embedded in general history. There is an extended treatment of the period before 1871 in A. Stern, *Geschichte Europas 1815–1871*, 10 vols. (1894–1924). For the period after 1871, *Histoire diplomatique de l'Europe 1871–1914*, 2 vols. (1929), edited by H. Hauser, is still the best, despite the faults inevitable in a collective work. For particular countries, there are R. W. Seton-Watson, *Britain in Europe 1789–1914* (1937), not much use after 1880; E. M. Carroll, *French Public Opinion and Foreign Affairs 1870–1914* (1931); A. F. Pribram, *England and the International Policy of the European Great Powers 1871–1914* (1931), a very good summary; E. M. Carroll, *Germany and the Great Powers 1866–1914* (1938); H. Oncken, *Das deutsche Reich und die Vorgeschichte des Weltkrieges*, 2 vols. (1933); and E. V. Tarle, *Evropa v Epokhu Imperializma* (1927).

Special Topics, arranged more or less chronologically.

Much remains to be done on the diplomacy of *the revolutionary year and the reaction*. De Guichen, *Les grandes questions européennes et la diplomatie des puissances dans la seconde république*, 2 vols. (1925–9), is an anthology of quotations from the archives rather than an analysis. D. M. Greer, *L'Angleterre, la France et la révolution de 1848* (1925), does not exhaust the subject. P. Flaad, *England und die Schweiz* (1935), is interesting on this side-issue. There is nothing on Poland or Sleswick-Holstein. H. Precht, *Englands Stellung zur deutschen Einheit 1848–52* (1925), is not very satisfactory. E. Scharff, *Die europäischen Großmächte und die deutsche Revolution* (1942), argues, unconvincingly, that France and Russia would have forbidden the unification of Germany. Italy is better provided for: A. J. P. Taylor, *The Italian Problem in European Diplomacy 1847–49* (1934), and R. Moscati, *La diplomazia europea e il problema italiano del 1848* (1947), using Italian archives. Bourgeois and Clermont, *Rome et Napoléon III* (1907), covers the period from 1849 to 1870. The reaction in Italy is described by R. Moscati, *Austria, Napoli e gli stati conservatori italiani 1849–52* (1942). On Hungary, R. A. Averbukh, *Tsarskaya interventsiya v borbe s vengerskoi revolyutsiei* (1935); E. Horvath, *Origins of the Crimean War* (1937); and C. Sproxton, *Palmerston and the Hungarian Revolution* (1919), rather slight.

Crimean war. A. M. Zaionchkovsky, *Vostochnaya voina*, 2 vols. (1908–12), very good; Shebunin, *Rossiya na Blizhnem Vostokye* (1926); S. M. Goriainov, *Le Bosphore et les Dardanelles* (1910), an important collection of documents covering the entire period; all give the Russian side. V. M. Puryear, *England, Russia and the Straits Question 1844–56* (1931) and *International Economics and Diplomacy in the Near East 1834–53* (1935), have novel, if unreliable, ideas. Guichen, *La guerre de Crimée et l'attitude des puissances* (1936), is another anthology. E. Bapst, *Les origines de la guerre de Crimée* (1912), has important French material. The outstanding English work is H. W. V. Temperley, *England and the Near East: the Crimea* (1936). There is an odd study of public opinion in Kingsley Martin, *The Triumph of Lord Palmerston* (1924). All these go only to the outbreak of war. The war diplomacy has to be followed in G. B. Henderson, *Crimean War Diplomacy* (1947), a collection of most valuable essays. There are some good books on the diplomacy of the central Powers: H. Friedjung, *Der Krimkrieg und die österreichische Politik* (1907), now rather out of date: K. Borries, *Preußen im Krimkrieg* (1930), with Prussian documents; and F. Eckhart, *Die deutsche Frage und der Krimkrieg* (1931), good on Austrian policy. F. Valsecchi, *L'alleanza di Crimea* (1948), is excellent for the Italian side until the alliance of January 1855. The immediate aftermath of the war is in E. G. East, *The Union of Moldavia and Wallachia* (1927), and T. W. Riker, *The Making of Roumania* (1929).

After the Crimean war. Some very good books here. Charles-Roux, *Alexandre II, Gortchakoff et Napoléon III* (1913), covers 1856 to 1870, but is most valuable for the years before 1863; there are many quotations from French sources. E. Schüle, *Rußland und Frankreich 1856–59* (1935), is a more detailed survey, which exhausts the subject. C. Friese, *Rußland und Preußen vom Krimkrieg bis zum polnischen Aufstand* (1931), is equally good. B. Nolde, *Die Petersburger Mission Bismarcks 1859–62* (1936), does not add much.

War of 1859. F. Valsecchi, *L'unificazione italiana e la politica europea 1854–59* (1939), is a useful collection of documents which are otherwise rather hard to come by. M. Mazziotti, *Napoleone III l'Italia* (1925), does not go deep. One is reduced to works of detail: F. Valsecchi, *La mediazione europea . . . alla vigilia della guerra del 1859* (1938); F. Engel von Janosi, *L'ultimatum austriaco del 1859* (1938); W. Deutsch, *Habsburgs Rückzug aus Italien* (1940); A. Zazo, *La politica estera del regno delle due Sicilie nel 1859–60* (1940). Problems after the war in J. Trésal, *L'annexion de la Savoie à la France* (1913); L. M. Case, *Franco-Italian relations 1860–65* (1932). The diplomatic history of Italian unification on a modern basis is still to be written. F. Valsecchi's book on the Crimean alliance, referred to above, promises to be the first volume of this general history.

The Austro-Prussian conflict. To be complete this would have to include all the works on German unification. I have kept to those in which diplomacy predominates. A. O. Meyer, *Bismarcks Kampf mit Österreich am Bundestag zu Frankfurt* (revised 1939), is very good, though it judges too narrowly from the Prussian side. K. Kaiser, *Kaiser Napoleon III. und der polnische Aufstand von 1863* (1932), is useful. L. D. Steefel, *The Schleswig-Holstein Question* (1932), is excellent, though written before the publication of the Prussian and Austrian documents. The Austrian archives were used by C. W. Clark, *Franz*

Joseph and Bismarck (1934). The classic account, still important despite errors of detail, is H. Friedjung, *Der Kampf um die Vorherrschaft in Deutschland* (1897; abbreviated Eng. 1934). H. von Srbik, *Deutsche Einheit*, 4 vols. (1935–42), ranges far back, but the last two volumes give a detailed summary of diplomacy between 1859 and 1866. F. Beiche, *Bismarck und Italien 1866* (1931), does not add much. R. Stadelmann, *Das Jahr 1865* (1933), puts the case for Bismarck as being in favour of compromise. Bortolotti, *La Guerra del 1866* (1941), gives the Italian side.

Franco-Prussian war. A modern treatment is still to seek. Schierenberg, *Die deutsch-französische Auseinandersetzung und die Luxemburger Frage* (1936), and A. Lamberti, *Die Bündnisverhandlungen Napoleon IIIs* (1939), are crude summaries. R. Fester, *Briefe und Aktenstücke* (1913) and *Genesis der Emser Depesche* (1915), have much valuable material. D. N. Raymond, *British Policy and Opinion During the Franco-Prussian War* (1921), is now out of date. Eddleston, *Italian Neutrality in the Franco-German War of 1870* (1935), is useful. K. Rheindorf, *Die Schwarz-Meer (Pontus) Frage* (1925), illuminates Russian policy to some extent. But we must still rely on Sorel, *Histoire diplomatique de la guerre franco-allemande* (1873).

1871–5. The outstanding book is W. L. Langer, *European Alliances and Alignments 1871–90* (new edition, 1950), with a magnificent bibliography. It is centred rather too much on Bismarck and tends to accept his version of events; but there is nothing to compare with it, except Langer's own later volume. There is a splendid analysis of the background of Italian policy in F. Chabod, *Storia della politica estera italiana dal 1870 al 1896*, vol. i, *Le premesse* (1951). S. W. Halperin, *Italy and the Vatican at War* (1939), is also good on this. So is F. Cataluccio, *La politica estera di Visconti Venosta* (1940). H. Holborn, *Bismarcks europäische Politik zu Beginn der siebziger Jahre und die Mission Radowitz* (1925), is important for the war-scare of 1875.

The Eastern Crisis 1875–8. General summary in M. D. Stojanović, *The Great Powers and the Balkans 1875–78* (1939). Russian policy in B. H. Sumner, *Russia and the Balkans 1870–80* (1937), a wonderful book. Further material in Goriainov, *La question d'Orient* (1946). British policy and internal politics in R. W. Seton-Watson, *Disraeli, Gladstone and the Eastern Question* (1935). Austro-Hungarian policy in G. H. Rupp, *A Wavering Friendship: Russia and Austria 1876–78* (1941), rather clumsy. F. Leidner, *Die Außenpolitik Österreich-Ungarns 1870–79* (1936), has important material. D. Harris, *A Diplomatic History of the Balkan Crisis of 1875–78. The First Year* (1936) and *Britain and the Bulgarian Horrors of 1876* (1939), are both good for the beginning of the crisis. D. W. Lee, *Great Britain and the Cyprus Convention* (1934), is also important for British policy. W. N. Medlicott, *The Congress of Berlin and After* (1938), and C. E. Black, *The Establishment of Constitutional Government in Bulgaria* (1943) cover the end of the crisis.

Bismarck's alliances. W. Windelband, *Bismarck und die europäischen Großmächte 1879–85* (1940), is the most thorough recent account. A. O. Meyer, *Bismarcks Friedenspolitik* (1930), is too favourable. M. Müller, *Die Bedeutung des Berliner Kongresses für die deutsch-russischen Beziehungen* (1927), has some good points. S. Skazkin, *Konets avstro-russko-germanskogo soiuza 1879–84* (1928), is very important for Russian policy. A. C. Coolidge, *The Origins of the Triple Alliance* (1926), is good though rather out of date. L. Salvatorelli, *La triplice alleanza 1877–1912* (1939), is a more recent study. Bismarck's relations with the western Powers are in R. H. Wienefeld, *Franco-German Relations 1878–85* (1929) a dull summary; P. B. Mitchell, *The Bismarckian Policy of Conciliation with France* (1935); W. O. Aydelotte, *Bismarck and British Colonial Policy* (1937), which leaves the problem unsolved; and A. J. P. Taylor, *Germany's First Bid for Colonies* (1938), which tries to solve it. S. E. Crowe, *The Berlin West African Conference* (1942) is also useful.

1885–90. J. V. Fuller, *Bismarck's Diplomacy at its Zenith* (1922), is distinguished by its hostility to Bismarck. V. Khvostov, *Ocherki istorii vneshnei politiki germanskoi imperii* (1940), is a good Russian study; P. Pavlovich, *Avantyury russkogo tsarizma v Bolgarii* (1935), full of revelations. Trützschler von Falkenstein, *Bismarck und die Kriegsgefahr des Jahres 1887* (1924), still has value. L. Israel, *England und der orientalische Dreibund 1887–1896* (1938), is good for the Mediterranean agreements. H. Krausnick, *Holsteins Geheimpolitik in der Ära Bismarcks* (1942), tells, at excessive length, the story of Holstein's intrigues against Bismarck's balancing policy.

1890–7. W. L. Langer, *The Diplomacy of Imperialism 1890–1902* (1951), though as thorough as its predecessors, sees everything through German eyes and is excessively unsympathetic, for example, to the Franco-Russian alliance. E. Brandenburg, *From Bismarck to the World War* (1927; enlarged German edition, 1939), is not much more than a summary of German documents, despite its title and reputation. G. Hallgarten, *Imperialismus vor 1914*, 2 vols. (1951), promises more than it performs; it is really a sociological study of German policy with some exaggeration. W. L. Langer, *The Franco-Russian Alliance 1890–94* (1929), is more accurately an account of the effect of the alliance on the central Powers. G. Michon, *L'alliance franco-russe* (1927), is an attack on the alliance. A. J. Marder, *British Naval Policy 1880–1905* (1940), is very useful, especially between 1889 and 1896. D. C. Blaisdell, *European Financial Control in the Otto-*

man *Empire* (1929), is also important. More generally, H. Feis, *Europe: the World's Banker 1870–1914* (1930), is rich in details of financial imperialism. So is E. Staley, *War and the Private Investor* (1935). H. Preller, *Salisbury und die türkische Frage im Jahre 1895* (1930), is interesting. There is an admirable study of German policy in A. Yerusalimskii, *Vneshniaia politika i diplomatsia germanskogo imperializma v kontse XIX veka* (1948). W. Schinner, *Der Österreichisch-italienische Gegensatz auf dem Balkan 1875–96* (1936), is good.

Anglo-German relations 1898–1914. R. J. Sonntag, *Germany and England, Background of Conflict 1848–94* (1938), is an agreeable general account. O. J. Hale, *Publicity and Diplomacy* (1940), analyses Anglo-German relations between 1890 and 1914 with an excessive emphasis on the anti-German influence of *The Times*. Ross Hoffmann, *The Anglo-German Trade Rivalry* (1933), also exaggerates the importance of his subject. Pauline Anderson, *The Background of Anti-British Feeling in Germany 1890–1902* (1939), is not much more successful. F. Meinecke, *Geschichte des deutsch-englischen Bündnis-Problems 1890–1901* (1927), laments the lost alliance. G. Ritter, *Die Legende von der verschmähten englischen Freundschaft 1898–1901* (1929), argues that it was not there to lose. R. I. Lovell, *The Struggle for South Africa* (1934), is the best book on the subject. H. Hallmann, *Krugerdepesche und Flottenfrage* (1927), is important for the beginning of the great German navy. His later book, *Der Weg zum deutschen Schlachtflottenbau* (1933), is eclipsed by E. Kehr, *Schlachtflottenbau und Parteipolitik* (1930), a wonderful book, despite its exaggeration of the sociological factors. For later years, E. L. Woodward, *Great Britain and the German Navy* (1935), is the only book of any importance; it is a beautiful composition, though rather thin after 1912.

The Far East. G. F. Hudson, *The Far East in World Politics* (1939), is a model of brief exposition. Another good summary, though less brilliant, is P. Renouvin, *La question d'extrême Orient* (1946). For earlier years, W. C. Costin, *Great Britain and China 1833–60* (1937), and V. H. Kiernan, *British Diplomacy in China 1880–85* (1938) are both admirable. P. Joseph, *Foreign Diplomacy in China 1894–1900* (1928), is useful, though weak on the Russian side. The essential Russian book is B. A. Romanov, *Rossia v Manchzhurii 1892–1906* (1938). B. H. Sumner, *Tsardom and Imperialism in the Far East and Middle East* (1942), is invaluable in its short compass. F. von Steinmann, *Rußlands Politik im fernen Osten und der Staatssekretär Bezobrazov* (1931), is also useful for Russian policy. E. H. Zabriskie, *American-Russian Rivalry in the Far East* (1946), is important for both countries. A. Galperin, *Anglo-iaponskii soiuz* (1947), is the best book on the subject. O. Becker, *Der ferne Osten und das Schicksal Europas 1907–1918* (1940), is useful for the later period.

The Triple Entente. M. B. Giffen, *Fashoda* (1930), is not very satis-factory on the crisis of 1898. J. J. Mathews, *Egypt and the Formation of the Anglo-French Entente* (1939) is a bare summary. There is not much in C. W. Porter, *The Career of Théophile Delcassé* (1936); nor in A. Néton, *Delcassé* (1952). J. A. Tyler, *The British Army and the Continent* (1938), is of value for the military conversations. R. P. Churchill, *The Anglo-Russian Convention of 1907* (1939), is reasonably good. C. Michon, *La préparation à la guerre* (1935), is an attack on the French three-year service.

Morocco. F. R. Flournoy, *British Policy towards Morocco in the Age of Palmerston* (1935). and E. F. Cruickshank, *Morocco at the Parting of the Ways* (1935), give the background. H. T. Williamson, *Germany and Morocco before 1905* (1937), explodes the German economic grievances. H. von Huene-Hoeningen, *Untersuchungen zur Geschicte der deutschenglischen Beziehungen 1898–1901* (1934), draws attention to the importance of Morocco. E. N. Anderson, *The First Moroccan Crisis* (1930), is good, though written before the publication of the French documents. I. Barlow, *The Agadir Crisis* (1940), is rather too innocent.

American relations with the European Powers. There are some good books on this subject which I have rather neglected. R. H. Heindel, *The American Impact on Great Britain 1898–1914* (1940); L. M. Gelber, *The Rise of Anglo-American Friendship 1898–1906* (1938); A. Vagts, *Deutschland und die Vereinigten Staaten,* 2 vols. (1935); J. H. Ferguson, *American Diplomacy and the Boer War* (1939).

Balkans and Near East 1908–14. For the Bagdad railway, E. M. Earle, *Turkey, the Great Powers and the Bagdad Railway* (1923); J. B. Wolf, *The Diplomatic History of the Baghdad Railway* (1936); and F. H. Bode, *Der Kampf um die Bagdadbahn 1903–14* (1941). The springs of Russian policy are revealed in N. Mandelstam, *La politique russe d'accès à la Méditerranée au XXᵉ siècle* (1934). B. Schmitt, *The Annexa-tion of Bosnia* (1937), exhausts the subject; and makes M. Nintchitch, *La crise bosniaque* (2 vols., 1937), unnecessary. Austro-Hungarian policy is outlined in A. F. Pribram, *Austrian Foreign Policy 1908–1918* (1923); A. F. Pribram, *Austria-Hungary and Great Britain 1908–1914* (1951); and O. H. Wedel, *Austro-German Diplomatic Relations 1908–1914* (1932), all three rather drab diplomatic accounts. W. C. Askew, *Europe and Italy's Acquisition of Libya 1911–12* (1942), and E. C. Helmreich, *The Diplomacy of the Balkan Wars* (1938), are sound diplomatic narratives, without much consciousness of the under-lying rivalries between the Great Powers. H. N. Howard, *The Parti-tion of Turkey 1913–23* (1931), covers the Balkan wars as well as the plans for the partition during the World war.

Outbreak of the World war. There are many books which begin with a general background and then discuss the crisis of July 1914 in detail. Even the most scholarly tend to have a propagandist character, the more dangerous when it is concealed by an air of impartiality. The best statements of the German views are in A. von Wegerer, *Der Ausbruch des Weltkrieges*, 2 vols. (1939), and E. Anrich, *Europas Diplomatie am Vorabend des Weltkrieges* (1937); of the French view P. Renouvin, *Les origines immédiates de la guerre* (1927), and C. Bloch, *The Causes of the War* (1935). J. Isaac, *Un débat historique* (1933), criticizes his French colleagues. S. B. Fay, *The Origins of the World War*, 2 vols. (1930), has long enjoyed a great reputation. It relies mainly on the German sources and is, in my opinion, unfair to both Serbia and Russia. B. E. Schmitt, *The Coming of the War*, 2 vols. (1930), seems to me free from these faults and is incomparably the best account; but it is, of course, twenty years behind in its sources. A more recent study is L. Albertini, *Le origini della guerra del 1914*, 3 vols. (1943), which is now being translated into English (1952 et seq.). The first volume treats of the background with a rather unsatisfactory concentration on Austria-Hungary and Italy; the two later volumes treat of July 1914 with much new detail. But even this book is now more than ten years behind the times; and a convincing analysis of the origins of the World war remains to be written. On special topics there deserve to be mentioned J. B. Bredt, *Die belgische Neutralität und der Schlieffensche Feldzugsplan* (1929); E. Anrich, *Die englische Politik im Juli 1914* (1934); G. Franz, *Rußlands Eintritt in den Weltkrieg* (1930).

The World war. There is no satisfactory diplomatic history. A. Pingaud, *Histoire diplomatique de la France pendant la grande guerre*, 3 vols. (1938–41), is very useful, especially for its material from unpublished French sources. M. Toscano, *Il patto di Londra* (1934) and *Gli accordi di San Giovanni di Moriana* (1936), are adequate summaries. H. W. Gatzke, *Germany's Drive to the West* (1950), is excellent on German war-aims. E. Dahlin, *French and German Public Opinion on Declared War Aims* (1933) is also good. Kent Forster, *The Failures of Peace* (1941), is competent, but marred by its pacifist sympathies. There is a good deal on the peace-manœuvres of 1917: E. O. Volkmann, *Die Annexionsfragen des Weltkrieges* (1929); R. Fester, *Die Politik Kaiser Karls* (1925) and *Die politischen Kämpfe um den Frieden* (1938); A. Chatelle, *La paix manquée?* (1936); F. von Lama, *Die Friedensvermittlung Papst Benedict XV.* (1932); and H. J. T. Johnson, *Vatican Diplomacy in the World War* (1933). On American policy the best books are C. Seymour, *American Diplomacy during the World War* (1934), and H. Notter, *The Origins of the Foreign Policy of Woodrow Wilson* (1937). Wilson is attacked in W. Millis, *Road to War* (1935), and in C. C. Tansill, *America Goes to War* (1938).

INDEX